INTRODUCTION TO BIBLICAL INTERPRETATION

INTRODUCTION TO BIBLICAL INTERPRETATION

DR. WILLIAM W. KLEIN

DR. CRAIG L. BLOMBERG

DR. ROBERT L. HUBBARD, JR.

THOMAS NELSON
Since 1798

NASHVILLE   DALLAS   MEXICO CITY   RIO DE JANEIRO

Introduction to Biblical Interpretation (revised & expanded)

Published in Nashville, Tennessee, by Thomas Nelson, Inc.

Library of Congress Cataloging-in-Publication Data

Introduction to biblical interpretation (revised & expanded) / William W. Klein, Craig L. Blomberg, and Robert L. Hubbard, Jr.
cm.
   Includes bibliographical references and indexes.
   Bible—Hermeneutics.   I. William W. Klein, Dr.   II. Craig L. Blomberg.   III. Robert L. Hubbard, Jr..
   220.6'01—dc20   93-20099
   ISBN-10: 0-7852-5225-8   (formerly 0-8499-0774-8)
   ISBN-13: 978-0-7852-5225-2   CIP

Printed in the United States of America

13 14 15 16 — 20 19 18 17

Dedicated to our esteemed mentors:
Donald W. Burdick (†)
D. A. Carson
David A. Hubbard (†)
A. Berkeley Mickelsen (†)

TABLE OF CONTENTS

PART III—UNDERSTANDING LITERATURE

PART V—THE FRUITS OF INTERPRETATION

LIST OF ABBREVIATIONS

Abbreviations in the following lists occur throughout the text of the book and in the footnotes. Abbreviations are also found in the concluding bibliography, which lists extensive sources.

General Abbreviations

abbrev.	abbreviated
ad loc.	*ad locum,* at the place
ANE	Ancient Near East
ca.	*circa,* about
cent.	century
cf.	*confer,* compare
chap.(s)	chapter(s)
contra	in contrast to
diss.	dissertation
ed.(s)	edited by, editor(s)
e.g.	*exempli gratia,* for example
esp.	especially
et al.	*et alii,* and others
ET	English translation
f., ff.	following [verse(s); page(s)]
fem.	feminine
FS	*Festschrift*
Ger.	German
Gr.	Greek
Heb.	Hebrew
hiph.	hiphil
Hith.	Hithpael
id.	*idem,* the same
i.e.	*id est,* that is
lit.	literally
loc.	locative
loc. cit.	*loco citato,* the place cited
MS(S)	manuscript(s)
masc.	masculine
n.d.	no date
niph.	niphal
no.	number
n.s.	new series
orig.	original
p., pp.	page, pages
pace	with due respect to, but differing from
par.	parallel (to)

para.	paragraph
pass.	*passim,* throughout
pl.	plural
Q	*Quelle* (Ger. "sayings" source for the Gospels)
repr.	reprint(ed)
rev.	revised, reviser, revision
sing.	singular
s.v.	*sub verbo,* under the word
tr.	translator, translated by
UBS	United Bible Societies
unpubl.	unpublished
upd.	updated
v., vv.	verse(s)
viz.	*videlicet,* namely
vol.	volume
vs.	versus
X	times (as in 3X = three times)

Versions and Translations of the Bible

ASV	*American Standard Version* (1901)
CEV	*Contemporary English Version* (1995)
ESV	*English Standard Version* (2001)
GNT	*Good News Translation* [formerly *Good News Bible* = TEV] (1976)
HCSB	*Holman Christian Standard Bible* (NT, 2000)
KJV	*King James Version (Authorized Version)* (1611)
LBP	*Living Bible Paraphrased* (1971)
NASB	*New American Standard Bible* (1995)
NCV	*New Century Version* (1987)
NEB	*New English Bible* (1970)
NIV	*New International Version* (1983)
NKJV	*New King James Version* (1982)
NLT	*New Living Translation* (1996)
NRSV	*New Revised Standard Version* (1990)
Phillips	J. B. Phillips, *The New Testament in Modern English* (1959)
REB	*Revised English Bible* (1989)
RSV	*Revised Standard Version* (1952, 1971)
TEV	*Today's English Version* (= GNT) (1976)
TNIV	*Today's New International Version* (NT, 2001)

Periodicals, Reference Works, and Serials

ABD	*The Anchor Bible Dictionary,* ed., D. N. Freedman
AnBib	Analecta Biblica
ANET	*Ancient Near Eastern Texts Relating to the Old Testament,* ed., J. B. Pritchard

AnOr	Analecta Orientalia
ATANT	Abhandlungen zur Theologie des Alten und Neuen Testaments
ATD	Das Alte Testament Deutsch (German Old Testament)
BA	*Biblical Archaeologist*
BBR	*Bulletin for Biblical Research*
BDB	F. Brown, S. K. Driver, and C. A. Briggs, *Hebrew and English Lexicon of the Old Testament*
BDF	F. Blass, A. Debrunner, and R. W. Funk, *A Greek Grammar of the New Testament and Other Early Christian Literature*
BHS	*Biblia Hebraica Stuttgartensia*
Bib	*Biblica*
BibInt	*Biblical Interpretation*
BJRL	*Bulletin of the John Rylands University Library of Manchester*
BNTC	Black's New Testament Commentary
BSac	*Bibliotheca Sacra*
BT	*The Bible Translator*
BTB	*Biblical Theology Bulletin*
BZAW	Beihefte zur *ZAW*
CBNT	Coniectanea Biblica New Testament Series
CBQ	*Catholic Biblical Quarterly*
CBQMS	CBQ Monograph Series
CHB	*Cambridge History of the Bible*
Chr Cent	*Christian Century*
CRBS	*Currents in Research: Biblical Studies*
CSR	*Christian Scholars Review*
CT	*Christianity Today*
CTR	*Criswell Theological Review*
EcR	*Ecclesiastical Review*
EDNT	*Exegetical Dictionary of the New Testament*, ed., H. Balz and G. Schneider
EvQ	*The Evangelical Quarterly*
EvT	*Evangelische Theologie*
ExpT	*The Expository Times*
FOTL	Forms of Old Testament Literature
FRLANT	Forschungen zur Religion und Literatur des Alten und Neuen Testaments
GNT	Greek New Testament
GTJ	*Grace Theological Journal*
HALOT	*The Hebrew and Aramaic Lexicon of the Old Testament*, ed. Koehler, Baumgartner, and Stamm
HBT	*Horizons in Biblical Theology*
HDR	Harvard Dissertations in Religion
HTR	*Harvard Theological Review*
IB	*Interpreter's Bible*
IBMR	*International Bulletin of Missiological Research*
ICC	International Critical Commentary

IDB	*The Interpreter's Dictionary of the Bible*, ed., G. A. Buttrick
IDBS	*Interpreter's Dictionary of the Bible, Supplement*
Int	*Interpretation*
ISBE	*International Standard Bible Encyclopedia*, ed., G. W. Bromiley
JAAR	*Journal of the American Academy of Religion*
JBL	*Journal of Biblical Literature*
JBR	*Journal of Bible and Religion*
JETS	*Journal of the Evangelical Theological Society*
JLT	*Journal of Literature and Theology*
JPT	*Journal of Pentecostal Theology*
JSJ	*Journal for the Study of Judaism*
JSJSup	JSJ Supplements
JSNT	*Journal for the Study of the New Testament*
JSNTSup	JSNT Supplements
JSOT	*Journal for the Study of the Old Testament*
JSOTSup	JSOT Supplements
JTS	*Journal of Theological Studies*
KB	*Lexicon in Veteris Testamenti Libros*, ed., L. Koehler and W. Baumgartner
M&M	J. H. Moulton and G. Milligan, *The Vocabulary of the Greek New Testament*
NAC	New American Commentary
NCB	New Century Bible
NICNT	New International Commentary on the New Testament
NICOT	New International Commentary on the Old Testament
NIGTC	New International Greek Testament Commentary
NIDNTT	*New International Dictionary of New Testament Theology*, ed., C. Brown
NIDOTTE	*New International Dictionary of Old Testament Theology and Exegesis*, ed., W. VanGemeren, et al.
NovT	*Novum Testamentum*
NT	New Testament
NTL	New Testament Library
NTA	*New Testament Abstracts*
NTS	*New Testament Studies*
OT	Old Testament
OTA	*Old Testament Abstracts*
OTL	Old Testament Library
PNTC	Pillar New Testament Commentary
PRS	*Perspectives in Religious Studies*
RSP	*Ras Shamra Parallels: The Texts from Ugarit and the Hebrew Bible*
SBET	*Scottish Bulletin of Evangelical Theology*
SBLDS	Society of Biblical Literature Dissertation Series
SBLMS	SBL Monograph Series
SBLSP	SBL Seminar Papers
SBT	Studies in Biblical Theology
SJOT	*Scandinavian Journal of the Old Testament*

SNTSMS	Society for New Testament Studies Monograph Series
St.VladThQ	*St. Vladimir's Theological Quarterly*
SUNT	Studien zur Umwelt des Neuen Testament
TBü	Theologische Bücherei
TDNT	*Theological Dictionary of the New Testament,* ed., G. Kittel and G. Friedrich
TDOT	*Theological Dictionary of the Old Testament,* ed., G. J. Botterweck and H. Ringgren
THAT	*Theologisches Handwörterbuch zum Alten Testament,* ed., E. Jenni and C. Westermann
Theol	*Theology*
TLZ	*Theologische Literaturzeitung*
TNTC	Tyndale New Testament Commentaries
TOTC	Tyndale Old Testament Commentaries
TrinJ	*Trinity Journal*
TU	Texte und Untersuchungen
TWOT	*Theological Wordbook of the Old Testament,* ed., R. L. Harris, et al.
TynB	*Tyndale Bulletin*
USQR	*Union Seminary Quarterly Review*
VoxEv	*Vox Evangelica*
VT	*Vetus Testamentum*
VTSup	VT Supplements
WBC	Word Biblical Commentary
WTJ	*Westminster Theological Journal*
WMANT	*Wissenschaftliche Monographien zum Alten und Neuen Testament*
ZAW	*Zeitschrift für die alttestamentliche Wissenschaft*
ZNW	*Zeitschrift für die neutestamentliche Wissenschaft*
ZPEB	*Zondervan Pictorial Encyclopedia of the Bible,* ed., M. C. Tenney.

Books of the Bible and Other Works

Old Testament

Gen	1 Kgs	Eccl	Obad
Exod	2 Kgs	Song	Jonah
Lev	1 Chr	Isa	Mic
Num	2 Chr	Jer	Nah
Deut	Ezra	Lam	Hab
Josh	Neh	Ezek	Zeph
Judg	Esth	Dan	Hag
Ruth	Job	Hos	Zech
1 Sam	Psa (Pss)	Joel	Mal
2 Sam	Prov	Amos	

New Testament

Mt	2 Cor	1 Tim	2 Pet
Mk	Gal	2 Tim	1 Jn
Lk	Eph	Titus	2 Jn
Jn	Phil	Phlm	3 Jn
Acts	Col	Heb	Jude
Rom	1 Thes	Jas	Rev
1 Cor	2 Thes	1 Pet	

Apocrypha

1 Macc	1 Maccabees
2 Macc	2 Maccabees
Sir	Ecclesiasticus (Wisdom of Jesus the son of Sirach)
Wis	The Wisdom of Solomon

Pseudepigrapha, Other Jewish and Patristic Writings

Ant.	Josephus, *Antiquities of the Jews*
Ag. Apion	Josephus, *Against Apion*
Barn	Barnabas
1–2 Clem	1–2 Clement
Did	Didache
H.E.	Eusebius, *Historia Ecclesiastica,* History of the Church
Strom	*Stromateis* (Clement of Alexandria)

Rabbinic Writings

b. B. Bat.	Babylonian Talmud, Tractate Baba Bathra
b. Sanh.	Babylonian Talmud, Tractate Sanhedrin

Texts and Ancient Versions

DSS	Dead Sea Scrolls
LXX	Septuagint
MT	Masoretic Text of the Old Testament

Preface to Second Edition

Much has happened within the discipline of biblical interpretation in the years since the first edition of this book appeared in 1993. Many worthy volumes and innumerable articles, essays, and chapters have appeared steadily over the years. Clearly this remains a "hot topic," as it should. In addition, the landscape of biblical studies and biblical interpretation has changed in many ways. We are faced with new understandings of how language functions, the rise and demise of several approaches to evaluating texts, differing attempts to assess the nature of meaning, and the increased influence of postmodernism, to name a few. Several important translations and versions of the Bible have appeared.

We have been gratified to witness the widespread use of the first edition of this book since it was published. It has served as a textbook in many classes in colleges and seminaries. It has been translated into several other languages and is used widely. But, given the changes over these past years, we welcomed the opportunity to alter the way we said some things, to rearrange some of the parts, to bring some issues from the appendix into the main text, and, *very importantly*, to bring the discussions of many issues, the footnotes, and the annotated bibliography up to date. We have read many reviews of the book and have learned from reviewers and users their assessments of its strengths and weaknesses. As we approached the process of revision, we solicited and received targeted and extremely helpful comments from several valued colleagues in other institutions who have used the book regularly in their classes. We appreciate very much the time and effort they gave us in their assessments.

We offer this volume to advance the practice of biblical interpretation—also called hermeneutics—in this generation. A comprehensive yet readable text, it covers all the key issues in interpreting the Bible. We have incorporated insights from beyond biblical studies themselves—philosophy, linguistics, the social sciences, and literary criticism, among others. We have written this book not merely to collate and report others' findings—though we have certainly done much of that—but also to propose our own strategy for this crucial venture of interpretation. The book brims with biblical examples to demonstrate the principles under discussion. We strive to show students not merely what interpretation is all about, but *how* to interpret.

How did such a book emerge, and how do three authors write a book together? Initially Dr. Klein proposed the idea of a new volume on hermeneutics and wrote the original outline. Soon he realized how formidable a task this would be, so he recruited three colleagues, all professors at Denver Seminary, and they divided the tasks of research and writing equally among themselves. Unexpectedly, other Seminary responsibilities forced Dr. Kermit Ecklebarger to withdraw from the project. He was able to provide input for the chapters on the history of interpretation, general rules of hermeneutics, and application. The task fell to the remaining three—Dr. Klein and Dr. Blomberg covered the New Testament field, and Dr. Hubbard represented Old Testament studies.

To maximize the value of our backgrounds and expertise, we decided that all three would be involved in everything produced. So each wrote his assigned sections and then read the others' drafts. We made extensive comments and suggested revisions, deletions, or insertions. Where genuine differences and disagreements surfaced we discussed the issues until a consensus was reached; we wanted to produce a text that all could affirm. Ultimately, Dr. Klein served as the final editor with freedom to alter and edit as necessary to produce the final manuscript.

Since the first edition appeared, Robert Hubbard moved from Denver to take up a teaching post at North Park Theological Seminary in Chicago. Drs. Blomberg and Klein remain at Denver Seminary. We three employed the same approach in this revision as we did in the initial writing. We returned each chapter to its original author to perform the initial revision—taking into consideration all the reviews and comments we received. We circulated each revised chapter to the other two authors for comments, critique, suggestions for revisions, and corrections, and then returned it to the author for a rewrite in view of these reactions. We were more ruthless with each other than before. When we were satisfied that we had the best product, William Klein again did the final editing. We hope that the resulting volume weds the best of our individual and joint competencies. We have verified the truth of the proverb, "As iron sharpens iron, so one man sharpens another" (Prov 27:17). By absorbing each other's critical comments, we grew to appreciate one another's abilities and understanding of God's truth. We have remained good friends, and we believe our joint efforts have produced a volume that will yield a rich harvest of faithful interpreters and doers of God's Holy Word.

We wish to thank Wayne Kinde, Associate Publisher of Reference & Electronic Publishing at Thomas Nelson, for enthusiastically agreeing to produce this second edition. As well, it was a pleasure to work directly with Lee Hollaway, Managing Editor of Nelson Reference and Professional Books, who helped oversee the project in a hands-on way. We were again assisted and blessed by the efforts of several colleagues at Denver Seminary—with research assistance by Prof. Elodie Emig and the word processing and indexing skills of Ms. Jeanette Freitag. Our research also benefited from sabbaticals granted by our schools, from their fine libraries and expert staffs, and from the input of teaching assistant Paul Corner of North Park Theological Seminary. We also thank the theological faculty of the University of Tübingen, Germany for its hospitality and the use of its excellent libraries during one sabbatical.

No book surfaces apart from the contributions of numerous people beyond the author or, in this case, authors. Dr. Timothy P. Weber graciously read the chapter on the history of interpretation. Dr. M. Daniel Carroll R. provided extensive comments on the chapters on the Old Testament. Our numerous references readily acknowledge the work of our colleagues in the scholarly arena. No doubt many others contributed to our thinking, but we were unaware of their input, gained as it was over the years, and are unable to acknowledge it beyond this admission. Yet four individuals—not adequately featured in the footnotes—have made a lasting impression on our lives. They were our first mentors in graduate biblical studies. They not only honed our skills in interpretation, but they also ignited an enduring love for the Bible. Each stressed the need to know not only *what* the Bible says, but also what the Bible *means* by what it says. We pray that we can pass on the same mindset to our students. We rededicate this second edition to these mentors, three of whom now reside in the presence of their Lord. So we laud Donald W. Burdick (†), D. A. Carson, David A. Hubbard (†), and

A. Berkeley Mickelsen (†). Well might the writer of Hebrews have spoken of this quartet when he admonished:

> "Remember your leaders, who spoke the word of God to you. Consider the outcome of their way of life and imitate their faith" (Heb 13:7).

Thank you, brothers, for what you have meant to us.

—William W. Klein
Craig L. Blomberg
Robert L. Hubbard, Jr.
31 October 2003

INTRODUCTION

Almost daily, the average Christian is challenged to obey God's Word. How well we sense the urgency of Jesus' words to that Israelite woman of long ago, "Blessed rather are those who hear the word of God and obey it!" (Lk 11:28 NRSV). And James' words ring out in our minds: "Do not merely listen to the word, and so deceive yourselves. Do what it says" (Jas 1:22).[1] The Psalmist assures us, "Your word is a lamp to my feet and a light for my path" (Psa 119:105). We believe we can grow in our relationship with God, we can develop into more spiritually-wise disciples, and we can become increasingly useful servants of God—if we will only believe and follow God's instructions in the Bible. How much more effective we could be—how much more Christ-like—if we would make Bible study and application integral parts of our lives. We face the challenge to become *biblical* Christians: Christians who learn what God's Word says, and who humbly, obediently, put it into practice.

But how are we to learn what the Bible says? How do we mine its resources? What are we to learn and how are we to respond? Can we know if we have understood the message correctly? Our goal in writing this book is to help answer these questions, to unravel some of the mysteries of biblical interpretation.

Admittedly, it can be daunting to face a voluminous Bible full of alien genealogies, barbaric practices, strange prophecies, and eccentric epistles. It would be so much simpler if the "experts" would simply assemble God's instructions for us in a nice systematic list. But God himself did not provide a mere list of principles and practices. Dare we reduce the Bible to such a level? However much we might prefer that God's revelation came in a different form, we bow to his wisdom in giving us the Bible as it stands. We are convinced that when we understand the nature of the Bible and what God has done in providing it, we will see that it cannot be reduced to a list of beliefs to espouse, attitudes to adopt, actions to pursue, nor the corresponding opposites to avoid. In his wisdom, God has given his people the kind of revelation he decided would be best for us. Our task is to understand and respond to what God has communicated in ways that demonstrate our obedience and faithfulness to that revelation. We have to come to terms with the Bible *as it is!* And that is precisely what we intend to help the reader accomplish.

But in order to execute the task of correct biblical interpretation, we must first understand what biblical interpretation is. Thus, in *Part I* we define hermeneutics and demonstrate the crucial need for careful and valid hermeneutical principles. To understand how to interpret the Bible today requires an appreciation of our predecessors in the biblical faith. So we investigate the various approaches and techniques people have employed to understand Scripture throughout history. We want to learn from them—appropriating what is valid and valuable while avoiding their mistakes and pitfalls.

---

1 Unless otherwise noted, all Scripture references are from the Holy Bible, New International Version (NIV), copyright © 1973, 1978, 1984, International Bible Society and are used by permission.

In recent years, some biblical scholars and interpreters have issued a call for a radical shift in the focus of interpretation. Several new, and in some cases esoteric, methods have arisen in both literary-critical (e.g., structuralism) and social-scientific (e.g., feminist hermeneutics) studies. While some readers of this textbook may not add all of these tactics to their arsenals of interpretative methods, they offer some definite assistance to interpreters. In addition, their presence on the modern scene requires us to provide students with some assessment of their procedures and usefulness.

A most valuable legacy of our spiritual ancestors is the biblical canon. We provide insight and perspective on the formation of the Bible. In addition, we will consider the phenomenon of Bible translation and seek to help readers navigate through the maze of competing versions available today.

In *Part II* we will consider first the interpreter—the qualifications and presuppositions that are necessary and appropriate for the task of biblical interpretation. Hermeneutics has long been concerned with unraveling the meaning of the ancient texts. But until recently sufficient attention was not given to those seeking to understand that meaning—to the interpreters themselves. Interpreters are not blank slates or empty sponges; who they are contributes greatly to the entire enterprise of understanding. So beyond qualifications and presuppositions, we investigate the concept of "preunderstanding"—what interpreters bring with them to the task of interpretation. Having described the interpreter we will then raise the question of the *goal* of interpretation—what it is that we seek. Is the goal to determine the meaning the authors intended, the meaning in the texts themselves, or the meaning produced when text and modern interpreter interact? Can we say that a text has (or produces) only one possible meaning, or should we seek different meanings or levels of meaning within it? Or, to ask it differently, can texts have meanings that their authors intended while containing an additional meaning or meanings placed there by the Holy Spirit to be recovered by subsequent readers? Can we assure that our interpretations are valid? These are foundational questions, and their answers have enormous implications for our task because issues of life and eternity are determined by a proper understanding of God's message.

In *Part III* we proceed to establish basic, commonly-accepted principles for understanding how literature—both prose and poetry—functions. The Bible is fundamentally a literary document, and we must understand it as such. We survey the various literary, cultural, social, and historical issues involved in interpretation. Since languages function according to specific rules and principles, interpreters must understand these rules in order to study the texts properly. The goal is not to complicate matters, but to achieve better understanding. We aspire to the greatest precision and accuracy in the process of interpretation.

Part IV introduces the reader to the specific kinds of literature (or genres) found in the Bible, and gives an overview of the appropriate methodologies for understanding the meaning conveyed by each. We describe each genre—Law (the Bible's legal material), OT historical narrative, poetry, prophecy, wisdom literature, OT apocalyptic, Gospels, NT historical narrative (Acts), Epistles, and Apocalypse—and show how the interpreter needs to study each one to comprehend its message fully.

Undoubtedly, readers have a variety of reasons for wanting to study the Bible. *Part V* seeks to make accessible the practical wealth of the Bible by investigating, briefly, the various ways it ministers to God's people. Whether they use the Bible to help others (in teaching, preaching, or counseling a friend), or to seek for personal spiritual encouragement, or simply to worship the God of the universe, the Bible has proved its value since its origin. What is more, the Bible serves as the source book for the Church's theology—for its understanding of God's perspective on life and his will for his people.

In essence, the Bible is God's written revelation to his people. It records in human words what God has mandated for them. Thus, a significant question for every student of the Bible is: How can we *apply* the Bible to our lives today? *Part V* considers this essential question of personal application. This task is not easy, for the Bible message moves across centuries and cultures. And precisely because the Bible came to people within their own cultures and experiences thousands of years ago, modern Christians are not always sure how literally they should implement what the Bible commands. They are puzzled about how to move from the principles in a passage to appropriate modern application. When we read what God required of the ancient Israelites or the first-century Christians, we puzzle over his expectations for us today. If pork and shrimp were forbidden for God's people in 1200 B.C. (Lev 11:7, 10-12), on what basis, if any, can we rescind that prohibition today? If Paul required women in the Corinthian church of A.D. 57 to wear appropriate head coverings (1 Cor 11:4–6, 13), may twenty first-century women disregard his instructions? Why do we insist on following Jesus' instructions to his disciples: "This is my body given for you; *do this* in remembrance of me" (Lk 22:18)? Should we not also perform his other clear instruction: ". . . you also should wash one another's feet. I have set you an example that *you should do* as I have done for you" (Jn 13:14–15)? These are pivotal issues for the Christian who sincerely wants to apply the Bible correctly to his or her life.

To aid biblical interpreters, whether novice or experienced, we have provided an Annotated Bibliography of suggested helps. As carpenters, secretaries, or surgeons require tools to do their work, so interpreters need specific tools. Throughout the book we argue for a responsible approach to discerning the meaning of the biblical texts. That approach often requires insights and information accumulated by specialists. In this final section we show why appropriate tools are necessary; we explain how to use them; and then we list those we feel interpreters will find most useful. The Bibliography is a practical list for students to *use* in Bible interpretation. For the more technical details and documentation of the approach to biblical interpretation developed in this book, readers can consult the footnotes at appropriate points.

We have a final word to teachers who employ this as a textbook: each chapter was designed to be self-contained in scope. The chapters can be assigned for study in various sequences, for each can stand on its own. This also means there is some minor overlap and repetition in the discussions of a few topics. We usually cross-reference topics to alert readers to locations where an issue receives more detailed discussion.

PART I—THE TASK OF INTERPRETATION

1

THE NEED FOR
HERMENEUTICS

Correctly understanding Scripture is an arduous and often puzzling task. Consider some of the difficult tensions we face in this task:

♦ The Bible is God's Word, yet it has come to us through human means. The commands of God appear to be absolute, yet they are set in such diverse historical contexts that we are hard-pressed to see how they can be universally normative.

♦ The divine message must be clear, yet many passages seem all too ambiguous.

♦ We acknowledge the crucial role of the Holy Spirit, yet scholarship is surely necessary to understand what the Spirit has inspired.

♦ The Scriptures present the message God wants us to hear, but that message is conveyed within a complex literary landscape with varied genres and over a huge span of time.

♦ Proper interpretation requires the interpreter's personal freedom, yet that freedom comes with considerable risks of bias and distortion. Is there some role for an external, corporate authority?

♦ The objectivity of the biblical message seems essential to some readers, yet on the one hand, presuppositions surely inject a degree of subjectivity into the interpretive process, while, on the other, postmodernity calls the very concept of objectivity into question.[1]

No doubt every student of the Bible could add his own list of troublesome and perplexing issues. How can we be successful in our attempts to understand the Scriptures correctly? We need a well-thought-out approach to interpreting the Bible. And that is precisely where hermeneutics comes in.

---

1 Adapted from M. Silva, *Has the Church Misread the Bible?* (Grand Rapids: Zondervan, 1987), 37–38.

Hermeneutics describes the task of explaining the meaning of the Scriptures. The word derives from the Greek verb *hermeneuein* that means "to explain, interpret or to translate," while the noun *hermeneia* means "interpretation" or "translation." Using the verb, Luke informs us that Jesus *explained* to the two disciples on the Emmaus road what the Scriptures said about him (Lk 24:27). Paul uses the noun in 1 Cor 12:10 to refer to the gift of *interpretation* of tongues. In essence, then, hermeneutics involves interpreting or explaining. In fields like biblical studies or literature, it refers to the task of explaining the meaning of a piece of writing. Hermeneutics describes the principles people use to understand what something means, to comprehend what a message—written, oral, or visual—is endeavoring to communicate.

WHY HERMENEUTICS?

But what does hermeneutics have to do with reading and understanding the Bible? Haven't God's people through the millennia read and understood the Scriptures without recourse to hermeneutics? Actually, the answer to this second question is, no. For though we might not always be conscious of it, without an organized approach or means to understanding we would not be able to comprehend anything.

Think of normal everyday life. We engage in conversations or read a newspaper, and we unconsciously interpret and understand the meanings we hear or read. When we watch a television program, listen to a lecture, or read an article about a familiar subject in our own culture and language, we interpret intuitively and without consciously thinking of using methods. Though unaware of it, we employ methods of interpretation that enable us to understand accurately. This explains why normal communication "works." If there were no system, understanding would occur only randomly or occasionally, if at all.

But is reading the Bible like this? Can we understand the Bible correctly merely by reading it? Some Christians are convinced that we can. One seminary professor tells how a crying student once interrupted a seminar on principles for understanding the Bible. Fearful that he might have offended the student, the teacher asked if anything was wrong.

Sobbing, the student responded, "I am crying because I feel so sorry for you." "Why do you feel sorry for me?" The professor was perplexed. "Because," said the student, "it is so hard for you to understand the Bible. I just read it and God shows me the meaning."

While this approach to biblical interpretation may reflect a commendable confidence in God, it reveals a simplistic (and potentially dangerous) understanding of the illumination of the Holy Spirit and the clarity of Scripture. As we will see, the role of the Spirit in understanding God's Word is indispensable. The Spirit convinces God's people of the truth of the biblical message, and then convicts and enables them to live consistently with that truth. The Spirit does not inform us of Scripture's *meaning.* That is, the Spirit's help does not replace the need to interpret biblical passages according to the principles of language communication. Through the centuries, if people have correctly understood God's Word, it is because they have employed proper principles and methods of interpretation. That does not mean, of course, that they all had "formal" biblical training. Rather, they were good readers—they used common sense and had enough background to read accurately. What this book aspires to do, then, is to surface and clarify what makes a "good reader" and to provide the principles to enable Bible-readers to read well and avoid mistakes.

The need for such principles becomes more obvious in an unfamiliar domain—such as a lecture on astrophysics or a highly technical legal document. Terms, expressions, and concepts are strange and perhaps incomprehensible. We immediately perceive a need for help in deciphering the message. How are we to make sense of antiquarks, the weak anthropic principle, or neutrinos? Who can tell us how to distinguish a *habeas corpus* from a *corpus delicti?* It will not do simply to make up our own meanings, nor merely to ask anyone who might be readily at hand. We need the help of a specialized dictionary. Taking a physics class might help in the first situation, while consulting a lawyer would be helpful in the second.

At times even the most straightforward communication is not so straightforward. For example, to understand a father's statement to his daughter, "You will be home by midnight, won't you?" will probably require decoding various cues beyond the simple meanings of individual words. To determine whether this is an inquiry, an assumption, or a command will require a careful analysis of the entire situation. How much more complicated this task is when one seeks to decode an ancient text written by people in centuries past! What does Gen 1:2 have in mind when it says, "Now the earth was formless and empty, darkness was over the surface of the deep"? What lies behind John's words when he writes the simple words, "Jesus wept" (Jn 11:35)? Just think of the great distances of time and culture between those ancient writers and us.

If the goal is correct understanding of communication, we need an approach and methods that are appropriate to the task. Hermeneutics provides the means for acquiring an understanding of the Scriptures. To avoid interpretation that is arbitrary, erroneous, or that simply suits personal whim, the reader needs methods and principles for guidance. A deliberate attempt to interpret based on sensible and agreed-upon principles becomes the best guarantee that an interpretation will be accurate. When we consciously set out to discover and employ such principles, we investigate hermeneutics. Thus, the basic goal of this book will be to establish, explain, and demonstrate guidelines and methods to guide those who want to understand Scripture correctly.

HERMENEUTICS DEFINED

The Art and Science of Interpretation

Interpretation is neither an art nor a science; it is *both* a science *and* an art. Every form of communications uses "codes" of some sort—cues in sounds, spelling, tone of voice, etc.—to convey meaning. We use rules, principles, methods, and tactics to "decode" them when we enter the worlds of the historian, sociologist, psychologist, and linguist—to name a few. Yet, human communication cannot be reduced solely to quantifiable and precise rules. No mechanical system of rules will ever help one understand correctly all the implications or nuances in the three words "I love you" as spoken by a teenage girl to her boyfriend, a husband to his wife of twenty-five years, a mother to her child, or an aging baby boomer to his mint-condition '54 Chevy. This is where the "art" of interpretation enters in. Adults may think they understand the words "awesome," "sweet," or "dude"[2] (or any popular teenage word), but without knowing the codes of a specific youth subculture, they may be wide of the mark. Similarly, youth may find words of their parents like "far out" or "smashing"—words common in their youth—unintelligible.

In light of this, how much more must modern biblical interpreters seek to bridge the linguistic, historical, social, and cultural gaps that exist between the ancient and

---

2 Is a "dude" a cowboy, a guy, or merely a sentence starter akin to "man" in "Man, is that a cool shirt"? It all depends on the context.

modern worlds so that they may understand what texts mean. We assume that people communicate in order to be understood, and this includes the authors of the Scriptures. Hermeneutics provides a strategy that will enable us to understand what an author or speaker intended to communicate.

Of course, this presumes that there is only one possible meaning of a text or utterance, and that our goal is to understand the author's intention in writing that text. But it is not that simple. Perhaps, given a specific text, we must ask whether it has only one correct meaning or whether it may accommodate several or even an infinite number of possible meanings (perhaps at different levels). On one end of the spectrum, some say that the only correct meaning of a text is that single meaning the original author intended it to have.[3] On the other end stand those who argue that meaning is a function of readers, not authors, and that any text's meaning depends upon the readers' perception of it.[4] Readers, they say, actually "create" the meaning of a text in the process of reading it. Between the two stand other options. Perhaps meaning resides independently in the texts themselves, regardless of what the author meant or of what later readers understand from them. Or perhaps meaning results from some dynamic, complex dialogue between a reader and a text. These issues are crucial because our definition of the task of hermeneutics will depend on our answer to where meaning resides—in a text, in the mind of the reader, or in some combination of the two?[5]

---

3 The name often associated with the stress on meaning as a function of authorial intention is E. D. Hirsch. He articulates and defends this view in *Validity in Interpretation* (New Haven: Yale University Press, 1967) and *The Aims of Interpretation* (Chicago: University of Chicago, 1976). An early proponent in the field of biblical studies was K. Stendahl, "Implications of Form Criticism and Tradition Criticism for Biblical Interpretation," *JBL* 77 (1958): 33–38.

4 A key figure among the several we could mention is S. E. Fish. See his seminal work *Is There a Text in This Class? The Authority of Interpretive Communities* (London and Cambridge, MA: Harvard University Press, 1980).

5 Two points require clarification here. First, in this volume we are using the term hermeneutics in what might be called its traditional sense: a systematic study of principles and methods of interpretation. Seminal thinkers like Schleiermacher, Dilthey, Heidegger, Fuchs, Ebeling, Gadamer, and Ricoeur use hermeneutics in a more philosophical sense to identify how something in the past can "mean" today or become existentially significant in the modern world. The term "new hermeneutic" describes this program to move hermeneutics from mere rules for understanding texts to a more far-reaching understanding of understanding. Its practitioners would say they have shifted hermeneutics out of the realm of merely explaining, to providing an in-depth understanding of human existence. To fathom the intricacies of the "new hermeneutic" requires a separate discussion that lies beyond our scope here. Some further perspectives will be presented in the chapters that follow. We refer readers to A.C. Thiselton, *The Two Horizons: New Testament Hermeneutics and Philosophical Description with Special Reference to Heidegger, Bultmann, Gadamer, and Wittgenstein* (Exeter: Paternoster; Grand Rapids: Eerdmans, 1980); id., *New Horizons in Hermeneutics* (Grand Rapids: Zondervan, 1992); E.V. McKnight, *Meaning in Texts* (Philadelphia: Fortress, 1978); and K. J. Vanhoozer, *Is There a Meaning in This Text?* (Grand Rapids: Zondervan, 1998). Second, readers will sometimes encounter the singular term "hermeneutic." Typically, this refers to a specific and self-acknowledged standpoint or frame of reference that an interpreter adopts to interpret a text or utterance. Usually this approach implies an established ideology, specific attitudes, and a definite approach. Thus, a "feminist hermeneutic" will adopt a way of reading a text that conforms to the premeditated confines of a feminist ideology. Substitute "womanist," "African-American," "Marxist," "*mujerista*," "liberation," "homosexual," or "Freudian" for the word "feminist" and you can see how adopting a frame of reference will program a reading or hermeneutic of the text.

The Role of the Interpreter

What role does the interpreter play in the hermeneutical process? We must realize that just as the biblical text arose within historical, personal processes and circumstances, so interpreters are people in the midst of their personal circumstances and situations. For example, the phrase "white as snow" may strike a resident of Colorado as comprehensible but rather inconsequential; more important are details about packed snow on wintry ski slopes. In contrast, the phrase will be totally incomprehensible to a tribesman from Kalimantan who has no idea what snow is, much less what color it is. Then the resident of Chicago will have another perspective, wistfully recalling what used to be white while grumbling about the dirty, rutted, frozen snow that impedes the commute to work. In other words, people understand their world on the basis of what they already know or have experienced. Does this mean that because we live in an age and location far removed from people of the Bible we are doomed to misunderstand its message? No, we simply need approaches and tools that will guide us to interpret it as accurately as possible—that is, to become better readers—and we need to take into account the presuppositions and preunderstandings we bring to the task of interpretation. To fail to do so leaves us open to distortion and misunderstanding.

Thus, while hermeneutics must give attention to the ancient text and the conditions that produced it, responsible interpretation cannot ignore the modern context and the circumstances of those who attempt to explain the Scriptures today. No one interprets in a vacuum: everyone has presuppositions and preunderstandings. Dr. Basil Jackson, a leading Christian psychiatrist, learned this hermeneutical lesson during his youth when a Plymouth Brethren elder in Ireland told him, "Wonderful things in the Bible I see, most of them put there by you and me."[6] To what extent is this a problem?

On the other hand, no one can interpret without some preunderstanding of the subject.[7] Yet no one should approach biblical interpretation with only preunderstanding. Those who read the Bible only from the perspective of their immediate personal circumstances, who forget that the passage was originally written to somebody else, cut short the interpretive process and, thus, miss some of what the text says. They understand the message strictly in terms of the events going on in their own lives and ignore the perspective of the text and its original recipients. This results in serious misunderstanding like that reported by a Christian counselor. A woman explained to her therapist that God had told her to divorce her husband and marry another man (with whom she was romantically involved). She cited Paul's command in Eph 4:24 (KJV), "Put on the new man," as the key to her "divine" guidance. As humorous as this sounds, she was absolutely serious.[8] Although modern translations clarify that Paul was instructing believers to replace their sinful lifestyle with a Christian one, this woman, preoccupied with her marital problems, read her own meaning into the passage. Is what she did wrong? Can't we discover our own meaning in the Bible, and if not, why not?

Is an accurate analysis of the Bible, then, simply a matter of applying with absolute honesty and accuracy certain precise techniques? Things are not so simple. When we try to understand each other's communication, scientific precision seems to elude our

---

6 B. Jackson, quotation from a lecture at Denver Seminary, March 1991.

7 On these points see the classic article by R. Bultmann, "Is Exegesis Without Presuppositions Possible?" in *Existence and Faith,* ed. S. Ogden (London: Hodder and Stoughton, 1961), 289–96.

8 H. L. Bussell, *Unholy Devotions* (Grand Rapids: Zondervan, 1983), 119.

grasp. In fact, even the so-called objective or hard-science researchers recognize the influence of values. D. Tracy observes,

> Former claims for a value-free technology and a history-free science have collapsed. The hermeneutical character of science has now been strongly affirmed. Even in science, we must interpret in order to understand.[9]

No one comes to the task of understanding as an objective observer. All interpreters bring their own presuppositions and agendas, and these affect the ways they understand as well as the conclusions they draw.[10] In addition, the writer or speaker whom the interpreter wishes to understand also operates with a set of presuppositions. We humans mediate all our understanding through a grid of personal history and bias. Our prior experiences and knowledge—our total background—shape what we perceive and how we understand. So can we study Scripture texts objectively and accurately? Though we will argue that objective certainty in interpretation will always elude our grasp, we do propose a critical hermeneutical approach that will provide standards and tactics to guide us in navigating through the variable and subjective human factors.

The Meaning of the Message

Any type of oral or written communication involves three expressions of meaning: (1) what the speaker or writer meant by what he or she said; (2) what the recipient actually understood by the statement; and (3) in some abstract sense, what meaning is actually encoded in the text or utterance itself.[11] Another helpful way to define a text occurs in Vanhoozer: "A text is a complex communicative act with *matter* (propositional content), *energy* (illocutionary force), and *purpose* (perlocutionary effect)."[12] Authors may occasionally unconsciously convey more than they intended, but the point is that they normally determine *what* they will say, *how* they will encode their message, and what *results* they hope to achieve. Of course when we seek to understand the meaning of a biblical text, all we have is the text itself. The author's intended meaning cannot be fully

---

9 D. Tracy, *Plurality and Ambiguity: Hermeneutics, Religion, Hope* (San Francisco: Harper, 1987), 33.

10 Those who believe that women can be ordained ministers have no difficulty detecting those biblical passages that emphasize the crucial role women played in biblical history. Yet those who argue for the traditional understanding of the role of women in the Church that precludes ordination point to those passages they believe teach the subordination of women. Presuppositions and agendas clearly influence what evidence interpreters value more highly. A classic documentation of this phenomenon occurs in W. Swartley, *Slavery, Sabbath, War, and Women* (Scottdale, PA: Herald Press, 1983).

11 Following a more semantically based model, G. B. Caird investigates the phenomenon of meaning in some detail in *The Language and Imagery of the Bible* (Philadelphia: Westminster, 1980), especially pp. 32–61. Under "meaning" he assesses referential meaning, sense, value, entailment, and intention. The overlap with our three categories is clear. The meaning encoded in the text itself probably relates most closely with referential meaning, though that in no way exhausts what a text "means." For valuable discussions of these semantic relations see J. Lyons, *Semantics*, 2 vols. (Cambridge: Cambridge University Press, 1977) and id., *Linguistic Semantics: An Introduction* (Cambridge: Cambridge University Press, 1996).

12 Vanhoozer, *Is There a Meaning?* 228.

uncovered since he or she is no longer available to explain what was "meant." The first hearers or readers remain equally inaccessible, so we cannot ask them to tell us how they understood the message. Only by means of the written text itself can we reconstruct the meaning the author most likely intended and the meaning the first recipients most likely understood. Any appraisal of "meaning," then, must take into consideration this complex coalition of text, author, and audience.

The Text

How can the utterance or text itself help in discovering the message the author intended to convey or the message the hearers understood? Clearly, one basic factor is to determine the meanings of the terms that are used. We must adopt an approach to understanding the meaning of words that considers precisely their referential, denotative, connotative, and contextual meanings. Briefly, *referential* meaning specifies what some words or terms "refer to." In other words, part of the meaning of the word "tree" is a large leafy plant growing outside that bears apples in the fall. Denotative and connotative meanings speak of complementary aspects of a word's meaning. Words may denote a specific meaning. A biologist could provide a specific, scientific definition of tree[13] that would represent its *denotative* meaning. But in a specific instance the word "tree" might take on special definitive meanings or *connotations*, as when Peter observes that Jesus died on a tree (1 Pet 2:24). In that instance the term comes to have a unique significance for Christians for whom "tree" warmly recalls what Jesus did for them in giving his life. Connotations, then, are a word's emotional overtones—the positive or negative associations it conjures up beyond what the word strictly denotes. The "hanging tree" used for executing criminals also conveys connotative meaning—a sad, sober feeling for crimes and their victims. In these uses, tree means more than the biologist's explanation, just as that scientific explanation pales before the picture or view of a mighty oak tree in the yard. Peter's use also illustrates *contextual* meaning, for when we read his words we quickly conclude that he does not refer to a literal tree at all. In the context, tree means "cross."

Of course words do not occur in isolation in a text. All languages present their words in a system of grammatical and literary structures—sentences, paragraphs, poems, discourses, and whole books. We must understand how the biblical languages function if we are to understand what the writers meant to say. A larger dimension involved in understanding an utterance is the specific literary genre or writing style the author employed to convey his or her message (illocutionary force). We interpret the words in a poem differently from those in a letter when we know we are looking at a poem rather than a letter, or vice versa. We expect ambiguity or figures of speech to convey a meaning in poetry that is different from the more concrete sense of words in a historical narrative.

In fact, much recent study has focused upon the literary dimensions of the Bible, of both individual passages and whole books, and any responsible procedure to interpret Scripture must address this dimension.[14] When we receive a letter in the mail, we

---

13 For example, a tree is a woody perennial plant at least several feet high that has a single erect main stem and side branches growing out of the stem.

14 For an introduction to the Bible's literary features, see our later chapters on prose, poetry, and genres.

expect it to follow a fairly standard format. For the most part, the biblical writers also used and adapted literary forms and conventions that were standard at the time they wrote. Thus, in order to understand the books of the Bible as literary documents and to appreciate the various dimensions—both cognitive and aesthetic—of what God has given us in the Scriptures, we need to employ the insights and methods of literary criticism. The use of literary critical (or historical) methods to understand the biblical writings need not diminish our conviction that they are the divine Word of God. Their uniqueness as Scripture pertains to their content as God's revelation and to the process God employed to convey his truth. Part of that process included the specific and varying literary features.

What does it mean to study the Bible from a literary standpoint? L. Ryken provides some help. Speaking of the literary dimensions of the NT, he argues that we must be "alive to the images and experiential concreteness of the New Testament" (and the OT, we would hasten to add) while resisting "the impulse to reduce literary texts to abstract propositions or to move beyond the text to the history behind it." Further, "this means a willingness to accept the text on its own terms and to concentrate on reliving the experiences that are presented."[15] To take a literary approach to the Bible means entering, living, and understanding its world before we move beyond it to abstract meaning. It also means that we study the texts in terms of their genres, that is, in keeping with their own conventions and intentions. It requires that we appreciate the artistry and beauty of texts, that we savor the nuances of language, and that we apply appropriate techniques for teasing out the meaning in the extensive poetic sections. Ryken summarizes his principle in the formula "meaning through form." This simply confirms that "we cannot derive the meaning of the New Testament (or the OT) without first examining its form."[16] Part of the meaning recorded in the Bible derives from the forms the authors employed in their writing. We risk missing much of significance if we attempt merely to formulate abstract propositions from the texts we analyze. As we noted above, the meaning of a text embodies not merely "content" but also how it is constructed and to what end. How much of the artistic elegance of passages such as Psa 23 or 1 Cor 13 we will miss if we extract only theological statements. To grasp the text fully—and, more important, to *be grasped* by it fully—means to enjoy the "pleasure of the text," to engage it joyfully and adventurously with our mind, emotions, and imagination.[17]

The Author and the Audience

Although we cannot ask the authors directly for a clue to the meaning they intended to convey, an examination of their respective contexts (general living conditions and specific life circumstances), when known, can provide helpful information for interpretation. Knowing all the conditions that surround the recipients of the original message

---

15 L. Ryken, *Words of Life: A Literary Introduction to the New Testament* (Grand Rapids: Baker, 1987), 22–23.

16 Ryken, *Words of Life*, 24.

17 We borrow the phrase from R. Barthes, *The Pleasure of the Text* (New York: Hill & Want, 1975).

provides further insight into how they most likely understood the message,[18] as does the relationship between the author and recipients at the time of writing.[19]

Of course, if we are seeking the meaning intended by the author to the original recipients, that meaning *must* be the meaning they could understand at that time, not the meaning we would determine based on our position of advanced historical developments. Obviously, we have access to the full canon of Scripture. We know how the whole story turned out, so to speak. However, in seeking to understand the meaning of a given text, we cannot impose insight that is based on later revelation. For example, it would be out of bounds to apply information known from the NT in interpreting an OT text. The first readers could never have known that information. At least we must admit that the human author could not have intended in his message what we know only from subsequent revelation. Further, almost two millennia of history have passed since the last NT book was written. Again, we cannot impose on a biblical author information that we possess because of our accumulated current knowledge. If we read into the biblical texts information the authors could not possess, we distort their meaning. For example, when a biblical writer speaks of the "circle of the earth" (Isa 40:22), he may well employ a flat earth model (that is, as seen from God's heavenly throne, the earth looks like a flat, round disk). To hear him on his terms requires that we resist the temptation to impose our scientific, global worldview upon the text. That is, we must not assume that the word circle implies that the author believed the earth was completely round. Because we know "the rest of the story," we have to make a special effort to recreate how the writers understood things and the impact their words had on their original recipients who lacked our knowledge.

This works on another level as well, because the Bible contains not only the words of the final authors or editors of each book but also the words of people whose stories they report. We may be intensely interested in what the historical Jesus said on specific occasions, but we do not have transcripts of the actual words he spoke (probably in Aramaic).[20] We have only the Evangelists' Gospels, originally written in Greek and now

---

18 Through his analysis of Mark's Gospel, R. H. Stein, "Is Our Reading the Bible the Same as the Original Audience's Hearing It?" *JETS* 46 (2003): 63–78, identifies six key features that describe its intended readers. One crucial finding, one that interpreters often forget, is that Mark's audience originally consisted of *hearers*; they did not read the gospel silently (as you are now reading this footnote). Of course this is true for most of the books in the Bible: they were composed to be heard aloud. How might this affect how we interpret? Among other points, Stein suggests that this likely precludes all the very elaborate structures that scholars sometimes "find" in the biblical books (e.g., book-length chiasms). Normal, unlearned, common believers in the first century had "to process the information being read to them, *as it was being read* " (p. 74). See also, id., "The Benefits of an Author-Oriented Approach to Hermeneutics," *JETS* 44 (2001): 451–66. On the other hand, Stein may be overly cautious here. If books were designed to be read and reread repeatedly, the author could choose to embed more subtle structures.

19 For example, the situation of some NT epistles is simpler than, say, that of OT prophetic oracles. In the former we may be able to isolate such information to aid our understanding of the written text. In the latter we may have little or nothing to help us understand the relationship between a prophet and the original audience who heard his or her spoken message. Likewise, we may be able to discover little if anything about the relationship between the author or editor of the final form of a book of the Bible and the readers—whether an OT prophecy or one of the Gospels. These points illustrate the larger problem with which we must deal as interpreters.

20 Unfortunately, "red letter" editions of the Gospels may give the (mistaken) impression that we have direct quotes.

translated into modern languages. To achieve their purposes for writing, they selected and recast Jesus' words and actions in their unique ways. We do not mean that the Evangelists distorted or misconstrued what Jesus said, nor as some Bible scholars aver, that the Evangelists actually attributed words to Jesus that he never said. Our point is simply that we must take the Bible as it is.

The report that God sent Saul an "evil spirit" (1 Sam 16:14–16, et al.) illustrates how easily we may read later information into our reading of the Old Testament. In the NT an "evil spirit" is a demon (e.g., Mk 1:26 par.), so we naturally assume that the same term identifies the tormentor of Saul as a demon. This assumption overlooks two points of background: to read the OT phrase as "an evil spirit from God" implies that God sends demons on people, a theological assumption unsupported by Scripture because it conflicts with the biblical teaching that God does not associate with "evil." In addition, it wrongly assumes that the OT has an awareness of the demonic world, which does not seem to be the case. Instead, we might better translate the Hebrew as "bad spirit" (i.e., "foul mood" or "depression"; cf. Judg 9:23). Jesus' parable of the Good Samaritan also illustrates our tendency to read a later understanding into our interpretation of biblical texts. When we call the Samaritan "good," we betray how far removed we are from sensing the impact the parable had on the Jewish legal expert who first heard this memorable story (Lk 10:25). We must remember that the Jews despised the Samaritans as half-breeds. How shocked the lawyer would be when Jesus made a hated Samaritan the hero of his story—as shocked as Jews of today would be if one of their storytellers portrayed a Palestinian as more heroic or sympathetic than leading Jewish figures! Accurately understanding the Bible requires that we take into account any preconceptions we carry that could distort the text's meaning. Our goal remains to hear the message of the Bible as the original audiences would have heard it or as the first readers would have understood it.

We must avoid the tendency to regard our own experience as the standard for interpreting what we see and read. All of us seem to suffer from the same malady: to view our own experiences of the world as normative, valid, and true. Naturally, we are inclined to read the Bible through the lens of this tendency. For example, though today we readily see slavery as an abhorrent evil, it is amazing how many leading Christians defended this inhuman institution prior to the U.S. Civil War. Using the book of Philemon, Hopkins defended slavery in the nineteenth century saying:

> He [Paul] finds a fugitive slave, and converts him to the Gospel, and then sends him back again to his old home with a letter of kind recommendation. Why does St. Paul act thus? Why does he not counsel the fugitive to claim his right to freedom, and defend that right . . . ?
>
> The answer is very plain. St. Paul was inspired, and knew the will of the Lord Jesus Christ, and was only intent on obeying it. And who are we, that in our modern wisdom presume to set aside the Word of God?[21]

---

21 J. H. Hopkins, *A Scriptural, Ecclesiastical, and Historical View of Slavery, from the Days of the Patriarch Abraham, to the Nineteenth Century* (New York: W. I. Pooley & Co., 1864), 16, as quoted in Swartley, *Slavery, Sabbath, War, and Women*, 37.

Based on his own worldview and experiences, Hopkins believed slavery was a commendable and biblically sanctioned institution.

Like Hopkins, we may unconsciously assume that our own experiences parallel those of the ancients—that life and landscape are the same now as then. In one sense no one can avoid this outlook. But when we simply allow our unchallenged feelings and observations to distort or determine what the Bible means, our experiences have become the measure for what a text can mean.[22] We must adopt an approach to interpretation that confronts this danger, for Scripture alone constitutes the standard of truth for Christians, and we must judge our values and experiences based on its precepts, not vice-versa. It follows, then, that any valid approach to interpretation must concern itself with two crucial dimensions: (1) an appropriate methodology for deciphering what the text is about, and (2) a means of assessing and accounting for the readers' present situation as we engage in the interpretive process. We must account for both ancient and modern dimensions. In our view, historical and grammatical methods offer us the best means to understand the contours of the ancient world of the text. At the same time, we must somehow delineate the impact that interpreters themselves produce in the process of interpretation.

SOME CHALLENGES OF BIBLE INTERPRETATION

Distance of Time

One word summarizes some of the greatest challenges (and frustrations) the Bible interpreter will face—*distance*. Consider first the distance of *time* that exists between the ancient texts and our modern world. The writings and events recorded in the Bible span many centuries, but more than 1900 years have passed since its last words were written. Simply put, the world has changed in substantial ways since then. Further, most of us lack essential information about the world as it was when the Bible was written. We may be at a loss to understand what a text means because it involves subjects beyond our time span. Even a cursory glance at Hos 10 points to many references that remain incomprehensible to most modern readers: calf-idol of Beth Aven (v. 5); Assyria (v. 6); Ephraim (v. 6); "ashamed of its wooden idols" (v. 6); "the high places" (v. 8); "Did not war overtake the evildoers in Gibeah?" (v. 9); "as Shalman devastated Beth Arbel on the day of battle" (v. 14). What was a calf-idol? Where was Beth Aven, or Assyria, or Ephraim located? What's this about Gibeah? How do we determine the meaning behind historical features that are so far removed in time?

Another time span that must be considered in interpreting the Bible involves the gaps that existed—more or less in various places—between the time the Bible events occurred and the time when those events were actually written down in the texts we now possess. Since the chronology in Genesis goes all the way to the death of the patriarch Joseph, earlier sections like Gen 12—25 probably were written long after their main

---

22 We in the West face the danger of reading the Bible through our experience of prosperity and technology. Is not the "health and wealth gospel"—that God wants all his children to be healthy and wealthy—a prime example of this bias? How many so-called Third World Christians would assume the Bible taught this? Are there no godly and faithful believers in the poverty-stricken areas of the world? Yet the phenomenon is real: consider the differing impact the story of the abused concubine (Judg 19) has on men versus women due to what they *bring* to the text.

character, Abraham, died. When God created the universe (Gen 1), he was the only one there the first five days, and since Hebrew as a distinct language probably emerged ca. 1000 B.C., obviously someone wrote the report later than that. We may date the ministry of the prophet Amos to the mid-eighth century B.C., but it is very likely that his words were collected into the biblical book known by his name by someone else at a later date. Though Jesus' ministry probably spanned the years A.D. 27–30, our Gospels were not written until at least several decades later. This means that our interpretation must reckon both with the situation on the day Amos or Jesus originally spoke and with the situation (i.e., date, purpose) in which later people wrote down and compiled their words. Certainly, both the Jewish and Christian traditions cared deeply about preserving and transmitting information accurately. Yet the authors' unique perspectives and their goals for writing would influence what they felt was important, what deserved emphasis, or what might be omitted. In this process the writers would consider their readers and the effects they hoped to produce in them.

Certainly, some of the biblical authors were eyewitnesses and wrote strictly out of their own experiences. Others incorporated additional sources into their own accounts. Still others had little or no personal contact with the people and events about which they wrote.[23] Once we recognize that many of the biblical writers employed or edited preexisting materials (and sometimes, several renditions alongside each other), we must evaluate the roles and motives of these editors. So, for example, after learning from one biblical historian that Solomon, not David, would build the temple (2 Sam 7:12–13), and reading that he in fact did so four years after David's death (1 Kgs 2:10; 6:1), the Chronicler's long report of David's extensive preparations for the temple's construction and worship system comes as a complete surprise (1 Chr 22—26; 28—29; cf. 2 Chr 8:14; 29:25; 35:15).[24] Apparently, while the editor of Kings omitted David's temple preparation, the Chronicler makes David the virtual founder of temple worship, in our view, to root restored, post-exilic temple worship in the Davidic covenant. Similarly, if we are aware that Matthew hoped to persuade Jews in his locale not to repeat the mistake of Jesus' Jewish contemporaries, we have a better understanding of his constant use of OT quotes and allusions. His message to that particular audience shouts: Jesus is the Messiah, and you must acknowledge him. The books of the Bible are literary pieces, carefully crafted to sound their themes, not transcripts or merely scissors-and-paste collections put together naively, haphazardly, or even chronologically.

Cultural Distance

Another challenge of distance that must be considered is the *cultural* distance that separates us from the world of the biblical texts. The biblical world was essentially agrarian,

---

23 Luke admits this last category in his introduction to the third Gospel (Lk 1:1–4). There he informs Theophilus that he "carefully investigated everything from the beginning." In our estimation, the "we" sections in Acts (16:10–17; 20:5–15; 21:1–18; 27:1—28:16) indicate that Luke participated with Paul in some of the incidents recorded there. If we adopt the commonly accepted explanation of the origin of the Gospels, we must conclude that when writing their Gospels both Luke and Matthew employed several sources. See R. H. Stein, *Studying the Synoptic Gospels: Origin and Interpretation*, 2d ed. (Grand Rapids: Baker, 2001) for a sane appraisal of this issue.

24 Notice also that the Chronicler, writing two centuries after the completion of Kgs (ca. 350 B.C.), seems aware that his portrait of David differs from that of the latter because he twice takes pains to explain that David made those preparations because of Solomon's youth and experience (1 Chr 22:5; 29:1).

made up of landowners and tenant farmers using machinery that was primitive by our standards and methods of travel that were slow and wearying. On the pages of the Bible we encounter customs, beliefs, and practices that make little sense to us. Why would people in the ancient world anoint priests and kings, and sick people, with oil? What is the sandal custom for the redemption and transfer of property mentioned in Ruth 4:6–8? What was the point of the Levitical purity laws or the many other seemingly pointless requirements? For example, Lev 19:19 seems to rule out most of the garments we wear today: "Do not wear clothing woven of two kinds of material." What about today's polyester and wool blends? And why were tattoos forbidden in Lev 19:28? Are they still?

In addition, our understanding of ancient customs might be so colored by what we think they mean that we miss their significance. For example, what does "head covering" mean in 1 Cor 11:4–16? Are we to understand this in terms of a hat? It is possible that after reading some translations we will instinctively assume that Paul refers to veils, so we envision the veil that Middle Eastern Muslim women wear today. Yet hats or veils may not be in view at all. We may need to research further to properly understand the subject and its significance. Likewise, a western concern for cleanliness might not help (it might even hinder) our understanding of the Pharisees' practice of ceremonial washing (Mk 7:3–5). We must discipline ourselves to determine carefully the significance of the customs and concepts of the biblical world that are foreign to us. We cannot simply pick up the Bible and read it like today's newspaper.

Finally, we must be aware that the grid of our cultural values and priorities sometimes may inadvertently affect our interpretation and cause us to establish a meaning that may not be in the text at all.[25] For example, in the West individualism so pervades our thinking that even in the Church we encounter interpretations that focus on individuals and never think about testing whether the text may actually have more corporate intentions.[26] For instance, readers familiar with modern contests between individuals might view the battle between the boy David and the Philistine Goliath as simply two enemies going "one-on-one" (1 Sam 17). In fact, the episode follows the ancient custom of "representative combat" in which armies let a winner-take-all contest between two soldiers decide the victorious army rather than slaughter each other on the battlefield. Each contestant competes as if he were the whole army. Similarly, some readers conclude that in 1 Cor 3:16–17 Paul's reference to God's temple indicates instructions to individual Christians. Hence they explore how Christians can build proper qualities in their personal lives. They read individualism into the passage despite clear references in the context that Paul is referring to the corporate Body of Christ as a temple in which God's Spirit dwells. Individual Christians form one temple—on a local or worldwide level—not many individual ones.[27]

---

25 For a handy introduction to the cultural values of the U.S. in the latter decades of the twentieth century, see R. Bellah, et al., *Habits of the Heart. Individualism and Commitment in American Life*, 2d ed. (Berkeley: University of California Press, 1996).

26 For further insight on corporate elements in the Bible see, e.g., E. Best, *One Body in Christ* (London: SPCK, 1955); B. J. Malina, *The New Testament World*, 3d ed. (Louisville: Westminster John Knox, 2001); R. Shedd, *Man in Community* (London: Epworth, 1958); H. W. Robinson, *Corporate Personality in Ancient Israel* (Philadelphia: Fortress, 1964); and W. W. Klein, *The New Chosen People: A Corporate View of Election* (Grand Rapids: Zondervan, 1990; Eugene, Oregon: Wipf & Stock, 2001).

27 See A. C. Thiselton, *The First Epistle to the Corinthians*, NICNT (Carlisle, UK: Paternoster; Grand Rapids: Eerdmans, 2000), 316.

In the metaphor, Paul cooperates in building the Church (3:10). As in this instance, a cultural value has inadvertently produced an interpretation that is not inherent in the text at all.

Geographical Distance

Another challenge to correct Bible interpretation is *geographical* distance. Unless we have had the opportunity to visit the places mentioned in the Bible, we lack a mental, visual data bank that would aid our understanding of certain events. Of course, even if we could visit all the accessible sites (and many Christians have), few of them retain the look (and none, the culture) they had in biblical times. In other words, we have difficulty picturing why the NT speaks of people going "up" to Jerusalem from Caesarea (Acts 21:12) or "down" from Jerusalem to Jericho (Lk 10:30) unless we know the differences in elevation. Perhaps less trivial, though in many parts of the world we dig graves "down" into the earth, in Palestine graves were often dug into limestone outcroppings (or existing caves were used and were sealed with a stone). So the phrase, "he was gathered to his people/fathers" (Gen 49:29, 33; 2 Kgs 22:20), may have originated from the practice of collecting the bones of the deceased after the flesh had decomposed and putting them in a location with those of the ancestors. Likewise, knowledge of geography helps us understand why Jonah, in seeking to avoid God's call to prophesy against Assyria (way east), headed for Tarshish (way west).

Distance of Language

The task of biblical interpretation is further challenged by a *language* gap between the biblical world and our own. The writers of the Bible wrote in the languages of their day—Hebrew, Aramaic, and Greek—languages that are inaccessible to most people today. Hebrew has different forms for masculine and feminine nouns, pronouns, and verbs, so English "you" hides whether the Hebrew word it translates is singular or plural and masculine or feminine. The plural "they" is expressed in one gender or the other. We are also relatively unfamiliar with the literary conventions of the ancient authors. We depend upon trained biblical scholars to translate the biblical languages and their literary devices into our native tongues, but their work is necessarily interpretive. Note, for example, the difference in translations of 1 Cor 7:1 in a variety of versions. The NIV renders the final clause, "It is good for a man not to marry." Compare this with the KJV/RSV, "It is good (or well) for a man not to touch a woman"; Phillips, "It is a good principle for a man to have no physical contact with women"; and NEB, "it is a good thing for a man to have nothing to do with women." Finally, the revision of the NIV, the TNIV, puts forward what is probably the most likely meaning: "It is good for a man not to have sexual relations with a woman."[28] The verb translated "touch" is a euphemism for sexual intercourse (cf. "sleep with" today), so the versions that capture that point are likely to be correct. Since these versions diverge so markedly, how would an English reader understand what Paul really meant apart from some help with the cultural situation? In addition, the desire to supply "gender neutral" versions makes the translation process even more complex. In both Hebrew and Greek the word translated "man" (masc. sing.) often refers to both males and females. For example, when Paul

---

28 On this point see G. D. Fee, *The First Epistle to the Corinthians*, NICNT (Grand Rapids: Eerdmans, 1987), 275.

says, "if any man be in Christ" (2 Cor 5:17 KJV), he clearly does not mean that only males can be saved. So one may rightly translate the phrase, "if anyone is in Christ" (e.g., NIV, NRSV; cf. Deut 19:16; 21:1). The distances between the various biblical worlds and our own require careful historical study if we are to understand those worlds and what people wrote in the Bible.

ETERNAL RELEVANCE—THE DIVINE FACTOR

Though the Bible originates through human agents in the most human circumstances of life, it is first and foremost God's word to his people; it has an "eternal relevance."[29] While we have demonstrated the humanness of the Bible and have emphasized that we must treat it in many ways like other books, this does not diminish in any way its quality as a divine book. We assert that critical methods of interpretation alone will never do complete justice to Scripture if they exclude its theological and spiritual dimensions from consideration. To affirm that the Bible is God's Word does not mean we believe God dictated a series of propositions out of heaven for people simply to receive intact and obey. The presence of the many writing styles and genres within its pages refutes any such conclusion. Historically, Christians have affirmed that God inspired human authors to compose the Scriptures as a means to convey his truth, albeit through the matrix of human words reporting human circumstances and events and through diverse kinds of literature. Paul speaks of the Scriptures as "God-breathed" or inspired (2 Tim 3:16), while Peter avers that in Scripture people spoke God's message as they were "carried along" by the Holy Spirit (2 Pet 1:21). Verses like these assert the Bible's "divine factor," God's sovereign shaping of *all* its dimensions—human, theological, and spiritual. Historical and rational methods of interpretation have a proper place in unfolding its human dimension; however, they can take us only so far in the interpretive process. We must consider in more detail below, when we discuss the qualifications of the interpreter, those factors we believe will enable readers better to appreciate and understand the "spiritual dimensions" of the biblical text.

No doubt, the mere mention of historical and rational methods of interpretation raises questions in the minds of many sincere Christians. They may feel with some justification that the scholars and their historical-critical methods have done great damage to a high view of the Bible and to the faith of countless people. They may view scholarship as a subtle threat or even as a hostile enemy. At best, they perceive it as largely irrelevant to the faith of believers and the mission of the Church in the world. No doubt, many academics contribute to this perception, for they do their work with no concern for the faithful who believe that the Bible is God's Word. They may even leave the impression that their mission is to dispel religious myths and to show that the Bible is merely a human book that records the religious beliefs and aspirations of a disparate array of ancient Jewish and Christian writers.[30]

---

29 G. D. Fee and D. K. Stuart, *How to Read the Bible for All It's Worth,* 2d ed. (Grand Rapids: Zondervan, 1993), 17.

30 One of the avowed objectives of the "Jesus Seminar" is to wrest the Bible from dogmatic interpretations. It seeks to determine using critical scholarly methods which of the 176 events in the Gospels that record words and deeds of Jesus actually occurred. Their consensus is that only 16% of the deeds and 18% of the words did. See R. W. Funk, *The Acts of Jesus. The Search for the Authentic Deeds* (San Francisco: HarperCollins, 1998).

However, the fact that some scholars employ critical methods in what many Christians perceive as destructive ways should not drive us to reject such methods. The culprit (if there is one) is not historical or rational methods per se, but rather the *presuppositions* of some of those who use them. Believers, we assert, must not ignore the insights that accurate and precise critical methods bring, for Christians are committed to the truth. Biases that distort the texts' meaning have no place in our work. Admittedly, some scholars have biases that do not allow for supernatural occurrences, while others have biases that accept them. Some seem to exclude any role for a God who interacts with his creation and with his people, while others strongly affirm such a deity. As we will examine in more detail below, all interpreters come with preunderstandings and presuppositions. None comes to interpret with "disinterested objectivity." The danger, however, is that some believers may refuse to acknowledge the usefulness of any scholarly achievements.[31] Instead, we suggest that they should welcome valid historical and rational methods that properly control the impact of unwarranted and truth-distorting biases.

When the methods of scholars uncover what is true, as believers we are committed to welcome and incorporate these findings into own interpretations.[32] On the other hand, we may deem unacceptable other conclusions or conjectures where an interpretation simply accounted for historical and literary dimensions of the text in purely rationalistic terms. We believe valid interpretation must account for the "divine factor" of the text (i.e., all its dimensions) and accept what God says through it to his people. Though we never will condone believing what is untrue, we affirm that rationalistic scholarship alone cannot fully discover truth in the Bible.

The Goal of Hermeneutics

We would be misguided if we limited hermeneutics to the factors and issues that concern our understanding of the ancient text. People do not usually seek to understand the Bible as a mere intellectual exercise. Certainly, the biblical authors never intended their writings to be objects of such study. Nor do historians who aspire to understand the causes or the results of the ancient Punic Wars attempt to apply what they discover to their personal lives.[33] However, Christian believers study the Bible precisely because

---

31 Some conservative scholars appear to decry the very presence of historical criticism: R. L. Thomas and F. D. Farnell, ed., *The Jesus Crisis: The Inroads of Historical Criticism into Evangelical Scholarship* (Grand Rapids: Kregel, 1998). We think this is misguided.

32 Admittedly, a key question arises: how do we determine what is true? Surely a scholarly consensus contributes to assurances that results are true or correct. When accepted historical or literary methods display results that honest and thoughtful scholars acknowledge, we can have confidence that they are true. But we must remain aware of the influence of presuppositions (discussed more fully later). In other words, when some scholars say that the miracles attributed to Elijah in 1 Kgs 17–18 can only be myths or legends, we must protest. Similarly we object when some form critics conclude that Jesus could never have said the words that Matthew attributes to his lips in 28:19–20, because they reflect the Church's later concerns and thus could only have been formulated in subsequent decades. Given our presuppositions, we believe genuine history can include miracles and genuine prophecy of future events can occur, even though others with rationalistic commitments will not accept the validity of such phenomena.

33 Of course, later strategists may indeed study the tactics of previous military generals and apply useful principles of warfare.

they believe it does have something to say to their lives. Indeed, we intend to argue that one cannot thoroughly understand the Bible's message simply through the exercise of historical and grammatical methods that disclose the original meaning of a text. We insist that the goal of hermeneutics must include detecting how the Scriptures can affect readers today. This means that true interpretation of the Bible combines both an exercise in ancient history and a grappling with its impact on our lives. Indeed, to truly understand what a text meant to its original recipients requires that we apprehend something of that original impact ourselves.

At the same time, if we admit that "applying" the Bible is a primary reason people read or study it, then we must answer a crucial question: how do we know *what* to apply and how do we apply it? In other words, if Christians believe that the Bible is God's Word to all people (see our discussion of this presupposition below), then to say to ourselves or to those we teach, "The Bible says . . . ," carries the implication that this is what God says. And if so, we must believe it and do it or reject God's will to our own peril. This is no inconsequential matter. It becomes exceedingly critical to understand as well as we possibly can what God means by what he says in the Bible. We must understand correctly so we can believe and act correctly. There is no benefit to following—even with great and earnest sincerity—a mistaken point of view. To paraphrase a line from a recent movie, we prefer not to lie to ourselves to make ourselves happy.

Because proper hermeneutics helps us understand God's will, it is crucial to faithful application. Satan tried to convince Jesus to misapply Scriptures in one of the temptations (Lk 4:9–12). Quoting from Psa 91:11–12, he urged Jesus to apply the Scriptures literally and throw himself down from the Temple mount with the assurance that God's Word promised divine protection. In response, Jesus accused Satan of bad hermeneutics. Jesus showed that Satan did not understand the full context of God's promise but needed to understand Psa 91 in light of the principle of not putting God to the test (see Deut 6:16). Neither extraordinary faith nor great sincerity will necessarily save a person who jumps from a tall building from a tragic death. Psa 91 promised God's protection when unexpected or accidental harm threatened (and even then not *always*), not from self-inflicted foolishness. Since Satan misconstrued the intention of Psa 91, the application of a bad interpretation would have had unfortunate—even deadly—results. Thus, since we desire to obey God's will, we need to understand how to interpret the Scriptures, which reveal his will, correctly.

CONCLUSION

Hermeneutics is essential for a valid interpretation of the Bible. Instead of piously insisting that we will simply allow God to speak to us from his Word, we contend that to insure we hear God's voice rather than our culture's voice or our own biases we need to interpret the Scriptures in a systematic and careful fashion. We need to practice proper hermeneutics. Why?

1. *To discern God's message.* If we are to understand God's truth for ourselves (and to teach or preach it to others), we must discover precisely what God intended to communicate. A careful system of hermeneutics provides the means for the interpreter to arrive at the text's intention, to understand what God intended to communicate through human minds and hands. A careful approach to hermeneutics provides the means for the interpreter to arrive at what God intended to communicate. Some conservative

Christians abuse the Bible by their "proof-texting." They use the Bible like a telephone book of texts they cite by chapter and verse to prove their viewpoint. This can lead to many distortions and errors that could be avoided by using hermeneutics. Hermeneutics safeguards the Scriptures against misuse by people who, deliberately or not, distort the Bible for their own ends. Proper hermeneutics provides the conceptual framework for interpreting correctly by means of accurate exegesis.[34] Exegesis puts into practice one's theory of interpretation. Thus good hermeneutics will generate good exegetical methods.

2. *To avoid or dispel misconceptions or erroneous perspectives and conclusions about what the Bible teaches.* Ideally, correct interpretation would undermine erroneous teachings that people use to support aberrant beliefs and behavior. One reads all too often in our newspapers of sincere and well-meaning parents who withhold medical intervention for their children because with the best of motives they believe they should trust God for healing. Though we do not deny God's ability to heal today or his invitation to pray for what we need, we believe that a correct interpretation of the relevant biblical texts mandates prayer for healing *and* medical intervention. God can use a variety of means to effect healing. Failure to seek appropriate medical help may be akin to jumping from the Temple. Or to go in another, more controversial direction, ought Christians be more concerned to support the nation of Israel (based on such texts as Gen 12:3; 27:29) or Palestinian Christians who happen to live in that land today (Mt 10:42; 25:40, 45)? How one interprets these texts drives one's concerns. Gen 12:3 does not mention the political state of Israel, only Abraham's seed or descendants, and Paul clearly equates Abraham's seed with Christians (e.g., Rom 4:16; Gal 3:29)! A huge percentage of Christians in Israel today happen to be Palestinian.[35]

3. *To be able to apply the Bible's message to our lives.* God has chosen to reveal most of his truth through the medium of written language, and this message is both univocal and analogical. As Carnell puts it, "terms may be used in one of three ways: with but one meaning (univocally), with different meanings (equivocally), and with a proportional meaning—partly the same, partly different (analogically)."[36] In other words, in places the Bible speaks to us univocally. That is, though its message was written to ancients, many features remain the same—human existence, the realities of angels, demons, God, and Jesus as God's Son, to name a few. As Paul notes concerning truth in the Scriptures, certain factual affirmations about past events always remain true (1 Cor 15:3–5). These statements are univocal, having the same meaning for Paul as for us, though we may apply that single meaning in a variety of ways.

---

34 From the Greek word *exēgeomai*, exegesis means to "lead out" the meaning of a text or passage. Here we agree with G. R. Osborne (*The Hermeneutical Spiral* [Downers Grove: InterVarsity, 1991], 6) who says, "Hermeneutics is the overall term, while exegesis and 'contextualization' (the cross-cultural communication of a text's significance for today) are the two aspects of that larger task."

35 On this controversial point see, C. Chapman, *Whose Promised Land?* 2d ed. (Grand Rapids: Baker, 2002) and G. Burge, *Who Are God's People in the Middle East?* (Grand Rapids: Zondervan, 1993).

36 E. J. Carnell, *An Introduction to Christian Apologetics* (Grand Rapids: Eerdmans, 1948), 144. Univocal meaning is single, having only one sense. We learn by analogy when we make inferences from what we learn or know in one sphere and apply it to another sphere.

At the same time, the Bible conveys truth to us analogically in its didactic sections, poetry, apocalypses, and narratives though they were uttered or written to people long ago. We learn by analogy when we discover that truth in the Bible applies to life and situations in the modern world. Jesus told his followers, "You are the light of the world" (Mt 5:14). Since people in Bible times and people today both have an understanding of how a light functions to provide illumination to everyone in the house (whether by means of candles, lamps, torches, electric or battery-operated lights), we understand the analogy. We learn that Jesus wants his followers to "brighten up" their world, which Jesus elaborates to mean, among other things, doing good deeds (5:16).

Today we can only read about God's actions and those of his people in the past, but because parallels and commonalities link the worlds of the ancients and ours, we can comprehend the analogies and learn from them. Our task is more difficult in places where an author or speaker does not clearly spell out the lesson to be learned or the nature of the analogy. For example, what precisely should we learn from the story of Joseph's life and his exploits in Egypt? Or from the inspiring narratives about David's friendship with Jonathan? What are the points of analogy between Israel's circumstances and ours? What does God expect us to learn from psalms written by an ancient king to express his frustrations or joys in life? How can we profit from the erotic love poems in the Song of Songs? The basic goal of this book is to help readers discover God's message to Christians today from the teachings and stories "back then."[37]

---

37 Indeed, we wish to take seriously Paul's words to his Roman readers, "For everything that was written in the past was written to teach us, so that through endurance and the encouragement of the Scriptures we might have hope" (Rom 15:4)

2

THE HISTORY OF INTERPRETATION

As will soon become apparent, we believe one must interpret Bible passages in their original historical context—a view that descends from a long line of intellectual ancestors, both Jewish and Christian, who have sought to interpret the Bible properly. A brief survey of the history of Bible interpretation is beneficial in several ways. First, it introduces key issues that are pertinent to Bible interpretation, which, in turn, prepares the student to understand the approach to these issues that we present.

Second, it sensitizes readers to the opportunities and pitfalls involved in trying to contextualize Bible teachings in the present. A critical assessment of the major interpretive methods practiced throughout history challenges readers to develop a personal approach to Bible interpretation that maximizes the opportunities and minimizes the pitfalls. Finally, knowledge of the history of interpretation cultivates an attitude of humility toward the interpretive process. Certainly we want to avoid the methods that history has judged as mistaken or faulty. At the same time, the history illustrates how complex the process is and how inappropriate is arrogance in the pursuit of it.[1]

JEWISH INTERPRETATION

The Bible's first interpreters were those who first possessed its writings—ancient Israelites who studied and edited what later became the Hebrew Scriptures. Their identity and the history of their work remain obscure, but the Hebrew Scriptures still show the thumbprints of their work.[2] One such anonymous writer, for example, ended Deuteronomy with this interpretation of the unique significance of Moses: "Since then,

---

1 With a few exceptions, our survey limits itself to the history of interpretation by Western Christianity or, after the Reformation, primarily to Protestant interpretation. For a good overview of the most relevant features of Eastern Christianity's hermeneutics for evangelicals, see G. R. Osborne, "The Many and the One: The Interface between Orthodoxy and Evangelical Protestant Hermeneutics," *St. VladThQ* 39 (1995): 281–304.

2 Recent investigations have brought this "inner-biblical exegesis" to light. For an excellent overview, see D. A. Carson and H. G. M. Williamson, eds., *It is Written: Scripture Citing Scripture* (Cambridge: Cambridge University Press, 1988), 25–83. For OT examples, see M. Fishbane, *Biblical Interpretation in Ancient Israel* (Oxford: Clarendon, 1984) for his discussion of inner-biblical exegesis in the OT; for NT examples, see R.B. Hayes, *Echoes of Scripture in the Letters of Paul* (New Haven: Yale University Press, 1989). Recent studies include G. Gakuru, *An Inner-Biblical Study of the Davidic Covenant and the Dynastic Oracle*, Mellen Biblical Press Series 58 (Lewiston, NY: Mellen, 2000); R. Nurmela, *Prophets in Dialogue: Inner-Biblical Allusions in Zechariah 1–8 and 9–14* (Åbo: Åbo Academis Förlag, 1996); and S. L. Harris, *Proverbs 1–9: A Study of Inner-Biblical Interpretation*, SBLDS 150 (Atlanta: Scholars Press, 1995).

no prophet has risen in Israel like Moses, whom the Lord knew face to face" (Deut 34:10).[3] Similarly, the books of 1-2 Chronicles offer, in part, a reinterpretation of 1-2 Kings from a post-exilic perspective. Such interpretations sought to apply then-extant biblical materials to contemporary concerns.

The first known interpreters by name were Levites who assisted Ezra the scribe. When the Israelites returned from exile (late sixth century B.C.), they spoke the Aramaic of Babylon instead of the Hebrew of their Scriptures. So, when on a solemn occasion Ezra publicly read the Mosaic Law, Levites explained to the crowd what he was reading (Neh 8:7–8). Probably, their explanations involved both translation of the text into Aramaic and interpretation of its content. According to rabbinic tradition, this incident spawned a new Jewish institution, the Targum (i.e., translation-interpretation).[4]

In fact, that institution was one of two formative activities involving biblical interpretation in intertestamental Judaism. In that period, Jewish worship included the oral Targums—i.e., the translation and interpretation of Hebrew scripture readings in Aramaic. Eventually, scribes reduced these oral Targums to writing in order to perpetuate their use, which continues to the present.[5] At the same time, scribes and rabbis vigorously pursued the study and teaching of the Hebrew Scriptures, especially the Pentateuch. They worked to solve problems raised by the texts, explaining obscure words and reconciling conflicting passages. More important, they sought to apply the Scriptures to the issues of daily life raised by their contemporaries.

A grave cultural crisis fueled their intensive scripture study. In the late intertestamental era, domination by the Greek and Roman empires forced Jews to define and preserve their own religious identity in the face of foreign cultural values and religions. They found refuge in the study of their ancient Scriptures. In the process, they honed their methods of interpretation to a fine edge. As Kugel points out, the influence of these largely anonymous figures proved far-reaching:

> They established the basic patterns by which the Bible was to be read and understood for centuries (in truth, up until the present day), and, what is more, they turned interpretation into a central and fundamental religious activity.[6]

---

3 For discussion of the date and concerns of its writer(s), see conveniently R. E. Clements, *Deuteronomy* (OT Guides; Sheffield: JSOT Press, 1989), 69–83.

4 *Palestinian Talmud, Megillah* 4, 74d; G. Vermes, "Bible and Midrash: Early Old Testament Exegesis," in *The Cambridge History of the Bible: From the Beginnings to Jerome*, 3 vols., ed. P. R. Ackroyd and C. F. Evans (Cambridge: At the University Press, 1970), 1:201 (henceforth, *CHB I*). Cf. the insight of M. Hengel, "The Scriptures and Their Interpretation in Second Temple Judaism," in *The Aramaic Bible: Targums in their Historical Context*, ed., D. R. G. Beattie and M. J. McNamara, JSOTSup 166 (Sheffield: Sheffield Academic Press, 1994), 161, that Ezra "concluded the time of revelation and opened up the era of scribal learning."

5 For general background on Targums, see P. Grelot, *What are the Targums?* (Collegeville, MN: the Liturgical Press, 1992); J. Bowker, *The Targum in Rabbinic Literature* (Cambridge: Cambridge University Press, 1969), 3–28.

6 J. L. Kugel, "Early Interpretation: The Common Background of Late Forms of Biblical Exegesis," in *Early Biblical Interpretation*, ed. J. L. Kugel and R. A. Greer (Philadelphia: Westminster, 1986), 13.

By the NT period, amid this intense hermeneutical activity three distinctive approaches to Scripture began to coalesce. Each approach was associated with a geographical center of Jewish religious life and a different school of thought. For our purposes, their importance lies in the background they provide on the way NT writers interpreted the OT.[7]

Hellenistic Judaism

In 333 B.C. Alexander the Great completed his conquest of the Persian Empire including Palestine. He and his successors began to impose Greek culture throughout their domain. Greek influence proved to be particularly strong on the large Jewish community in Alexandria, the city in Egypt named for the great emperor. There, Hellenistic Judaism flourished, a movement which sought to integrate Greek philosophy, especially that of Plato, with Jewish religious beliefs.[8]

Eventually, Greek replaced Hebrew as the common language among Jews outside of Palestine. So about 285 B.C., Alexandrian Jewish scholars produced a remarkable Greek translation of the Pentateuch (the remaining Hebrew Scriptures were translated later).[9] Eventually called the Septuagint (i.e., "70"; abbrev. LXX) because, according to tradition, seventy scholars translated it, it later became the Bible of the early Church.[10] More important for our purposes, in the fertile intellectual soil of Alexandria flowered a major school of biblical interpretation, one that enjoyed wide influence among Jews scattered throughout the Roman Empire and in Jerusalem itself.

The major distinctive of this school was its allegorical method, which was rooted in platonic philosophy. Plato taught that true reality actually lay behind what appeared to the human eye.[11] Applied to literature, this view of reality suggested that a text's true meaning lay behind the written words. That is, the text served as a kind of extended

---

7 A comprehensive collection of interpretations by these (and other) schools is available in L. H. Schiffman, *Texts and Traditions: A Source Reader for the Study of Second Temple and Rabbinic Judaism* (Hoboken, NJ: KTAV, 1998), 121–761. For a useful introduction to the variety of literature produced by Jews outside the Hebrew Bible, see L. R. Helyer, *Exploring Jewish Literature of the Second Temple Period* (Downers Grove: InterVarsity, 2002). Besides introducing subjects like the apocrypha, pseudepigrapha, apocalyptic, Dead Sea Scrolls, Mishnah, Targums, Josephus, and Philo, it also shows their value for students of the NT.

8 Kugel, 'Early Interpretation,' 40–44. For an overview of Hellenistic Judaism, see M. Hengel, *The Hellenization of Judaea in the First Century After Christ* (London: SCM, 1989).

9 The translation of the Pentateuch was particularly remarkable because the very process of its completion created, in the words of Lamarche, "a whole religious language . . . that would find its culmination in the New Testament and in the works of the Fathers"; cf. P. Lamarche, "The Septuagint: Bible of the Earliest Christians," in *The Bible in Greek Christian Antiquity*, P. M. Blowers, ed. (Notre Dame, IN: University of Notre Dame, 1997), 18.

10 The alleged story of its origin and purpose told in the *Letter of Aristeas* is now thought unreliable by scholars; cf. Lamarche, "The Septuagint: Bible of the Earliest Christians," 15–33. For excellent introductions, see N. F. Marcos, *The Septuagint in Context* (Leiden: Brill, 2001); and K. H. Jobes and M. Silva, *Invitation to the Septuagint* (Grand Rapids: Baker, 2000).

11 To illustrate, Plato compared human perception of reality to the experience of being in a dimly lit cave. There one sees only shadowy figures (the "forms"), but true reality (the "ideas") lies behind them. For more on platonic philosophy, see J. Coppelston, *A History of Philosophy*, 8 vols. (Paramus, NJ: The Newman Press, 1971), 1:127–206.

metaphor that pointed to the ideas hidden behind it.[12] With respect to the Hebrew Scriptures, the master practitioner of allegory was the brilliant Alexandrian Jewish thinker, Philo (20 B.C. - A.D. 54), who sought to reconcile the Hebrew Scriptures with the philosophy of Plato.[13]

For Philo, a Bible passage was like a human being; it had a body (i.e., a literal meaning) and a soul (an allegorical meaning).[14] He accepted the literal meaning of many Scriptures (e.g., observance of the Mosaic Law), but he also believed that only the allegorical method could reveal the true inner meaning that God had encoded in them. He developed a set of rules to recognize when a text's allegorical meaning was its true meaning. In his view, one could disregard a text's literal meaning when it (1) said anything unworthy of God, (2) contained some insoluble difficulty, unusual grammar, or unique rhetoric, and (3) involved an obvious allegorical expression.

Further, Philo believed that hidden meaning lay behind numbers and names. More ingeniously, he also found it by playing with the many possible meanings of the same word and by regrouping the words of a biblical passage. In Philo's interpretation of Gen 2:10 ("A river flows out of Eden to water the garden, and from there it divides and becomes four branches" NRSV), he determined that the Edenic river represented goodness, while the other four represented the four great virtues of Greek philosophy—prudence, temperance, courage, and justice.[15] In other words, the number four in the biblical text suggested to him four items from Greek philosophy.[16]

From hindsight, the strengths and weaknesses of Philo's approach appear evident. On the one hand, he rightly recognized the limitations of human language to convey the profound mysteries of spiritual reality and the nature of God, and he attempted to integrate biblical ideas with those of the dominant philosophy of his day in order to relate biblical faith to contemporary culture—a difficult challenge people of faith in every generation must face. On the other hand, from a modern viewpoint, Philo's approach too often seems dependent on subjectivity, arbitrariness, and artificiality. One might ask, for example, why the Edenic river represents goodness and its tributaries four other virtues. To someone else, the former might represent the stream of human life and the latter four major ethnic groups of humanity. Again, Philo tends to ignore the real differences between biblical ideas and those of Greek philosophy. It is hard to escape the conclusion that ultimately Philo's interpretation depended more upon platonic philosophy than

---

12 The Greeks had honed this interpretive method to a fine edge from the sixth century B.C. It allowed them to find value in Greek classical literature (e.g., Homer, etc.), some of whose ideas (e.g., the morality of the gods) the philosophers found offensive. The Platonists at Alexandria used allegory to teach platonic philosophy from classical Greek literature.

13 For Philo's life and thought, see P. Borgen, *Philo of Alexandria: An Exegete for His Time* (JSNT 86; Leiden: Brill, 1997); E. R. Goodenough, *An Introduction to Philo Judaeus*, rev. ed. (New York: Barnes & Noble, 1963); B. Smalley, *The Study of the Bible in the Middle Ages* (New York: The Philosophical Library, 1952), 1–6.

14 *De Vita Contemplativa*, x. 78. For a translation, see C. D. Yonge, *The Works of Philo: Complete and Unabridged* (Peabody, MA: Hendrickson, 1995).

15 *Legum Allegoriarum*, 1.63–64.

16 On the other hand, in keying on insoluble textual difficulties, by appealing to the multiple meanings of single words, and by rearranging words, Philo's method closely resembles that of midrash.

upon the Bible.[17] Nevertheless, one scholar rightly judges him as "probably the most influential Jewish biblical scholar and theologian of the ancient Jewish diaspora."[18]

The Qumran Community

A branch of Judaism—probably the Essenes—flourished at Qumran, a site on the northwestern shore of the Dead Sea, about 150 B.C.- A.D. 68. Its now famous literary legacy, the Dead Sea Scrolls, reveals the community's self-identity and reason for being. It regarded the Judaism centered in Jerusalem as apostate. So, led by its founder, a mysterious figure called the Teacher of Righteousness, its members withdrew to the wilderness of Judea to form a monastic community to prepare for the coming of the messianic age. Specifically, they awaited God's imminent judgment, which they expected to fall on their apostate religious competitors, and they anticipated his renewal of the covenant with the only true, pure Israel—themselves. They saw themselves as the final generation about whom biblical prophecy speaks.[19]

The interpretation of Hebrew Scriptures played a prominent role at Qumran.[20] If the Law of Moses entranced the rabbis, the OT prophets preoccupied the Qumranians. Alleging special divine inspiration, the Teacher of Righteousness claimed to show that events of that day, especially those involving the Qumran community, fulfilled OT prophecies. This explains why so many of the scrolls consist of copies of OT books and why Qumran produced so many commentaries on them. For our purposes, the latter are most important, for they show the principles of biblical interpretation that the community followed.

To be specific, the community practiced a method called *pesher*.[21] Three interpretive techniques typified this approach. Interpreters might actually suggest a change in

---

17 Whether Philo's thought owes more to Greek philosophy than to Judaism or vice versa remains a hotly contested issue among scholars. For a convenient summary, see D. Hagner, "Philo," in *New Dictionary of Theology*, ed. S. B. Ferguson and D. F. Wright (Downers Grove: InterVarsity Press, 1988), 509–510; cf. also Borgen, *Philo of Alexandria*, 282–87.

18 R. E. Olson, *The Story of Christian Theology: Twenty Centuries of Tradition and Reform* (Downers Grove: InterVarsity, 1999), 49. For Philo's influence on later patristic interpreters, see F.Ó. Fearghail, "Philo and the Fathers: The Letter and the Spirit," in *Scriptural Interpretation in the Fathers: Letter and Spirit*, ed. T. Finan and V. Twomey (Dublin: Four Courts Press, 1995), 39–59. A less philosophical hermeneutical approach appears in the writings of Philo's Jewish contemporary, Josephus (A.D. 37–100?), whose principal works are *The Antiquities of the Jews* and *The Jewish Wars*. As an apologetic mainly for Jewish detractors, his interesting paraphrastic retelling of biblical texts occasionally seems to rewrite them. For a comprehensive study of his biblical materials, see L. H. Feldman, *Studies in Josephus' Rewritten Bible*, JSJSup 58 (Leiden: E.J. Brill, 1998); cf. also S. Mason, *Josephus and the New Testament* (Peabody, MA: Hendrickson, 1992).

19 Kugel, "Early Interpretation," 61–62. For an English translation of the scrolls with Hebrew text and notes, see F. Garcia Martinez and E. J. C. Tigchelaar, *The Dead Sea Scrolls Study Edition*, 2 vols. (Grand Rapids: Eerdmans, 1999); for background to interpretation, see G. Vermes, *An Introduction to the Complete Dead Sea Scrolls* (Minneapolis: Fortress, 2000); M. A. Knibb, *The Qumran Community* (Cambridge: Cambridge University Press, 1987).

20 For an overview of their interpretive methods, see M. Berstein, "Interpretation of Scriptures," in *Encyclopedia of the Dead Sea Scrolls*, ed. L. H. Schiffman and J. C. VanderKam (Oxford: Oxford University Press, 2000), 1:376–83.

21 On the nature of *pesher*, see M. P. Horgan, *Pesharim: Qumran Interpretations of Biblical Books*, CBQMS 8 (Washington, D.C.: The Catholic Biblical Association, 1979), 229–59.

the biblical text (textual emendation) to support an interpretation. They would select a known alternate textual reading of the phrase in question and offer the interpretation. Lacking an existent variant, Qumran interpreters were not averse to creating one that suited their interpretive purposes! For example, Hab 1:13a reads, "Your eyes are too pure to behold evil, and you cannot look on wrongdoing" (NRSV). The Pesher rightly comments that the words address God and describe his holiness. One expects a similar treatment for v. 13b: "why do you look on the treacherous, and are silent when the wicked swallow those more righteous than they?" (NRSV). But the commentary interprets the "you" pronouns as plural, not singular, and as such they refer not to God but to the house of Absalom—a religious group that the Qumranians disliked.[22]

Again, commentators might contemporize a prophecy, claiming to find a prophecy's fulfillment in events either of their own day or of the immediate future. For example, one writer sought to contemporize Hab 1:6, "For I am rousing the Chaldeans, that fierce and impetuous nation" (NRSV). Originally, the line predicted that the Babylonian army would come to punish sinful Judah, but according to the Pesher, "this refers to the Kittim [Romans] who are indeed swift and mighty in war."[23] In other words, the commentator interpreted the ancient prophecy about the Babylonians as predicting the coming of Qumran's enemies, the Romans.

Finally, interpreters might use an atomization approach, dividing the text into separate phrases, then interpreting each one by itself regardless of the context. For example, in explaining Hab 2:4 (literally "Look, his soul shall be swollen . . .") the Pesher says, "they will pile up for themselves a double requital for their sins." The idea of double punishment derives from the word "swollen" (Heb. 'pl), which the commentator arbitrarily reads as "to be doubled" (Heb. kpl).[24]

In sum, Judaism sought to relate its ancient Scriptures to the realities of its contemporary experience. Rabbinic Judaism found in the application of the Mosaic Law a refuge to protect Jewish identity. Rather than resist outside influences, Hellenistic Judaism tried to accommodate its beliefs to those of platonic philosophy. And the ascetic Qumranians mined OT prophecies to explain their involvement in the events of their own day. In part drawing on this rich, complex stream of interpretation, and in part parallel to it, flowed a new interpretive current—Christian interpretation.

Rabbinic Judaism

Centered in Jerusalem and Judea, this branch of Judaism promoted obedience to the Hebrew Scriptures, especially the Torah, in the face of mounting pressure to accommodate to Greco-Roman culture.[25] The interpretive approach of rabbinic Judaism is

---

22 Horgan, *Pesharim*, 15, 32–34; W. H. Brownlee, *The Midrash Pesher of Habakkuk*, SBLMS 24 (Missoula, MT: Scholars, 1979), 91–98.

23 Brownlee, *Midrash Pesher*, 59–62; Horgan, *Pesharim*, 13, 26.

24 The translation follows Brownlee, *Midrash Pesher*, 122–24 ("a pun"); cf. Horgan, *Pesharim*, 17, 39 ("probably an interpretation").

25 G. Boccaccini, *Roots of Judaism: An Intellectual History from Ezekiel to Daniel* (Grand Rapids: Eerdmans, 2002), explores the roots of the rabbinic system in the Second Temple period (B.C. 515–A.D. 70), a system that in his view (xiv–xv) came to prominence no earlier than the 3d century A.D. For an excellent analysis of how a spectrum of Jewish sources handled controversial interpretive test cases, see I. Kalimi, *Early Jewish Exegesis and Theological Controversy*, Jewish and Christian Heritage 2 (Assen: Van Gorcum, 2002).

evident in the massive amounts of literature it inspired. It contains two basic types of content. *Halakah* (Heb. "rule to go by") involves the deduction of principles and regulations for human conduct derived specifically from OT legal material. *Haggadah* (Heb. "a telling"), by contrast, draws on the whole OT offering of stories and proverbs to illustrate biblical texts and to edify readers.[26]

Rabbinic Judaism produced three main literary works. The Mishnah presents the once-oral teachings of leading rabbis from the time of the famous competitors, Hillel and Shammai (late first century B.C. to early first century A.D.). Published about A.D. 200, the Mishnah presents many individual tractates arranged under six topics (e.g., feasts, women, holy things, etc.).[27] About fifty years later, another document called Abot (lit., "the Fathers") affirmed that what the Mishnah writers taught was part of the oral law received by Moses at Mt. Sinai. Most of its content is halakah.

The Palestinian and Babylonian Talmuds (ca. A.D. 400 and 600, respectively) essentially offer commentary (also known as Gemara) on the Mishnah by later rabbis. Topically organized, each Talmudic section quotes a passage of Mishnah, which is followed by citations of rabbis and portions of Scripture. The frequent citation of Scripture implies that the Talmud's purpose was to give biblical support for the interpretations of the Mishnah.[28] At times like modern biblical commentaries but often very different, the Midrashim (from Heb. *dāraš*, "to search") provide interpretation of biblical books, sometimes explaining passages almost verse-by-verse while often addressing only selected verses. The commentary—which may provide parallel or even competing perspectives—follows the quotation of a verse or phrase from Scripture. Though written no earlier than the second century A.D., some of their interpretive material probably derives from the pre-Christian era, and most of their content is haggadah.[29]

The interpretation of Scripture in rabbinic Judaism shows several distinct features. First, it depends heavily upon rabbinic interpretive tradition. Interpretation amounts to citing what earlier revered rabbis say about a passage. For example, consider how the Mishnah cites two ancient rabbis to resolve a possible conflict between two important OT legal teachings.[30] The Law taught that the people of Israel must not work on the Sabbath (Deut 5:12–15) and must circumcise newborn sons on their eighth day of life

---

26 *Halakah* and *haggadah* also refer to the genres of rabbinic traditions themselves, whether they are legal or narrative in form; cf. Kugel, "Early Interpretation," 67–72. For an introduction to Rabbinic Judaism, see J. Neusner, *Rabbinic Judaism: Structure and System* (Minneapolis: Fortress, 1995).

27 For a standard edition, see H. Danby, *The Mishnah* (Oxford: Oxford University Press, 1964). Cf. also the general comments and examples in J. Neusner, *From Testament to Torah: An Introduction to Judaism in Its Formative Age* (Englewood Cliffs, NJ: Prentice Hall, 1988), 45–65.

28 Cf. the excellent introduction with examples in Neusner, *From Testament to Torah*, 72–99. Schiffman (*Texts and Traditions*, 619–70) offers additional examples.

29 Kugel, "Early Interpretation," 78; B. Chilton, "Varieties and Tendencies of Midrash: Rabbinic Interpretation of Isaiah 24.23," in *Studies in Midrash and Historiography*, vol. 3 of *Gospel Perspectives*, ed. R. T. France and D. Wenham, (Sheffield: JSOT Press, 1981), 9–11 (henceforth *GP III*). Conveniently, Neusner (*From Testament to Torah*, 100–15) provides a useful overview and examples.

30 Two recent studies explore in-depth the rabbinic interpretation reflected in the Mishnah; cf. J. N. Lightstone, *Mishnah and the Social Formation of the Early Rabbinic Guild: A Socio-Rhetorical Approach*, Studies in Christianity and Judaism 11 (Waterloo, ON: Wilfrid Laurier University Press, 2000); and A. Samely, *Rabbinic Interpretation of Scripture in the Mishnah* (Oxford: Oxford University Press, 2002).

(Lev 12:3; cf. Lk 1:59; 2:21). But suppose the eighth day falls on a Sabbath? The Mishnah resolves the conflict by appealing to rabbinic tradition:

> R. Eliezer says: If they had not brought the circumcision knife on the eve of Sabbath it may be brought openly on the Sabbath; and in time of danger a man may cover it up in the presence of witnesses. R. Eliezer said moreover: They may cut wood [on the Sabbath] to make charcoal in order to forge an iron implement. R. Akiba laid down a general rule: Any act of work that can be done on the eve of Sabbath does not override the Sabbath, but what cannot be done on the eve of Sabbath overrides the Sabbath.[31]

Second, rabbinic commentators often interpret Scripture literally (Heb. *peshat*, "plain sense"). At times, taking the plain sense of Scripture produced a rather wooden interpretation. For example, Deut 21:18–21 legislated the legal recourse of Israelite parents who have a rebellious son. By taking the text quite literally, the Mishnah defined the circumstances under which an accused son would escape condemnation:

> If either of them [i.e., the son's parents] was maimed in the hand, or lame or dumb or blind or deaf, he cannot be condemned as a stubborn and rebellious son, for it is written, *Then shall his father and his mother lay hold on him*—so they were not maimed in the hand; *and bring him out*—so they were not lame; *and they shall say*—so they were not dumb; *this is our son*—so they were not blind; *he will not obey our voice*—so they were not deaf.[32]

The central feature of rabbinic interpretation, however, is the practice of *midrash*. Basically, midrash aims to uncover the deeper meanings that the rabbis assumed were inherent in the actual wording of Scripture. Ultimately, their motives were pastoral—to give logical biblical teaching for situations not covered directly by Scripture. To do so, the rabbis followed a system of exegetical rules (Heb. *middôt*) carefully worked out over the years. Hillel listed seven such rules by which an interpreter might draw inferences from a passage.[33] Most of the rules employed assumptions that we still deem valid—e.g., the use of analogous words, phrases, or verses from biblical cross-references to illumine the text under study. On the other hand, they sometimes used cross-references in ways that we consider questionable (e.g., citing words, etc., without regard to their context).

As the Mishnah and Midrashim attest, the application of these rules resulted in a fragmentary approach to exegesis. Interpreters first break up the Scripture quotation

---

31 Shabbath 19.1 (from Danby, *The Mishnah*, 116); cf. also J. Neusner, *The Mishnah* (New Haven/London: Yale University Press, 1988), 202.

32 Sanhedrin 8.4 (from Danby, *The Mishnah*, 394, his italics); cf. Neusner, *The Mishnah*, 601.

33 For Hillel's list, see C. K. Barrett, "The Interpretation of the Old Testament in the New," *CHB I*, 383–84. Tradition also attributes lists of thirteen and thirty-two rules to later rabbis. Cf. the excellent treatment of midrashic interpretation in I. Jacobs, *The Midrashic Process: Tradition and Interpretation in Rabbinic Judaism* (Cambridge: Cambridge University Press, 1995); R. N. Longenecker, *Biblical Exegesis in the Apostolic Period*, 2d ed. (Grand Rapids: Eerdmans, 1999), 18–24.

into separate short phrases, then interpret each one independently without regard for its context. Thus, they tend to make much of a text's incidental details that may or may not have been intended to convey such meanings. For example, one Gemara in the Mishnah biblically defends Jewish agricultural practices as follows:

> Whence do we learn of a garden-bed, six handbreadths square, that five kinds of seed may be sown therein, four on the sides and one in the middle? Because it is written, *For as the earth bringeth forth her bud and as the garden causeth the seeds sown in it to spring forth* [Isa 61:11]. It is not written *Its seed*, but the *seeds sown in it*.

By breaking down Isa 61:11 into parts, the Gemara explains why Jews should sow five kinds of seed in the same small garden:

> R. Judah said: "The earth bringeth forth her bud"; "bringeth forth"—one; "her bud"—one; making two. "Seeds sown" means (at least) two more; making four; "causeth to spring forth"—one; making five in all.[34]

Such interpretations may strike modern readers as ingenious manipulations of Scripture. In fairness, however, one must remember that the rabbis had a high view of Scripture: they assumed that divine truth resided both within and behind its words. Further, their motive was the same as that of any modern pastor—to apply Scripture to the pressing problems of a contemporary audience. On the other hand, the rabbis were the first to model the cross-reference strategy in biblical interpretation. In that respect, modern Bible students remain in their debt.[35]

THE APOSTOLIC PERIOD (ca. A.D. 30–100)

Continuity and discontinuity mark the comparison between Jewish and early Christian interpretation. As devout Jews, the first Christian interpreters—the apostles— regarded Jesus as Israel's promised Messiah and the small religious community he left behind as the true fulfillment of Judaism's ancient hopes. They appealed to the OT Scriptures to support their beliefs, interpreting them by many of the same principles as

---

34 Shabbath 9.2 (from Danby, *The Mishnah*, 108, including n. 8); cf. Neusner, *The Mishnah*, 190.

35 A common scholarly claim is that Paul occasionally interpreted the OT in midrashic ways similar to those of the ancient rabbis. An oft-cited example is Galatians 3:16 where he bases his interpretation of the word "seed" in the Abrahamic promise (e.g., Gen 12:2–3; 17:1–11) as a reference to Christ on one detail—the fact that the word is singular (i.e., "seed" not "seeds")—in apparent violation of the original context (i.e., "seed" means collectively "descendants"). However common, this claim is anachronistic, since Paul's wrote long before the Midrashim and Targumim reached written form. Further, it fails to reckon sufficiently with two facts: (1) Paul's interpretation accords well with some Jewish tradition that interpreted "seed" as a reference either to Israel as a nation or to a specific individual (i.e., Isaac), and (2) Gal 3:29 shows Paul's awareness of the collective sense of "seed." Instead, Paul probably appeals to the biblical understanding of corporate solidarity, whereby Jesus the Messiah represents both Abraham's true descendant and Israel as a nation; cf. R. N. Longenecker, *Galatians*, WBC 41 (Dallas, TX: Word, 1990), 131–32. For a good assessment of Paul's OT exegesis, see the excursus in B. Witherington III, *Grace in Galatia: A Commentary on St Paul's Letter to the Galatians* (Edinburgh: T & T Clark, 1998), 219–24.

other Jewish religious groups.[36] On the other hand, they revered Jesus as the new Moses and the authority of Jesus as superior even to that of the Law of Moses—a decisive departure from their Jewish roots. Also, they interpreted the OT from a radically new perspective—in light of the Messiahship of Jesus and the new age inaugurated by his coming.[37]

Indeed, Jesus' *literal fulfillment* of OT prophecy was their fundamental hermeneutical principle. In this they followed the example of Jesus himself.[38] Jesus launched his ministry by claiming in a Galilean synagogue that he personally fulfilled Isa 61:1-2 (Lk 4:18–21; cf. Mk 1:15). Later, when John doubted that Jesus was the Messiah, Jesus appealed to his healing of the blind, the lame, and the deaf just as Isa 35:5–6 had forecast (Lk 7:21-23). Along those same lines, the apostles found the prophetic fulfillment of the OT in Jesus and his teaching about the kingdom of God. In other words, they understood the OT christologically. According to Paul, to read the Law of Moses without Christ is like reading it through a veil (2 Cor 3:14–16; cf. Exod 34:33–35). The reader simply cannot see what it really means.

To remove that veil of ignorance, however, the apostles did not limit themselves to the literal interpretation of OT prophecies; in fact they employed at least three other interpretive approaches. First, they often mined OT historical and poetic sections to find predictions of the work of Christ and the Church. Their method was that of *typological* interpretation—to find events, objects, ideas, and divinely inspired types (i.e., patterns or symbols) represented in the OT that anticipate God's activity later in history.[39] The assumption is that the earlier event/object/idea repeats itself in the later one. This technique sought to persuade the apostles' first-century Jewish audience of the similarities between the OT and NT ideas and events as well as the superiority of the latter to the former. The point was to show Christianity as the true culmination of the OT worship of God.[40]

Two NT books, Matthew and Hebrews, best illustrate the typological approach.[41] For example, Mt 2:17 writes that Herod's killing of young Jewish boys fulfills Jer 31:15:

---

36 R. A. Greer, "The Christian Bible and Its Interpreters," in Kugel and Greer, *Early Biblical Interpretation,* 128. For details and examples, see Longenecker, *Biblical Exegesis in the Apostolic Period,* 36–198; more briefly, D. Dockery, *Biblical Interpretation Then and Now* (Grand Rapids: Baker, 1992), 34–44. F. F. Bruce, *The New Testament Development of Old Testament Themes* (Grand Rapids: Eerdmans, 1968), still offers an excellent broad thematic treatment.

37 Cf. Barrett, "Interpretation," 399–401.

38 Dockery, *Biblical Interpretation,* 23–26, summarizes interpretation of the OT, especially as regards Jesus himself; cf. R. M. Grant and D. Tracy, *A Short History of the Interpretation of the Bible,* 2d ed. (Philadelphia: Fortress, 1984), 8–38.

39 Grant and Tracy, *Short History,* 36–38. The classic study of NT typology remains L. Goppelt, *Typos: The Typological Interpretation of the Old Testament in the New* (Grand Rapids: Eerdmans, 1982); cf. also the good overviews in C. A. Evans and J. A. Sanders, eds., *Early Christian Interpretation of the Scriptures of Israel,* JSNTSup 148 (Sheffield: Sheffield Academic Press, 1997); id., *The Function of Scripture in Early Jewish Christian Tradition,* JSNTSup 154 (Sheffield: Sheffield Academic Press, 1998); and S. Moyise, *The Old Testament in the New* (New York: Continuum, 2001).

40 In fact, recent studies have shown that, in using typology, the NT writers followed an approach evident within the OT itself; cf., F. Ninow, *Indicators of Typology Within the Old Testament: The Exodus Motif* (Frankfurt am Main: P. Lang, 2001); C. Seitz, *Figured Out: Typology and Providence in Christian Scripture* (Louisville: Westminster John Knox Press, 2001). More on this to follow.

> A voice is heard in Ramah,
>   weeping and great mourning,
> Rachel weeping for her children
>   and refusing to be comforted,
> because they are no more.

In the context of Jeremiah, the verse refers to the exile of Israel to Babylon in the sixth century B.C. It invokes the ancient image of Rachel, the Israelite mother par excellence (cf. Ruth 4:11), as a symbol of corporate Israel's intense maternal grief. Matthew believed Herod's violence fulfilled the lines from Jeremiah in a typological sense: history had, as it were, repeated itself in that both the earlier and later events shared similar features indicating God's sovereign hand at work in both events. This repetition signaled to Matthew that Herod's bloodshed fulfilled Jeremiah's words and thus implied that Jesus was the Messiah.[42]

A second apostolic approach that departed from seeking only how Jesus fulfilled the OT literally could be called *literal-contextual* interpretation. This approach interpreted OT Scriptures more broadly according to their normal meaning within their original contexts. Here again, their method followed Jesus' example. Jesus rebutted Satan's clever but twisted use of OT passages with straightforward OT quotations (Deut 6:16 in answer to Psa 91:11-12; cf. Mt 4:5–7). Twice Jesus invoked the normal sense of Hos 6:6 ("For I desire steadfast love and not sacrifice" NRSV) to answer the Pharisees' criticism of him or his disciples (Mt 9:13; 12:8).

The epistles offer several examples of this approach. Primarily, the apostles cited OT texts interpreted literally (that is, their normal senses in context) to support their instruction on Christian morals.[43] In Rom 12, Paul taught his readers not to seek revenge on those who had wronged them (vv. 17–21). To back up his point, he cited Deut 32:35 ("Vengeance is mine, I will repay, says the Lord" NRSV) and Prov 25:21-22 ("If your enemies are hungry, give them bread to eat" NRSV) according to their natural meaning. Along the same line, Peter instructed believers to treat each other with humility, quoting Prov 3:34 for support: "God opposes the proud, but gives grace to the humble" (1 Pet 5:5 NRSV). If you do this, he concludes (v. 6 NRSV), God "may exalt you in due time."

A third apostolic method is *principle/application*. In this method they did not interpret an OT passage literally; rather, they interpreted it by applying its underlying principle to a situation different from, but comparable to, the one in the original context. For example, Paul sought to prove that God wants to save both Jews and Gentiles by quoting Hos 2:23:

> I will call them 'my people'

---

41 Cf. Grant and Tracy, *Short History*, 28–35.

42 Cf. D. A. Hagner, *Matthew 1–13*, WBC 33A (Dallas: Word, 1993), 38, who believes that the tradition of Rachel's burial near Bethlehem "was initially responsible for [Matthew's] utilization of the quotation."

43 Barrett, "Interpretation," 396–97; for specifically Pauline practice, see Longenecker, *Biblical Exegesis in the Apostolic Period*, 98–109.

who are not my people;
and I will call her 'my loved one'
who is not my loved one"
(Rom 9:25 NIV; cf. 9:26 with Hos 1:10)

Originally, Hosea's words referred to the nation of Israel—specifically to Israel's reconciliation with God after a period of divine rejection. "Not my people" and "not beloved" were actually the names of Hosea's children that symbolized that rejection. To make his case, Paul extracted a theological principle from Hosea's words—God can lovingly make those into his people who were not so before—then he used that principle to justify the full membership of Gentile believers in the people of God.

Paul's defense of the apostles' right to earn a living from their ministry provides another classic example of this approach (1 Cor 9:9; cf. 1 Tim 5:17–18). This practice may have needed justification because Jewish custom prohibited rabbis from receiving payment for their services.[44] He quoted Deut 25:4 ("You shall not muzzle an ox while it is treading out the grain" NRSV), a text that, one's initial impression notwithstanding, actually contributes to the theme of Deut 24–25—in Thiselton's words, "*human* sensitivity and *humane compassion* toward the suffering or defenseless."[45] On one level, from the ox citation Paul defended apostolic financial support ("when the plowman plows and the thresher threshes, they ought to do so in the hope of sharing in the harvest," 1 Cor 9:10 NIV). For Paul the underlying principle was: if human labor benefits anyone (and gospel ministry *does*), it should at least benefit those who perform it (here, the apostles). On another more important level, however, understood as originally promoting human compassion, the citation also served Paul's wider, long-term purpose—to cultivate the mature, Christ-like character that God desires of the entire Christian community.

In summary, apostolic interpretation both compares with and departs from the contemporary Jewish interpretive method.[46] The apostles' primary method is typology, especially when defending the Messiahship of Jesus and the ministry of the Christian Church. Significantly, they were the last notable interpreters with Jewish roots. From here on, Greco-Roman influences displace Jewish ones and dominate Christian biblical interpretation.

THE PATRISTIC PERIOD (ca. A.D. 100–590)

The death of the last apostle, John, ushered in a new era for the Church. It lasted until Gregory I became pope in A.D. 590. We call it the "patristic period" because it features the contribution of the so-called Church Fathers—the prominent leaders during

---

44 Greer, "The Christian Bible," 130. According to Longenecker (*Biblical Exegesis in the Apostolic Period*, 109–110), Paul's method here is allegorical in that it subordinates the OT's literal sense in order to tease out an additional meaning. But Thiselton persuasively argues that Paul's application of Deut 25:4 actually pursues "a more complex hermeneutical strategy"; cf. A. C. Thiselton, *The First Epistle to the Corinthians*, NIGTC (Grand Rapids: Eerdmans, 2000), 686.

45 Thiselton, *First Corinthians*, 686 (his italics), on whose careful discussion (686–88) our comments here draw.

46 A full treatment of this important subject is available in D. A. Carson and G. K. Beale, eds., *Commentary on the Use of the Old Testament in the New* (Grand Rapids: Baker, forthcoming).

the initial four centuries after the apostolic period.[47] During most of the patristic period, the writings of the apostles circulated among the churches but had not yet been collected into a canonical companion to the OT. Thus, while the Church considered many of the books and letters that later became our NT to be on a par with the OT, it still regarded the OT as its primary authoritative collection of Scriptures.[48]

As we shall see, however, during this period another authority—church tradition—began to exercise significant influence on the definition of church doctrine. Indeed, this development definitively shaped the practice of biblical interpretation until the Protestant Reformation fourteen hundred years later. When church councils finally agreed on the precise contents of the Christian canon of Scripture, this period came to an end.

The Apostolic Fathers (ca. A.D. 100–150)

We divide the patristic period into three main subperiods. The first, that of the apostolic fathers, gives us a glimpse of biblical interpretation during the first half-century after the apostle John's death. Our sources are the writings of early church leaders like Clement of Rome, Ignatius, Polycarp, and a pseudonymous writer who calls himself Barnabas. Other important writings include the *Didache* (from Gk. "teaching"), the *Shepherd of Hermas*, the *Epistle to Diognetus*, and various fragments that help round out the picture.[49] The fathers address two primary audiences—Christians in the churches and Jews opposing them—and their writings serve two corresponding purposes—to instruct believers in Christian doctrine and to defend the faith against Jewish arguments.

Several methods of interpretation are evident among the early Church Fathers.[50] Occasionally, they use *typology* to relate the OT to the NT, especially with regard to teachings about Jesus. For example, the *Epistle of Barnabas* (12:1-7) sees two OT passages as types of the cross of Christ—the outstretched arms of Moses, which gave Israel victory over Amalek (Exod 17), and the bronze serpent, which Moses lifted up in the wilderness (Num 21; cf. Jn 3:14). The Christian writer implies that both of these types teach that there is no hope of salvation outside of Jesus. Similarly, according to *First Clement*, a letter from the church in Rome to the church in Corinth, the scarlet color of the cloth that Rahab hung in Jericho to signal Joshua's spies foreshadowed the blood of Jesus (1 Clem

---

47 For an overview, see C. A. Hall, *Reading Scripture with the Church Fathers* (Downers Grove: InterVarsity Press, 1998); R. P. C. Hanson, "Biblical Exegesis in the Early Church," *CHB I*, 412–53. More detailed treatment appears in Blowers, ed., *The Bible in Greek Christian Antiquity*, and Dockery, *Biblical Interpretation*, 45–73.

48 For further study of biblical interpretation by the early church fathers we commend the emerging Ancient Christian Commentary on Scripture series edited by T. C. Oden (InterVarsity Press, 1998–). The series projects thirteen volumes for the OT, two for the apocrypha, and twelve for the NT, each providing a kind of *glossa ordinaria* (on this see below)—the biblical texts artfully elaborated with ancient reflections and insights.

49 For translation and commentary see M. W. Holmes, ed., *The Apostolic Fathers*, upd. ed. (Grand Rapids: Baker, 1999).

50 Greer, "Biblical Interpretation," 137–42. For a more detailed, classic treatment of the larger period, see also J. Pelikan, *The Emergence of the Catholic Tradition (100–600)* (Chicago: University of Chicago Press, 1971).

12:7). In this letter's view, by choosing that signal, the spies showed that "through the blood of the Lord redemption will come to all who believe and hope in God."[51]

On other occasions, typology helps the writer to teach about Christian living from the OT. So, the *Epistle of Barnabas* 10:3 finds in Moses' prohibition against eating pork a warning against associating with inconsistent Christians. The reason is that, like pigs, "when they are well off, they forget their Lord, but when they are in need, they acknowledge the Lord."[52]

The most popular interpretive approach among the fathers, especially when handling the OT, was that of *allegory*.[53] Apparently, several factors led them to adopt this approach. They wanted to support their teachings from the OT Scriptures, presumably to give their doctrine more credibility, and at the time, the allegorical method was the most popular way to interpret literature in general. Hence, it was natural for them to take up the accepted literary method of the day and apply it to the Scriptures. Despite some awareness of the history of interpretation, modern readers tend to do the same thing.

Consider, for example, the interpretation that Barn 7–8 gives the OT ritual of the red heifer (Num 19). Typical of allegory, it draws great spiritual significance from the details of the procedure. So, the writer says the red heifer represents Jesus, and the children who sprinkle its ashes "are those who preached to us the good news about the forgiveness of sins . . . , those to whom he [Jesus] gave the authority to proclaim the gospel" (i.e., the apostles). Similarly, for Barnabas the seven days of creation provide the interpretive key to the future of history. The six days symbolize that the world will last six thousand years, the seventh day symbolizes the second coming of Christ, followed by the eighth day—"the beginning of another world" (15:3–9).[54]

At times the early fathers employ a *midrashic* interpretive approach reminiscent of the rabbis and the Qumran sectarians. The interpretation of Gen 17:23–27 in Barn 9:7–8 provides a classic example. Here Barnabas cites as "Scripture" a brief paraphrase of the Genesis report of Abraham's inauguration of the observance of circumcision, arbitrarily including in the citation the number 318 from Gen 14:14 as the total number circumcised that day. By clever (though to us opaque) midrashic treatment of the number 318, Barnabas surprisingly finds a reference to Jesus and his cross:

> Now the (number) 18 (is represented) by two letters, J = 10 and E = 8—thus you have "JE," (the abbreviation for) "JEsus." And because the cross, represented by the letter T (= 300), was destined to convey special significance, it also says 300. He makes clear, then, that JEsus

---

51 The translation is from Holmes, *The Apostolic Fathers*, 43. Cf. also his treatment of the epistle's author and background (22–27).

52 Holmes, *The Apostolic Fathers*, 301.

53 In our view, this is certainly evident in A. Louth, ed., *Genesis 1–11*, ACCS OT 1 (Downers Grove: InterVarsity, 2001). That allegory was less popular in commentary on the NT, however, seems also evident in, e.g., G. Bray, ed., *1–2 Corinthians*, ACCS NT 7 (Downers Grove: InterVarsity, 1999).

54 Translation of Holmes, *The Apostolic Fathers*, 295, 317.

is symbolized by the two letters (JE = 18), while in the one letter (T = 300) is symbolized the cross.[55]

Finally, the fathers show early signs of an interpretive principle that was to dominate biblical interpretation until it was rejected during the Reformation. In the second century, an increasing number of heretical groups arose within the Church. Most prominent among them were the Gnostics who, like the others, supported their unorthodox views by appealing both to the Scriptures and to so-called sayings of Jesus—sayings they claimed Jesus taught his disciples in private.[56] The lack of a finished, canonical collection of apostolic writings placed leaders of the orthodox branch of the Church at a disadvantage. They felt that their only recourse to rebut the heresies was to appeal to the authority of tradition handed down from the apostles.

This established a new hermeneutical principle in the Church called *traditional interpretation*. The Church came to regard the traditional interpretation of a biblical passage (that which the churches taught) as its correct interpretation.[57] Without a completed canon of Scripture, church tradition offered the only firm basis for explaining what the apostles had taught. It enabled the Church to defend its teaching against the Gnostics and the early heretics. Later, even with a settled canon in place, traditional interpretation still served positively as a kind of interpretive "rule of thumb" to explain what biblical texts meant.[58] The danger, of course, is that in practice church tradition may attain a status almost equal with that of Scripture as the Church's ultimate authority for doctrine. Further, by making church leaders official adjudicators of the apostolic tradition, the practice froze their doctrinal rulings as the correct interpretation of many biblical passages. Eventually, abuses of the otherwise useful principle of traditional interpretation (e.g., its application to support the payment of medieval indulgences) contributed to the rise of the Protestant Reformation.

The Alexandrian School (ca. A.D. 150–400)

With the passing of the early Church Fathers from the scene, the patristic period entered its second main era as a new generation took up the task of interpreting the Bible, especially the OT, to meet the needs of the Christian community. Though not a clear-cut "method" per se (the early Church, in fact, lacked such), its approach was to interpret all of Scripture in light of one single key theological idea.[59] At the Christian

---

55 Translation of R. A. Kraft, *The Apostolic Fathers*, 4 vols., ed. R. M. Grant (New York: Nelson, 1964), 1:109.

56 For a popular treatment of Christian Gnosticism, see J. Dart, *The Jesus of Heresy and History: The Discovery and Meaning of the Nag Hammadi Gnostic Library* (San Francisco: Harper & Row, 1988). More recently, see R. Roukema, *Gnosis and Faith in Early Christianity: An Introduction to Gnosticism* (Harrisburg, PA: Trinity International Press, 1999).

57 Cf. W. H. C. Frend, *The Rise of Christianity* (Philadelphia: Fortress, 1984), 134–39, 231; and Pelikan, *The Emergence of the Catholic Tradition*, 7–10.

58 The so-called "rule of faith" taught by Irenaeus (A.D. 120–200)—i.e., the rejection of any view that did not agree with the preaching of the apostles—articulates this idea; cf. Dockery, *Biblical Interpretation*, 68-70.

59 We gratefully acknowledge the conceptual and bibliographic advice of Dr. D. Fairbairn, a patristics scholar and our former student, in the revision of this section.

catechetical school at Alexandria that prevailing idea was the person of Christ,[60] and among the reading strategies available from the fathers it adopted that of allegory, the exegetical method of the Alexandrian Jewish scholar, Philo, and one long promoted by Alexandrian thinkers among Jews and Neoplatonic philosophers. With the prestige of Alexandria as a center of learning behind it, the use of allegory came to dominate Christian biblical interpretation until the dawn of the Renaissance (A.D. 15th cent.). By adapting the interpretive methods of their contemporaries, Christian teachers at Alexandria undoubtedly hoped to gain credibility for their interpretations among their non-Christian peers. More important, they regarded the method as the best way to bring Scripture to bear in a positive way on the life of the expanding Church and its members.[61]

Two articulate spokesmen present the case for reading the Bible allegorically. The first is Clement of Alexandria who taught there from A.D. 190 until 203 when the persecution of Christians by the Roman emperor Septimius Severus drove him into exile.[62] Like Philo, Clement taught that Scripture has a twofold meaning: like a human being, it has a body (literal) meaning as well as a soul (spiritual) meaning hidden behind the literal sense. Clement regarded the hidden, spiritual sense as the more important one. His allegorical method is evident in his interpretation of the parable of the prodigal son.[63] Typical of those who allegorize, he attributed Christian meaning to the story's various details. So, the robe that the father gave to the returned prodigal represents immortality; the shoes represent the upward progress of the soul; and the fatted calf

---

60 I.e., "the person of Christ, the revelation of Christ, and the ecclesial reality established by Christ constitute the fundamental and indispensable hermeneutic principle and method for the complete and perfect interpretation and understanding of the prophecy of Isaiah and any other Old Testament prophecy"; cf. Metropolitan D. Trakatellis, "Theodoret's Commentary on Isaiah," in *New Perspectives on Historical Theology: Essays in Memory of John Meyendorff*, ed. B. Nassif (Grand Rapids: Eerdmans, 1996), 341. This christological principle also applied to the interpretation of non-prophetic OT books.

61 Here we follow recent patristics scholarship that no longer contrasts the "Alexandrian" and "Antiochene" schools as proponents of, respectively, allegorical (thought "bad") and grammatical-historical methods (thought "good"). The idea of a unique Antiochene school of interpretation proves in reality to have been the creation of nineteenth-century scholarship, whereas the current consensus believes both Alexandrians and Antiochenes shared a common approach, albeit with identifiable differences. For details, see D. Fairbairn, *Grace and Christology in the Early Church* (New York and Oxford: Oxford University Press, 2003); B. Nassif, " 'Spiritual Exegesis' in the School of Antioch," in Nassif, *New Perspectives*, 343–77; and F. Young, "The Rhetorical Schools and Their Influence on Patristic Exegesis," in *The Making of Orthodoxy: Essays in Honour of Henry Chadwick*, ed. R. Williams (Cambridge; New York: Cambridge University Press, 1989), 182-99. Cf. Hall, *Reading Scripture With the Church Fathers*, 156–176. For a more traditional scholarly view of Alexandria and Antioch, cf. K. Froehlich, *Biblical Interpretation in the Early Church* (Philadelphia: Fortress, 1984), 19–20.

62 Our discussion follows the treatment in Grant and Tracy, *Short History*, 52–56. For further in-depth discussion, see E. Osborn, "The Bible and Christian Morality in Clement of Alexandria," in Blowers, ed., *The Bible in Greek Christian Antiquity*, 112–30.

63 A. R. Roberts and J. Donaldson, eds., *The Ante-Nicene Fathers*, 10 vols. (New York: Charles Scribner's Sons, 1913), 2:581–82 (sermon fragment). Though Philo undoubtedly influenced Clement, a recent assessment concludes that the great Jewish exegete shaped his interpretation of Scripture very little (Osborn, "The Bible and Christian Morality in Clement of Alexandria," 114).

represents Christ as the source of spiritual nourishment for Christians. In Clement's view, therefore, a text's literal sense is but a pointer to its underlying spiritual truth.

The second spokesman is Clement's successor, the distinguished scholar Origen (A.D. 185–254). In his extensive writings, Origen argued that just as humans consist of body, soul, and spirit, so Scripture has a threefold meaning.[64] Origen expanded Clement's twofold body and soul view by separating the soul into soul and spirit, adding a third or "moral" meaning: ethical instructions about the believer's relationship to others. He also refined the idea of a spiritual sense into a doctrinal sense, i.e., truths about the nature of the Church and the Christian's relationship to God.

Thus, said Origen, the wise interpreter of Scripture must move from the events of a passage (its literal sense) to find the hidden principles for Christian living (its moral sense) and its doctrinal truth (its spiritual sense). As an example, consider Origen's interpretation of the sexual relations between Lot and his daughters (Gen 19:30–38).[65] According to Origen, the passage has a literal sense (what actually happened), but its moral meaning is that Lot represents the rational human mind, his wife the flesh inclined to pleasures, and the daughters vainglory and pride. Applying these three elements yields the spiritual (or doctrinal) meaning: Lot represents the OT Law, the daughters represent Jerusalem and Samaria, and the wife represents the Israelites who rebelled in the wilderness.

From a modern perspective, such interpretation seems to play fast and loose with the text. One might argue that Origen is simply reading his own Christian ideas into the text rather than drawing them from it. Anticipating such criticism, Origen contended that God had inspired the original biblical writer to incorporate the allegorical meaning into his writing. Thus, what Origen considered the highest meaning of Scripture—its deeper spiritual truth—was already implicit in Scripture, not something invented by the interpreter. Of course, Origen's was not the only view at this time; voices asserting alternate views were occasionally heard. For example, the later Alexandrian, Cyril (A.D. 378–444), understood the anarchistic and arbitrary tendencies of allegory and rejected the method in favor a more grammatically based approach.[66] Similarly, Theodore of Mopsuestia (ca. A.D. 350–428), thought to be the greatest interpreter among those associated with Antioch, wrote that only four psalms (2; 8; 45; 110) truly contained messianic prophecy about the incarnation of Christ and the Church. He also departed from the traditional allegorical interpretation of the Song of Songs as symbolizing Christ's love for the Church or the Christian's devotion to Christ, reading it instead as a love poem written by Solomon to celebrate his marriage to an Egyptian

---

64 R. Heine, "Reading the Bible with Origen," Blowers, ed., *The Bible in Greek Christian Antiquity*, 135–39; cf. also J. W. Trigg, *Origen* (London: Routledge, 1998), 32–35; Dockery, *Biblical Interpretation*, 87–97; M. F. Wiles, "Origen as Biblical Scholar," *CHB I*, 454–89.

65 "Genesis Homily V," in *Origen: Homilies on Genesis and Exodus*, The Fathers of the Church 71 (Washington, D.C.: Catholic University of America Press, 1982), 112–20. For Origen's interpretation of Jesus' triumphal entry that sought to reconcile differing gospel accounts, see D. L. Dungan, *A History of the Synoptic Problem* (New York: Doubleday, 1999), 78–80.

66 J. O'Keefe, "Christianizing Malachi: Fifth-Century Insights from Cyril of Alexandria," *Vigiliae Christianae* 50 (1996): 138–139. Cyril's interpretation of Malachi illustrates two phenomena typical of this period: how a single theological concern (i.e., the life of the Christian community) dominated biblical interpretation, and how both Alexandria and Antioch shared a common concern about the excesses of allegory.

princess.[67] Nevertheless, Origen's allegorical approach would shape Christian interpretation for more than a millennium.[68]

Church Councils (ca. A.D. 400–590)

The era of the church councils marks the third and final phase of the patristic period. With the conversion of the Roman emperor Constantine in A.D. 312, politics exercised a profound influence on the Church's interpretation of Scripture. In the emperor's view, doctrinal disputes between the orthodox mainstream and its heretical tributaries threatened the empire's political stability. So he pressured the Church to settle its differences and to standardize its disputed doctrines. This proved to be a difficult task for two reasons. First, simple appeals to Scripture in defense of orthodoxy produced nothing but a doctrinal stalemate. The reason was that the unorthodox groups also supported their views from Scripture, often very persuasively.

Second, orthodox theologians themselves could not agree on the proper way to interpret Scripture. Worse, even the heretics quoted Scripture to support their views, a fact that led the early church father Tertullian (ca. A.D. 200) to question their right to such appeals since in his view the Scripture belonged only to a church holding to apostolic teaching.[69] The Church desperately needed some authority to determine with finality the meaning of Scripture. It found the answer in the apostolic succession of church leadership.

Above, we noted how the apostolic fathers appealed to traditional interpretation in response to heresies like Gnosticism. Under Constantine, orthodox church leaders took up that argument again, affirming their "apostolicity"—i.e., that only they, the apostles' successors, were the true interpreters of Scripture since only they had directly received the apostolic teaching. To implement this principle, church leaders convened a series of church councils to define official church doctrine.

Their decisions defined correct Christian beliefs and defended orthodox views against those of the heretics. Since all sides cited Scripture as support, the conciliar pronouncements tried to spell out what, according to apostolic tradition, was the correct interpretation of the Scriptures and wherein lay the heretics' misunderstandings. The importance of the councils lies in their description of "orthodoxy," the mainstream Christian beliefs consistent with properly interpreted Scripture and the apostles' teaching. Those beliefs distinguished orthodoxy from the views of the heretics.

Early in this period, the great church leader Augustine became the first orthodox Christian in the western Church to articulate an original and comprehensive

---

67 For more on Theodore, although from an older scholarly perspective, see M. F. Wiles, "Theodore of Mopsuestia as Representative of the Antiochene School," *CHB I*, 489–510. Trakatellis ("Theodoret's Commentary on Isaiah," 313–42) claims to find a synthetic interpretive approach, albeit with obvious differences, in the commentaries of Theodore's student, Theodoret (ca. A.D. 393–460), and in the sermons of John Chrysostom (ca. A.D. 347–407). For a very nuanced discussion of the hermeneutical idea of *theoria* (Gk. "insight") among the so-called "Antiochenes," see Nassif, "Spiritual Exegesis,'" 345–77.

68 Most modern interpreters feel ambivalence, if not antipathy, toward this approach. But for a recent, balanced Roman Catholic assessment of patristic exegesis as the stream of tradition that also shapes modern Catholic exegesis in some ways, see P. S. Williamson, *Catholic Principles for Interpreting Scripture*, Subsidia Biblica 22 (Rome: Pontificio Istituto Biblico, 2001), 137–47.

69 Dockery, *Biblical Interpretation*, 71.

hermeneutics.[70] His complex, nuanced interpretive approach emerges in his sermons, biblical commentaries, the famous *Confessions*, and especially his *On Christian Doctrine* (A.D. 397). Augustine's first principle of interpretation specifies that it aims to lead readers to love God and other people (i.e., the goal of Scripture itself).[71] Proper interpretation seeks to cultivate a proper, ethical, and devout Christian life. According to Augustine, to interpret the Bible properly one must focus on a text's literal or historical meaning, by which he meant its "real meaning" or what the text intended to say.[72] But what does one do when Scripture does not make good literal sense? For example, taken literally, the phrase "the image of God" (Gen 1:27) might imply that God has some physical substance, if not a physical body just like humans.[73] In such cases, Augustine (a highly trained rhetorician) sought a figurative or allegorical meaning in the text (e.g., that "image" refers to humanity's spiritual side). To guard against the subjective excesses of allegory, he offered three interpretive principles for finding the figurative meaning of difficult texts.

First, one consults what other, clearer passages of Scripture say on the subject, and second, one consults the "rule of faith" or the Church's traditional interpretation of the text. Third, if conflicting views meet both criteria, one should consult the context to see which view best commends itself. One cannot overstate Augustine's momentous contribution to the study of the Bible. His thought profoundly influenced later thinkers (e.g., Aquinas, Erasmus, Luther), and Bible students still follow his principles of proper interpretation.[74]

Another important event toward the close of the patristic period involving another influential thinker merits mention. Church leaders finally persuaded the learned scholar, Jerome (A.D. 331-420), to translate the OT and NT, as well as the Apocrypha, into Latin.[75] This translation from Hebrew and Greek manuscripts, known as the

---

70 F. Van Fleteren, "Principles of Augustine's Hermeneutics: An Overview," in *Augustine: Biblical Exegete*, ed. F. Van Fleteren and J. C. Schnaubelt (New York: P. Lang, 2001), 1–32; cf. T. Williams, "Biblical Interpretation," in *The Cambridge Companion to Augustine*, ed. E. Stump and N. Kretzmann (Cambridge: Cambridge University Press, 2001), 59–70. Augustine's commentaries on Genesis and Psalms offer especially important clues to his interpretive approach.

71 *On Christian Doctrine*, I, 40–41. For translation and commentary, see J. E. Rotelle, ed., *The Works of Saint Augustine: A Translation for the 21st Century*, Vol. 11 (Hyde Park, NY: New City Press, 1996).

72 Van Fleteren, "Principles of Augustine's Hermeneutics," 10; Augustine, *On Christian Doctrine*, 1.41. Cf. the convenient overview of Augustine and his thought in Hall, *Reading Scripture With the Church Fathers*, 116–25; Dockery, *Biblical Interpretation*, 136–46; and G. Bonner, "Augustine as Biblical Scholar," *CHB I*, 541–63.

73 Indeed, according to Hall (*Reading Scripture With the Church Fathers*, 119–20), Augustine's North African contemporaries held such a materialistic view of God based on a wooden, literal hermeneutic. Augustine found temporary intellectual refuge among the more flexible (but heretical) Manichees, but eventually the preaching of Ambrose with its allegorical approach won his return to the ecclesiastical mainstream. Later he rebutted the Manichees' criticisms of orthodox hermeneutics and interpreted Genesis' figures of speech in his *Two Books on Genesis Against the Manichees* (Hall, 122–23).

74 Cf. Van Fleteren's characterization of him ("Principles of Augustine's Hermeneutic," 22) as "the philosopher-theologian upon whom the West was constructed."

75 Jerome received a rigorous education in classics at Rome and later learned Greek and Hebrew (cf. Dockery, *Biblical Hermeneutics*, 129: "the most learned person in the Latin-speaking church of the late fourth century"). In a letter, he once described himself as "trilinguis, Hebraeus, Graecus, Latinus" (quoted from Hall, *Reading Scripture With the Church Fathers*, 110).

Vulgate (from the Latin word for "common"), became the official Bible of the western Church. Its unique contribution was to provide the Latin-speaking world a translation of the OT based on the original text rather than on a translation (i.e., the Septuagint).[76] Unfortunately, from that time the western Church's study of the Bible in the original Hebrew and Greek ceased for all practical purposes until revived during the Renaissance. Instead, the western Church came to depend upon the Vulgate translation for all doctrinal discussions. In some instances, Jerome's dynamic-paraphrase method of translation gave renderings that were not as accurate in reflecting the original languages as they could have been (e.g., in Lk 1:28, "Hail Mary, full *of grace* . . ." [cf. Gk. "favored one" NRSV; "highly favored" NIV]). Thus the Church moved still another step away from dependence upon the original Scripture text itself as the source for its teachings.[77]

THE MIDDLE AGES (ca. A.D. 590–1500)

As the name implies, the Middle Ages is the millennium that falls between the patristic period, dominated by church fathers and councils, and the new courses charted by the Reformation. In a sense, it constitutes a transitional phase between the two. The Middle Ages mark the decline of some features of the former and lay the groundwork for the emergence of the latter. Popular impression sees the period as a dark, oppressive one, and that portrait is largely consistent with historical reality.[78] Ignorance plagued both Christian clergy and laity, and morally bankrupt church leaders stopped at nothing to preserve their ecclesiastical power. At the same time, and usually hidden behind cloister walls, a millennium-long, lively, and rich dialogue with the Bible quietly advanced and produced tools for its continuing study that profoundly shaped the practice of biblical interpretation in the following centuries.[79]

Three approaches typify biblical interpretation in the Middle Ages. Interpreters continued to depend heavily upon *traditional* interpretation—the views of the fathers passed down over centuries. The primary resource for this method remained the written *catena* (Lat. "chain") or chain of interpretations, i.e., long collections of interpretive comments compiled from the commentaries of the Church Fathers.[80] Significantly, while premedieval catenas cited a variety of commentators, medieval ones featured fathers like Augustine and Jerome, who expressed the Church's accepted doctrinal views. In other words, interpreters using catenas tended to conform their interpretations to the Church's

---

76 Cf. Dockery, *Biblical Hermeneutics*, 131, who also notes that the later Wycliffe (14th cent. English) and Douai (16th cent.) versions were translated from the Vulgate.

77 J. N. D. Kelly, *Jerome: His Life, Writings, and Controversies* (New York: Harper and Row, 1975), offers in-depth biographical treatment of him; cf. also H. D. F. Sparks, "Jerome As Bible Scholar," *CHB I*, 510–40.

78 For an overview, see J. H. Dalmus, *The Middle Ages* (Garden City, NY: Doubleday, 1968). Cf. also C. A. Volz, *The Medieval Church* (Nashville: Abingdon, 1997).

79 For an insightful survey of the contours of this dialogue, see C. Ocker, "Medieval Exegesis and the Origin of Hermeneutics," *SJT* 52 (1999): 328–45.

80 R. E. McNally, *The Bible in the Early Middle Ages* (Atlanta: Scholars Press, 1986), 30–32. The *Catena Aurea* compiled by medieval scholar, Thomas Aquinas, exemplifies this practice; cf. the English translation in M. F. Toal, *The Sunday Sermons of the Great Fathers* (San Francisco: Ignatius Press, 2000).

doctrinal norms. As McNally puts it, during this period "[e]xegesis became almost synonymous with tradition, for the good commentator was the scholar who handed on faithfully what he had received."[81]

The catena spawned one important interpretive offspring during the Middle Ages. Medieval monks developed the practice of the *interpretive gloss,* Scripture annotations or commentaries from the fathers that were written in the margins or between the lines of the Bible (8th–9th cent.). By the late eleventh century, this practice became widespread in medieval schools, eventually took on a uniform design, and finally saw publication in glossed Bibles in Paris (ca. 1220). About the same time, the *Glossa Ordinaria* (lit. "ordinary tongue") also appeared, a massive multi-volume compilation of comments and glosses on individual biblical books that soon became the standard medieval commentary on the Bible.[82]

As noted earlier, of all the methods of biblical interpretation in the Middle Ages, the *allegorical* method dominated. Indeed, in contrast to Origen's threefold sense of Scripture, many medieval scholars believed every Bible passage had four meanings. A popular rhyme (in Latin, that is) that circulated widely in the Middle Ages summarizes them:

> The letter teaches deeds;
> allegory, what you should believe;
> the moral sense, what you should do;
> and the anagogical sense, what to hope for.[83]

Thus, the Bible's four senses are: literal (or historical), allegorical (or doctrinal), moral (or tropological), and anagogical (or eschatological). For example, medieval Bible scholars commonly took the word "Jerusalem" to have four senses:

Literal:	the ancient Jewish city
Allegorical:	the Christian Church
Moral:	the faithful soul
Anagogical:	the heavenly city[84]

---

81 McNally, *The Bible in the Early Middle Ages,* 29. For a major, more positive recent assessment, see H. De Lubac, *Medieval Exegesis: The Four Senses of Scripture,* Vol. 1 (Grand Rapids: Eerdmans, 1999).

82 Smalley, *Study of the Bible,* 46–66 (with a photograph); Ocker, "Medieval Exegesis," 329–32, who notes its "tremendous influence within scholastic exegesis" (332). J. Swanson, "The *Glossa Ordinaria,*" in *The Medieval Theologians,* ed. G. R. Evans (Oxford: Blackwell, 2001), 156–67, provides a convenient recent discussion of its history, calling it "an intermediate textbook" that schooled students and enabled scholars to develop their own interpretations (166–67, quote 167). For further developments in scholastic exegetical literature (i.e., the improvements on the *Glossa Ordinaria* in the *Historia Scholastica,* the *postilla* [a kind of running commentary], and Latin Bible concordances), see Ocker, "Medieval Exegesis," 332–36.

83 Williamson, *Catholic Principles,* 172, who credits the couplet to Augustine of Denmark (13th cent.). For a slightly different, rhyming version, see Grant and Tracy, *Short History,* 85.

84 Both the expansion to a four-fold sense of Scripture and Jerusalem as an example go back to the writings of John Cassian (early 5th cent.); cf. Ocker, "Medieval Exegesis," 338–39. For a detailed discussion of this approach from a modern Catholic perspective, see Williamson, *Catholic Principles,* 161–215.

This suggestion of Scripture's "senses" might strike the modern reader as a cliché, if not plain nonsense. But Ocker rightly reminds us that this apparent cliché rests on an important (and obvious) assumption—the depth and complexity of Scripture—in other words,

> . . . that biblical texts and nouns yielded historical meanings more remote from the reader or the reader's world and other meanings that touched on present religious life—the church, the moral condition of the soul, the future. The four-fold sense indicated a process of abstraction and the possibility of lithe movement, seldom if ever a procedure for chopping Bible passages into quarters.[85]

The third method of medieval interpretation was *historical* interpretation. Some medieval interpreters sought to find the historical sense of Scripture by consulting with Jewish authorities. The biblical commentaries written by Andrew of St. Victor (12th cent.), abbot of an English abbey at Wigmore, exemplify this approach.[86] Unlike his contemporaries, Andrew excluded spiritual commentary and theological questions from his interpretation. Instead, he concentrated on a text's historical or literal sense, drawing often on Jewish interpretation. Though a minority figure on the larger historical landscape, Andrew reminds us that some medieval scholars kept alive the tradition of earlier exegetes like Jerome and Augustine for whom Scripture's literal sense was primary.

Eventually a more influential proponent of the literal approach emerged, the movement called *scholasticism*.[87] Scholasticism was a pre-Renaissance intellectual awakening in Europe that began in the monastic schools and later spread to the universities (12th to 13th cent.). Its main concern was to sort out the relationship between the Christian faith and human reason. Two factors provided the fertile seed bed from which this movement sprouted and spread.

First, Europe enjoyed several centuries of relative political stability and peace that allowed scholars to pursue their questions without distraction. Second, the rediscovery of pre-Christian classical philosophers, especially Aristotle, provided the intellectual tools for the task. Aristotelian philosophy was the primary tool.[88] Forerunners of scholasticism like Anselm and Peter Abélard (11th cent.) used its method of logical analysis and syllogisms to raise great "cathedrals of ideas" on various theological topics.[89] More importantly, Aristotle's

---

85 Ocker, "Medieval Exegesis," 339; cf. the similar sentiment in R. A. Muller and J. L. Thompson, "The Significance of Precritical Exegesis: Retrospect and Prospect," in *Biblical Interpretation in the Era of the Reformation*, ed. R. A. Muller and J. L. Thompson (Grand Rapids: Eerdmans, 1996), 344.

86 Smalley, *Study of the Bible*, 120–72.

87 Below we draw on the fine discussions in Olson, *The Story of Christian Theology*, 311–15; J. González, *The Story of Christianity* (San Francisco: Harper and Row, 1984), 1:301–23; and K. S. Latourette, *A History of Christianity* (New York: Harper & Row, 1953), 495–98.

88 Interestingly, some access to Aristotle came through Arabic and Syriac translations of his Greek writings (so Latourette, *History of Christianity*, 497).

89 This phrase comes from Olson, *The Story of Christian Theology*, 312, who also offers an illuminating discussion of these two theologians (316–30); cf. G. R. Evans, "Anselm of Canterbury," and L. O. Nielsen, "Peter Abelard and Gilbert Poitiers," in Evans, *The Medieval Theologians*, 94–101 and 102–14 (respectively).

theory of causation (i.e., that events may have multiple causes) subtly reshaped the thought-world of exegetes in the late Middle Ages (14th cent.). Applied to the Bible, it led them to consider the possibility of multiple causes behind the Bible itself (e.g., God, the human authors, their intentions as determiners of textual meanings, etc.). Further, they began to see that, in Ocker's words, "a quality of thought *beyond* speech [i.e., the basis for multiple senses] in fact was a quality of thought *of* speech."[90] That insight ultimately undermined the long-held distinctions assumed between Scripture's various "senses" and led to a more holistic understanding of its meanings.

The most articulate spokesman for scholasticism was the brilliant Christian thinker, Thomas Aquinas (13th cent.).[91] His massive *Summa Theologica* synthesized the intellectual fruits of three centuries of intense academic discussion. It gave the Christian faith a rational, systematic expression, and eventually became the standard summary of theology in the Roman Catholic Church. More than any of his contemporaries, Aquinas propounded the importance of the literal meaning of Scripture. For him it represented the basis on which the other senses (allegorical, anagogical, etc.) rested. Indeed, he argued that the literal sense of Scripture contained everything necessary to faith.[92]

In summary, practitioners of allegory still abounded in the Church of the Middle Ages, and dependence upon traditional interpretation remained heavy.[93] At the same time, the method's long hegemony within the Church declined, various other approaches to interpretation flourished, and a reformulation of how the supposed four senses interrelated emerged. The scholastic application of philosophical tools to theology also tended to anchor the interpretation of Scripture to more rational, objective moorings. As Muller and Thompson observe, "an increasing interest in both the text and its literal sense" positioned medieval exegesis "along a trajectory pointing toward the Reformation rather than away from it."[94] The intellectual stage, thus, was set for the next step in the long saga of how the Church would interpret its Bible.

THE REFORMATION (ca. A.D. 1500–1650)

Despite popular impression, the step from the Middle Ages into the Protestant Reformation was neither as radical nor as obvious as is often thought. The historical forces that caused it are many, but one in particular merits mention because of its relevance to our subject. During the late Middle Ages, conflict arose between the more

---

90 Ocker, "Medieval Exegesis," 341. We are indebted to his remarkably insightful discussion and citation of medieval writers reflecting this changed outlook (338–44).

91 Olson, *The Story of Christian Theology*, 331–47, who judges Aquinas to be "the single greatest theologian of the Western Catholic tradition between Augustine in the fifth century and Karl Rahner of Austria in the late twentieth century" (331); cf. F. Kerr, "Thomas Aquinas," in Evans, *The Medieval Theologians*, 201–220.

92 G. Bray, *Biblical Interpretation Past and Present* (Downers Grove: InterVarsity, 1996), 152–53.

93 Perhaps the epitome of the persistence of the allegorical method in this period is the eighty-six sermons on the Song of Songs by the mystic, Bernard of Clairvaux (12th cent.); cf. Bray, *Biblical Interpretation*, 160–64.

94 Muller and Thompson, "The Significance of Precritical Exegesis," 344.

traditional scholastics and the so-called new learning of Christian humanists like Erasmus.[95]

With some justification, the latter derided what he deemed the hair-splitting, convoluted logic of scholastic theology.[96] According to the humanists, such theology offered no spiritual food for hungry Christian souls, and many writers openly yearned for the simple faith and devotion of the early Church. Erasmus proposed that the regnant theology of sterile speculation give way to what he called the "philosophy of Christ," genuine spirituality and concern for ethics centered on the teaching of Christ.[97] Since scholastic systematic theology provided traditional orthodoxy with its rational buttress, many saw scholasticism as a fortress that needed to fall.

Further, a renewed interest in studying the Bible in its original Hebrew and Greek languages provided scholars with a fresh glimpse of the Scriptures. In 1506, the controversial philologist Johann Reuchlin published a rudimentary Hebrew grammar, thereby founding the modern study of Hebrew.[98] In 1516, Erasmus published the first modern edition of the Greek New Testament with a fresh Latin translation appended to it. This increasing interest in the early manuscripts exposed many translation errors in the Latin Vulgate and undermined the absolute authority it had enjoyed in supporting church doctrine. Since the Catholic Church had staked its own authority in part on the Vulgate, doubts concerning the authority of the latter also cast shadows of doubt on the authority of the former.[99]

Again, growing dissatisfaction with the allegorical method fueled a desire for a better interpretative approach. At the end of the fifteenth century, a man named Geiler of Kaiserberg observed that abuse of the allegorical method had made Scripture a "nose of wax" to be turned interpretively any way the reader wanted.[100] Many rued the arbitrary, speculative nature of allegory.

---

95 What follows draws on O. Chadwick, *The Reformation* (Baltimore: Penguin Books, 1972), 29–39. "Humanists" were scholars who devoted themselves to the study of classical literature during this period. For an excellent discussion of the continuity and discontinuity between medieval and reformation interpretation, see R. A. Muller, "Biblical Interpretation in the Era of the Reformation," in Muller and Thompson, *Biblical Interpretation*, 8–16. For an insightful analysis of the crucial paradigm-shifts in intellectual thought that contributed to the Reformation and later to modern biblical criticism, see Dungan, *Synoptic Problem*, 146–58.

96 He described his opponent as "academic theology, corrupted as it is by philosophic and scholastic quibbling"; quoted from M. Hoffmann, *Rhetoric and Theology: The Hermeneutic of Erasmus* (Toronto: University of Toronto Press, 1994), 7. Hoffmann offers a thorough, rigorous assessment of Erasmus' approach to biblical interpretation (esp. 95–167, 211–27).

97 Olson, *The Story of Christian Theology*, 315, 362; cf. the expanded treatment of J. L. Carrington, "Desiderius Erasmus," in *The Reformation Theologians*, ed. C. Lindberg (Oxford: Blackwell, 2002), 37–39.

98 B. K. Waltke and M. O'Connor, *An Introduction to Biblical Hebrew Syntax* (Winona Lake, IN: Eisenbrauns, 1990), 38, 39; for details, see O. Chadwick, *The Early Reformation on the Continent* (Oxford: Oxford University Press, 2001), 25–30.

99 Dungan (*Synoptic Problem*, 185–90) details the history of how Erasmus' Greek New Testament, despite its flaws, won acceptance as the *textus receptus*—"the received (i.e., only true) text" from which the King James Version was translated—and how the emerging method of textual criticism eventually undermined its credibility (191–97).

100 B. Hall, "Biblical Scholarship: Editions and Commentaries," in *Cambridge History of the Bible: The West from the Reformation to the Present Day*, ed. S. L. Greenslade (Cambridge: At the University Press, 1963), 48 (henceforth *CHB II*).

According to a popular saying in the sixteenth century, "Erasmus laid the egg and Luther hatched it."[101] Indeed, Martin Luther was one of two figures whose careful exegesis aligned the best of the medieval approach with the new ecclesiastical reality of the sixteenth century and led Christian hermeneutics into new paths. First, Luther affirmed that only Scripture has divine authority for Christians. In so doing, Luther broke with the long-held principle that church tradition and ordained church leaders held virtually the same weight of doctrinal authority as the Bible.[102] He, thus, laid down the foundational premise of the Reformation, the principle of *sola scriptura* (Scripture alone). As a corollary, Luther also affirmed the principle that Scripture itself is its own best interpreter; consequently, readers no longer needed to depend as heavily on patristic commentary and church authorities to understand the Bible as before.

Second, Luther followed those medievalists who rejected the allegorical method of interpretation because, in his view, it amounted to empty speculation. Instead, with Aquinas he affirmed that Scripture had one simple meaning, its historical sense. This is discerned, Luther said, by applying the ordinary rules of grammar in the light of Scripture's original historical context. At the same time, Luther echoed a theme of the Church Fathers and the medievalists: he read the Bible through Christocentric glasses, claiming that the whole Bible—including the OT—taught about Christ.[103] Thus, while rejecting allegory, Luther took up again the typological interpretation typical of the NT.

But Luther stressed that proper interpretation also has a subjective element. By this he meant that the illumination of the Holy Spirit guides Christians in applying their personal experience to biblical interpretation. It enables the Bible reader to understand accurately what a given passage teaches about Christ. The resulting interpretation is, thus, a truly "spiritual interpretation."[104]

The other figure that led the hermeneutical transition was John Calvin.[105] Like Luther and Aquinas, Calvin rejected allegory in favor of a historical interpretation of

---

101 Olson, *The Story of Christian Theology*, 367. Cf. the treatment of Luther's life in Chadwick, *The Reformation*, 40–75. For an excellent biography of Luther, see R. Bainton, *Here I Stand: A Life of Martin Luther* (New York: Mentor Books, 1950).

102 E. Cameron, *The European Reformation* (Oxford: Oxford University Press, 1991), 136–37. As Latourette points out (*History of Christianity*, 704), Luther learned the nominalistic philosophy of William of Occam, who taught that one had to accept Christian beliefs by faith, not by reason, following the authority of the Church and the Bible.

103 Cameron, *The European Reformation*, 137–38, 140; Bray, *Biblical Interpretation Past and Present*, 167. The doctrine of justification by faith, a central theme in Luther's thought, also influenced his reading of Scripture. This interpretive lens in part accounts for his well-known characterization of the Epistle of James as "an epistle of straw."

104 Grant and Tracy, *Short History*, 94–95. For more on Luther's spiritual interpretation, see R. C. Gleason, " 'Letter' and 'Spirit' in Luther's Hermeneutics," *BSac* 157 (2000): 468–85. K. Hagen, "*Omnis homo mendax*: Luther on Psalm 116," in Muller and Thompson, *Biblical Interpretation*, 85–102, offers an illuminating glimpse of Luther as exegete, highlighting elements of his continuity and discontinuity with medieval exegesis and calling into question any ties of Luther's work to Enlightenment approaches.

105 For an overview of his life and work, see R. C. Zachman, "John Calvin (1509–1564)," in Lindberg, *The Reformation Theologians*, 184–97; Chadwick, *The Reformation*, 82–96. Cf. also B. Cottret, *Calvin: A Biography* (Grand Rapids: Eerdmans, 2000).

Scripture. With Luther, he also affirmed the Scripture as the Church's only ultimate authority, an authority to be accepted by faith. Again, Calvin believed in a subjective element in interpretation—what he called "the internal witness of the Holy Spirit." In Calvin's view, this witness served not to illuminate the process of interpretation but to confirm in the Christian's heart that an interpretation was correct.[106]

In brief, the Reformation further developed the emphasis of some medievalists on the primacy of Scripture's literal sense. Also, while cherishing and often invoking church tradition and the interpretations of church fathers, the Reformers set the teachings of Scripture over both as their ultimate authority. They affirmed that the Bible itself was both "perspicacious" (i.e., clearly understandable) and its own best interpreter. If many past exegetes applied allegory to dig out Scripture's alleged multiple meanings, the Reformers followed Aquinas in accepting Scripture's plain, simple, literal sense as the basis for all its treasury of meanings. Small wonder, then, that both Luther and Calvin produced commentaries on numerous biblical books, commentaries still prized by Bible students today.

The Reformers' consensus on "how" to understand Scripture, however, proved no guarantee of their concurrence on "what" it says. In fact, they disagreed on the meaning of many biblical texts. For example, at a now famous meeting in 1529 Luther and H. Zwingli, a leading Swiss Reformer, failed to agree on what the Bible taught about the Lord's Supper.[107] Indeed, the episode anticipated the many interpretive differences that soon divided "Lutherans" and "Calvinists" in the post-Reformation era, divisions that remain today. Such disagreements, however, both confirm the complexity of the process of interpretation (including the fact that interpreters still work within traditions) and affirm the centrality of the Bible as the primary source of Christian doctrine.

Indeed, like most movements, the Reformation also birthed a more extreme expression—the so-called "Radical Reformation."[108] In hermeneutics, groups like the Anabaptists and Mennonites took seriously the Reformation principles of *sola scriptura* and of the perspicacity of Scripture, although they applied them in ways that other Reformers strongly opposed. They gave priority to the NT, which they read literally, appealing to the Holy Spirit for illumination, and they sought to establish relatively

---

106 T. H. L. Parker, *Calvin: An Introduction to His Thought* (Louisville: Westminster/John Knox Press, 1995), 24–27; cf. R. C. Zachman, " 'Do You Understand What You Are Reading?' Calvin's Guidance for the Reading of Scripture," *SJT* 54 (2001): 1–20; and id., "John Calvin," 191, 193. The collection of essays in R. C. Gamble, ed., *Calvin and Hermeneutics* (New York: Garland, 1992), further explores Calvin's interpretive method as reflected in his *Institutes of the Christian Religion* and his commentaries. S. E. Schreiner, " 'The Spiritual Man Judges All Things': Calvin and the Exegetical Debates about Certainty in the Reformation," in Muller and Thompson, *Biblical Interpretation*, 189–215, provides a fascinating glimpse of exegesis by Calvin and other Reformers amid the heated debates over the certainty of faith.

107 Both rejected *transubstantiation*, the Catholic teaching that in the Mass the bread and wine become literally the body and blood of Christ and automatically convey grace when consumed. Luther argued that communion comprised a sacrament involving Christ's "real presence" in the sacrament, while Zwingli believed that, since the physical Christ was in heaven, communion was a symbolic sacred meal (later called an "ordinance"); cf. Olson, *The Story of Christian Theology*, 404–408; G. J. Miller, "Huldrych Zwingli," in Lindberg, *The Reformation Theologians*, 161–63.

108 G. H. Williams, *The Radical Reformation*, 3d ed. (Kirksville, MO: Sixteenth Century Journal Publishers, 1999).

autonomous Christian communities patterned after the NT church. They only baptized adults by immersion, appointed Spirit-led lay leaders, separated themselves from both the world and the established churches, and refused to pay taxes or serve as soldiers. Thought rebellious and seditious by other Christians at the time, thousands of them were cruelly martyred—in retrospect truly a dark day for the Reformation.[109] They bequeathed to Christendom, however, a vibrant fifth stream of western Bible interpretation and Christian community alongside the more established Catholic, Lutheran, Calvinist, and Anglican ones. More importantly, they put the Bible and its interpretation in the hands of lay leadership and, through the groups' community gatherings, made the Bible an ongoing part of the lives of ordinary Christians.

Ironically, in the late sixteenth century the spiritual children of Calvin and Luther seemed to lapse back into a Protestant form of scholasticism.[110] Esoteric doctrinal disputes bordering on hair-splitting tended to preoccupy the emerging Lutheran and Calvinist churches. For example, in Geneva the idea of predestination preoccupied Calvin's successor, Theodore Beza, who led speculation by theologians concerning the logical order of God's decrees.[111] To outside observers, the Reformed churches departed from Luther and Calvin in one respect: they appeared to place more importance on intellectual agreement with Protestant dogma than on the practice of warm, lively, personal piety. In their preoccupation with Protestant orthodoxy, they sadly seemed to resemble the very scholasticism against which the Reformation movement had revolted. Their shared piety failed to bridge the doctrinal chasms between them. On the broader scene, Catholicism still held sway in Spain, France, Italy, Austria, and Poland; in England the newly formed Anglican Church, a stepchild of the Reformation, ruled; Lutherans dominated Germany, Denmark, Sweden, Norway, and Finland; Calvinists controlled Scotland and most of Switzerland; and the Anabaptists held small pockets in Germany, Poland, and Hungary.[112]

The decisions of the Council of Trent (1545–63) marked the official Catholic response to the Reformation. Against the Protestant principle of *sola scriptura*, it reaffirmed, among other things, the Roman Catholic tradition of biblical interpretation

---

109 The well-known story of the German town of Münster illustrates the extremes to which this movement could go. Claiming prophetic inspiration, a series of authoritarian leaders took over the town, compelled the populace to accept rebaptism or else, executed dissenters, and attempted to set up a "New Jerusalem" patterned, in this reconstruction, mainly after the OT, including the practice of polygamy. Only a siege organized by the local bishop ended the Anabaptist rule sixteen months later (1534–1535); cf. T. Howard, "Charisma and History: The Case of Münster, Westphalia, 1534–1535," *Essays in History* 35 (1993): 49–64.

110 Olson, *The Story of Christian Theology*, 455–60; Latourette, *History of Christianity*, 739–40; Hall, "Biblical Scholarship," 76–77; and N. Sykes, "The Religion of the Protestants," *CHB III*, 175–76. R. A. Muller, *Post-Reformation Reformed Dogmatics*, vol. 1 (Grand Rapids: Baker, 1987), 13–97, examines the development of the doctrines of God and Scripture after the Reformation.

111 Beza argued for *supralapsarianism* (Lat. *supra* "before" + *lapsus* "fall"), the idea that God's decree to predestine the salvation/damnation of humans logically preceded his decrees to create and to allow them to fall into sin. By contrast, according to *infralapsarianism* (Lat. *infra* "later"), the former decree follows the latter two decrees.

112 See the illuminating map in S. Ozment, *The Age of Reform 1250–1550* (New Haven: Yale University Press, 1980), 373.

that combined Scripture and tradition, the latter including the doctrinal decisions of popes and church councils. It also upheld the authenticity of the Vulgate and forbade anyone to interpret Scripture out of harmony with church doctrine.[113] As a result, from the momentous events of the sixteenth century flowed two distinct streams of biblical interpretation, one Protestant and one Catholic. Nearly four centuries would pass before their approaches drew closer together again.

THE POST-REFORMATION PERIOD
(ca. A.D. 1650–1800)

The Reformation was not the only revolutionary movement spawned by the late Middle Ages. The Renaissance (1300–1600) featured a reborn-interest in classical Greek and Roman art and philosophy. The revived interest in Hebrew and Greek that aided the Reformation derived from the spirit of the Renaissance. If renewed Christian faith drove the Reformation, an increasing reliance on human reason spurred on the Renaissance. Consequently, important movements flowing from both the Reformation and the Renaissance influenced the interpretation of the Bible in the Post-Reformation period.

From the Reformation emerged the movement called *pietism*. Pietism began in Germany in the seventeenth century and later spread to Western Europe and America.[114] It represented a reaction to the arid intellectual dogmatism of Protestant scholasticism and the sterile formalism of Protestant worship services. Pietism sought to revive the practice of Christianity as a way of life through group Bible study, prayer, and the cultivation of personal morality. Its leader was Philip Jacob Spener (1635–1705), a German pastor who preached the necessity of personal conversion to Christ and an intimate, personal relationship with God. Against the purely doctrinal interests of their contemporaries, Spener and the German Pietists stressed the devotional, practical study of the Bible. Their method featured a literalistic, "common sense" approach applied to careful grammatical study of the ancient Hebrew and Greek texts, always, however, with an eye for their devotional or practical implications. In England, another pietistic movement, the Methodism of John Wesley (1703–91), also sought to recover a vibrant personal piety and holy life through Bible study and prayer.[115] Both movements took advantage of a ground-breaking innovation of the early Renaissance—the translation of the Bible into the spoken languages of the people (e.g., the KJV in 1611). Today's widespread practice of small-group Bible studies and prayer groups continues their practice.

The renowned New England preacher Jonathan Edwards (1703–58) represents pietism in America. Unlike Spener and Wesley, Edwards approached the Bible with an

---

113 Ozment, *The Age of Reform*, 407–409; cf. also the account of the Council of Trent in Chadwick, *The Reformation,* 273–81. In fairness, Trent's decisions also responded positively to Protestant criticisms, authorizing bishops to pastor their flocks more closely and promoting active, personal spirituality among laity. On the other hand, on the heels of Trent, Catholic biblical scholars sadly retreated to the safety of patristic and medieval interpretive paths and showed little originality for three hundred years (Bray, *Biblical Interpretation*, 208–209).

114 Olson, *The Story of Christian Theology*, 473–92; González, *The Story of Christianity,* 204–216; cf. more briefly, Sykes, "The Religion of the Protestants," 190–93.

115 For a recent scholarly reassessment of the Wesleyan movement, see J. Kent, *Wesley and the Wesleyans* (Cambridge: Cambridge University Press, 2002); cf. also González, *The Story of Christianity*, 209–216; Olson, *The Story of Christian Theology*, 510–16.

eye both for its practical application as well as for its doctrinal teachings. As for method, Edwards resorted to typology to draw out practical applications from Scripture. Consider, for example, his interpretation of Gen 29:20: "So Jacob served seven years for Rachel, and they seemed to him but a few days because of the love he had for her" (NRSV). In enduring hard work out of love for Rachel, according to Edwards, Jacob was a type of Christ who endured the cross out of love for the Church.

The spirit of the Renaissance gave birth to the important intellectual movement called *rationalism*.[116] Rationalism regarded the human mind as an independent authority capable of determining truth. The roots of rationalism lay in the Christian humanism of scholars like Erasmus. In the service of the Church, they employed human reason to study the Bible in its original languages. They also believed that the use of reason to investigate the Bible helped Christians to establish their faith. In the seventeenth and eighteenth centuries thinkers applied this tool of reason not only against the authority of the Church but also against the Bible itself. Subtly, their work set the stage for the complete overthrow of both.

In Neil's words, rationalism "was not a system of beliefs antagonistic to Christianity, but an attitude of mind which assumed that in all matters of religion reason is supreme."[117] Three thinkers, two of them philosophers, illustrate the approach of seventeenth-century rationalism to the Bible. In his *Leviathan* (1651), the Anglican philosopher Thomas Hobbes argued from internal evidence that Moses lived long before the Pentateuch was completed and, hence, could not be its author.[118] In his *Critical History of the Old Testament* (1678), the French secular priest Richard Simon reached a similar conclusion, stating that some parts of the OT reflect confusion in chronology.[119]

It was the thoughts of Jewish philosopher Bernard Spinoza, however, that most significantly undercut the authority of Scripture.[120] In his originally anonymous *Tractatus Theologico-Politicus* (1670), Spinoza argued for the primacy of reason in the interpretation of Scripture. In other words, Scripture should be studied like any other book—by using the rules of historical investigation. For example, reason understands scriptural claims to God's direct intervention in history to be simply a common Jewish way of speaking, not actual revelation. Miracle stories thus become nothing more than a powerful way to move ignorant people to obedience. By implication, Spinoza subjected Scripture to the authority of the human mind rather than the other way around.

Thus, the Post-Reformation period brought the fragmentation of approaches to biblical interpretation. On the one hand, the pietists continued to search the Scriptures

---

116 Cf. the extensive survey in Sykes, "Religion of the Protestants," 193–98; W. Neil, "The Criticism and Theological Use of the Bible 1700–1950," *CHB III*, 128–65; and Grant and Tracy, *Short History*, 100–109.

117 Neil, "Criticism and Theological Use," 239. Cf. also the useful historical analysis in Dungan, *Synoptic Problem*, 171–76.

118 T. Hobbes, *Leviathan,* III, chap. 33. This denial, of course, ran counter to the longstanding opinion of the day.

119 Sykes, "Religion of the Protestants," 194; Bray, *Biblical Interpretation*, 239–40. Later scholars would look back to Simon as the father of modern biblical criticism.

120 Grant and Tracy, *Short History*, 105–108. For a detailed analysis of Spinoza's thought, including his political agenda to promote modern secular democracy, see Dungan, *Synoptic Problem*, 198–260.

to feed their hungry souls and to guide their quest for virtuous lives. On the other hand, whereas Aquinas had sought the integration of philosophy and theology, the rationalists promoted the radical divorce of each from the other. Though rationalism had declined in popularity by the mid-eighteenth century, it spawned a series of influential biblical handbooks written along the critical lines of Spinoza and enjoyed an even greater renaissance in the next century.[121]

THE MODERN PERIOD (ca. A.D. 1800–PRESENT)

The Nineteenth Century

On many fronts, the nineteenth century was a revolutionary one. Latourette calls it "The Great Century" because it saw an unprecedented expansion in missions,[122] but ironically, at the same time it witnessed a skeptical repudiation of Christianity among intellectuals. Radical advances in human science created popular confidence in the scientific method, which in turn produced a revolutionary and more scientific method for studying history. Also, in the nineteenth century, developmentalism—the idea that evolving historical progress underlies everything—became widespread as the dialectical philosophy of G. W. F. Hegel, which shaped the social philosophy of Karl Marx, and the evolutionary theory of Charles Darwin attest.

The Bible did not escape the impact of these changes. Scholars, especially those teaching in German universities, sought to approach the Bible similarly through so-called objective, scientific means.[123] Thus was born the approach known as *the historical-critical method,* an interpretive method guided by several crucial philosophical presuppositions.[124] It inherited the rationalistic assumption from its seventeenth-century intellectual ancestors, that the use of human reason, free of theological limitations, is the best tool with which to study the Bible. Therefore, scholars treated the Bible as they would any other literature, not as God's special revelation to humanity.

In addition, the historical-critical method presupposed a naturalistic worldview that explained everything in terms of natural laws and excluded the possibility of supernatural intervention. Thus, scholars accounted for biblical miracles by means of the laws of physics, biology, and chemistry. Again, the approach believed that all history happens as an evolutionary process of development. Thus, its practitioners interpreted the history that the Bible reports along that line, viewing earlier eras as "primitive" and later ones as "advanced." The historical-critical method further regarded the Bible's

---

121 Influential writings during this period included the introduction to the NT by J. D. Michaelis (1750) and an introduction to the OT by J.G. Eichhorn (1780–1783); cf. Bray, *Biblical Interpretation,* 245, 248.

122 Latourette, *History of Christianity,* 1061; cf. González, *The Story of Christianity,* 239–93, whose excellent treatment especially tracks the expansion in America, Latin America, and Europe.

123 For details, see Neil, "Criticism and Theological Use," 255–65; González, *The Story of Christianity,* 282–93.

124 Cf. the summary in Bray, *Biblical Interpretation,* 251–53. According to Harrisville and Sundberg, as the offspring of the political chaos birthed by the Reformation, the purpose of historical criticism was "to nullify the arbitrary political power of those [i.e., princes and priests] who used the Bible to legitimate their authority"; cf. R. A. Harrisville and W. Sundberg, *The Bible in Modern Culture: Theology and Historical-Critical Method from Spinoza to Käsemann* (Grand Rapids: Eerdmans, 1995), 264–66 (quote 266).

ideas as time-bound truths not timeless ones (the Bible merely records what people thought at the time). Finally, scholars assumed that the Bible's greatest contribution lay in its moral and ethical values, not in its theological teachings or historical claims.

These presuppositions brought about two decisive shifts in the focus of biblical interpretation. First, rather than seek to discern what a text meant, many scholars sought instead to discover the sources behind it—the method called *source criticism*.[125] Second, rather than accept the Bible as divine revelation, some scholars sought to retrace the historical development presumed to underlie it. The work of three influential German scholars illustrates these shifts in biblical interpretation.

F. C. Baur, professor of historical theology at the University of Tübingen (1826–1860), argued that Paul's letters reflect a deep division in apostolic Christianity.[126] On one side, said Baur, stood the church of Jerusalem (led by Peter and other original disciples) that taught a Jewish form of Christianity. On the other, stood Paul and his Gentile converts who insisted that the gospel actually abolished the legalistic demands of Judaism. More important, Baur inferred that NT books that did not reflect early Christianity as divided must be post-apostolic in origin. On this premise he dated both Acts and the Gospels to the second century, in effect denying their authority as sources of information for the life and ministry of Jesus and the apostles. In short, Baur and his disciples, the so-called Tübingen School, applied only critical human reason to the study of the NT and claimed to find a historical scenario implicit in the NT that differed from the impression the documents themselves gave. The resulting portrait of the history of early Christianity departed radically from portraits commonly accepted by their contemporaries.

In OT studies, Julius Wellhausen concluded a long scholarly discussion about the written sources of the Pentateuch. In his monumental *Prolegomena to the History of Israel* (1878), Wellhausen argued that behind the Pentateuch stood four separate sources written between 850 and 550 B.C.[127] Several crucial implications derived from that claim: (1) Moses could not have written any of the Pentateuch; (2) the Law originated *after* the historical books, not *before* them; and (3) the actual history of Israel differed markedly from the history the OT books narrate.

The last German scholar whose work typifies nineteenth century thought is Adolf von Harnack. Probably more than any other book, his *What Is Christianity?* (1901) summarized the liberal theology that dominated nineteenth century Protestantism and

---

125 For a detailed history of this method and its assumptions as applied to the origin of the Gospels, see Dungan, *Synoptic Problem*, 302–41.

126 Bray, *Biblical Interpretation*, 321–24; cf. F. F. Bruce, "The History of New Testament Study," in *New Testament Interpretation*, ed. I. H. Marshall (Grand Rapids: Eerdmans, 1977), 42–43. For a larger account, see the still-valuable volume by P. C. Hodgson, *The Formation of Historical Theology: A Study of Ferdinand Christian Baur* (New York: Harper and Row, 1962). B. E. Shields, "The Hermeneutics of Alexander Campbell," *RestQ* 43 (2001): 169–72, 178–79, briefly compares the hermeneutical principles of Baur with those of his American contemporary, Alexander Campbell, leader of the Restoration Movement.

127 Originally in German, its English translation appeared as J. Wellhausen, *Prolegomena to the History of Israel* (Edinburgh: Adam and Charles Black, 1885; Atlanta: Scholars Press, 1994). The application of source criticism in NT studies produced the now widely accepted theory that two main documents (Mark and a collection of Jesus' sayings called "Q") lay behind the present Synoptic Gospels; cf. Bruce, "History," 53–55.

shaped its biblical interpretation.[128] Harnack called for Protestants to return to the religion of Jesus, the religion he claimed lay hidden behind the Church's later portrait of him in the NT. For Harnack, three essential teachings summarize Jesus' religion: (1) the coming of the kingdom of God; (2) the fatherhood of God and the infinite value of the human soul; and (3) the commandment of love.

In sum, Baur, Wellhausen, and Harnack claimed that historical criticism unearthed a complex literary and religious history behind sections of the present Bible. As many critics pointed out, if true, their views severely undermined the historical reliability of the Bible and, hence, its authority as a document of divine revelation. More important, their work radically redefined the object of biblical interpretation. Its purpose was not to determine the meaning of the present text but to find the sources and history lurking behind it. The implication was that only at the earliest stages of the tradition could one encounter accurate and authoritative history.

Though dominant, their views did not pass unchallenged. As one would expect, German Confessional scholars strongly criticized the rationalism of the new historical criticism and promoted academically credible alternative interpretations of both Testaments.[129] Other scholars, including the highly respected H. Ewald and M. Kähler, similarly charted their own interpretive paths in opposition to their more radical colleagues.[130] In the United Kingdom, the academic stature of S. R. Driver and W. Robertson Smith, who wrote the preface to the English translation of Wellhausen's *Prolegomena*, helped the latter's views gain entry there, but J. B. Lightfoot's now-classic translation of the apostolic fathers disproved several of Baur's key assumptions and essentially discredited his theory.

In North America, figures like B. B. Warfield, W. H. Green, and W. J. Beecher not only ably critiqued the assumptions of the new criticism but promoted an alternative, vibrant new criticism of their own, thus winning a standoff if not actually reversing the inroads of European criticism.[131] Against the latter's skepticism, they defended their

---

128 The English translation of the German original is A. von Harnack, *What Is Christianity?* (New York: Putnam, 1901); cf. the discussion in Grant and Tracy, *Short History*, 116–17. For liberalism, see A. Richardson, "The Rise of Modern Biblical Scholarship and Recent Discussion of the Authority of the Bible," *CHB III*, 311–18.

129 Certainly the formative leader in OT studies was E. W. Hengstenberg, but others sympathetic and contributory included C. F. Keil, J. C. K. von Hofmann, and F. Delitzsch. In fairness, however, one must state that these scholars represented a spectrum of views and degrees of openness to the method; cf. the definitive study by J. Rogerson, *Old Testament Criticism in the Nineteenth Century: England and Germany* (London: SPCK, 1984), 79–90 (Hengstenberg, Keil), 104–120 (Hofmann and Delitzsch). Significant opposing NT scholars included A. H. Cremer (1834–1903), J. P. Lange (1802–84), B. Weiss (1827–1918), and M. Baumgarten (1812–1889); cf. Bray, *Biblical Interpretation*, 332–33, 335.

130 Rogerson (*Old Testament Criticism*, 91) regards Ewald as "one of the greatest critical Old Testament scholars of all time" and devotes an entire chapter to his contribution (91–103). Another example is C. C. J. von Bunsen (Rogerson, *Old Testament Criticism*, 121–29). For Kähler, see Bray, *Biblical Interpretation*, 335.

131 Cf. Bray, *Biblical Interpretation*, 324–25; M. A. Noll, *Between Faith and Criticism: Evangelicals, Scholarship, and the Bible in America*, SBL Confessional Perspective Series (San Francisco; Cambridge, UK: Harper & Row, 1986), 11–31, 62–90. Prominent among the casualties were Presbyterian scholars C. A. Briggs, H. P. Smith, and A. C. McGiffert, who either lost a denominational judicial hearing for their views or chose to resign to avoid one. In Scotland, W. R. Smith also lost his professorial post but retained his ordination in the Free Church of Scotland. Noll's concluding assessment of the American scene (31) is that, as the 19th century ended, both the "strongholds of the new criticism" and "conservative evangelical scholarship" remained secure, the latter maintaining its place in the wider academic world and its "theological grounding"—a situation not true a generation later.

straightforward inductive approach to biblical interpretation by appealing to the epistemology of the so-called Scottish Common Sense philosophy—the view that common sense rightly recognizes some ideas as true and needing no defense.[132] Meanwhile, away from academia the Anabaptist theme of a return to primitive NT Christianity reappeared in two new movements that, as one might expect, gave new priority to the NT in interpretation. The Restoration Movement led by B. W. Stone and Alexander Campbell based itself on the interpretation of Acts and the epistles, with Campbell developing a hermeneutical approach that remarkably anticipated that of twentieth century evangelicals.[133] At the same time, Pentecostal revivals in the late nineteenth century convinced many that God had supernaturally baptized them in the Holy Spirit and that their supernatural experiences had recovered the essence of the NT church.[134] How their experiences related to the interpretation of the Bible would become a topic of discussion among their spiritual descendants in the next century.

The Twentieth Century

The dawn of this century witnessed the flowering of two interpretive approaches that grew out of the late nineteenth century. The first was that of the *history of religions*.[135] Baur and Wellhausen had claimed to uncover the "true history" of the Israelite and Christian religions through internal biblical evidence. But during the nineteenth century, archaeologists had unearthed numerous written texts from ancient Egypt, Syro-Palestine, Babylonia, and Assyria. These texts gave scholars fresh new insights into religions contemporary to the Bible. Inevitably, scholars came to compare them with biblical religion. Such comparisons soon gave birth to the history-of-religions approach, a method that tried to trace the historical development of all ancient Near Eastern religions. Specifically, it professed to show how ancient neighboring religions had profoundly influenced the religious practices of the Israelites. Sometimes its adherents went to unwarranted extremes in their approach, as when F. Delitzsch famously tried to argue that the OT contained nothing more than warmed-over Babylonian ideas.[136]

The history-of-religions approach left two lasting influences on biblical interpretation. First, its comparative research suggested that many biblical ideas had originated

---

132 Cf. M. A. Noll, "Common Sense Traditions and Evangelical Thought," *American Quarterly* 37 (1985): 216–238; and his criticism of evangelical dependence on this philosophy in id., *The Scandal of the Evangelical Mind* (Grand Rapids: Eerdmans; Leicester: InterVarsity, 1994), 94–107.

133 Cf. Shields, "Hermeneutics," 175–79; and T. H. Olbricht, "Hermeneutics in the Churches of Christ," *RestQ* 37 (1995): 1–24. Present-day Disciples of Christ, the Christian Church, and the Churches of Christ trace their roots to this movement. For recent discussion of this movement's inductive method of hermeneutics and its possible response to postmodernism, see D. L. Little, "Inductive Hermeneutics and the Early Restoration Movement," *Stone-Campbell Journal* 3 (2000): 5–18.

134 K. J. Archer, "Pentecostal Hermeneutics: Retrospect and Prospect," *JPT* 8 (1996): 64.

135 For its story, see H. F. Hahn and H. D. Hummel, *The Old Testament in Modern Research* (Philadelphia: Fortress, 1970), 83–118. J. Riches, *A Century of New Testament Study* (Valley Forge, PA: Trinity Press International, 1993), 14–49, reviews its impact on NT studies. For developments since World War II, see P. D. Miller, "Israelite Religion," in *The Hebrew Bible and Its Modern Interpreters*, ed. D. A. Knight and G. M. Tucker (Philadelphia: Fortress, 1985), 201–37; cf. id., *The Religion of Ancient Israel* (London: SPCK; Louisville: Westminster John Knox, 2000).

136 F. Delitzsch, *Babel and Bible* (New York: G. P. Putnam's Sons, 1903).

earlier than scholars like Wellhausen had thought. For example, the discovery of ancient law codes implied that at least some of the OT's ethical demands might be ancient, perhaps even derived from Moses, rather than from the religious creativity of the prophets. Second, it firmly established what came to be known as "the comparative principle." Henceforth, proper biblical interpretation would require consultation with relevant cultural evidence from the ancient world of the Bible in order better to tune into its cultural milieu.[137]

The second interpretive approach was the new literary method called *form criticism*.[138] The father of form criticism was Hermann Gunkel, a German OT scholar best known for his study of the Psalms. Form criticism sought to recover the shorter oral compositions from which the Bible's written sources supposedly derived. It also aimed to determine the specific cultural life-setting in which each originated. Thus, Gunkel and his disciples claimed that the original setting of most of the psalms was the temple in Jerusalem.

Eventually, OT form criticism began to focus more on the literary types of the present written text rather than on the Bible's oral pre-stages.[139] For that reason form criticism remains an invaluable method in the toolbox of all serious Bible students. Our survey of OT literary genres later in this book bears witness to the lasting legacy of Gunkel's approach, and, as we shall see, in the hands of NT scholars it also profoundly shaped the interpretation of the Gospels in this century.[140]

Post-World War I

To a great extent, the twentieth century's two world wars provide the key markers in biblical interpretation during that century. The disastrous events of World War I devastated Europe and destroyed the naive optimism that had supported liberal theology. The horrors of the war also seemed to stir up both a reaction against the exclusive hegemony of science and an increasing interest in the existentialist philosophies of figures like Søren Kierkegaard and Martin Heidegger. Like the proverbial phoenix, new directions in biblical interpretation arose from the ashes of world conflict. Two towering figures, men who today still cast long shadows of influence, initially charted those new directions.

---

137 Krentz has rightly pointed out the sinister downside of late nineteenth century "scientific" thought, both history-of-religions and historical criticism in general. By elevating historical knowledge in opposition to Christian faith, such thinking removed the academic study of the Bible from any accountability to the church and denigrated Christian use of the Bible that was not "historical" by its definition; cf. E. Krentz, *The Historical-Critical Method*, Guides to Biblical Scholarship (Philadelphia: Fortress Press, 1975), 28–30.

138 Cf. Hahn and Hummel, *Old Testament*, 119–56; more briefly, Neil, "Criticism and Theological Use," 289–91.

139 Gunkel's own definitive research on the psalms certainly reflects this change. An English translation of his introductory work is available in H. Gunkel, J. Begrich, and J. Nogalski, *Introduction to the Psalms: The Genres of the Religious Lyric of Israel*, Mercer Library of Biblical Studies (Macon, GA: Mercer University Press, 1998); cf. also his classic study of narratives, *The Stories of Genesis* (n.p.: D & F Scott Publishers, 1998).

140 For a standard introduction to the method, see G. M. Tucker, *Form Criticism* (Philadelphia: Fortress, 1971). Cf. also the critical assessment of M. J. Buss, *Biblical Form Criticism in Its Context*, JSOTSup 274 (Sheffield: Sheffield Academic Press, 1999). See also the volumes in the Forms of Old Testament Literature (FOTL) series published by Eerdmans. For NT form criticism, see below.

The first was the Swiss country pastor, Karl Barth (1886–1968), whose commentary on Romans (1919) severely critiqued the mistakes of liberalism and sought to reassert long-lost emphases of his Reformation heritage.[141] Specifically, he reemphasized the authority of Scripture as the Word of God and the necessity of a personal encounter with the living God of whom it speaks. The idea of such a personal encounter reflected the influence on Barth of Kierkegaard. Barth's later multi-volume *Church Dogmatics* fueled a lively renaissance in Protestant systematic theology and exemplified how penetrating biblical interpretation could enrich theology.[142]

The second imposing shadow on the twentieth-century landscape was the noted NT scholar, Rudolf Bultmann (1884–1976).[143] As Kierkegaard helped to shape Barth's theology, so Heidegger's brand of existentialism formed the philosophical foundation of Bultmann's work. The history of biblical interpretation remembers Bultmann for two distinct developments. First, he applied the method of form criticism to the study of the Gospels and their historical development. As Gunkel had done magisterially with the psalms, Bultmann classified the Gospels' individual episodes (pericopes) into various literary types (e.g., miracle story, pronouncement story, etc.) and suggested an original setting for each.[144] Bultmann also judged the historical reliability of certain literary forms depending upon their setting. He especially doubted those types that, in his view, seemed colored by the later beliefs of the early Christian community. Thus, in Bultmann's hands, form criticism raised serious questions concerning the historical reliability of the Gospels. Bultmann distinguished between the "Jesus of history" (the person who actually lived) and the "Christ of faith" (the person in Christian preaching). On the other hand, using modern historical-critical methods, British scholars like C. H. Dodd, T. W. Manson, and Vincent Taylor ably defended the substantial historical reliability of Gospel accounts.

---

141 For an English translation based on the 6th German edition, see K. Barth, *The Epistle to the Romans* (London: Oxford University Press, 1968). Cf. Richardson, "The Rise of Modern Biblical Scholarship," 319–23; S. Neill and T. Wright, *The Interpretation of The New Testament 1861–1986*, 2d ed. (Oxford: Oxford University Press, 1988), 215–27.

142 The English translation is K. Barth, *Church Dogmatics*, 4 vols. (Edinburgh: T & T Clark, 1956–1969). For an overview of Barth's thought, see G. W. Bromiley, *An Introduction to the Theology of Karl Barth* (Edinburgh: T & T Clark, 2000); and T. F. Torrance, *Karl Barth, Biblical and Evangelical Theologian* (Edinburgh: T & T Clark, 1990). A recent assessment of his hermeneutics is available in N. B. MacDonald, *Karl Barth and the Strange New World Within the Bible* (Carlisle, UK: Paternoster, 2000).

143 Cf. the appreciative treatments in Harrisville and Sundberg, *The Bible in Modern Culture*, 203–237; Neill and Wright, *The Interpretation of the New Testament*, 237–51. T. Larsson, *God in the Fourth Gospel*, CBNT 35 (Stockholm: Almqvist and Wiksell, 2001), 168–212, assesses his influential work on the Gospel of John.

144 For a translation of the ground-breaking work originally published in 1921, see R. Bultmann, *The History of the Synoptic Tradition* (New York: Harper & Row, 1963). Cf. also the influential form critical work of Bultmann's contemporary, M. Dibelius, *From Tradition to Gospel* (New York: Charles Scribner's Sons, 1965 [Germ. orig. 1919]). E. V. McKnight, *What Is Form Criticism?* (Philadelphia: Fortress, 1969) provides a convenient introduction to the method.

Second, Bultmann sought to "demythologize" the Bible, to recover the *kerygma* or "message" currently couched in its (in his view) outmoded mythological worldview.[145] Like Barth, Bultmann was concerned that the Bible speak to the needs of modern people. He wanted to make the Bible's message understandable and relevant to his contemporaries. In his view, the prevailing scientific worldview had undermined the faith of many intelligent Christians. They had trouble believing the Bible because of what he called its mythological language—for example, its three-storied universe, its claims that Jesus "descended" from and "ascended" to heaven, and its miracles.

Bultmann's approach requires that one read the Bible with an existentialist hermeneutic.[146] Most readers expect to derive objective information from the Bible, and Bultmann conceded that the text does provide much of that, but he also allowed that readers may disregard anything they deem as prescientific (e.g., primitive cosmology, myths, etc.). Further, he argued that one should read the Bible subjectively to let its understanding of human existence clarify one's own existential predicament. Indeed, Bultmann affirmed that the Bible becomes revelation when it confronts us with such a challenge. He determined that people can understand the Bible only when they understand what he called their "unauthentic existence" and the possibilities of making it more authentic. In other words, he proposed a primarily subjective, existentialist reading of the Bible—one uprooted from any first-century historical event.

Between the two world wars, the work of Barth and Bultmann spawned a new theological movement called *neo-orthodoxy* (or dialectical theology). Dominated by Barth and another Swiss theologian, Emil Brunner, three basic assumptions guided the approach of neo-orthodox theologians to biblical interpretation. First, God is regarded as a subject not an object (i.e., a "Thou" not an "It"). Thus, the Bible's words cannot convey knowledge of God as abstract propositions; one can only know him in a personal encounter. Such encounters are so subjective, mysterious, and miraculous that they elude the objective measurements of science. Second, a great gulf separates the Bible's transcendent God from fallen humanity. Indeed, he is so transcendent that only myths can bridge this gulf and reveal him to people. Thus, rather than read biblical reports of events as in some way historical, neo-orthodoxy interpreted them as myths meant to convey theological truth in historical dress. Critics, of course, pointed out that the effect of this approach was to downplay the historicity of biblical events.

Third, neo-orthodox theologians believed that truth was ultimately paradoxical in nature, so they accepted apparently conflicting statements in the Bible as paradoxes for which a rational explanation would be both inappropriate and unnecessary. By accepting apparently opposite biblical ideas as paradoxes, critics noted, neo-orthodoxy in effect seemed to cast doubt on the assumption that rational coherence underlies and binds together the diverse ideas of Scripture.

---

145 The translation of the 1941 German original is R. Bultmann, "New Testament and Mythology," in *Kerygma and Myth*, vol. 1, ed. H. W. Bartsch (London: SPCK, 1957), 1–44; cf. also his *Jesus Christ and Mythology* (New York: Charles Scribner's Sons, 1958). Bray, *Biblical Interpretation*, 438–41, and Neill and Wright (*Interpretation of the New Testament*, 241–51) provide insightful retrospective assessments of Bultmann's work.

146 Hence, the chapter title, "The Development of An Existential Interpretation of the Bible," in Riches, *A Century of New Testament Study*, 70–88; cf. Richardson, "Modern Biblical Scholarship," 327–39.

Post-World War II

If World War I gave birth to neo-orthodoxy and Bultmann's program, World War II also fathered significant offspring. In postwar America, a flood of publications showed a revival of interest in biblical theology, a revival that Childs calls the *Biblical Theology Movement*.[147] In 1947, the journal *Interpretation* began publication to promote positive reflection on theology and the Bible. Three years later, SCM Press launched its scholarly series "Studies in Biblical Theology." While historical-critical matters had formerly dominated biblical commentaries, now the commentaries featured discussions of the theology and message of biblical books.

According to Childs, five major emphases typified the movement: (1) the rediscovery of the Bible's theological dimension; (2) the unity of the whole Bible; (3) the revelation of God in history; (4) the distinctiveness of the Bible's mentality (i.e., a Hebrew way of thinking in contrast to a Greek way); and (5) the contrast of the Bible to its ancient environment. Though criticism of the movement cast doubt on many of those emphases, in the late 1960s it nevertheless served to revive study of the theological dimension of the Bible, a dimension that had become a casualty of historical criticism in the late nineteenth century.[148]

The postwar era also saw the birth of what proved to be an influential new method. The nineteenth century passed on interpretive methods that tended to highlight the Bible's diversity and disunity. With source criticism, for example, biblical interpretation amounted to a kind of academic autopsy. It was enough for the interpreter simply to catalog the parts of the textual cadaver. Again, by focusing on individual forms and their transmission, form criticism tended to bog down in a similar tedious analysis. In both cases, scholars simply ignored the larger literary context (the present, final text of the Bible) of which the sources and forms were a part.

But in the mid-1950s, *redaction criticism* emerged as a complementary discipline to form criticism. Essentially, redaction criticism seeks to discern the distinctive theological and thematic emphases that the individual biblical writers or editors gave their

---

147 The term "biblical theology" refers to the theology that the Bible itself shows as opposed to that of philosophers or systematic theologians. B. S. Childs, *Biblical Theology in Crisis* (Philadelphia: Westminster, 1970), 13–60, provides details on the Biblical Theology Movement. But see also J. D. Smart, *The Past, Present, and Future of Biblical Theology* (Philadelphia: Westminster, 1979), 22–30, who denies the movement's existence.

148 Despite this contribution, Childs pronounced the movement "dead" and proposed that the canon provides the only viable context for Christian exegesis and theology (on his "canon criticism" see below). Nevertheless, as Mark Twain might say, news of biblical theology's demise seems premature. The Overtures to Biblical Theology series continues to publish volumes (most recently, D. L. Smith-Christopher, *A Biblical Theology of Exile* [Minneapolis: Fortress, 2002]), and the journal *Ex Auditu* still publishes the papers of the annual Theological Symposium held at North Park Seminary in Chicago. Two of Childs' former students (B. C. Birch and D. L. Petersen) recently teamed with T. E. Fretheim and W. Brueggemann to produce a new genre, *A Theological Introduction to the Old Testament* (Nashville: Abingdon, 1999). Evangelicals stand at the forefront of this lively field of study, as attested by the recent major work by C. H. H. Scobie, *The Ways of Our God: An Approach to Biblical Theology* (Grand Rapids: Eerdmans, 2003). The "New Studies in Biblical Theology" series edited by D. A. Carson (InterVarsity Press) seeks to fill the gap left when the earlier Studies in Biblical Theology (SBT) was discontinued. Obviously, scholarly interest in biblical theology remains very much alive.

materials.[149] It assumes, for example, that—however it came to be—each context or book reflects the editorial design of its author/editor, a design that aims to emphasize certain themes. Redaction criticism first appeared in studies of the Gospels,[150] but OT scholars have used a similar approach in studying sections of the Hebrew canon.[151]

Two other postwar interpretive developments trace their intellectual genealogy to the work of Bultmann. The first is the movement among Bultmann's students called the "new quest for the historical Jesus."[152] They reacted vigorously against his rigid denial that one could know much of anything historical about Jesus. They (and many others) asked how one could have an authentic Christian faith without an actual historical Jesus. They wondered whether Bultmann's agnosticism about Jesus might actually undermine the faith. So, in the 1950s and 1960s they cautiously sought to sketch from the Gospels what they thought could be known historically about Jesus.[153] Bultmann's critics had accused him of Docetism, the heresy that Jesus only appeared to suffer and die but did not actually do so because he was not human. Consequently, his students paid particular attention to the history of the crucifixion because of its importance in Christian theology. Conservative scholars might regard their conclusions as rather meager, but they at least narrowed the gap between the "Jesus of history" and the "Christ of faith."[154]

The second development, the so-called *new hermeneutic*, also involved Bultmann's academic children.[155] From the field of linguistics it drew on new views about human language. Specifically, it understood language to be an actor (i.e., something that sets things in motion) rather than a label one attaches to passive objects. Thus, each use of language

---

149 For the method, see the introduction by NT scholar N. Perrin, *What is Redaction Criticism?* (Philadelphia: Fortress, 1969). E. V. McKnight, "Form and Redaction Criticism," in *The New Testament and Its Modern Interpreters*, ed. E. J. Epp and G. W. McRae (Philadelphia: Fortress, 1989), 149–174, ably treats the method's subsequent refinement and application.

150 E.g., W. Marxsen, *Mark the Evangelist: Studies on the Redaction History of the Gospel* (Nashville: Abingdon, 1969); and H. Conzelmann, *The Theology of Saint Luke* (New York: Harper & Row, 1961).

151 E.g., most recently, J. A. Wagenaar, *Judgment and Salvation: The Composition and Redaction of Micah 2–5*, VTSup 85 (Leiden: Brill, 2001); N. L. deClaissé-Walford, *Reading from the Beginning: The Shaping of the Hebrew Psalter* (Macon, GA: Mercer University Press, 1997); and G. A. Rendsburg, *The Redaction of Genesis* (Winona Lake, IN: Eisenbrauns, 1986).

152 The expression derives from the book title of J. M. Robinson, *A New Quest of the Historical Jesus*, SBT 25 (London: SCM; Naperville, IL: Allenson, 1959), a title that echoes the English title of an important book written by A. Schweitzer more than fifty years earlier (*The Quest of the Historical Jesus* [New York: MacMillan, 1910; recently, Minneapolis: Fortress, 2001]). For a survey of the quest, see Neill and Wright, *Interpretation of the New Testament*, 288–312, 397–98.

153 The monograph by Robinson (*A New Quest of the Historical Jesus*) pointed the way. Other important contributors included the 1953 lecture by E. Käsemann, "The Problem of the Historical Jesus," published in translation in his *Essays on New Testament Themes*, SBT 21 (London: SCM; Naperville, IL: Allenson, 1964), 15–47; and G. Bornkamm, *Jesus of Nazareth* (New York: Harper & Row, 1960).

154 According to Neill and Wright (*Interpretation of the New Testament*, 379–403), a "Third Quest" for the historical Jesus has recently superseded both the "first" (i.e., A. Schweitzer's) and the "new" quests. Its distinctives are: (1) use of extra-biblical evidence to reconstruct the cultural milieu of Jesus; (2) a renewed interest in Jesus' Jewishness; and (3) discussion about why Jesus was crucified. See below.

155 For an overview, see W. G. Doty, *Contemporary New Testament Interpretation* (Englewood Cliffs, NJ: Prentice-Hall, 1972), 28–51; and the essays in J. M. Robinson and J. B. Cobb, eds., *The New Hermeneutic* (New York: Harper & Row, 1964). The movement's master theoretician is H. G. Gadamer, *Truth and Method* (London: Sheed and Ward, 1975).

brings a new entity into being—what movement spokesmen like E. Fuchs and G. Ebeling call a "word-happening" or "language-event." Each speech-event communicates its own unique truth—and this is the crucial point—in light of the hearer's own experience.

Applied to biblical interpretation, this new concept of language implied a different view of the biblical text. Up to now, interpreters presumed it to be an object that passively responded to their interpretive questions, an object over which they were master. By contrast, the new hermeneutic assumed that, when read, the text created, as it were, a new language-event that mastered the reader. In other words, the biblical text interprets the reader, not vice versa, confronting him or her with the Word of God at that moment. Thus, in the new hermeneutic the text, not the interpreter, guides biblical interpretation. In interpretation, the text and its intention must grip the reader rather than the reader's questions controlling the text.

The new hermeneutic made several positive contributions to biblical interpretation. First, it stimulated a refreshing revival of theoretical reflection on the subject. Biblical hermeneutics used to focus on the various interpretive techniques a reader employed to draw out meaning from a text. The new hermeneutic, however, underscored the complex relationship that links readers and written texts. Second, it rightly drew attention to the effect a text has on the reader. Previously the assumption was that the interpreter controlled interpretation, that the text was a passive object to be analyzed. Now the interpreter is challenged to reckon with the scrutiny that the text imposes on him or her. In essence, by drawing readers into its world, the text actively interprets their world.

Third, the concept of language-event in the new hermeneutic properly emphasized that Scripture must relate to the meaningful existence of its contemporary audience. In other words, besides defining what the text meant originally, interpretation also entails relating the historical meaning of Scripture to the issues of contemporary life.

As for its weaknesses, the new hermeneutic tends to deemphasize a text's historical meaning and its contribution to the language-event. Hence, it runs the risk of losing its roots in the biblical text. Again, while opening up new interpretive insights, in effect its existentialist orientation limits what a text can say to the reader, namely, it can offer insights into human existence. Readers may not gather biblical insights, for example, into history, science, culture, the nature of God, etc.

The postwar Biblical Theology Movement also left a methodological offspring: the method of *canon criticism*. To remedy the movement's weaknesses, B. S. Childs proposed a new context for doing theology—the canonical status of the Bible.[156] Canon criticism regards biblical books as canonical, that is, as the authoritative writings of the Jewish and Christian communities. It also presumes that theological convictions guided those who compiled these books. Hence, it seeks to find their theological meaning by analyzing their canonical shape—the editorial design of their present form.[157]

---

156 Childs, *Biblical Theology in Crisis*, 99–107. For an introduction to the approach, see J. A. Sanders, *Canon and Community: A Guide to Canonical Criticism* (Philadelphia: Fortress, 1984). See our further analysis in chapter 3.

157 Childs himself pursued this task in his *Introduction to the Old Testament as Scripture* (Philadelphia: Fortress, 1979), his *The New Testament as Canon: An Introduction* (Philadelphia: Fortress, 1984), and his *Biblical Theology of the Old and New Testaments* (London: SCM, 1992). For recent developments and examples, see C. Seitz and K. Greene-McCreight, eds., *Theological Exegesis: Essays in Honor of Brevard S. Childs* (Grand Rapids: Eerdmans, 1999).

Finally, the late twentieth century saw the emergence of two important new developments whose influence still continues. First, academic discussions of hermeneutics from a Pentecostal perspective began to appear. In 1979 the Society for Pentecostal Studies launched a major journal, *Pneuma* (Leiden: E. J. Brill), as a forum for international scholarly discussion of Pentecostal and charismatic issues. In 1992, Sheffield Academic Press began the *Journal of Pentecostal Theology* (*JPT*) to promote constructive theological discussion across many faith traditions.[158] Though no hermeneutical consensus has yet emerged, lively discussion has surfaced several key questions: Is the use of a rational evangelical hermeneutic helpful or harmful to experience-based Pentecostal life? How does the experienced work of the Holy Spirit relate to biblical interpretation? According to the NT, is the central authority of the Christian community to be the Bible or Christ addressing it through the Spirit?

Second, beginning in the early 1980s the appearance of several major studies on Jesus led some NT scholars to hail them as the "Third Quest for the Historical Jesus."[159] New archaeological data concerning first-century Palestine, refinements in scholarly methods, and newly discovered manuscripts like the *Gospel of Thomas* provided new perspectives from which to interpret him. The Jesus Seminar, a self-appointed select group of North American scholars, developed a set of highly controversial criteria allegedly necessary to differentiate what Jesus actually said or did from later embellishments. Recent publications by a spectrum of scholars have portrayed Jesus in a variety of ways (i.e., as an itinerant Cynic philosopher, an eschatological prophet, a prophet of social change, a wise sage, a marginal Jew, and a Jewish messiah). The lively discussion continues and, along with the "heat" of controversy, has shed some new "light" on our understanding of Jesus. The long-term significance of this "quest" remains to be seen.

In conclusion, the twentieth century saw the emergence of new methods of interpretation as well as rigorous philosophical and theological reflection on the nature of the interpretive process.[160] In its last two decades, other new methods joined the ranks of those discussed above. Literary approaches—the new literary criticism, reader-response criticism, and deconstruction—generated intriguing interpretations and lively scholarly discussion. Sociological approaches, including explicit hermeneutics adopted by various advocacy groups (e.g., feminist and liberationist hermeneutics), also gained a wide hearing. The ascendancy of these methods has been so rapid, and in some early twenty-first century circles have become so dominant, that we devote the entire next chapter to them.

---

158 Sheffield is publishing a new scholarly commentary series, The Pentecostal Commentary, written by and for Pentecostals. For its first volumes, see J. C. Thomas, *The Johannine Epistles* (Sheffield: Sheffield Academic Press, 2003); and R. Skaggs, *1 & 2 Peter and Jude* (Sheffield: Sheffield Academic Press, 2003). For hermeneutics, see especially the essays in *Pneuma* 15 (1993); K. J. Archer, "Pentecostal Hermeneutics: Retrospect and Prospect," *JPT* 8 (1996): 63–81; M. J. Cartledge, "Empirical Theology: Towards An Evangelical-Charismatic Hermeneutic," *JPT* 9 (1996): 115–26; and J. K. A. Smith, "The Closing of the Book: Pentecostals, Evangelists, and the Sacred Writings," *JPT* 11 (1997): 49–71.

159 For a convenient introduction and helpful evaluation, see B. Witherington III, *The Jesus Quest: The Third Search for the Jew of Nazareth* (Downers Grove: InterVarsity, 1995).

160 Here we refer readers to the definitive discussion of contemporary biblical interpretation in A. C. Thiselton, *New Horizons in Hermeneutics* (Grand Rapids: Zondervan, 1992). The 21st century is seeing the emergence of a new series, Scripture and Hermeneutics (Zondervan/Paternoster), whose volumes treat state-of-the-art issues.

3

RECENT LITERARY AND SOCIAL-SCIENTIFIC APPROACHES TO INTERPRETATION

Most of this book considers what one might call traditional hermeneutics, that is, common-sense wisdom for interpreting the Bible combined with the methodological precision given to that wisdom by the last two centuries of modern biblical criticism. As we saw in chapter 2, it also embraces the more sophisticated tools of source, form, and redaction criticism—tools whose foundational concepts substantially predate the terms themselves. Today, however, many Bible scholars, particularly those outside of evangelical circles, have called for nothing less than a paradigm shift in hermeneutics.[1] They found the old ways sterile, limiting, or misleading and believed it was time to do something new. The suggestions they have made for replacing the more common approach to interpretation—traditional historical-grammatical analysis—primarily revolve around two areas of study: (1) modern literary criticism and (2) social-scientific analysis.[2] The first of these in certain aspects recovers a healthy emphasis on the literary nature of the Bible that has been lost in our scientific age. We dispute that it is a case of *either* the old ways *or* the new ways.[3] We grant that these new arenas of study can afford important insights to supplement traditional hermeneutics, but they also offer dangerous pitfalls when abused.

---

1 The concept comes originally from T. S. Kuhn, *The Structure of Scientific Revolutions*, 2d ed. (Chicago: University of Chicago Press, 1970). A paradigm shift occurs when one model of interpreting data is almost entirely replaced by a quite different model.

2 For an excellent example, see C. H. Talbert's unnecessarily scathing review of J. Fitzmyer (*The Gospel According to Luke*, 2 vols. [Garden City: Doubleday, 1981–85] in *CBQ* 48 (1986): 336–38), in which Talbert essentially faults Fitzmyer for having written a traditional, historical-critical commentary of a kind that Talbert believes is now passé, that is, in an age when he thinks literary-critical paradigms should predominate. For a more positive call for a paradigm shift to a social-scientific perspective, see B. J. Malina, *Christian Origins and Cultural Anthropology* (Atlanta: John Knox, 1986).

3 An excellent defense and discussion of the complementarity of historical and literary methods appears throughout M. A. Powell, *What Is Narrative Criticism?* (Minneapolis: Fortress, 1990). For the blend of historical and social-scientific methods, see J. H. Elliott, *What Is Social-Scientific Criticism?* (Minneapolis: Fortress, 1993).

LITERARY CRITICISM

"Literary criticism" means different things to different people. Aída Spencer has compiled a list of no less than fifteen distinct definitions, many of which are best treated under different headings.[4] Such topics include analysis of authorship, date, place of writing, original audience, linguistic style, sources, tradition and redaction, integrity, and purpose. All of these are necessary components of the analysis of any work of literature. But while all at various times in the past have been considered a part of literary criticism, now they are usually treated under *historical* criticism. What critics who are calling for a shift in biblical studies usually mean by literary criticism today is largely *ahistorical* in nature—methods that require an examination only of the final form of the text. We treat two such methods later in this volume: genre criticism, which analyzes the literary classification of an entire biblical book, and that portion of form criticism that describes the form or subgenre of a given part of a biblical book. Under genre criticism we note also the growing tendency to classify the nature of the rhetoric of the writer—what is often called rhetorical criticism.[5] This still leaves three major areas of literary criticism, however, that we need to discuss: narrative criticism, reader-response criticism, and deconstruction.

The history of literary criticism correlates closely with the three dimensions of hermeneutical analysis we introduced in chapter 1—the author, the text, and the reader. While traditionally literary critics have attempted to determine an author's original intent, the approach in the first half of the twentieth century of "formalism" or "new criticism" in literary studies more generally focused on a coherent interpretation of the text in its entirety apart from any historical background information. Seeking to avoid committing what they called the "intentional fallacy," such critics stressed that readers usually do not have access to the mental states or intentions of authors, often long separated in time and place from contemporary readers. In addition, the written, historical information that does exist about the circumstances of the composition of a document may not be adequate to enable us to discern authorial intention. Moreover, authors may write something other than what they mean to say or there may be additional dimensions of the meanings of their texts than those they recognized initially.[6]

Focusing on texts independent of their authors then spawned two subdisciplines—narrative criticism and structuralism. Narrative criticism focused on a close reading of what became known as the surface structure of a text—elements like plot, theme, motifs, characterization; or, in poetry, meter, rhyme, parallelism, and so on. Structuralism analyzed the so-called "deep structures" of a text—consistent elements perceptible beneath the surface of the narrative, related to, for example, how a "sender" attempts to communicate an "object" to a "receiver" by means of a "subject," who may be aided to a "helper" and/or hindered by an "opponent." Or, it might analyze how

---

4 A. B. Spencer, "Literary Criticism," in *New Testament Criticism and Interpretation*, ed. D. A. Black and D. S. Dockery (Grand Rapids: Zondervan, 1991), 235–36.

5 A term first given widespread currency and used in a broader context, to overlap with some of the concerns we will treat under narrative criticism, by J. Muilenburg, "Form Criticism and Beyond," *JBL* 88 (1969): 8.

6 See, classically, W. K. Wimsatt and M. C. Beardsley, "The Intentional Fallacy," in *The Verbal Icon*, ed. W. K. Wimsatt (Lexington: University of Kentucky Press, 1954), 2–18.

narratives, especially in religious myths, try to mediate between and resolve the conflict generated by pairs of opposites. In biblical studies, this method generated an intense flurry of specialized studies in the 1970s and 1980s, but the highly esoteric terminology and the sense that few exegetical insights resulted not already available by other methods led to its demise. Today one finds very few scholars doing much of anything with structuralism.[7]

Instead, attention has turned to two kinds of "poststructuralism"—reader-response criticism and deconstruction—which focus on the role of the reader in the interpretive process. Narrative criticism, however, continues to generate considerable interest; hence, the three main subheadings of this half chapter on literary criticism.[8]

Narrative Criticism

Narrative criticism is that branch of modern literary criticism that most closely resembles what readers of the world's great literary classics have done for centuries. Its predecessor was the study of the Bible as literature, a profitable exercise often undertaken in public school and university settings. Studying the Bible as literature focuses on the questions one would ask of Shakespeare or Cervantes, Sophocles or Cicero, Aesop or Goethe. Of particular value for works of narrative genre, this approach analyzes plot, theme, motifs, characterization, style, figures of speech, symbolism, foreshadowing, repetition, speed of time in narrative, point of view, and the like. It focuses more on an appreciation of the aesthetic value of the work than on its theological or moral value. If the latter are studied too, one still approaches the work only from the point of view of a sympathetic outside observer, not as the devotee of a particular religion.[9]

Applications

Such an approach to a portion of Scripture can have great value. Noting how a character is developed may help one understand whether the author wants readers to identify with that character or to avoid imitating that person. In other instances, characterization may be deliberately ambiguous. Thus, it is arguable that, despite the complexities of characterization, Samson's heroic death, like his repeated filling by the Holy Spirit throughout his life (Judg 13–16), marks him out ultimately as someone to emulate, though not in

---

7 For representative surveys of applications in OT and NT studies, respectively, see D. Jobling, *The Sense of Biblical Narrative: Structural Analyses in the Hebrew Bible*, 2 vols. (Sheffield: JSOT, 1986); R. F. Collins, *Introduction to the New Testament* (Garden City, NY: Doubleday, 1983), 231–71. The scholar in the U.S. who perhaps did the most with the method was D. Patte. For an introduction to his approaches, see his *What Is Structural Exegesis?* (Philadelphia: Fortress, 1976). For sample applications, see id., *Structural Exegesis: From Theory to Practice* (Philadelphia: Fortress, 1978).

8 For an excellent, thorough overview of these three periods of attention to author, text, and reader in literary criticism and biblical studies, see S. E. Porter, "Literary Approaches to the New Testament: From Formalism to Deconstruction and Back," in *Approaches to New Testament Study*, ed. S. E. Porter and D. Tombs (Sheffield: Sheffield Academic Press, 1995), 77–128.

9 Good introductions to the method include M. A. Powell, *What Is Narrative Criticism?* and D. Marguerat and Y. Bourquin, *How to Read Bible Stories: An Introduction to Narrative Criticism* (London: SCM, 1999). Perhaps the best anthology is R. Alter and F. Kermode, eds., *The Literary Guide to the Bible* (Cambridge: Harvard University Press, 1987). From an explicitly evangelical perspective, cf. esp. L. Ryken and T. Longman, III, eds., *A Complete Literary Guide to the Bible* (Grand Rapids: Zondervan, 1993). Also very helpful is L. Ryken, *Words of Delight: A Literary Introduction to the Bible* (Grand Rapids: Baker, 1987).

every aspect of his life. Conversely, for all of Saul's redeeming characteristics, Scripture ultimately seems to portray him as a tragic figure, losing what he could have had while knowing better, and thus someone not to emulate (1 Sam 9—2 Sam 1).[10] In between these two stands Nicodemus who appears three times in the Fourth Gospel (Jn 3:1-15; 7:50–52; 19:39). But here the reader is not given enough data to know if Nicodemus, like Joseph of Arimathea with whom he finally appears (19:38), eventually became a disciple of Jesus or not. He can be viewed as a model of someone who came to faith against the pressure of his peers, and hence more slowly and secretively than others, or as one who failed to make a decisive break from his past, which true discipleship requires. Perhaps John deliberately refuses to satisfy our curiosity so that we might take whatever steps are necessary to enter the kingdom, whether or not Nicodemus did.[11]

Focusing on the surface features of plot, theme, episode, and so on, can also demonstrate the unity of a text, which older historical criticism often segmented into complex layers of tradition and redaction. David Clines, for example, broke fresh ground with his study of themes in the Pentateuch by showing how the five books of Moses were united by the common theme of the partial fulfillment of the promise to or blessing of the patriarchs—which in turn contained the three aspects of posterity, divine-human relationship, and land. In so doing Clines undermined important bases that had led critics to postulate J, E, D, and P (Jahwist, Elohist, Deuteronomist, and Priestly writers) among whom the Pentateuch could be parceled out.[12] So too, Alan Culpepper, in his fine literary analysis of the unity of style and literary features of John, appears to have superseded his earlier work on a Johannine school as the composite author through several successive stages of redaction of the Fourth Gospel.[13]

Of course, this kind of narrative criticism may presuppose an earlier tradition history in which a text gained its current form over a long period, but it may also offer a more radical challenge too. As G. W. Coats explains in his analysis of the Joseph narrative (Gen 37–50), if "the story stands as a unit in at least one stage of its history," then "the burden of proof lies therefore on the person who wants to argue that the unity is synthetic" (i.e., brought about by a redactor imposing that unity on disparate sources).[14] And even when literary critics do not recognize this point, their concern to focus on the final, unified form of the text makes possible many discussions across theological lines (most notably evangelical-mainline), since historical questions are simply

---

10 For both of these assessments see D. M. Gunn, *The Fate of King Saul,* JSOTSup 14 (Sheffield: JSOT, 1980).

11 Cf. esp. J. M. Bassler, "Mixed Signals: Nicodemus in the Fourth Gospel," *JBL* 108 (1989): 635–46. For a striking contrast between Nicodemus in John 3 and the Samaritan woman in John 4, see C. L. Blomberg, "The Globalization of Biblical Interpretation—A Test Case: John 3–4," *BBR* 5 (1995): 1–15.

12 D. J. A. Clines, *The Theme of the Pentateuch*, JSOTSup 10 (Sheffield: JSOT, 1978). The suggestion that Genesis through Deuteronomy is actually a compilation of the works of four different anonymous authors (usually called J, E, D, P), centuries after the life of Moses, represents the famous "documentary hypothesis," which has dominated the last hundred years of Pentateuchal criticism.

13 R. A. Culpepper, *Anatomy of the Fourth Gospel* (Philadelphia: Fortress, 1983). Cf. id., *The Johannine School* (Missoula: Scholars, 1975).

14 G. W. Coats, *From Canaan to Egypt: Structural and Theological Context for the Joseph Story* (Washington, DC: CBAA, 1976), 60.

bracketed as irrelevant for the matters at hand. In other words, even if one scholar may accept that a certain narrative tells the story as it actually happened, while another may dispute that claim, both may agree on what the story means and how it functions.

Studying the Bible as literature further helps us to focus on major emphases and not get sidetracked with peripheral details. For example, once we understand the theme of the Pentateuch as the partial fulfillment of God's promises despite various obstacles, apparent digressions such as Abraham's twice-aborted attempts to pass Sarah off as his sister (Gen 12:10–20; 20:1-18) make more sense in their context. Along this line, neither story has a particular "moral" in its own right—for example, to speak for or against half-truths or deceiving an enemy. Rather, thematically, they reflect potential impediments to the fulfillment of God's desire to bless Abraham with the Holy Land and promised seed. As Abraham's schemes fail, we learn more of God's sovereignty and how he is working to assure that his promises do not fail.[15]

Yet again, this kind of literary criticism can explain the purposes of repetition better than traditional source criticism. For example, two passages that might have been viewed as doublets (two similar sounding accounts believed to reflect only one original, historical event, which was then narrated differently in two or more different documents), and as clues to discerning separate sources, can now both be seen as authentic. Thus, the similarities between Isaac's meeting Rebekah and Jacob's first encounter with Rachel, both at a well, involving the watering of flocks, and leading ultimately to a return to the woman's home and a betrothal, fit into a conventional "type-scene" of ancient oral and literary narrative.[16] In other words, as in form criticism, because of the currency of stereotypic forms in which people expected those stories to be told, they often sounded more similar than they would have if additional details had been narrated. This means, then, that Bible readers should not assume that only one historical event has been repeated in two or more different ways. Rather, the similarities in the stories help them to recognize the "form" or "subgenre" of the passage and thereby how to interpret it (see our chapter on OT genre criticism). Then, to discover the unique emphasis of any given text, readers should pay attention to those areas in which the stories, notwithstanding convention, diverge. With this strategy in mind, the reader will see how Jacob is much more assertive than Isaac, a feature that continues throughout the patriarchal narratives. Conversely, Rebekah proves more discerning than Rachel. These observations fit the greater prominence given to Jacob (Rebekah's coconspirator for the blessing) than to either his father or his wife. Thus, the narrative gives clues as to the characters with whom we should most identify and from whom we should most learn.

A careful study of plot and character development also helps us to identify the climax or most important idea of a passage. Too, we may recognize where a surprise or shock effect would have driven home certain truths with extra force or poignancy to the original biblical readers. Dan Via has helpfully categorized the parables as comic or tragic, based on their endings.[17] ("Comic" here refers, of course, to a positive resolution of a plot conflict,

---

15 B. K. Waltke, *Genesis: A Commentary* (Grand Rapids: Zondervan, 2001), 212–17, 282–89. Particularly helpful in interpreting OT historical narrative is J. Goldingay, *Approaches to Old Testament Interpretation*, 2d ed. (Toronto: Clements, 2002).

16 See esp. R. Alter, *The Art of Biblical Narrative* (New York: Basic, 1981), 49–56.

17 D. O. Via, Jr., *The Parables: Their Literary and Existential Dimension* (Philadelphia: Fortress, 1967).

not to a sense of humor.) Hence, even though the parables of the wedding banquet (Mt 22:1–14) and the wicked tenants (Mt 21:33–46) have similar structures and much of the identical imagery, the former ends on a note of destruction and the latter on a note of victory. Modern teaching based on these passages should reflect similar emphases: warning those who too glibly think that they are right with God and encouraging those who fear that God's purposes may fail.

We can similarly categorize the Minor Prophets. Although many of them preach judgment throughout a majority of their books, often a climactic, final look to the eschatological restoration of God's people reverses the reader's focus to the ultimate "good news" beyond the "bad news" (e.g., Hos 14:4–8; Amos 9:11–15; Zeph 3:14–20). The amount of discussion of a topic may not prove as significant as the placement of that discussion within a given book. On the other hand, Micah seems consistently to alternate between sections of good and bad news, as if to balance them.[18]

Literary criticism has done many other things. It identifies characters as flat, stock, or round, or as agents, types, or full characters, depending on how complex and lifelike they are portrayed.[19] Those developed the most—as with Jacob, Joseph, and his brothers in Gen 37–50—are most likely the characters on which the story's writer wanted his audience to center most attention.[20] In 2 Kgs 5 Naaman evokes sympathy because of the complex or round nature of his character. Elisha too is round, alternately tolerant and intolerant, which makes the reader hold him at arm's length. Literary criticism delineates ways in which writers attempt to achieve empathy, as with the introduction and conclusion to the story of Simeon and Levi's revenge for the rape of Dinah (Gen 34), or to "justify God's ways to man."[21] Gehazi as a "flat" representative of mere greed inspires only antipathy.[22] Plot analysis can dovetail with redaction criticism in helping to understand the outline and ideological emphases of a narrative author. The central plot of Matthew's Gospel, for example, unfolds around the growing hostility of the Jewish leaders against Jesus.[23] Matthew's placement of certain passages, different from the other Gospels, then makes sense against this backdrop.[24] But what is today increasingly called "narrative criticism," while adopting all of these devices from the study of Bible as literature, usually goes one important step further.

Narrative criticism today typically adopts an analytical framework that distinguishes the *real author* of a particular writing from the *implied author,* who is again distinguished from the *narrator.* The real author is the person who actually wrote the text.

---

18 Cf. M. J. Buss, "Tragedy and Comedy in Hosea," *Semeia* 32 (1984): 71–82; and N. K. Gottwald, "Tragedy and Comedy in the Latter Prophets," *Semeia* 32 (1984): 83–96.

19 One of the most thorough studies of characterization is A. Berlin, *Poetics and Interpretation of Biblical OT Narrative* (Sheffield: Almond, 1983). For the Gospels cf. D. Rhoads and K. Syreeni, *Characterization in the Gospels* (Sheffield: Sheffield Academic Press, 1999).

20 W. L. Humphreys, *Joseph and His Family: A Literary Study* (Columbia: University of South Carolina Press, 1988), 68–92.

21 See, respectively, M. Sternberg, *The Poetics of Biblical Narrative* (Bloomington: Indiana University Press, 1985), 445–75, 484.

22 Marguerat and Bourkin, *How to Read Bible Stories*, 61–62.

23 R. A. Edwards, *Matthew's Story of Jesus* (Philadelphia: Fortress, 1985).

24 See the suggested outline and headings in C. L. Blomberg, *Matthew,* NAC (Nashville: Broadman, 1992).

The implied author is the picture of the real author that emerges from the text without any additional background information. The narrator is the person in the narrative who actually tells the story. Similarly, one may separate the *real readers* from the *implied readers* (the picture of the readers emerging from the text alone) and the *narratées* (the persons in the text to whom the story is told). The real author and readers are often inaccessible from the written text alone.[25] Narrators and narratées might well be fictional characters, as, for example, with the narrator, Ishmael, in Herman Melville's *Moby Dick*. Thus, those who believe that Luke-Acts was not written by Paul's "beloved physician" but by a second-generation Christian to an end-of-the-first-century church might distinguish between the real author and readers (as just described), the implied author and readers (the picture of Luke derivable from the text, who was perhaps purporting to write to a pre-A.D. 70 congregation), and the narrator and narratée (the historical Luke and Theophilus).[26]

For an OT example, in the Minor Prophets several different real authors seem to resemble one and the same implied author; several groups of real readers correspond to one implied reader.[27] Thus, it is not so crucial to determine the exact historical settings of books like Joel and Obadiah, which pose notorious problems for traditional historical critics. The real authors (or editors) are not concerned to divulge much information about themselves because they share a common, almost timeless concern—to warn God's people about particularly well-entrenched patterns of sin. They prophesy judgment with the possibility of subsequent restoration contingent on repentance. In this instance literary criticism allows Bible students more closely to approximate the interpretations of average Bible readers who never bothered with much historical background in the first place. There are obviously strengths and weaknesses in such a situation. But when students discover proposals of modern narrative criticism that fit with the results of more traditional historical criticism, they may be able to accept both with greater degrees of confidence.

In still other cases, narrative criticism reminds us to distinguish between the presumably reliable narrator of a biblical book and an unreliable speaker whose words are reported within that book. The apparent contradiction between 1 Sam 31, in which Saul has his armor bearer help him commit suicide, and 2 Sam 1, in which an Amalekite boasts that he has killed Saul, is resolved when we understand that the Amalekite was lying in hopes of gaining some reward from David, whom he assumed would be grateful to learn of his archenemy's death. In other instances, it is harder to be sure of what the narrator is doing. It is interesting, for example, to compare the quite different analyses by Y. Amit, on the one hand, and Gunn and Fewell, on the other hand, of the role of Judah in Gen 38 where he has sex with Tamar believing her to be

---

25 Most scholars credit the development of this method in literature more generally to W. Iser, *The Implied Reader* (Baltimore: The Johns Hopkins University Press, 1974).

26 New Testament narrative criticism has largely focused on the Gospels and Acts, with one pioneering study dominating the analysis of each of the four Evangelists: J. D. Kingsbury, *Matthew as Story* (Philadelphia: Fortress, 1986); D. Rhoads and D. Michie, *Mark as Story* (Philadelphia: Fortress, 1982); R. C. Tannehill, *The Narrative Unity of Luke-Acts,* 2 vols. (Philadelphia and Minneapolis: Fortress, 1986–90); and Culpepper, *Anatomy.*

27 Sternberg, *Poetics,* 75. The Minor Prophets are not, for the most part, historical narratives, but many narrative critics apply their methods to all genres of literature.

a prostitute. Depending on which elements one focuses on, Judah can be seen as thoroughly ignoble or somewhat redeemed.[28]

Critique

To the extent that narrative criticism engages a close reading of texts with a view to understanding their plots, themes, characterizations, and other features of the "surface structure" of biblical books as literature, we may enthusiastically welcome the discipline. Additionally, in avoiding both the intentional and affective fallacies (which affirm, respectively, that meaning is wholly in the mind of an author or wholly in the perception of readers), narrative criticism offers a more sophisticated and valid model of where the meaning of a text resides—namely, in that text! We may speak of authorial intention as a key to hermeneutics only to the extent that real authors have been transparent in equating their narrators with their implied authors and making both reveal substantial information about the real authors themselves. We may speak of readers creating meaning only to the extent that real readers correctly identify the roles of narratee and implied readers.[29] As Stephen Mailloux puts it, intentions are best described or defined in terms of "the intended structure of the reader's response."[30] Moreover, narrative criticism's focus on the final form of the text, taken as a unity, and with an intentional analysis of how narratives work, all comport well with evangelical theology *for theology as well as method*.[31] After all, it is the final literary form of any biblical book we believe to be inspired and therefore authoritative.

But there are more serious pitfalls with narrative criticism, whether in its more traditional form as "the Bible as literature" or in its more rigorous, recent analytical form of distinguishing various kinds of authors and readers. Narrative critics often assume when they study the Bible as literature that the texts must be viewed as fiction.[32] This seems to result, however, not from the nature of the method itself but from a misunderstanding of the number of features that historical and fictional texts share in common. Students of ancient historiography helpfully stress how few literary characteristics actually enable a reader to distinguish what we today would call historical fiction from well-written, interesting history.[33] And Norman Petersen has applied literary criticism

---

28 For the more positive take, see Y. Amit, *Reading Biblical Narratives* (Minneapolis: Fortress, 2001), 91–92. For the negative take, see D. M. Gunn and D. N. Fewell, *Narrative in the Hebrew Bible* (Oxford: Oxford University Press, 1993), 34–45.

29 Cf. further Blomberg, *Parables,* 156–59, and the literature there cited.

30 S. Mailloux, *Interpretive Conventions: The Reader in the Study of American Fiction* (Ithaca: Cornell University Press, 1982), 112.

31 F. Watson, "Literary Approaches to the Gospels: A Theological Assessment," *Theol* 99 (1996): 125–33.

32 E.g., D. A. Robertson, *The Old Testament and the Literary Critic* (Philadelphia: Fortress, 1977); D. A. Templeton, *The New Testament as True Fiction* (Sheffield: Sheffield Academic Press, 1999).

33 See esp. C. H. Gempf, "Historical And Literary Appropriateness in the Mission Speeches of Paul in Acts" (Ph.D. Thesis, University of Aberdeen, 1988); cf. id., "Public Speaking and Published Accounts" in *The Book of Acts in Its Ancient Literary Setting*, ed. B. W. Winter and A. D. Clarke (Carlisle: Paternoster; Grand Rapids: Eerdmans, 1993), 259–303. From the perspective of modern literature, cf. esp. T. J. Roberts, *When Is Something Fiction?* (Carbondale, IL: Southern Illinois University Press, 1972).

to the epistle to Philemon, showing how even the nonfictional and nonnarrative material we find in a letter can have an unfolding plot, point of view, climax, and so on.[34] Thus, it does not follow that narrative and fiction must be synonymous.

Second, narrative critics often depreciate the religious value of a text in favor of its aesthetics, even if sometimes this is done to correct a past imbalance in the other direction. But again, it seems this abuse can be divorced from the method itself. A genuine appreciation of the beauty, power, and style of a biblical book should lead a believer in its inspiration and canonicity to treasure it that much more.[35] Third, narrative critics may employ modern, anachronistic theories of the composition of literature that do not work well with ancient texts. James Dawsey, for example, remains wholly unconvincing in his book-length attempt to defend the thesis that the narrator of Luke is unreliable because there are numerous contradictions between what the real author wants to communicate and what his narrator actually does communicate.[36] Again, the problem resides with Dawsey's analysis more than with the model of narrative criticism itself.

In general, narrative criticism holds the most promise of all of the subdisciplines of literary criticism, since it focuses on the "surface structure" or literary features of the final form of the text that all readers have to come to grips with. Sadly, many literary critics have not stopped here, however, but have moved on to the discipline known as "poststructuralism." Here we cannot be as enthusiastic about scholarly developments. But in some circles, poststructuralism is so popular that serious Bible students must familiarize themselves at least briefly with its methods.

Poststructuralism

Poststructuralism refers to developments that built on but went beyond structuralism (and, for that matter, narrative criticism). Both share a concern to move past the focus of these disciplines on meaning as residing in a text to a consideration of meaning residing in individual readers. Increasingly, poststructuralism is linked ideologically to postmodernism in general. Postmodernism is a broad term, used in different ways by different authors. But it usually involves a cluster of such convictions and values as: 1) an ideological pluralism in which no one religion or worldview contains absolute truth; 2) the impossibility of objectivity in interpretation and the treasuring of value-laden approaches; 3) the importance of human communities in shaping ourselves and our interpretive perspectives; 4) a rejection of the negative modernist evaluation of religion and spirituality; 5) an emphasis on the aesthetic, the symbolic, and ancient tradition; 6) the formative role of narrative in understanding our own life-pilgrimages and those of others, along with the rejection of the existence of any overarching "meta-narrative" that can give meaning to all individual stories; and 7) language as determinative of thought and meaning.

---

34 N. R. Petersen, *Rediscovering Paul: Philemon and the Sociology of Paul's Narrative World* (Philadelphia: Fortress, 1985).

35 Powell, *What Is Narrative Criticism?* 88–89.

36 J. M. Dawsey, *The Lukan Voice: Confusion and Irony in the Gospel of Luke* (Macon: Mercer, 1986).

Clearly postmodernism offers evangelicals a mixed bag of bane and blessing.[37] We should welcome the rejection of modernism's dependence on human autonomy, reason, and science and technology as the be-all and end-all of life, for in its most thoroughgoing forms it led inexorably to skepticism and atheism. Christians in general (and the Bible in particular) have historically valued narrative, symbolism, the aesthetic, a value-laden interpretation, and the importance of community. Christians once too enamored with modernism are increasingly recapturing many of these dimensions thanks to postmodernism.

On the other hand, we must dispute the postmodernists' denial of absolute truth, their claim that no religion or ideology can ultimately be superior to any other, much less the "one true way," their denial of any overarching meta-narrative (like the one portrayed in the Bible), and the inability of humans to transcend their cultural or linguistic conditioning. One of the major problems with respect to hermeneutics, to which postmodernism has called attention, is the impossibility of human interpreters ever to fully capture (or to know they have fully captured) someone else's meaning in any communicative act. This much Christians should readily accept because of our beliefs that humans are both finite and fallen. But there is a middle ground between claiming absolute objectivity and denying that in many cases we can attain *adequate* understanding of the meaning of a text. N. T. Wright and B. Meyer have both argued persuasively that interpreters should embrace "critical realism," an approach that involves the dialogical process between interpreter and texts in which one successfully approximates true meaning, even if never comprehensively capturing it (or knowing that one has).[38] The image of a hermeneutical spiral—like a cone-shaped tornado zeroing in on one small spot on the ground—or that of an asymptote of a hyperbola, coming very close to the vertical or horizontal lines of its axes without ever actually touching them, helps us to visualize this model.[39] The flip side of this approach is that while we may not always be able to determine one and only one correct or even simply the most correct interpretation of a given text, we can usually rule out many as improbable.[40]

Returning to literary criticism more narrowly, the two major categories of postmodern or poststructural analysis are reader-response criticism and deconstruction. Reader-response criticism is the less radical of the two, affirming that meaning derives

---

37 Critiques multiply rapidly; particularly helpful on its strengths is S. Grenz, *A Primer on Postmodernism* (Grand Rapids: Eerdmans, 1996); on its weaknesses, D. R. Groothuis, *Truth Decay: Defending Christianity Against the Challenges of Postmodernism* (Downers Grove: InterVarsity, 2000). An anthology of various responses that cumulatively captures perhaps the right balance is D. S. Dockery, ed., *The Challenge of Postmodernism: An Evangelical Engagement* (Wheaton: Victor, 1995). With respect to the philosophical issue of pluralism, an outstanding resource is D. A. Carson, *The Gagging of God: Christianity Confronts Pluralism* (Grand Rapids: Zondervan, 1996).

38 N. T. Wright, *The New Testament and the People of God* (London: SPCK; Minneapolis: Fortress, 1992), 32–37; B. F. Meyer, *Reality and Illusion in New Testament Scholarship: A Primer in Critical Realist Hermeneutics* (Collegeville: Liturgical, 1994).

39 Cf., respectively, G. R. Osborne, *The Hermeneutical Spiral* (Downers Grove: InterVarsity, 1991); A. O. Bellis, "Objective Biblical Truth Vs. the Value of Various Viewpoints: A False Dichotomy," *HBT* 17 (1995): 30.

40 See esp. U. Eco, *Interpretation and Overinterpretation* (Cambridge: Cambridge University Press, 1992).

from the interaction between a text and its readers. Deconstruction, when consistently applied, despairs of finding coherent meaning at all, apart from readers' own diverse perceptions and experiences.

Reader-Response Criticism[41]

As the label suggests, reader-response criticism focuses primarily not on authors' intentions or the fixed meaning of texts but on the diverse ways readers respond to a text (see also our discussion in chap. 6). Reader-response criticism itself breaks down into two major approaches, though they are not always clearly distinguished from each other (just as narrative criticism sometimes includes both text- and reader-centered approaches).[42] A more conservative form was pioneered by Wolfgang Iser, who also developed the concepts of implied authors and readers (see above), thus generating further overlap between methods. But the distinguishing feature of "conservative" reader-response criticism is that the text still provides important constraints on interpreters. This form of analysis may try, for example, to reproduce the experience of a "first-time" reader of a passage, so that what one learns from a later portion of a text cannot yet influence the understanding of an earlier portion.

Robert Fowler comes close to a traditional evangelical hermeneutic when he refuses to endorse a popular, modern reading of the feedings of the 5000 and 4000 (Mk 6:30–44; 8:1-10) as eucharistic, because the Last Supper (Mk 14:12–26) had not yet occurred at the time of those miracles. A reader may use the feeding miracles to interpret the Last Supper but not vice versa. But Fowler is not applying historical criticism to limit the interpretation of an event to data derived from previous events; he is taking the point of view of a reader coming to Mark for the first time, who has not yet read of the Last Supper.[43]

Interestingly, this strategy of sequential reading perhaps agrees better with the standard process in the ancient world in which written texts were read aloud to gathered groups. Hearing a text only once afforded the listener no luxury to look ahead to the end or to reread a section already forgotten. Perhaps traditional historical-grammatical analysis, with all its cross-references to uses of words and concepts throughout a document, has often found too much meaning in texts, which a one-time listener could not catch![44]

A more conservative reader-response criticism, further, helpfully explores the "gaps" in a text, in which a reader must supply his or her own meaning. For example, why does the account of David's sin with Bathsheba begin with kings going out to war, while David (the

41 Good introductions to reader-response criticism appear in J. L. Resseguie, "Reader-Response Criticism and the Synoptic Gospels," *JAAR* 52 (1984): 307–24 (limited to the Gospels); R. M. Fowler, "Who Is 'The Reader' in Reader Response Criticism?" *Semeia* 31 (1985): 5–23 (on Scripture more generally); and J. P. Tompkins, ed., *Reader-Response Criticism* (Baltimore: Johns Hopkins University Press, 1980) (on literature more generally).

42 J. Barton, "Thinking About Reader-Response Criticism," *ExpT* 113 (2002): 147–51; K. J. Vanhoozer, *Is There a Meaning in This Text?* (Grand Rapids: Zondervan, 1998), 152.

43 R. M. Fowler, *Loaves and Fishes: The Function of the Feeding Stories in the Gospel of Mark,* SBLDS 54 (Chico, CA: Scholars, 1981), 140–41.

44 S. D. Moore, *Literary Criticism and the Gospels* (New Haven: Yale University Press, 1989), 84–88. R. H. Stein, "Is Our Reading the Bible the Same as the Original Audience's Hearing It? *JETS* 46 (2003): 63–78, also makes this point.

king) stays home (2 Sam 11:1)? Why does David send Uriah home to sleep with his wife after David has committed adultery with her? When Uriah refuses to go, is it because he knows what David has done and refuses to participate in his attempted cover-up? Or is it just that he is so virtuous he will not avail himself of any privileges that his fellow-soldiers still on the battlefield cannot share, as he explicitly claims (v. 11)? When he does not go home, does David suspect that Uriah knows his ploy? At each stage of this narrative, the reader must make some assumptions to fill in these "gaps." How we answer these questions will considerably color our perspectives on the main characters in the story.[45] If Uriah is being less than straightforward with David, then we cannot identify with him quite so much as the innocent victim. If we had additional historical information to enable us to answer these kinds of questions, we would be engaging simply in historical criticism. Absent these, we must make inferences from other features of the text itself, so that the process becomes part of literary criticism.

A more radical reader-response criticism focuses on meaning as that which is entirely, or almost entirely, the product of the individual reader. Meaning (like beauty) is in the eye of the beholder. The only reason similarities and interpretations arise in the first place, according to this view, is because various readers belong to "interpretive communities" with shared conventions that lead them to read texts in similar ways. But apart from these shared conventions, there is no objective meaning in the symbols of the texts themselves.

Stanley Fish is the putative founder of this wing of reader-response criticism that delights in showing how even texts that seem most clearly to communicate objective, recoverable meaning can be plausibly understood in quite different ways.[46] For example, one could read the story of God's interactions with Saul and David as a largely secular "novel" of an arbitrary, capricious God who raises up and brings down rulers without good reason—a story that Jews and later Christians then domesticated into an edifying religious tale.[47] One might understand the parable of the prodigal son so that the prodigal, his father, and the older brother correspond respectively to Freud's understanding of id, ego, and super-ego.[48] We do not encounter a large number of such readings of biblical texts, i.e., apart from readings by interpreters who identify with specific advocacy movements, which we discuss in the second half of this chapter.[49]

The main weaknesses of more radical reader-response criticism lie in its relativism. On the one hand, if nothing more than shared interpretive conventions account for similarities in readings of given texts, reader-response critics should not object to readings very different from their own, and yet many still attempt to defend their interpretations as better

---

45 Sternberg, *Poetics,* 193–213. Cf. M. Garsiel, "The Story of David and Bathsheba: A Different Approach," *CBQ* 55 (1993): 244–62.

46 S. E. Fish, *Self-Consuming Artifacts* (Berkeley: University of California Press, 1972); id., *Is There a Text in This Class?* (Cambridge: Harvard University Press, 1980).

47 K. L. Noll, "Is There A Text in This Tradition? Readers' Response and the Taming of Samuel's God," *JSOT* 83 (1999): 31–51.

48 M. A. Tolbert, "The Prodigal Son: An Essay in Literary Criticism From a Psychoanalytic Perspective," *Semeia* 9 (1977): 1–20.

49 For some of the main reasons, see S. E. Porter, "Why Hasn't Reader-Response Criticism Caught On in New Testament Studies?" *JLT* 4 (1990): 278–92. Cf. the response by P. R. Noble, "Fish and the Bible: Should Reader-Response Theories 'Catch On?' " *HeyJ* 37 (1996): 456–67.

than others! And those who do not at least want people to understand their intended meaning in normal kinds of human discourse—not to mention the articles or books they write! On the other hand, one could argue, theologically, that all humans—created in God's image—share common interpretive conventions that allow for objective meaning to transcend individual perceptions. In the former scenario, reader-response criticism is self-defeating; in the latter it collapses back into some more traditional text-centered hermeneutic. What is more, radical reader-response criticism cannot account for how texts transform readers, generating interpretations and behavior that cut against the grain of their preunderstandings, presuppositions, and social conditioning.

In some cases, what pass for competing *interpretations* should probably be viewed as alternative *applications.* As we will argue, original meaning remains fixed, even as contemporary significance varies. Alternately, using the language of "speech-act theory,"[50] we may say that the illocution (the act of speaking) remains the same even as the perlocution (the effect[s] of speaking) changes.[51] At the very least, reader-response criticism has done all interpreters a service in reminding them of the truly significant influence of their preunderstandings (as we will discuss further below). But we must subject our cherished preconceptions of the meanings of texts to the challenges of new data and new perspectives that acknowledge the potential of objectivity.[52]

Deconstruction

Even more widespread in literary circles, including biblical studies, is the second brand of poststructuralism: deconstruction. Ideologically, deconstruction derives from Nietzsche and his modern-day disciple, Jacques Derrida. It is an anarchistic, hyper-relativistic form of criticism designed to demonstrate how all texts, indeed all human communication, ultimately "deconstructs" or undermines itself.[53] In the words of T. K. Seung, its avowed purpose is one of "generating conflicting meanings from the same text, and playing those meanings against each other."[54] Nor is this just a new variation on the old theme of pointing out

---

50 For an excellent introduction to the discipline and its application to biblical studies, see R. S. Briggs, "The Uses of Speech-Act Theory in Biblical Interpretation," *CRBS* 9 (2001): 229–76.

51 Vanhoozer, *Is There A Meaning in this Text?* 261.

52 For as appreciative a critique as exists among evangelicals, but one that nevertheless points out some of these and other problems with reader-response criticism, see A. C. Thiselton, "Reader-Response Hermeneutics, Action Models, and the Parables of Jesus," in R. Lundin, A. C. Thiselton, and C. Walhout, *The Responsibility of Hermeneutics* (Grand Rapids: Eerdmans, 1985), 79–113. From a Roman Catholic perspective, cf. esp. T. J. Keegan, "Biblical Criticism and the Challenge of Postmodernism," *BibInt* 3 (1995): 1–14. We too adopt a somewhat open stance, while insisting on the constraints we defend under the concept of "validation" below.

53 Two standard introductions to deconstruction in literature more generally are J. Culler, *On Deconstruction: Theory and Criticism After Structuralism* (Ithaca: Cornell University Press, 1982); and C. Norris, *Deconstruction: Theory and Practice* (New York: Methuen, 1982). R. Briggs ("Gnats, Camels and Aporias: Who Should Be Straining Out What? Christianity and Deconstruction," *VoxEv* 25 [1995]: 17–32) adopts a less sweeping definition of deconstruction as merely an approach that asserts the existence of meaning that cannot finally be pinned down to the words that carry it. He is thus able to find more virtue in it than most evangelicals have, but his does not seem to be the most common understanding of the concept.

54 T. K. Seung, *Structuralism and Hermeneutics* (New York: Columbia University Press, 1982), 271. For application to biblical studies, see A. K. M. Adam, *What Is Postmodern Biblical Criticism?* (Minneapolis: Fortress, 1998).

apparent contradictions in Scripture.[55] Rather, deconstruction normally seeks subtle, often unwitting, ideological inconsistencies or ambiguities in a text that seem hard to resolve and that prevent interpreters from claiming that it has a fixed meaning. Motives for such analysis range from an innocuous desire to be creative to a preoccupation with denying any absolute claims of the text over interpreters.

Obviously, no one with anything like a traditional Christian view of Scripture's inspiration, accuracy, clarity, or authority should accept deconstruction as an ideological package. Still, focusing on underlying tensions in a text may surface some part of its meaning, particularly in the more cryptic parts of Scripture—even if we might wish to go on to propose resolutions to those tensions. For example, it is intriguing to read how Esther, in essence, has to lose her "Jewishness" in order to save it. Only as the Persian queen, hiding her ethnic identity from her husband-king, can she rescue the Jewish people from the pogrom Haman planned for them.[56] Perhaps this presents a salutary reminder of the ambiguities and compromises inherent in trying to live life as a person of God in the political arena of fallen humanity.

Again, consider Job. After all the many speeches of Job and his counselors, God ultimately vindicates Job against his friends: "I am angry with you and your two friends, because you have not spoken of me what is right, as my servant Job has" (Job 42:7). His friends, in essence, have tried to vindicate God as justly punishing sinners and rewarding the righteous, whereas Job has repeatedly protested that God is unfairly persecuting him. However, if God is right in supporting Job, then God must be unjust because Job seemed to accuse him of being unjust.[57] The solution may be that when God declares Job right, he is not referring to every single thing that Job said. Again we are cautioned against imitating Job's friends with too facile or simplistic explanations of why people suffer. Here is one more example on the very conservative end of the deconstructive spectrum (which, by definition, is not very conservative!). Werner Kelber has helpfully called attention to how John's Gospel comprises words about "the Word" (*ho logos*) incarnate, who is Jesus. Careful attention to these words and the Word will direct oneself away from written (or oral) words to a Person. The more one takes seriously the medium of John's message, the more one will be pointed away from that message to a living relationship with the one about whom the message is spoken.[58] To a certain degree, the text undermines its own unique authority. And doubtless, many Christians do need regular reminders that they worship a Person and not a book.[59]

---

55 Though in some instances, this is how the term gets applied. See esp. D. Seeley, *Deconstructing the New Testament* (Leiden: Brill, 1994).

56 D. J. A. Clines, "Reading Esther from Left to Right," in *The Bible in Three Dimensions,* ed. D. J. A. Clines, S. E. Fowl, and S. E. Porter, JSOTSup 87 (Sheffield: JSOT, 1990), 31–52.

57 Id., "Deconstructing the Book of Job," in D. J. A. Clines, *What Does Eve Do To Help? And Other Readerly Questions to the Old Testament,* JSOTSup 94 (Sheffield: JSOT, 1990), 106–23.

58 Kelber is cited in Moore, *Literary Criticism and the Gospels,* 152–57, and refers to a forthcoming work by Kelber in which this discussion is to appear. Apparently the work never appeared.

59 Cf. G. A. Phillips, " 'You Are Either Here, Here, Here, or Here': Deconstruction's Troublesome Interplay," *Semeia* 71 (1995): 193–213. Phillips argues that if deconstruction attends to texts to discover evidence for and disclose more about the fullness and depth of meaning beyond an original author's intent or audience's understanding, then it can lead us back to the Other behind the text that modernism and strictly author- or text-centered approaches disallowed.

Far more characteristic of deconstruction, however, are its much more radical applications. Dominic Crossan, for example, has written quite a bit about the parables in which his own cleverness rather than validity in interpretation seems to be his goal, as summarized by his term, "freeplay."[60] In one place, he declares, "Since you cannot interpret absolutely, you can interpret forever."[61] Thus, he reads the parable of the prodigal son (Lk 15:11-32) as an allegory of Western consciousness' path from mimetic (realistic) to ludic (playful) allegory.[62] He sees the parable of the treasure in the field as teaching, among other things, that one must abandon all for the sake of the kingdom, which includes abandoning the parable, and, ultimately, abandoning abandonment![63] Quite understandably, D. A. Carson critiques this type of deconstruction by calling it "so anachronistic as to make a historian wince,"[64] to which Crossan would probably reply, "Of course, I wasn't attempting to please a historian!" Even more bizarre is Stephen Moore's entire book on Mark and Luke that uses the wordplays (in English!) between Mark and "mark" as the stroke of a letter on a piece of paper, and between Luke and "look," meaning "to see." Moore then proceeds to discuss Mark and Luke in association with a wide range of modern literature as two Gospels that stress written marks and the art of seeing, respectively.[65]

From an OT perspective, Peter Miscall argues that any attempt to assess the positive or negative characterizations of David and his associates in 1 Sam 16–22 runs aground on conflicting data so that it is impossible to make definitive statements about the significance of these characters or the events with which they were involved.[66] If Miscall is right, then we cannot identify characters whose behavior we are to emulate or avoid quite as easily as most readers have thought.

Advocates of deconstruction ought to ask where all this would lead us if adopted on a widespread scale. Those who have replied to this question do not give us satisfying answers.[67] Although some argue that deconstruction is here to stay, ordinary people do not and cannot live as if human conversation were ultimately relativistic and self-defeating. More likely, poststructuralism will prove to be a passing fad. Deconstruction will one day deconstruct itself. The rapid decline in the number of studies from this perspective in the early years of the twenty-first century (as compared to the prior decade) suggests this is already starting to happen. But what will take its place?

Supporters of poststructuralism reject the idea of a giant eclecticism or meta-criticism in which the valid insights of all the various new critical tools will cooperate with more traditional hermeneutics. But it seems to us that we need something precisely like this.

---

60 See esp. J. D. Crossan, *Cliffs of Fall: Paradox and Polyvalence in the Parables of Jesus* (New York: Seabury, 1980), 25–104.

61 Crossan *Cliffs*, 102.

62 Crossan, *Cliffs*, 101.

63 Id., *Finding Is the First Act* (Philadelphia: Fortress, 1979), 93.

64 D. A. Carson, "Matthew," in *The Expositor's Bible Commentary*, ed. F. E. Gaebelein, vol. 8 (Grand Rapids: Zondervan, 1984), 329.

65 S. D. Moore, *Mark and Luke in Poststructuralist Perspectives* (New Haven and London: Yale, 1992). For a deconstruction of John, see P. C. Counet, *John—A Postmodern Gospel: Introduction to Deconstructive Exegesis Applied to the Fourth Gospel* (Leiden: Brill, 2000).

66 P. D. Miscall, *The Workings of Old Testament Narrative* (Chico, CA: Scholars; Philadelphia: Fortress, 1983).

67 Most notably, Moore, *Literary Criticism and the Gospels*, 171–78.

Cultural anthropologists, for example, have for nearly two decades renounced relativism in favor of seeking meta-models that remain valid atop cross-cultural diversity.[68] Interestingly, the method that some hail as the next panacea for biblical criticism is a social-scientific analysis that draws heavily on anthropological models.[69] To date, such analysis has not always accepted its place as one limited method among many. As with new ideas more generally, its supporters tend to hail it as the best approach of all. But in time, less grandiose claims will no doubt prevail. Meanwhile, we must survey this new methodological arena of biblical scholarship and see what promise it offers a study of hermeneutics.[70]

SOCIAL-SCIENTIFIC APPROACHES TO SCRIPTURE

Many of the same factors that spawned discontent with traditional historical-critical methods and gave rise to literary criticism of the Bible have also led scholars to propose new, social-scientific models of interpretation. Discontent with the status quo, a realization of the modern presuppositions imported into historical criticism, opportunities for creativity and fresh insights, and the growing interdisciplinary dialogue in the universities all have contributed. Hence, many biblical scholars are delving deeply into the study of sociology, anthropology, economics, and political science, using the findings of their studies to add new dimensions to the discipline of biblical hermeneutics.

Classification

These social-scientific studies fall into two broad categories: research that illuminates the social history of the biblical world and the application of modern theories of human behavior to scriptural texts.[71]

---

68 P. G. Hiebert, "Critical Contextualization," *IBMR* 11 (1987): 104–12.

69 Note particularly how B. J. Malina ("Reader Response Theory: Discovery or Redundancy?" *Creighton University Faculty Journal* 5 [1986]: 55–66) sees social-scientific analysis as the appropriate successor to a bankrupt reader-response criticism.

70 Additional key literature on modern literary criticism of the Bible, not already mentioned in the preceding footnotes of this section, includes T. Longman, III, *Literary Approaches to Biblical Interpretation* (Grand Rapids: Zondervan, 1987)—an evangelical survey and sympathetic critique; N. Frye, *The Great Code: The Bible and Literature* (New York: Harcourt, 1982)—a major study of archetype and symbol by a leading literary critic; E. V. McKnight, *The Bible and the Reader* (Philadelphia: Fortress, 1985)—a survey of reader-centered approaches, but including structuralism and more traditional forms of literary criticism as well; S. Bar-Efrat, *Narrative Art in the Bible* (Sheffield: Almond, 1989)—on narration, characters, plot, time and space, and style in the Hebrew Bible; A. K. M. Adam, ed., *Postmodern Interpretations of the Bible—A Reader* (St. Louis: Chalice, 2000)—deconstructive or reader-response analyses of all the major sections of the Bible; and D. Jobling, T. Pippin, and R. Schleifer, eds., *The Postmodern Bible Reader* (Oxford: Blackwell, 2001)—a more thematically organized collection of similar studies.

71 Good overviews of recent research include, for the OT, T. W. Overholt, *Cultural Anthropology and the Old Testament* (Minneapolis: Fortress, 1996); C. E. Carter and C. L. Meyers, eds., *Community, Identity, and Ideology: Social Science Approaches to the Hebrew Bible* (Winona Lake: Eisenbrauns, 1996); C. E. Carter, "Opening Windows Onto Biblical Worlds: Applying the Social Sciences to Hebrew Scripture," in *The Face of Old Testament Studies: A Survey of Contemporary Approaches*, ed. D. W. Baker and B. T. Arnold (Grand Rapids: Baker; Leicester: InterVarsity, 1999), 421–51. For the NT, see Elliott, *What Is Social-Scientific Criticism?*; P. F. Esler, *The First Christians in Their Social Worlds: Social-Scientific Approaches to New Testament Interpretation* (London and New York: Routledge, 1994); and D. G. Horrell, ed., *Social-Scientific Approaches to New Testament Interpretation* (Edinburgh: T. and T. Clark, 1999).

Social History

This category could easily comprise a special branch of historical background research. But, for the most part, modern students of the Bible have not focused on the significantly different social world and dynamics of Bible times. Today we in the West live in a highly individualistic culture with many opportunities for choices in life—concerning spouses, jobs, places to live, and so on. More often than not, ancient Middle Eastern cultures were rooted more strongly in the various groups to which an individual belonged, and these—family, ethnicity, gender, occupation—usually determined the opportunities for choosing a spouse, or changing a career or place of residence (or in the case of women, even having education or a career "outside the home"). Careful attention to the social world explicit or implicit in various biblical texts often casts new light on them and/or gives the lie to popular misinterpretations.[72]

This obvious but often neglected truth captured the attention of one of us in a conversation about married life that he had with a Singaporean friend in graduate school. The author marveled at how he could speak so calmly and pleasantly about extended families living together—including newlyweds moving into the home of one of their parents! He ventured to tell him that the Bible suggested a different model— "a man will leave his father and mother and be united to his wife" (Gen 2:24). The Singaporean quickly replied that this could not mean physical, geographical separation, since Bible cultures more often than not resembled his experience in traditional Chinese society. Rather, this verse must refer to a change in ultimate allegiances (after marriage the interests of spouse supersede those of parents even if all live under the same roof). The author left the conversation feeling rather foolish.

Sensitivity to this kind of social history can illumine numerous other passages. Mk 3:31–35, for example, then stands out as remarkably radical. Jesus lived in a culture that prized familial loyalties above all other human relationships (a virtue often lacking today). So for him to ignore his biological family while teaching the crowds that his disciples ("whoever does God's will") were "my brother and sister and mother" would have shocked and offended many of his listeners. What is more, these words suggest that Jesus was creating not only new, intimate personal relationships with his followers but also an extended family that would involve detailed obligations for care and commitment among these new "family" members.[73] An understanding of kinship ties can also explain how entire households were converted simultaneously (e.g. Acts 16:14–15, 31–34). Modern missionaries, encountering non-Western tribes or clans in which religious commitments made by leaders were binding on whole groups of people, have been too slow to recognize the validity and biblical precedent for such response.[74] Conversion must be personal, but it is not always individual.[75]

---

72 Particularly helpful in stressing these points, in his application of "group/grid" analysis to modern versus biblical cultures, is Malina, *Christian Origins and Cultural Anthropology.*

73 See esp. D. M. May, "Mark 3:20–35 from the Perspective of Shame/Honor," *BTB* 17 (1987): 83–87.

74 See esp. D. Tidball, *Social Context of the New Testament: A Sociological Analysis* (Grand Rapids: Zondervan 1984), 84–85.

75 A concept particularly associated with the modern church growth movement and pioneered by D. McGavran first in *Bridges of God* (New York: Friendship, 1955).

Modern American separation of church and state also clouds our understanding of ancient cultures that knew no such divisions. To say, for example, that Jesus brought a spiritual message without political implications—or that religion is purely a private matter—would introduce a division foreign to the first century (and to many people today). The various Jewish authorities combined governmental and religious roles in their communities and nation. If they perceived Jesus as a threat to their authority in the one realm, that threat naturally carried over to the other. Conversely, Rome (more naturally associated in modern eyes with the political authority) would eventually include within its purview religious claims ("Caesar is Lord"). Christians could not offer the imperial sacrifice, even though the rest of the empire viewed these claims as little more significant than our pledge of allegiance or salute to the flag. For first-century Christians such "patriotism" implied blasphemous associations of deity with human emperors. Consequently, their "civil disobedience" led to numerous outbreaks of persecution and to the writing of several NT documents (e.g., Hebrews, 1 Peter, and Revelation).[76]

The number of areas in which a better understanding of the social history of the biblical cultures can illuminate the text is almost endless.[77] The large topic of honor and shame helps us understand why a man rousted from his sleep by a midnight visitor would be so concerned to provide hospitality for him, even if it required considerable inconvenience (Lk 11:5–8); his reputation in the village was at stake.[78] Jephthah showed the seriousness of his commitment to defend the honor of his people against

---

76 For the various points in this paragraph, cf. esp. R. A. Horsley, *The Liberation of Christmas* (New York: Crossroad, 1989). It is worth asking if "Christian patriotism" today ever elevates country above God.

77 For a wide-ranging survey, see R. L. Rohrbaugh, ed., *The Social Sciences and New Testament Interpretation* (Peabody: Hendrickson, 1996).

78 V. H. Matthews and D. C. Benjamin ("Social Sciences and Biblical Studies," *Semeia* 68 [1994]: 7–21) offer an excellent summary of applications of these concepts, which we quote at length. "Honor entitled the household to life. Honorable households ate moderately, did not get drunk, worked hard, made good friends, sought advice before acting, held their temper, paid their taxes, and imposed fair legal judgments. They were careful in dealing with one another during menstruation, sexual intercourse, childbirth, and death. And they were equally conscientious about what food they ate, what clothes they wore, what animals they herded, and what crops they planted in their fields. Honorable households could care for their own members and were prepared to help their neighbors. They were households in good standing, licensed to make a living in the village and entitled to its support. Only honorable households were entitled to buy, sell, trade, marry, arrange marriages, serve in assemblies, and send warriors to the tribe. Only honorable households were entitled to make wills, appoint heirs, and serve as legal guardians to care for households endangered by drought, war, and epidemic. Honorable households were in place and functioning well.

"Shame sentenced the household to death by placing its land and children in jeopardy. Shamed households ate too much, drank too much, were lazy, quarrelsome, selfish, and thought nothing about lying to the village assembly. They were thoughtless in their sexual relationships, and disrespectful of the newborn and the dead. Their herds were mangy, and their farms rundown. Shamed households did not fulfill their responsibilities to their own members or their neighbors. Shamed households were on probation. They were out-of-place and not functioning properly. Consequently, both their contributions to the village and their eligibility for its support were suspended. The label downgraded the status of a household, until it demonstrated that it was once again contributing to the village" (11–12).

their enemies by vowing to sacrifice "whatever comes out of the door" of his house to meet him when he returned triumphantly from battle (Judg 11:31). Tragically, that turned out to be his daughter, whose striking reply (v. 36) showed her understanding of the need to keep a vow, however rash it may have been.[79]

Issues of ritual purity dominated the life of ancient Israel, which explains the highly symbolic divisions of the Jerusalem temple into progressively more sacred space as one drew closer to the holy of holies, and as fewer people could enter each successive court. A particularly damaging form of impurity resulted from a curse. One interesting belief widely held in ancient Mediterranean cultures (and still present in places to this day) was that certain people had the ability to cast a spell on others merely with the power of a malignant stare—known as "the evil eye." In several places in the Gospels, the literal translation of the text refers to this belief. For example, in Matt 6:23 Jesus spoke of those whose eyes are evil, corrupting their entire selves. To avert the curse, one must seek to look at the world in wholesome ways, and then one's entire life will be pure (vv. 22–24).[80]

The social system of patronage, in a world largely without the concept of state-sponsored welfare, linked well-to-do benefactors with groups of clients for whom periodic employment and financial care were provided in return for private favors and public, political support. Paul's care not to ask for or accept money for ministry except in very specific situations (see esp. 1 Cor 9:1–18) stemmed from his concern not to be perceived as giving his supporters anything that might compromise his freedom to preach and minister precisely as he believed God was leading him. The reciprocal expectations of patron-client relations also explain why Paul avoided too direct an expression of thanksgiving in Phil 4:10–20. He did convey his gratitude to the Philippian church for their monetary gift, but he did not want to be perceived as becoming indebted to them in any inappropriate fashion.[81]

To understand some dynamics in ancient Israel require an awareness of cultural practices of the surrounding nations. Many aspects of Elisha's healing ministry could have conjured up images of shamanism in other Ancient Near Eastern (ANE) cultures, but Elisha clearly attributed his powers to Yahweh, the God of Israel.[82] The patriarchy of the OT was considerably muted compared to that of the nations around Israel, and the Song of Songs depicts the woman's right to initiate and experience sexual delight with her beloved in a way that stands out even within the OT.[83] The political and economic dimensions of sexual

---

79 V. H. Matthews and D. C. Benjamin, *Social World of Ancient Israel 1250–587 BCE* (Peabody: Hendrickson, 1993), 19-21. Cf. also T. S. Laniak, *Shame and Honor in the Book of Esther*, SBLDS 165 (Atlanta: Scholars, 1998).

80 Cf. further J. H. Elliott, "The Evil Eye and the Sermon on the Mount," *BibInt* 2 (1994): 51–84.

81 For wide-ranging applications of this cultural system, especially with respect to the Pauline epistles, see B. W. Winter, *After Paul Left Corinth: The Influence of Secular Ethics and Social Change* (Grand Rapids and Cambridge: Eerdmans, 2001); and A. D. Clarke, *Serve the Community of the Church: Christians as Leaders and Ministers* (Grand Rapids and Cambridge: Eerdmans, 2000).

82 T. W. Overholt, *Cultural Anthropology and the Old Testament* (Minneapolis: Fortress, 1996), 24–68.

83 D. Bergant, " 'My Beloved is Mine and I Am His' (Song 2:16)": The Song of Songs and Honor and Shame" *Semeia* 68 (1994): 23–40.

behavior in other texts must also be noted. Amnon's rape of Tamar is not merely a case of incest but a claim on David's throne, which also explains the extent to which Absalom, the rival claimant, goes to avenge his brother's sin (2 Sam 13).[84]

Like other items of historical background, the value of a study of the history of social interaction in a given culture depends directly on the accuracy of the data and the appropriateness of their application to specific texts. Scholars agree on most of the above examples. In other cases, interpretations prove more controversial. For example, many people assume that Jesus and his followers came from the substantial majority of the Galilean populace who were poor, marginalized, peasant workers. Recent study has reassessed the role of tradesmen, like carpenters and masons in Galilean villages. Such study focuses attention on details such as the mention in Mk 1:20 that Zebedee's family had "hired men" or servants. A growing number of scholars thus suggests that Jesus and his troupe may have included a fair number of the tiny "middle class" of their society (though even then we may not import the affluence attributed to Western middle class people into our picture of first-century life).[85] Equally groundbreaking but less secure is the attempt to divide the prophets into Ephraimite and Judean categories, in which the former are identified as "peripheral" to their society, and working for social change, and the latter as "central" to their human environment, working for social stability.[86] Given that appeals to the laws of Moses dominate the messages of both groups of prophets, one wonders if theological emphases do not overshadow sociological distinctives.

Good resources now exist, however, to familiarize students with the most secure results of social-historical analysis of the biblical world. For OT study, pride of place must go to King and Stager's *Life in Biblical Israel*. A distinctively evangelical survey, only slightly less comprehensive, and occasionally more speculative, is Matthews' and Benjamin's, *Social World of Ancient Israel 1250–587 BCE*. More selective still is the anthology of Carroll R., *Rethinking Contexts, Rereading Texts*, but the essays are well-conceived and Carroll's own overviews provide an excellent introduction to the literature. For NT study, Bell provides a succinct, introductory overview in *A Guide to the New Testament World*, de Silva's *Honor, Patronage, Kingship and Purity* covers a wide swath of key cultural issues, while Hanson and Oakman's *Palestine in the Time of Jesus* offers a thorough introduction to the first-century world of Israel and relevant background for studying the Gospels. Hanson also provides a thorough bibliography to social-scientific analysis of both Testaments in a separate work.[87]

---

84 Matthews and Hamilton, *Social World of Ancient Israel*, 182-86.

85 See the discussion of past and present study in J. P. Meier, *A Marginal Jew*, 4 vols. (New York and London: Doubleday, 1991–), 1: 278–85. There is also a fair consensus today that a significant minority of the first Christians came from the small, middle, and upper classes of the Roman Empire, especially as the Jesus-movement spread into predominantly Gentile territories.

86 R. R. Wilson, *Prophecy and Society in Ancient Israel* (Philadelphia: Fortress, 1980).

87 Full information on the sources cited in this paragraph is, respectively, P. J. King and L. E. Stager, *Life in Biblical Israel* (Louisville and London: Westminster John Knox, 2001); Matthews and Benjamin, *Social World of Ancient Israel*; M. D. Carroll R., ed., *Rethinking Contexts, Rereading Texts: Contributions from the Social Sciences to Biblical Interpretation* (Sheffield: Sheffield Academic Press, 2000); A. A. Bell, Jr., *A Guide to the New Testament World* (Scottdale and Waterloo: Herald, 1994); D. A. de Silva, *Honor, Patronage, and Purity: Unlocking New Testament Culture* (Downers Grove: InterVarsity, 2000); K. C. Hanson and D. E. Oakman, *Palestine in the Time of Jesus: Social Structures and Social Conflicts* (Minneapolis: Fortress, 1998); and K. C. Hanson, "Greco-Roman Studies and the Social-Scientific Study of the Bible: A Classified Periodical Bibliography (1970-1994)," *Forum* 9 (1993): 63-119.

Perhaps the most valuable upshot of the new interest in studying social history is that it gives interpreters new sets of questions to ask of the biblical texts. Howard Kee helpfully enumerates a long list of these; sample items include: to what groups do various individuals in the Bible belong? What are the social dynamics of those groups? What are their goals? How might they accomplish them? What are the roles of power within the group and the means of attaining them? Are age groups or sex roles defined? What are the key formative experiences of the group, including initiation, celebration, and stages of transition? What are the boundaries of acceptable behavior that one may or may not transgress? And there are many more.[88] Asking new questions of a text will certainly elicit new answers and yield fresh insights.

Application of Social-Scientific Theories

Under this heading we turn to a different kind of social-scientific analysis. Here scholars use theories about human behavior developed in modern studies of various cultures, including the so-called primitive cultures, to shed fresh light on what may have been the dynamics of social interaction in biblical times. In other words, even where we have no reliable data from the Bible or other ancient texts about the ways in which people interacted in certain settings, perhaps analogies from other cultures in other times and places can enable us to make plausible inferences as to those dynamics.

So, for example, scholars have expended much energy in the attempt to account for the social forces involved in the rise of ancient Israel as a political state, from a loose confederation of tribes to a people who demanded and received a king (the story narrated in 1 Samuel–2 Kings). The three most popular theories have proposed analogies, respectively, from the later development of the Greek nation out of independent city-states, from peasant revolts in other ancient cultures, and from the rise of modern socialism or communism.[89] From the Greek concept of "amphictyony" (an association of neighboring states) has come the hypothesis that during the days of the judges Israel was a very loose confederation of tribes unified only by the single Shiloh sanctuary. An alternate explanation of the settlement period theorizes that "Israel" came into being by a rebellion of nomadic tribesmen already living in Canaan who overthrew their urban oppressors. On a quite different front, studies of ritual taboos in traditional cultures have offered widely accepted explanations for why certain animals were considered unclean in ancient Israel: they deviated from some established norm that was the symbol of ritual purity.[90]

Again, the study of Melanesian "cargo" cults in the South Pacific led to a popular proposal about a people's response to "failed prophecy" (a bit of a misleading term), as when the OT prophets repeatedly predicted "the day of the Lord is at hand" (see esp.

---

88 H. C. Kee, *Knowing the Truth: A Sociological Approach to New Testament Interpretation* (Minneapolis: Fortress, 1989), 65–67.

89 These three views are classically associated, respectively, with M. Noth, *The History of Israel* (New York: Harper, 1958); G. E. Mendenhall, *The Tenth Generation: The Origins of the Biblical Tradition* (Baltimore: Johns Hopkins University Press, 1973); and N. K. Gottwald, *The Tribes of Yahweh: A Sociology of the Religion of Liberated Israel 1250–1050 B.C.E.* (Maryknoll: Orbis, 1979).

90 See esp. M. Douglas, *Purity and Danger: An Analysis of Concepts of Pollution and Taboo* (London: Routledge & Kegan Paul, 1966); cf. id., *Leviticus as Literature* (New York/Oxford: Oxford University Press, 2001).

Zeph), even though centuries passed without its fulfillment. Perhaps this phenomenon recurred in the experience of first-generation Christians who may have expected Christ's return within their lifetime (see esp. 2 Thessalonians). Among other things, this proposal suggests that a religious group whose members discover that "the end" has not come as soon as they first believed "saves face" by engaging in more vigorous proselytizing or evangelism. As more people flock to the movement, then, it regains its credibility and can revise its expectations without threatening the existence of the group.[91]

Study of recurring patterns of institutionalization in the development of religious groups or sects has proved influential in accounting for the development of the first-century Church. Itinerant charismatics often give way to more settled and organized forms of leadership. Office replaces charisma. Many NT scholars identify such a pattern of institutionalization in the movement from Jesus and his first followers (the "wandering charismatics"), to Paul (who promoted settled charismatic worship—1 Cor 12–14), to post-Pauline literature (esp. 1 Tim 3, with its criteria for office-holding, believed by most to be written a generation later than Paul; or Jude 3, seen as a classic example of "early catholic" institutionalization of "the faith that was once for all entrusted to the saints").[92] In the OT, some suggest that charismatic prophets eventually yielded to forces that institutionalized or "routinized" their leadership. The latest writing prophets (e.g., Haggai, Malachi) thus may resemble the preachers in the emerging synagogue more than their iconoclastic predecessors (e.g., Amos, Jeremiah).[93]

Employing sociological analysis some view the divisions at Corinth (1 Cor 1:10–17) in light of socio-economic divisions, in which the more wealthy apparently brought extra to eat and drink but did not share enough of their provisions with the poor who came empty-handed (cf. 11:20–21).[94] Others see 1 Peter as an extended tract encouraging the Church to become "a home for the homeless" (referring to literal refugees).[95] Still others view miracle-stories in the Gospels and Acts as responses to the frustration of a marginalized existence in this life.[96]

How should the student of hermeneutics respond to this plethora of proposals? Numerous items are certainly worthy of consideration, but we must subject this program to careful analysis by asking key questions. First, is the specific sociological theory reductionistic or deterministic?[97] That is to say, does it rule out God, the supernat-

---

91 Cf. esp. J. G. Gager, *Kingdom and Community: The Social World of Early Christianity* (Englewood Cliffs, NJ: Prentice-Hall, 1975); and R. P. Carroll, *When Prophecy Failed: Cognitive Dissonance in the Prophetic Traditions of the Old Testament* (New York: Seabury, 1979).

92 Cf. esp. G. Theissen, *The Sociology of Early Palestinian Christianity* (Philadelphia: Fortress, 1978). Theissen builds on the more wide-ranging studies of the growth of religions from sect to institution by M. Weber.

93 R. E. Clements, "Max Weber, Charisma and Biblical Prophecy," in *Prophecy and Prophets*, ed. Y. Gitay (Atlanta: Scholars, 1997), 89–108; J. Blenkinsopp, "The Social Roles of Prophets in Early Achaemenid Judah," *JSOT* 93 (2001): 39–58.

94 G. Theissen, *The Social Setting of Pauline Christianity* (Philadelphia: Fortress, 1982), 145–74.

95 J. H. Elliott, *A Home for the Homeless: A Sociological Exegesis of 1 Peter* (Philadelphia: Fortress, 1981). See now also his *1 Peter*, AB (New York and London: Doubleday, 2000).

96 H. C. Kee, *Miracle in the Early Christian World* (New Haven: Yale University Press, 1983).

97 A criticism frequently leveled by E. Yamauchi in his important analytical survey, "Sociology, Scripture and the Supernatural," *JETS* 27 (1984): 169–92.

ural, or human freedom as possible and even primary agents? Several of the explanations for the establishment of the Israelite nation or for belief in Jesus' miracles involve precisely such presuppositions. The open-minded inquirer cannot accept those that rule out God or human freedom.

Second, does the theory require rejecting part of the biblical text as it stands or reconstructing a set of historical events at odds with the claims of the text itself? Many of the theories involving the transition from judges to kingship assume that the data of Scripture are almost wholly unreliable and must be replaced with a different reconstruction of events.[98] Theissen's view that Jesus' first followers in Palestine were almost exclusively itinerant charismatics requires that we trust only a handful of Q-sayings as the oldest and most authentic portion of the gospel tradition, often *at the expense* of other sayings. Other perspectives require a denial of the stated authorship of biblical books (e.g., Ephesians). To the extent that such theories assume the unreliability of the Bible as we have it, we believe that they are ill-founded.

Third, is a given proposal based on a valid theory commonly accepted by other social scientists? A popular view of the rise of apocalyptic literature proposes that it stems from times of acute social crisis among the communities in which it arises. But recent study has shown that more crucial is the *perception* of crisis—which may or may not correspond to reality. In this case we may not speak with as much confidence about the social origins of every scriptural use of apocalyptic as consistently due to the oppression of the people of God.[99] A popular explanation for group dynamics in OT times has been the notion of "corporate personality" (hence, e.g., all Israel could be punished for the sins of Achan—Josh 7),[100] but more recent research suggests that while corporate responsibility (as in the Achan story) may indicate some kind of corporate solidarity, it does not necessarily require the "psychical unity" so often postulated as a unique feature of the ancient Hebrew mind.[101]

Fourth, if the theory is valid elsewhere, are the parallels or analogies with the biblical material close enough to warrant its application to this new context? Twentieth-century South Pacific islanders may be too far removed in time and space from the ancient Middle East to provide much help for interpreting the missionary movements in ancient Judaism and early Christianity!

Fifth, does the theory fit the biblical data as well as do alternatives that are more traditional? For example, one may read 1 Peter as a call to "seek the welfare of the city"

---

98 W. G. Dever, *What Did the Biblical Writers Know and When Did They Know It? What Archaeology Can Tell Us about the Reality of Ancient Israel* (Grand Rapids: Eerdmans, 2001).

99 See esp. A. Y. Collins, *Crisis in Catharsis: The Power of the Apocalypse* (Philadelphia: Westminster, 1984). On the origins of OT Apocalyptic, see classically P. D. Hanson, *The Dawn of Apocalyptic* (Philadelphia: Fortress, 1975).

100 Due in large measure to H. Wheeler Robinson, "The Hebrew Conception of 'Corporate Personality' in the Old Testament," in *Werden und Wesen des Alten Testaments* (Berlin: Topelmann, 1936), 49–62; rev. and repr. as *Corporate Personality in Ancient Israel* (Philadelphia: Fortress, 1980; Edinburgh: T. & T. Clark, 1999).

101 See esp. J. W. Rogerson, "The Hebrew Conception of Corporate Personality: A Re-examination," *JTS* 21 (1970): 1–16. For helpful correctives to Rogerson see R. A. di Vito, "Old Testament Anthropology and The Construction of Personal Identity," *CBQ* 61 (1999): 217–39; and J. S. Kominsky, "The Sins of the Fathers: A Theological Investigation of the Biblical Tension Between Corporate and Individualized Retribution," *Judaism* 46 (1997): 319–33.

(cf. Jer 29:7) at least as plausibly as a mandate to care for the needy within the Church.[102] Or, it is hard to find much fit between peasants' revolts within a nation and the Israelites' establishment of themselves in the land from outside.[103] The story of exodus, covenant, and conquest, however one conceives it, seems far more plausible.

Notwithstanding all of these caveats suggesting that we may need to temper, if not reject outright, some of the more popular social-scientific theories, numerous proposals do improve on older, commonly held opinions. Viewing ritual cleanliness and uncleanliness in light of religious taboos or an understanding of order versus disorder seems more appropriate than the popular view that these laws reflected some kind of primitive understanding of hygiene.[104] Wayne Meeks' research on "the first urban Christians," a study of the major cities in which Paul ministered, helpfully compares and contrasts Pauline churches with other socio-religious groups, including trade guilds. He demonstrates that the Church might often have been perceived as a similar voluntary association that held the potential, from the viewpoint of Roman leadership, to be subversive to the state.[105] Because of the abundance of written material on life in ancient Greece and Rome from extrabiblical sources, theories here are much more likely to be valid than those, say, relating to periods of Israelite history for which little but ambiguous archeological evidence exists to confirm or contest biblical detail. In viewing early Palestinian Christianity as a rural-based renewal movement of local communities within the existing but diverse forms of Judaism, Richard Horsley offers a devastating critique of the wandering charismatic theory of Christian origins and provides a more plausible model.[106] William Herzog applies research into the social stratification of ancient and modern pre-capitalist empires to show the probable percentages of people in each of the socio-economic brackets of the Roman world.[107]

These kinds of evaluations or "judgment calls" obviously require some familiarity with the social sciences. We advise theological or "pre-seminary" students to take introductory courses in sociology, psychology, anthropology, economics, and the like, in order to be familiar with the basic terms and theories that these disciplines employ. They will still need to rely on helpful literature that evaluates the methods employed in these disciplines, especially when applied to the Bible.[108] But even the relative novice

---

102 See esp. D. L. Balch, *Let Wives Be Submissive: The Domestic Code in I Peter* (Chico, CA: Scholars, 1981); B. Winter, *Seek the Welfare of the City: Christians as Benefactors and Citizens* (Carlisle: Paternoster; Grand Rapids: Eerdmans, 1994), 11–23.

103 Cf. esp. N. P. Lemche, *Early Israel: Anthropological and Historical Studies on the Israelite Society Before the Monarchy* (Leiden: Brill, 1985).

104 See esp. the appropriation of Douglas' research throughout G. J. Wenham, *The Book of Leviticus,* NICOT (Grand Rapids: Eerdmans, 1979).

105 W. Meeks, *The First Urban Christians: The Social World of the Apostle Paul* (New Haven: Yale University Press, 1983).

106 R. A. Horsley, *Sociology and the Jesus Movement* (New York: Crossroad, 1989).

107 W. R. Herzog II, *Parables as Subversive Speech: Jesus as Pedagogue of the Oppressed* (Louisville: Westminster John Knox, 1994), 53–73. Herzog's comparison is compelling because the model largely fits what primary source data we do have from the Roman Empire itself.

108 Cf. esp. B. Holmberg, *Sociology and the New Testament: An Appraisal* (Minneapolis: Fortress, 1990). To date, no comparable, comprehensive critique of the methodologies of a broad cross-section of OT sociology exists.

can sift theories that incorporate biblical data as valid source material from those that depend largely on reconstructions of ancient history that contradict the testimony of Scripture.[109] In our judgment, even the most valid social-scientific study will never replace the classic historical-grammatical tools of analysis, but it can provide important supplementary information and correctives to past mistakes in interpretation.

Advocacy Groups

Within the broad arena of social-scientific interest in the Bible several subdisciplines have taken on whole lives of their own, both in the sheer volume of literature published and in the ideological stances they represent. Traditionally, biblical scholarship promoted a certain detachment by its practitioners as a laudable goal. Precisely because the use of the Bible in church and synagogue has usually involved theological motives and biases, scholars in academic institutions have tried to distance themselves from particular ideologies as they study Scripture. But various practitioners of social-scientific analysis now seek to reverse this trend. In the 1970s and 1980s the two main representatives of this perspective were those who practiced liberation and feminist hermeneutics. In the 1990s the former largely gave way to broader forms of cultural criticism, while the latter has continued unabated. Each of these movements shares a common commitment to the liberation of the disenfranchised of this world and views "detached objectivity" as both a myth and a weakness. In other words, if one is not part of the solution, he or she is part of the problem! If biblical scholars do not join the marginalized in their quest for full equality, human rights, and a decent life for all, irrespective of gender, race, sexual orientation, nationality, and so on, then they *de facto* remain aligned with the inhuman, oppressive, sexist, and racist powers of this world. There are, of course, numerous other strands of Christian theology, both traditional and avant-garde, that remain activistic in nature.[110] But no other systems of thought employ so unique a set of hermeneutical axioms nor remain as influential internationally as the following three. So we turn to each briefly for some special analysis.

Liberation Hermeneutics

Liberation theology initially developed as an engaged, Roman Catholic response in Latin America to centuries of oppression of the impoverished majority of poor, mostly native American residents by ruling élites in government, society, and even the Church.[111] Liberation hermeneutics developed a three-part agenda. In opposition to the stated objectives of many forms of classical theology, experience takes precedence over theory. The dominant experience of a majority of people in the Two-Thirds World, in which liberation theology emerged, is the experience of poverty—suffering,

---

109 For NT study three like-minded works in commentary format provide easy access to a wide range of hypotheses that should be tested. See B. J. Malina and R. L. Rohrbaugh, *Social-Science Commentary on the Synoptic Gospels* (Minneapolis: Fortress, 1992); B. J. Malina and J. J. Pilch, *Social-Science Commentary on the Book of Revelation* (Minneapolis: Fortress, 2000); and Eerdmans' *Socio-Rhetorical Commentaries* on Mark, Acts, Romans, Corinthians, and Galatians, by B. Witherington, and on Hebrews by D. De Silva. Some of the interpretations prove problematic but a significant number provide valuable, legitimate insights.

110 E.g., one thinks, respectively, of mainstream Protestant liberal reformers and proponents of New Age or pantheistic worldviews.

111 The widely acknowledged founder of this movement is G. Gutiérrez, with his *A Theology of Liberation: History, Politics, and Salvation*, 2d ed. (Maryknoll: Orbis, 1988 [orig. Spanish 1968]).

malnutrition, lack of access to basic human rights, education, clean water, medicine, and the like. Hence, first, a liberation hermeneutic begins with the experience of the injustice of poverty. Second, it attempts to analyze or assess the reasons for this impoverished existence. Third, actions take precedence over rhetoric. Liberationists seek to determine a course of corrective measures based on their previous observation, insight, and judgment.[112] In the liberationist hermeneutic, the Bible does not normally come into play in step one of the three-part agenda outlined above but only to aid in steps two and three. Particularly by focusing on the biblical narratives of liberation from oppression, with the exodus as the OT paradigm, and a socio-political understanding of God's kingdom as the NT paradigm, the liberationist takes heart from his or her conviction that God has a "preferential option for the poor."[113] God sides with the oppressed against their oppressors and calls believers today to do the same in working for a more humane society on this earth.

How to bring about this new society, God's kingdom, remained a topic on which liberationists disagreed. Some have labored within the framework of Western democracies but believed that we need more socialist checks and balances on a capitalism run amok.[114] Some have strongly eschewed violence but endorsed social protest and civil disobedience *à la* Martin Luther King, Jr.[115] Still others have endorsed both violence and Marxism as necessary means to more desirable ends.[116] Most all have agreed that the current disparities between the haves and have-nots of this world cannot continue to widen, as they have so considerably under current forms of capitalism. Most all have believed that the Bible itself promotes peace and justice in ways that require a modification of current economic and political structures in society.

As clearly as any liberationist writer, José Miranda equated Christianity with communism, believing that it is taught throughout the Bible.[117] It is indeed striking that both "halves" of Marx's manifesto come straight from the book of Acts: "from each according to his ability" (Acts 11:29) and "to each according to his need" (4:35). The OT Jubilee laws were designed to prevent the perpetuation of extreme disparities in the distribution of wealth, as debts had to be forgiven in the Sabbath and Jubilee years. A major theme of the Law and Prophets is the denunciation of injustice against the powerless and a call to help the poor. The communal living and redistribution of goods depicted in Acts 2:42–47 and 4:32–5:11 serve as indictments of contemporary Western forms of Christianity. And Luke's summary statements make it clear that he viewed this fellowship as exemplary and not the mistake (2:47, 5:14) some modern-day Christians

---

112 A good, detailed introduction to liberationist hermeneutics (as distinct from liberation theology more generally) is C. Rowland and M. Corner, *Liberating Exegesis: The Challenge of Liberation Theology to Biblical Studies* (Louisville: Westminster John Knox, 1989).

113 A slogan that emerged in the late 1960s from Vatican II and subsequent Catholic bishops' conferences as the rallying cry and starting point for the vast majority of liberation theology.

114 E.g., R. J. Sider, "An Evangelical Theology of Liberation," *ChrCent* 97 (1980): 314–18; and J. A. Kirk, *Theology Encounters Revolution* (Leicester: InterVarsity, 1980).

115 E.g., R. J. Cassidy, *Jesus, Politics and Society* (Maryknoll: Orbis, 1978); and J. M. Ford, *My Enemy Is My Guest: Jesus and Violence in Luke* (Maryknoll: Orbis, 1984).

116 E.g., J. H. Cone, *A Black Theology of Liberation*, 3d ed. (Maryknoll: Orbis, 1990); and J. L. Segundo, *The Liberation of Theology* (Maryknoll: Orbis, 1976).

117 J. P. Miranda, *Communism in the Bible* (Maryknoll: Orbis, 1982).

have thought it was. Paul too outlined radical requirements for Christian stewardship of money (2 Cor 8–9), in which, following the model of God's provision of manna in the wilderness, "he who gathered much did not have too much, and he who gathered little did not have too little" (2 Cor 8:15; Exod 16:18). The goal was "that there might be equality" (2 Cor 8:13).[118]

We observe two major problems, however, with a hermeneutic that proceeds from the conviction that Christianity is inherently socialist, at least in the forms that have evolved since the days of Marx. First, such a hermeneutic tries to impose on society ethics that were originally limited to God's people. Neither in OT Israel nor in the NT church were "believers" mandated to make God's laws or principles the laws of every nation. Second, the liberationist hermeneutic usually plays down the voluntary nature of NT giving (2 Cor 9:7; cf. Acts 4:32). Texts like these show that the Christians retained personal property. In short, as with the good news of the kingdom itself, no one is forced to be a good steward of his or her God-given resources who does not want to![119] But, having said this, many Bible scholars, evangelicals included, now agree with liberationists that models of Western church life have much to learn from the paradigms of fellowship and stewardship of the Bible. As well, in certain respects the Bible's paradigms may more closely approximate socialist (or social democratic) rather than purely capitalist structures.[120]

Liberationist hermeneutics pose other problems. They often do not seem adequately to preserve the "spiritual" element of salvation. Mk 8:36 stands out poignantly: "What good is it for you to gain the whole world, yet forfeit your soul?" (TNIV). They may overlook that "the poor" in Scripture are consistently not *all* the physically dispossessed or oppressed but those who in their need turn to God as their only hope.[121] In so doing they create a *de facto* "canon within the canon" and ignore or deem as not as authoritative those texts that do not support their agenda. At the same time, more traditional forms of theology have proved equally blind to the parts of Scripture the liberationists stress. So as a corrective to one imbalance, though not as the sum total of the scriptural witness, liberation theology proves extremely significant.

Rereading other Scriptures from a perspective of a commitment to help the disenfranchised of this world can thus shed significant new light on them. The Exodus account reminds us that God is concerned about sociopolitical as well as spiritual freedoms.[122] We may rightly see Esther as a model of one who risked the penalties of civil

---

118 From a different perspective, see also C. L. Blomberg, *Neither Poverty Nor Riches: A Biblical Theology of Possessions* (Leicester and Downers Grove: InterVarsity, 1999); cf. also id., " 'Your Faith Has Made You Whole': The Evangelical Liberation Theology of Jesus," in *Jesus of Nazareth, Lord and Christ*, ed. J. B. Green and M. Turner (Grand Rapids: Eerdmans, 1994), 75–93.

119 For important critiques of liberation hermeneutics, cf. E. A. Nuñez, *Liberation Theology* (Chicago: Moody Press, 1985); R. C. Hundley, *Radical Liberation Theology: An Evangelical Response* (Wilmore, KY: Bristol Books, 1987); and R. Nash and H. Belli, *Beyond Liberation Theology* (Grand Rapids: Baker, 1992).

120 Cf., e.g., T. D. Hanks, *God So Loved the Third World* (Maryknoll: Orbis, 1984); A. Kirk, *The Good News of the Kingdom Coming* (Downers Grove: InterVarsity, 1983).

121 See esp. W. Heard, "Luke's Attitude Toward the Rich and the Poor," *TrinJ* n.s. 9 (1988): 47-80; cf. S. Gillingham, "The Poor in the Psalms," *ExpT* 100 (1988): 15–19.

122 See esp. J. S. Croatto, *Exodus: A Hermeneutics of Freedom* (Maryknoll: Orbis, 1981).

disobedience to stand up for her people rather than as one who was duly submissive to the authorities in her world.[123] We should view Jesus, as already noted above, as a challenge to political as well as religious authorities and structures in his society.[124] And in perhaps the most important biblical document that requires us to wrestle with the liberationist agenda, the epistle of James, we discover a community of largely poor, Christian day-laborers being oppressed by their wealthy, often absentee landlords—a frightening parallel to the situation of many Third-World laborers today. Many of them are Christian believers denied a decent wage and basic human rights by the large multinational corporations or corrupt national governments that employ them as virtual slave labor.[125] Yet many conservative Christians explicitly and implicitly continue to support right-wing regimes and ultra-capitalist policies that only exacerbate the physical suffering of their Christian brothers and sisters. Whatever else we may question in a liberationist hermeneutic, we obviously have much still to learn from it. We must listen to the voices of the disenfranchised, test each claim against the Scriptures, and see if either their or our presuppositions have obscured the true meaning or significance of the text.[126]

Cultural Criticism

The collapse of Communist regimes in Eastern Europe and Asia at the beginning of the 1990s dealt a near-deathblow to those forms of liberationist hermeneutics that were closely wedded to socialist economics.[127] Indeed, comparatively little has been written since, under the explicit banner of "liberation theology." Also, at the grassroots level, the poor in Latin America have been converting to evangelical and especially Pentecostal Christianity in large numbers. As these branches of Christianity mature in their recognition of a holistic gospel—meeting needs of body and soul alike—the impetus swings away from liberation theology as well. What remains of a liberationist hermeneutic appears far more toned down, but perhaps that much more balanced and legitimate as a result.[128] For example, E. Tamez, in her recent commentary on Ecclesiastes, reads from a context of "hopelessness" of many Third-World poor at the start of the twenty-first century, and derives four major principles from the text that afford hope for the future: (1) there is a time and season for everything (3:1–8); (2) real life has a rhythm to it that dehumanizing social forces ignore; (3) one must fear God as one recognizes the finite limited human condition (12:13–14); and (4) discernment and wisdom in everyday tasks can lead to a solidarity with fellow sufferers that encourages God's people in the midst of a radically individualistic, "save-your-own-skin" world.[129]

---

123 O. E. Costas, "The Subversiveness of Faith: Esther as a Paradigm for a Liberating Theology," *EcR* 40 (1988): 66–78.

124 Cf. further H. C. Waetjen, *A Reordering of Power: A Socio-Political Reading of Mark's Gospel* (Minneapolis: Fortress, 1989).

125 See esp. P. U. Maynard-Reid, *Poverty and Wealth in James* (Maryknoll: Orbis, 1987); and E. Tamez, *The Scandalous Message of James*, 2d ed. (New York: Crossroad, 2002).

126 A good anthology to help in such a process is R. S. Sugirtharajah, ed., *Voices From the Margin* (London: SPCK, 1991).

127 Cf. D. B. Forrester, "Can Liberation Theology Survive 1989?" *SJT* 47 (1994): 245–53.

128 Cf. S. K. George, "From Liberation to Evangelization: New Latin American Hermeneutical Keys," *Int* 55 (2001): 367–77.

129 E. Tamez, *When the Horizons Close: Rereading Ecclesiastes* (Maryknoll: Orbis, 2000), 143.

At the same time as the near demise of liberationism, however, has come the upsurgence of a flood of biblical and theological studies under the rubric of "cultural" or "intercultural" criticism.[130] Common to such study is an emphasis on reading Scripture through the eyes of those raised in traditionally marginalized cultures. Some cultural criticism closely resembles liberationist exegesis in that it selectively accepts those portions of Scripture that it believes humanize or give dignity to the oppressed, while rejecting parts believed to be inherently dehumanizing. R. C. Bailey, for example, studies the OT polemic against the Canaanite peoples for their sexual sin. He believes it functions to dehumanize Israel's enemies to pave the way for their (unjustifiable) genocide.[131] Somewhat paradoxically, this approach uses Judeo-Christian morals, found in certain parts of Scripture to critique and even condemn the contents of other parts, and it still presupposes the modernist conception that some absolute truths exists, in this case that genocide is always wrong.

Increasingly, however, cultural criticism is joining hands with postmodernism so that it exists not only as a subset of social-scientific analysis but also as one category of reader-response criticism. Here, claims that are more modest surface. Practitioners suggest readings merely as viable alternatives to traditional ones, not as inherently correct or even better.[132] But this perspective leaves inadequately addressed questions such as: "Why should liberating interpretations be preferred to oppressive ones?" The very approach undercuts convictions that biblical texts should aid in the advocacy of certain causes versus others.

Some cultural criticism appears merely as a form of application of biblical texts and themes to cultures and contexts not often previously addressed. For example, the apostles in Acts 6:1-7 seek to redress the neglect of the Hellenist widows in the early church in Jerusalem by having the Hellenistic branch of the church appoint its own leaders to address the problem. Here is a possible mandate for doing all we can to empower indigenous leadership in each new culture that accepts the gospel.[133] Likewise, the situation of repatriated Jewish exiles presupposed by Isa 56–66 closely parallels the experiences of Chinese Christians in Hong Kong after its return to China. So lessons from these chapters apply quite directly in this contemporary context.[134] But these are merely cross-cultural applications or "contextualizations"[135] of the Bible, a practice followed

---

130 For both of these terms, see F. F. Segovia, "And They Began to Speak in Other Tongues: Competing Modes of Discourse in Contemporary Biblical Criticism," in *Reading From this Place*, ed. F. F. Segovia and M. A. Tolbert, 2 vols. (Minneapolis: Fortress, 1995), 1: 7; and id., "Toward Intercultural Criticism: A Reading Strategy From the Diaspora," in *Reading From this Place*, 2: 303–30.

131 R. C. Bailey, "They're Nothing But Incestuous Bastards: The Polemical Use of Sex and Sexuality in Hebrew Canon Narratives," in *Reading From this Place*, 1: 121–47.

132 Again, see esp. F. F. Segovia throughout his contributions to *Reading From this Place*, 2 vols. Cf. id., *Decolonizing Biblical Studies: A View From the Margins* (Maryknoll: Orbis, 2000).

133 J. L. González, "Reading From My Bicultural Place: Acts 6:1–7," in *Reading From This Place*, 1:139–47.

134 A. C. C. Lee, "Exile and Return in the Perspective of 1997," in *Reading From This Place*, 2:97–108.

135 On which, see esp. T. E. van Spanje, "Contextualization: Hermeneutical Remarks," *BJRL* 80 (1998): 197–217.

in varying ways throughout church history and one to which we will return in a later chapter, but hardly a new hermeneutical method.

One important branch of cultural criticism that has been widely discussed is "postcolonialism." Whereas liberation theology initially grew out of the distinctive Latin American political history, postcolonialism has emerged in former Asian and African colonies. Liberation for them was politically achieved in most cases by no later than the 1960s, but Western religious and economic forces still keep them from being fully "decolonized" in those arenas. One definition of the task of postcolonialism in the late 1990s could have been a central objective of liberation theology in its heyday:

To ensure that the yearnings of the poor take precedence over the interests of the affluent; that the emancipation of the subjugated has primacy over the freedom of the powerful; and that the participation of the marginalized takes priority over the perpetuation of a system which systematically excludes them.[136]

But postcolonialism often goes one distinctive step further—accepting a pluralism among religious worldviews which relativizes its own claims. M. W. Dube, for example, objects to the "one-way" theology of the Gospel of John, with its emphasis on Jesus' unique divinity and absolute claims on the world. This sounds too much like the ideology that supported colonization, she argues, and so it must be rejected.[137] Sugirtharajah provocatively identifies the various saviors in religions that have influenced Asia as all on the side of good versus the Satanic dehumanizing forces of secularism:

> In a multireligious context like ours, the real contest is not between Jesus and other savior figures like Buddha or Krishna, or religious leaders like Mohammed, as advocates of the "Decade of Evangelism" want us to believe, it is between mammon and Satan on the one side, and Jesus, Buddha, Krishna, and Mohammed on the other. Mammon stands for personal greed, avariciousness, accumulation, and selfishness, and Satan stands for structural and institutional violence. The question then is whether these religious figures offer us any clue to challenge these forces, or simply help to perpetuate them, and how the continuities rather than contrasts among these savior figures may be experienced and expressed.[138]

Less radically, G. M. Soares-Prabhu compares the Great Commission of Mt 28:18–20 to a famous Buddhist scripture that commands monks to go into the world with the teaching of the *ehamma*—the good in the beginning, middle and end of everything—as "the Lord" does, based on the spiritual liberation the monk has experienced,

---

136 R. S. Sugirtharajah, "A Postcolonial Exploration of Collusion and Construction in Biblical Interpretation," in *The Postcolonial Bible*, ed. R. S. Sugirtharajah (Sheffield: Sheffield Academic Press, 1998), 113.

137 M. W. Dube, "Savior of the World but Not of This World: A Postcolonial Reading of the Spatial Construction in John," in *The Postcolonial Bible*, 118–35.

138 R. S. Sugirtharajah, *Asian Biblical Hermeneutics and Postcolonialism: Contesting the Interpretations* (Maryknoll: Orbis, 1998), 119.

and out of compassion for the world and for the happiness of many. By juxtaposing two such partly parallel mandates, the differences also stand out more clearly. The Asian familiar with Buddhism will recognize more clearly even than Christians from other contexts would the distinctive Christological (Christ-centered) rather than anthropological (person-centered) focus of Jesus' commission.[139]

The most valid and helpful results of cultural (or multicultural) exegesis, however, involve the recognition of genuine dimensions of meaning or background of biblical texts drawn from non-Western settings that more closely parallel the biblical world than typical Western culture. This often enables readers, particularly from the Two-Thirds World, to pick up something that First World readers miss or unwittingly distort.[140] African readers of the OT, for example, will probably recognize that polygamy in the biblical world, as on their continent, was not primarily about sex but about status, having large families to provide for basic needs, and even peace between rival tribes through intermarrying.[141] African-Americans are more likely to recognize a theological and literary unity to the book of Daniel because of their historic appeal both to Daniel's this-worldly salvation in chaps. 1-6 and to its other-worldly rescue in the more apocalyptic chaps. 7–12. Both sections speak powerfully to people marginalized in society; no historical-critical dissection into separate documents need be postulated, as white liberal scholars so often have done.[142]

Turning to the NT, Spanish readers will quickly observe the links between "righteousness" and "justice" because they have only one word to use—*justicia*—to translate the one Greek word *dikaiosunē*. They are more likely to understand, when Paul speaks of imputing God's righteousness to believers, that he employs a holistic concept that involves spiritual salvation and social justice. As the Spirit then works in believers' lives, they should be equally concerned with both tasks.[143] Likewise, Two-Third-World readers of Rev 17–18, accustomed to economic oppression by the minority of well-to-do people in their society, including those in political and religious positions of power, will more quickly note the economic dimensions of the exploitation by the great, evil, end-times empire depicted in these chapters. They will thus more likely point to the increasingly anti-Christian, enormously wealthy West and its multinational corporations with their exploitative sweatshops in Third World

---

139 G. M. Soares-Prabhu, "Two Mission Commands: An Interpretation of Matthew 28:16–20 in the Light of a Buddhist Text," *BibInt* 2 (1994): 264–82.

140 So explicitly D. Smith Christopher, "Introduction," in *Text and Experience: Towards a Cultural Exegesis of the Bible*, ed. D. Smith Christopher (Sheffield: Sheffield Academic Press, 1995), 12–22. Cf. C. L. Blomberg, "The Globalization of Biblical Hermeneutics," *JETS* 38 (1995): 581–93; id., "The Globalization of Biblical Interpretation—A Test Case: John 3–4," *BBR* 5 (1995): 1–15. Good guidelines for pursuing this objective appear also in T. Okure, "Reading From This Place: Some Problems and Prospects," in *Reading From This Place*, 2: 52–66.

141 K. Holter, *Yahweh in Africa: Essays on Africa and the Old Testament* (New York: Peter Lang, 2000), 77–90.

142 J. Kampen, "The Genre and Function of Apocalyptic Literature in the African American Experience," in *Text and Experience*, 43–65.

143 Cf. E. Tamez, *The Amnesty of Grace: Justification by Faith From a Latin American Perspective* (Nashville: Abingdon, 1993). Interestingly this English title actually better captures this holism than the title of the Spanish original: *Contra Todo Condenado* ("Against Everything Condemned").

countries than to largely impoverished Middle Eastern or formally Soviet countries for the closest contemporary parallels.[144]

Of course, even contemporary cultures more akin to biblical ones are not identical, and the danger remains of interpreting an ancient text in light of current cultural practices, however traditional, where the ancient and modern cultures do not match. Thus while it is fascinating to consider traditional African taboos on counting as bringing bad fortune as possible background for why God condemned David's census (2 Sam 24:1),[145] it was probably the practice of counting people for the sake of military conscription in Israel that displeased God when he had not commanded David to go to war (thus explicitly v. 2). Even more clearly mistaken is the attempt to make *Yahweh Elohim* ("the Lord God") in the OT mean "Yahweh [is] the gods" in a polytheistic context, just because that is what it could mean in certain African contexts and might well have meant even in various Ancient Near Eastern contexts.[146] The significant differences between Israel and the nations even in the earliest stages of its developing monotheism, not to mention consistent OT usage, are overlooked in the process.

Thus we may study traditional cultures analogous to biblical ones to identify a correct interpretation of a scriptural text. On the flip side we can use such parallels to expose an incorrect interpretation found among Western commentators. This challenges the common tendency to read into the text modern and alien (to the Bible) cultural prejudices. Stereotypes concerning African slaves in American history may lead white readers to assume blindly that Onesimus was a runaway who had committed some crime, perhaps stealing Philemon's goods. In fact, that is only one of several possible inferences from the text. Some commentators suggest that Onesimus may have gone to Paul in Rome voluntarily as a respected friend and mediator for both parties, following an ancient Roman convention for resolving conflict. If so, then Onesimus may not have been at fault at all.[147] More controversially, assuming that the Cushites of the OT were black Ethiopians (as seems probable), do white readers of Amos 9:7 overlook the apparent synonymous parallelism of the verse comparing the positive deliverance of Israel from Egypt with God's attitude to Cush? They may in fact inappropriately conclude that God is negatively judging both peoples when he says, "Are not you Israelites the same to me as the Cushites?"[148] But the context of vv. 1–6 and

---

144 D. R. Fernández, "The Judgment of God on the Multinationals: Revelation 18," in *Subversive Scriptures: Revolutionary Readings of the Christian Bible in Latin America*, ed. L. E. Vaage (Valley Forge, PA: Trinity Press International, 1997), 75–100.

145 So S. Githuku, "Taboos on Counting," in *Interpreting the Old Testament in Africa*, M. Getui, K. Holter and V. Zinkuratire, eds. (New York: Peter Lang, 2001), 113–17.

146 T. L. J. Mafico, "The Divine Name Yahweh Elohim From an African Perspective," in *Reading From This Place*, 2:21–32.

147 For the evidence for both sides, see in detail J. A. Fitzmyer, *The Letter to Philemon* (New York and London: Doubleday, 2000), 12–24. The African-American scholar A. D. Callahan (*Embassy of Onesimus: The Letter of Paul to Philemon* [Valley Forge: Trinity Press International, 1997]) goes one step further, arguing that the references to slavery and Philemon are metaphorical and that Philemon and Onesimus are actually blood brothers in need of reconciliation. This view does not do justice to the grammar or use of *doulos* ("slave") in Philemon, but the suggestion was worth considering, and it was unlikely to have arisen from a culture not afflicted with slavery.

148 So Holter, *Yahweh in Africa*, 115–25.

8–9 is entirely one of judgment. So perhaps it is not racial prejudice that led to the more negative interpretation.

This last example, however, points to an additional unique contribution of African and African-American cultural analysis. While no one can argue fairly that East Asians, Latin Americans, or native Americans appear in the Bible, set as it is in the Ancient Near and Middle East, there are certainly black and African characters in Scripture, who are not necessarily so recognized by white readers—or even by black readers trained by white teachers! Cain Hope Felder, perhaps the most prolific African-American practitioner of cultural criticism, has a helpful survey of these characters, including Hagar, Egyptian pharaohs, Moses' Cushite wife, Eli's son Phineas (the Nubian), Zephaniah son of Cushi, the Queen of Sheba, Candance Queen of Ethiopia, Simeon called Niger in the church at Antioch, the Ethiopian eunuch, and so on. Some of these characters are positive; others negative, so one can scarcely use them for purposes of reverse discrimination. But there clearly is a positive black presence in the Bible that readers must recognize. Even the color and features of Jews in the first century, prior to centuries of intermarrying with Europeans, would have been more akin to contemporary Palestinian or Lebanese peoples. Using the terminology of modern polls and censuses, Jesus would have checked a box marked "non-white." But centuries of Euro-American artwork have portrayed all biblical characters, but especially Jesus, more as members of their own white cultures, so few readers of the Bible really have a true picture in their minds.[149]

On top of all the strengths and weaknesses of the various methods of cultural and intercultural criticism that we have surveyed, perhaps the most significant consequence of the movement is the reminder that all interpreters are the products of their own cultures and subcultures. Thus we must always be aware of imposing an alien culture onto the biblical text. Norman Gottwald suggests that theological students in particular should self-consciously reflect on the following eighteen factors that have shaped their experiences: (1) their denominational history or tradition, (2) norms or standards valued besides the Bible; (3) their working theology, (4) ethnicity, (5) gender, (6) social class, (7) educational background, (8) community priorities, (9) explicit political position, (10) implicit political stances, (11) customary exposures to the Bible, (12) Bible translations used, (13) use of other Bible study tools, (14) past exposure to biblical preaching, (15) orientation toward biblical scholarship, (16) family influences, (17) life crises, and (18) spirituality and divine guidance.[150] Students may then reflect on how they have consciously or unconsciously prioritized these various factors in their lives and how these factors may help or hinder valid biblical interpretation.[151]

---

149 Cf. C. H. Felder, *Troubling Biblical Waters: Race, Class, and Family* (Maryknoll: Orbis, 1989). Of course, art in all cultures often portrays Jesus in culturally compatible terms, so we are not only picking on Christians in the West.

150 N. K. Gottwald, "Framing Biblical Interpretation at New York Theological Seminary: A Student Self-Inventory on Biblical Hermeneutics" in *Reading From This Place*, 1: 251-61.

151 In addition to works already noted in the footnotes for this subsection on cultural criticism, see esp. M. D. Carroll R., *Contexts for Amos: Prophetic Poetics in Latin American Perspective* (Sheffield: JSOT, 1992); K. K. Yeo, *What Has Jerusalem to Do with Beijing: Biblical Interpretation from a Chinese Perspective* (Harrisburg: Trinity Press International, 1998); G. O. West, *The Academy of the Poor: Towards a Dialogical Reading of the Bible* (Sheffield: Sheffield Academic Press, 1999); and J. R. Levison and P. Pope-Levison, eds., *Return to Babel: Global Perspectives on the Bible* (Louisville: Westminster John Knox, 1999).

Feminist Hermeneutics

Feminism may be viewed as one particular branch of liberation theology or cultural criticism, but it too has developed a life and literature all its own. Indeed, depending on which writers one reads, it may be considered as a subset of social-scientific analysis or as an alternative to it. It may also function as one of many viable readings of a passage, in keeping with postmodern, pluralist versions of reader-response criticism. Or it may be viewed as the most viable, most necessary reading of a text, in keeping with modernism. In the 1980s, Rosemary Reuther identified three major directions in contemporary feminism: liberal, socialist/Marxist, and romantic/radical. The liberal element saw a model of progress within capitalist society and worked for political reform, equal rights, and improved working conditions. It tended to benefit middle-class women more than poor or minority women. The socialist feminists who followed Marxist assumptions believed that women could achieve full equality only by the full integration of labor and ownership. They argued that capitalism in typical patriarchal cultures placed a double burden on working women: not only did they work outside the home, they also remained the major source of domestic labor. The romantic or radical view upheld the notion of women and feminist values as inherently superior to men and patriarchal values.[152] Still other writers advocated some combination of two or three of these positions.

With the demise of Communist socialism in so many parts of the world, feminist studies in the 1990s and more recently, like liberation theology, turned largely to different emphases. A better categorization of more recent feminist studies involves the role the Bible and Christianity play in their hermeneutics. Evangelical or biblical feminists believe that Scripture, at least in Gen 1-2 (before the Fall) and in the NT (after redemption), promotes full equality of the sexes and does not delineate any unique, timeless roles for husband vs. wife or male vs. female.[153] Nonevangelical Christian feminists agree with more traditional Christians that parts of the Bible, even before the Fall or after redemption, promote patriarchalism and bar women from certain roles in the family and in the Church (e.g., Eph 5:22–33; 1 Tim 2:11–15). But because of their prior commitment to a world-view that permits no such discrimination and seeks human liberation from all forms of oppression, these feminists will not accept such portions of Scripture as authoritative. Instead, they focus on other texts that do teach complete equality (e.g., Gen 1; Gal 3:28), regarding them as more "programmatic." They believe that "biblical revelation and truth are given only in those texts and interpretative models that transcend critically their patriarchal frameworks and allow for a vision of Christian women as historical and theological subjects and actors."[154] A third category

---

152 R. Reuther, *Sexism and God-Talk: Toward a Feminist Theology* (Boston: Beacon, 1983), 41–45, 216–32.

153 E.g., G. Bilezikian, *Beyond Sex Roles: A Guide For the Study of Female Roles in the Bible* (Grand Rapids: Baker, 1985); and A. B. Spencer, *Beyond the Curse: Women Called to Ministry* (Nashville: Thomas Nelson, 1985). A major organization, Christians for Biblical Equality, has been organized to reflect this perspective. Cf. esp. *Discovering Biblical Equality: Complementarity Without Hierarchy*, ed. R. M. Groothuis, R. W. Pierce, and G. D. Fee (Downers Grove: IVP, 2003).

154 E. Schüssler Fiorenza, *In Memory of Her: A Feminist Theological Reconstruction of Christian Origins* (New York: Crossroad, 1983), 30. Schüssler Fiorenza is generally held to be the primary founder of this wing of feminist hermeneutics. She has arguably also been its most prolific spokesperson, continuing to publish into her retirement. See, recently, her *Wisdom Ways: Introducing Feminist Biblical Interpretation* (Maryknoll: Orbis, 2001).

of feminists finds Scripture so irredeemably chauvinist that they have abandoned any recognizable forms of Judaism or Christianity in favor of other religions, most notably, reviving an interest in the goddess worship of many ancient pagan cults.[155]

We may divide nonevangelical Christian feminism, which produces by far the largest quantity of feminist biblical scholarship, into three categories. The first is the "revisionist" or "neo-orthodox," well represented by Letty Russell and Rosemary Reuther, who distinguished the central contents of scripture from its larger patriarchal form and believe that God speaks *through* the text of the Bible but that not all of Scripture is itself inspired. The second category involves those who hold to a "remnant" perspective, as particularly with Phyllis Trible, retrieving texts overlooked or distorted by patriarchal hermeneutics, while recognizing that a majority of Scripture does (unacceptably, in their view) promote male headship in the domestic and religious spheres. Finally, there is the "reconstructive" or "liberationist" approach of Elisabeth Schüssler Fiorenza, which views the societies of OT Israel and NT Christianity as more liberating than the later Jewish and Christian communities that grew out of them. So they view more repressive portions of Scripture as stemming from transitional periods in which these liberating dimensions were already starting to be lost.[156]

Ironically, nonevangelical Christian feminists rarely ever acknowledge the existence of evangelical feminism, but lump all conservatives together (usually calling them fundamentalists) as hopelessly loyal to the entrenched patriarchy of the Bible. Conversely, those evangelicals who do believe the Bible promotes male headship as a timeless absolute often label evangelical feminists as simply liberals, without recognizing the vast difference in their use of Scripture as compared with nonevangelical feminists.[157] One of those huge differences is the general refusal of the evangelical feminists to speak of God as female, even while recognizing feminine metaphors for God here and there in Scripture.[158] Thus biblical feminists become doubly marginalized. Even the term "feminist" has become so misleading that some who embraced it a decade or two ago now simply prefer to be called "egalitarian"—supporting the equality of the sexes. To compare liberal and evangelical feminist perspectives, under whatever label, on any given passage of Scripture, read the treatments of those texts in the respective one-volume women's Bible commentaries now available from those two scholarly communities: from a more liberal perspective see C. A. Newsom and S. H. Ringe, eds., *Women's Bible Commentary: Expanded Edition*,[159] and from a more conservative perspective

---

155 Most notably, N. R. Goldberg, *Changing the Gods: Feminism and the End of Traditional Religions* (Boston: Beacon, 1979), from a Jewish background; and M. Daly, *Quintessence: Realizing the Archaic Future—A Radical Elemental Feminist Manifesto* (Boston: Beacon, 1998), from a Christian background. But both authors have virulently renounced their religious roots.

156 E.g., C. Osiek, "The Feminist and the Bible: Hermeneutical Alternatives," in *Feminist Perspectives on Biblical Scholarship*, ed. A. Y. Collins (Chico, CA: Scholars, 1985), 93–105. This categorization is still largely endorsed today. See, e.g., E. K. Wondra, "By Whose Authority? The Status of Scripture in Contemporary Feminist Theologies," *ATR* 75 (1993): 83–101; and J. O. H. Amador, "Feminist Biblical Hermenetucs," *JAAR* 66 (1998): 39–57. Our summary is a synthesis of the taxonomies found in these three sources.

157 See esp. the various writings of W. Grudem, most recently and explicitly articulated in "Is Evangelical Feminism a New Liberalism? Some Disturbing Indications" (Toronto: ETS, 2002).

158 See esp. V. R. Mollenkott, *The Divine Feminine: The Biblical Imagery of God as Female* (New York: Crossroad, 1983).

159 (Louisville: Westminster John Knox, 1998).

C. C. Kroger and M. J. Evans, eds., *The IVP Women's Bible Commentary*.[160] (Evangelicals who believe in some form of male headship increasingly prefer the less pejorative term "complementarian," believing that men's and women's roles complement each other while not remaining identical.[161])

Feminists of all these various classifications have challenged numerous traditional interpretations of Scripture. They have argued that a better translation of "a helper suitable for" Adam (Gen 2:18) is "a partner corresponding to" (or even "superior to") him.[162] They interpret 1 Tim 2:11–15 in the context of women teaching heresy, promoting fertility rites, or murdering men, and hence not mandating a timeless prohibition that women are not "to teach or have authority over a man" (v. 12).[163] They have called upon Bible readers to focus on the women in various texts, to read their stories through feminine eyes, so that we agonize over the rape of Tamar (2 Sam 13) or the dismemberment of the unnamed woman of Judg 19,[164] or so that we reflect theologically on metaphors involving divine violence directed toward promiscuous women in the OT.[165] They ask us to question why five women appear in Matthew's genealogy of Jesus (Mt 1:1–18), all of whom are famous in Scripture for finding themselves in morally ambiguous situations. One plausible answer—with which we agree—suggests that Matthew intends to stress that even the Messiah had such women in his ancestry and came to identify with and remove the stigma attached to them.[166] Feminists point out paradigms of wisdom, leadership, and authority like Ruth, Deborah, and Huldah, inviting readers to identify with the desire of these women for justice or their loyalty to family.[167] They may even come up with solutions to otherwise baffling problems, as with Lot's bizarre behavior in offering his virgin daughters to an unruly and seemingly homosexual mob. Was this an attempt to do something so jarring that it would defuse tension in a setting in which Lot knew the crowd was not interested in the young women but in which he also had the obligation to protect his heavenly sent houseguests (Gen 19)?[168]

---

160 (Downers Grove: InterVarsity, 2002).

161 For recent, articulate defenses of both perspectives within evangelicalism see J. R. Beck and C. L. Blomberg, eds., *Two Views on Women in Ministry* (Grand Rapids: Zondervan, 2001).

162 Spencer, *Beyond the Curse*, 25.

163 C. C. Kroeger has promoted each of these views in a succession of articles. All may now be found in her book, co-authored with R. C. Kroeger, *I Suffer Not a Woman: Rethinking 1 Timothy 2:11–15 in Light of Ancient Evidence* (Grand Rapids: Baker, 1992). The Kroegers conclude that the best option for rendering 1 Tim 2:12 is "I do not allow a woman to teach nor to proclaim herself the author of man" (p. 103).

164 P. Trible, *Texts of Terror: Literary-Feminist Readings of Biblical Narratives* (Philadelphia: Fortress, 1984).

165 J. C. Exum, "The Ethics of Biblical Violence against Women," in *The Bible in Ethics*, ed. J. W. Rogerson, M. Davies and M. D. Carroll R. (Sheffield: Sheffield Academic Press, 1995), 248–71.

166 C. L. Blomberg, "The Liberation of Illegitimacy: Women and Rulers in Matthew 1–2," *BTB* 21 (1991): 145–50. Cf. J. Schaberg, *The Illegitimacy of Jesus* (San Francisco: Harper & Row, 1987), 33, who, much more implausibly, goes on to argue that Jesus was in fact illegitimately conceived by Mary and another man (not Joseph).

167 T. Cavalcanti, "The Prophetic Ministry of Women in the Hebrew Bible," in *Through Her Eyes*, ed. E. Tamez (Maryknoll: Orbis, 1989), 118–39.

168 L. M. Bechtel, "Boundary Issues in Genesis 19:1–38," in *Escaping Eden: New Feminist Perspectives on the Bible*, ed. H. C. Washington, S. L. Graham, and P. Thimmes (Washington Square, NY: New York University Press; Sheffield: Sheffield Academic Press, 1999), 22–40.

As with liberation theology more generally, a feminist hermeneutic combines certain objectionable (to us) features with other highly commendable ones.[169] When nonevangelical feminists create a canon within a canon to reject the authority of texts with which they disagree, they replace the Bible with some other external standard as their ultimate authority and, hence, differ from the perspective on Scripture we have defended in this volume. When biblical feminists argue for lexically dubious interpretations of certain words (such as "suitable" meaning "superior" or "have authority" meaning "to engage in fertility rites"), they raise suspicions that their eagerness to make the text say something other than what they find objectionable has overwhelmed exegetical rigor, not to mention common sense. More liberal feminists have also rightly criticized more conservative ones for so stressing the liberating strands of the NT that the OT—and Judaism more generally—appear in an unnecessarily and inappropriately negative light.[170]

At times the fallacies are subtle and can trap even well-intentioned interpreters. From a liberal perspective, Susan Durber, for example, notes that both the parables of the lost sheep and the lost coin presuppose a male audience, even though the protagonist in the latter is a woman. She deduces this from the fact that Jesus introduces the first parable by asking, "which of *you* [second person plural] . . . ?" but begins the second by asking, "which *woman* [third person] . . . ?" So she concludes that any woman reading Lk 15 is "emasculated" (forced to read as if she were a man) and that alternative feminist readings are not viable.[171] But these subtleties were almost certainly lost on an ancient audience, used to such male-oriented language, but doubtless stunned by Jesus' choice of a woman to justify his own behavior and, in some sense, to represent God. Jesus' parables are actually far more amenable to feminist concerns than Durber recognizes.[172] But the last decade of nonevangelical feminist scholarship has increasingly moved away from an appreciation of the radical nature of various texts *in their original contexts* to a (somewhat unfair) criticism of their failure to throw off all vestiges of patriarchy.

These critiques notwithstanding, all Bible students, particularly those from more conservative backgrounds, would do well to reread Scripture through the windows of various feminist perspectives. They must be open to see if they have read texts in light of their own prevailing, patriarchal cultural biases (that is, traditionalists have preunderstandings, too, as we will discuss in chap. 5). For example, when biblical writers use the term "sinner" to describe men, no particular sin necessarily comes to mind. So why

---

169 The most important and detailed critique of modern Christian and particularly evangelical feminism is J. Piper and W. Grudem, eds., *Recovering Biblical Manhood and Womanhood* (Wheaton: Crossway, 1991). On the 1 Tim material, an important response to the Kroegers is A. J. Köstenberger, T. R. Schreiner and H. S. Baldwin, *Women in the Church: A Fresh Analysis of 1 Timothy 2:9–15* (Grand Rapids: Baker, 1995).

170 E.g., J. Plaskow, "Anti-Judaism in Feminist Christian Interpretation," in *Searching the Scriptures*, vol. 1: *A Feminist Introduction*, ed. E. Schüssler Fiorenza (New York: Crossroad, 1993), 117–29.

171 S. Durber, "The Female Reader of the Parables of the Lost," *JSNT* 45 (1992): 59–78.

172 Cf., by way of contrast, the positive affirmation of the value of these texts in particular and of parables in general in N. Slee, "Parables and Women's Experiences," *Religious Education* 80 (1985): 232–45.

did traditional readings of Lk 7:36–50 almost automatically assume that the female "sinner" who anoints Jesus is a prostitute? The text itself scarcely demands that interpretation.[173] They must learn to hurt where oppressed women hurt and work together with them for a more just and compassionate world. They have to ask if elements of passages traditionally assumed to be universally timeless are indeed culture-bound instead. That is quite different, however, from applying an interpretive canon-within-a-canon. We seek to acknowledge *every* text of Scripture as inspired and authoritative but recognize that both interpretations and applications often vary from one culture to the next. Today most Christians do not believe it is necessary for women to keep their heads covered while praying in the modern Church, any more than that all believers ought literally to wash each other's feet. Might there be equally good reasons for not insisting that women refrain from teaching or having authority over men? The principles taught by each text must be applied today in culturally appropriate ways (see further our chapter on application).

Just as importantly, we need to recognize that women may read the Bible differently than men. Both may discover unique insights that emerge more clearly because of their specific gender. Both, too, may be "blinded" in some contexts because of their gender. In other words, there are two issues at stake. First, the biblical texts themselves are culturally conditioned by the overwhelmingly patriarchal societies of their day. They reflect the world as it existed "back then." Interpreters must consider when this conditioning coincides with normative, divinely intended values and when it does not. Second, all readers are conditioned by their culture and gender and must exercise great care not to impose anachronistic, alien grids from high profile agenda items of modern society onto ancient texts.

Further, we encourage readers for whom some of these ideas are new or possibly scandalous not to reject them without sensitive study of the authors who propose them. In many cases, liberationist and feminist hermeneutics emerge out of suffering of a kind and scale that most Americans, particularly white males, have never experienced or even observed firsthand. When writers reflect the double marginalization of "womanist" (African-American feminism) or "*mujerista*" (Hispanic or Latina feminism) or other Two-Thirds world feminist theology, white men and women alike in the privileged West should try to read with great empathy, whether or not they ultimately agree with every hermeneutical detail.[174] All the writers of this textbook can personally testify that extensive travel in Third-World cultures, as well as among the urban poor of North America, invariably has made us question standard but culturally biased interpretations of various passages. For example, one of us was particularly challenged by a Third-World Christian who called his attention to the oft-abused passage, "the poor you will always have with you" (Mk 14:7)—a quote by Jesus of a text from the Law

---

173 Thus rightly T. J. Hornsby, "Why Is She Crying? A Feminist Interpretation of Lk 7.36–50," in *Escaping Eden*, 91–103.

174 See esp. R. J. Weems, "Womanist Reflections on Biblical Hermeneutics," in *Black Theology: A Documentary History*, 2 vols., ed. J. H. Cone and G. S. Wilmore (Maryknoll: Orbis 1993), 1: 216–24; A. M. Isasi-Díaz, "Mujerista Narratives: Creating a New Heaven and a New Earth," in *Liberating Eschatology*, ed. M. A. Farley and S. Jones (Louisville: Westminster John Knox, 1999), 227–43; M. W. Dube, *Other Ways of Reading: African Women and the Bible* (Atlanta: SBL; Geneva: WCC, 2001); and H. Kinukawa, *Women and Jesus in Mark: A Japanese Feminist Perspective* (Maryknoll: Orbis, 1994).

commanding generous care for the poor (Deut 15:11). Even the most sensitive North American Christian is likely to read this text from the viewpoint of the benefactor—we always have time and obligation to help the needy. Quite differently, the impoverished Third-World Christian living in a regime that abuses human rights will more likely see it as a tragic reminder that there will always be oppressors in the world for God to judge! We must take the time to listen to divergent readings of Scripture from our Christian brothers and sisters around the globe, and particularly from women, minorities, and the poor. As we do so, we will be both convicted and renewed.[175]

Like the literary readings surveyed in the first half of this chapter, we will have to assess each social-scientific reading on a case-by-case basis according to its own merits. Not all will prove legitimate or helpful but those that do can expand our horizons of biblical understanding considerably.

---

175 Additional important feminist works not already footnoted include L. M. Russell, ed., *Feminist Interpretation of the Bible* (Philadelphia: Westminster, 1985); A. L. Laffey, *An Introduction to the Old Testament: A Feminist Perspective* (Philadelphia: Fortress, 1988); L. Schottroff, S. Schroer, M. T. Wacker, *Feminist Interpretation: The Bible in Women's Perspective* (Minneapolis: Fortress, 1998); and A. Brenner and C. Fontaine, eds., *A Feminist Companion to Reading the Bible: Approaches, Methods and Strategies* (Sheffield: Sheffield Academic Press, 1997). See also the ongoing series of commentaries from Sheffield Academic Press entitled *A Feminist Companion to the Bible.* For an annotated bibliography and critical introduction, see M. P. Walsh, *Feminism and Christian Tradition* (Westport, CT: Greenwood, 1999). For a detailed bibliography of the sociology of the NT, see D. M. May, *Social-Scientific Criticism of the New Testament: A Bibliography* (Macon: Mercer, 1991).

4

THE CANON AND TRANSLATIONS

THE BIBLICAL CANON

The word "canon" comes from the Greek *kanōn,* meaning "list," "rule," or "standard." The canon of Scripture refers to the collection of biblical books that Christians accept as uniquely authoritative. We accept it, but how do we know we have the right collection of books? Why do these sixty-six writings command our attention but not others? Did any other books ever "compete" for inclusion in the canon, and if so, why were they excluded? The question of which books belong in the Bible becomes crucial for a study of hermeneutics that asserts that certain documents, and only those documents, remain normative for all believers. Our discussion becomes all the more urgent because Protestants, Catholics, and Orthodox Christians have never agreed on the extent of the OT. What is more, many Christians from mainline denominations today suggest that, although all branches of Christianity traditionally have agreed on the contents of the NT (since at least the fourth century), the criteria for that agreement may no longer be acceptable. Some would argue that other ancient Christian and even Gnostic writings are as valuable as parts of the canonical NT.[1] In the first half of this chapter we will sketch, in turn, the rise of the OT canon, the development of the NT canon, the criteria of canonicity, and the implications for hermeneutics of the methodology known as canon criticism.

THE CANON OF THE OLD TESTAMENT

The Development of the Canon

Since the Reformation, Protestants have accepted the thirty-nine books, from Genesis to Malachi, that appear in the standard editions of the Bible in print today. Roman Catholics and Eastern Orthodox Christians, however, preserve various so-called

---

1 Important recent studies of the formation of the Christian Bible that challenge the legitimacy of the ancient criteria of canonicity are H. von Campenhausen, *The Formation of the Christian Bible* (Philadelphia: Fortress, 1972) (mildly); H. Y. Gamble, *The New Testament Canon: Its Making and Meaning* (Philadelphia: Fortress, 1985) (moderately); and L. M. McDonald, *The Formation of the Christian Biblical Canon,* 2d ed. (Peabody: Hendrickson, 1995) (significantly). R. W. Funk (*Honest to Jesus: Jesus for a New Millennium* [San Francisco: HarperSanFrancisco, 1996], 99–120), founder of the Jesus Seminar, has forthrightly called for a reassessment of the biblical canon with a view to changing some of its contents. Sectarian groups like the Mormons, of course, add entirely different books to their canons of Scripture.

apocryphal (from the Greek word for "hidden") or deutero-canonical (a "second canon") books that were influential throughout the first 1500 years of church history.[2] These books include such works as 1 and 2 Esdras, Tobit, Judith, the Wisdom of Solomon, Ecclesiasticus (also called the Wisdom of Jesus ben Sira[ch], and not to be confused with Ecclesiastes), Baruch, the Letter of Jeremiah, the Prayer of Azariah and the Song of the Three Young Men, Susanna, Bel and the Dragon, the Prayer of Manasseh, and 1 and 2 Maccabees. Some of these works are historical in nature: 1 and 2 Macc describe the history of key portions of second-century B.C. Israel, while 1 Esdras largely reduplicates material found in Chronicles, Ezra, and Nehemiah. 2 Esdras is an apocalypse of secret revelations purportedly given to Ezra. The two books of Wisdom somewhat resemble the canonical book of Proverbs. Baruch resembles parts of the prophecy of Jeremiah, and the Letter of Jeremiah could be characterized as an impassioned sermon based on the canonical text of Jer 11:10. Devotional literature is represented by the two Prayers. The remaining books are (at least partially) legendary novels illustrating virtue and vice by means of their main characters. The three works known as Susanna, the Prayer of Azariah and the Song of the Three Young Men, and Bel and the Dragon all appear as subsections within a longer form of the book of Daniel. Apocryphal additions to Esther also exist.[3]

Protestants have defended the shorter OT canon, asserting that these thirty-nine books were the only books that the Jews of the time of Christ and the apostles accepted into their canon of Scripture. The other books, presumably though not demonstrably all of Jewish origin (some exist now only in Greek or Latin and not Hebrew), date from the intertestamental period after the time of Malachi. The Jews never believed they were inspired in the same way as the earlier biblical books. In fact, widespread testimony in later rabbinic literature (primarily from the second through fifth centuries after Christ), as well as in Josephus (a first-century Jewish historian), outlines the Jewish belief that prophecy (or at least divinely inspired writings) ceased after the time of Ezra, Nehemiah, and the latest of the minor prophets: Haggai, Zechariah, and Malachi (see esp. Josephus, *Ag. Apion* 1.40–41; *b. Sanh.* 22a). This means that no book dated later than about 450–400 B.C. could be considered part of the Hebrew Scriptures, and therefore, part of the Christian OT. Such claims should not unduly denigrate the apocryphal books, for they provide valuable information about historical and theological developments between the Testaments and often prove inspiring, even if not inspired, reading (for the evidence for the actual contents of the OT canon, see below). One should remember that Roman and Orthodox belief in some of these works as authoritative

---

2 For a complete list of the OT canons of the Roman Catholic Church and each of the various Eastern Orthodox churches, see H. P. Rüger, "The Extent of the Old Testament Canon," *BT* 40 (1989): 301–8.

3 A standard edition of the Apocrypha can be found in the *The New Oxford Annotated NRSV Bible with the Apocrypha*, ed. M. D. Coogan, et al., 3d ed. (New York: Oxford University Press, 2001). Two excellent recent introductions and surveys of these books are D. J. Harrington, *Invitation to the Apocrypha* (Grand Rapids and Cambridge: Eerdmans, 1999); and D. A. de Silva, *Introducing the Apocrypha* (Grand Rapids: Baker, 2002). One major commentary series, *The Anchor Bible* (Garden City: Doubleday), is somewhat unique in including volumes on the Apocrypha as well as the OT and NT.

stems from a later period, removed by at least a century from the NT era, when Christianity had largely lost sight of its Jewish roots.[4]

Since the pioneering work of A. C. Sundberg, however, it is often argued that, because the NT reflects widespread use of the Septuagint (the Greek OT, abbreviated LXX), which included much of the Apocrypha, first-century Christians must therefore have believed in the canonical status of apocryphal works.[5] However, the NT authors never quote these works directly as they do the rest of the OT. With LaSor, Hubbard, and Bush, "it is probably safe to assume that the Old Testament they used was identical with that known today."[6] The evidence of Philo and Josephus points in the same direction. Lee McDonald disputes these claims, citing numerous possible allusions to the Apocrypha in the NT,[7] but none appears as unequivocally as the numerous direct quotations of undisputed OT literature. What is more, not even the fairly obvious allusions to apocryphal books (e.g., Wis 15:7 in Rom 9:21 or Sir 51:23–27 in Mt 11:28–30) convincingly prove that early Christians viewed these works as canonical. Paul, for example, alluded to Greek poets and prophets (Acts 17:28; Tit 1:12) and Jude quoted the pseudepigrapha (other Jewish intertestamental literature) on two different occasions (vv. 9, 14), even though Christians never claimed canonicity for any of these sources.[8]

In fact, Christians often came to value the Apocrypha for hermeneutically illegitimate reasons. Even as early Christian interpreters often read into OT texts allegorical and Christological meaning that the original authors could not have intended (see chap. 2), so also the apocryphal books were often preserved and cherished because of "Christian readings" of them, which in retrospect we can see were not valid. For example, the Wisdom of Solomon contains the verse, "Blessed is the wood through which righteousness comes" (14:7). In context it refers to Noah's ark, but early Christians prized it as an apparent prediction of the cross of Christ. Baruch 3:36–37 speaks of God who "found the whole way to knowledge," which "afterward appeared on earth and lived among people." In context, the author personifies God's knowledge as a woman, much as wisdom appears in Prov 9, but many church fathers interpreted the passage as a reference to Christ's incarnation. From the second century onward, a majority of them increasingly accepted the apocrypha as canonical, although a minority (including esp. Jerome) argued for following the Jewish canon. But the sixteenth-century Reformation returned resoundingly to the Jewish Bible of Jesus and the apostles.

---

4 The fullest, most recent exposition of the traditional Protestant defense is R. Beckwith, *The Old Testament Canon of the New Testament Church* (Grand Rapids: Eerdmans, 1985), to which this paragraph is largely indebted.

5 A. C. Sundberg, *The Old Testament of the Early Church* (Cambridge, MA: Harvard University Press, 1964).

6 W. S. LaSor, D. A. Hubbard, F. W. Bush, *Old Testament Survey* (Grand Rapids: Eerdmans, 1982), 21. Curiously, the newer 1996 edition so revises the treatment of canon that this sentence never appears.

7 McDonald, *Canon*, 45, 259–67 (this list also contains possible allusions to the pseudepigrapha—other intertestamental Jewish literature never canonized by anyone). A more modest and convincing list and discussion of possible allusions appears in B. M. Metzger, *An Introduction to the Apocrypha* (New York: Oxford, 1957), 158–70.

8 For a response to the view that the earliest church fathers viewed the Apocrypha as canonical, see Beckwith, *Canon*, 386–95.

The patristic misreadings of the Apocrypha already noted seem harmless enough, but in other instances the question of whether or not the Apocrypha should be viewed as canonical takes on greater significance. Probably the most famous example comes from 2 Macc 12:44–45, which extols the virtue of praying for the dead to help make atonement for them. From this text, more than from any other, developed the Roman Catholic practice of praying for those who died, in hopes of speeding their way through purgatory and on to heaven. No NT text, however, clearly speaks of the existence of purgatory, so Protestants reject its existence.[9] Both Paul (Phil 1:23) and the thief on the cross (Lk 23:43) expected to be with Christ immediately after death.

Modern scholars, Protestant and Catholic alike, often admit that some ancient Christian uses of the Apocrypha were inappropriate.[10] Nevertheless, many still challenge the inviolability of the Protestant canon.[11] Again, particularly since Sundberg, many claim that the Jews of Jesus' day did not have a fixed collection of authoritative Scriptures.[12] All agree that the five books of the Law (Genesis to Deuteronomy) became canonical at least by the time of Ezra's reading of the Law or the time of the Samaritan schism with Israel (because Samaritans accepted only the Law as canonical) ca. 500–400 B.C. The writings of the Prophets, which included Joshua, Judges, Samuel, and Kings, as well as Isaiah through Malachi (minus Daniel), were probably all recognized as uniquely authoritative at least by 200 B.C. All appear, for example, among the Dead Sea Scrolls at Qumran, which date from that time onward. They were translated into Greek (the Septuagint or LXX) as part of the Hebrew Scriptures by 198 B.C., and the prologue to Ecclesiasticus, probably written no later than the mid-100s B.C., refers to both Law and Prophets as Scripture.[13] Certainly conservatives and liberals differ widely as to the authorship and, therefore, dating of many of the OT books.[14] But even if the dates of the acceptance of the Law and Prophets are as late as the critical consensus outlined here claims, they still well predate Jesus and the apostles, and the traditional Protestant argument remains persuasive.[15]

More intense controversy attends the third traditional division of the Hebrew Scriptures: the Writings. This catch-all category includes all of the books not classified

---

9 An exception is evangelical J. L. Walls, "Purgatory for Everyone," First Things 122 (April 2002): 26–30, who argues theologically for the probability of purgatory. See also id., *Heaven: The Logic of Eternal Joy* (Oxford: Oxford University Press, 2002).

10 See esp. the introductions and annotations to the apocryphal books and the above-cited texts in Metzger, ed., *Apocrypha*. This edition (and only this one) is accepted by Protestants and Catholics alike.

11 See, e.g., most of the contributors to the section on OT canon in L. M. McDonald and J. A. Sanders, eds., *The Canon Debate* (Peabody: Hendrickson, 2002).

12 Sundberg, *Old Testament*, 107–69.

13 See esp. E. E. Ellis, *The Old Testament in Early Christianity: Canon and Interpretation in the Light of Modern Research* (Tübingen: Mohr, 1991; Grand Rapids: Baker, 1992).

14 E.g., contrast the evangelical text by R. B. Dillard and T. Longman, III, *An Introduction to the Old Testament* (Grand Rapids: Zondervan, 1994) with the liberal standard by J. A. Soggin, *Introduction to the Old Testament*, 3d ed. (Louisville: Westminster John Knox, 1989).

15 The fullest survey of recent proposals appears in S. B. Chapman, *The Law and the Prophets: A Study in Old Testament Canon Formation* (Tübingen: Mohr, 2000). Chapman also argues that a core of the Law and Prophets began to emerge together as canonical Scripture already in the mid-sixth century B.C

as Law or Prophecy: Ruth, Chronicles, Ezra, Nehemiah, Esther, Job, Psalms, Proverbs, Ecclesiastes, Song of Songs, Lamentations, and Daniel. Many argue that the Writings may have included at different times any or all of the Apocrypha, and that the canon of the OT was not limited to the books Protestants now accept until after the proceedings of a Jewish council at Jamnia (also spelled Jabneh or Javneh) in approximately A.D. 90 (and perhaps considerably later than that).[16] In other words, some assert that the OT canon was not decisively determined within Judaism until the end of the writing of the NT books. This view may agree that it is logical to follow Jesus' lead in treating as Scripture what he, with Jews of his day, accepted as Scripture. But they insist that we simply cannot know which books he would have embraced.

Though this view of the OT canon often prevails in some scholarly circles today, it is improbable. A closer examination of what occurred at Jamnia shows that, more likely, discussions there dealt with challenges to and questions about books that were already widely established as canonical.[17] A variety of quotations from writers no later than the mid-first century A.D. strongly suggests that the Writings as well as the Law and Prophets were already fixed in number at an earlier time. Josephus speaks of "only 22" books "containing the record of all time and justly accredited" (*Ag. Apion* 1:38–41). He goes on to specify the five books of Moses (the Law) and thirteen books of prophecy and history, which from later Jewish lists we can reconstruct as Joshua, Judges and Ruth (as one book), 1 and 2 Samuel (as one), 1 and 2 Kings (as one), 1 and 2 Chronicles (as one), Ezra and Nehemiah (as one), Esther, Job, Isaiah, Jeremiah and Lamentations (as one), Ezekiel, Daniel, and the 12 minor prophets (as one). "The remaining four books," Josephus concludes, "contain hymns to God and principles of life for human beings." These would be Psalms, Proverbs, Ecclesistes, and Song of Songs.

Lk 24:44 recognizes a similar threefold division of the Hebrew canon ("the Law of Moses, the Prophets, and the Psalms"), as does the earlier first-century Jewish writer Philo ("the Laws, and Oracles given by inspiration through the Prophets, and the Psalms and the other books whereby knowledge and piety are increased and completed," *De Vita Contemplativa* 25). The Greek prologue to the important apocryphal book of Jewish Wisdom, Ecclesiasticus, already in the mid-second century B.C. specified "the Law and the Prophets and the other books of the fathers." At Qumran thirty-eight of thirty-nine OT books (except Esther) have been found, but only three of the Apocrypha—Tobit, small fragments of Ecclesiasticus and a few lines of the Letter of Jeremiah—though of course the existence of a book within the Dead Sea sect's library does not by itself prove (or disprove) its canonicity. And one of the most recently translated Dead Sea Scrolls (4Q397) refers to the need to understand "the books of Moses [and] the book[s of the pr]ophets and Davi[d . . .]." Of course we cannot be sure of the exact contents of those sections summed up as "David" (or in Luke or Philo as "the Psalms").

The interpretation of this and other evidence remains disputed, but Sid Leiman, from a Jewish perspective (followed by Roger Beckwith from a Christian perspective), sets out

---

16 Most recently, cf. A. C. Sundberg, Jr., "The Septuagint: The Bible of Hellenistic Judaism," in *Canon Debate*, 68–90.

17 See *esp.* J. P. Lewis, "Jamnia After Forty Years," *HUCA* 70–71 (1999-2000): 233–59.

all the texts in great detail, including many later rabbinic discussions.[18] Leiman and Beckwith plausibly conclude that the entire twenty-two book canon (following Josephus' enumeration) was already well-established before the writing of Ecclesiasticus in the mid-second century B.C. Even more common are references to twenty-four books, but ancient lists make it clear that this number results simply from dividing Judges and Ruth, and Jeremiah and Lamentations, into two parts. Attempts to deny the significance of widespread belief in the cessation of prophecy (again found as early as the second century B.C. in, e.g., 1 Macc 9:27) point out that not every Jew shared this belief.[19] But such attempts do not successfully dislodge the convincing Protestant claim that most first-century Jews recognized no inspired and canonical writers after the fifth-century B.C.[20] Less certain, but still plausible, is the additional proposal of Leiman and Beckwith that the final collection of these books and the separation of the Prophets and Writings into distinct categories occurred at the time of and under the influence of the great Jewish revolutionary hero, Judas Maccabeus, in the 160s B.C. (cf. 2 Macc 2:13–15).[21]

On this view, later rabbinic debates focus more on matters of interpretation than of canonization. The five books that appear in those discussions are Proverbs, Ecclesiastes, Ezekiel, Song of Songs, and Esther. Rabbis raised questions about these books because of the apparent contradiction in Prov 26:4–5, the tension between Ezekiel's picture of the new temple (Ezek 40–48) and early biblical commands about God's sanctuary, the seeming "secularity" of Ecclesiastes and Song of Song, and the lack of reference to God in Esther coupled with its institution of a new, non-Mosaic festival (Purim). The only apocryphal book discussed was Ecclesiasticus, which the Rabbis deemed too late to be canonical.[22] To be sure, in later centuries, after the writing down and codification of the oral law (first in the Mishnah about A.D. 200 and then in the greatly expanded Jerusalem and Babylonian Talmuds of the fourth and fifth centuries), there was a sense in which these works too were treated as canonical. But all this substantially postdates NT times, and even then most rabbis apparently still accorded a privileged place to the original written Torah (our OT).[23]

---

18 S. Z. Leiman (*The Canonization of Hebrew Scripture: The Talmudic and Midrashic Evidence* [Hamden, CT: Archon, 1976], 51–124) lays out all the rabbinic texts. Beckwith (*Canon*, 16–104) discusses the nature of the witnesses and their sources.

19 See esp. F. E. Greenspahn, "Why Prophecy Ceased," *JBL* 108 (1989): 37–49.

20 See esp. B. D. Sommer, "Did Prophecy Cease? Evaluating a Reevaluation," *JBL* 115 (1996): 31–47.

21 Leiman, *Canonization*, 29; Beckwith, *Canon*, 152. S. Dempster (" 'An Extraordinary Fact': *Torah and Temple* and the Contours of the Hebrew Canon," *TynB* 48 [1997]: 23–56, 191–218) has pointed to phenomena particularly at the beginning and end of each of the three parts of the Hebrew canon that suggest one discrete stage of conscious, thematic editing of a final, canonical form of the Hebrew Bible at the end of the biblical period itself. Even allowing for a late date for Dan, this, too, would place us no later than the mid-second century B.C. Even more speculative, but nevertheless intriguing, is J. W. Miller's appeal to the same text in 2 Macc, along with the contents of Sir 44–49, to suggest the existence of a three-part OT canon begun already at the time of Ezra and Nehemiah (*The Origins of the Bible* [New York: Paulist, 1994]).

22 Beckwith, *Canon*, 283–91, 318–23.

23 D. Kraemer, "The Formation of Rabbinic Canon: Authority and Boundaries," *JBL* 110 (1991): 613–30. Kraemer's interpretation also implies that one need not resort to Leiman's somewhat artificial and confusing distinction between inspired and uninspired canonical works in the rabbis' discussion of Apocrypha and later Jewish writings. Interesting, too, is the characteristic rabbinic term for Scripture's effect on those who touched it: it "defiled the hands" (because the profane was coming in contact with the sacred).

The Order of the Canon

It is reasonable, therefore, to conclude that the Jews agreed upon the boundaries of the Hebrew canon in NT times. The order of its books, however, is less clear, largely because at that time individual documents were still written on separate scrolls. One ancient Jewish tradition, possibly the oldest, puts the order as: the Law (Genesis-Deuteronomy), the Prophets (Joshua, Judges, Samuel, Kings, Jeremiah, Ezekiel, Isaiah, and the Twelve [minor prophets]), and the Writings (Ruth, Psalms, Job, Proverbs, Ecclesiastes, Song of Songs, Lamentations, Daniel, Esther, Ezra-Nehemiah, and Chronicles) (*b. B. Bat.* 14b). This arrangement sometimes proceeds chronologically (Joshua-Kings; Daniel-Nehemiah), and sometimes thematically (Ruth ends with David's genealogy, a fitting introduction for the Psalms of David; Chronicles sums up almost all of OT history).

Modern Hebrew Bibles preserve the order, Law, Prophets, and Writings, but change the sequence of some of the books within the last two categories.[24] English Bibles are based on the arrangement of the Greek translation of the OT (the Septuagint—LXX), in which the Prophets and Writings are interspersed within each other in order to create a past-present-future sequence: Genesis through Esther describes the history first of the human race and then of Israel from creation to the fifth century B.C.; Job through Song of Songs includes psalms and wisdom for present living; and Isaiah through the Twelve preserves that form of prophecy that is mostly proclamation (foretelling and forthtelling) rather than historical narrative.[25] The order of these books of prophecy sometimes follows chronological considerations and sometimes decreasing length of the documents.

THE CANON OF THE NEW TESTAMENT

The Development of the Canon

Clearly one may not appeal to the teaching of Jesus to determine which books belong in the NT even if he did hint of future Spirit-inspired Scripture (note a possible inference from Jn 14:26; 15:26). One might expect, therefore, less agreement among Christians as to the boundaries of the NT than to the limits of the OT, but in fact, historically, there has been much more unanimity. Still, agreement did not appear instantly in the formation of the NT canon.[26]

---

24 For details see F. F. Bruce, *The Canon of Scripture* (Leicester and Downers Grove: InterVarsity, 1988), 29.

25 The reason Jews could include historical books as part of "prophecy" stems from their understanding of a prophet, more broadly, as an accredited teacher of moral law. See esp. J. Barton, *Oracles of God: Perceptions of Ancient Prophecy in Israel After the Exile* (Oxford: Oxford University Press, 1986). For one plausible explanation of the sequence of the twelve minor prophets, see P. R. House, *The Unity of the Twelve* (Sheffield: Almond, 1990), 63–109. House sees a progression from the themes of covenant and cosmic sin in Hos through Mic to covenant and cosmic punishment in Nah to Zeph climaxing in hope for restoration in Hag to Mal.

26 The best overviews are Bruce, *Canon*; D. G. Dunbar, "The Biblical Canon," in *Hermeneutics, Authority, and Canon*, ed. D. A. Carson and J. D. Woodbridge (Grand Rapids: Zondervan, 1986), 315–42; and B. M. Metzger, *The Canon of the New Testament: Its Origin, Development, and Significance* (Oxford: Clarendon, 1987).

Since the first Christians inherited a "complete" Bible from the Jews, it might seem surprising that they were willing to add *any* books to what they termed Scripture. But in viewing Jesus as the fulfillment and authoritative interpreter of the Hebrew Scriptures (based on Jesus' own claims in Mt 5:17–48), they already had relativized somewhat the value of those writings. Increasingly, the story of Jesus and the preaching of the gospel took on greater significance. So it was natural for them to write down the story and message about Jesus and, within a generation or two, to view them at least as authoritatively, if not more so, than the previous writings, which they believed had prepared the way for that gospel. OT history provided a precedent with Deuteronomy and the Prophets as commentators or "appliers" of the earlier Law of Moses.[27] The concept of covenants proved instructive, too. Jeremiah had prophesied about a coming new covenant (Jer 31:31-34), which Jesus and the NT writers claimed that his death established (Lk 22:20; 2 Cor 3:6; Heb 8:8–13). If the older covenant with Moses led to a collection of written Scriptures, it would be natural to expect God to guide Christian writers to inscribe a newer collection of Scriptures. This kind of reasoning seems to be implied by the discussions near the end of the second century in Tertullian (*Against Marcion* 4:1) and Clement of Alexandria (*Strom.* 1:9; 3:11; 4:21; 5:13).

But belief in the Gospels, Acts, Epistles, and Revelation as Scripture began to emerge much earlier than the second century. Two of the later NT writings refer to earlier Christian works as Scripture (1 Tim 5:18, quoting Lk 10:7;[28] 2 Pet 3:16, referring to an unknown number of Paul's epistles). Although some critics date 1 Timothy and 2 Peter well into the second century, a growing number of scholars recognize that late first-century dates are more probable, and in our view, the traditional views that put them in the sixties still commend themselves.[29]

The earliest noncanonical Christian literature dates from about A.D. 90 through the mid-second century and is referred to as the apostolic fathers.[30] (This title is somewhat misleading because it refers to the generations immediately *following* the apostolic era.) These works include numerous epistles from early church leaders to various Christian individuals or communities.[31] Like the NT epistles, these letters give instruc-

---

27 The independence of the OT writing prophets from the Law has often been asserted, but see Brevard S. Childs, *Biblical Theology of the Old and New Testaments* (Minneapolis: Fortress, 1992), 174–75.

28 Some would argue that "Scripture" applies only to the quotation of Deut 25:4 in the first half of 1 Tim 5:18, but this is not a natural reading of the verse. I. H. Marshall (*A Critical and Exegetical Commentary on the Pastoral Epistles*, with P. H. Towner [Edinburgh: T&T Clark, 1999], 615) comments, "for the author the second citation had equal authority with the OT."

29 For the Pastorals, see esp. L. T. Johnson, *Letters to Paul's Delegates* (Valley Forge: Trinity Press International, 1996); expanded in id., *The First and Second Letters to Timothy*, AB (New York and London: Doubleday, 2001). For 2 Pet, see D. Guthrie, *New Testament Introduction*, 3d ed. (Leicester and Downers Grove: InterVarsity, 1990), 811–42; cf. J. D. Charles, *Virtue amidst Vice: The Catalog of Virtues in 2 Peter 1* (Sheffield: Sheffield Academic Press, 1997), 11–37.

30 The best introduction and translation is that of J. B. Lightfoot and J. R. Harmer, rev. and ed. M. W. Holmes, *The Apostolic Fathers* (Grand Rapids: Baker, 1989).

31 E.g., from Clement of Rome to Corinth; from Ignatius to Ephesus, Magnesia, Tralles, Rome, Philadelphia, Smyrna, and to St. Polycarp; from Polycarp to the Philippians; from an unknown author to one Diognetus; and from an unknown author taking the pseudonym of Barnabas to a general Christian audience.

tion concerning various aspects of Christian living. For the most part they follow the teaching of the NT writers, though newer developments emerge, for example, a growing preoccupation with the virtue of martyrdom or an increasing emphasis on an episcopal church hierarchy. Additional works include a more or less historical narrative of *The Martyrdom of St. Polycarp*; a manual called *The Teaching of the Twelve Apostles* (or the *Didache*) on church order, especially regarding baptism, the Eucharist, and false prophets; and a series of commands, parables, and visions allegedly given by God to a Christian writer known as Hermas the Shepherd, replete with instruction on the themes of purity and repentance.

In various parts of the Roman Empire, the writings of Barnabas, Hermas, and perhaps Clement seem to have gained a brief following among some Christians who prized them as highly as other books that eventually became part of our NT. But this status never included a majority of Christians and was relatively short-lived. A study of most of the apostolic fathers in fact reveals that their authors were conscious that they lacked the authority of the apostolic writings.[32] In addition, they liberally quoted and alluded to those earlier books in ways that acknowledged their greater authority and, at times, their scriptural status. For example, Ignatius, bishop of Smyrna, wrote to the Trallians in the early second century, "I did not think myself qualified for this, that I . . . should give you orders as though I were an apostle" (3:3). A generation or two later 2 Clem 2:4 quoted Mk 2:17 verbatim, after a citation of Isaiah, with the introduction "another Scripture says." Not surprisingly, the apostolic fathers most often cited the words of Jesus in ways that suggested they viewed them as of the highest authority.[33]

In the middle of the second century, the first major impetus to the explicit discussion of a Christian canon came from the heretic Marcion.[34] Marcion believed that Jesus and the God of the OT were opposites, and that anything in Christian writings that smacked of Judaism ought to be expunged. He therefore promoted a "canon" of edited versions of the Gospel of Luke and various epistles of Paul, but nothing else. The rise of Gnostic writings, also beginning about the mid-second century, provided a further stimulus. Many of these purported to contain secret revelations from Jesus, following his resurrection, to one or more of his followers (most notably James, Peter, John, Thomas, Philip, and Mary).[35] Also, as persecution against Christians intensified, especially toward the close of the second century and periodically in the third, it became more crucial for Christians to agree on what books they were willing to die for (when they defied orders to burn all their holy books). So, beginning about A.D. 150, and continuing without complete agreement for another 200 years, they produced a series of lists of Christian books to be treated as Scripture. But the testimony of Irenaeus, during this period in which the false teachers were "perverting the Scriptures" (see esp.

---

32 The evidence for the last three sentences is scattered throughout each of the works cited in n. 26. See esp. Dunbar, "Canon," 323–28. More generally, cf. Metzger, *Canon*, 39–73.

33 The significance of the evidence of the apostolic fathers has regularly been exaggerated by conservatives and unduly denigrated by liberals. Particularly balanced, though somewhat limited in scope, is D. A. Hagner, "The Sayings of Jesus in the Apostolic Fathers and Justin Martyr," in *Gospel Perspectives V*, ed. D. Wenham (Sheffield: JSOT, 1984), 233–68.

34 See Bruce, *Canon*, 134–44.

35 The standard collection and translation is J. M. Robinson, ed., *The Nag Hammadi Library*, 3d ed. (Leiden: Brill, 1996).

Against Heresies 3.12.12), suggests an already existing canon even before the publication of the various lists.

Probably the earliest of these lists is the so-called Muratorian fragment from the late second century.[36] It includes the four Gospels, Acts, all thirteen letters attributed to Paul, two letters of John, the letter of Jude, and Revelation. It also curiously refers to the Wisdom of Solomon, and it notes that in Rome the Apocalypse of Peter was read, though some questioned it, as in fact some did the Apocalypse of John (Revelation). Around this time Irenaeus, bishop of Lyons, recognized a similar collection with the addition of 1 Peter.[37] At the turn of the third century, Tertullian first used the Latin *testamentum* in referring to the NT. He was translating the concept of a Greek *diathēkē* ("covenant"), which should not be interpreted, as we often understand "testament" in English, as referring to a will. Tertullian recognized twenty-three of our NT books as authoritative, omitting James, 2 Peter, and 2 and 3 John, about which he mentions nothing.[38] Early in the third century, Origen refers to all twenty-seven, but notes that six are disputed: Hebrews, James, 2 Peter, 2 and 3 John, and Jude (as quoted in Eusebius, *H.E.* 6:25.8–14).[39] This situation seems to have persisted until the fourth century.

Like the rabbinic discussions about certain OT books, however, questions about these six writings focus more on internal evidence (issues arising from the texts themselves) than on external evidence (doubts about their inspiration or the conditions under which they were written). The one exception is Hebrews. Some believed it came from Paul; others proposed different authors or pled ignorance. But in the case of James, then as later, questions focused on harmonizing his view of faith and works with that of Paul. Doubts about 2 Peter focused on the differences from 1 Peter in style and contents. Arguably, some deemed 2 and 3 John too personal to be universally relevant. Jude's quotation of the intertestamental Jewish apocalypse known as 1 Enoch and his apparent allusion to an apocryphal work known as the Assumption of Moses puzzled some. A seventh book also came under some fire, as the millennial theology of Revelation troubled many who were becoming increasingly amillennial in outlook. These internal problems, thus, led some to doubt the inspiration and canonicity of these last six books mentioned.

Athanasius, bishop of Alexandria, in his Easter-time festal letter of A.D. 367, is the earliest-known Christian writer to endorse without hesitation the twenty-seven books that now comprise our NT. The subsequent Councils of Hippo (A.D. 393) and Carthage (A.D. 397) ratified his views. Only minor debates persisted after that time. Due to these debates, some writers argue that the NT canon was not closed until the time of the Protestant Reformation and the Roman Catholic Council of

---

36 For its contents and significance, see Bruce, *Canon*, 158–69. A 4th-century date for this fragment has been defended by G. M. Hahneman, *The Muratorian Fragment and The Development of the Canon* (Oxford: Clarendon, 1992). But see the rebuttal by C. E. Hill, "The Debate over the Muratorian Fragment and the Development of the Canon," *WTJ* 57 (1995): 431–52.

37 Irenaeus nowhere gives one definitive list of these works, but one may be pieced together from a variety of references presented and discussed in Bruce, *Canon*, 170–77.

38 Again, Tertullian's views reflect a mosaic of sources. See Bruce, *Canon*, 180–83. Around the same time, Clement of Alexandria may have begun to use the Greek *diathēkē* in the same way.

39 At the same time, Eusebius himself accepted Hebrews but not Revelation. Origen doubted the Pauline authorship of Heb, but not its inspiration.

Trent in the mid-1500s, if even then.[40] Such a position leaves the door open, then, for certain sects, most notably Mormons, to add their own formative documents to the canon.[41] But while it is true that one cannot prove either Christian or Jewish canons ever to have been so conclusively closed as to preclude all further discussion, it is abundantly clear that no later sectarian literature could ever pass the early Church's criteria for canonicity (see below). Most obviously, such writings could not meet the criterion of widespread use from the earliest days of the faith to the present.

Even though the NT canon has remained well-established since the fourth century, numerous voices today clamor for a reconsideration of its boundaries. Particularly noteworthy are those students of ancient Gnosticism who argue that texts like those found at Nag Hammadi (esp. the Gospel of Thomas, the Gospel of Truth, the Apocryphon of James, the Gospel of Philip, and the Treatise on the Resurrection) preserve traditions of Jesus' teaching at least as valuable as those found in our canonical Gospels, and that they date from at least as early a time period, that is, the mid-first century.[42] Almost certainly these scholars date every one of these non-canonical sources (except Q) at least seventy-five years too early! No clear evidence for the existence of those documents predates the mid-second century, and a careful comparison of their teachings with those of the Gospels shows them to be mostly later than and, where they run parallel, dependent on the canonical four. It is possible, to be sure, that otherwise unparalleled but authentic sayings of Jesus may have occasionally been preserved in these texts, but a substantial percentage of them reads more like later Gnostic revisions and corruptions (if not outright fabrications) of earlier traditions of Jesus' words and deeds.[43]

---

40 This is one of the complaints of M. J. Sawyer, "Evangelicals and the Canon of the New Testament," *GTJ* 11 (1991): 29–52, against the traditional Protestant defense of the canon, which leads him to appeal for a return to the Reformers' emphasis on the witness of the Holy Spirit. But it is not clear he appreciates the degree of subjectivity (far greater than that of the standard criteria discussed below) that this introduces into the discussion when it is made the *primary* criterion.

41 See esp., S. E. Robinson, *Are Mormons Christians?* (Salt Lake City: Bookcraft, 1991), 45–56.

42 See esp. R. W. Funk, R. W. Hoover, and the Jesus Seminar, *The Five Gospels: The Search for the Authentic Words of Jesus* (New York and Oxford: Macmillan, 1993); R. W. Funk and the Jesus Seminar, *The Acts of Jesus: The Search for the Authentic Deeds of Jesus* (San Francisco: HarperSanFrancisco, 1998). J. D. Crossan (*The Historical Jesus* [San Francisco: Harper & Row, 1991], 427–50) locates in age and authenticity Thomas, the Egerton Gospel, the Gospel of Hebrews, sources for the Gospel of Peter, and Q all to the first layer of tradition (A.D. 30–50), Mk in the second layer (A.D. 60–80), and Mt and Lk later still (A.D. 80–120).

43 See esp., C. Tuckett, *Nag Hammadi and the Gospel Tradition* (Edinburgh: T. & T. Clark, 1986); and J. P. Meier, *A Marginal Jew: Rethinking the Historical Jesus*, 4 vols. (New York: Doubleday, 1991), 1: 112–66. For a more specialized study, cf. C. L. Blomberg, "Tradition and Redaction in the Parables of the Gospel of Thomas," in *Gospel Perspectives V*, 177–205. For a more recent update, cf. J. H. Charlesworth and C. A. Evans, "Jesus in the Agrapha and Apocryphal Gospels," in *Studying the Historical Jesus: Evaluations of the State of Current Research*, ed. B. Chilton and C. A. Evans (Leiden: Brill, 1994), 479–533.

The Order of the Canon

As with the OT, the final arrangement of NT books combined chronological and topical concerns with issues of length of documents.[44] The Gospels were naturally placed first, as they described the origins of Christianity in the life of Jesus. Matthew assumed first place because, as the most Jewish of the Gospels, it provided the clearest link with the OT.[45] Then Mark, Luke, and John most commonly followed in the order in which presumably they were composed.[46] Even though Acts was Luke's second volume, it was separated from his Gospel by John's work when the four Gospels were all grouped together. But it naturally came next as the historical sequel to the events of Jesus' life.

After Acts came the Epistles. As Paul was the premier apostle to the Gentile world and the most prolific epistle writer, his letters were naturally placed first. As the order of the books became increasingly standardized, Paul's epistles were then divided into letters to churches (Romans—2 Thessalonians) and letters to individuals (1 Timothy—Philemon). Within these two sections the Epistles were arranged in order of decreasing length, except that books written to the same church or person were kept together even when this pattern was broken (1 and 2 Thessalonians, 1 and 2 Timothy).[47] Even though it is just slightly shorter, Galatians may have been placed before Ephesians as a frontispiece to the collection of Prison Epistles (Ephesians, Philippians, Colossians) because of its use of the term *kanōn* or "rule" (Gal 6:16).[48] Hebrews was placed immediately after the avowedly Pauline epistles because many thought it came from Paul, but it was not placed within the collection since it was anonymous, and many others disavowed Pauline authorship. The writings of James, Peter, John, and Jude were then added in that order, also in generally decreasing length but probably also in descending order of the prominence of their authors in the earliest church. James the brother of Jesus also was originally the head of the Jerusalem church (Acts 15). Eventually, after Peter arrived in Rome, he supplanted James in empire-wide significance, but in the earliest years he seems to have been subordinate to James.[49] John the son of Zebedee was another one of Jesus' inner three apostles (with Peter and James his brother). Jude, another brother of Jesus, clearly figures least prominently in early Christian writings. Finally, Revelation, with its focus on the end of history, formed a fitting conclusion to the canon.[50]

---

44 As in the OT, early groupings of NT books took a variety of orders, though as far as we know the Gospels, Epistles of Paul, and General Epistles were always discrete groupings, despite variations in sequence within each section. Interestingly, initially Acts was often put at the head of the General Epistles. For key lists, see Metzger, *Canon*, 295–300.

45 Some would also argue that it was written first, though that discussion is beyond our scope. See the NT introductions in the bibliography at the end plus the standard commentaries on the Synoptic Gospels.

46 Cf. M. Hengel, *The Four Gospels and the One Gospel of Jesus Christ* (London: SCM; Harrisburg: Trinity Press International, 2000), 38–47.

47 Metzger, *Canon*, 297.

48 This last point is by far the most dubious but is a plausible suggestion of W. R. Farmer in *The Formation of the New Testament Canon*, with D. M. Farkasfalvy (New York: Paulist, 1983), 79–81.

49 Numerous recent studies have rehabilitated the historical James to the place of prominence he once held. Many of these are conveniently summarized in H. Shanks and B. Witherington, III, *The Brother of Jesus* (San Francisco: HarperSanFrancisco, 2003), 89–223.

50 See esp., R. W. Wall, *Revelation* (Peabody: Hendrickson, 1991), 25–32, who takes an explicitly canon-critical approach (on which see below).

CRITERIA OF CANONICITY

The reasons the Jews came to accept the thirty-nine books of the Hebrew Scriptures as arranged in modern enumeration are largely lost in antiquity. The main reason given in the rabbinic discussions revolves around their inspiration. But this only throws the question back one stage—i.e., why were these books believed to be inspired or "God-breathed" (cf. 2 Tim 3:16)? Conservative scholars have often tried to link inspiration and canonicity to prophecy. The Law was given by God to Moses, they argue, and he was also called a prophet and was largely responsible for the composition of the Pentateuch. Moses, they claim, anticipated a succession of divinely accredited prophets (Deut 18:17–19) who composed the books the Jews included among the Prophets. What is more, even many of the Writings come from prophetic authors (e.g., David [cf. Acts 2:30] and, for some of the Psalms, Asaph the seer).[51] But this view fails to account for all of the biblical books and probably pushes the evidence for prophetic authorship (even of the books it does account for) farther than is defensible.

A second view links canonicity to the concept of covenant. The Law established God's covenant; the historical narratives described Israel's obedience and disobedience to the covenant; the prophets called people back to a proper relationship to the covenant; and the Wisdom Literature expanded the theme of obedience to it.[52] This theory has fewer holes in it than the previous one, but it also remains rather broad in nature and without much ancient testimony to corroborate it. While plausible, it must remain a theory. Christians will probably have to rest content with the traditional Protestant argument outlined above. To state it rather colloquially, "What was good enough for Jesus (as a representative Jew of his day) is good enough for us."

More evidence survives that suggests criteria for the canonicity of the NT. Again, inspiration is more a corollary of canonicity than a criterion of it.[53] But other criteria may helpfully be classified under three headings: apostolicity, orthodoxy, and catholicity. All of the NT writings were believed to have apostolic connections. Though not necessarily written by one of the original twelve apostles (this would apply only to Matthew, John, and Peter), they came from the apostolic age (first century) and could be closely associated with those who were considered apostles (including Paul), or closely associated with Jesus (such as the epistles of his brothers, James and Jude). Thus, Mark was traditionally associated with Peter, Luke with Paul, and Hebrews, if not from Paul himself, then with one of his intimate companions.[54] Although many of these traditional authorship claims are widely disputed today, a cogent case can still be made for each of them.[55]

---

51 See esp. R. L. Harris, *Inspiration and Canonicity of the Bible*, 2d ed. (Grand Rapids: Zondervan, 1965).

52 See esp. M. G. Kline, *The Structure of Biblical Authority* (Grand Rapids: Eerdmans, 1972).

53 Bruce, *Canon*, 268.

54 Suggestions from the first centuries of the church's history include Paul, Barnabas, Luke and Clement of Rome; at the time of the Reformation, Luther suggested Apollos; A. Harnack in the 19th century suggested Priscilla and Aquila. Modern scholars have added several other proposals.

55 See esp. Guthrie, *Introduction*; D. A. Carson, D. J. Moo, and L. Morris, *An Introduction to the New Testament* (Grand Rapids: Zondervan, 1992), both ad loc. Some would argue today that the other criteria for canonicity are adequate so that not as much depends on authorship for the modern church as for the ancient church.

Second, Christians believed that the theology and ethics promoted by the NT books as a whole cohered in shared orthodoxy—beliefs not held by most of the Gnostic challengers. To call all the NT writings orthodox does not preclude a wide measure of diversity among them, but it does imply that none of the texts actually contradicts another one. Although this claim is widely rejected today,[56] it remains thoroughly defensible.[57]

Third, books were preserved that had proved useful for a large number of churches from the earliest generations of Christianity. Closely related was the widespread recognition of a book's authority. One can only speculate as to why the first letter Paul wrote to the Corinthians, before our 1 Corinthians (see 1 Cor 5:9), was not preserved. It obviously was apostolic and presumably orthodox, but quite plausibly was not as relevant for other groups of believers outside of Corinth. Christians often ask the tantalizing question, "What would happen if such a letter were discovered and proved highly relevant?" This question is in fact just a specific form of the broader question: "Is the Christian canon open or closed?" Now since we believe that no church tradition is on a par with Scripture, so that authoritative church pronouncements of the fourth and fifth centuries cannot ultimately determine the canon, we must say that the canon *theoretically* remains open—if some additional document could meet all the criteria for canonicity. But *practically,* the canon is closed, since a work that had not been used for nearly twenty centuries could not meet the criterion of catholicity and would almost certainly not command the acclaim of more than a minority of Christians today.[58]

CANON CRITICISM

In response to the often atomistic approaches of traditional historical criticism, a new form of biblical analysis developed, particularly in the 1980s and 1990s, known as canon or canonical criticism. Initially due to the extensive writings of Yale professor Brevard Childs, canon criticism seeks to move beyond standard source, form, and redaction criticism, and to interpret the biblical texts in their "canonical shape" (i.e., their final form).[59] Canon criticism does not reject the reconstructions of modern historical criticism as to how the various documents developed, but it finds little value in these methods for preaching or ministry in the life of the church. Rather, it calls the Christian community to accept the wisdom of its ancestors and to interpret passages and books of Scripture as they finally took shape. Many of these developments may be welcomed.

In some cases, canon criticism is difficult to distinguish from the renewed emphasis in literary criticism on interpreting possibly composite documents as unities (see

---

56 Just about every nonevangelical NT theology is predicated on the assumption of irreconcilable diversity. Of recent works, cf. esp. U. Schnelle, *The History and Theology of the New Testament Writings* (Minneapolis: Fortress, 1998); and G. Strecker, *Theology of the New Testament* (Berlin: de Gruyter; Louisville: Westminster John Knox), 2000.

57 For detailed demonstration of this defensibility, see D. Guthrie, *New Testament Theology* (Downers Grove: InterVarsity, 1981); and G. E. Ladd, *A Theology of the New Testament*, rev. and ed. D. A. Hagner (Grand Rapids: Eerdmans, 1993). For methodological discussion, see P. Balla, *Challenges to New Testament Theology* (Tübingen: Mohr, 1997).

58 See esp. Metzger, *Canon*, 271–75.

59 See esp. B. S. Childs, *Introduction to the Old Testament as Scripture* (Philadelphia: Fortress, 1979); id., *The New Testament as Canon: An Introduction* (Philadelphia: Fortress, 1984).

above). So, for example, one reads Genesis as a literary unity, looking for the themes that cut across the supposed layers of tradition that modern OT source criticism has usually identified (J, E, D, P—from the so-called Jahwist, Elohist, Deuteronomistic, and Priestly writers). Within a canonical framework Isa 1-39 and 40–66 are read as a unified piece of literature rather than parceled out to different periods of time separated by over 200 years as historical criticism often does. Likewise, 2 Corinthians is treated as a coherent whole—not broken down into chapters 1-7, 8, 9, and 10–13 as separate documents. In this respect canon criticism does what evangelical scholars have done all along, because, at least in the United States, evangelicals were initially reluctant to accept the modern theories of source criticism.

In other instances, canon criticism focuses on agreements rather than disagreements among allegedly divergent texts. Again, the claims of more liberal scholars are not rejected but simply set to one side. Childs, for example, believes with many that the two gospel infancy narratives (Mt 1-2 and Lk 1-2) contradict each other in numerous places. But instead of following redaction critics who focus on those distinctives as keys to Matthew's and Luke's emphases, he prefers to stress the features the texts have in common: the Spirit-influenced virgin birth, the child who is to bring salvation, the fulfillment of OT prophecy, and the need to accept and adore the Christ-child.[60]

Canon criticism also tempers the urge to absolutize one of two or more competing strands of biblical theology. Exodus, for example, presents a supernatural view of God's intervention in the lives of his people, whereas Genesis provides a much more "naturalistic" understanding of God's providence acting in ordinary human events (Gen 50:20).[61] Liberals have often rejected the former picture and conservatives have often neglected the latter. Canon critics, however, call interpreters to balance the two.[62] Again, evangelicals may reject the claims that such examples really involve outright contradiction, but they should welcome a renewed emphasis on the unity of the Scriptures and a balanced appropriation of their diverse themes and theological perspectives.

Sometimes, for canon critics the final form of the text does not mean the final form of an individual book of Scripture; rather, the final form indicates its theological role in the context of the later, completed canons of the OT and NT. That is, canon criticism brackets *all* historical issues. Thus Acts can be studied, not as the sequel to Luke's Gospel as it was originally intended, but as an introduction to the epistles that follow. For example, Acts may well describe and legitimize the ministries of Paul to Gentiles as well as of James and Peter to Jews, even while showing how "Paul's Gospel" ultimately became more dominant. This reading paves the way for an understanding of the legitimacy of the epistles of both Paul and James, but it also explains why, historically, Paul enjoys more prominence, even as the position of his letters in the NT canon

---

60 Childs, *New Testament*, 161–65.

61 In fact, some suggest that a gradually diminishing role of God's direct intervention in human affairs is a unifying feature of the narrative of Genesis itself. See R. Cohn, "Narrative Structure and Canonical Perspective in Genesis," *JSOT* 25 (1983): 3–16.

62 J. A. Sanders (*Canon and Community* [Philadelphia: Fortress, 1984], 50) gives the humorous example of Balaam's talking donkey. Liberals denied the donkey could really talk; conservatives defended that it could, but neither asked the more important question of what the account was meant to teach in the context of Num 22–24!

suggests.[63] So, too, in the OT, even though many of the psalms originally were composed in unrelated contexts, their position in the collection of the 150 may shed some light on how the "canonical community" interpreted them. Most obviously, Psa 1, with its classic contrast of righteous and wicked, seems to establish the theme for the entire collection. Pss 144–150, all praise psalms, form a fitting climax and point to activity that should be the culmination of the life of all God's people.[64]

In sum, canon criticism's focus on the "final form" of a text can mean two quite different things. It can refer to what the actual author or final editor of a given book wrote or put together—roughly equivalent to what we mean by the "autograph" of a particular biblical document. To the extent that evangelical doctrines of inspiration focus on the autographs alone and not on their previous tradition-histories,[65] this pre-occupation of canon criticism offers a welcome corrective to those who find only certain, supposedly oldest layers of a text authoritative or most significant (e.g., the most authentic words of Jesus in a given Gospel or the oldest Jahwist stratum in a book of the Law).[66]

But when "final form" or "canonical shape" refers to how a completed book of Scripture was interpreted centuries after its composition, when it was combined with other Scriptures, then we simply have an observation, often rather speculative, from the history of exegesis.[67] More often than not, these interpretations deflect attention from the original intention of the texts. As Metzger helpfully explains, the canon is "a collection of authoritative texts," not an "authoritative collection of (authoritative) texts."[68] In other words, the canonical placement of the books was not inspired; only the writing of the books was. The most important lesson of a study of canon criticism, therefore, is occasionally a lesson in how *not* to interpret the Scriptures! But to the extent that such study helps us focus on the biblical autographs as literary unities, or on the biblical canon as a theological unity, or on important details within individual texts that might not otherwise be stressed, then it is most surely to be welcomed.[69]

---

63 R. W. Wall, "The Acts of the Apostles in Canonical Context," *BTB* 18 (1986): 1–31.

64 For these and other examples from the Psalms, see G. H. Wilson, "The Qumran Psalms Manuscripts and the Consecutive Arrangement of Psalms in the Hebrew Psalter," *CBQ* 45 (1983): 377–88.

65 The evangelical OT scholar who has most extensively employed this form of canon criticism is J. H. Sailhamer, esp. his *Introduction to Old Testament Theology: A Canonical Approach* (Grand Rapids: Zondervan, 1995). The two evangelical NT scholars who have worked the most with this kind of canon criticism are R. W. Wall and E. E. Lemcio, esp. their *The New Testament as Canon: A Reader in Canonical Criticism* (Sheffield: JSOT, 1992).

66 Cf., respectively, J. Jeremias, *New Testament Theology*, vol. 1 (London: SCM; NY: Scribner, 1971), esp. 3–37; and H. Bloom, *The Book of J* (New York: Grove Weidenfeld, 1990), esp. 3, 16, 316–22. The former is a common approach among certain NT scholars; the latter more unusual for OT commentary.

67 See several of the chapters in Wall and Lemcio, *The New Testament as Canon*, that speculate on the interpretive significance of juxtaposing the collections of Gospels and Letters or by placing Acts in between them, or by grouping Paul's and others' epistles into separate collections.

68 Metzger, *Canon*, 282–84.

69 For a more philosophical critique of canon criticism, see esp. P. R. Noble, *The Canonical Approach: A Critical Reconstruction of the Hermeneutics of Brevard S. Childs* (Leiden: Brill, 1995).

James Sanders practices a quite different form of canon criticism, one that probably ought to have a different name.[70] Sanders' study focuses on canon not so much as a *product* but as a *process*. Canonical hermeneutics, in this program, refers to the way in which one biblical writer read, rewrote, and/or reapplied earlier Scripture, for example, Deuteronomy's reworking of the laws of Exodus and Leviticus, the Chronicler's rewriting of parts of the Samuel-Kings narrative, or the NT quotations of and allusions to the OT. But these topics are not new, and they are probably best studied under other headings such as redaction criticism, midrash criticism, and the history of exegesis.

What may be more significant is Sanders' claim that the hermeneutics used in these scriptural interpretations themselves should be normative for believers. This question surfaces, for example, whenever one asks, Can Christians today interpret the OT in the same way the NT writers did? Sanders believes the answer is clearly, yes. We offer our qualified agreement, though we often disagree with him in his actual assessment of the methods employed (see chap. 6 below).

TEXTS AND TRANSLATIONS

Ideally, students would interpret the autographs of Scripture—the original documents penned by the various biblical writers. However, since none of these exists, the next best choice is to read and interpret the modern critical editions of the Hebrew, Aramaic, and Greek texts: the *Biblia Hebraica Stuttgartensia* (*BHS*, now in its 5th edition) for the OT, and the Nestle-Aland (27th edition) or United Bible Societies' (4th rev. edition) *Greek New Testament* (*GNT*). The *BHS* follows the text of Codex Leningradensis—a well-preserved tenth-century A.D. manuscript of the Masoretic family of texts, the dominant orthodox Hebrew tradition of scribal activity from ca. A.D. 600–900. A critical apparatus presents textual variants in the footnotes, including readings of older Hebrew texts (primarily the Dead Sea Scrolls [DSS]) and other older translations (esp. the LXX). The *GNT* chooses from among all the ancient manuscripts and versions of the NT to reconstruct what those autographs most likely contained.[71] However, many Bible interpreters do not have the language skills to read these documents either, so they must rely on translations of Scripture into their native tongues.

How then does one choose among the many available translations? Students should consider two factors. First, to what extent does a given translation utilize the most reliable findings of modern textual criticism reflected in works like the *BHS* or *GNT*? Second, what kind of translation is it? Is it highly literal, highly paraphrastic, or somewhere in-between? To help the student answer these two questions we will discuss several pertinent issues.

---

70 For an article-length autobiographical reflection on his method, see J. A. Sanders, "Scripture as Canon for Post-Modern Times," *BTB* 25 (1995): 56–63. For fuller treatment, see esp. id., *Canon and Community*; and id., *From Sacred Story to Sacred Text* (Philadelphia: Fortress, 1987).

71 There is still plenty of room, however, for questioning the choices of individual readings at numerous places, as stressed in R. R. Reeves, "What Do We Do Now? Approaching the Crossroads of New Testament Textual Criticism," *PRS* 23 (1996): 61–73. A very tiny minority of textual critics supports what is called the Majority Text that largely lay behind the textual choices of the translators of the King James Version of the Bible, despite the discoveries of numerous older and more reliable manuscripts in the centuries since 1611. See further below.

Textual Criticism

Since this is not a manual on exegesis (interpreting the Bible in its original languages), we will discuss textual criticism only briefly.[72] Much of the work of textual critics involves tedious and painstaking comparisons of dozens of ancient OT manuscripts and versions, and hundreds (thousands if one includes small fragments) of portions of Greek NT texts from the early centuries of the Christian era. The vast majority of the differences between the manuscripts stem from the mechanics of copying by hand the contents of a written document. A brief introduction to that process will enable readers to understand why manuscripts were not always copied perfectly.

Ancient writing on scrolls and codices (manuscripts in book form) did not look much like print in modern books. In the oldest manuscripts words were written in capital letters with no use of lower case and no spacing between words. Nor was there punctuation, hyphenation, paragraphing, section headings, or any of the other devices of modern writing.[73] In addition, in the case of Hebrew and Aramaic, generally only consonants were written out. The vowels (later represented by symbols underneath or above the consonants) were supplied by the Masoretic scribes much later, centuries after the books were written and the canon was complete. To imagine what this might look like for an English reader, we might conceive of the NIV of Gen 1:1-2 as appearing:

NTHBGNNNGGDCRTDTHHVNSNDTHRTHNDTHRTH-
WSFRMLSSNDMPTYDRKNSSWSVRTHSRFCFTHDPNDTH-
SPRTFGDWSHVRNGVRTHWTRS.

John 1:1-2 would not look quite so bad because vowels were included in Greek manuscripts:

INTHEBEGINNINGWASTHEWORDANDTHEWORD-
WASWITHGODANDTHEWORDWASGODHEWASWITH-
GODINTHEBEGINNING.

Naturally one wonders how anybody could read such writing. But those who read these languages had learned the method from childhood, and in the case of Hebrew had learned what vowels should be added to the consonants mentally or orally. Nevertheless, modern readers do well to remember that the original Scripture texts looked quite different from our own. No one dare claim inspiration for chapter and

---

72 Helpful introductory guides include P. K. McCarter, Jr., *Textual Criticism: Recovering the Text of the Hebrew Bible* (Philadelphia: Fortress, 1986); E. R. Brotzman, *Old Testament Textual Criticism: A Practical Introduction* (Grand Rapids: Baker, 1994); J. H. Greenlee, *Introduction to New Testament Textual Criticism*, 2d ed. (Peabody: Hendrickson, 1995); and D. A. Black, *New Testament Textual Criticism: A Concise Guide* (Grand Rapids: Baker, 1994). More technical but more thorough studies are E. Tov, *Textual Criticism of the Hebrew Bible*, 2d ed. (Assen: Royal Van Gorcum; Minneapolis: Fortress, 2001); and K. Aland and B. Aland, *The Text of the New Testament*, 2d ed. (Grand Rapids: Eerdmans; Leiden: Brill, 1989*)*.

73 This is demonstrable for the oldest NT documents. For OT texts, even the oldest existing copies indicate word division in various ways, but also show signs that they were copied at some stage from texts without such division. See Tov, *Textual Criticism of the Hebrew Bible*, 208–9.

verse references (these were added in the Middle Ages),[74] punctuation and NT word division (which began about the sixth century), or Hebrew vowels (finalized in writing in about the ninth century).

When manuscripts began to be copied, many of the differences among them, therefore, resulted from the ambiguities of the older documents, especially with respect to word division. However, the context usually clarified the correct reading. But unintentionally, scribes introduced other mechanical errors: letters, words, or whole lines were accidentally omitted or repeated as the copyist's eye jumped back to the wrong place in the text being copied. Spelling variations or mistakes intruded, when two adjacent letters were reversed, or when one letter was substituted for another that was similar in appearance. Sometimes scribes intentionally altered texts they copied—e.g., in the direction of "orthodoxy" or to harmonize a text with another one. But most of these errors are trivial, detectable, and correctable, and do not significantly affect the overall meaning of the larger passages in which they appear. Occasionally, there are interesting exceptions. For example, should 1 Thes 2:7 read "we were *gentle* among you" or "we were *little children* among you?"[75] The two readings in the Greek differ only by an additional *n-* to begin the second word: *egenēthēmen ēpioi* "we became gentle" vs. *egenēthēmen nēpioi* "we became infants."[76] Is it more likely that a scribe accidentally (or intentionally) added or omitted the *n-*?[77]

Or should Gen 49:26 read, "Your father's blessings are greater than the blessings of the ancient mountains" or ". . . greater than the blessings of my progenitors" (i.e., "those who conceived me")? The phrase "the ancient mountains" (הַרְרֵי עַד; *harᵃrê ʿad*) in Hebrew looks similar to "those who conceived me" (הוֹרַי עַד; *hôray ʿad*), if one letter (ר; *r*) is replaced with a similar looking letter (ו; *ô*).[78]

Obviously, textual variants in verses of great doctrinal significance introduce important ambiguities. Usually Psa 2:12 has been seen as messianic, in keeping with the traditional rendering of the Hebrew (נַשְּׁקוּ־בַר; *naśśᵉqû-bar*), as "Kiss [i.e., reverence] the Son" (NIV). But the last two letters (בַר *bar*, reading from right to left) are not the

---

74 Chapter divisions were introduced by the Archbishop of Canterbury, Stephen Langton, at the beginning of the 13th century; verses, by Robert Estienne (Stephanus), in the mid-16th century.

75 Most modern English translations adopt the former, but most textual critics favor the latter. But see now TNIV which follows the textual-critical consensus.

76 Recall originally these were written in all capitals with no spaces. They would differ only in the presence of an extra *-n*. Compare *ΕΓΕΝΗΘΗΜΕΝΗΠΙΟΙ* (we were gentle) with *ΕΓΕΝΗΘΗΜΕΝΝΗΠΙΟΙ* (we became infants).

77 The standard source for explaining the cases for and against the major textual variants in the New Testament is B. M. Metzger, *A Textual Commentary on the Greek New Testament*, 2d ed. (New York: UBS, 1994). Particularly useful is Metzger's description of how the five-member committee that produced the UBS *GNT* arrived at its decisions to rank a certain reading with an {A}, {B}, {C}, or {D} level of confidence. In this particular example, the committee adopted the reading *nēpioi* (infants) and gave it a {B} rating indicating that the text is almost certain. (An {A} indicates that the text is certain; {C} that the committee had difficulty in deciding which variant to place in the text; and {D} that the committee had great difficulty with its decision, an option occurring rarely.)

78 On which, see e.g. V. P. Hamilton, *The Book of Genesis, Chapters 18–50* (Grand Rapids: Eerdmans, 1995), 682–83, n. 19. The former reading lies behind the LXX; the latter, the Hebrew (MT).

normal Hebrew for "Son" (which is בֵּן *bēn,* as in verse 7), and the LXX translates the command into Greek as "take hold of discipline," which cannot be extracted from these Hebrew letters at all. Modern translators, therefore, have sometimes supposed that these six letters, along with those of the preceding two words, were at some point rather dramatically rearranged from an original נַשְּׁקוּ בְרַגְלָיו בִּרְעָדָה (*naššᵉqû bᵉraglāyw birʿādâ*) to the existing MT וְגִילוּ בִּרְעָדָה נַשְּׁקוּבַר (*wᵉgîlû birʿādâ naššᵉqû-bar).* They propose a non-messianic rendering: "Kiss his feet" (RSV referring to God). Thus instead of "Serve the Lord with fear and rejoice with trembling, Kiss the son," Psa 2:11–12a then reads, "Serve the Lord with fear, with trembling kiss his feet."[79]

Less complex, but equally significant, is a NT example from Lk 22:19b-20. Did a later scribe add the words, "given for you. This do in remembrance of me. And likewise the cup, after supper saying, this cup is the new covenant in my blood shed for you"? Or were these words accidentally omitted in the exemplar (an influential manuscript widely copied for a large number of other manuscripts) behind the manuscripts that lack this material, and so the scribe merely added what ought to be present?[80] We could multiply examples. But we insist that no doctrine of Christianity rests solely on textually disputed passages.[81] There are numerous other messianic psalms and prophecies besides Psa 2:12, and there are three other accounts of Jesus' words at the Last Supper, one of which very closely agrees with the wording of Luke's disputed text (1 Cor 11:24–25).

The science of textual criticism nevertheless has a crucial place in proper hermeneutics. All of the other methods described in this book are somewhat inconsequential if we cannot determine with reasonable probability what the original words of the Bible actually were. The good news is that the vast majority of the Bible is textually secure.[82] Readers of English translations, especially of the NT, need not wonder if textual variants lurking behind every verse they read would drastically change the meaning of the passage. Estimates suggest between 97 and 99 percent of the original NT can be reconstructed from the existing manuscripts beyond any measure of reasonable doubt. The percentage for the OT is lower, but at least 90 percent or more. But good editions of the various modern English translations contain footnotes that alert readers to most of the significant textual variants (as well as important alternate translations). Serious students of the Bible would be wise to obtain such editions of the Scriptures.

Even with all of this help, Christians often ask two important questions for which there are no simple answers. First, why did God in his providence not insure that an

---

79 For details and alternative proposals see C. Vang, "Ps 2, 11–12—A New Look at An Old Crux Interpretum," *SJOT* 9 (1995): 162–85; and S. Olofsson, "The Crux Interpretum in Ps 2, 12," *SJOT* 9 (1995): 185–99.

80 For details, see I. H. Marshall, *Last Supper and Lord's Supper* (Grand Rapids: Eerdmans, 1980), 36–38.

81 For this and related points, and for an excellent introductory survey to the theological issues surrounding textual criticism for the evangelical, particularly with reference to the more difficult OT issues, see B. K. Waltke, "How We Got the Hebrew Bible: The Text and Canon of the Old Testament," in *The Bible at Qumran: Text, Shape, and Interpretation,* ed. P. W. Flint (Grand Rapids: Eerdmans, 2001), 27–50.

82 Brotzman (*Old Testament Textual Criticism,* 23) notes that much of the OT text exists without any variation.

inerrant, inspired original was also inerrantly *preserved?*[83] Second, how do we as Christians deal with those portions of traditional translations (like the KJV) that modern discoveries have shown were not part of the original autographs? The first question takes on added significance in light of other religions that claim, however speciously, that their sacred writings have been perfectly preserved (most notably the Book of Mormon and the Qur'an/Koran). To be sure, we do not know God's hidden motives. Perhaps he did not want us to idolize a book but to worship the God who became incarnate in Jesus. Leaving the transmission of Scriptures to fallible human beings parallels leaving the proclamation of those Scriptures to sinful and potentially rebellious disciples. God does not choose to override free will in either case, and he reveals and inspires only at particular moments in human history. At the same time we can discern his providence in the amazing extent to which the texts have been preserved.

The second question becomes particularly acute with regard to the two longest passages (printed in most Bibles) that almost certainly did not appear in the original manuscripts: Mk 16:9–20 (an additional account of Jesus' resurrection) and Jn 7:53–8:11 (the story of the woman caught in adultery). The necessary approach should be clear—whatever was most likely in the original texts should be accepted as inspired and normative; what was not in those texts should not be given equal status. But application proves more difficult. As noted elsewhere in this book, Jn 7:53–8:11 may be a true story, from which we can derive accurate information about Jesus' view of the Law, even if it did not originally form part of John's Gospel. On the other hand, there is almost no evidence to support Jesus ever having said, "Whoever believes and is baptized will be saved" (Mk 16:16; as if baptism were necessary for salvation), or for the promise that believers may pick up snakes, drink their venom, and yet not be harmed (Mk 16:18). One unnecessarily risks suicide by treating that text as normative! But in both Mark and John, the textual evidence is very strong for rejecting these passages as inspired Scripture.[84]

The OT creates different problems. Some books are so different in Hebrew and Greek forms that we probably must speak of two different editions of these books. The clearest example is Jeremiah, which is nearly one-sixth shorter in the LXX. Now that fragments of a Hebrew copy of Jeremiah that resemble the LXX have been found among the DSS, it seems likely that the Hebrew version of Jeremiah underwent successive revisions. But, whatever we make of this process of development, there is no evidence that Judaism ever treated the shorter Jeremiah as authoritative, once the longer revised version was available. So it is this final Jeremiah, on which our English translations are based, that we should continue to treat as canonical.[85]

---

83 The fact that no two known manuscripts are identical refutes any claim that God did preserve an inerrant manuscript. To identify any particular manuscript as without error is an act of sheer faith that all the empirical evidence contradicts. See esp. D. B. Wallace, "The Majority-Text Theory: History, Methods and Critique," *JETS* 37 (1994): 185–215.

84 The UBS *GNT* gives an {A} rating (its highest) for not including this material in each instance.

85 See esp. Tov, *Textual Criticism of the Hebrew Bible*, 319–27. For the more general debate regarding method when OT texts or passages seem to have existed in different forms from very early on, see K. H. Jobes and M. Silva, *Invitation to the Septuagint* (Grand Rapids: Baker; Carlisle: Paternoster, 2000), 120–24. This book is also now perhaps the best introduction to the LXX more generally.

In other instances, however, the DSS have provided textual variants—sometimes completely new, sometimes matching the LXX—that probably reflect the original autographs more closely than the MT. English translations like the NIV and NRSV periodically include in their footnotes references to readings found among the DSS. Probably the most celebrated example involves additional texts at the beginning of 1 Sam 11 in 4QSam that seems likely to have been original and later accidentally omitted.[86] The NRSV has thus added it in, rendering it:

> Now Nahash, king of the Ammonites, had been grievously oppressing the Gadites and the Reubenites. He would gouge out the right eye of each of them and would not grant Israel a deliverer. No one was left of the Israelites across the Jordan whose right eye Nahash, king of the Ammonites, had not gouged out. But there were seven thousand men who had escaped from the Ammonites and had entered Jabesh-gilead.

These changes remind us again that our knowledge of the original text of the Bible is not 100 percent secure, and new discoveries may lead to still more revisions. But it is also important to stress that our ability to reconstruct the probable original far outstrips that of any other document from the ancient world.[87]

A different kind of hermeneutical issue raised by textual criticism involves verses in which the NT quotes the OT but follows the Septuagint, even though the meaning in the Greek translation does not accurately reflect the Hebrew of traditional OT manuscripts. These differences prove more difficult to assess. As we have noted, the traditional Hebrew versions date from no earlier than the A.D. 800–900s. The existing Septuagint manuscripts go back an additional half a millennium or more. It is possible, therefore, that at times the LXX accurately translated a Hebrew original that later became corrupted. Portions of OT books found among the DSS from as long ago as 200 B.C. suggest that occasionally, though not often, this was exactly what happened. Compare, for example, Heb 1:6, which quotes a longer form of Deut 32:43 found only in the LXX and DSS.[88]

Aramaic Targums, which combined free translation with occasional explanatory additions and commentary, may at times also account for NT renderings of OT texts. Interpreters, for example, have often wondered how to account for the end of Eph 4:8, "he gave gifts to his people," (NRSV) when the Hebrew of Psa 68:18 that Paul quotes reads "receiving gifts from people" (NRSV). But at least one early Targum contains Aramaic wording that parallels how Paul rendered this verse, so it is quite possible that Paul is following a similar tradition. Jews and Christians have often speculated that God received tribute in order to return those gifts as blessings to his people. Whether

---

86 Tov, *Textual Criticism of the Hebrew Bible*, 342–44.

87 For some comparative data, see P. D. Wegner, *The Journey from Texts to Translations* (Grand Rapids: Baker, 1999), 233

88 On which, see esp. J. de Waard, *A Comparative Study of the Old Testament Text in the Dead Sea Scrolls and in the New Testament* (Leiden: Brill, 1965), 13–16; G. L. Cockerill, "Hebrews 1:6: Source and Significance, *BBR* 9 (1999): 51–64.

or not Paul reasoned in this way, the Targum at least shows that Paul based his interpretation on an acceptable Jewish reading and did not simply manipulate the psalm willy-nilly.[89]

Because the LXX was the common Bible for first-century Jewish readers outside Israel, in some instances the NT may quote from it even when it differed from the Hebrew, so long as it did not mitigate the point at stake. Thus, James in Acts 15:17 quotes the LXX of Amos 9:11-12 in which the Greek, "that the remnant of men may seek the Lord, and all the Gentiles who bear my name," is quite different from the Hebrew, "so that they may possess the remnant of Edom and all the nations that bear my name." Yet James' point can be justified from either version—when God restores Israel, Gentiles will become an integral and united part of his new chosen people along with Jews.[90] Of course, not every NT use of the LXX can be explained in these ways. (For additional discussion, refer to the section on the use of the OT in the NT in chapter 6).

Perhaps the most important hermeneutical principle to learn from textual criticism is that one must not derive theological or ethical principles solely from passages that are textually uncertain. When significant textual variants appear in a given passage, the sensible Bible reader will derive interpretations and applications that can be defended no matter which version of the text one follows. So, too, students should always base syntheses of biblical doctrine and practice on textually certain passages.

Techniques of Translation

Translation techniques constitute the second criterion by which readers ought to evaluate modern versions of the Bible. It helps to arrange the various English translations along a spectrum from highly literal to highly paraphrastic.[91] There is no perfectly literal translation from one language to another of any extensive piece of writing because the structures and vocabularies of languages vary considerably. The literal word-by-word equivalent of the Spanish "una piñata pequeña rompí yo" in English would be "a piñata small broke I." But English does not allow such a sentence; we have to say, "I broke a small piñata." What is more, piñata is not an English word (though many English speakers have come to understand it), and we have no one-word English equivalent. One would have to replace the one Spanish word with a long English phrase like, "a large, colorful papier-mâché animal stuffed with candy and hung from the ceiling for people to bat at in a game." Likewise, even the KJV, often viewed as the most literal of Bible translations, occasionally

---

89 For this and other attempts to resolve the problem, see P. T. O'Brien, *The Letter to the Ephesians* (Grand Rapids: Eerdmans; Leicester: InterVarsity, 1999), 289–93. For more detail on the use of Psa 68:19 in early non-rabbinic sources see, H. H. Harris, III, *The Descent of Christ: Ephesians 4:7–11 and Traditional Hebrew Imagery* (Leiden: Brill, 1996; Grand Rapids: Baker, 1998), 96–122.

90 This is the approach frequently taken and well defended by D. L. Bock, *Proclamation from Prophecy and Pattern: Lucan Old Testament Christology*, JSNTSup 12 (Sheffield: JSOT, 1987). For the textual details here, cf. D. W. Baker, "Language and Text of the Old Testament," in *Interpreting the Old Testament: A Guide for Exegesis*, ed. C. C. Broyles (Grand Rapids: Baker, 2001), 79.

91 On the theory and practice of translation, see esp. E. A. Nida, *Toward a Science of Translating* (Leiden: Brill, 1964); J. Beekman and J. Callow, *Translating the Word* of God (Grand Rapids: Zondervan, 1974); and J. de Waard and E. A. Nida, *From One Language to Another: Functional Equivalence in Bible Translating* (Nashville: Thomas Nelson, 1986).

resorts to paraphrase, as in 1 Pet 1:18, where the one Greek word *patroparadotou* ("father-tradition") must be rendered "received by tradition from your fathers." The most literal "translations" are interlinear Bibles, but by themselves they are often virtually unintelligible, as the Spanish example above. They are actually not translations at all, but merely decode literally the biblical words into English equivalents.

Nevertheless, certain versions try to adhere as closely to Hebrew or Greek grammar and syntax as possible, while still being understandable in English. We call these *formally equivalent* translations. The NASB is a prime example. Other versions seek to reproduce thought-for-thought rather than word-for-word—called *dynamically* (or functionally) *equivalent* translations. They seek to produce the same effect on readers today that the original produced on its readers. These versions are less concerned to translate consistently a given Greek or Hebrew word with the same English word. Dynamically or functionally equivalent translations often reword a passive sentence into an active sentence, reflecting better English style ("I was hit by him" would equal "he hit me."). For example, "Blessed are those who mourn, for they will be comforted" (Mt 5:4), becomes in the GNB, "Happy are those who mourn; God will comfort them!" Idioms and figures of speech often become more intelligible by means of modern equivalents or nonidiomatic language ("laying down one's neck" [see KJV] in Rom 16:4 might become "risking one's neck" [see NRSV] or even "risking one's life" [see NIV]).

Paraphrases go one step further; they add explanatory words or phrases that do not correspond to anything in the original text and are not necessary to preserve the sense of the passage, but which, nevertheless, give the text added freshness and impact. One example is Eugene Peterson's rendering of 1 Cor 13:4–7 in *The Message*:

> Love never gives up. Love cares more for others than for self. Love doesn't want what it doesn't have. Love doesn't strut, doesn't have a swelled head, doesn't force itself on others, isn't always "me first," doesn't fly off the handle, doesn't keep score of the sins of others, doesn't revel when others grovel, takes pleasure in the flowering of truth, puts up with anything, trusts God always, always looks for the best, never looks back, but keeps going to the end.

Compare this with the more literal versions. Many times, the more a reader seeks formal correspondence the less understandable the text becomes. On the other hand, paraphrases that are the easiest to read and the liveliest run the greatest risk of departing from the text's original meaning. Many translators thus believe that the ideal is to try to strike a balance between preserving the original form and preserving the meaning.[92]

---

92 One popular way of striking this balance among fairly conservative translations is to render unknown terms as literally as possible and then to supply an explanatory phrase in parentheses or a footnote. For additional discussion and debate on the larger philosophical issues at stake, see D. J. Hesselgrave, "Contextualization and Revelational Epistemology," with responses by M. A. Inch and W. A. Grudem, in *Hermeneutics, Inerrancy, and the Bible*, ed. E. D. Radmacher and R. D. Preus (Grand Rapids: Zondervan, 1984), 691–764.

The Major English Translations[93]

Since its completion in 1611, the King James Version of the English Bible has dominated the field. The first "authorized" version, after previous efforts by men like John Wycliffe, Miles Coverdale, and William Tyndale ran aground of ecclesiastical authorities, the KJV was a masterpiece of formal equivalence rendered into the common vernacular of seventeenth-century England. A team of scholars commissioned by James VI bypassed the Latin Vulgate, which had dominated Christianity for 1000 years, compared prior English translations with the best couple dozen Hebrew and Greek manuscripts available to them, and produced a painstaking, monumental version of the Scriptures.[94] But the English language has changed dramatically in the last 400 years, and the discovery of many, new Bible manuscripts much older than those available in 1611, make the KJV far less valuable today. The KJV, of course, has been revised frequently; no edition in print today reads exactly like the original. The most famous twentieth century edition of the KJV, the Scofield Reference Bible, contains numerous marginal notes to indicate where it updates obscure English. The New King James Version (NKJV) offers an even more thorough rewrite.

The textual base in each of these editions and versions of the KJV, however, remains unchanged. A handful of textual critics continues to defend the so-called Majority Text (the 80 percent or so of NT manuscripts that roughly agrees with the KJV). They argue that if this were not the earliest text-form, it would not have survived in so many manuscripts.[95] But, in fact, most of these manuscripts come from the "Byzantine" family of texts (a collection of manuscripts with similar readings and geographic origins suggesting that they all derived from one or a few exemplars) associated with the world power that ruled from Constantinople (formerly called Byzantium) after the fall of Rome. So naturally their manuscripts of the NT were most widely copied and well-preserved. But none of the oldest manuscripts, most of which were discovered since 1611, come from this tradition, and so our knowledge of what the biblical writers themselves actually wrote has improved greatly since the days of the KJV. We really ought to be thankful, for example, that Mark did not write the KJV rendering of Mk 16:18 (see above), but readers who limit themselves to the KJV will never know this. Readers of the NKJV will know about the differences among manuscripts, if they read the footnotes, but they will naturally conclude that the better readings are those of the KJV. For this reason, we cannot endorse the widespread use of these versions when alternatives are available.[96]

---

93 The two best surveys are S. Kubo and W. Specht, *So Many Versions? Twentieth Century English Versions of the Bible.* 2d ed. (Grand Rapids: Zondervan, 1990); and J. P. Lewis, *The English Bible from KJV to NIV*, 2d ed. (Grand Rapids: Baker, 1991). More selective but more recent is B. M. Metzger, *The Bible in Translation* (Grand Rapids: Baker, 2001).

94 On the incredible achievement of the production of the KJV, also called the Authorized Version (av), see A. Nicolson, *God's Secretaries. The Making of the King James Bible* (New York: HarperCollins, 2003).

95 See esp., Z. C. Hodges and A. L. Farstad, eds., *The Greek New Testament According to the Majority Text* (Nashville: Nelson, 1982).

96 For a detailed defense of these claims, see D. A. Carson, *The King James Version Debate* (Grand Rapids: Baker, 1979); and J. R. White, *The King James Only Controversy* (Minneapolis: Bethany, 1995).

Revision of the KJV based on new textual discoveries in both Testaments began with the British Revised Version (RV) in 1885 and the American Standard Version (ASV) in 1901. But the most dramatic manuscript discoveries, including the DSS, occurred since then. The first truly modern translation, still highly literal (or formally equivalent, direct) but abreast of the scholarly state of the art, was the Revised Standard Version (RSV) completed in 1952. Unfortunately, it received unduly negative press in some conservative circles because of occasional controversial renderings. Most famous was its use of "young woman" instead of "virgin" in Isa 7:14. Others criticized the RSV because of its somewhat liberal use of conjectural emendation (proposing different consonants in the Hebrew text, even when no known variants support those proposals) in seemingly garbled OT passages (as in the illustration from Psa 2:12 above).[97] But, when it appeared, the RSV was far superior in fluency and accuracy to any other English version available. The RSV was updated in 1971, and in 1990 a New Revised Standard Version (NRSV) appeared. One of the prominent changes is the use of inclusive language instead of masculine nouns and pronouns when both men and women are in view. An inclusive language lectionary (a collection of Scriptures for weekly reading in liturgical churches that adopt a fixed calendar of texts to be read on specific Sundays) using the NRSV that employs inclusive language for the Godhead was also produced—a much more controversial move.

After the RSV first appeared, many English and American readers began to feel the need for versions of Scripture that were easier for the average, biblically illiterate person to read. Paraphrases, produced by individuals rather than the larger committees that worked together on the other versions, began to appear. J. B. Phillips published his NT in England in 1958. An American, Ken Taylor, published his "Living Letters" in 1962. Taylor eventually completed the Living Bible Paraphrased (LBP) in 1971. Phillips and Taylor were often harshly criticized for taking undue liberties with the text. In the LBP, Psa 119:105 (literally translated, "your word is a lamp to my feet") became, anachronistically, "Your words are a flashlight to light the path ahead of me." In Acts 4:36, "Joseph . . . called Barnabas (which means Son of Encouragement)" turned into the rather slang, "Joseph nicknamed 'Barny the Preacher' "! And Phillips' rendering of Acts 8:20 (usually translated, "May your money perish with you") became shocking to many ("To hell with you and your money!"), even though Phillips correctly comments in a footnote that this is a quite defensible and a highly literal translation of the Greek. In the 1990s, however, the publishers of the LBP convened a large committee of scholars to revise Taylor's work to make it a legitimate, functionally equivalent translation. This New Living Translation (NLT) first appeared in 1996.[98] On the other hand, Eugene Peterson's *The Message* (completed in 2002) is a far freer paraphrase than even the original LBP, but a group of scholars has assessed it for theological accuracy and it has proved very popular because of its strikingly fresh language. Critics often overlooked that these versions were not produced to replace translations that are more traditional; rather, they aimed to make the Bible come alive and to be read by people who

---

97 For a good summary of most of the complaints that led certain evangelicals to seek new, alternate translations to the RSV, see P. J. Thuesen in *Discordance with the Scriptures* (Oxford: Oxford University Press, 1999), 67–144.

98 The NLT and the NKJV rank third after the NIV and KJV in international distribution, far outstripping all of the remaining newer translations in this respect.

would not otherwise read Scripture at all. To that extent they succeeded remarkably. More distinctive is the Amplified Bible, which often places several synonyms for particular words in parentheses right in the text itself. Unfortunately, uninformed Bible readers may think that all of these words are equally plausible translations or that the original terms actually meant everything that appears in parentheses simultaneously! Neither of these is true, of course.

Translations that sought dynamic equivalence as a middle ground between formal equivalence and paraphrase include, most notably, Today's English Version (TEV) of the NT (1966), which ten years later was expanded to become the Good News Bible (GNB), along with most of the newer translations being published by the United Bible Societies in languages other than English. The British produced the New English Bible (NEB; NT in 1961 and OT in 1970), which falls somewhere between dynamic equivalence and paraphrase but often relies on idiosyncratic textual criticism. Improvements, revisions, and the addition of some inclusive language to the NEB resulted in the Revised English Bible (REB) of 1990. The American Bible Society has issued a new translation entitled the Contemporary English Version (CEV, completed in 1995). A widely used children's Bible proved so popular with adults that it was revised and "upgraded" for a wider audience as the New Century Version (NCV). It, too, employs inclusive language for people, dynamic equivalence translation principles, and uses the simplest English of all the new versions.

Many evangelicals were unhappy with one or another feature of the first efforts to improve on the KJV and ASV. Either they suspected liberal bias or found paraphrases too free, but they agreed updating was desperately needed. So two translations stemming from evangelical teams of scholars were produced—the first by Americans, the second by an international group. The former, a revision of the ASV, was called the New American Standard Bible (NASB) and was completed in 1971; the latter, the New International Version (NIV), was finished in 1978. The NASB is highly literal, to the point of being rather stilted occasionally. The NIV falls in between formal and dynamic equivalence and has become by far and away the translation of choice in evangelical circles, much as the RSV and NRSV have in ecumenical circles.[99] A simplified version known as the New International Readers' Version (NIRV) particularly geared for children or adults just learning to read has proved very popular. Sadly, no translation has appeared, nor (to our knowledge) is one being planned, that would combine the best of evangelical and ecumenical scholarship. Since all translations reflect at times a certain theological bias, not all Christians are likely soon to agree on an "authorized" successor to the KJV.

The most controversial issue concerning Bible translation in evangelical circles today involves inclusive language for humanity. As long as the practice was limited to translations that were more ecumenical or to paraphrastic renderings of the text, few evangelicals paid much attention. In 1996, however, Hodder and Stoughton in London issued the NIV Inclusive Language Edition (NIVI), which consistently uses substitutions

---

99 The importance of these two translations has led to entire books about their production: K. L. Barker, ed., *The NIV: The Making of a Contemporary Translation* (Grand Rapids: Zondervan, 1986); and B. M. Metzger, R. C. Dentan, and W. Harrelson, *The Making of the New Revised Standard Version* (Grand Rapids: Eerdmans, 1991).

like "brothers and sisters" for "brothers"; "person" for "man"; and even "they" or "you" for "he" when the terms in question were deemed generic in their original context. Vigorous protests from certain very conservative American evangelicals led to the suspension of plans to publish a highly similar American edition.[100] But the NIV's "Committee on Bible Translation" (CBT) continued to work and in 2002 released Today's NIV (TNIV) with similar revisions. Sadly, criticism of the TNIV has often been based on misunderstandings of linguistics in general and the CBT's philosophy of translation in particular[101] and seem to have polarized the evangelical community in the U.S. into two large groups, who are either staunchly opposed or solidly in favor of the methodology. Those opposed have also produced their own more formally equivalent and gender-exclusive translations, most notably the English Standard Version (2001). A uniquely Southern Baptist venture called the Holman Christian Standard Bible (NT, 2000) is more like the NIV in balancing formal and functional equivalents but also more gender exclusive than the NIVI or TNIV. [102]

Choosing a Translation

Which translation is the best to use? The basic answer is that it depends on your purpose or occasion in reading the Bible. If, for the sake of doing word studies or outlining a passage, you want a version that generally tries to reflect the actual structure of the biblical language and that translates key terms with the same English word as often as possible, then follow the NASB or, with a few more exceptions, the ESV or NRSV. Deciding among those three might depend on your view of the inclusive language issue. If you are looking for an accurate translation with fresh thoughts and insights for a young or beginning reader in simple and vivid language, consider the NLT or the NCV. For sheer arresting paraphrase and innovation, check out *The Message*. For the best overall balance between directness and readability, consult the NIV or TNIV (or NIVI), the latter particularly to avoid misleading modern readers not used to thinking generically when they see words like "brother," "men," or "he." But beyond even that point, the

---

100 See further C. L. Blomberg, "Today's New International Version: The Untold Story of a Good Translation," forthcoming.

101 For overviews of the debate, contrast D. A. Carson, *The Inclusive Language Debate: A Plea for Realism* (Grand Rapids: Baker; Leicester: Intervarsity, 1998) (generally favorable to inclusive language for humanity) with V. S. Poythress and W. A. Grudem, *The Gender-Neutral Bible Controversy: Muting the Masculinity of God's Words* (Nashville: Broadman and Holman, 2000) (generally opposed).

102 We could say much more about other modern translations. Briefly, in Roman Catholic circles the two most important are the New Jerusalem Bible and the New American Bible. Both break with the traditional Catholic practice of following the Latin Vulgate and go back instead to the Greek and Hebrew. The NAB is reasonably similar to the NIV in its place on the spectrum of literal vs. free translation; the NJB is closer to the REB. In Judaism, The New Jewish Version is a significant modern rendering of the Hebrew Scriptures into contemporary English. Various pseudo-Christian sects use their own versions. The New World Translation of the Jehovah's Witnesses is widely known because of its unjustifiable translations of passages that teach Christ's deity or the personality of the Holy Spirit (both of which the Jehovah's Witnesses deny). The Mormons rely on their own edition of the KJV, since the Book of Mormon often quotes the Bible in the King James text-type, even when older manuscripts prove that the original Scripture writers wrote something different. This fact alone disproves the Book of Mormon's claim to be a reliable translation of tablets predating the KJV by fifteen centuries or more. The NET Bible is a unique, electronic edition that bridges the gap between formal and functional equivalents, surrounded by a huge apparatus of textual and interpretive annotations.

gender-sensitive versions open up to all readers the inclusive intent of many texts otherwise easily overlooked and help readers who do not know the biblical languages see how to adjudicate between generic uses of "man" and male uses. For dramatic and poetic readings in classic Elizabethan English, dust off the KJV!

Above all, whenever you are serious about studying a passage intensively, especially when you are teaching it to others or dealing with controversial exegetical or theological issues, consult more than one translation. For memorization, choose the translation you prefer and use it consistently. But for valid interpretation, if you cannot read the biblical languages, you must compare several versions lest you miss an important possible translation. Indeed, comparing translations is probably the best way to discover where significant textual differences or ambiguous wording occurs in the Hebrew or Greek originals. Editions that print four parallel columns from different versions are particularly helpful in this respect.[103] Numerous computer programs also allow for the quick comparison of standard texts and translations.[104]

---

103 E.g., *Today's Parallel Bible* [NIV, NASB, KJV, NLT] (Grand Rapids: Zondervan, 2000). Particularly useful is the verse-by-verse listing of interesting translations and paraphrases that comprises *The Bible from 26 Translations* (Grand Rapids: Baker, 1988).

104 Logos and BibleWorks software are two of the perennially most popular, but many other publishers offer a wide range of Bible versions in their packages.

PART II—THE INTERPRETER
AND THE GOAL

5

THE INTERPRETER

Suppose two chemists decided to conduct a similar experiment. While one carefully followed the experimental design with accuracy and precision, the other worked carelessly and failed to follow the procedures or make the measurements precisely. Which of these two chemists would obtain the more valid results? Without doubt, the chemist who worked with accuracy and precision would get the nod. The same is true of Bible interpretation. If interpretation is to succeed, the interpreter must possess certain competencies and must work with correct and accurate methodology. Careful and accurate work produces the best results, regardless of the practitioner. It is our goal to present responsible, careful methods for accurate interpretation and understanding of the Scriptures. Those who practice these methods with rigor and care will have the best possible prospects of success in this endeavor. The techniques furnish correct insights regardless of who utilizes them.

However, we are still faced with a dilemma, for in addition to accurate methodology, the interpreter's set of convictions or presuppositions about the nature of Scripture and about the precise nature of the task of interpretation profoundly affects his or her work. In chapter 1 we stressed that interpretation was both a science and an art. An art critic who analyzes a painting for the first time would observe the focus of attention, mood, use of color and shadow, perspective, etc., in additional to the more technical or mechanical details. The artist's own commitments affect the assessment of these features. Likewise, to cite a stark example, the biblical interpreter who rejects the possibility of resurrection must explain all such biblical "events" as myth or legend—certainly not as literal history. Whatever these passages may convey to modern readers, said interpreter will reject the reality of such events. So the two topics, qualifications and presuppositions, go hand in hand. In this chapter we will discuss qualifications first and then will consider presuppositions. Then, building on that foundation, we will consider the role of preunderstanding in the interpretive process.

QUALIFICATIONS OF THE INTERPRETER

We believe that the following set of qualifications puts the interpreter in the best position to obtain valid interpretations of the biblical text.[1]

---

1 Vanhoozer lists three additional "interpretive virtues" that we will assume without explicitly stressing them: honesty (acknowledging one's personal stance and commitments), openness (willingness to hear and consider others' views), and attention (having a focus on the text). See K. J. Vanhoozer, *Is There a Meaning in This Text?* (Grand Rapids: Zondervan, 1998), 376–77.

A Reasoned Faith

All understanding requires a framework or context within which to interpret. Thus, to understand a lecture about the properties of antiquarks, one must have at least some knowledge of theoretical physics. The more knowledge the listener has about theoretical physics, the more understanding he or she will gain from the lecture. Returning to the art world, the more one understands the effects and uses of lighting, perspective, textures, the other works of a period or school of painting, etc., the more "qualified" that person will be to appraise a painting. Likewise, if the Bible is God's revelation to his people, then *the essential qualification for a full understanding of this book is to know the revealing God.* To know God we must have a relationship with him. The Bible uses the term "faith" to describe the essential element in this relationship: "And without faith it is impossible to please God, because anyone who comes to him must believe that he exists and that he rewards those who earnestly seek him" (Heb 11:6). Only the one who believes and trusts in God can truly understand what God has spoken in his Word. This makes sense, for how can one understand a text from the Bible that purports to be a word from God if one denies that there is a God or that the Bible is from God? How can one really understand someone with whom she is only vaguely familiar or whom he or she does not trust?

Paul makes clear in 1 Cor 2:14 that the ability to apprehend God's truth in its fullest sense belongs only to the "spiritual person." This is true because the substance is "spiritual" in nature—i.e., it concerns God who is spirit—and so requires a reader who can more fully tune in to that dimension. So while excellence in methodology is a necessary qualification, we allege that excellence alone does not suffice for understanding the Bible. Such understanding comes only through possessing the spiritual sensitivity that God gives to those who have faith in him, to those who believe. Thus, faith is foundational for a full comprehension of the Scriptures. It is not the only qualification, nor does it guarantee correct interpretation, but it is the foundation for correct interpretation.

Do not misunderstand. We do not arrogantly assert that one who does not believe cannot understand the Bible. Unbelievers, even skeptics, can grasp much of its meaning. They may discover what it asserts or claims even when their own beliefs or value systems lead them to deny those claims. Thus, a competent, unbelieving scholar may produce an outstanding technical commentary on a biblical book—perhaps even better written than many believing Christian scholars could write. But that unbelieving scholar cannot understand and portray the true *significance*[2] of the Bible's message, for he or she is not ultimately committed to the Bible as divine revelation. So we do not assert that a believing interpreter will always be right in an interpretation or that an unbelieving interpreter will necessarily be wrong. Indeed, as we have noted, a liberal

---

2 The difference between the findings of unbelieving versus believing scholars is often one of volition, not cognition. Through their careful work, both may come to the same understanding of a text's *meaning.* But due to their different faith commitments, only the believer will perceive the text's true *significance* and be willing to obey the truth conveyed. We take this perspective partly from our understanding of 1 Cor 2:14, on which see C. L. Blomberg, *1 Corinthians,* NIVAC (Grand Rapids: Zondervan, 1995), ad loc. We discuss the distinction between meaning and significance later. In addition, one's faith commitment opens a believer's mind to listen more carefully under the guidance of the Holy Spirit. See the next point.

scholar might produce a finer and more accurate exegesis of a given text than his or her conservative counterpart. Equally, the believer must defend his or her specific interpretation and demonstrate its validity. We simply argue that even when scholars apply the same methodology, their differing presuppositions will open the way to potentially different results. If a scholar says, "The Gospel account states that the man was possessed by a demon, though we now know demons don't exist and there is a psychological explanation for his behavior," the scholar is permitting modern values or philosophical positivism to lead to a rejection of a teaching of the Bible. On the other hand, those who accept the Bible as God's revelation expect it to provide true information, and they would not utter such a statement. They may puzzle over what the Bible teaches; they may disobey its instructions; but they are bound to acknowledge it as the true Word of God.

Since an unbelieving scholar does not accept the Bible as God's revealed truth, he or she may feel justified in arriving at conclusions critical of Scripture, may reject depictions of miracles as fables or myth, and may account for "God-language" as a prescientific way of explaining the unexplainable. But if through a study of the Scripture this unbelieving scholar should become convinced of its truthfulness, he or she would need to become a believer: one who confesses Christ as Lord and submits to the truth of God's Word. Only when a person comes to that position can he or she understand the Bible's message as "God's personal word to *me*."

If interpreters choose to work within the Bible's own framework (e.g., the existence of an all-powerful, all-knowing God; the reality of the supernatural; and the fact that God speaks in the Bible), the results will be of one kind. Interpretations will correspond to the affirmations the biblical writers themselves make. Such interpreters will engage in detailed and scholarly research on all kinds of issues. Religious language (e.g., God, angels, demons, faith, kingdom of God) will be appropriate and valid. However, if an interpreter operates within a modern, secular, naturalistic viewpoint, then he or she will exclude certain categories out of hand. For example, such a perspective cannot pronounce on resurrection from the dead or other "supernatural" phenomena since no one can confirm the truth of these phenomena by scientific criteria. From a postmodern point of view, a supernatural reading of the Bible may be "valid," but no more so than a psychological or existentialist one. Read it any way you want!

In other words, two scholars, a conservative and a liberal, might both research literary elements in the Gospel narratives. They might come to similar conclusions about most issues—say the background of the pericope in the life of Jesus, the editorial work of an Evangelist, et al. But how would they handle the mention of "demons"? The conservative scholar is disposed to admit the existence of such creatures, if for no other reason than that the Bible affirms their reality. The other scholar may state that ancient peoples attributed certain infirmities to demons, but today we "know" better and ascribe them to psychological causes.

Modern scientists cannot study miracles for they are beyond the orbit of scientific analysis. Biblical scholarship built solely on the foundation of rationalism and science is compelled to find naturalistic explanations for the biblical accounts of miracles. Evangelicals, on the other hand, accept the miraculous in the Bible as factual.[3]

---

3 We discuss the phenomenon of miracles in the section devoted to the Gospels in the chapter on the genres of the NT. See key literature in Blomberg, *Historical Reliability,* 73–112.

However, evangelicals cannot defend their position simply by resorting to dogmatic pronouncements. No amount of protesting can dislodge the scientists, for, according to their presuppositions, miracles do not occur.

As evangelicals, we can conduct a defense of our position. We concede the validity of rational, historically defensible arguments. We are committed to being logical. We bind ourselves to the facts of history, but we insist this does not obligate us to a non-supernatural explanation of the biblical record.[4] However, it does force us to engage in careful historical argumentation to show that the biblical accounts are defensible and historically credible, even if in the end they cannot be scientifically proven.[5] When the sources prove reliable where they can be tested, we give them the benefit of the doubt where they cannot be, even apart from presupposing inerrancy. We insist that to hold evangelical presuppositions is neither to commit intellectual suicide nor to relegate ourselves to a hopelessly obscurantist dogmatism. The evangelical faith is committed to a defensible, historically credible explanation of the Bible—within the bounds of the Bible's own claims about itself and its origins. Rather than reject logic and reason, the evangelical study of the Bible welcomes any method or approach that enables the Bible's meaning and significance to be understood.

Obedience

A second requirement, following close upon the requirement of faith, is the *willingness to put oneself "under" the text, to submit one's will to hear the text in the way its author intended.* Hermeneutics cannot be limited to the grammatical-historical techniques that help the interpreter understand the original meaning of the text. More precisely, the work of technical scholars may become so caught up in a world of academic inquiry that the significant issues the original biblical authors were trying to communicate become lost or are determined irrelevant. N. Lash states the point forcefully, "If the questions to which ancient authors sought to respond in terms available to them within their cultural horizons are to be 'heard' today with something like their original force and urgency, they have first to be 'heard' as questions that challenge us with comparable seriousness."[6]

---

4 As an example, see the massive weight of the historical evidence for Jesus' miracles in the Gospels defended by J. P. Meier, *A Marginal Jew: Rethinking the Historical Jesus,* vol. 2 (New York et al.: Doubleday, 1994), esp. 509–644.

5 In addition to the literature cited in defense of Scripture's truthfulness cited above, see for the OT, V. P. Long, D. W. Baker, and G. J. Wenham, eds., *Windows into Old Testament History: Evidence, Argument, and the Crisis of "Biblical Israel"* (Grand Rapids: Eerdmans, 2002); W. G. Dever, *What Did the Biblical Writers Know and When Did They Know It? What Archaeology Can Tell Us about the Reality of Ancient Israel* (Grand Rapids: Eerdmans, 2001); and W. C. Kaiser, *Are the Old Testament Documents Reliable and Relevant?* (Downers Grove, IL: InterVarsity, 2001). For a helpful introduction to the role of the historical method in NT studies see D. A. Hagner, "The New Testament, History, and the Historical-Critical Method," in *New Testament Criticism and Interpretation,* ed. D. A. Black and D. S. Dockery (Grand Rapids: Zondervan, 1991), 73–96. Hagner concludes his essay with several valuable modifications of the historical-critical method that will counter its unwarranted negative conclusions (89–91). On the historical veracity for the Gospels, see also I. H. Marshall, *I Believe in the Historical Jesus* (Grand Rapids: Eerdmans, 1977); and id., *Luke: Historian and Theologian,* 3d ed. (Downers Grove, IL: InterVarsity, 1998) on Luke more specifically.

6 N. Lash, "What Might Martyrdom Mean?" *Ex Auditu* 1 (1985): 17.

This means that true interpretation of the Bible can never be merely an exercise in ancient history. We cannot genuinely understand what a text meant without it affecting our lives. Interpretation involves a crucial dialectic between the historical origin of a text and the perspective of the modern reader or interpreter. To focus only on the former consigns the Bible to the status of an ancient and irrelevant artifact. Yet to abandon the historical reference and seek only for some felicitous significance for today is equally misguided. Scripture loses all normativeness if all "readings" of its text can claim equal validity. Genuine interpretation requires a fusing of the ancient and modern horizons where the meaning of the ancient text helps interpreters come to new understandings of themselves.[7] As Lash properly insists, "the articulation of what the text might 'mean' today, is a necessary condition of hearing what that text 'originally meant.'"[8] Though Lash does not take the point this far, we insist that full understanding comes only to the sincere follower of the God who revealed—the follower who diligently seeks to practice the message of the text studied.[9]

Illumination

For his part, God provides the resource for such obedient understanding of his truth: the illumination of the Holy Spirit. A corollary of the requirement of faith is the *regeneration of the Holy Spirit.* That is, once people have committed their lives in faith to Jesus as Lord, the Bible speaks of a work that God performs in them. This internal operation enables believers to perceive and take hold of spiritual truth, an ability unavailable to unbelievers (cf. 1 Cor 2:6–16; 2 Cor 3:15–18). This illuminating work of the Spirit does not circumvent nor allow us to dispense with the principles of hermeneutics and the techniques of exegesis. That is, the Spirit does not alter the meaning of the text or reveal secret meanings. Illumination means that a dynamic comprehension of the *significance* of Scripture and its *application to life* belongs uniquely to those indwelt by the Holy Spirit. Though scholars possess an arsenal of methods and techniques with which to decipher the meaning of the biblical texts, interpretation falls short of its true potential without the illumination of the Spirit. Neither methodology nor the Spirit operates in isolation from the other. Neither is sufficient in itself. For though we admit it is possible that the Spirit may supernaturally grant to a reader the true meaning of a text independent of any study, we posit that the Spirit rarely, if ever, operates in this manner. On the other hand, methods alone are not sufficient to understand profoundly and exactly the true meaning and significance of Scripture. Then how are methodology and illumination interwoven?

First, consider whether one can depend simply upon the Holy Spirit for understanding the Bible apart from methods and techniques. Origen (ca. A.D. 200) might have been the earliest defender of this practice, but if so, he was certainly only the first in a long line

---

7 We borrow the image of the fusing of horizons from A. C. Thiselton, *The Two Horizons* (Grand Rapids: Eerdmans, 1980), who in turn builds on H. G. Gadamer whose work Thiselton thoroughly analyzes.

8 Lash, "Martyrdom," 18.

9 The writer of Psa 119:97–104 exemplifies the perspective of the obedient believer. The psalmist desires that God's commands be "ever with me." Speaking to God, his practice remains to "meditate on your statutes," and he seeks to "obey your precepts." "I have not departed from your laws," he says to his God.

that continues to this day. The reasoning often goes like this: if the Holy Spirit inspired the original writers, then certainly he can impart his meaning without recourse to such means as historical or grammatical study. C. H. Spurgeon (1834–92), England's best-known preacher for most of the second half of the nineteenth century, countered such pretension with some advice to budding preachers in "A Chat about Commentaries":

> Of course, you are not such wiseacres as to think of ways that you can expound Scripture without assistance from the works of divines and learned men who have labored before you in the field of exposition. If you are of that opinion, pray remain so, for you are not worth the trouble of conversion, and like a little coterie who think with you, would resent the attempt as an insult to your infallibility. It seems odd, that certain men who talk so much of what the Holy Spirit reveals to themselves, should think so little of what he has revealed to others.[10]

In the pulpit today this error may sound like this:

> Dear friends, I have consulted no other books, human sources, or worldly wisdom. I have considered no commentaries. I have gone right to the Bible—and only the Bible—to see what it had to say for itself. Let me share with you what God showed me.

As B. Ramm, who invented a similar quote, observes, "This sounds very spiritual," but in fact "it is a veiled egotism" and a "confusion of the inspiration of the Spirit with the illumination of the Spirit."[11] The Spirit's work of illumination does not grant new revelation.[12]

Unfortunately, some deeply spiritual people have declared some obviously incorrect interpretations of the Bible. Being indwelt by the Spirit does not guarantee accurate interpretation. Though we have no desire to diminish the creative work of the Spirit, the Spirit does not work apart from hermeneutics and exegesis. Rather, he provides the sincere believer that indispensable comprehension of the text (that "Aha!") by working within and through methods and techniques.[13] An encounter occurs between the Spirit of the Word and the human spirit. Swartley says,

---

10 C. H. Spurgeon, *Commenting and Commentaries* (Grand Rapids: Baker, repr. 1981, orig. 1876), v. Of course, in his day virtually all scholars and preachers were "men."

11 B. Ramm, *Protestant Biblical Interpretation*, 3d ed. (Grand Rapids: Baker, 1970), 17–18.

12 One of the striking features of most heresies or cults is their use of Jesus' words recorded in Jn 14–16, esp. 14:26, 15:26, and 16:5–16. In fact, Jesus does not promise that the Holy Spirit will provide new truth or revelation to all succeeding Christians throughout the Church Age. Rather he refers to the inspiration of the Spirit in providing the NT canon of Scripture through the apostles. The Spirit's role in relationship to believers today is not to reveal new truth; he did that in producing the NT. His role now is to speak through Scripture to enable believers to apprehend and apply its truth. On these Johannine texts see D. A. Carson, *The Gospel According to John*, PNTC (Grand Rapids: Eerdmans, 1991), ad loc.

13 We do not wish to deny that God works in the lives of unbelievers, even through the Scriptures. We merely stress the Holy Spirit's illumination in the lives of believers in keeping with 1 Cor 2:14–16.

> In the co-creative moment, text and interpreter experience life by the power of the divine Spirit. Without this experience, interpretation falls short of its ultimate potential and purpose.[14]

Certainly, we cannot "program" this creative encounter; it requires a stance of faith and humility before the Lord of the universe who has revealed his truth on the pages of Scripture. Yet in seeking to hear his voice, the interpreter becomes open to true understanding—to allow the text to fulfill God's purposes for it. *Prayer puts one in the position to hear and understand.* For the Christian, prayer is an indispensable ingredient for the proper understanding of Scripture. We must ask God to assist our study and to speak to us through it so that we might understand his truth and will for our lives. We do not substitute prayer for diligent exegetical work. We pray that we will do our work well, that we will be sensitive to the Spirit's direction, and that we will be obedient to the truth of what we discover. We openly admit our bent to sin, error, and self-deception, and our finitude; we ask for an openness to receive what God has revealed and a willingness to learn from others throughout the history of interpretation.

Membership in the Church

As Bible interpreters we must be wary of the trap of individualism. *We need to recognize our membership in the Body of Christ, the Church.* First, the Church (and we mean local as well as universal) is the arena in which many of the significant requirements for truly hearing the text can be nurtured. We do not work in a vacuum; we are not the first ones to puzzle over the meaning of the Bible. We require the enrichment, endeavors, and assistance of our fellow believers to check our perceptions and to affirm their validity. Likewise, our conclusions, if they are correct, have importance for others. The Church throughout the ages, constituted by the Spirit, provides accountability; it offers the arena in which we can formulate our interpretation. Such accountability guards against maverick and individualistic interpretations.[15] It provides a check against selfish and self-serving conclusions by those who lack the perspective to see beyond their own circumstances. And since the Church of Jesus Christ is a worldwide fellowship, it crosses all cultural boundaries and parochial interests—a reality we deny if we limit our interpretations and formulations of God's truth to personal (or parochial) attempts to understand Scripture. If we discover the meaning of God's revelation, it will make sense or ring true to others in Christ's worldwide Body when they openly assess the evidence we used to reach our conclusions.

Appropriate Methods

The final qualification has been assumed, but we wish to make it explicit: *we need methods that are appropriate to the task of interpretation.* This task requires diligence and commitment, hard work and discipline. It requires the pursuit of excellence and learning in all dimensions (language, history, culture, theology) that relate to the study of the Scriptures.

---

14 W. Swartley, *Slavery, Sabbath, War, and Women* (Scottdale, PA: Herald Press, 1983), 224.

15 For a provocative appeal to situate interpretation in the community, see S. Hauerwas, *Unleashing the Scripture: Freeing the Bible from Captivity to America* (Nashville: Abingdon, 1993).

If the best interpretation involves a merging of the horizons of the ancient text and those of the modern interpreter, then interpreters must be aware of their own worlds as well as those of the texts—the worlds of the Ancient Near East or the Roman Empire of the first century A.D., as well as the modern world of the twenty-first century. There is no substitute for diligent study and the use of available tools. The interpreter must cultivate a sensitivity to hear and learn from all the data available. This requires study and practice.

Interpreters cannot settle issues that concern factual matters by an appeal to prayer or the illumination of the Holy Spirit. One cannot know through prayer that Baal was a fertility god worshipped by the Canaanites or that the Jews of Jesus' day regarded Samaritans as hated half-breeds. One cannot determine the identity of the "sons of God" in Gen 6:1–4 or the "spirits in prison" in 1 Pet 3:18–22 simply by reading and rereading these texts in a prayerful and humble way. One must study history and culture to discover the nature of the "high place" at Bethel (2 Kgs 23:15) and the "head coverings" in first-century Corinth (1 Cor 11:2–16). Today the Bible interpreter is privileged to have numerous, excellent tools that provide facts and information about the ancient world and the biblical texts. Capable interpreters become acquainted with such research tools and use them to the best of their ability. If the first goal of interpretation is to determine the meaning the text had for its original author and recipients, then the diligent interpreter must be committed to using historical sources.

As well, since the Bible comes to us as literature—and in a variety of literary genres—those who would understand its message must become competent readers of literature. We must apply methods that will unpack for us what each level of the text and each kind of genre requires for understanding—whether historical narrative, epic, parable, prophetic denunciation, epistle, or apocalypse. On the lowest levels of language we must understand lexicography and syntax and then proceed to the levels of paragraph, discourse, genres, literary analysis, book, and finally to an understanding of the entire canon.

Does this mean that without a competence in biblical languages and a mastery of all the critical historical and linguistic tools no one can understand God's message in the Bible? No, for certainly no one can attain total proficiency, and even were it obtainable, it would not guarantee correct interpretation. Without doubt, a simple, sincere, and uneducated believer can comprehend the central truths of the Bible. The diligent Christian with even an average education who is willing to study, and who has access to the fine tools now available, can arrive at the central meaning of virtually every passage in the Bible. The believer who can acquire expertise in the biblical languages in addition to further training in biblical studies, history, culture, and theology, will become that much more qualified to explain the meaning of most verses and even many of the more obscure or controversial texts. Finally, the scholars who have advanced training and specialized skills are able to perform closely reasoned and technical studies, write commentaries, engage in textual criticism to determine the original texts, translate and evaluate ancient literature that sheds light on the Bible, and produce modern versions of the Bible.

PRESUPPOSITIONS FOR CORRECT INTERPRETATION

The computer industry has popularized a basic truth, immortalized in the acronym, GIGO—"garbage in, garbage out." That is, what you get out directly depends on what you put in.[16] This principle is especially true in interpretation. The aims and presuppositions of interpreters govern and even determine their interpretations. When cartoon character Charlie Brown expects to find the shapes of ducks and sheep in the clouds overhead, he finds them! Like Charlie Brown, many interpreters find in a text precisely the meaning, and *only* the meaning, they expected (and wanted!) to find—as anyone who has read or listened to debates over biblical scholarship will attest.

No one interprets anything without a set of underlying assumptions. When we presume to explain the meaning of the Bible, we do so with a set of preconceived ideas or presuppositions. These presuppositions may be examined and stated, or simply embraced unconsciously. But anyone who says that he or she has discarded all presuppositions and will only study the text objectively and inductively is either deceived or naïve. Therefore, as interpreters we must discover, state, and consciously adopt those assumptions we agree with and can defend, or else we will uncritically retain those we already have, whether or not they are adequate and valid.[17]

Indeed, interpretation depends not only upon the methods and qualifications of interpreters but also upon their presuppositions. Thus, the development of an approach to hermeneutics involves two components: (1) an essential set of presuppositions that constitutes its starting point and (2) a deliberate strategy involving methods and procedures that will determine viable interpretations and assess competing alternatives. Such a strategy will also require some means of verifying that the preferred interpretation is superior to the alternatives.

That is why we present here the assumptions or presuppositions that we believe are necessary for an accurate interpretation of the Bible. Not all interpreters or readers will align themselves with this position, though we hope that many do (and that others will be persuaded to).

Presuppositions about the Nature of the Bible

Inspired Revelation

The view of the nature of the Bible that an interpreter holds will determine what "meaning" that interpreter will find in it. If the Bible owes its origin to a divine all-powerful being who has revealed his message via human writers, then the objective of interpretation will be to understand the meaning communicated through the divinely inspired document. If the interpreter adopts an alternative explanation of the Bible's origin, then he or she will prescribe other goals in interpreting the text.[18] We adopt the

---

16 Paul comprehended that principle well in expressing his counsel to the Philippians: "whatever is true, whatever is noble, whatever is right . . . —think about such things" (Phil 4:8).

17 This has some parallels to what D. A. Carson calls "distantiation," the need to stand back from the text to study it critically (in *Exegetical Fallacies*, 2d. ed. [Grand Rapids: Baker, 1996], 23–24). The failure to undertake this step often leads to *eisegesis*—the "reading into" a text the meaning the interpreter prefers.

18 If the Bible records the religiously inspired thinking of pious Jews and Christians but is not divine revelation itself, then interpreters may feel free to handle it precisely and only as they do other ancient religious books. Such interpreters may seek to explain on the basis of sociological or anthropological models (among others) how the Jewish or Christian religious communities came into existence and how they formulated myths such as the crossing of the Red Sea (Sea of Reeds) or Jesus' resurrection to explain their religious experiences and longings.

presupposition that *the Bible is a supernatural book, God's written revelation to his people given through prepared and selected spokespersons by the process of inspiration.* This has been the Church's universal creed throughout its history.[19]

Our defense of this view derives from the Bible's view of itself. The NT describes the OT as "inspired," using a term literally meaning "God-breathed" (2 Tim 3:16), an allusion to Gen 2. It further affirms that the Holy Spirit carried along the writers as they spoke the words of God (2 Pet 1:20–21). The OT language affirms divine inspiration with quotations like, "The Lord says, . . ." (e.g., Gen 6:7; 26:2; Exod 6:2; 12:43; 1 Sam 9:17; 1 Kgs 9:3; Zech 4:6), indicating that the speakers believed they were uttering God's message, not simply their own. When the NT writers quote the OT, they demonstrate their belief that the OT derives from God himself (e.g., 2 Cor 6:16/Lev. 26:12; Mt 19:5/Gen 2:24; Acts 4:25/Psa 2:1; Rom 9:17/Exod 9:16).

In addition, various NT writers' views of other portions of the NT disclose their verdicts about the nature of the Bible. Peter clearly views Paul's writings or letters in the same category as the "other Scriptures" (2 Pet 3:16). After employing the introductory formula, "for the Scripture says," Paul proceeds to quote from both Deuteronomy and (possibly) Luke (1 Tim 5:18/Deut 25:4; Lk 10:7).[20] In places Paul seems to express the recognition that the apostles' teaching parallels that of the OT writers (1 Cor 2:13). John identifies his words with the "true words of God" (Rev 19:9).[21]

Of course, we do not argue that because the Bible claims to be God's Word the question of its claims is settled. That would simply beg the question. Christians do not accept the Qur'an's view of itself, or that of the Book of Mormon. Though someone claims to be a fish, he or she remains a human. We cannot conduct the necessary apologetic defense of the Scriptures here but we do argue that the general reliability of those historical portions of Scripture that can be verified lends credence to the Bible's overall truthfulness. Further, Jesus accepted the authority of the OT (Jn 10:35), and we are inclined to follow his lead.[22]

---

19 For a classic defense of this statement, see J. D. Woodbridge, *Biblical Authority* (Grand Rapids: Zondervan, 1982). Key volumes students may want to consult on this evangelical view of the Bible include: M. J. Erickson, *Christian Theology*, 2d. ed. (Grand Rapids: Baker, 1998), esp. 196–259; D. S. Dockery, *Christian Scripture: An Evangelical Perspective on Inspiration, Authority and Interpretation* (Nashville: Broadman & Holman, 1995); P. E. Satterwaite and D. F. Wright, eds. *A Pathway into the Holy Scripture* (Grand Rapids: Eerdmans, 1994); C. F. H. Henry, "The Authority of the Bible," in *The Origin of the Bible*, ed. P. W. Comfort (Wheaton: Tyndale House, 1992), 13–27; A. E. McGrath and D. Wenham, "Evangelicalism and Biblical Authority," in *Evangelical Anglicans: Their Role and Influence in the Church Today*, ed. R.T. France and A. E. McGrath (London: SPCK, 1993); and C. F. H. Henry, *God, Revelation, and Authority*, 6 vols. (Waco: Word, 1976–83).

20 Admittedly, Paul's quotation of the words that appear in Luke may derive from a collection of Jesus' sayings, rather than a written version of Luke's Gospel itself.

21 For a thorough treatment of how biblical writers viewed their writings as Scripture, see W. A. Grudem, "Scripture's Self-Attestation and the Modern Problem of Formulating a Doctrine of Scripture," in *Scripture and Truth*, ed. D. A. Carson and J. D. Woodbridge (Grand Rapids: Zondervan, 1983), 19–59.

22 On these two points in defense of Scripture's truthfulness see, first, C. Armerding, *The Old Testament and Criticism* (Grand Rapids: Eerdmans, 1983); K. A. Kitchen, *Ancient Orient and the Old Testament* (Chicago: InterVarsity, 1966); E. M. Yamauchi, *The Stones and the Scriptures* (Grand Rapids: Baker, 1981); C. L. Blomberg, *Historical Reliability of the Gospels* (Downers Grove: InterVarsity, 1987); id., *Historical Reliability of John's Gospel* (Downers Grove: InterVarsity, 2002); C. J. Hemer and C. H. Gempf, ed., *The Book of Acts in the Setting of Hellenistic History* (Winona Lake, IN: Eisenbrauns, repr. 1990); and, second, J. Wenham, *Christ and the Bible*, 2d ed. (Grand Rapids: Baker, 1994).

We accept, then, that the Bible is God's Word in written form—that it records God's self-disclosure, as well as his people's varied responses to his person and his acts in history. Also the Bible is a human book. Certainly human writers composed the Scriptures in the midst of their own cultures and circumstances, writing out of their own experiences and with their own motives for their readers. Yet, somehow, God superintended their writing so that what they wrote comprised his message precisely. The Bible is God's Word, and the Holy Spirit speaks through it. As S. Grenz and J. Franke rightly underscore, "We acknowledge the Bible as scripture in that the sovereign Spirit has bound authoritative, divine speaking to this text. We believe that the Spirit has chosen, now chooses, and will continue to choose to speak with authority through the biblical texts."[23]

Authoritative and True

It follows from the first presupposition that *the Bible is authoritative and true.* Being divine revelation through which God speaks, the Bible possesses ultimate authority. For this reason, it must constitute the standard for all human belief and behavior. It speaks truthfully about who we are and how we are to live, so rejecting the message of the Bible means rejecting the will of God.

What God says must be true, for God cannot lie nor will he mislead.[24] Some conservative scholars have maintained that inspiration implies inerrancy—that what God authored of necessity must contain no errors.[25] Others emphasize the Bible's "infallibility," its Spirit-driven ability to achieve God's purposes, and allow that a greater amount of imprecision is present in the Bible.[26] Some prefer to defend a more "limited inerrancy" in which the biblical authors did not err in what they intended to teach theologically, but may have erred in other incidental (to their purposes) issues.[27] These and others may locate the authority of the Bible in what it accomplishes in readers rather than in the biblical text itself.[28] The so-called neo-orthodox theologians argue that the Bible only becomes the Word of God as believers faithfully read, preach, and apprehend its

---

23 S. J. Grenz and J. R. Franke, *Beyond Foundationalism. Shaping Theology in a Postmodern Context* (Louisville: Westminster John Knox, 2001), 65.

24 The author of Num 23:19 distinguishes between God and humans in their ability to lie: God does not. See also 1 Sam 15:29; Tit 1:2; and Heb 6:18. James 1:13 asserts that God never tempts people to do evil. Rather, God does only what is good. Assuming, then, that the entire Bible is God's revelation, this revelation cannot mislead, nor can it present what is untrue. R. Nicole provides a helpful appraisal of how both Testaments present the nature of truth as factuality, faithfulness, and completeness: "The Biblical Concept of Truth," in *Scripture and Truth,* ed. Carson and Woodbridge (Grand Rapids: Zondervan, 1983), 287–298.

25 The classic exposition is B. B. Warfield, *Revelation and Inspiration* (Oxford: Oxford University Press, 1927). Another example of this position is C. F. H. Henry, *God, Revelation, and Authority,* 6 vols. (Waco: Word, 1976–79). More recently see M. J. Erickson, *Christian Theology,* esp. 196–259.

26 See, e.g., I. H. Marshall, *Biblical Inspiration* (Grand Rapids: Eerdmans, 1982), 66.

27 J. B. Rogers and D. K. McKim, *The Authority and Interpretation of the Bible* (New York: Harper, 1979).

28 Vanhoozer denies that "all parts of Scripture need be factually true" (*Is There a Meaning?* 425). He prefers to speak of the Bible's efficacy: "the power to produce results" (427). Grenz and Franke take a similar position: "It is not the Bible as a book that is authoritative, but the Bible as the instrumentality of the Spirit; the biblical message spoken by the Spirit through the text is theology's norming norm" (*Beyond Foundationalism,* 69).

message.[29] These various views may be combined in different fashions especially as the genres of Scriptures vary. John Goldingay, for example, argues that Scripture as "witnessing tradition" best fits narrative material, that Law and instruction form an "authoritative canon," that an "inspired word" best applies to prophecy, and that wisdom and poetry can be characterized as "experienced revelation."[30] Finally, scholars that are more liberal affirm that the Bible is great, inspired religious literature in the same sense that the world's great literature is inspired. Hence, they accord it no divine status or privileged claim to truth and study it alongside other ancient (religious) documents.[31] For some of them the Bible has at best only limited authority (perhaps no more than other classic documents or writings).

For us, the Bible is a trustworthy communication by Spirit-guided interpreters and is true in all it intends to teach. Its statements convey what is factual given its literary conventions; its record is faithful and reliable. This includes all its individual parts as well as its overall message. This is not the place for an exhaustive defense of the Bible's truthfulness, but several NT texts, in our estimation, assume this conclusion (e.g., Mt 5:18; Jn 10:35; 17:17; Tit 1:2). The psalmist likewise affirms that God's commands are utterly perfect (119:96). We believe that this represents the position of the Church throughout its history.[32] We also believe this presupposition alone does justice to the Bible's character and its claims of truthfulness.

We realize that while only a minority of scholars today hold this presupposition, it is customary for thoughtful, believing Christians worldwide (and not only fundamentalists) and throughout church history. How do we handle apparent contradictions or errors? Following our supposition of truth, we are bound to look for viable solutions or admit that with the present state of our knowledge we cannot find a solution. This does not mean that no solution exists; it simply means that we do not know how to solve the problem at this time. When responsible exegesis can suggest a possible solution, we claim some vindication, even if we cannot be confident that our solution is certain. It means that the charge of "error" is not mandated. And when every possible solution seems contrived or tendentious, we consciously adopt a more "agnostic" stance toward the problem: we frankly admit that at present we do not know the best way to solve the problem. In fact, in the vast majority of cases, plausible solutions to alleged problems or contradictions *do* exist so that our withholding judgment in certain instances is not simply special pleading.[33] This is no more presumptuous than assuming a modern, scholarly, critical omniscience about such questions.[34] Our presupposition of truthfulness disposes us to reject the

---

29 K. Barth remains the prime example: *Church Dogmatics* (Edinburgh: T. & T. Clark, 1936, 1956), I/1, 98–140; I/2, 457–537. For a helpful appraisal of how Barth puts his treatment of Holy Scripture within his larger treatment of the Word of God see G. W. Bromiley, *An Introduction to the Theology of Karl Barth* (Grand Rapids: Eerdmans, 1974), 3–53; esp. 34–44.

30 J. Goldingay, *Models for Scripture* (Grand Rapids: Eerdmans, 1994).

31 See J. Barr, *Holy Scripture: Canon, Authority, Criticism* (Philadelphia: Westminster, 1983).

32 L. Morris, *I Believe in Revelation* (Grand Rapids: Eerdmans, 1976), defends the inherent authority of the Bible, though Rogers and McKim, *Authority and Interpretation*, dispute the claim that the church always affirmed inerrancy.

33 To see how often this is the case in the Gospels, see Blomberg, *Historical Reliability.*

34 D. R. Hall, *The Seven Pillories of Wisdom* (Macon, GA: Mercer University Press, 1990), provides an excellent and witty exposure of how much faulty reasoning occurs in the guise of scholarship.

position that the Bible errs and to assume, rather, in such instances that the data, our knowledge, or our theory to explain the evidence remains deficient.

A Spiritual Document

A second conclusion follows from the view that God has revealed his message in the Bible: *the Bible manifests unparalleled spiritual worth and a capacity to change lives.* The Bible has the unique power to affect the reader spiritually. Scripture results from the living word of the living and all-powerful God, a word that has inherent power (see particularly Isa 55 and Heb 4:12–13). This makes the Bible a unique book in human history—useful in ways unlike any other book. Various individuals (the average Christian reader, theologian, professor, preacher, Sunday school teacher) use the Bible in different ways and for different purposes (devotion/nurture, corporate worship, preaching, teaching, ethical guidance). As we will see, such Christian interpreters share many hermeneutical principles and methods in common with those who expound other kinds of literature. But we acknowledge this added spiritual dimension for the Bible and seek to take it into account in interpreting (rather than deny its presence as do many critical scholars).

By terming the Bible "spiritual," we affirm the role of the Holy Spirit who applies its message to readers. With the Spirit's aid we explore the Scriptures and find life-giving and life-changing meaning. As we respond in faithful obedience, we grow in maturity; we worship and praise the God of the Bible. The Spirit-energized reading of the Scriptures gives direction to our thoughts and guidance to our lives. They have an animating and uplifting effect as the Spirit of God uses their truth in the lives of the faithful. To treat the Bible in any other way (merely like an inspiring book) robs it of its central purpose as God's revelation to his creatures.

Characterized by both Unity and Diversity

We also affirm that the Bible is a unit, yet it is diverse.[35] Throughout most of the history of the church, Christians assumed the unity of Scripture and downplayed its diversity. Readers harmonized apparent contradictions or tensions within the Bible, or resorted to typology, allegory, or the principle of the *regula fidei* ("the rule of faith") to interpret difficult texts in the light of clearer ones. Since the Enlightenment, however, many scholars regularly deny the unity of the Bible, and, especially in the last two centuries, many interpreters claim there are irreconcilable conflicts among the authors of Scripture that preclude any claims to unity. Today only evangelicals and advocates of canonical criticism defend a unity in Scripture. First, what can we say about the Bible's unity?

As for the OT, various proposals have emerged for a unifying center. Some defend the prevalence of a single theme, for example, covenant, promise, the mighty acts of God, communion, the life of God's people, dominion, justice, or righteousness. Others find pairs of themes, for example, law and promise, election and obligation, creation and covenant, the rule of God and communion with humankind, or salvation and

---

35 On many of these points see C. L. Blomberg, "Unity and Diversity of Scripture" in *New Dictionary of Biblical Theology*, ed. T. D. Alexander, and Brian S. Rosner (Downers Grove: InterVarsity, 2000), 64–72. What follows draws upon this analysis.

blessing. Other suggestions involve polarities, such as the presence versus the absence of God, or the legitimation of structure versus the embracing of pain. Some writers point simply to Yahweh, or God, as the sole unifying element within the older Testament.[36]

On the NT side, some suggest single themes as a center for the NT: kingdom, gospel, righteousness, justification, reconciliation, faith, new creation, salvation or salvation history, eschatology, Israel or the new Israel, the cross and/or the resurrection, the love of God, existential anthropology, covenant, and, most common of all, Jesus (or Christology more generally). Others suggest various combinations of themes, often some kerygmatic summary of essential Christian doctrine.[37]

Assessing the unity of the entire Bible, the most common suggestions are promise–fulfillment, type–antitype, salvation history, a relationship with the living God, intertextuality, and Christology. Some aver narrower themes such as monotheism, God's covenant faithfulness, God's reign, righteousness, the covenants, election, grace and the response of obedience, the people of God, Exodus and new Exodus, creation and new creation, or sin and salvation. We also encounter multiplex solutions, for example, the existence of God, God as creator of a good world, the fall of humanity, and the fact of election. P. Stuhlmacher offers the following narrative summary of the story of both Testaments:

> The one God who created the world and chose Israel to be his own people has through the sending, the work, and the death and resurrection of his only Son, Jesus Christ, sufficiently provided once and for all the salvation of Jews and Gentiles. Jesus Christ is the hope of all creation. Whoever believes in him as Reconciler and Lord and obeys his instruction may be certain of their participation in the kingdom of God.[38]

This last suggestion, treating the Bible as *narrative*, suggests a useful model for seeing the unfolding unity and diversity within Scripture. We may summarize the plot line of the story, recognizing that various literary genres of Scripture occur within this larger "historical" framework. Despite their diversity, the books within Scripture present a rather coherent chronological sequence, each building upon what precedes in an apparently conscious and straightforward fashion. The four major periods in the Bible's overall narrative portray the creation, the fall, redemption, and the consummation of all God's purposes. In line with this, the non-narrative portions of the Bible—the Law, the Prophets, the wisdom, and the epistolary literature—depict how God's people should conduct themselves as this narrative proceeds to fulfillment.

---

36 Among the variety of relevant works, the reader might consult H. H. Rowley, *The Unity of the Bible* (Philadelphia: Westminster, 1953), who weighs recurring themes in the Bible. W. Eichrodt, *Theology of the Old Testament*, 2 vols. (Philadelphia: Westminster, 1961, 1967), champions the promise/fulfillment approach. A leading proponent of a typological approach is G. von Rad, *Old Testament Theology*, 2 vols. (New York: Harper, 1965), esp. 2: 319–35. Certainly, the canon itself makes a fundamental statement of God's intention. See our discussion of canon criticism in chapter 4. For an ambitious and compelling proposal, see E. A. Martens, *God's Design: A Focus on Old Testament Theology*, 3d ed. (N. Richland Hills: D & F Scott, 1998).

37 For example, see A. M. Hunter, *Introducing New Testament Theology* (London: SCM, 1957), 66.

38 *How to Do Biblical Theology* (Allison Park: Pickwick, 1995), 63.

On the other hand, the Bible exhibits marked diversity.[39] This takes several forms. It exists as two very different "Testaments" written in three languages, in different cultures, over a vast span of time. The Bible embodies a diverse collection of kinds of literature: legal, historical, poetic, prophetic, gospel, epistolary, and apocalyptic. Added to all this, the various authors write with distinct purposes, to different audiences, on different topics, and with varying emphases. As well, in places, different portions of Scripture so closely parallel each other that most readers postulate a literary relationship between them and assume that their differences are motivated theologically or to achieve stylistic variation. Deuteronomy consciously modernizes various laws of Exodus and Leviticus for a later time. Chronicles rehearses significant portions of the Deuteronomistic history, focusing more on life in the southern kingdom. The four Gospels clearly adopt individual perspectives on Jesus and his ministry. The letter of 2 Peter appears to revise and adapt Jude for a different situation. All of this, and more, illustrates numerous differences as one compares writings within a Testament and between Testaments, not to mention across the centuries. Now no one would question the fact of the Bible's diversity; that it would have unity is more difficult to imagine.

In conclusion, we must acknowledg—e both the Bible's unity and its diversity, and hold them in the proper balance. Often more conservative scholars emphasize the former almost to the exclusion of the latter, while scholars who are more liberal do the opposite. We suggest we must uphold both. The Bible's unity provides the authoritative foundation for Christian faith and practice; this has been the historic Christian perspective. Yet an acknowledgement of the Bible's diversity allows interpreters to appreciate each text, book, and author on its own terms, thereby differentiating what God intended to say to his people at each point in their history. Scripture's unity also helps circumscribe what is the "Christian faith," in contrast to alternatives; its diversity reminds the church that different expressions of that "faith" may have a claim to legitimacy.

An Understandable Document

We affirm that the Bible is *understandable*; it is an accessible book. It presents a clear message to anyone willing to read it, and that is why people throughout history have understood its teachings. This does not imply that it is a simple book or that anyone may grasp easily everything it contains. The doctrine of the perspicuity or clarity of the Scriptures, so stressed in the Protestant Reformation, always referred to that which was essential for right doctrine or living—not to every sentence of the Bible.[40] Its profundity exhausts the human mind, for it derives from God himself and deals with the most important and urgent issues of human existence, now and eternally. Yet, the Bible is not a puzzle or cryptogram whose solution remains hidden from all but an

---

39 See esp. J. Goldingay, "Diversity and Unity in Old Testament Theology," *VT* 34 (1984): 153–168; and J. D. G. Dunn, *Unity and Diversity in the New Testament* (London: SCM; Philadelphia: Fortress, 1977.

40 See J. P. Callahan, "*Claritas Scripturae*: The Role of Perspicuity in Protestant Hermeneutics," *JETS* 39 (1996), 353–72, and id., *The Clarity of Scripture* (Downers Grove, IL: InterVarsity, 2001).

elite group who know the code.[41] Written so that common people could apprehend its truth, the Bible's central message still speaks clearly to human hearts even after scores of intervening centuries.

Forming the Canon of Scripture

As Protestant scholars, *we accept the 66 books of the canon as the entirety of God's scriptural record to his people.* Canon has the figurative sense of "ruler," "measuring rod," and therefore refers to a norm or standard.[42] We use it here to speak of the list of authoritative books that comprise Holy Scripture. Though not a very "tidy" matter, canonicity affirms that, guided by the Spirit through various historical processes over a span of several centuries, the Church separated out and accepted certain books due to their apostolic origin or basis in Jesus' life and ministry. As well, they canonized these books because they were useful for specific purposes (e.g., preaching, catechetical training, refuting heretics, worship), or because of their consistency with the orthodox teaching of Jesus and of the apostles. Added to the completed "Old Testament" canon (established by the Church's Jewish predecessors), this process enabled the Church to fix the extent of the canon. The canon marks the boundaries of God's written revelation. The procedure of Scripture formation stands completed. In interpretation the Church does not seek new revelation that would add to the Bible, for that process ceased. Rather, the Church seeks to understand what was revealed and collected in the canon. As a hermeneutical starting point, this implies we give priority to these 66 books in interpretation and in authority; they form the literary and theological context—the "boundary," as it were—in which to interpret any given passage.

We presuppose, as well, that the science of textual criticism has given us the best approximations possible of the autographs of the original canon, given the current state of knowledge. In other words, though we do not possess the original copies of any of the books (or even parts) of the Bible, textual critics have taken us very close to what they must have said. Thus the *Biblia Hebraica Stuttgartensia* and the Nestle/Aland *Novum Testamentum Graece,* 27th edition (which is virtually identical to the United Bible Societies' *The Greek New Testament,* 4th edition) are surely very close to the original documents of the Bible. Together these volumes constitute our canon.

Presuppositions about Methodology

The qualification of a "reasoned faith" and the presuppositions about the nature of the Bible naturally lead to this next item. We want to employ any method or technique that enables us to discover the meaning of a text, regardless of who developed

---

41 This underscores the essential fallacy in such works as M. Drosin and D. Vitstum, *The Bible Code* (New York: Simon and Schuster, 1998) and others in this genre. Often certain fundamentalists treat prophetic or apocalyptic portions of the Bible as if they alone hold the keys that unlock the codes. Unwittingly, theirs is the ultimate in reader-response interpretation of which we say more below.

42 Catholics and Orthodox Christians, of course, include the Apocrypha in their canon. For additional details, see our discussion of canon and textual criticism in chapter 4 and the literature cited in the footnotes.

or perfected it.[43] In short, we believe we must be willing to use whatever methods yield accurate understanding. This goes with the qualification of intellectual honesty.

Because we believe the Bible owes its origin to the inspiration of the Holy Spirit (2 Pet 1:21), it would be illegitimate to subject it to methods that deny or reject its divine status. A literary example will illustrate. A poetic line in Psa 96:12 reads: "Then all the trees of the forest will sing for joy." Literary criticism recognizes that one cannot apply literary canons for interpreting one kind of literature (say historical narrative) to another genre (poetry). One might get an "interesting" reading by a "nonpoetic" interpretation of that line from the psalm, but it would be beyond the bounds of what the text seeks to convey. In the true sense of the word, that would not be a *literal* reading of the poem.[44] Similarly, we believe that our presuppositions about the nature of Scripture preclude avenues of study that deny its essential character. But this also obtains for historical issues.

We affirm that the Bible is a human document that we must read and study like other human documents (given the caveats above about its character as a spiritual document). A key question emerges, however: did the events the Bible records actually happen as recorded—even when they involve the supernatural? Israel remembered her past as genuine history (see Deut 26:5–9; Josh 24:2–13; Psa 78). Paul insisted that the Scriptures record Jesus' resurrection as true and factual history (1 Cor 15:3–8, 17–20). This great apostle argued for the significance of the factuality of this central Christian event in history. We assume, therefore, that the honest historian ought to be free of preconceived notions that simply deny the possibility that an all-powerful God could act in such ways in human history. Hence, we must be open to what we call miracles and supernatural explanations of biblical reports of the miraculous. This need not be circular reasoning. Rather, it constitutes an attempt to understand the Bible on its own terms.[45]

It follows that an interpreter who operates with our presuppositions about the nature of the Bible may well employ certain techniques of form or redaction criticism to discover the unique perspectives of the OT story of Joseph or of one of the Gospels. However, that same interpreter will reject the results of these same methods in the hands of other practitioners whose inherent stance presumes that a "miraculous" incident that appears in a gospel account really originated decades later in the life of the early Church. Such an *ideological* form critic may insist that miracles as recorded in the

---

43 Contra E. Linnemann, *Historical Criticism of the Bible* (Grand Rapids: Kregel, 2001); and R. L. Thomas and F. D. Farnell, ed., *The Jesus Crisis: The Inroads of Historical Criticism into Evangelical Scholarship* (Grand Rapids: Kregel, 1998).

44 Literal interpretation in this sense means understanding a text in the manner intended by the author.

45 We stressed this point above. Additionally, N. T. Wright mounts an impressive campaign to demonstrate that the NT writers' presentations are historically credible when understood in light of first-century Jewish worldviews: *The New Testament and the People of God* (Minneapolis: Augsburg Fortress, 1992; *Jesus and the Victory of God* (Minneapolis: Augsburg Fortress, 1996); and *The Resurrection of the Son of God* (Minneapolis: Augsburg Fortress, 2003). At the same time, we do not take all literature "on its own terms," as, for example, the "legends" contained in extra-biblical literature. As stated above, we presume the inspiration and authority of the biblical documents. But there is historical evidence to support making these kinds of distinctions, as we have already noted.

Gospels simply did not happen. These issues are presuppositional. So, if a method or technique is "neutral" and productive (obvious and noncontroversial examples are grammatical and lexical analyses), we do not object to using it to understand the meaning of a text.[46] However, where the use of a method adopts a basic stance or presupposition that is inconsistent with our views about Scripture, then we find *that use* of the method unacceptable or at least requiring modification. Some rational methods without a substructure of (what we deem to be) proper presuppositions will yield results antithetical to an evangelical view of Scripture. We reject any methods that we find unacceptable—including those deriving from the humanistic or naïve (often fundamentalistic) position that scientific or presuppositionless interpretation is desirable or even possible.

We embrace historical methods in our investigation of the meaning of Scripture.[47] Since faith is connected to what happened in history, we commit ourselves to know biblical history, even where it conflicts with subsequent church tradition.[48] We agree with the affirmation of 2 Pet 1:16: "We did not follow cleverly invented stories." Thus, historical and literary methods become essential to understand and explain the biblical record. We reject the kind of "faith" that simply believes what it wants to believe. Faith and history need not be at odds; they ought to and do inform each other.[49] If Jesus did not truly rise from the dead, then the Christian faith, Paul argues correctly, is groundless and fraudulent!

This means that as Christian interpreters we walk a tightrope, but we do it self-consciously and openly. No interpretation occurs apart from presuppositions. We approach the Bible with commitments, and they influence our choice of methods. We affirm the Bible's uniqueness, and we acknowledge this commitment before we begin the process of interpretation. At the same time, we drink deeply at the well of rational methods and seek to exegete each passage with integrity, accuracy, and sincerity. We want to employ whatever techniques help us understand the Bible accurately.

---

46 As examples, R. Funk and W. Bauer were extremely liberal yet their grammar and lexicon, respectively, have become standards that all scholars employ. See the bibliography at the end for details.

47 D. A. Hagner puts it well: "Because revelation comes to us in and through history, historical criticism is not an option but a necessity. 'Criticism' here means the making of informed judgments. In this sense no one who attempts to interpret or explain the Bible in any way can avoid the 'critical' method" ("The New Testament," 75). For a recent discussion of historiography from an evangelical viewpoint, see V. P. Long, *The Art of Biblical History*, Foundations of Contemporary Interpretation 5 (Grand Rapids: Zondervan, 1994).

48 The Catholic Church's historical claim that the Gospels' mention of Jesus' brothers and sisters (e.g., Mk 3:31ff. parallels; 6:3; Jn 7:3–5; cf. 1 Cor 9:5) refers to cousins not siblings derives, we argue, from its dogma concerning Mary's perpetual virginity, rather than a precise understanding of the texts' meanings. See the frank assessment of that issue from a Catholic scholar of the first rank, J. P. Meier, *A Marginal Jew. Rethinking the Historical Jesus*, vol. 1 (New York: Doubleday, 1991), 318–32. He concludes, "if . . . the historian or exegete is asked to render a judgment on the New Testament and patristic texts we have examined, viewed simply as historical sources, the most probable opinion is that the brothers and sisters of Jesus were true siblings" (331). Of course, this is not merely a Catholic problem; Protestants sometimes succumb to the same errors, e.g., the claim by some groups, based on Acts 2:38, that baptism should be performed only in the name of Jesus Christ rather than the Trinity.

49 Marshall, *Luke: Historian and Theologian,* defends this third Gospel against the charge that theology and history are mutually exclusive categories. For OT history, see the essays in Long, Baker, Wenham eds., *Windows into Old Testament History*.

Therefore, we reject a gullible naïveté that simply believes what it wants to believe. Yet rationalism is not the final word.

Presuppositions about the Ultimate Goal of Hermeneutics

As we will argue in the next chapter, we are convinced that the goal of hermeneutics is to enable interpreters to arrive at *the meaning of the text that the biblical writers or editors intended their readers to understand.* The authors and editors produced literature of various kinds. Adopting our view of the nature of the Bible, we believe that through the divine/human concurrent activity that resulted in the Bible, God has communicated with his people. Thus, all biblical texts convey meaning through both their human and divine dimensions. Yet to understand the original "historical meaning" of the text is not the sole goal of the hermeneutical process.

In our view, biblical interpretation succeeds, first, when it enables modern readers to understand the meaning of the original biblical texts—the meaning the people at the time of the texts' composition (author, editor, audience, readers) would have most likely understood—and only then seeks its significance for Christians today. In some instances the original meaning is readily apparent. Without much help a reader of the Bible can understand the narration: "One day Elisha went to Shunem. And a well-to-do woman was there, who urged him to stay for a meal. So whenever he came by, he stopped there to eat" (2 Kgs 4:8). It would fill out our understanding to know more about the prophet Elisha and where Shunem was located, but even apart from such insights the text makes clear sense. In other places we may need a detective's extraordinary skills to discern a text's meaning, as in the section that informs us that Christ "was put to death in the body but made alive by [in] the S[s]pirit, through whom also he went and preached to the spirits in prison" (1 Pet 3:18–19). In any case, we seek to understand the text. Only when we grasp the meaning in the original text, to the best of our ability, may we proceed to the second crucial component of the hermeneutical enterprise: to investigate its significance for us today.

It follows as a presupposition for us that God's design in inspiration assures that the Bible spoke not only to its original readers or to hearers, but also to us today.[50] An inspired and authoritative Bible has significance and relevance beyond its original circumstances. Further, we assume that the significance God wants it to have today grows out of the original meaning. On the basis of the solidarity of the human race and the spiritual plight we share, the ancient meanings will speak more or less directly to the human condition as they are applied appropriately today. The questions the Bible addresses concern ultimate issues, in addition to merely localized or immediate matters. As we learn God's mind, expressed by human authors long ago, we find understanding and significance for our concerns today. Any quest for other "meanings" from the Bible lacks that objectifying basis in God's revelation. The meaning found in the text alone provides this foundation. Vanhoozer terms it, "determinative textual meaning."[51]

---

50 Paul affirmed as much about the OT to his Roman readers: "For whatever was written in former days was written for our instruction, so that by steadfastness and by the encouragement of the scriptures we might have hope" (Rom 15:4 NRSV). The principle applies to the NT as well.

51 Vanhoozer, *Is There a Meaning?* 300.

PREUNDERSTANDINGS OF THE INTERPRETER

Snow falls regularly during the winter months at the seminaries where we teach. Several years ago we found it humorous when one of our newly arrived African students expressed shock at seeing snow fall from the sky during our first snowstorm in Denver that winter. Her only previous encounter with snow had been in pictures, and she assumed that snow somehow came up out of the ground like dew. Arguably, it was a logical assumption, though it turned out to be false. Similarly, we all have certain suppositions or assumptions of the world based upon our prior experience, training, and thinking, and we interpret our experiences based on these presuppositions. They may be true or false—or partly true or false—but they filter or color everything we encounter. Knowingly and unknowingly, we construct a body of beliefs and attitudes that we use to interpret or make sense of what we experience. These beliefs and attitudes are called "preunderstandings," and they play a significant role in shaping our view of reality. No one is free from them; it is impossible to interpret reality in a "totally objective" way. It does not follow from this, however, that what readers bring to a text determines the meaning of that text. The textual meaning is fixed; but readers will have more or less baggage to account for as they seek to understand that meaning.

All we know has been molded in some way by the preunderstandings that we bring to the process of interpretation. In the past, the discipline of hermeneutics concentrated on the ancient world of the texts and the techniques for understanding what texts meant "back then." Now we recognize that we must give far more attention to what the interpreter brings to the interpretive process. We need to know ourselves, as well as the object of our inquiry. Thiselton observes, "historical conditioning is two-sided: *the modern interpreter, no less than the text, stands in a given historical context and tradition.*"[52] He adds, "Hermeneutics cannot proceed without taking account of the existing horizons of the interpreter."[53] Borrowing the metaphor of "horizon" from Gadamer (the limits that a point of view or understanding presents), Thiselton argues that "the goal of biblical hermeneutics is to bring about an active and meaningful engagement between the interpreter and text, in such a way that the interpreter's own horizon is re-shaped and enlarged."[54]

Definition of Preunderstanding

The term *preunderstanding* describes what the interpreter brings to the task of interpretation. D. S. Ferguson provides a succinct definition: "Preunderstanding may be defined as a body of assumptions and attitudes which a person brings to the perception and interpretation of reality or any aspect of it."[55] It is the basic and preparatory starting point for understanding. Our preunderstanding constitutes where we begin as

---

52 Thiselton, *Two Horizons,* 11 (emphasis his). He goes on to observe, "Everything is understood in a given context and from a given point of view" (105).

53 Thiselton, *Two Horizons,* 237.

54 Thiselton, *Two Horizons,* xix. We disagree with his mentor, H.-G. Gadamer (*Truth and Method* [New York: Seabury, 1975], 359), however, who infers that since meaning is a "fusion" of the horizons of the text and interpreters, a text does not have a single correct interpretation. We believe meaning resides in the text, not merely in a given "reading" of a text. We have more to say on this in the next chapter.

55 D. S. Ferguson, *Biblical Hermeneutics: An Introduction* (Atlanta: John Knox, 1986), 6.

we currently are. Indeed, preunderstanding is desirable and essential.[56] Certain background knowledge and experiences can be pertinent to understanding other experiences or situations. For example, most of us can make only limited sense out of a medical prescription. We know it prescribes that a determined quantity of a specific medication should be taken at definite times, but apart from that limited preunderstanding, we are probably in no position to understand more about the medical terms and symbols. Possessing a more complete preunderstanding, a medical doctor or pharmacist reads the "text" with more meaning. Similarly, our African friend now understands pictures of snow better because her firsthand experiences of falling snow enlarged her preunderstanding.

What are the various elements that constitute preunderstanding, and how are they derived? Preunderstanding consists of the total framework of being and understanding that we bring to the task of living: our language, social conditioning, gender, intelligence, cultural values, physical environment, political allegiances, and even our emotional state at a given time. These elements construct and govern our individual worlds. They formulate the paradigm that helps us function and make sense of the world.

Ferguson discerns four categories of preunderstanding: (1) *informational:* the information one already possesses about a subject prior to approaching it; (2) *attitudinal:* the disposition one brings in approaching a topic, also termed prejudice, bias, or predisposition; (3) *ideological:* both generally, the way we view the total complex of reality (world view, frame of reference) and particularly, how we view a specific subject (point of view, perspective); and (4) *methodological:* the actual approach one takes in explaining a given subject. Possible approaches include scientific, historical, and inductive. Different approaches will influence the type of results obtained, though in another sense interpreters employ specific methods precisely to guard against undue interpretive bias.[57]

We cannot avoid or deny the presence of preunderstanding in the task of biblical interpretation. Every interpreter comes to study the Bible with preconceptions and prior dispositions. If we ask about the origin or basis of our preunderstanding, we will find it in our prior experiences, conditioning, and training—political, social, cultural, psychological, and religious—in short, all our lives up to this point. Even our native language influences our view of reality. All these color and in many senses determine how we view the world. Each individual processes all these factors.

The Role of Preunderstanding

Obviously, preunderstanding plays an enormously influential role in the process of interpretation. For example, as we noted above, those whose *ideology* (to use Ferguson's third category) allows science alone to settle matters of fact will tend to reject supernatural explanations of the biblical record.[58] For example, scientism's ideology influences the interpretive

---

56 Before we go further, we need to insist that preunderstanding be distinguished from bias or prejudice. Indeed, bias is only one element of a person's preunderstanding. We will take up these distinctions further below.

57 Ferguson, *Biblical Hermeneutics,* 12. He admits there are degrees of overlap between them and that a single act of preunderstanding contains elements of all four.

58 It should be clear here that our prior discussion of presuppositions overlaps that of preunderstanding. Part of the total preunderstanding an interpreter brings to the task consists of his or her presuppositions.

results, just as adopting the Bible's own world-view allows for alternative explanations of the data. Speaking of the epistemological stance of the scientific method, David Tracy observes, "Scientism has pretensions to a mode of inquiry that tries to deny its own hermeneutical character and mask its own historicity so that it might claim a historical certainty."[59] On the other hand, some postmodern interpreters do not object to supernatural "readings" of a biblical text since there are no privileged readings anyway. Readers make whatever sense of a text they wish. We could cite many other examples of ideological influence on interpretation. On the attitudinal dimension of preunderstanding, Wellhausen's anti-Judaism led him to denigrate the Law.[60] It seems likely that Hegel's ideological influence underlay Wellhausen's view that Israel's history evolved through three distinct phases.[61] Gunkel's form criticism—a methodological element—significantly affected a whole generation of OT scholarship.[62] Dever catalogs what he sees as huge biases affecting how many contemporary OT scholars read the evidence of archaeology.[63] Likewise, canon criticism has opened up important insights on the interpretation of the Psalms.[64]

In an extremely insightful essay, "Our Hermeneutical Inheritance," Roger Lundin traces the historical and philosophical roots of contemporary approaches to understanding.[65] He compares the deductive approach of Descartes with the more inductive one of Bacon. He then shows how American Christians in the nineteenth century combined Scottish common-sense-realism with the scientific approach of Bacon to develop their basic hermeneutical approach. Lundin observes, "To get at the meaning of the Bible, they merely employed the inductive techniques exploited with considerable success by the natural scientists."[66] He argues that "inductive Bible study" was very much the product of historical processes, particularly the assimilation of Enlightenment thought in America, and not necessarily the only, or a self-evident and universally supe-

---

59 *Plurality and Ambiguity: Hermeneutics, Religion, Hope* (San Francisco: Harper & Row, 1987), 31. For many scholars this "certainty" excludes the possibility of the miracles recorded in both Testaments, as we saw in our consideration of presuppositions above.

60 See Lou H. Silberman, "Wellhausen and Judaism," *Semeia* 25 (1982): 75–82; and Moshe Weinfeld, *Getting At the Roots of Wellhausen's Understanding of the Law of Israel on the 100th Anniversary of the Prolegomena* (Jerusalem: Institute for Advanced Studies, 1979).

61 R. N. Whybray, *The Making of the Pentateuch: A Methodological Study,* JSOT Sup 53 (Sheffield: JSOT, 1987), 43.

62 D. A. Knight, "The Pentateuch," in *The Hebrew Bible and Its Modern Interpreters,* ed., D. A. Knight, et al. (Philadelphia: Fortress and Chico, CA: Scholars, 1985), 264, who observes, "it is now inconceivable to conduct critical exegesis without attention to form, genre, Sitz im Leben and intention."

63 W. Dever, *What Did the Biblical Writers Know?*

64 G. H. Wilson, *The Editing of the Hebrew Psalter,* SBLDS 76 (Chico, CA: Scholars, 1985), 139–228; and B. S. Childs, *Introduction to the Old Testament as Scripture* (Minneapolis: Augsburg Fortress, 1979), 504–25.

65 In R. Lundin, A. C. Thiselton, and C. Walhout, *The Responsibility of Hermeneutics* (Grand Rapids: Eerdmans; Exeter: Paternoster, 1985), 1-29. See also Lundin's essay, "Hermeneutics," in *Contemporary Literary Theory. A Christian Appraisal* (Grand Rapids: Eerdmans, 1991), 149–71; Vanhoozer, *Is There a Meaning?* 16–35; and D. A. Carson, *The Gagging of God* (Grand Rapids: Zondervan, 1996), 57–92. The most exhaustive treatment is A. C. Thiselton, *New Horizons in Hermeneutics* (Grand Rapids: Zondervan, 1992).

66 Lundin, Thiselton, and Walhout, *The Responsibility of Hermeneutics,* 21.

rior method.[67] Interestingly, Lundin observes how this fascination with the inductive approach to biblical interpretation opened the door for any individual, group, denomination, or cult to sanction its beliefs based on its own exacting study of the Scriptures.[68]

Lundin concludes that, in reality, no one reads Scripture—or any literature, for that matter—in a completely disinterested way, even though "many of us cling stubbornly to our belief that we can approach a text with Cartesian cleanliness and Baconian precision."[69] Alluding to the philosophical tradition of Heidegger, Wittgenstein, Gadamer, and Ricoeur, Lundin concludes, "The idea of a disinterested interpretation of a literary text becomes an impossible one for hermeneutical theory."[70]

It would seem, then, that one may view preunderstanding as either a desirable asset or a dangerous culprit. Alas, asset or culprit may be in the eye of the "preunderstander"! Of course, to the extent that the interpreter requires some preunderstanding prior to coming to a text, it is indispensable. But equally, the preunderstanding may distort the reader's perception of reality and function like an unconscious prejudice adversely affecting the interpreter's ability to perceive accurately. It certainly determines how the reader will understand the task of reading the Bible.

We must take into consideration that we do not always consciously adopt or clearly recognize our preunderstandings or the role they play in the interpretive process. As the proverbial goldfish remains unaware of the water in which it swims, we are not always conscious of our views of reality. Nor do we realize how extremely idiosyncratic *our* own preunderstandings may be—no one else sees the world as we do.

These preunderstandings may be more or less influential on the process of interpretation depending upon their relevance to the issue at hand. For example, our African student's misunderstanding of the origin of snow probably made little difference in her understanding of the text, "Though your sins are like scarlet, they shall be as white as snow" (Isa 1:18). On the other hand, an ideology—like Wellhausen's anti-Judaism on the one hand or a "politically correct" aversion to any anti-Judaism on the other—will exert a major influence on how one interprets the accounts of Jesus' negative critique of certain "Jews" as reported in the Gospels. The one may be prone to conclude that all Jews are "bad guys." The other may dismiss the Evangelists as anti-Semites and seek to cleanse the accounts of such stains (and modern translations that persist in retaining such "biases"). These two examples also illustrate that some preunderstandings may have more far-reaching implications than others may. One affects (and risks distorting)

---

67 We do not mean to imply here that we reject the possibility of an inductive approach to Bible study, nor do we declare that an interpreter should not be systematic and methodical in study. We argued for appropriate methods above.

68 Lundin, Thiselton, and Walhout, *The Responsibility of Hermeneutics,* 22. This leads Hauerwas to opine that we need to take the Bible out of the hands of individual Christians in North America who think they are qualified to interpret the Bible on their own, and leave that task to "spiritual masters who can help the whole church stand under the authority of God's word" (*Unleashing the Scripture,* 16).

69 Lundin, Thiselton, and Walhout, *The Responsibility of Hermeneutics,* 23.

70 Lundin, Thiselton, and Walhout, *The Responsibility of Hermeneutics,* 24; also see Lundin, "Hermeneutics," 158–63.

our reading only of texts that concern snow. The other regulates how we read every incident or claim in both Testaments that speak negatively about Jews.

In the face of new evidence, our African student did not hesitate to adjust her erroneous preunderstanding about the origin of snow. One of our challenges as interpreters is not simply to identify and take into account our preunderstandings but also to adjust or revise them, or courageously jettison those that prove to be erroneous. We must learn to recognize our preunderstandings and to evaluate their worth. We must have a basis on which to amend them or judge them unchangeable.

A Philosophy of Interpretation as Preunderstanding

We have to make a decision about our basic stance in interpreting the Bible. When most people think of biblical interpretation, they think of understanding ancient documents. Indeed, up until the 1940s or so the essential concerns of hermeneutics were to investigate the world of the biblical author or editor, the resulting texts, and the original readers of those texts. That is, in biblical interpretation one was concerned with the historical locus of the text—what happened in the ancient world that resulted in what was written in the text. More recently, however, scholars have come to understand that *historical methods* prove useful only when one's objectives focus on recovering what happened or was written in history. If one chooses to ignore the history a biblical text reports and focus on the text only—particularly the interaction between text and reader—then different methods and different conclusions will follow.

So while Morgan does not intend a literary approach to supplant or deny the results of historical or linguistic study, he argues that in today's pluralistic and rationalistic world, literary (i.e., not author/text-based) approaches "allow a large range of legitimate interpretations of the Bible."[71] Morgan believes that to attempt to find "the single correct answer" (i.e., *the* correct interpretation of a text) would result in a hopelessly fragmented Bible that "would offer from the distant past various pieces of information with little relation to the present."[72] In other words, he implies that because people bring to the Bible various preunderstandings and they use the Bible for various purposes, no one has the right to say only one approach, if any, is valid or true or even at least better. Then are we left with a kind of hermeneutical cafeteria where we must grant legitimacy to every method of interpretation and to all interpreters? May people simply choose how they want to read the Bible, then employ appropriate methods, and finally display their conclusions?

Since in this pluralistic age we live with many truth-claims—those of the Buddhist, Muslim, Jew, and Christian, to name a few—Morgan believes it simply will not do to claim arrogantly that a correct historical reading of the Bible supports solely one's own religious perspective. Thus, he argues, if we read the biblical accounts as literature, religious people can simply affirm their views and positions on other grounds and not make a historical use of the Bible serve that function. Morgan does not want to expunge historical-critical exegesis; rather, he seeks to relegate it to its proper place of fine-tuning existing theological formulations and keeping honest those who already base their religion on the Bible.

---

71 R. Morgan with J. Barton, *Biblical Interpretation* (Oxford: Oxford University Press, 1998), 286.

72 Morgan and Barton, *Biblical Interpretation*, 286.

As noted above, someone may adopt a certain philosophical position and proceed to interpret through that grid. For example, building on a framework of existentialism,[73] Heidegger and Bultmann argue that the biblical texts have meaning only when we as subjects can engage those texts and their significance for our being.[74] Though their point has clear merit, they severely limit truth or reality to what corresponds to our personal experience. Their vantage point *determines* what the text means, rather than giving the author the right to mean what he or she intended. What can justify such a presumption? Of course, a reader can do anything he or she wishes with a text. But as we will argue in the next chapter, this willy-nilly tactic is not the appropriate way to read a text. And as we argued above, since the Bible is qualitatively different from other literature, as God's authoritative revelation its categories and its content surpass our existential human condition. To perceive its resident meaning should be our goal.

As we saw in chapter 2, the so-called *new hermeneutic* followed upon Bultmann's more existential understanding of hermeneutics.[75] Instead of employing a methodology or process for determining the meaning of texts (i.e., what they historically intended to communicate), practitioners of the new hermeneutic focused attention on the modern situation—how the ancient text speaks with power and freshness today.

Likewise, *liberation theology* illustrates the importance of preunderstanding.[76] The role the Church should perform in bringing justice to the poor (initially in Latin America) determined the starting point for this approach. These theologians do not simply study the Bible based on a set of principles; they interpret the Bible based on an agenda with the goal of justice for the poor. Often Marxist, this ideological base becomes for these theologians the preunderstanding for interpreting the Bible and for developing their political agenda. In a similar vein some readers now welcome gay (or queer) readings of the Bible that apply the tools of "queer theory" and gender

---

73 For a rather exhaustive treatment of these existential approaches, including Gadamer and Bultmann, see Thiselton, *Two Horizons*. Also consult the review of *Two Horizons* by W. W. Klein in *Trinity Journal*, n.s. 2 (1981): 71–75.

74 Thiselton cites Bultmann's declaration that "it is valid in the investigation of a text to allow oneself to be examined by the text, and to hear the claim it makes" (Thiselton, *Two Horizons,* 191). Additionally, Bultmann argues that to believe in the cross of Christ "does not mean to concern ourselves . . . with an objective event (*ein objektiv anschaubares Ereignis*) . . . but rather to make the cross of Christ our own, to undergo crucifixion with him" (211). Finally, Thiselton says, "Bultmann insists that through history the interpreter comes to understand *himself*. His relationship to the text is not theoretical but *existentiell*. Only thus does the text 'speak' " (287). Rightly Bultmann has been criticized because he places so much emphasis on the existential dimension that for him it matters little if any objective or historical events recorded in the NT even occurred. This is a serious flaw for, though Christ's death or resurrection may be inspiring mythical events, if they did not actually occur in history, how can they provide objective atonement or assure the Christian's own resurrection (cf. 1 Cor 15:17)?

75 Representatives include: J. M. Robinson and J. Cobb, eds., *The New Hermeneutic* (New York: Harper & Row, 1964); R. W. Funk, *Language, Hermeneutic and Word of God* (New York: Harper & Row, 1966); and G. Ebeling, *God and Word* (Philadelphia: Fortress, 1967).

76 See our detailed discussion in chapter 3.

studies to biblical texts.[77] Through such studies a new (often termed "more accurate") understanding of the biblical texts emerges that eradicates the Bible's proscription of homosexual behavior. Self-consciously and unashamedly, these readers apply to their interpretation of the Bible their preunderstanding that homosexual behavior is acceptable. Similarly, *process theologians* adopt a stance or preunderstanding through which they view the Bible. Following philosopher A. N. Whitehead, they understand reality as a process, a maelstrom of causes and effects in which humans make sense out of their world.[78] George Lucas suggests, "Process philosophy is distinguished from other movements by its stress on the primacy of change, becoming, and the event character of reality, in opposition to what Whitehead termed the static or 'vacuous' actualities of traditional substance metaphysics."[79]

According to these theologians, language is fluid, imprecise, and capable of a variety of meanings. Thus, understanding language cannot be exact for it conveys reality by way of abstraction. Since all reality exists in such a state of fluctuation, the meaning of a text in Scripture cannot be precise or authoritative. Neither the author's intention nor some historical meaning of a text determines the goal of understanding for process hermeneutics. Process interpreters do not search for propositional truth; they simply process what the reader has encountered in the text. Their preunderstanding is clearly self-conscious and becomes a grid through which they understand the Bible.[80]

---

77 A few examples include: S. Kader, *Openly Gay, Openly Christian: How the Bible is Gay Friendly* (San Francisco: Leyland, 1999); R. E. Goss and M. West, eds., *Take Back the Word: A Queer Reading of the Bible* (Cleveland: Pilgrim, 2000); W. Wink, *Homosexuality and Christian Faith* (Minneapolis: Augsburg Fortress, 1999); S. D. Moore, *God's Beauty Parlor: And Other Queer Spaces in and Around the Bible* (Palo Alto: Stanford University Press, 2001); and K. Stone, *Queer Commentary and the Hebrew Bible* (Cleveland: Pilgrim, 2001). For a critique of this hermeneutical stance see R. A. Gagnon, *The Bible and Homosexual Practice* (Nashville: Abingdon, 2001).

78 Some representatives include D. Brown, R. E. James, and G. Reeves, eds., *Process Philosophy and Christian Thought* (New York: Bobbs-Merrill, 1971); J. B. Cobb and D. R. Griffin, *Process Theology: An Introductory Exposition* (Philadelphia: Westminster, 1976); and J. B. Cobb, *Process Theology as Political Theology* (Manchester: University Press; Philadelphia: Westminster, 1982). See also A. N. Whitehead, *Science and the Modern World* (New York: Macmillan, 1927). Again we risk, yet attempt to avoid, caricatures in what follows. The essays in C. H. Pinnock, ed., *The Openness of God: A Biblical Challenge to the Traditional Understanding of God* (Downers Grove, IL: InterVarsity, 1994), seek to distinguish an open view of God from process theism.

79 G. R. Lucas, *The Genesis of Modern Process Thought: A Historical Outline with Bibliography* (Metuchen, NJ: Scarecrow Press and the ATLA, 1983), 5. This book provides a basic survey of process thinking with extensive bibliographies. See also id., *The Rehabilitation of Whitehead* (Albany: The State University of New York Press, 1989); J. R. Sibley and P. A. Y. Gunter, eds., *Process Philosophy: Basic Writings* (Washington, DC: University Press of America, 1978), which compiles twenty-one essays on various aspects of process thinking in five parts: epistemology, metaphysics, science, ethics, and aesthetics; and T. Trethowan, *Process Theology and the Christian Tradition* (Petersham, MA: St. Bede's Publications, 2002), who argues that the idea of an eternal yet changeable God is part of the Christian heritage.

80 In R. Nash, ed. *Process Theology* (Grand Rapids: Baker, 1987), various evangelical scholars respond to different facets of process philosophy and theology. They provide helpful assessments that compare process theology to classical theism and various theological and philosophical issues and offer personal judgments of the usefulness of process thought.

What we have described under these various more recent developments signals a distinct shift in the practice of biblical interpretation—part of the movement sometimes termed postmodernism. They illustrate the swing from author- and text-centered interpretation to reader-centered approaches. In fact E. V. McKnight contends that the nature of the modern reader's preunderstanding has led to a fundamental shift in the hermeneutical task. In his view, "A *reader-oriented approach* acknowledges that the contemporary reader's 'intending' of the text is not the same as that of the ancient author and/or ancient readers."[81] He observes, further, "Biblical texts are perceived and interpreted in quite different ways as a result of changes in world view and in social surroundings within any given world view."[82] In a later paragraph he summarizes: "Readers *make* sense. Readers may perform their role constrained by their cultural contexts and critical assumptions and remain unaware of their potential as creative readers."[83] For McKnight, the modern interpreter's ability to read the biblical texts "creatively" is a major gain. Such readers attain a new freedom because they are "no longer constrained by traditional dogmatic and/or historical-critical goals of reading and interpretation."[84] Clearly, McKnight's postmodern view greatly relativizes the Bible's teachings. Since for McKnight the Bible's teachings are the product of a series of ancient cultures and their primitive or precritical world-views, then they can have no necessarily abiding authority for modern people. In this view whatever authority or application the Bible may have for people today must pass through this grid: that the Bible comprises culturally and historically conditioned documents, and that its cultures and ours today are radically different. For McKnight, the reader's perception of the text, *not the text itself*, is the ultimate basis of authority for the meaning of the text.

But what about the objective message conveyed in the Bible? Is the message that is relayed to the hearer in any sense the correct message? What about the meaning the text had for its original readers? Ferguson's critique of such postmodern approaches is well-founded:

> What, for example, happens to history as a means of God's self-disclosure? Once again, it would appear that the content of the *kerygma* as an object of faith has been obscured. There is little recognition that the crucifixion and resurrection are historical events themselves creative of language, not merely "language events." Language as the only hermeneutical guide fails to do full justice to history.[85]

We conclude that these calls for a hermeneutic more committed to pluralistic openness leaves interpreters liable to the grave danger of subjectivism and relativism. If the greatest virtue is tolerance or avoiding interpretations that offend those of other religions, then do we simply abandon the search for truth? Do we set aside the Bible

---

81 E. V. McKnight, *Postmodern Use of the Bible: The Emergence of Reader-Oriented Criticism* (Nashville: Abingdon, 1988), 150 (our emphasis).

82 McKnight, *Postmodern Use,* 149.

83 McKnight, *Postmodern Use,* 161.

84 McKnight, *Postmodern Use,* 161.

85 Ferguson, *Biblical Hermeneutics,* 174.

when we seek what is true?[86] Further, some ideas like anti-Semitism or racism are simply very bad ideas that, if left unchallenged, threaten society with dangerous consequences. Morgan recognizes this inherent danger, but calls only for the critical voice of well-trained historians and linguists "to call rubbish by its name."[87] But it is not clear how, if all literary approaches are equally welcome and readers make meaning, the historians and linguists can sufficiently challenge as rubbish a specific "literary reading" of a text. For if the historical perspective—what the author intended the text to mean at the time written—does not have the major and controlling influence, then various "readings" might be termed equally legitimate, and even desirable, whether they be capitalist, Marxist, gay, liberationist, process, feminist, or African-American.[88] Postmodernism may welcome this state of affairs because its approach puts the reader in charge. We wish to welcome and employ literary methods that enable us to understand and appreciate the Bible's literary dimensions. But in using literary methods we cannot abandon the texts' historical moorings. We insist that the "historical" focus provides the best avenue to a legitimate "literary" reading. We do not want an either-or approach.[89] We reject any preunderstandings that replace the historical meaning of a text with a modern "reading" of it.

Testing Preunderstandings

How can we know if our preunderstandings correspond to truth? Gordon Lewis argues that one can assess one's presuppositions so that the interpretive task is not hopelessly mired in a vicious hermeneutical circle.[90] Lewis observes, "Presuppositions carry

---

86 Historically, Christianity has claimed that it is uniquely true—that in Jesus we have the way, truth, and life, the only way to God (Jn 14:6; Acts 4:12). In a well-reasoned book H. A. Netland defends this wildly unpopular assertion of Christian exclusivism. He asserts, "Where the claims of Scripture are incompatible with those of other faiths, the latter are to be rejected as false" (*Dissonant Voices: Religious Pluralism and the Question of Truth* [Grand Rapids: Eerdmans; Leicester: InterVarsity, 1991], 34). Netland's point is *not* that all the claims or teachings of other religions are false, or that they possess no value, or that Christians can learn nothing from them. Rather, when religions make conflicting claims to truth, the Christian position is the true one. Netland's work presents a compelling defense of the historic Christian faith. All missiologists and philosophers of religion will need to examine what Netland has presented. See also L. Newbigin, *The Gospel in a Pluralist Society* (Grand Rapids: Eerdmans; Geneva: WCC, 1989).

87 Morgan and Barton, *Biblical Interpretation*, 289.

88 We will take up below our understanding and defense of author-based textual meaning as the primary goal of hermeneutics.

89 To be fair, neither does Morgan argue for literary methods to replace historical ones. He realizes how subjective any interpretation can be, even those that purport to be "historical." He wants a historical framework to govern only those studies whose aims are historical (*Biblical Interpretation*, 287). But, argues Morgan, where one's aims are religious or theological, other methods (i.e., literary) need to provide the framework. History, for Morgan, takes the back seat. But, we protest, theological beliefs *must* also be rooted in history, as the apostle Paul argues concerning Jesus' resurrection in 1 Cor 15:13–23. For our alternative approach of "critical realism" see below.

90 G. R. Lewis, "Response to Presuppositions of Non-Evangelical Hermeneutics," in *Hermeneutics, Inerrancy, and the Bible*, eds. E. D. Radmacher and R. D. Preus (Grand Rapids: Zondervan, 1984), 613–26. Scholars employ the technical term "hermeneutical circle" in at least two ways: (1) asking questions of the text whose answers subsequently reshape the questions that are then posed to the text, and (2) the phenomenon by which one cannot understand constituent parts of a whole without some comprehension of the whole, while at the same time recognizing that an understanding of the whole comes by combining an understanding of its component parts (see Thiselton, *Two Horizons,* 104). In neither instance are we doomed to subjectivity; indeed, the burden of this book is to enable understanding to proceed with some measure of objectivity, a "critical realism," a phrase coined by N. T. Wright and adopted

only provisional authority until adequately tested and affirmed."[91] One test of our pre-understandings is whether they correspond to the biblical data. Yet a critic may ask why the Bible assumes the role of ultimate authority. Any answer requires some further explanation. Why do Christians presuppose that the Bible is foundationally true?

Thoughtful Christians insist that accepting the Bible's truthfulness is not merely a prejudiced dogmatism, an undefended presuppositionalism that simply assumes its stance. That is to say, we do not position ourselves in the camp of those whom apologists technically call "presuppositionalists" (e.g., C. Van Til). In this view, one starts by assuming such tenets as God's existence or the truthfulness of revelation in the Bible.[92] We are happier with a modified evidentialist or verificationalist stance.[93] N. T. Wright calls this approach "critical realism," and with him we agree.[94] That is, we believe we must start with certain hypotheses that we test and either accept or reject. We must evaluate the evidence for the Christian claims in light of all the alternative truth claims.

We believe that such an approach establishes the viability and defensibility of the historic Christian faith. It explains the issues of existence and reality with fewer difficulties than all competing alternatives. We do not claim proof in any scientific sense. Nevertheless, in Carnell's words, "the Christian finds his system of philosophy in the Bible, to be sure, but he accepts this, not simply because it is in the Bible, but because, when tested, it makes better sense out of life than other systems of philosophy make."[95] We soundly reject a view that the Christian position is merely a "leap in the dark" opinion, no better (or worse) than alternatives that many people "sincerely believe." Postmodern western culture exalts relativism and pluralism as great virtues, almost non-negotiable axioms rooted in human freedom. We believe, in contrast, that absolute truth exists, and that "truth" cannot be relativized so that contradictory claims are accepted as equally valid. We believe that to accept the Bible's veracity best accords with the evidence.

---

by Vanhoozer. In fact, as we will show below, perhaps changing "circle" to "spiral" alters the image enough to see we are not doomed to a "vicious circle." Also see G. R. Osborne, *The Hermeneutical Spiral* (Downers Grove: InterVarsity, 1991), 6, 14.

91 Lewis, "Response," 620.

92 In Van Til's words, "To argue by presupposition is to indicate what are the epistemological and metaphysical principles that underlie and control one's method. The Reformed apologist will frankly admit that his own methodology presupposes the truth of Christian theism" (C. Van Til, *The Defense of the Faith* [Philadelphia: Presbyterian and Reformed Publishing Co., 1955], 116). Van Til took issue with his colleague B. B. Warfield who taught that apologetics was a prior and separate discipline to establish the truth of Christianity before one moved to the other theological subjects. Rather, Van Til says, "All the disciplines must presuppose God, but at the same time presupposition is the best proof" (C. Van Til, *An Introduction to Systematic Theology* [Phillipsburg, NJ: Presbyterian and Reformed, 1974], 3). At this point we find ourselves more in sympathy with Warfield than Van Til.

93 See E. J. Carnell, *An Introduction to Christian Apologetics* (Grand Rapids: Eerdmans, 1948), 103–121, for a helpful discussion of what constitutes verification in apologetics. See also the verificational method of doing theology defended by B. Demarest and G. Lewis, *Integrative Theology* (Grand Rapids: Zondervan, 1996), 10–13.

94 Wright, *New Testament*, 32–46.

95 Carnell, *Introduction*, 102.

A Christian Preunderstanding [96]

As responsible interpreters we seek to employ whatever rational methods will enable us to understand the correct meaning of the biblical texts. But when it comes to making judgments about the "theological" significance of those texts, we must go beyond our analytic methods. Though we share many of the critical methods of the secular historians, we do so with our own preunderstanding of the significance of the documents we are studying.

Secular historians may view the Bible only as a collection of ancient religious texts. To treat it as such—which often occurs in academia or among theologically more liberal critics—is unlikely to lead to valid conclusions about the religious value or significance of the Bible. In fact the results may seem "sterile" compared to those of a believing scholar. However, as authors of this book we believe that the Bible is the divine Word of God. Only from that stance can we use our historical and critical methods and arrive at theologically meaningful and pertinent results. Hirsch puts it forcefully: "An interpreter's notion of the type of meaning he confronts will powerfully influence his understanding of details."[97] We posit that our stance provides the best basis for a valid understanding of the biblical texts. Richardson makes this point succinctly,

> That perspective from which we see most clearly all the facts, without having to explain any of them away, will be a relatively true perspective. Christians believe that the perspective of biblical faith enables us to see very clearly and without distortion the biblical facts as they really are: they see the facts clearly because they see their true meaning.[98]

We are members of the worldwide evangelical community. We have committed ourselves to the faith understood as traditionally "Christian." This informs our preunderstanding and provides the boundaries for our reading of the Bible. Though we must always submit to the teachings of the Bible as our sole and final authority, our actual preunderstanding of the Bible as God's revelation guides our interpretation of its pages. We insist, as well, that our commitment to the authority of the Bible derives from our prior conviction of its truthfulness and our assumption of its divine inspiration. This is an informed circularity, an outgrowth of "critical realism," to borrow again Wright's phrase.

Can we avoid being jaundiced by our preunderstanding? Is there a way to critique and correct our preunderstanding when it so completely encompasses all that we are? If Christians are committed to being thoroughly biblical, then one solution is to sub-

---

96 As we have indicated at various points already, we position ourselves in the evangelical tradition, within the framework described, for example, by the Lausanne Covenant or the basic affirmations of the National Association of Evangelicals. Yet what follows need not be limited to "our circle" of Christians. The principles and methods we employ will yield significant understanding regardless of the practitioner, though readers with differing presuppositions and preunderstandings will admit or reject our results in varying ways. To the extent that methods are neutral (and we insist most are), the results will be similar.

97 E. D. Hirsch, Jr., *Validity in Interpretation* (New Haven: Yale University Press, 1967), 75.

98 A. Richardson, *Christian Apologetics* (New York: Harper & Row, 1947), 105.

ject our views to the scrutiny of Scripture. That is, we can aspire to have a biblically based and determined preunderstanding. In other words, where beliefs and commitments derive from our culture that contradict or oppose biblical truth, we must identify them, and, somehow, specify and control their effects in the interpretive process. The Christian community, guided by the Spirit, comprises the optimal arena for such self-analysis.

We must anchor our subsequent discussion of how to understand texts to this discussion of preunderstanding. A document consisting of words on a page remains an inert entity. What are ink and paper, after all? The significance we give to those words depends to a large extent upon us: what significance do we *want* to give to the words? Postmodern readers can do anything they please; no court of law restricts how texts can be used or abused (though, of course, libel is punishable by the courts—a flagrant misrepresentation of someone's printed views). We must decide if we want to hear the words in terms of what they most likely meant at the time they were written, or whether we want to use, or handle, or employ them in other ways. The authors, editors, or communities that formulated the biblical texts obviously cannot plead their case. Nor can the first readers be consulted for their input. As ongoing debates in political circles about interpreting the U.S. Constitution illustrate, people today decide how they will use old documents.[99] The biblical texts or the creeds of the church may well claim inspiration for the Scriptures, but interpreters today still decide how they will handle those claims. Are theology and Christian practice to be based upon what the biblical texts seem to communicate, upon the objectives, concerns, and agendas of the modern community that interpret those authors, or upon some combination of the two? Evangelicals may insist (correctly, we believe) upon a focus on the original meanings of the biblical texts; however, as we have seen, the history of interpretation clearly demonstrates the pervasive (sometimes harmful) influence of the interpreter's agenda or preunderstanding. What is the optimum Christian preunderstanding? For us it is the one that derives from the set of presuppositions listed earlier in this chapter.

Preunderstandings Change with Understanding

At the same time that we speak of this biblically determined preunderstanding, we acknowledge that it will never be static, nor should it be if we are growing as Christians in our spiritual understanding because of our Bible study. Interpreters approach texts with questions, biases, and preunderstandings that emerge out of their personal situations. Inevitably, those preunderstandings influence the answers they obtain. However, the answers also then affect the interpreter: the text interprets the interpreter who becomes not only the subject interpreting but the object interpreted. Recall our African student with her preunderstandings about snow. Once she realized that snow fell from above, that it did not emerge out of the earth, she revised her understanding about this

---

99 Is our concern to apply the Constitution in the way its original framers intended, or in view of current understandings and realities? Parallel to the phenomenon of postmodern biblical interpretation, some argue that today the courts have usurped from the Constitution the authority for governing. They determine what is legal or not in how they "interpret" the founding documents of the republic. For this view, see the musings of the editors, "The End of Democracy? The Judicial Usurpation of Politics" and "To Reclaim Our Democratic Heritage," *First Things* 69 (1997): 25–28.

type of precipitation. In her adjusted understanding it fit in the same category as rain, rather than in the category of dew.

This scenario has led interpreters to speak of a hermeneutical circle, or better, a hermeneutical spiral.[100] Every interpreter begins with a preunderstanding. After an initial study of a biblical text, that text performs a work on the interpreter. His or her preunderstanding is no longer what it was. Then, as the newly interpreted interpreter proceeds to question the text further, out of this newly formed understanding further—perhaps, different—questions and answers emerge. New understanding results. The interpreter does not merely go around in circles. Not a vicious circle, this is, rather, a progressive spiral of development. The meaning of the text has not changed, but rather the interpreter's enhanced (we sincerely hope) ability to understanding it (more) correctly.

HERMENEUTICAL SPIRAL

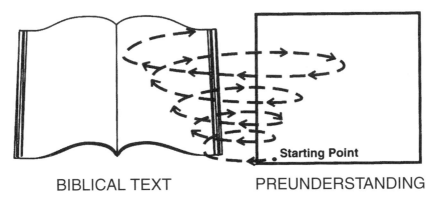

BIBLICAL TEXT   PREUNDERSTANDING

Admittedly, there is an inevitable circularity in interpretation. When we posit the requirement of faith to understand the Bible fully and then we go to the Bible in order to understand God's self-revelation in Christ in whom we have faith, the process has a definite circularity. In defense we insist that an appropriate level of preunderstanding is necessary for any kind of knowledge. This, as we have seen, is the nature of all inquiry. Thus, one must have some knowledge of God even to arrive at the preunderstanding of faith. Then that stance of faith enables the Christian to study the Bible to come to a deeper understanding of God and what the Scriptures say. As we learn more from our study of Scripture, we alter and enlarge our preunderstanding in more or less fundamental ways. In essence, this process describes the nature of all learning: it is interactive, ongoing, and continuous. When believers study the Bible they interact with its texts (and with its Author), and, as a result, over time they enlarge their understanding.

---

100 Cf. Osborne, *The Hermeneutical Spiral*, 10, 324; W. J. Larkin, Jr., *Culture and Biblical Hermeneutics* (Grand Rapids: Baker, 1988), 302; and R. C. Padilla, "Hermeneutics and Culture: A Theological Perspective," in *Gospel and Culture*, ed. J. R. W. Stott and R. T. Coote (Pasadena: William Carey Library, 1979), 63–78. Carson, *The Gagging of God*, 121–122, proposes a mathematical model, the asymptote. Our knowledge can increasingly approximate though never attain complete (divine) knowledge.

Preunderstandings and Objectivity in Interpretation

Following such a discussion of preunderstanding, some may still wonder if we are doomed to subjectivity in interpretation. Can we ever interpret the Bible in an objective fashion, or do we simply detect in its pages only what we want or are predisposed to see? Must we say with the postmodernists only what is "true for me" and despair of or abandon the quest of finding truth that is universal or absolute? These questions hinge on the validity of our presupposition that the Bible communicates truth and constitutes God's revelation to us, and that interpreters are capable of discovering it. If God has revealed truth in the Bible, then it seems reasonable also that he has made us capable of apprehending that truth, or at least some measure of it—and that it is God's message that we ought to seek (not our own "reading" of it). Thus, though we inevitably bring preunderstandings to the texts we seek to interpret, this does not mean that we cannot apprehend the meaning the text intends to impart. Particularly if our goal is to discover the meaning the texts conveyed at the time they were written, we have some objective criteria to validate our interpretations.[101]

Thus we rebuff any charge that our view simply jettisons all inductive assessment of the facts or data of the text and its situation. Recognizing the role of our preunderstanding does not doom us to a closed circle—that we find in a text what we want to find in a text—though that looms as an ever-present danger. The honest, reflective, humble interpreter remains open to change, even to a significant transformation of preunderstandings. This is the hermeneutical *spiral.* Since we accept the Bible's authority as mediated through the Spirit, we remain open to correction by its message. There are ways to verify interpretations or, at least, to validate some interpretive options as more likely than others. It is not a matter of simply throwing the dice. There is a wide variety of methods available to help us find what the original texts most likely meant to their initial readers. Every time we alter our preunderstanding as the result of our interaction with the text we demonstrate that the process has objective constraints, otherwise, no change would occur; we would remain forever entombed in our prior commitments.

W. Larkin makes the valid point that because God made people in his own image they have the capacity to "transcend preunderstanding, evaluate it, and change it."[102] People are not so captive to their preconceptions that they cannot transcend them. One of the tactics, Larkin believes, that fosters the process of evaluating and transcending our preunderstanding as interpreters is to "seek out the definite and fixed meaning intended by the author of the text and to use Scripture as the final critical authority for judging extrabiblical thought-patterns."[103] This is our goal.

---

101 See the section on "reading and critical realism" in Wright, *New Testament,* 61–69.

102 Larkin, *Culture and Biblical Hermeneutics,* 299.

103 Larkin, *Culture and Biblical Hermeneutics,* 300. However, as we will defend in detail below, we are on safer ground to set as a goal to detect the historically based (and author-centered) meaning of a given text rather than the more abstract "meaning an author intended." Also, Larkin may be overly optimistic when he assures us, "interpreters who consciously set aside their cultural preunderstanding can be confident that the grammatical-historical-literary context will enable them to find the plain and definite meaning of the text" (301). Whether we can set aside our cultural preunderstandings remains a huge question. A good starting point is simply to try to identify them and to assess their influence.

The hermeneutical spiral can illustrate a very positive experience as God through his Holy Spirit brings new and more adequate understanding of his truth and its application to believers' lives. If the Bible is true (and this takes us back to our presuppositions), then subscribing to its truth constitutes the most adequate starting point for interpreting its content. But alone that would be insufficient to comprehend the Bible. To understand the Bible's message adequately demands appropriate methodology and the willingness of interpreters to allow the Bible to alter or clarify their preunderstandings. As Ferguson has said: "all knowledge is elusive, and to grasp it demands a great deal of effort on our part, not the least of which is keeping a watchful eye on our own personal and societal forms of preunderstanding."[104] The metaphor of a spiral suggests the healthiest approach to an adequate comprehension of the Bible.

---

104 Ferguson, *Biblical Hermeneutics*, 17.

6

THE GOAL OF
INTERPRETATION

When we communicate, we seek to convey a message to others. Implicitly, those who hear or read that message will seek to understand its meaning. We usually say that communication succeeds when the meaning received corresponds to the meaning sent. Human communication actually comprises a "speech act."[1] When an author composes a text (this is what Austin called the "locution," the act of writing), then, he or she engages in a communicative act. As a communicative act, the text has content, energy or power ("illocutionary force"), and purpose ("perlocutionary effect"). To communicate an author encodes some propositional content in a specific literary form. The form (i.e., genre) may well be chosen because it best provides the "energy" to accomplish the desired purpose, that is, to produce the intended effect in the readers, whether to persuade, promise, inform, warn, guide, exhort, etc. To explain the "meaning" in a text requires an understanding of these aspects of communication.

Within the scope of written communication, we can talk about three potential aspects of meaning: (1) the meaning the author intends to convey [content, effect], (2) the grammatical and lexical meaning of the words configured on the page, and (3) the meaning the reader understands. We may assume that what an author intends to communicate corresponds precisely to the meaning of the text; however, an author may not frame the message correctly or put on paper precisely what he or she meant. In those cases, the author's intended meaning will match only to a certain degree what the words on the page mean. Likewise, what a reader understands will not necessarily correspond with either the author's intention or the text's meaning. For these reasons we distinguish among authorial intention, textual meaning, and perceived meaning.

---

1 Speech act theory was developed by J. L. Austin, *How To Do Things with Words*, ed. J. O. Urmson and M. Sbisa, 2d. ed. (Cambridge: Harvard Univ. Press, 1975), and J. Searle, *Speech Acts: An Essay in the Philosophy of Language* (Cambridge: Cambridge Univ. Press, 1969). To "say" or "write" something is in reality something that is "done." So they argued we must analyze what a text 'does' if we are to discern appropriately its meaning. See the perceptive application to biblical studies provided by K. J. Vanhoozer, "The Semantics of Biblical Literature," in *Hermeneutics, Authority, and Canon*, ed. D. A. Carson and J. D. Woodbridge (Grand Rapids: Zondervan, 1986), 49–104. For more on speech act theory and biblical studies, see the entire issue of *Semeia* 41 (1988), and A. C. Thiselton, *New Horizons in Hermeneutics* (Grand Rapids: Zondervan, 1992), 283–312. Finally, see various articles that address these issues in C. Bartholomew et al., ed., *After Pentecost: Language and Biblical Interpretation* (Grand Rapids: Zondervan, 2001).

Though one may never completely understand all dimensions and nuances of a specific speech act, normally the recipient in communication seeks to understand what the author/speaker intended. Yet, when we read a literary text or listen to an oral message, we cannot read the author's or speaker's mind; we can work only with the written or verbal message. In biblical interpretation, when we have only the written text to study, our goal is to understand the meaning (again, content, energy, and intended effect) of that text. For this reason we dare not disregard the author's role and intention. Each individual text was written at some time in history in a specific culture by a person with a personal framework of preunderstandings. The author or editor intended to communicate a message to a specific audience to accomplish some purpose. Our goal is to discover that meaning of the text in those terms.[2]

So the common-sense approach to interpreting assumes that meaning resides in the message or text and that the author or speaker encoded this meaning in that text. Semanticists may rightly insist that meaning concerns the interaction between human beings. Yet, our role as interpreters of a document (as in a biblical text) is auxiliary to that of the original author or editor. The author encoded the meaning in the text, and our objective is to discover it, at least to the extent that we are able to recover it in the text. As we usually perceive their role—and as normal human communication intuitively works—interpreters seek to understand what the author had to say, not to take the text and do something inventive with it that the author never intended. In Vanhoozer's words, "What an act counts as is not a matter of how it is taken, but of how it was meant."[3] This is true, because, he goes on, "The author is the one whose action determines the meaning of the text—its subject matter, its literary form, and its communicative energy."[4] Osborne puts it this way, "The implied author and the implied reader in the text provide an indispensable perspective for the intended meaning of a text."[5] The whole point of developing an arsenal of appropriate interpretive methods and skills is that we are listeners or receivers of a message. We do not create the message; rather, we seek to discover what is already there—whether consciously or unconsciously intended by the authors or editors.

These points may seem rather straightforward to some readers, but not all interpreters would agree with them. Of course, the biblical writers are not around to insist that we seek only the meaning they intended, nor can they verify that after all our efforts we have interpreted the meaning correctly (even when we discover meaning that goes beyond their intentions). This leads us to several pointed questions in our discussion of the goal of interpretation. Can a modern reader discover "new meaning" in a biblical text (or any text, for that matter)? Are texts capable of more than one meaning,

---

2 Attempting to comprehend written texts is as close as we can get to their authors' intended meanings. On the other hand, authors may write more than they intended, for modern studies have shown that much of what humans communicate occurs unconsciously (e.g., body language). So, again, finding textual meaning is a worthy goal.

3 See K. J. Vanhoozer, *Is There a Meaning in This Text?* (Grand Rapids: Zondervan, 1998), 229.

4 Vanhoozer, *Is There a Meaning?* 230.

5 G. R. Osborne, *The Hermeneutical Spiral* (Downers Grove: InterVarsity, 1991), 414. See also W. R. Tate, *Biblical Interpretation*, rev. ed. (Peabody, MA: Hendrickson, 1997), 196–208, for his discussion of "Author-Centered Interpretation."

even if their authors intended only a single meaning? And is the author's intention any more significant than other possible meanings in a text?

Obviously, modern interpreters can do anything they please with a text. Even if the author were present to protest, we could play with a text or manipulate it in any way we chose. We could impose on it modern categories or could view it through a grid of our own choosing, as we saw in the previous chapters. We could ask our own questions of it, or demolish and reconstruct it to our liking. We could try to find meaning in the patterns of blank spaces on the printed page. No court of law prevents us from using the texts in many different ways, as we please.[6] But the issue we must decide is: what is our objective as evangelical interpreters in handling the biblical texts? If we seek to hear what the biblical text means, then this restricts our approach and our methods of interpretation. If our goal is author/text centered, then historical, grammatical, literary, and cultural methods (to name some representatives) must be central. To help us establish an accurate methodology of interpretation we need to consider some strategic questions that relate to the meaning of the text.

LEVELS OF MEANING

Does the Text Have One Fixed Meaning or Several Levels of Meaning?

Does a text have only one possible meaning, several meanings, or an infinite number of meanings? Some scholars insist that the only correct meaning of a text is that meaning (or that set of meanings) the original author intended it to have. A vigorous defender of meaning as a function of authorial intention is E. D. Hirsch, Jr.[7] In this sense, meaning precedes interpretation. As we noted above, however, others argue that meaning is a function of readers not authors, and that any text's meaning depends upon the readers' perception of it. Representatives of those who defend such "reader-response" approaches to meaning include Jacques Derrida, Roland Barthes and Stanley Fish.[8] In their approach meaning does not reside within a text because the author put it there; rather, readers bring meaning to a text. Thus, a specific author does not predetermine meaning, for readers may decipher a variety of possible meanings from a written text. Most of these postmodern critics would not argue that readers can make a text say anything they please, but rather that a text may have many possible meanings. Such interpreters reject any concept of a single or normative meaning of a biblical text.

---

6 Before we throw off all restraints, we stress that in fact some boundaries *do* exist in how we use others' words. The courts have a category of "libel" that recognizes that we are not completely free in how we use words.

7 See esp. E. D. Hirsch, Jr., *Validity in Interpretation* (New Haven: Yale University Press, 1967) and id., *The Aims of Interpretation* (Chicago: Univ. of Chicago Press, 1976). We should note here that Hirsch vacillated between seeking meaning in what the author intended versus what the text meant. We opt for the latter though with all possible constraints based on the former. Our goal is the text's meaning because that is all that we may recover. At the same time we hope that textual meaning provides a fair approximation of the author/editor's intention. That is a better goal than the alternatives, as we shall see.

8 We have more to say about this methodology below. For examples see J. Derrida, *Of Grammatology* (Baltimore: Johns Hopkins Univ. Press, 1976); R. Barthes, *S/Z* (London: Jonathan Cape, 1975); and S. Fish, *Is There a Text in this Class? The Authority of Interpretive Communities* (Cambridge, MA; London: Harvard University Press, 1980).

But is a text capable of more than one meaning? Morgan rightly argues that interpretation needs the checks provided by history, exegesis, and other rational controls to keep it from becoming arbitrary. Yet he espouses a potentially problematic view when he argues that "without the possibility of finding new meaning in a text, an authoritative scripture stifles development."[9] In other words, to encourage hermeneutical creativity he posits the need to continually find new meanings in the texts. For Morgan, to deny the possibility of finding new meaning increases the likelihood that "theologically motivated scholars are likely to become either biblicist conservatives opposed to any development or ultra-liberals who have little use in their own theologies for what they learn from the Bible."[10] Though we reject the stance of the ultra-liberals, we doubt that biblicist conservatives constitute an equally abhorrent alternative. Indeed, that is precisely where we position ourselves! We seek to be conservative in retaining what the biblical texts actually *mean*, rather than imposing modern (and perhaps alien) meanings upon them. Then we seek imagination and relevance in finding *significance and application* for biblical principles. Morgan seeks to retain "theological flexibility," and this requires what he calls "hermeneutical creativity." But at what price come such flexibility and creativity? Does the Bible present normative truth? Is meaning constant or is it only in the eyes of the beholder? Where are the checks and balances?

Let us focus the question further. Suppose someone read a text from a given author and then presented the author with a meaning that the reader had "discovered" in the text. The author might admit that the "discovered" meaning was not intended even though it is apparent in the text. The text means more than the author intended. Does this episode imply that when language leaves the mind of an author, it is in the public domain and capable of meaning a number of different things depending upon who reads it? Does the meaning of a text rest solely in what the author consciously intended to convey, or does meaning somehow result from the interaction between the text (language) and the reader?

The biblical authors or the creeds of the Church may well claim inspiration and authority for the Scriptures, but modern interpreters still decide how they will handle those claims. Will we base theology and Christian practice upon what the Spirit communicates through biblical texts or upon the current objectives, concerns, and agendas of the modern individuals and communities that interpret them? We may insist too glibly upon the former when the history of interpretation clearly demonstrates how often the latter has been the case. Indeed, some argue it should be the case, or that it cannot be otherwise. How we define the task of hermeneutics depends, therefore, on determining our goal. Where does meaning reside? Is it in the speech act of the biblical text or in the reader's creative interaction with it?

Before we can determine whether our goal in interpretation is the meaning resident in the original text or something else, we must consider the possibility of multi-

---

9 R. Morgan with J. Barton, *Biblical Interpretation* (Oxford: Oxford University Press, 1988), 182.

10 Morgan and Barton, *Biblical Interpretation*, 182. We doubt that "development," to use Morgan's term, is a desirable item on the interpreter's agenda. Where the goal is to understand God's revelation—as it is for us—development smacks of adding to Scripture, an enterprise that for the last book of the Bible, at least, was specifically condemned (Rev 22:18–19). If development means to enlarge our understanding of the text's meaning and its various significances, we embrace the idea.

ple meanings within a biblical text. We may suspect multiple meanings exist in a text when we see how a NT writer employs an OT text. When Matthew says that Jesus' protection from Herod's murderous designs *fulfills*[11] the prophecy, "Out of Egypt I called my son" (Mt 2:15; cf. Hos 11:1), did he presume that Hosea's words themselves had more than one meaning? In the book of Hosea the writer referred to a past event: God's rescue of Israel from Pharaoh. But is his reference to God's "son" also a prediction about a circumstance in the Messiah's life? Did Matthew think that Hosea was speaking of Christ or did he just "make up" a new meaning he wanted to find in Hosea's text? Did Matthew convey or perhaps uncover a meaning the Holy Spirit intended even though Hosea was not aware of this meaning? How did Matthew arrive at his interpretation? It seems we have several options to consider.

1. *An author intends only one meaning for a text;* so this original, historical meaning is the legitimate object of exegesis. In this case, Hosea's intent focused on God's rescue of Israel (the historical meaning). That is the only meaning in this text. If so, that raises a question: Can a NT writer discover more meaning in an OT text than what the original writer intended? Walter Kaiser ardently insists that no NT writer ever finds more, or a different, meaning in an OT text than was originally intended by that OT writer.[12] Kaiser does not object to saying that a NT writer might variously apply or develop implications of the OT text that the original OT writer did not intend. That is on the level of *significance.* Kaiser rejects the idea that a NT author finds additional or different *meaning.*[13]

However much some may laud this stance, it raises major questions. Perhaps most troublesome to Kaiser's view are the data themselves: can we demonstrate that all NT uses of the OT disclose only that meaning the original OT author actually intended? Though Kaiser has done an admirable job of defending his case in several problematic texts, we doubt that he has succeeded in each instance, or that it is possible to demonstrate that the OT writers did in fact intend all the meaning that NT writers later found.[14] We are convinced, with most, that there are instances where NT authors

---

11 The verb "fulfill" also occurs in verses 17 and 23 in this chapter. It occurs five times in chapters 1–2. All present problems for understanding Matthew's use of the OT. See C. L. Blomberg, "Matthew," in *Commentary on the Use of the Old Testament in the New,* ed. D. A. Carson and G. K. Beale (Grand Rapids: Baker, forthcoming).

12 For Kaiser's defense and explanation see, esp., *The Uses of the Old Testament in the New* (Chicago: Moody, 1985; repr. Eugene, OR: Wipf and Stock, 2001). For a view different from Kaiser's see C. A. Evans and J. A. Sanders, *Early Christian Interpretation of the Scriptures of Israel* (Sheffield, UK: Sheffield Academic Press, 1997).

13 Here Kaiser depends heavily on the work of E. D. Hirsch who said, "*Meaning* is that which is represented by a text; it is what the author meant by his use of a particular sign sequence; it is what the signs represent. *Significance,* on the other hand, names a relationship between that meaning and a person, or a conception, or a situation, or indeed anything imaginable" (*Validity in Interpretation,* 8). He argues that the meaning of a text remains the same while its significance may change a great deal, even to the author.

14 D. J. Moo evaluates Kaiser in "The Problem of *Sensus Plenior,*" in *Hermeneutics, Authority, and Canon,* eds. D.A. Carson and J. D. Woodbridge (Grand Rapids: Zondervan, 1986), csp. on pp. 198–201. Another critic is P. B. Payne, "The Fallacy of Equating Meaning with the Human Author's Intention," *JETS* 20 (1977): 243–52, though it is not accurate to say that Kaiser always commits this fallacy.

found meaning in an OT text that the OT author did not intend. Moo opines that God as the divine author may intend meaning beyond what the human writer intended, but we will take up that suggestion more below.[15]

Note, for example, how the writer of Hebrews speaks as if Psa 45:6–7 was specifically written about Jesus:

> But about the Son he says, "Your throne, O God, will last for ever and ever, and righteousness will be the scepter of your kingdom. You have loved righteousness and hated wickedness; therefore God, your God, has set you above your companions by anointing you with the oil of joy" (Heb 1:8–9).

Some argue that Psa 45 might contain messianic overtones,[16] but what about, more astonishingly, the quote from Deut 32:43 (found in the LXX and the Dead Sea Scrolls!): "And again, when God brings his firstborn into the world, he says, 'Let all God's angels worship him'" (Heb 1:6)? For a different example, Peter employs Pss 69:25 and 109:8 as in some sense predicting what Judas did and the apostles' need to replace him in their company: "'For,' said Peter, 'it is written in the book of Psalms, "May his place be deserted; let there be no one to dwell in it," and, "May another take his place of leadership"'" (Acts 1:20). Did these OT writers *intend* these references as "deeper" meanings to their words? We have no means to affirm that they did.

We doubt that in such examples the NT writers discovered the original meanings of the texts they interpreted. To return to our initial example, we still must account for what Matthew does with the text. Though we may generally concur that an author intends a single meaning (sense), at least in a given text, what do we make of instances where it appears a later biblical writer finds a sense beyond the surface historical sense? What other options do we have?

2. *An author may intend a text to convey multiple meanings or levels of meaning—for instance, a literal level and a spiritual level.*[17] Possible examples of multiple meanings occur in apocalyptic literature and predictive prophecy. In both Daniel and Revelation, the same mythical beasts convey meanings about different nations and leaders. Also, Isaiah's prophecy of an upcoming birth (Isa 7:14) was fulfilled on two levels: in the immediate future, in our view (Isa 8:1–10), and in the distant future (Mt 1:23). Are these examples of authors who intended multiple meanings?

In fact, when a later writer finds additional significance in an earlier prophecy (as Matthew did with Isa 7:14), we are hard-pressed to prove that the original text contained that meaning on an additional level. There may be a few instances where we find some contextual clues to an author's intention to signify multiple meanings. Yet, methodologically we struggle to devise ways to uncover multiple levels apart from explicit statements, or at least very marked clues, in the text.[18] That is, if the author did

---

15 Moo, "The Problem of *Sensus Plenior*," 199.

16 See M. J. Harris, "The Translation of *Elohim* in Psalm 45:7–8," *TynB* 35 (1984): 65–89.

17 Recall our discussion about some of the church fathers like Origen.

18 For some examples of such contextual clues see C. L. Blomberg, "Interpreting Old Testament Prophetic Literature in Matthew: Double Fulfillment," *TrinJ* 23 NS (2002): 17–33, esp. 20–21.

intend multiple levels of meaning, he or she alone can identify intended meanings beyond the historical-grammatical meaning that exegetical methods uncover from the written text.[19] So this proposal, too, provides little help for the process of exegesis.

But some may object, "Can't a text be applied to a wide variety of situations?" The answer is, yes, if the question is *application,* but, no, if the issue is *multiple meanings.* When we try to make the Bible relevant today, we are not saying that the Bible can have multiple meanings—the original that the author intended and the ones we find pertinent for ourselves. Ideally, a given text bears the meaning its author intended it to have. Though in isolation a text may conceivably have a variety of possible meanings, were the author present to adjudicate, the "correct" meaning of a text would be that which the author intended for it. However, that same meaning can have a variety of valid significances for different readers who read it in their own time and place. An example will help explain this.

Jesus told many parables during his ministry. Subsequently, the Evangelists incorporated various ones in their Gospels to serve their purposes for their readers. Throughout the history of the Church countless interpreters have employed these same parables, as we do today in our study and teaching. Does the meaning that Jesus intended when he spoke a specific parable change throughout its history? No, we argue, but that meaning impacts different situations in distinct ways.[20] For example, the parable of the workers in the field (Mt 20:1–16) is truly puzzling. How outrageous to pay the same wage to laborers who worked one hour and to those who had slaved the entire day! True, one denarius for a day's work was fair, but do not those who worked more deserve to be paid more? What was Jesus' point? What *meaning* did he intend? It could well be to show that salvation is undeserved; God gives his grace to those who do not deserve it.

In the context of Mt 19–20, though, the author (i.e., Matthew) juxtaposes this parable with the disciples' faithfulness in serving Christ. Peter had said, "We have left everything to follow you! What then will there be for us?" (19:27). The frames at both ends of this parable make essentially the same point: the first will be last and the last will be first. The meaning Matthew intended may be that disciples ought to assess their motives in serving Christ. Alternatively, perhaps the issue for Matthew's community was the increasing priority and quantity of Gentiles as compared to Jews in the emerging Church.[21] What were the Christians, especially Jewish ones, to make of this development? The meaning is single—God gives rewards at his discretion—but it has several possible significances. Ryken notes, "In the kingdom of God where generosity is the foundational premise, ordinary human standards have been abolished."[22] The single meaning is capable of several possible significances through history.[23]

---

19 Of course, a writer might agree to a "meaning" that a later reader found in the author's work, as we noted above.

20 A. C. Thiselton, "Reader-Response Hermeneutics, Action Models, and the Parables of Jesus," in R. Lundin, A. C. Thiselton and C. Walhout, *The Responsibility of Hermeneutics* (Grand Rapids: Eerdmans, 1985), 79–113, recasts this in terms of multiple speech acts or multiple perlocutions in one speech act.

21 On this point see D. A. Hagner, *Matthew 14–28,* WBC 33B (Dallas: Word, 1995), 566–72.

22 L. Ryken, *Words of Life* (Grand Rapids: Baker, 1987), 70.

23 Of course, the meaning of parables may involve several points, all of which may find a variety of applications. We discuss later both how to interpret and how to apply parables. For further help see C. L. Blomberg, *Interpreting the Parables* (Downers Grove: InterVarsity, 1990).

Our point should now be clear. Though a text may find a wide variety of significances—both in the original context and forever after—we cannot confuse *significance* with *meaning*. In other words, unless we can demonstrate that the authors *intended* multiple meanings for a text, we can never assume they did. The possibility and presence of multiple applications or significances must be distinguished from what authors or speakers intend to communicate. Apart from clear clues in the context or the genre employed, we must expect that authors intend single meanings.[24] What other options should be considered?

3. *A later reader could simply invent or read into a biblical text a meaning not intended by the original author.* In other words, in the process of reading a text, interpreters may introduce some meaning that suits their purposes. Returning to Matthew's use of Hosea, the difference from the previous option lies in the purported connection to Hosea. Here, Hosea's text exists only as a jumping-off point for Matthew to devise the later (and perhaps minimally connected) meaning.

Some interpreters believe this is the only way to understand how people actually read texts.[25] Once texts exist in writing, readers not only can but do treat them as they please. Understanding involves text plus reader, and each reader produces a different reading. Note what W. G. Jeanrond says:

> The reading of a text is, rather, a dynamic process which remains in
> principle open-ended because every reader can only disclose the sense
> of a text in a process and as an individual. This signifies in its turn
> that reading is in each case more than the deciphering of the signs
> printed on paper. Reading is always also a projection of a new image
> of reality, as this is co-initiated by the text and achieved by the read-
> er in the relationship with the text in the act of reading.[26]

In this view, given the conventions of the interpretive community of which he was a member (Jewish-Christian), Matthew simply read Hosea in ways that were appropriate for his concerns.[27] That is, through that group's Christian and Christological glasses, he could read Hosea and "see" Christ as the Son whom God also protected in Egypt. Interpreters

---

24 An example of a double meaning identified in the context occurs in Jn 3:3 in Jesus' use of *anōthen* with its double entendre "again" and "from above." The Greek word *pneuma* "wind" and "spirit" continues the scheme. Clearly these are intentional. See D. A. Carson, *The Gospel of John* (Grand Rapids: Eerdmans, 1991), ad loc.

25 Such an approach is one of several, often termed "reader-response" criticism, which we mentioned above. See esp. W. Iser, *The Act of Reading: A Theory of Aesthetic Response* (Baltimore: Johns Hopkins University Press, 1978); U. Eco, *The Role of the Reader* (Bloomington: Indiana University, 1979); S. Croatto, *Biblical Hermeneutics: Toward a Theory of Reading as the Production of Meaning* (Maryknoll: Orbis, 1987); E. V. McKnight, *The Bible and the Reader* (Philadelphia: Fortress, 1985); id., *Post-Modern Use of the Bible: The Emergence of Reader-Oriented Criticism* (Nashville: Abingdon, 1988); and A. K. Adam, *What Is Postmodern Biblical Criticism?* Guides to Biblical Scholarship (Minneapolis: Augsburg Fortress, 1995).

26 W. G. Jeanrond, *Text and Interpretation as Categories of Theological Thinking* (New York: Crossroad, 1988), 104.

27 S. Fish defends this perspective: "It is interpretive communities, rather than either the text or the reader, that produce meanings and are responsible for the emergence of formal features" (*Is There a Text?* 14).

today enjoy the same privileges, such reader-response critics insist. One may put on Marxist, liberationist, gay, or feminist glasses to discover different, equally legitimate readings of a text.[28]

In violent reaction to this approach to interpretation, Steinmetz explains what he thinks of the modem tendency to make texts mean anything readers want: "Indeed, contemporary debunking of the author and the author's explicit intentions has proceeded at such a pace that it seems at times as if literary criticism has become a jolly game of ripping out an author's shirt-tail and setting fire to it."[29] He makes a legitimate point that we cannot simply ignore the author or the historical meaning of the ancient text. Yet we cannot scorn the modern reader's role either, for it is only in the process of reading that the meaning of a text emerges. To paraphrase an old philosophical question, if there is a book in the forest but no one around to read it, does it have any meaning? Once more we stress an important point: meaning is not indeterminate awaiting some reader to produce it. Meaning was encoded in the author's speech act. However, meaning is not discerned until a reader understands it. As we saw earlier, Thiselton employs a useful image in entitling his book on hermeneutics, *The Two Horizons*.[30] Understanding occurs when the horizon of the text fuses with the horizon of the modern interpreter, but only after some "distantiation" occurs—unlike the "no holds barred" approach that occurs with many reader-response critics. It is worth quoting Carson at length where he defines more carefully what is at stake.

> Whenever we try to understand the thought of a text . . ., if we are to understand it critically . . . we must first of all grasp the nature and degree of the differences that separate our understanding from the understanding of the text. Only then can we profitably fuse our horizon of understanding with the horizon of understanding of the text—that is, only then can we begin to shape our thoughts by the thoughts of the text, so that we truly understand them. Failure to go through the distantiation before the fusion usually means there has been no real fusion: the interpreter thinks he knows what the text means, but all too often he or she has simply imposed his own thoughts onto the text.[31]

The historical meaning of the text must play the controlling role. S. D. Moore makes the crucial point, "If our texts do not contain such [i.e., invariant] properties, what prevents interpretive anarchy in the academy (or in general)?"[32] We cannot simply dispense with the historical sense and do what we please with texts. We doubt that Matthew simply engaged in some arbitrary reader-response reading of Hosea. Then

---

28 Some pointed examples include L. M. Russell, ed., *Feminist Interpretation of the Bible* (Philadelphia: Westminster, 1985); and L. D. Richesin and B. Mahan, eds., *The Challenge of Liberation Theology: A First-World Response* (Maryknoll: Orbis, 1981). See the more careful assessment above.

29 D. Steinmetz, "The Superiority of Pre-Critical Exegesis," *Theology Today* 37 (1980): 38.

30 A C. Thiselton, *The Two Horizons* (Grand Rapids: Eerdmans, 1980).

31 D. A. Carson, *Exegetical Fallacies*, 2d. ed. (Grand Rapids: Baker, 1996), 23–24.

32 S. D. Moore, *Literary Criticism and the Gospels. The Theoretical Challenge* (New Haven and London: Yale University Press, 1989), 68.

what did he do? Is it possible in any way to replicate his methods? Before we respond to these questions we have further options to consider.

4. *Along with the literal sense intended by the human author, the Holy Spirit may encode a hidden meaning not known or devised at all by the human author.* Thus, in the process of inspiration God could make Matthew aware of a meaning *in Hosea's prophecy* previously intended by the Holy Spirit even though Hosea had no idea his words had that meaning. Matthew recognized that "fuller" sense, sometimes called the *sensus plenior.* In J. R. McQuilkin's thinking, "The second (hidden or less apparent) meaning . . . might have been only in the mind of the Holy Spirit, who inspired the author."[33] The question, then, is whether (some) OT texts possess a surface intentional meaning (intended by both human and divine authors) and an additional underlying meaning or meanings—a *sensus plenior*—intended by the Holy Spirit and unknown to the human author. Further, expanding the question beyond certain OT texts later cited in the NT: Can Scripture more generally be said to have this "deeper level" of meaning? Is there a "fuller sense" intended by the divine author beyond what the human author intended that a modern interpreter of the Bible might discover?[34]

Almost by definition, traditional historical, grammatical, and critical methods of exegesis cannot detect or understand such a fuller sense. That is, such methods can distinguish only the meaning of the text, not some secret sense embedded in the text that even its author did not intend. If this is true, on what basis might the existence of such a sense even be defended? Do all biblical texts have a deeper meaning? And, if all texts do not have this *sensus plenior*, how do we know which ones do? And how would we discover what it is?

Of course, one response is to simply reject the existence of a *sensus plenior* and confine exegesis to what we can defensibly study.[35] If there are no satisfactory answers to the questions posed in the previous paragraphs, we are safer simply to reject that possibility altogether. Safer, to be sure, but we have no way of knowing if we have thus lost an opportunity for legitimate understanding. Another option is to admit, provisionally, the existence of such a sense but to insist that only inspired NT writers, under the

---

33 J. R. McQuilkin, *Understanding and Applying the Bible,* 2d. ed. (Chicago: Moody, 1992), 45.

34 The volume by J. DeYoung and S. Hurty, *Beyond the Obvious* (Gresham, OR: Vision House, 1995), seeks to demonstrate that Christians today can duplicate Matthew's kind of "reading" of the OT. They believe we can discover new meaning as we are sensitive to the revelatory work of the Holy Spirit in interpreting the Bible, in keeping with its overarching theme—which they deem to be the kingdom of God. While their enterprise is admirable in many ways, they admit their case is very sketchy at present, and, despite their attempts, their method supplies no real interpretive controls. Such an approach runs the risk of miring the interpretive enterprise in subjectivism, for who can either prove or question whether an interpreter's new meaning is genuinely a product of new revelation from the Spirit?

35 In various places W. C. Kaiser rejects the concept of *sensus plenior.* e.g., "Legitimate Hermeneutics," in *Inerrancy,* ed. N. L. Geisler (Grand Rapids: Zondervan, 1979), 117–47; *Uses of the Old Testament*; and "The Current Crisis in Exegesis and the Apostolic Use of Deuteronomy 25:4 in 1 Corinthians 9:8–10," *JETS* 21(1978): 3–18. For an analysis of Kaiser's position see D. L. Bock, "Evangelicals and the Use of the Old Testament in the New," part 1, *BSac* 142 (1985): 210–12.

guidance of the Holy Spirit, could find a fuller sense.[36] This position must still verify the existence of a deeper level of meaning in the Bible, even when it admits our inability to replicate what the NT writers did with the OT texts. In other words, that interpretive option is not available to us who are not inspired (in the technical sense) interpreters of the Bible. These first two options result in the same approach to exegesis for the modern evangelical interpreter. We must limit ourselves to historical-grammatical methodology. A third solution is to welcome a deeper meaning to Scripture, to find it, defend it, and explain it.

Scholars who defend the existence of a *sensus plenior* range from Roman Catholics to evangelicals.[37] Catholics typically limit the presence of this fuller sense to that which is confirmed either by revelation in subsequent Scripture (viz., the NT) or via the authority of the Roman Catholic Church. Protestants typically limit their admission of a fuller sense to subsequent revelation in the NT alone, though D. A. Oss, adopting a canonical approach, attributes the fuller sense to what derives from a given text's organic relation to the rest of the canon.[38]

How is it possible, when God inspired writers of Scripture, that he intended a sense separate and different from what the human authors conceived and intended? In reply Moo argues that God could "have intended a sense related to but more than that which the human author intended."[39] Larkin goes even further in asserting that "many uses of the OT material in the New seem unrelated to the meaning intended by the original writer."[40] Similarly LaSor asks, "Is it not possible for God to present to the author a revelation which by its very nature contains a deeper significance?"[41] Whatever understanding the human author might have had about what he wrote, LaSor claims

---

36 In a noteworthy section near the end of his work, R. N. Longenecker argues that we can reproduce the exegesis of the NT authors only where they employ historico-grammatical methods to understand the OT. We cannot replicate their methods since the NT writers' use of the OT depended upon the Holy Spirit's inspired analysis. See *Biblical Exegesis in the Apostolic Period*, 2d ed. (Grand Rapids: Eerdmans, 1999), xxxiv–xxxix; 193–98.

37 A leading Catholic proponent was R. Brown, *The 'Sensus Plenior' of Sacred Scripture* (Baltimore: St. Mary's University, 1955); id., "The History and Development of the Theory of a Sensus Plenior," *CBQ* 15 (1953): 141–62; and id., "The *Sensus Plenior* in the Last Ten Years," *CBQ* 25 (1963): 262–285. Evangelicals include Moo, "*Sensus Plenior*," 175–212; J. D. Kunjummen, "The Single Intent of Scripture—Critical Examination of a Theological Construct," *GTJ* 7 (1986): 81–110; D. A. Oss, "Canon as Context: The Function of *Sensus Plenior* in Evangelical Hermeneutics," *GTJ* 9 (1988): 105–27; and W. S. LaSor, "Interpretation of Prophecy," in *Hermeneutics*, ed., B. Ramm (Grand Rapids: Baker, 1987), 94–117. Finally, see Steinmetz, "Pre-Critical Exegesis," who traces how belief in a fuller sense of Scripture characterized many scholars throughout the history of exegesis.

38 Oss, "Canon as Context," 107–8.

39 Moo, "*Sensus Plenior*," 204. Of course, the question is not whether God could have intended a deeper sense, but whether he did and whether we have any means to verify such an intention.

40 W. J. Larkin, *Culture and Biblical Hermeneutics* (Grand Rapids: Baker, 1988), 257. He goes on to cite such examples as Mt 27:9–10/Zech 11:12–13 and Jer 32:6–9; Acts 15:16–17/Amos 9:11–12; Rom 10:6–8/Deut 9:4 and 30:12–14; 1 Cor 2:9/Isa 64:4; 1 Cor 9:9/Deut 25:4; Heb 3:7–11/Psa 95:7–11. Of course, simply because the meanings seem rather unrelated is no reason to account for the new sense as a *sensus plenior*. As well, we wonder if Larkin really means the NT writers' uses of the OT texts are completely unrelated to the sense intended by the OT writers.

41 LaSor, "Interpretation," 108. Again, possibilities are not the issue here.

that he did not intend to convey a deeper level of meaning or fuller sense to his hearers. "But at a later date," he argues, "in the light of further revelation, the fuller meaning becomes clear to readers under the influence of the Spirit who inspired the original author."[42]

Yet, even Moo admits that the construct of *sensus plenior* does not handle all the NT's use of the OT. At times the NT writers appeal to what the OT human author said,[43] even though the meaning the NT author derives is not apparent to us after we subject the OT text to traditional historical methods. And we believe that LaSor mitigates his view of a deeper sense when he also attributes a fuller sense to great poets, philosophers, and other creative thinkers who express a fuller meaning that their disciples develop into schools or systems of thought.[44] This does not argue, then, for a deeper meaning in the texts intended by the Holy Spirit. If LaSor is correct, the fuller sense merely develops further implications or consequences of what the author originally meant.

5. There is a final option, which itself consists of alternative elements. *A biblical author may have intended a text to have only a single meaning, but a later biblical author may have discovered an additional meaning in that text.* In other words, if Matthew was performing strict historical-grammatical exegesis of the Hosea quote, he could never assert that it spoke of the Messiah. But, unlike the previous option, the Holy Spirit encoded no hidden meaning that bore such messianic overtones. It was Matthew's doing, using a "creative" exegetical method, that devised the additional sense. If so, from where did this additional meaning come? Is this option open to modern interpreters?

A common answer to the former question alleges that some NT writers made use of interpretive techniques that derived from their background in Judaism. In other words, they used some of the methods of the rabbis or the interpreters at Qumran, such as "midrash" and "pesher."[45] Scholars do not easily arrive at definitions of these practices, but several comments will help us understand them better. J. Goldin says of midrash:

> All Midrashic teaching undertakes two things: (1) to explain opaque or ambiguous texts and their difficult vocabulary and syntax . . .; (2) to contemporize, that is, so to describe or treat biblical personalities

---

42 LaSor, "Interpretation," 108.

43 Moo cites the example of Peter's use of Psa 16 in his Pentecost sermon (Acts 2:25–28) in "*Sensus Plenior*," 204. Was the human David speaking about Jesus' resurrection?

44 LaSor, "Interpretation," 108.

45 For an introduction to these and other Jewish methods, see our earlier discussion of Jewish interpretive methods. The key literature includes J. L. Kugel, ed., *Studies in Ancient Midrash* (Cambridge, MA: Harvard Univ. Press, 2001); M. A. Fishbane, ed., *The Midrashic Imagination: Jewish Exegesis, Thought, and History* (Albany, NY: State Univ. of NY Press, 1993); J. L. Kugel and R. A. Greer, *Early Biblical Interpretation* (Philadelphia: Westminster, 1986), esp. 52–106; R. Kasher, "The Interpretation of Scripture in Rabbinic Literature," in *Mikra*, ed. M. J. Mulder and H. Sysling, *Compendia Rerum Judaicarum ad Novum Testamentum*, sec. 2, pt. 1 (Philadelphia: Fortress, 1988), 560–77; R. T. France and D. Wenham, eds., *Gospel Perspectives III. Studies in Midrash and Historiography* (Sheffield, UK: JSOT, 1983); and C. L. Quarles, *Midrash Criticism: Introduction and Appraisal* (Lanham, MD: University Press of America, 1997).

and events as to make recognizable the immediate relevance of what would otherwise be regarded as only archaic.[46]

To further clarify the nature of midrash: "It was a way of delving more deeply than the literal meaning of the word of Scripture, and a method of linking the various parts of the Bible together by the discovery of typological patterns, verbal echoes, and rhythms of repetition."[47] There appear to be several examples of the use of midrashic methods in the NT. One is the well-known technique of *gezerah shawah* (combining various texts that have some verbal correlations) as in Acts 2:25–34.[48] Or note the many uses of the kind of argumentation called *qal wahomer* (from the lesser to the greater) as at Mt 10:25; Lk 11:13; and 12:28. At times such methods seem completely responsible and reflect good common sense. In other instances in the hands of rabbis, they opened the door to rather fanciful connections and interpretations.[49]

The method of pesher had a distinctive trait: "The authors of the *pesharim* believed the scriptural prophecies to have been written for their own time and predicament, and they interpreted the biblical texts in the light of their acute eschatological expectations."[50] Hence their use of the introductory phrase, "Its interpretation refers to" or more precisely, "This is that." The Qumran sectarians who produced the Dead Sea Scrolls were particularly enamored of the pesher technique as evidenced in their Habakkuk Commentary. Longenecker observes,

> Biblical interpretation at Qumran was considered to be first of all revelatory and/or charismatic in nature. Certain of the prophecies had been given in cryptic and enigmatic terms, and no one could understand their true meaning until the Teacher of Righteousness [Qumran's founder and early leader] was given the interpretive key.[51]

In their view the Teacher alone qualified to explain certain prophecies. What were the techniques that characterized the pesher method? Bruce answers: "The biblical text was atomized in the *pĕšārîm* so as to bring out the relevance of each sentence or phrase to the contemporary situation . . . . It is in this situation, not in the logical or syntactical sequence of the text, that coherence was found."[52] Some of the interpretations boggle the imagination of a modern reader.[53]

---

46 J. Goldin, "Midrash and Aggadah," in *The Encyclopedia of Religion*, ed. Mircea Eliade, 16 vols. (New York: Macmillan, 1987), 9:512.

47 R. J. Z. Werblowsky and G. Wigoder, eds., "Midrash," *The Encyclopedia of the Jewish Religion* (New York: Holt, Rinehart and Winston, 1965), 262.

48 Peter brings together Psa 16:8–11 and 110:1 to support Jesus' resurrection because both employ the phrase "at my right hand."

49 For examples see Longenecker, *Biblical Exegesis*, 21–24.

50 Werblowsky and Wigoder, eds., "Midrash," 298. See our brief treatment of Qumran exegesis in chapter 2.

51 Longenecker, *Biblical Exegesis*, 29. The "Teacher of Righteousness" was the putative leader of the Qumran Sect during the composition of much of its literature.

52 F. F. Bruce, "Biblical Exposition at Qumran," in *Gospel Perspectives*, 3: 81.

53 Bruce provides examples of their conclusions, 81–96.

Peter may have employed (or at least been influenced by) this technique when he used Joel in his Pentecost sermon: "*This is what* was spoken by the prophet Joel . . ." (Acts 2:16, emphasis added). Jesus may have engaged in something like pesher in his sermon recorded in Lk 4:16–21 where, quoting Isa 61:1–2, he says, "Today this scripture is fulfilled in your hearing" (4:21).[54]

Can such methods explain why some uses of the OT by NT writers seem to depart dramatically from what the OT appears to mean on the surface? In some cases, the answer may be, possibly, or even, yes.[55] Clearly the writers of the NT were convinced that they had entered a new era in redemptive history with the coming of Jesus. Naturally, they read the OT in a new light, a process Jesus himself encouraged (e.g., Lk 24:25–27).

The NT writers borrowed some methods of their Jewish counterparts, but they spurned others. That is, the NT writers, like Jewish interpreters, "appropriated" OT texts for their new situations—for example, "straightforward identification of one situation or person with another, modification of the text to suit the application, and association of several passages."[56] We doubt, though, that in these uses the NT authors were totally unconcerned about the original meaning of the OT texts.[57] We cannot lump together the apostles, the Qumran exegetes, and the rabbis as if they all operated in the same way. Where the apostles' interpretations seem to parallel methods of their Jewish forebears, their uses generally appear extremely restrained.

To the methods of midrash and pesher we must add another. *Typology* may be the best way to explain how NT writers most often used the OT. R. T. France sets out a clear definition of typology: "the recognition of a correspondence between New and Old Testament events, based on a conviction of the unchanging character of the principles of God's working."[58] K. Snodgrass prefers to describe this phenomenon as "correspondence in history"

---

54 See Longenecker, *Biblical Exegesis*, 54–58, 83–87, 113–116, where he makes a convincing case for further possible examples in the NT.

55 On the other hand, one point that the various articles in *Gospels Perspectives III* make repeatedly is, "very little that can confidently be traced back to the first century AD is 'midrash proper'" (France, "Postscript," 291). Thus, France goes on to express "real surprise that 'midrash' has been taken to be a major factor in the search for the literary affinities of the gospels" (291). We might add, "and for the rest of the NT."

56 Moo, "*Sensus Plenior*," 194. Their approach was restrained and guided by the historical events of their experience, though not by the historical events of the original text. France, "Postscript," 296, observes about the Gospel writers: "But the point where we have found it necessary to dissent from the attribution to the gospel writers of a 'creative midrash' which produced unhistorical stories in historical form out of the Old Testament texts is in the observation of the *secondary* role of the Old Testament texts in relation to the gospel traditions." That is, the historical events of Jesus' life and ministry provided the touchstone; the Evangelists did not creatively employ the OT to invent "history."

57 Clearly, in a textbook like this we cannot pursue the intricacies and implications that a thorough analysis of this issue requires. We must again direct the reader to the various essays in *Gospel Perspectives III* for the necessary clarification and defense of these assertions. See also S. E. Porter and C. A. Evans, *The Scrolls and the Scriptures* (Sheffield, UK: Sheffield Academic Press, 1997).

58 R. T. France, *The Gospel According to Matthew*, TNTC (Grand Rapids: Eerdmans, 1985), 40, quoting G. Lampe. His discussion is very helpful. Also, see L. Goppelt, *Typos: The Typological Interpretation of the Old Testament in the New* (Grand Rapids: Eerdmans, 1982); G. von Rad, "Typological Interpretation of the Old Testament," in *Essays on Old Testament Hermeneutics*, ed. C. Westermann and J. L. Mays (Richmond: John Knox, 1963), 17–39; and E. E. Ellis, "Biblical Interpretation in the New Testament Church," *Mikra*, ed. M. J. Mulder and H. Sysling, 716–20.

to distinguish it from abuses of the term typology.[59] The use of typology rests on the belief that God's ways of acting are consistent throughout history. Thus NT writers may, in places, explain phenomena in the new Messianic era in terms of their OT precursors. That is, they believed that many of God's former actions with Israel (or with others in the OT) were "types" of what he was now doing in Christ. For example, Peter speaks of the water that "saved" Noah and his family as a type of baptism that now saves Christians (1 Pet 3:20–21).[60] This need not imply that the OT authors actually intended, in a prophetic kind of way, the type that the NT writer later discovered. Typology is more a technique of a later writer who "mines" prior Scripture for similarities to God's present activities.[61] Theirs is no "no-holds-barred" reader-response reading of the OT; what they discover fits what they see are God's typical patterns of working.

Moo responsibly puts the subject of typology within the larger "promise-fulfillment" scheme for understanding the relationship between the Testaments. Thus, he says, "New Testament persons, events, and institutions will sometimes 'fill up' Old Testament persons, events, and institutions by repeating at a deeper or more climactic level that which was true in the original situation."[62] If this is true, then the OT writers were not always, if ever, conscious that what they were writing had typological significance. At the same time, NT writers assumed that God intended that his actions on behalf of Israel would one day find a kind of analogy or fulfillment in Christ and the Church.[63] Humanly speaking, these typological OT texts only had one level of meaning: the single meaning the human authors intended to convey. Yet God was at work too, and his past actions set the stage for what later writers would see as patterns of his working with people.[64]

This does not mean that the OT authors intended more than one meaning, nor even that the texts they wrote contained more than one meaning. Rather, it means that the OT as a whole (hence the value of canonical criticism) had a forward-looking dimension to it, sometimes (perhaps usually) unknown to the writers. Because God was at work in Israel and in the lives of his people, their writings reflected what he was doing. The subsequent writers of the NT perceived these divine patterns and made the typological connections. Craig Evans affirms this point:

---

59 K. Snodgrass, "The Use of the Old Testament in the New," in *Interpreting the New Testament: Essays on Methods and Issues*, ed. D. A. Black and D. S. Dockery (Nashville: Broadman and Holman, 2001), 215.

60 More precisely, Peter says that the water of baptism is the "antitype" (Greek: *antitypos*) of the water that saved Noah (1 Pet 3:21).

61 Snodgrass notes, "Later writers use exodus terminology to describe God's saving his people from Assyria (Isa 11:16) or salvation generally. The suffering of a righteous person (Ps 22) finds correspondence in the crucifixion of Jesus (Mt 27:39–46)" ("Use of the Old Testament," 215).

62 Moo, "*Sensus Plenior*," 196.

63 We do not presume here to know God's mind or intentions. Rather, we suspect that NT texts do refer back to OT incidents as types. As divine author of the Bible, the Holy Spirit directed the human authors to "see" the correspondences.

64 T. L. Howard, "The Use of Hosea 11:1 in Matthew 2:15: An Alternative Solution," *BSac* 143 (1986): 314–28, convincingly defends typology as the best approach to our example. He speaks of "analogical correspondence."

> The life, death, and resurrection of Jesus became for early Christians the hermeneutical key for their interpretation and application of the Jewish Scriptures. Since the Scriptures could be relied on for clarification of eschatological events, and since Jesus was the eschatological agent, there could be no doubt that the Scriptures were fulfilled in him.[65]

This view of typology helps us understand what often occurs when NT writers use the OT in what appear to be strange ways. Certainly they use the OT in ways that we do not recommend to students today! A typological framework recognizes that NT persons consciously considered their experiences to match the patterns of God's redemptive history that began with Israel. As they read the OT they became aware of the correspondences, even though their uses of the OT did not correspond—in such non-straightforward uses—to what the original writers probably intended, nor do they explain the historical-grammatical meanings of the texts themselves.

Do these "Jewish methods" imply that the meaning discovered by the NT writers was *actually in* the OT? Possibly, but only in some limited fashion. If the NT writers appropriated the OT because they observed some correspondences between an OT text and their new experiences in Christ, then perhaps in some narrow sense that meaning was discernible in the OT (though, of course, we have no way to demonstrate this). Yet, such later meaning was *not* present in the sense that the original OT author saw into the future and intended to refer to later realities. Nor would any contemporary reader of the OT have "seen" that meaning. More probably, the NT writers "brought" their interpretations to the OT texts in light of their experiences in Christ. At least we must say that their Christocentric preunderstanding predisposed them to interpretations that were not in the OT text.

Where does this leave us, then? Do biblical texts have one fixed meaning or several levels of meaning? We have set out the choices without coming to a firm conclusion. Perhaps a review of the options we have examined would be helpful before we proceed:

- Biblical authors intended *only one sense* (meaning), and this historical sense—what that text would have meant at the time written to its original readers—remains the sole legitimate object of exegesis. Whatever NT writers may have done with the OT, we must limit our exegesis to the original historical sense of the text.

- Biblical authors intended to convey *multiple meanings* or levels of meanings in at least some of their writings. These texts have several meanings that readers may subsequently discover.

- Biblical authors intended only one sense, but that sense need not limit how later readers understand a text since perception always involves a creative interaction between text and reader. Since all inter-

---

65 C. A. Evans, "The Function of the Old Testament in the New," in *Introducing New Testament Interpretation*, ed. S. McKnight (Grand Rapids: Baker, 1989), 193.

pretation is a "*reader-response*" enterprise, later readers—like the writers of the NT in their use of the OT—may invent meaning never envisioned in the original context. Interpreters may do the same today.

- Biblical authors intended only one sense, but unknown to them the Holy Spirit encoded in the text additional and hidden meaning(s). When NT writers employed OT texts, in places they were drawing out this fuller sense, the *sensus plenior*. Such a process may or may not be repeatable for modern interpreters.

- Biblical authors intended only one sense, though later readers may employ *creative exegetical techniques* to discover additional valid senses not intended by the original authors. Such techniques include Jewish methods like midrash, pesher, or typology. There probably was some connection between original text and later sense, though the connection may appear arbitrary, if not undecipherable, to others. The process may or may not be repeatable today.

Is one of these the preferred option? The answer is not simple; indeed it is complex!

AUTHOR-CENTERED TEXTUAL MEANING

What Kind of "Meaning" Ought to be the Goal of Interpretation?

Given our assumption that the Scripture constitutes God's Word to people, our goal in reading it is to discover the authors' meanings encoded in the texts they wrote. Following basic speech act theory, we believe the authors wrote texts to convey content and to effect responses in their readers. We believe God intended the Bible to function not as a mirror reflecting the readers and their meanings, but as a window into the worlds and meanings of the authors and the texts they produced. Therefore we posit the following: *the author-encoded historical meaning of these texts remains the central objective of hermeneutics.* We assume that the writers or editors of the Bible intended to communicate to their readers in the same way all people normally communicate. Thus, for the most part, they intended their messages to have only one sense (of course, they did use such devices as double entendre "words" occasionally, but our point is that the authors intended such devices to convey their meaning). They may have encoded them in metaphor, poetry, allegory, or apocalypse, in addition to more straightforward techniques, but they selected appropriate ways to convey their intended meaning. Beyond that, if the authors intended double or hidden meanings in their words, we have no means of discovering these apart from further clues, or perhaps from analogies based upon other examples in Scripture.[66] But this remains a problematic task. We must

---

66 For example, only with great reluctance do scholars offer possible explanations of John's code number 666 in Rev 13:18. Whatever the author intended to denote remains debatable at best to modern readers. Many conjecture it may be some kind of takeoff of the perfect digits 777 or a gematria pointing to Nero Caesar, or to someone else. See G. E. Ladd, *A Commentary on the Revelation of John* (Grand Rapids: Eerdmans, 1972), 186–87; R. Mounce, *The Book of Revelation*, NICNT, rev. ed (Grand Rapids: Eerdmans, 1998), 261–63; D. E. Aune, *Revelation 6–16*, WBC (Nashville: Nelson, 1998), 770–73; and G. K. Beale, *The Book of Revelation,* NIGNT (Grand Rapids: Eerdmans; Carlisle, UK: Paternoster, 1999), 718–28.

desist from affirming other levels of meaning without objective evidence. At most we may only tentatively suggest other possible meanings.

Clearly, two interpreters may disagree about what a biblical text means, and an author may admit seeing a meaning in a text he or she wrote that was not consciously intended. But we cannot allow these features to cloud the essential task of interpretation. Texts may indeed be polyvalent or polysemous.[67] A well-known example is: "Flying planes can be dangerous."[68] Its meaning would differ radically if said by a flying instructor to a new student pilot or by King Kong as he desperately clung to a precarious spot on the Empire State Building.[69] However, in our study of the Bible we presuppose that we seek to understand God's revelation. In the Bible, God has communicated a message to his people. Though a given passage may be capable of being understood in several ways, our goal is to determine what (of those various possible meanings) the text most likely would have meant to its author and to its original readers. This is why people communicate: they expect that what they express will be understood as they intended it. The original biblical text alone was inspired, for only its meaning was encoded in the original historical context. We seek, therefore, the original meaning of that original text. Furthermore, in light of the options of meanings noted above, if we can determine that the original text intended to convey more than one meaning, then those multiple meanings also comprise the goal of exegesis.[70]

Definition of Author-Centered Textual Meaning

What do we mean by textual meaning? The meaning of a text is *that which the words and grammatical structures of that text disclose about the probable intention of its author/editor and the probable understanding of that text by its intended readers.*[71] It is the meaning those words would have conveyed to the readers at the time they were written by the author or editor.

Of course, we do not know with certainty who wrote many of the biblical books. Furthermore, the composition of some books was probably due to a series of editors or "redactors" who put their own touches on the books until at some point the books acquired their canonical shape.[72] Truly, in some biblical texts we may have several "layers"

---

67 That is, texts, as well as words, may be capable of more than one meaning or sense. The word 'solution' affords a clear example on the lexical level. It can refer to either a liquid substance or the answer to a problem.

68 Another example of an ambiguous sentence is the sports headline that appeared in the 1970s: "Catfish Hunter Gets Perfect Game." *The New Yorker* (June 8, 1992, page 96) provided a humorous example from a flyer announcing a topic in the Lunch and Learn Series at Auburn University, Alabama: "Disciplining Children: Concrete Helps."

69 From the famous Hollywood movie originally made in 1933 and remade in 1976.

70 Readers will note that we employed "the NT use of the OT" as a kind of litmus test of what multiple meanings the OT can have, and by analogy what multiple meanings the rest of the Bible might display.

71 We are intentionally embracing together two options that some theorists split apart: an author-centered focus and a text-centered focus. We see liabilities in any attempt to select one of these over against the other as the sole focus of hermeneutics. We say more below.

72 The Pentateuch provides a clear example. We do not know who or how many "editors" put these books in the final form we now read. Clearly it was not Moses alone, since Deut 34 records his death and other indicators point to later times (e.g., Gen 12:6; 14:14; 22:14; 36:31). For a recent discussion

of authors. And though we encounter sayings of Jesus in the Gospels, in places we must distinguish Jesus' original point from the Evangelists' purposes as evidenced in their editing and placement. Further, where the Evangelists were not eyewitnesses to Jesus' remarks, presumably they obtained their material from other sources.[73]

In spite of these theoretical problems, we may conveniently speak of the person (or even group) who put the biblical book into its final form—the form the canon preserves. We likewise assume, along with most Christian confessions of faith, that this final form alone possesses the status of inspired revelation.[74] Our goal is to understand the meaning of the book (or texts) the human writer (the shaper of the book's final form) produced, while at the same time asserting that God's intention is also bound up in that inspired text. Can we be certain that a text expresses the intention of the author? On a strictly human level, perhaps we cannot. But for biblical texts, we assume that in the divine/human concursive activity of inspiration, God's influence assured that all biblical texts do indeed express the divine author's intentions.[75] God's purposes were not frustrated.

To repeat, in establishing the meaning of the biblical texts as our goal, we do not deny that some kinds of literature have meaning(s) beyond the surface level of the text, as in poetry or metaphorical language. In that case an author still intends a single meaning, but that meaning is conveyed through metaphors or symbols. Thus, a parable might appear to have two levels of meaning—the literal story and the "spiritual lesson"—but the author still intends to convey some specific meaning. Of course, that specific meaning might consist of several points or more than one lesson.[76] The parable's literal story conveys the author's intended meaning—the lesson(s). We seek only this intended meaning, though it could have several components. In other instances

---

concerning the origin of the Pentateuch, see G. Wenham, "Pondering the Pentateuch: The Search for a New Paradigm," in *The Face of Old Testament Studies*, ed. D. W. Baker and B. T. Arnold (Grand Rapids: Baker, 1999), 116–144; cf. also the enlightening study by D. Garrett, *Rethinking Genesis: The Sources and Authorship of the First Book of the Pentateuch* (Grand Rapids: Baker, 1991). Or, who wrote Ruth, and when was it written? Though the story derives from the period of the judges (1:1), internal references—such as the need to explain the "sandal ceremony" (4:7) and the genealogy at the end (4:18–22)—indicate that it was written much later to bolster the Davidic monarchy (see R. L. Hubbard, Jr., *The Book of Ruth*, NICOT [Grand Rapids; Eerdmans, 1988]). For the NT, the writers of the Gospels provide examples of editors who wove together the works and words of Jesus into coherent narratives.

73 On some of the issues that constitute the "synoptic problem," see R. H. Stein, *Studying the Synoptic Gospels: Origin and Interpretation* (Grand Rapids: Baker, 2001); and D. L. Dungan, *A History of the Synoptic Problem: The Canon, the Text, the Composition, and the Interpretation of the Gospels*, The Anchor Bible Reference Library (New York: Doubleday, 1999). The method of redaction criticism particularly focuses on the Evangelists as editors of the Gospels.

74 Even S. Grenz and J. Franke who reject foundationalism assume that the Bible is the unique book through which the Spirit speaks, constituting theology's norming norm (*Beyond Foundationalism* [Louisville: Westminster John Knox, 2001], esp. 63–75).

75 The classic texts on inspiration—2 Tim 3:16–17 and 2 Pet 1:20–21—do not even begin to exhaust the Bible's testimony to itself and to its divine origin and status as God's Word. For a detailed list and discussion of many such biblical texts see W. Grudem, "Scripture's Self-Attestation and the Problem of Formulating a Doctrine of Scripture," in *Scripture and Truth*, ed. D. A. Carson and J. D. Woodbridge (Grand Rapids: Zondervan, 1983), 19–64.

76 See Blomberg, *Interpreting the Parables*, esp. 162–67.

(what N. Perrin calls "tensive symbols"), metaphorical discourse may be deliberately open-ended or polyvalent.[77] Still, this results from an author's deliberate intention.

The Challenge of Reader-Oriented Interpretation

Obviously the interpreter or reader plays a crucial role in discovering meaning. In fact, based on their needs and inherent preunderstandings, readers and interpreters can find and "create" meanings in the text. Readers do *use* texts as mirrors and project their own meanings onto them. As we have seen, for some, our intention to restrict the goal of interpretation to an author-based textual meaning appears excessively and unnecessarily confining. McKnight observes that people have used the biblical writings throughout history to discover and create meaning for themselves.[78] Locating meaning in a reader-oriented process of interpretation requires that attention be paid to the "realities behind the text . . . in order to understand the text as a pattern of meaning that continues to have an effect on readers."[79]

Thus, a reader-oriented approach pays more attention to the role of the modern reader in the work of analyzing texts. Exegesis is "in part a creative construction of the reader, a construction of cause, which is a result of the effect of the text in the first place."[80] The original "causes" behind a text are relativized and placed in balance with what modern readers do with the text to create meaning. Instead of simply looking for facts from the Bible with which to create or inform theological systems, the reader-oriented approach attempts to create a new world within the reader in the process of reading the Bible, albeit a world that intersects with the world of the texts he or she is reading. The biblical text has challenged and modified the reader's starting points so that "the reader's self is being redefined in the process."[81]

Clearly there are perceived values and virtues in such an approach. It places the center of attention on Bible *readers*, who in fact ought to serve as the focal point of interpretation. Too readily do author- or text-based approaches get lost in the ancient world, as if having described the origin and world of a text or identified the text's form, we have completed the task. In addition, reader-centered approaches take seriously what readers bring to the process of interpretation: they often do so unashamedly and intentionally to produce their unique "readings" of a text.[82] And this has opened up biblical studies to other "voices," both ideological and geographical, and facilitated greater attempts to contextualize the fruits of those studies. Thus feminist or liberationist readings (to name just two) have helpfully and rightly directed attention to important issues of justice that might not have surfaced had not readers approached texts with such ideological concerns. Employing a hermeneutic of suspicion, they have

---

77 N. Perrin, *Jesus and the Language of the Kingdom: Symbol and Metaphor in New Testament Interpretation* (London: SCM, 1976).

78 E. V. McKnight, *Postmodern Use of the Bible: The Emergence of Reader-Oriented Criticism* (Nashville: Abingdon, 1988), 170.

79 McKnight, *Postmodern Use*, 175.

80 McKnight, *Postmodern Use*, 175.

81 McKnight, *Postmodern Use*, 176.

82 Even when such reader-centered approaches function unconsciously (as often done in conservative circles where readers avow they are merely reading what the Bible itself says), the result is a lively engagement with the text and a serious attempt to put its "message for me" into practice.

questioned long-standing interpretations assuming (perhaps rightly in some instances) that for too long western, northern, and male ideologies have controlled the outcomes of biblical interpretation.

Despite some of these benefits, we must register pointed cautions. A variety of reader-response approaches may find diverse meanings in a text (pointing out the subjectivity of the stance), but if the creativity of such readings goes beyond the author's meaning, they may be beside the point. We affirm that only the author-encoded meaning of the text, not one's reading of it, has any legitimate claim to acceptance as God's actual, authentic, and Spirit-inspired message. We can apply interpretive controls only if we seek as our primary goal the meaning that would have made sense to the original writer and readers. Though complete objectivity or certainty may elude all readers, the textual meaning represents a worthy ideal or target. We face the possibility that all other meanings may be subjective and merely reflect the whim of the interpreter. In a postmodern climate that may be acceptable and indeed desirable for some, but not for interpreters seeking to understand the biblical texts as divine revelation. Only textual meaning provides a fixed core of meaning for it represents the speech act of the author.

Does such an approach preclude studying the Bible as literature? No, it requires it. We have no desire to deny a legitimate place for a literary study of the Bible that may transcend historical approaches. We agree that interpreters may want to study and appreciate the literary dimensions of the text rather than seeking its propositional meaning or content.[83] Indeed, various literary theories and methods contribute immensely to our understanding and appreciation of Scripture. Morgan rightly notes, "One mark of great literature is its capacity to illuminate and enlarge the experience of successive readers in new social contexts."[84] We may read the Bible to obtain the information it contains, and we may read it for other purposes—for enjoyment, inspiration, courage, solace, or pleasure—that may go beyond the texts' original intentions. Surely we may "use" the Bible beyond its original intentions or meanings. These remain valid uses of the Bible. But there is a further point to be underscored.

We must study the various genres and parallel forms in the *literature* of the ancient world in order to shed light on the original meaning or intention of biblical texts. Indeed, a large part of this book is devoted precisely to that program. So if interpreters seek the historical meaning of the text, they will compare it with Jewish and Greco-Roman rhetoric, ancient Near Eastern sagas, law codes, biographies, letters, or plays, etc. to gain insight into what ancient authors—including those of the Bible—developed and produced in their

---

83 We give considerable space to deciphering the literary dimensions of the biblical texts, and particularly, literary criticism. See chapter 3. For additional insight see such works as A. Jefferson and D. Robey, eds., *Modern Literary Theory*, 2d ed. (London: B.T. Bratsford; Totowa, NJ: Barnes & Noble, 1986); and F. Lentricchia, *After the New Criticism* (London: Methuen, 1980). L. Ryken, *Words of Delight: A Literary Introduction to the Bible*, 2d ed. (Grand Rapids: Baker, 1993), provides good examples of how literary criticism works. For an introduction to OT narratives, see D. Gunn and D. N. Fewell, *Narrative in the Hebrew Bible* (Oxford: Oxford University Press, 1993); for poetry, see S. E. Gillingham, *The Poems and Psalms of the Hebrew Bible*, Oxford Bible Series (Oxford: Oxford University Press, 1994). T. Longman, III, *Literary Approaches to Biblical Interpretation* (Grand Rapids: Zondervan, 1987), furnishes a clear general introduction.

84 Morgan and Barton, *Biblical Interpretation*, 10–11.

writing.[85] All of this is to say that literary criticism subdivides into three areas: (1) focus on the author's intent in composing the text, (2) the conventions of the text that reflect that intent, and (3) the readers' response to the text.

Thus, we view literary approaches to studying the Bible, not as mutually exclusive with our historical concerns, but as complementary and equally legitimate. We must inquire about the historical basis of a text and its author's intentions in writing it; *and* we may seek to appreciate that author's writing as a literary product and how the writing conveyed the author's intentions. Since the texts function as "speech-acts," we seek to employ all tactics that uncover what they mean. But we insist that we must take seriously their authors' intentions and seek to understand them as such. Literary readings must enhance and clarify, not take over or subvert the meaning the author intended to convey.

The Question of Historicity

If an author writes an account as a historical report in the normal conventions of the time, then, assuming the author is a good historian, we are predisposed to accept it as true and interpret it in that light. If the account belongs to a different genre (say a parable or a fable) and its message is conveyed via the conventions consistent with that genre, then we interpret it on those terms. Either way we are seeking the author's intention as reflected in the resulting text. Recall our brief discussion of speech act theory: we aim to understand the text's propositional content, manner of presentation (e.g., genre), and the author's desired outcome or effect on the readers.

So as Christians in the evangelical tradition we want to retain the appropriate balance in evaluating the Bible in its character as literature. Literary approaches yield interesting and important insights into the nature of the documents; but we argue, even as literature, the biblical documents also record genuine history.[86] Of course, on the surface level of language, genuine history and historical fiction may appear indistinguishable. For example, did Nathan's story of the ewe lamb (2 Sam 12:1–4) really happen? What about the parable of the sower (Mt 13:3–8 par.)? Is the narrative of Job or the story of Jonah literal history or historical fiction that mixes both historical and nonhistorical elements? Are the early chapters of Genesis poetry or narrative? Are Luke's

---

85 Two important works in this regard are D. E. Aune, *The New Testament in Its Literary Environment* (Philadelphia: Westminster, 1987); and J. H. Walton, *Ancient Israelite Literature in Its Cultural Context: A Survey of Parallels Between Biblical and Ancient Near Eastern Texts* (Grand Rapids: Zondervan, 1989). See also the concluding bibliography.

86 Simply because the Bible is a religious document does not imply that it cannot report events as they really happened. Of course, neither may we merely assert that because the Bible records events, they happened as recorded. Historicity must he established on neutral ground. History and theology need not be mutually exclusive categories. For the OT, see W. G. Dever, *What Did the Biblical Writers Know & When Did They Know It?* (Grand Rapids/Cambridge, UK: Eerdmans, 2001); V. P. Long, *The Art of Biblical History*, Foundations of Contemporary Interpretation 5 (Grand Rapids: Zondervan, 1994); and K. L. Younger, Jr., *Ancient Conquest Accounts*, JSOTSup 98 (Sheffield: JSOT, 1990). For two NT examples, see the important discussion in I. H. Marshall, *Luke: Historian and Theologian*, 3d ed. (Downers Grove: InterVarsity, 1998); and C. L. Blomberg, *The Historical Reliability of John's Gospel* (Leicester: Apollos; Downers Grove: InterVarsity, 2001), esp. pp. 63–67. On establishing criteria of authenticity, see, e.g., N. T. Wright, *Jesus and the Victory of God* (London: SPCK; Minneapolis: Augsburg Fortress, 1996), esp. pp. 131–33.

reports of the speeches of Peter and Paul in Acts verbatim accounts, faithful epitomes, or pure fiction? What criteria help the interpreter decide? We must study the literary conventions as well as the accounts themselves for further clues.

Suppose we envision a continuum whose endpoints we label simplistically literal historical reports of events as they happened and pure fiction.[87]

historical   ⟵————————————————⟶   fictional
reporting   invention

We must analyze each biblical account to see where it falls between these endpoints. If a passage purports to record genuine history according to the literary and textual conventions of the day, then we may infer that the story actually happened. If, on the other hand, the literary and textual cues of genre point to inventiveness, then we must place the story toward the endpoint of fiction. The key issue is how the original writer intended the account to be read—how he or she and the first readers would have understood it. Individual narratives may fall somewhere along the continuum involving both factual and creative elements. In all cases the literary dimensions unfold for us important lessons and provide significant learning.[88]

We insist upon this historically plausible meaning because of our presumption that we must embrace the biblical authors' writings *on their terms*, not because we want to question their reliability or theological authority. This is a matter of integrity with the author's text. We would be just as misguided to insist that something intended as fictional (or somewhere in the middle of the continuum above) is historical as it would be to take something intended as historical to be fictional. Both would misconstrue the writer's intentions and impose alien readings on the biblical text, thereby making our modern preunderstanding the authority rather than the biblical text.

This brings us to the decision about what we will do with the biblical texts. We must decide whether we will seek the meaning in the texts or whether we will use, construe, or deconstruct the texts in other ways.[89] We believe that our task is to decode the speech acts of the texts in the way language normally functions in order to understand

---

87 D. Tovey, *Narrative Art and Act in the Fourth Gospel* (Sheffield, UK: Sheffield Academic Press, 1997), also employs this way of portraying the situation. Cf. C. L. Blomberg, *The Historical Reliability of John's Gospel.*

88 For insight into the complex issues of how narratives function, see R. Alter, *The Art of Biblical Narrative* (New York: Basic Books, 1981); A. Berlin, *Poetics and Interpretation of Biblical Narrative* (Sheffield: Almond Press, 1983); and M. A. Powell, *What Is Narrative Criticism?* Guides to Biblical Scholarship (Minneapolis: Augsburg Fortress, 1991); and J. P. Fokkelman, *Reading Biblical Narrative: An Introductory Guide* (Louisville: Westminster John Knox, 2000).

89 Deconstruction is a technical term that refers to a program of interpretation often identified with J. Derrida. Vanhoozer provides this definition: "Deconstruction is a painstaking taking-apart, a peeling away of the various layers—historical, rhetorical, ideological—of distinctions, concepts, texts, and whole philosophies, whose aim is to expose the arbitrary linguistic nature of their original construction" (*Is There a Meaning in This Text?*), 52. (We discussed this subject in more detail above.) For interpretive discussions, consult C. Norris, *Deconstruction: Theory and Practice* (London and New York: Methuen, 1982); J. Culler, *On Deconstruction: Theory and Criticism after Structuralism* (Ithaca: Cornell University Press, 1982); and Thiselton, *New Horizons*, 103–32.

their meaning. We will employ the usual exegetical procedures of lexical semantics,[90] grammar, genre criticism, and all appropriate tactics of historical and literary criticism. We will strive for the interpretation that is most plausible historically, given all the available data.

LEGITIMATE READER-RESPONSE INTERPRETATION

How Can We Assure that We Give the Reader Full Due?

We seek the meaning the texts had at the time they were written—the meaning the author/editor intended and that the original readers would most likely have acknowledged. But having stressed (repeatedly) this point, our reading of how NT writers employ the OT still leaves us reluctant to say that the historical meaning of a text can remain our sole concern. In our earlier discussion we noted that in places the NT writers found meanings in texts that the OT authors never intended—meanings that would not have occurred to the original readers of those OT texts. We doubt, however, that these phenomena suggest that the Holy Spirit inspired a *sensus plenior*, a fuller sense, which he then guided later writers to uncover. Though this may be a possible explanation of the data (and Moo's position may be the most defensible variety of a *sensus plenior*), we have no objective criteria to posit the existence of a *sensus*, or to determine where or when it might exist, or how one might proceed to unravel its significance.[91] In other words, if the human author of a text neither intended nor was aware of a deeper level of meaning, how can we be confident today that we are able to detect it? We may uncover analogies or types in how God works, and thus suggest additional meaning for a text (as we will explore below), but can we declare we have discovered an additional meaning that the Holy Spirit actually deposited within texts? We remain skeptical. *Sensus plenior* must remain an interesting construct, an attempt to make sense out of puzzling issues, but it provides little help for modern interpreters in the actual practice of understanding God's revelation.

So do readers bring any meaning to the interpretive process? At the risk of misunderstanding, we posit that in their interaction with the biblical text readers do "construct"

---

90 Lexical semantics comprises all the facets of doing responsible studies of words in their various historical and literary contexts to discover their meaning. The best introduction is M. Silva, *Biblical Words and Their Meaning: An Introduction to Lexical Semantics,* 2d ed. (Grand Rapids Zondervan, 1995). A helpful companion limited to the NT is E. A. Nida and J. P. Louw, *Lexical Semantics of the Greek New Testament Greek* (Atlanta: Scholars Press, 1992). Nothing comparable exists for the OT, but the ongoing Semantics of Ancient Hebrew Database project chaired by T. Muraoka may eventually fill the gap by publishing its results in electronic format.

91 See Moo, "*Sensus Plenior,*" 175–211. Moo argues for a multifaceted understanding of the variety of ways NT writers employ the OT. But in addition to the others he finds, he concludes, "it may be that some citations are best explained according to the traditional *sensus plenior* model: by direct inspired apprehension, the New Testament authors perceive the meaning in a text put there by God but unknown to the human author." Moo goes on to argue, "Even in this case, however, it is important to insist that this 'deeper meaning' is based on and compatible with the meaning intended by the human author" (210). Moo is at a loss, then, to find any usefulness for this approach in the exegete's interpretive work, unless the "deeper meanings" are clearly enunciated within Scripture itself. In our judgment, then, it remains a rather slippery and unproductive concept. DeYoung and Hurty's similar tactic seems equally unhelpful (*Beyond the Obvious*).

meaning. Though we have been mostly cautious due to its limitations, the reader-response approach merits thoughtful, though controlled, recognition. What do we mean? Understanding a biblical text is a creative enterprise, much like a conversation between friends. In a conversation each person is involved not only in analyzing (albeit subconsciously) the precise meanings of words and grammatical constructions, but also in understanding the other person. How each participant "reads" the other will depend upon prior experiences, as well as upon their individual situations. In Tate's words, "Individual interpretations . . . are individual conversations with the text and are always situated within some context. Interpretation is relational and involves understanding the text in light of who we are, and understanding ourselves in light of the text."[92] As we insisted above, readers do not change an author's meaning, but different readers will understand it differently.

But interpreters who remain committed to the Bible as divine revelation may allow only a limited range of possibilities for interpretation. The sky is not the limit for possible meanings, and here we must set ourselves clearly apart from other reader-response critics' work. Properly informed, readers may understand a text only in a way related to the intention of the author or its historical meaning. We believe Christians operate under the constraints of Jesus Christ—who he is, what he has done, and the community he has created—and the Holy Spirit, who inspired Scripture and illumines readers. Biblical texts must be understood within the context and confines of the believing community in which each interpreter resides, though, admittedly, these interpretations will differ among communities. How does this work?

For example, the NT presents the practice of baptism in the Gospels where John the Baptizer requires this rite of those repenting. In Mark's words, "And so John came, baptizing in the desert region and preaching a baptism of repentance for the forgiveness of sins" (Mk 1:4). Jesus continued and encouraged the practice (Jn 3:22; 4:1–2; Mt 28:19–20), and it became a central rite in the developing Church (Acts 2:38, 41; 8:12, 38; 9:18; 10:47f.; 16:15, 33; 18:8; 19:5; et al.). Some texts may indicate a certain method of baptism (e.g., often Acts 8:38–39 is cited to defend immersion), though most do not. The historical precedent among the Jews was evidently immersion in a *mikvah* (i.e., a tank for ritual baths).[93] Nevertheless, various believing Christian communities have come to understand the relevant texts in different ways. They view their community's practice in light of their "reading" of the relevant texts. Various immersionist groups appeal to the historical precedent of immersion as the rite of cleansing and initiation for the Jews. They insist that, while the spiritual message is of paramount importance, no other method of baptism correctly represents the biblical pattern.

---

92 W. R. Tate, *Biblical Interpretation* (Peabody, MA: Hendrickson, 1991), 211. The book's 2d edition appears to lack this quotation.

93 Though no archaeological evidence for these ritual immersion pools antedate Hellenistic times, Jewish tradition asserts that the practice of ritual cleansing in water goes back to Adam and was required for all Israelites prior to meeting God at the giving of the Law at Sinai; was practiced in the "well of Miriam" in the desert; was performed at the induction of Moses and Aaron and subsequent priests into the priesthood; was central to the ongoing Temple cult in Jerusalem; and became a requirement for all proselytes to Judaism. Traditionally, and up to the present time, immersion in water is a central feature of Jewish religious practice. See R. Slonim, *Total Immersion: A Mikvah Anthology* (Northvale, NJ: Jason Aronson, 1996); and A. Kaplan, *Waters of Eden: The Mystery of the Mikvah* (New York: NCSY/Union of Orthodox Jewish Congregations of America, 1976).

Others emphasize the spiritual significance of the rite, or its link to circumcision, and treat the mode—whether immersion, sprinkling, or pouring—as a secondary issue (though even some of these groups specify a single mode, e.g., sprinkling).

Do some texts "clearly" denote immersion, while others "clearly" teach sprinkling or pouring so that the groups pick or reject the ones they prefer? Or, to complicate the discussion, do some texts teach the baptism of *believers* while other texts teach the baptism of *infants*? Proponents of one side or the other often would insist upon affirmative answers, but the issues are not so simple. One matter is certain: various church traditions have decided what the relevant texts will *mean for them*. To cite a couple of examples, some Presbyterians decide to baptize infants and adult converts by sprinkling only; others sprinkle and/or immerse infants and adult believers—whatever the parents or converts prefer. Baptist groups typically insist upon the immersion of believers, though they must decide what "belief" means, especially in instances where children of a rather young age seek baptism. They also struggle over what to do if potential church members were baptized as believers but by another mode, or even by immersion in another denomination.

Does the Bible confirm these groups' practices of baptism? While each group would insist upon an affirmative answer, each one finds different meanings in the same baptismal texts. Most Presbyterians would never admit that the relevant texts "mean" immersion but that they choose to "apply" them by sprinkling (applying Hirsch's and our distinction between meaning and significance). Those who sprinkle babies may bring into the discussion the analogy of the OT practice of circumcision of infants. They note, of course, that the Church has employed the methods of sprinkling and pouring since the first or second century. Indeed, some paedobaptists may even admit that the pattern for baptism in the NT was immersion; sprinkling of infants is never taught in the Scriptures.[94] But, they are quick to add, that is because the NT writers never addressed the issue of children of believing parents. Infant baptism developed as a legitimate theological inference from other clear biblical teachings.[95] Or, says Bromiley, "The inclusion of the children of adult converts is so much in line with the thought and practice of the OT that it is taken for granted in the New, as the household baptisms of Acts suggest even if they do not prove."[96] He continues,

> Quite apart from the external evidence, the New Testament itself offers plain indications that the children of Christians are regarded as members of the divine community just as the children of Old Testament Israel were. In these circumstances the inference of an

---

94 See G. W. Bromiley, *Children of Promise. The Case for Baptizing Infants* (Grand Rapids: Eerdmans, 1979); and E. Ferguson, ed., *Conversion, Catechumenate, and Baptism In The Early Church* (New York: Garland, 1993).

95 R. R. Booth, *Children Of the Promise: The Biblical Case For Infant Baptism* (Phillipsburg, NJ: P&R Pub., 1995); and K. Stasiak, *Return To Grace: A Theology Of Infant Baptism* (Collegeville, MN: Liturgical, 1996). For a useful collection of essays on relevant biblical and church practice see S. E. Porter and A. R. Cross, ed., *Baptism, The New Testament And The Church: Historical And Contemporary Studies In Honour of R.E.O. White* (Sheffield, UK : Sheffield Academic Press, 1999).

96 Bromiley, *Children of Promise*, 2.

accepted practice of infant baptism is undoubtedly legitimate if not absolutely or bindingly so.[97]

Thus, such people interpret the texts concerning baptism with their preunderstandings. Biblical texts, principles and analogies, and historical tradition weigh heavily in their interpretation.[98]

Correspondingly, those who teach the immersion of adult believers also rely on biblical texts and their traditions. Opposing the baptism of infants, Beasley-Murray insists,

> It is not only that the New Testament is silent on the practice of infant baptism, but that the thought and practice of the primitive communities, as reflected in the New Testament documents, appear to be contrary to the ideas and practices that accompany infant baptism in the later Churches.[99]

Indeed, he insists that "infant baptism originated in a capitulation to pressures exerted upon the Church both from without and from within."[100] His take on the NT and historical issues seems radically different from Bromiley's. What is going on in the minds of such respected scholars?

What we are saying boils down to this: neither infant baptizers nor those who insist upon the immersion only of believers dismiss the Bible in defending their views. Indeed, both affirm their loyalty to its teaching and want to abide by what it says. Hence equally committed, sincere, and equipped interpreters in these two traditions arrive at different conclusions about the meaning of the biblical texts. Certainly, constraints must apply. For example, Presbyterians typically insist upon the need for each individual's personal faith in Christ. They do not teach that an infant's baptism secures his or her personal salvation; salvation, they affirm, depends upon each person's trust in Christ. In other words the total Bible's teaching about relevant issues provides the guidelines and restraints within which all legitimate interpretations must lie.

Another pertinent illustration is the theological topic of eschatology, which concerns the future or what are called the "end times." Since the earliest days of the Church, Christians have debated the various biblical texts that seem to indicate the intricacies of end-time events. What did the biblical writers say about future events, especially the conclusion of history? While we cannot engage in a thorough study of the issues surrounding eschatology, we can use this topic to illustrate a point about bringing meaning to the process of interpretation.[101]

---

97 Bromiley, *Children of Promise*, 4.

98 On some of the historical sources for infant baptism see J. Jeremias, *Infant Baptism in the First Four Centuries* (London: SCM, 1960). For the case against infant baptism from a Reformed theological position see P. K. Jewett, *Infant Baptism and the Covenant of Grace* (Grand Rapids: Eerdmans, 1978).

99 G. R. Beasley-Murray, *Baptism in the New Testament* (Grand Rapids: Eerdmans, 1973), 352.

100 Beasley-Murray, *Baptism*, 352.

101 Here we must limit our discussion to the views of those Christians who believe that biblical prophecies sketch out a well-developed future eschatology. For others who believe the Bible's teachings about the future to be less complete or clear, this example will be irrelevant.

One aspect of eschatology concerns the "millennium," or thousand-year reign of Christ.[102] Some theologians and Christian believers accept the view that this will entail a literal period of time (whether or not it spans precisely one thousand years). In one view, following his Second Coming, Christ himself will reign with believers on this present literal earth.[103] Others view the millennium more symbolically: they believe Christ and his followers currently reign in his kingdom, and at his glorious return Christ will bring history to a conclusion and usher in the eternal state, or age to come.[104] Proponents of a third but smaller group, adopting a literal view similar to the first, believe that this Church Age will develop into a final period of time—the millennium—after which Christ will return to begin the eternal state.[105]

As a test of these interpretations, we may scrutinize what two proponents say concerning Rev 20:4d-5, where the writer says of a group of people,

> They came to life and reigned with Christ a thousand years. (The rest
> of the dead did not come to life until the thousand years were ended.)
> This is the first resurrection.

Premillennialist G. Ladd argued that the phrase "came to life" refers to the literal resurrection of these believers, and that "it is not used of any 'spiritual resurrection' of the souls of the righteous at death."[106] Thus, he continued, "At the beginning of the millennial period, part of the dead come to life; at its conclusion, the rest of the dead come to life."[107] Finally, Ladd admits, "This is the only passage in the entire Bible which teaches a temporal *millennial* kingdom, and there is only one other passage in the NT which may envisage a temporal reign of Christ between his parousia and the *telos* [end]: 1 Cor 15:23–24."[108]

Yet in his commentary on these same verses amillennialist W. Hendriksen asserted, "In this entire passage there is not a single word about a resurrection of *bodies*."[109]

---

102 For a helpful introduction to the major competing options among conservative scholars, see R. Clouse, ed., *The Millennium: Four Views* (Downers Grove: InterVarsity, 1977); and C. A. Blaising, ed., *Three Views on the Millennium and Beyond* (Grand Rapids: Zondervan, 1999). For sane analyses of the options see S. J. Grenz, *The Millennial Maze* (Downers Grove: InterVarsity, 1992); and M. J. Erickson, *A Basic Guide To Eschatology: Making Sense Of The Millennium*, rev. ed. (Grand Rapids: Baker, 1999).

103 For obvious reasons such interpreters are called premillennialists. Christ returns to earth prior to his reign during the millennium.

104 Sometimes such theologians are called amillennialists, though that may be a misnomer. They do not deny a millennium; rather, they prefer to view it as realized in church history following Christ's victory over Satan at the cross. They expect no future millennium. Other amillennialists equate the millennium with the future state—the new heavens and the new earth.

105 We call these interpreters postmillennialists. According to this view, Christ returns following a literal millennium.

106 Ladd, *Revelation*, 265.

107 Ladd, *Revelation*, 266.

108 Ladd, *Revelation*, 267, his emphasis. Ladd also discusses this passage in his *Crucial Questions About the Kingdom of God* (Grand Rapids: Eerdmans, 1952), 135–150.

109 W. Hendriksen, *More Than Conquerors: An Interpretation of the Book of Revelation* (Grand Rapids: Baker, 1965), 230, his emphasis. Other excellent commentaries written from an amillennial perspective are D. E. Johnson, *Triumph of the Lamb: A Commentary on Revelation* (Phillipsburg, NJ: Presbyterian & Reformed, 2001); and S. J. Kistemaker, *New Testament Commentary: Exposition of the Book of Revelation* (Grand Rapids: Baker, 2001).

So "the thousand year reign takes place in *heaven*."[110] As to the binding of Satan during this millennial reign, "This work of *binding the devil* was begun when our Lord triumphed over him in the temptations in the wilderness, Mt. 4:1–11; Lk. 4:1–13."[111] For Hendriksen, Satan is now bound in this age—the millennial age in which Christ rules in heaven with his victorious saints.[112]

Meanwhile, R. Mounce seems to say something in-between. He distinguishes between the *form* of what the text of Revelation says and the *content* of meaning the author attempted to convey to his readers. Mounce observes, "In short, John described the millennium in temporal terms, but its essential meaning cannot be restricted to the form in which it was communicated."[113] In other words, the author may well have employed language that seems to indicate a literal period of time, and this probably originated in the dominant religious conceptions of the time of the author. But the "essential truth of prophecy" could well mean, says Mounce, that "we will cease to find in Revelation 20 the prediction of an *eschatological* era."[114]

Such divergent views naturally raise hermeneutical questions. Are the relevant passages of the Bible so unclear that sincere interpreters cannot agree whether they teach a future literal, lengthy reign of Christ on this earth or whether Christ will return before or after such a period, if it exists? How do such divergent views as these on baptism and the millennium develop? Is it because of a lack of *biblical evidence*? Are the data so obscure, imprecise, or minimal that any interpretation of what John meant is a stab in the dark? Can the data be assembled in several defensible ways? Is there not enough information to overturn any of the differing interpretations with certainty? One or more of these may certainly be true. More likely, we should attribute the variety of interpretations to the *interpreters*. Do interpreters want, perhaps even unconsciously, to read the evidence in certain ways? Are they blinded to alternatives, or is it perhaps a bit of *both*? These factors may explain some of the debatable issues in biblical studies; still, there may be another alternative at work here.

Perhaps one or more parties to these kinds of discussions are "creatively" interpreting the texts. This does not deny the above possibilities, but rather may legitimize the view that several options are not only possible but also valid in such interpretive stalemates. We are not advocating a position in which interpreters can simply read anything into a text, but in these examples, at least, variant interpretations have enjoyed long tenure in the history of the Church's interpretation. Certainly the substance and the spirit of the biblical revelation must constrain any meaning discovered within its pages. Patterns of God's working in the past and the significance of Christ in redemption as seen on the Bible's pages, for example, circumscribe allowable meaning. But we stress again that meaning always results from an encounter or "conversation" between two partners, in this case the biblical text and the interpreter. The preunderstanding and presuppositions of the interpreter contribute enormously to the results of the interpretive process. We might even say they determine the results. In this case perhaps both

---

110 Hendriksen, *Conquerors*, 231, his emphasis.

111 Hendriksen, *Conquerors*, 225, his emphasis.

112 Hendriksen, *Conquerors*, 229.

113 Mounce, *Revelation*, 370.

114 Mounce, *Revelation*, 369, his emphasis.

paedobaptists and immersionists can claim to have a correct interpretation. And premillennialists and amillennialists may both profess legitimacy.[115] But can both be "right" without opening the Pandora's box of postmodernism's text as mirror?

In some ways the process is circular, or as we have preferred to call it, a hermeneutical spiral. Interpreting texts helps us formulate our understandings and "systems." Out of those preunderstandings we continue to work at interpreting texts, and in the process revise our preunderstandings and systems.[116] No interpretation occurs apart from preunderstandings—which inevitably determine the outcomes of the interpretive process. They enable us to see, and yet they color what we see. Accordingly, we construct an interpretation of what we find in the text. Reformed theologians tend to discover that the Bible teaches infant baptism and amillennialism. Given their prior commitments and their historical traditions, they construct that understanding of the relevant texts. Readers in other traditions bring their preunderstandings and commitments to the process of interpreting the Bible, so their interpretation of the texts generates alternate understandings.

Without taking sides we could well argue that one of the positions in any debate provides a better or more likely understanding of the historical meaning of the relevant biblical texts and the intentions of their authors. As we have argued above, the historical meaning of the text remains our primary objective in interpretation. But as the writers of the NT did not always limit themselves to the literal historical sense of the OT texts they interpreted, we must be open to a possible place for our own "creative" use of biblical texts.[117] Might we say that even texts with a single locution (act of writing) can generate multiple perlocutions or effects even beyond the one the original

---

115 It intrigues us that on some deep level many Christian individuals and groups sense that we cannot allow such squabbles to divide us—almost as if to say that we acknowledge both our own inadequacies in getting at truth and an unwillingness to pass judgment on others by saying they are "wrong," at least about issues such as the ones we have used. How striking that major interdenominational evangelical agencies, including those affiliated with the National Association of Evangelicals and those who identify with Lausanne, agree that both of the doctrinal debates we have used as illustrations will not be included in the otherwise detailed list of crucial doctrinal affirmations. On the other hand, some denominations and entire wings of historic Christendom refuse the Lord's Supper to anyone not baptized under their aegis.

116 Of interest to some, in the early 1990s it became apparent that some dispensationalists were significantly revising their system. Some now call themselves "progressive dispensationalists," although the title is not wholly welcome to all. Yet one need only compare, for example, early versions of the *Scofield Reference Bible* (New York: Oxford University Press, 1909); L. S. Chafer, *Systematic Theology* (Dallas: Dallas Seminary Press, 1948); C. Ryrie, *Dispensationalism Today* (Chicago: Moody, 1965); and recent sessions of the "Dispensational Theology" group meeting in concert with the Evangelical Theology Society, to see ongoing and major shifts in how self-avowed members of this "system" have changed their understandings of biblical texts. For a sampling of studies proceeding from the recent developments among dispensationalists see D. Bock and C. Blaising, eds., *Dispensationalism, Israel, and the Church* (Grand Rapids: Zondervan, 1992); and H. W. Bateman, *Three Central Issues In Contemporary Dispensationalism: A Comparison Of Traditional And Progressive Views* (Grand Rapids: Kregel 1999). To change the issue, note the shift from Calvin's view of double-predestination (i.e., that God elected some to salvation and others to damnation) to the "single-predestination" Calvinism of many today that affirms only that God elected some to salvation. Is either option "true" Calvinism?

117 The laudable motive of replicating the interpretive techniques of the NT writers inspires DeYoung and Hurty (*Beyond the Obvious*) to devise their system, which, as we indicated above, we do not find convincing.

author intended? Or with the renewed interest in *Wirkungsgeschichte*, we might speak about the "history of the effects" of a text.

What can we learn from how the writers of the NT approached their reading of the OT? K. Snodgrass provides wise words of counsel on this issue:

> We have not completed the interpretive task until we have deter-
> mined how a text does or does not correspond with Jesus' ministry or
> the ministry of the church. The writers of the New Testament seem
> to have looked for patterns of God's working in the Hebrew
> Scriptures, in the life of Jesus, and in their own experience. Our read-
> ing of the Scriptures should do no less.[118]

Christ and his Church provided structures and trajectories for a new understanding of the events and texts in the OT Scriptures. They reread these texts and saw patterns and significance not apparent to non-Christians. In their Christian experience they perceived similarities to what God did with his covenant people in previous generations as recorded in the OT. So they interpreted those OT texts in light of their new insight. They did more than merely reapply the OT texts to new situations; they saw new meaning in those texts. The promised kingdom had arrived in the ministry of Jesus, and that made all the difference.

Have both paedobaptists and believers-only immersionists correctly perceived how God has worked with his people throughout history and how he is working among them today? They have taken the original author's meaning of the text (in the author's locution) and observed different perlocutions beyond the original purpose. Can many of the relevant texts be explained as a-, pre-, and post-millenarian depending upon what trajectories a reader chooses to follow? This may proceed along the lines of typology, as advocated above, but to admit that several options may claim validity suggests we have placed in the actions of readers the ability to generate perlocutions that go beyond the texts' original intentions, as typically happens in many speech acts.

If we are open to this, then we can follow in the footsteps of the biblical writers' exegesis, though the process requires due care and important controls. As we become aware of God's working and purposes, we may read texts in new lights and craft our plausible interpretations of the biblical texts we are studying, even though such interpretations were not strictly intended by the biblical authors.[119] *The fresh interpretation must be consistent with the text's historical meaning* (and with the Bible's total teaching—given our view of the Bible's unity), *but it need not be limited to that original sense.* Using one of our examples above, some argue that the likely historical meaning of the texts on baptism—based on the lexical meaning of *baptizō* (meaning "dip" or "immerse")—and the historical Jewish precedents of immersing proselytes and performing ritual cleansing by immersion—points to the practice of immersion in water of one with the capacity to repent and believe. Taking this as their cue, in some faith communities baptism functions as the rite of initiation and to baptize means "to immerse one who has faith in Christ." But in certain other faith communities the nature of God's covenant

---

118 Snodgrass, "Use of the Old Testament," 427.

119 Recall that we have no way of knowing with certainty what they intended; we only make inferences based on the texts that were preserved.

with his people—entrance into which was symbolized by the circumcision of sons in ancient Israel—plays a major role in their understanding of their relationship with God. Taking the analogy of circumcision and the importance of the covenant as their cues, for them baptism means "to sprinkle an infant who is joining the covenant community of believers." Since modes of baptism other than immersion (that is, pouring and sprinkling) can be traced back to early church practice, they feel justified in asserting that some of the pertinent NT texts could well be understood as using modes other than immersion.[120]

In such a scenario what have we witnessed? Given their preunderstandings and community commitments both groups embrace their own "perlocution" of specific texts. For one, when John baptized Jesus, he plunged him under the water (Mt 3:13–17 par.), and so the group "baptizes" by immersing believers in a pool of water, a lake, or a river. The other community envisions that Jesus and John were standing knee-deep in the Jordan, and John dipped a pot into the river and poured water on Jesus' head. So they "baptize" by pouring or sprinkling water (omitting here the issue of whether "candidates" ought to be believers or not). Is one interpretation of the incident correct and the other in error? (In the next chapters of this book we will discuss all the tactics of analysis that might help address this historical question.) Of course, a photograph of the event would show what really happened (or whether it happened in some way that differs from these two possibilities). If the hermeneutical spiral and our understanding of critical realism are to guide us, then the historical meaning of the text remains the central goal for all exegesis—even though we possess no photograph. The author intended some specific meaning, and historically, a specific event occurred. These, we believe, must be the goals of interpretation. But typically, different faith communities will play out that meaning differently. Both have a claim to validity given the history of the Church.

Let us sum up this discussion on baptism and the millennium in this way: (1) the authors' or texts' intents are not so clear as to exclude any of the competing options as heterodox or sub-biblical (i.e., none of the views promote heresy); (2) all the parties in the debates have gone beyond the clear authorial/textual intent and created additional meanings typically consistent with their historical and doctrinal trajectories; and precisely for these reasons; (3) we must agree to disagree in love on such topics and continue to fellowship and minister together. At the same time, we believe there are only two logical options concerning the historical meaning of texts, though epistemologically we may never be able to determine which applies in a given situation. Either (1) there *are* sufficient textual and historical data to support one view as more probable than another, in which case we ought to prefer that view even while allowing others to disagree without charging them with heresy or worse; or (2) there *are not* sufficient data to defend one view in which case we should admit that, refrain from passing judgment on others, and allow for the competing options. Differing interpretations of texts (such as occurs in the examples of baptism and the millennium that we have used) show that whatever the historical meaning of texts, faith communities have become vested in their own perlocutions. While we acknowledge that phenomenon, our goal as biblical inter-

---

120 One has only to consult iconography and other church art to see how frequently Jesus' baptism in the Jordan River is portrayed as John pouring water out of some vessel onto Jesus' head.

preters ought to be to minimize such perlocutions, wherever possible, while recognizing that we will never be able to do so. The goal of interpretation ought to be the perlocution the author intended.

VALIDATING OUR INTERPRETATION

How Can We Validate Our Interpretation?

In light of this discussion of variants within textual meaning, it seems appropriate to ask whether we can ever know if our understanding of a passage is correct, or at least within legitimate bounds. Can we ever be assured that we have perceived a text's meaning, much less an author's intention, accurately? Or where some have proceeded to follow in the footsteps of the biblical writers in arriving at other perlocutions of a text, how can we know whether they lie within the boundaries of acceptability? Indeed, are there such boundaries? We cannot ignore these questions. Even for Christian interpreters who affirm that the Bible is God's revelation, what value is an authoritative text if we cannot know that we have interpreted it correctly?

As stated earlier, in the absence of the author with whom we might consult, we are unable to assert with absolute confidence that we have precisely understood an author's intention in a given text. Nor can we in any way determine the extent to which a text was originally understood. But neither of these points implies that texts have no determinate meaning. Authors do determine meaning when they write. So we set as our goal the meaning of the resulting text in view of all we can discover about the original circumstances of its formulation. Consequently, we must deal in probabilities. Given all the evidence and all the factors at our disposal, we must ask more appropriately: Which interpretation is more likely to represent the text's original meaning? Which interpretations fall within the reasonable limits of a text's meaning for various faith communities? When might one's interpretation suggest that a faith community should modify its beliefs or practices, even long-established ones?[121] To verify an interpretation requires weighing two types of evidence: evidence pertaining to the text itself and evidence involving the interpreters.

E. D. Hirsch addresses the first concern.[122] He suggests four criteria to establish an interpretation as probable. The most probable reading:

---

121 This perennial problem faces interpreters: When is it proper to break out of the interpretive strictures of one's (or another's) faith community? For example, Protestants insist that Luther was correct in rejecting several texts' current meaning for the Roman Catholic faith community, to paraphrase what we have just written. Recent rapprochements between Catholics and evangelicals on the one hand, and Catholics and Lutherans on the other, appear to vindicate the correct biblical understanding of justification by faith alone. Catholic theology in the pre-Reformation period may well have veered away from the biblical moorings in the relevant texts' historical meanings. Or take Jesus' example of labeling some Pharisees' restrictive interpretations as old wineskins that were defective (Mt 9:17; par). We argue that both Luther and Jesus were justified on the basis of the historical meanings of the relevant texts. In these instances the "faith communities" had departed from the acceptable boundaries of God's teachings. They needed to be challenged and their erroneous views jettisoned. On what constitutes heresy in the NT, see C. L. Blomberg, "The New Testament Definition of Heresy (or When Do Jesus and the Apostles Really Get Mad?)," *JETS* 45 (2002): 59–72.

122 Recall that his book is entitled *Validity in Interpretation*. He discusses "Verification" on pp. 235–44, which he views as a procedure for establishing that a given reading or interpretation is more probable than any competing alternatives.

- is possible according to the norms of the language in which it was written;

- must be able to account for each linguistic component in the text;

- must follow the conventions for its type of literature; and

- must be coherent—it must make sense.[123]

In other words, the most probable interpretation of a text is the one that is consistent with language and literary genre in the ways that people typically use and understand them—at the time the texts were written.[124] We seek to understand a text in the normal and clear sense in which humans ordinarily communicate by that type of literature.[125] Indeed, Vanhoozer rightly affirms, "Scripture is composed of 'ordinary' language and 'ordinary' literature."[126]

Much of what is presented in this book expands and illustrates precisely those elements that enable interpreters to arrive at that "ordinary" meaning. We must address the issues of lexical analysis, historical and cultural background, literary criticism, genre, Hebrew and Greek grammar, and the like. We must consider, as well, the texts' contents, purposes, and force. An interpretation that seems at first to be coherent may turn out to be incorrect because we have misconstrued some evidence. But an incoherent or anachronistic interpretation is most certainly not correct. The more we know about the ancient world and the Bible itself, the more we increase the probability that from among the various viable alternatives we can select the correct interpretation. And if our interpretation is correct, others will be able to assess the study and agree with the conclusion.

Another locus of validation is the interpreters themselves. First, we must acknowledge the inevitable factors of human prejudice and parochialism, sinfulness and depravity, and our propensity to exonerate ourselves and blame others. Second, we must consider all the social, sexual, racial, political, economic, and religious factors that color our thinking. These indicate that no individual interpreter is in a position to judge rightly all the time, even given the above criteria. Is there a way to take into account our prejudices and preunderstandings so they don't skew the evidence? Can we recognize them

---

123 Hirsch, *Validity*, 236.

124 K. J. Vanhoozer, "The Semantics of Biblical Literature," in *Hermeneutics, Authority, and Canon*, ed. D. A. Carson and J. D. Woodbridge (Grand Rapids: Zondervan, 1986), 80, suggests, "Genre thus enables the reader to interpret meaning and to recognize what kinds of truth claims are being made in and by a text." While recognizing the importance of the modern reader's situation, Vanhoozer's magisterial *Is There a Meaning in This Text?* vigorously defends the crucial role of the author for establishing the meaning of a text.

125 See B. Ramm's clarification in *Protestant Biblical Interpretation*, 3d ed. (Grand Rapids: Baker, 1970), 119–27.

126 Vanhoozer, "Semantics," 85. His explanation of how literature "works" to communicate is fresh and provocative. Vanhoozer suggests than any analysis of biblical literature must take into account four crucial factors: (1) what the text is about—facts or issues; (2) why the text was written—its function or intention; (3) the form in which the message is "incarnated"; and (4) the power or force of the text that results from the combination of the first three elements (91–92). So, "As Christian readers, we ought to be interested not only in the propositions themselves but in the manifold ways these propositions are presented for our consideration" (92).

and take them into consideration in the interpretive process? Can we adopt some hermeneutic of distrust or suspicion that forces us to be aware of our biases and circumvent or account for them, at least as much as possible?[127]

Clearly, one tactic has always been at the disposal of those who seek to understand Scripture or any literature for that matter—to consider what others say. No reputable interpreter excludes the wisdom of Christians throughout the centuries. Those who want to understand Scripture must read widely and assess judiciously what others have learned about a text. Students must consider the findings of other reputable interpreters—preachers, teachers, and those who write various articles and other studies—all the while recognizing that not all of them share one's own presuppositions. Interpreters need to learn all they can from others. At the same time, they must be skeptical of any author (or speaker) who exclaims, "No one has ever discovered this truth about this passage before." Equally, interpreters should be cautious even when others *agree* with their preferred conclusions—until the evidence leaves no alternative. To paraphrase a proverb, "As iron sharpens iron, so one interpreter sharpens another" (see Prov 27:17). Indeed, to ensure "sharpening," we recommend that interpreters make it a practice always to consult others with whom they may *disagree* in order to test the validity of their conclusions.[128]

But considering what others say goes beyond reading only the "experts." Swartley suggests two other processes that can also help validate an interpretation. He proposes, first, that interpretations be validated in the "praxis of faith."[129] This criterion asks whether a proposed understanding of the text is workable in the lives of believers. Swartley suggests that interpreters apply this test "through personal and corporate *meditation* upon Scripture, through the witness of *preaching*, and through *living* the love, righteousness, reconciliation, and peace of the gospel."[130] Of course, this criterion alone cannot guarantee the accuracy of a given interpretation, for the history of the Church demonstrates that erroneous understandings can also be made to "work," though usually they do not meet all Swartley's tests.[131] But, given the nature of Scripture, correct understandings must work, and so this test can help validate them.[132]

---

127 We assume here, of course, that we do not simply celebrate our ideological stances and willingly read the texts so they mirror ourselves. We retain our objective to understand the historical, author-centered meaning of the texts.

128 An invaluable source for seeing how the earliest Christians interpreted biblical texts is the *Ancient Christian Commentary on Scripture* series, gen. ed. T. C. Oden (Downers Grove, IL: InterVarsity, 1998–). Twenty-seven volumes are projected to cover all the books of the Bible plus the Apocrypha.

129 W. Swartley, *Slavery, Sabbath, War, and Women* (Scottdale, PA: Herald Press, 1983), 223. He builds here upon the "hermeneutic of consent" articulated by P. Stuhlmacher, *Historical Criticism and Theological Interpretation of Scripture: Toward a Hermeneutic of Consent* (Philadelphia: Fortress, 1977).

130 Swartley, *Slavery*, 215; his emphasis.

131 With striking citations Swartley shows how thoughtful Christians employed the Bible to defend both sides of the four issues in his book: slavery, sabbath, war, and the role of women. In some sense both sides were made to "work" in the history of the Church.

132 On a practical level, if an interpreter cannot convince his or her Sunday school class that an alleged meaning of the text is at least an option, then it probably is not—unless the teacher is a lone evangelical in a liberal setting, or a "progressive evangelical" in a independent, fundamentalist church!

Second, Swartley suggests that interpreters need to secure the discernment of the believing community to check their conclusions. He says,

> The community, whether the local congregation or a churchwide body, assesses an interpretation's coherence with the central tenets of its traditional beliefs, its relationship to wider Christian beliefs, or the way the interpretation accords or conflicts with how the community discerns the Spirit to be moving.[133]

In other words, maverick or novel interpretations must be subjected to the critique of the corporate body of Christian believers. They must "ring true" in the Church.[134] Here is where theological acceptability informs the process. Interpretive communities draw boundaries around what they will admit. Rather than dismissing or denying this phenomenon, interpreters can take advantage of it. They can insist that interpretations be orthodox, that they conform to the community's preunderstanding. They will also understand why other communities adopt differing positions, "in spite of the clear evidence." Interpreters validate their understandings of the Bible in keeping with who they are.[135] It also means the Church rejects heresy.[136] The goal must always be the "better interpretation."

Yet this does not mean any interpretation is valid if some "faith community" adopts it.[137] Even well-accepted interpretations need to be subjected to the bar of the

---

133 Swartley, *Slavery*, 215.

134 Tragically, the guild of professional biblical scholars often ignores this criterion. It stands accountable to no one, usually in the name of objectivity. Increasingly this is now seen for what it is—arrogant modernism and elitism—and it has renewed interest in so-called "pre-critical exegesis" with its firm moorings in Church life; cf. the illuminating essays in R. A. Muller and J. L. Thompson, *Biblical Interpretation in the Era of the Reformation* (Grand Rapids/Cambridge: Eerdmans, 1996), especially the editors' concluding chapter (335–45).

135 See J. Schreiter, *Constructing Local Theologies* (Maryknoll: Orbis, 1985) for one study of the role of the community in adopting and shaping theology.

136 So, for example, orthodox Christians reject the heretical view of Jesus that Jehovah's Witnesses teach. Mainstream Christians refuse to admit interpretations of Jn 1:1 that suggest that Jesus was only "a god" (see the Jehovah's Witnesses *New World Translation*). In other words, some "creative" interpretations lie outside acceptable bounds; heresy is always intolerable even if some "faith community" accepts it (so Colossians and 1 John were written to champion the truth). Orthodox Christians might admit the possibility of alternative explanations of baptism or eschatology, as we saw above, but they agree that a Jesus who is less than deity is unacceptable. Christians refuse to tolerate heresy. In fact, they seek to persuade Jehovah's Witnesses of the truth about Jesus' deity using the very hermeneutical principles presented in this textbook. In our view, the Bible itself functions as the determiner of the select doctrines that *must* be defended. Sadly, even some Christian denominations now question positions that have been viewed as orthodox and essential throughout the history of the Church (e.g., Jesus' bodily resurrection or that salvation comes solely through Jesus' atonement).

137 Ironically, some fundamentalists fall prey to this error—while in the guise of faithfully reading the biblical text. That is, like the academic guild it scorns, fundamentalism also exercises ironclad community restraints on what texts can be allowed to mean. Their interpreters listen only to each other and ignore the scholarly consensus, even mainstream evangelicals, on many issues. They unwittingly adopt a reader-response reading of texts that allows the Bible to mean only what they want it to mean. A blatant example of this occurs in the essays in R. L. Thomas, and F. D. Farnell, ed., *The Jesus Crisis: The Inroads of Historical Criticism into Evangelical Scholarship* (Grand Rapids: Kregel, 1998). It is as closed-minded a fideism as the Jesus Seminar reflects. The better way is to embrace all good research to seek the truth.

worldwide Christian community. One way to examine the potentially distorting influence of our own preunderstandings is to listen to the insights of Christian brothers and sisters elsewhere, particularly those who differ from us. In the North American (or other so-called First World) contexts, this must include listening to the insights of believers who are poor, disenfranchised, persecuted, and oppressed. Likewise, developing-world interpreters can learn from their First-World colleagues. Correspondingly, men and women interpreters, those of different races, those who live in the inner cities and those in the suburbs, the urban and rural, the rich and poor, the white collar and blue collar, etc.—all need to listen to each other.

Interpreters can learn much about the meaning of the Bible from a multitude of sources, including non-Christian interpreters. Christian interpreters can gain insights from Jewish interpreters and Jewish interpreters can gain insights from Christian interpreters. In some instances unbelievers might shed crucial light on the meaning of biblical texts that believers might miss. But significance is another matter. Seeing the Bible's significance belongs to believers. The point is to exert all efforts to minimize our preferences and prejudices lest they blur our vision and obstruct our ability to see the truth in the Scriptures. The history of the interpretation of the Bible will dramatize to any reader just how easily even well-intentioned and pious believers can "squeeze the text into their own molds," to paraphrase translator J. B. Phillips' rendition of Rom 12:2. Individuals as well as communities of faith may currently adopt and prefer their pet interpretations of texts, but upon sane reflection and interaction with believers in other places, they might well decide that their views were prejudiced and ill-founded. They might even adjust their interpretations in keeping with the hermeneutical spiral. Honest and spiritually motivated reassessment of existing views can lead to their alteration if not abandonment. No individual or interpretive community is doomed to retain the errors of the past, no matter how passionately these views were embraced and defended. History also amply illustrates how individuals and communities have made such shifts.

What do we do when interpreters disagree? How do we proceed when well-intentioned Christians come to different interpretations about the meaning of a text or passage? First, we should set out precisely the nature of the difference—where, specifically, do the views depart from each other. Second, we should itemize the elements in the process of study that led each interpreter to his or her view. That is, returning to our textual criteria above, did either interpreter misconstrue some evidence or engage in shoddy reasoning, or were there other flaws in the process that indicate one of the positions must be relinquished?

Third, as we evaluate the options we must determine which one relies most on the historical meaning of a text using all the principles of sound hermeneutics, as opposed to any based on more creative extrapolations. Where one view more readily emerges from the historical sense of the text, it must stand. The *historically defensible interpretation has greatest authority*. That is, interpreters can have maximum confidence in their understanding of a text when they base that understanding on historically defensible arguments. If we are convinced that one interpretation precludes all alternatives (even if others adopt one or more of them), we may well reject the other view even if we do not believe the issue is central enough to make a big deal about it.

On the basis of these same hermeneutical criteria, however, we may conclude that Scripture does not provide enough data to exclude all competing views. At this point we acknowledge that differing interpretive communities do produce their differing meaning (perlocutions), largely on the basis of their own systems. We agree to live with this as long as the interpretations and the systems remain orthodox and biblical, that is, consistent with what is clearly revealed and acknowledged by the consensus of historical Christianity. What kind of alternatives might have a claim to such validity?

Going back to Matthew's use of Hos 11:1, it might not have reflected the prophet's intention or a historical understanding of the text to its original readers, but it "fit" typologically. That is, the Hosea text did express God's actions to protect his favored ones and to bring them out of Egypt, and that held true for the Messiah as well as for Jacob and his family.[138] Thus, we may adopt a creative interpretation if:

- it expresses or conforms to orthodox Christian theology;[139]

- it corresponds to typical paradigms of God's truth or activity as clearly revealed in historically interpreted sections of the Bible;[140]

- it works in the crucible of Christian experience—producing godliness and other valid Christian qualities, and advancing God's kingdom; and

- it finds confirmation along the full spectrum (racially, sexually, socioeconomically, et al.) of Christians within an orthodox faith-community.

Where a creative interpretation meets these criteria, it has a claim to validity—not as the historical meaning of the text, but as a valid "perlocution," that is, additional effect. Where one occurs in isolated sectors of the Church or derives from individual interpreters, it must remain seriously suspect and probably be rejected until it can meet the criteria.[141]

---

138 In other words, as we argued above, were the historical meaning of a text the only legitimate one, we might object to Matthew's use of Hos 11:1 in Mt 2:15. Therefore, the Bible seems to admit of two interpretations of Hos 11:1: the text's original historical meaning and Matthew's creative understanding and application of the text to the Messiah.

139 This excludes the Jehovah's Witnesses' interpretation of Jn 1:1 where they say the Word was "a god." It also excludes medieval Rome's inadequate understanding of justification by faith, against which the Reformers objected. And it excludes a postmodern interpretation of Jesus' resurrection as existential rather than physical.

140 Here we have "blended" typology and reader-response understandings. An acceptable reader-response must "fit" with how God works with his people, how the Church operates, and how Jesus exercises his Lordship.

141 Another example of an interpretation of selected texts that we put into the category of "must be rejected" is the so-called "health and wealth" message popular in some groups. We argue that it fails all four tests we set out. It is not orthodox in its theology, for the Bible and Christian history readily attest that God does not prefer health and wealth for his faithful people. It does not depend upon typical patterns, but elevates isolated miracles of healing to the status of the norm of how God treats his children if they simply had enough faith. It often does not promote godliness but promotes a seeking after God's gifts more than God himself. And, clearly, it lacks confirmation across the spectrum of orthodox Christians. Alas, its practitioners remain undaunted, and, we fear, dupe many.

What do we mean by "a claim to validity?" An original reader of Hos 11:1 would interpret his reminiscence in a valid way if he or she understood it to speak of God's past deliverance of the nation Israel. That was its historically valid meaning. Matthew's interpretation in Mt 2:15 was, by canonical definition, valid too, but not in the same historically defensible way. His was a creative perlocution. Presumably it would have met the four criteria we suggested.

We suggest such a perlocution to illustrate our point, but only in rough fashion. No NT writer quotes Psa 3. The psalmist writes:

> [1] O Lord, how many are my foes!
> Many are rising against me;
> [2] many are saying to me,
> "There is no help for you in God." *Selah*
> [3] But you, O Lord, are a shield around me,
> my glory, and the one who lifts up my head.
> [4] I cry aloud to the Lord,
> and he answers me from his holy hill. *Selah*
> [5] I lie down and sleep;
> I wake again, for the Lord sustains me.
> [6] I am not afraid of ten thousands of people
> who have set themselves against me all around.
> [7] Rise up, O Lord!
> Deliver me, O my God!
> For you strike all my enemies on the cheek;
> you break the teeth of the wicked.
> [8] Deliverance belongs to the Lord;
> may your blessing be on your people! *Selah*[142]

When we read it, we find images of enemies, divine protection, prayer, sleep, sustenance, deliverance, and blessing. All these themes find parallels in other Psalms that the NT writers use typologically of Jesus. Likewise, when we read Paul's letters and Luke's accounts in Acts of Paul's exploits, we observe God's manifold presence with Paul in many of these same ways. Thus an exposition of Psa 3 for Christians, after explicating the historical intent of the Psalm, could point out parallels in the lives of Jesus and the apostle Paul as part of the fuller meaning or perlocution of the Psalm. We might say the Psalm describes God's presence with his son and with the great apostle on the basis of these typological parallels. At the same time, there are no unique dimensions to this Psalm that necessarily point beyond what a faithful Jew then (or faithful Christian today) could experience, so, to repeat, any typological applications to Christ should not be our primary applications of the text. We have no warrant to proclaim that Psa 3 is a messianic psalm.

Preachers, teachers, and authors of books on biblical theology are all too aware of their attackers and detractors. Where interpreters have committed errors of methodology or

---

142 The quotation is from the NRSV.

judgment, they must be willing to learn and change their interpretations. As we have said already, and will continue to echo throughout this volume, determination and sincerity are no substitutes for accuracy. Nor are determination and sincerity rendered acceptable when mixed with large doses of piety! It may be an acceptable starting point in a small group Bible study for its members to opine, "What this verse says to me is . . . ," to suggest what the author might mean and to solicit the views of others to "sharpen" the group's understanding of the author's message. However, biblical interpretation cannot remain at the what-it-means-to-me level. Correct interpretation of the author's intended meaning in the text must always be our goal.

But once we have eliminated erroneous interpretations, what do we do when sincere believers adopt different or, in some cases, opposite explanations of the meaning of the same text? Here Christian grace must prevail. We must listen to each other and appreciate why others have arrived at alternative explanations. Consider again the millennial example. One of the views may be more historically defensible; it may better express the historical sense of the relevant texts. But all views are certainly acceptable within their respective interpretive communities and within the shared interpretive community of historic orthodox Christianity. The communities could make their claims that their views meet the four criteria for valid interpretation. That being the case, and given our mandate to maintain and promote the unity of the body of Christ, when alternative interpretations (or perlocutions) meet the requisite criteria, Christians should agree to avoid using such "interpretation" of texts to divide fellowship. Sadly, some Christian sects make an industry out of defining themselves by whom they are against and by separating from everyone else who does not agree with them. Beyond simple arrogance, as the history of interpretation shows, separating from other members of Christ's Church over these kinds of disputed texts causes great damage. Amillennialist and premillennialist Christians need to embrace each other and their postmillennialist fellow-believers, as should paedobaptists and believers-only baptists. One may say,

> I don't agree with your conclusions, but in light of who you are and your community of faith, in light of how these biblical texts have been interpreted throughout history, and in light of the diligence and care with which you attempt to understand and live in conformity to the Bible's teachings, I concede your interpretation. You have responded to the Bible in a valid manner.

Certainly this is preferable to accusing our brothers and sisters of shoddy work (at best) or dishonesty or heresy (at worst), and separating from them as if they were enemies. We ought to exert every effort to keep in line with Jesus' words: "Whoever is not against us is for us" (Mk 9:39), not to mention his prayer: "May [those who believe in me] be brought to complete unity to let the world know that you sent me and have loved them even as you have loved me" (Jn 17:23). If the cliché "Blood is thicker than water" has any validity, then even more valid is the truth that "Faith is thicker than either blood or water!" The landscape of Christian history exhibits tragic evidence of Christian brothers and sisters damaging each other and the cause of Christ over their preferred interpretations of the Bible. Hear us well: our plea is not to condone heresy, error, or harmful teaching in the guise of Christian toleration; rather, we plead for humility and the grace to treat other Christians as siblings and fellow-seekers for God's truth. Where sincere Christians come to two different interpretations on nonessentials of the faith, we must allow that both options are possible (as outlined above), "agree to disagree," and support each other as brothers and sisters in the life of faith.[143]

---

143 D. L. Bock, *Purpose-Driven Theology: Getting Our Priorities Right in Evangelical Conversations* (Downers Grove: InterVarsity, 2002), echoes these sentiments.

PART III—UNDERSTANDING LITERATURE

7

GENERAL RULES OF
HERMENEUTICS: PROSE

If the fundamental goal of interpretation is to discover the meaning of the biblical text, then the main objective of our task is to identify and explain the principles and procedures that are necessary to discern accurately that meaning. These include the principles that are necessary to understand language communication. The writers of Scripture expressed their divine message in human language. To know what they meant by the words used, we have to understand their message consistent with the way people ordinarily use language to communicate ideas.

It seems logical to surmise that the biblical writers intended for their original audiences to understand what they wrote. They did not convey their thoughts through secret codes. Though they occasionally used a riddle, parable, or apocalyptic symbol that might puzzle and challenge the reader, they intended to communicate clearly even through these. Like most writers, the authors wrote in a straightforward and direct manner so that readers would understand their message and live consistently with it.

Confident that the biblical authors adequately communicated the message, we have the obligation to interpret it correctly by following the conventions of language communication. In normal conversation we immediately understand what we hear with hardly a conscious thought. Our mental computer, the mind, automatically processes the information we hear. A lifetime of experience has programmed our memory bank to understand the meanings of words and sentences almost unconsciously. However, alas, this does not necessarily hold true when we read the Bible. For the Bible was originally written in foreign languages to people who lived a long time ago in different parts of the world with different ways of life. Statements that were quite clear to the initial readers may not communicate clearly to us at all. What was almost automatic comprehension for them takes considerably more effort for us.

For whenever we confront a statement we do not automatically understand, we have to stop and think about it. Hence, intentional interpretation requires that we raise the routine patterns of subconscious communication to the level of conscious analysis. We must deliberately analyze the unclear message according to the principles of language communication that normally function unconsciously. This basic premise underlies most of the principles of biblical interpretation that we will present in this book. Each hermeneutical guideline arises from and addresses some essential facet of overcoming these barriers to understanding the Bible.

How do we understand the written messages in the Bible? For effective communication to occur, the recipient (or any later reader) must understand the message consistent with the meaning indicators the writer used to express his or her thought. As we outlined in the previous chapter, for each speech act an author encodes a message that includes some (propositional) content presented via some medium (or genre) to achieve some effect in the readers. A valid interpretation of a communicative act will account for these elements in the best possible manner. The process of arriving at an accurate interpretation of written texts involves an understanding of five essential items: (1) literary context (that is, the immediate context in the book in which a specific text is located), (2) historical-cultural background, (3) word meanings, (4) grammatical relationships, and (5) literary genre (the global literary context of which the text is a part: letter, apocalyptic, narrative, parable, et al.). All the while we need to be sensitive to what the author is doing in the communicative act: e.g., informing, exhorting, encouraging, telling a story, establishing basic beliefs or worldview, threatening, connecting, soliciting, celebrating, et al. In other words, what is the author's way of thinking in the communicative act; what is he or she seeking to accomplish? (Understanding how poetry works poses additional and unique challenges, and we take them up in the next chapter.)

Writers normally communicate their thoughts through contextually coherent statements that use words according to their natural meanings in such contexts consistent with the historical-cultural setting. Each word's impact on the total thought of the sentence arises from its grammatical relationship to the other words. Therefore, regardless of the literary genre (a topic we will address in subsequent chapters), to discover what a writer meant, one must concentrate on four things: literary context, historical-cultural background, words, and grammar. An interpretation that is not faithful to all four of these aspects of the text is unlikely to be the meaning the writer intended.

LITERARY CONTEXT

A basic principle of biblical hermeneutics is that *the intended meaning of any passage is the meaning that is consistent with the sense of the literary context in which it occurs.* Hence, the first test that all proposed interpretations must pass is this: Is it consistent with the literary context? In literature, the context of any specific passage is the material that comes immediately before and after it. The context of a sentence is its paragraph, the context of a paragraph is the series of paragraphs that precede and follow it, and the context of a chapter is the surrounding chapters. Ultimately, the whole book in which a passage appears is its controlling context. In interpreting the Bible, the canon of all sixty-six books provides the largest literary context in which every passage must be understood.

The Importance of the Literary Context

Most of us know from personal experience the frustration of having something we said "taken out of context." Political leaders and public officials frequently complain that the news media have misrepresented their views. While acknowledging that the reporter's direct quote was technically accurate, they protest that their statement was given a totally different slant or emphasis because the context was omitted. In a politician's case the "taken-out-of-context" excuse may be a vain attempt to cover up an embarrassing slip of the tongue. Nevertheless the principle involved remains valid. Misunderstandings can certainly arise when people hear only part of what was said and base their understanding on it. The same is true of the Bible. Asserting that the Bible teaches "There is no God" by wrenching those words out of the context of Psa 14:1— "Fools say in their hearts, '*There is no God.*' They are corrupt, they do abominable deeds; there is no one who does good" (NRSV, emphasis added; cf. Psa 53:1)—clearly violates the intention of the quotation.

In fact, were the biblical writers alive they would undoubtedly protest loudly that they are "taken out of context" frequently when Christians quote individual Bible verses and apply them to their lives in violation of the biblical context. Misconstruing the context of a biblical passage has serious implications. We must interpret every passage consistent with its context for three main reasons.

Context Provides Flow-of-Thought

First, taking a passage out of context violates the writer's "flow-of-thought." A flow-of-thought is a series of related ideas an author organizes to communicate a specific concept. Most meaningful communication involves some type of logical thought-flow in which one thought leads naturally to the next in keeping with the genre of literature employed.[1] A preceding statement prepares for the one that comes after it. The words that follow grow out of what precedes. People communicate, not with a series of randomly selected ideas, but with related ideas linked together in a logical pattern. For example, consider this confusing account:

> I heard an interesting story on the news the other night. The quarterback faded back to pass. Carbon buildup was keeping the carburetor from functioning properly. The two-inch-thick steaks were burned on the outside but raw on the inside. Ten-feet-high snowdrifts blocked the road. The grass needed mowing. The elevator raced to the top of the one-hundred-story building in less than a minute. The audience booed the poor performance.

Grammatically, the sentences can occur together, but there is no evident logical continuity to link them; they are totally unrelated. People do not usually communicate ideas like this. Normally all sentences in a paragraph strive to develop a common theme. Each sentence carries or builds on the thought expressed in the previous sentence. Taken together, the sentences provide a continuity of subject matter that unifies the whole.

Since we normally communicate by a series of related statements, each sentence must be understood in light of the other ideas expressed in the context—in terms of the writer's train of thought. Any interpretation of a text that violates the point of its overall context is not likely to be the true one. It contradicts and ignores the normal way people use language to communicate.

Context Provides Accurate Meaning of Words

The second reason why an interpretation must agree with the general message of the context derives from the nature of words. Most words have more than one meaning.[2] The literary context presents the most reliable guide for determining the most likely meaning in that setting. In normal circumstances our minds automatically adopt the one meaning that best fits the subject at hand. Confusion or misunderstanding occurs when the literary context is vague or when several meanings fit equally well.

---

1 Of course, the kind of literature will determine the nature of the progression of thoughts. Certainly, the lines of poetry are "connected" differently than those of carefully reasoned prose, a narrative, or a parable.

2 Actually, semanticists say that words cover a "field" of meaning, or they have a semantic range of meaning.

Then a person must deliberately stop and think about the words' various possible meanings or analyze the context more carefully. Then he or she must select the one most likely intended by the writer.

For example, if we hear only the exclamation, "That was the largest trunk I ever saw!" we do not possess enough "literary context" (in fact we have none) to know what kind of "trunk" is meant. Does it refer to a type of luggage, the main stem of a tree, the rear storage area of a car (in American English), or the long nose of an elephant? Suppose, however, we read the statement in a book about animals at the zoo. Then we automatically picture an elephant's trunk. Given an article about the virtues of various automobiles, the image of a car's storage compartment would emerge. Yet neither of these meanings will come to mind if we are reading about the largest "trunk" seen in a California redwood forest. The literary context defines the precise meaning of the word.

Interpreters are not free to pick whichever meaning they choose for multiple-meaning words. We must understand each term according to the meaning that is consistent with the other ideas expressed in the literary context. This is how successful language communication works.

Context Delineates Correct Relationships Among Units

The third reason why correct interpretation must be consistent with context is that most biblical books were written and preserved as complete documents intended to be read as a unit. Biblical writers composed or edited individual sentences and paragraphs as parts of a larger document. Despite the "look" of many Bibles, the biblical writers did not intend verses to exist as isolated, independent entities. The sentences and paragraphs comprise individual units of larger literary works, and interpreters must understand them according to their relationship to the whole argument of the book.

A book like Proverbs may appear to be an exception in that it groups many different sayings that originated independently; apart from a few sections, we may see little connection between the proverbs that occur in sequence. But even here, where the immediate literary context before and after a given proverb may give little help in understanding its meaning, the context of the whole book becomes particularly important because the writer scattered many proverbs on the same topic throughout the book.[3] Thus the combined teaching of the book on each theme becomes the key to understanding the individual wisdom saying.

Ironically, the usually helpful chapter and verse divisions in our Bibles constitute one of the biggest hurdles to the process of Bible interpretation. We must remember that they were not in the original documents. Some verse divisions were in place in the early centuries A.D., though they fluctuated widely in various places. By the ninth and tenth centuries A.D. verse divisions began to appear in the Hebrew Bible of the Jewish Masoretes. F. F. Bruce says, "The standard division of the Old Testament into verses which has come down to our own day and is found in most translations as well as in the Hebrew original was fixed by the Masoretic family of Ben Asher about A.D. 900."[4]

---

3 Recent studies, however, have suggested that more design may underlie the collections in Proverbs than was previously thought. For details, see the introductory section on structure in B. K. Waltke, *Proverbs*, NICOT (Grand Rapids: Eerdmans, forthcoming).

4 F. F. Bruce, *The Books and the Parchments* (London: Pickering & Inglis, 1950), 118.

He adds, "The division into chapters, on the other hand, is much later, and was first carried through by Cardinal Hugo de Sancto Caro in 1244."[5] Others attribute the division into chapters to Stephen Langton, professor at the University of Paris and later Archbishop of Canterbury, in A.D. 1228. Three centuries later, in 1560, Robert Estienne (Stephanus), a Parisian printer and publisher, added the current verse numbering in his fourth edition of the Greek NT (which also contained two Latin versions).[6] His edition of the Latin Vulgate of 1555 was the first Bible of the modern era to use both the chapter and verse divisions. The Geneva Bible (1560) was the first English version to incorporate both the modern chapter and verse divisions. Although these divisions were meant to be helpful, even a casual reading of the Bible reveals that verse and chapter divisions are frequently poorly placed; new verses often begin in the middle of sentences,[7] and chapter changes occasionally interrupt the thought in a paragraph.[8]

The chapter and verse references do help us identify and locate passages quickly,[9] but unfortunately they have also contributed to the widespread practice of elevating individual verses to the status of independent units of thought. Each verse is treated like a complete expression of truth that, like a number in a phone book, has no connection to what precedes or follows—each is a "quote for the day" or "proof text" considered in isolation from its biblical context. This constitutes a grave danger, for in isolation a single verse might be as misleading as "There is no God." There is simply no justification for routinely treating individual verses as independent thought units that contain autonomous expressions of truth. As written communication, readers must understand biblical statements as integral parts of the larger units where they occur. Detached from their contexts, individual verses may take on meanings never intended by their writers. To qualify as the text's intended meaning, an interpretation must be compatible with the total thought and the specific intention of the immediate context and the book context.

Principles of Hermeneutics Relating to Context

Three important principles must guide our practice of interpretation. The first principle is: *Each statement must be understood according to its natural meaning in the literary context in which it occurs.* This is probably the single most important principle of

---

5 Bruce, *Books,* 118.

6 Cf. B. M. Metzger, *The Text of the New Testament,* 3d ed. (New York and Oxford: Oxford University Press, 1992), 103–04; and N. L. Geisler and W. E. Nix, *A General Introduction to the Bible* (Chicago: Moody, 1999), 229–33.

7 Metzger cites the no-doubt apocryphal story that "Stephanus marked the verse divisions while journeying 'on horseback,' and that some of the infelicitous divisions arose from the jogging of the horse that bumped his pen into the wrong places" (*Text,* 104).

8 For example, in light of the Servant Song that begins at Isa 52:13, dividing a new chapter at 53:1 is completely unwarranted. If a new chapter is required, it should occur at 52:13. Second Corinthians 2:1 falls in the middle of a paragraph explaining why Paul has not already made a return trip to Corinth. In modern versions that supply paragraphs, one notes how often the paragraphs do not correspond with either chapter or verse divisions. See how the beginnings of new chapters in Jeremiah come in the middle of thought units (e.g., 41, 42, 43). Cf. the NIV paragraph divisions at 1 Cor 11:2 (not 1), 12:31b (not 13:1), 2 Cor 7:2 (not 1), and Phil 4:2 (not 1) for other examples.

9 They enable us to avoid vague references like these found respectively in Heb 2:6; 3:7; and 5:6: "there is a place where someone has testified," introducing Psa 8:4–6; "as the Holy Spirit says," quoting Psa 95:7–11; or "and he [God] says in another place," indicating Psa 110:4.

217

hermeneutics since literary context is at the heart of all language communication. It affects the reader's understanding of both the meaning of individual words and the meaning of the complete statement. This guideline requires an interpreter not just to focus on the words of a passage but also to consider carefully the contribution of the passage to the literary work as a whole. It requires taking account of the illocutionary force of the context—what the author is seeking to accomplish in this context. It seeks to preserve the integrity of the line of thought being developed throughout the text.

The corollary principle is: *A text without a context may be a pretext.* Although an extension of the previous guideline, this principle puts it negatively and focuses on a serious abuse of Scripture. Here we define a "pretext" as an alleged interpretation that only appears valid; in reality it obscures the real state of affairs. This principle serves as a warning against the popular tendency to engage in invalid proof-texting: quoting biblical passages to prove a doctrine or standard for Christian living without regard for the literary context. As a ridiculous example one could string along three verses to "prove" that one ought to commit suicide: "Then he [Judas] went away and hanged himself" (Mt 27:5); "Jesus told him, 'Go and do likewise' " (Lk 10:37b); and "What you are about to do, do quickly" (Jn 13:27b). The disregard for context is evident! Unfortunately, other proof-texting does not appear so ridiculous but is equally invalid. Such proof-texts are merely "pretexts" when the interpretation fails the principle of literary context. There is nothing wrong with quoting verses to prove a point provided we understand them according to their contextual meaning (under the correct circumstances proof-texting can be valid). Before listing any verse in support of a position, we should first check the literary context to insure that the passage is about the same subject and really does have the meaning that proves the point. Otherwise the interpretation is only a pretext, using a passage that seems on the surface to prove some point when in actuality it does not. Such a pretext carries no divine authority for it subverts what the text really means.

The third principle (really a caution) is: *The smaller the passage being studied, the greater the chance of error.* Short texts usually contain very little information about the general theme of the larger passage. They give us less evidence about their meaning. Indeed, a phrase or a single sentence by itself could well convey several different meanings. Paul's words in Rom 8:28 provide a ready example: "And we know that all things work together for good to them that love God" (KJV). If someone were to assess the verse apart from its context in Rom 8 and the entire letter, he or she might incorrectly use it to convince a parent whose child has just died that the death was a good thing, since Paul promises good results from all circumstances. The surrounding context, however, provides crucial details about the subject that enable the reader to discount erroneous meanings. For Paul, all things are not good, but God will accomplish his salvific purposes (which are good) for his people, even though and when they suffer greatly. (A more accurate translation such as the NIV also helps: "And we know that *in all things* God works for the good of those who love him" [emphasis added]) Larger passages provide more facts about the topic and thus give the interpreter a clearer perspective for understanding each statement within it.

Simply stated, large passages have a built-in literary context; short passages do not. Normally speaking, the paragraph constitutes the basic unit of thought in prose.[10] Focusing

---

10 Of course, for poetry we must adopt other ways to distinguish complete thought units. Those might be, for example, couplets, stanzas, or the entire poem. For other genres we would think of entire oracles, epics, parables, or ballads, to name a few.

on the meaning of a paragraph rather than a verse, phrase, or single word (which unfortunately is the emphasis of some Bible teachers) increases the odds of discovering the accurate meaning. Only by concentrating on the theme of a paragraph and noting how each sentence contributes to the development of that theme can one discern the real meaning and significance of the individual sentences.

Circles of Contextual Study

To interpret a passage in its literary context one must examine different domains or circles of context:

- the immediate context
- the book context
- the author's corpus of writings context (where available)
- the pertinent Testament context
- the Bible context.

While these contextual domains interact, they need to be applied in a definite order of priority. Each provides significant insight into the intended meaning of the passage, but a decreasing relative importance and certainty exists as one moves from immediate context to the context of the rest of the Bible.

FIGURE 1: CIRCLES OF CONTEXT

1. Immediate Context 2. Entire Book Context 3. Context of the Bible

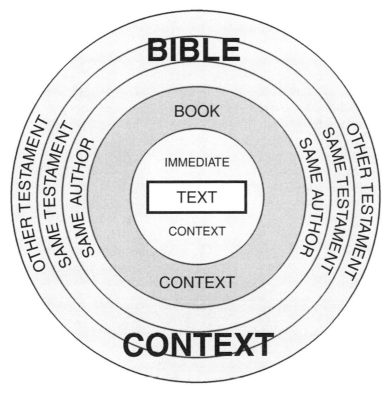

Immediate Context

The immediate context exerts the most important control over the meaning of a specific passage. We define the immediate context as the material presented immediately before and after the passage under study. In some instances this will be the preceding and succeeding sentences and paragraphs; in others it may be a subsection in the author's presentation, or possibly a major division of a book. The tactic of outlining a book helps the interpreter to discern its natural divisions and to establish the specific immediate context in which a passage occurs. A sequence of ideas links the ideas. The proximity of the materials to each other and the correlation of the materials with each other make the immediate context a more critical indicator of meaning than either the whole book or the whole Bible.

The investigation of the immediate context focuses on two things: *theme* and *structure*. To discover the *theme* or central idea of the entire section of the book where the passage under study occurs, the student must first determine the theme of the preceding section, the passage itself, and the following passage. Of course, this assumes that the passage for study does not occur at the beginning or end of a unit of thought. If it does, one can evaluate only what follows or precedes, respectively. Then the student must analyze these subjects to find the common theme that holds them together. This theme of the immediate context regulates the meaning of the individual words, phrases, clauses, and sentences within the specific passage under study.

Like any skill, learning how to recognize the main theme of a passage takes practice. The following steps illustrate the process. First, carefully read the preceding passage to determine the dominant subject. That is, find the topic to which everything in that paragraph or section refers. Second, write a topic sentence in your own words. A good topic sentence is both precise and concise. It is not enough to say that the theme of a passage is "love." Obviously, one passage does not tell everything there is to know about love. A precise topic sentence contains a brief summary of what the passage says about love. For example: Love is more than a feeling; it must be demonstrated by actions. In the interest of precision and brevity, the theme should be restricted to one sentence. Repeat this process for each part of the immediate context and then for the combined book context.

The second focus of the immediate context is *structure*. Passages are linked not only by a common theme but also by structure. A thorough interpreter investigates not only what a text says but also how the writer organizes the material. First, determine how the specific passage grows out of the preceding section and prepares for the following one. How does each paragraph contribute to the development of thought in the immediate context? These insights enable the interpreter to explain the relationship between the passage being studied and the surrounding paragraphs or sections. Just as one must understand each sentence in the given passage consistent with the general theme of the immediate context, so also one must interpret that sentence according to the paragraph's structural relationship with the adjoining material.

To arrange passages in sequential order writers employ many different structural relationships. In some sections paragraphs are arranged *chronologically*. Historical narratives typically proceed in this way, reporting events in the order in which they occurred. For example, note the beginning words in these paragraphs: "After they came down from . . . "; "Then Samuel took a flask . . . "; "Then you will go on . . . "; "After that you will go to . . . " (1 Sam 9:25; 10:1, 3, 5). Writers normally indicate such successions of events by temporal adverbs and conjunctions that indicate continuation: now, then, later, and afterwards. The OT books of Joshua, Kings and Chronicles narrate chronologically, whereas the patriarchal narratives (Gen 12–36) present loosely related episodes in a broad chronological structure.

Other texts group materials together in a context based on *thematic continuity.* For example, the Gospel writers sometimes clustered events or teachings that were of a similar nature even though they did not happen at the same time. The writer of Matthew probably gathered the parables in chapter thirteen to exemplify Jesus' teaching ministry.[11] In the OT Leviticus assembles diverse cultic contents in thematic sections, while Judges sounds its main theme (2:6–23), illustrates it in the exploits of the judges (chaps. 3–16), and offers other episodes to suggest that Israel needs a king (chaps. 17–21).

Logical order, another organizing principle, accounts for most of the sequential arrangement in the OT Prophets, NT Epistles, and Bible speeches. The logical arrangement of material takes many forms. Some of the more important structural patterns authors use in developing a logical line of thought are:

1.	Introduction	preparing for what follows
2.	Explanation	clarifying the meaning
3.	Illustration	citing an example or instance
4.	Causation	showing cause and effect
5.	Instrumentation	demonstrating the means to an end
6.	Interrogation	giving a question and answer
7.	Evidence	proving the stated point
8.	Particularization	stating the details
9.	Generalization	drawing a general principle from details
10.	Interchange	alternating sequence
11.	Cruciality	pivot marking change of direction
12.	Climax	indicating progression from lesser to greater
13.	Continuation	extending an idea
14.	Continuity	restating the same idea
15.	Repetition	restating the same words for emphasis
16.	Comparison	showing similarity to something else
17.	Contrast	showing difference from something else
18.	Summarization	reviewing main points briefly
19.	Conclusion	drawing inferences or bringing to an end

Occasionally conjunctions at the beginning of a paragraph indicate these logical connections. The writer's use of a specific logical connective between paragraphs simplifies the identification of the structural relationship, but, unfortunately, writers do not always use these logical connectives. In that case the interpreter has to infer the type

---

11 The parallel reports of some of these parables in the other Gospels show that they probably were not all taught during one phase of Jesus' ministry or necessarily in the order in which Matthew arranged them. The Sermon on the Mount in Mt 5–7 may indicate a similar thematic arrangement. Note also how Lk 15:1–2 introduces the theme for the parables that follow in vv. 3–32: "Now all the tax collectors and sinners were coming near to listen to him. And the Pharisees and the scribes were grumbling and saying, 'This fellow welcomes sinners and eats with them' " (NRSV).

of logical relationship from the nature of the contents. By determining how each paragraph functions in the logical flow of thought in the context, the interpreter gains perspective for appreciating the true significance of the passage.

Literary genre provides another clue to the organizational pattern of biblical materials. Biblical writers employed a wide variety of distinct types of literature that existed in biblical times. In recent years scholars have become increasingly aware of how much each different literary genre influences the meaning of the message it communicates.[12] We present the features of these specific literary formats and their significance for meaning in the subsequent chapters on literary genres.

In some instances the relationship between adjoining paragraphs may seem totally confusing. The student may discern no reason for the sequence of ideas—whether chronological, thematic, logical, or relative to the literary genre. We may explain such apparent "jumps" in thought between passages that the writer presents as related by a phenomenon called *psychological transfer.* This occurs when one subject triggers a psychological switch to a different subject. In the mind of the writer there is a connection between the thoughts but it is more psychological than logical. The relationship was clear to the writer but may not be immediately apparent to the reader. Before accusing the writer of a mental lapse in writing, the student should attempt to discover the writer's frame of reference and the likely connection.

An example of this may occur at 2 Cor 6:13. Following the paragraph of vv. 11–13, which ends with Paul's appeal that the readers "open wide your hearts also," he appears to interject a seemingly unrelated section, 6:14 – 7:1, that begins, "Do not be yoked together with unbelievers." Then at 7:2 he resumes where he left off at 6:13, repeating, "Make room for us in your hearts." The connection between sections may be psychological in nature. If you are to make room for me, Paul tells the Corinthians, you cannot "make room" for unrighteous associations with unbelievers. Paul believes their current unholy associations will subvert a genuine reunion between himself and the Corinthians.[13]

Finally, we may encounter an *abrupt transition* from one paragraph to another. When a writer introduces a new topic, a break in the thought flow will occur. Sometimes the writer prepares the reader for the transition;[14] at other times there is no

---

12 Recall we said much about this earlier; also the reader may consult such works as L. Ryken and T. Longman, III, ed., *A Complete Literary Guide to the Bible* (Grand Rapids: Zondervan, 1993); J. B. Gabel, et al., *The Bible As Literature*, 4th ed. (Oxford: Oxford University Press, 1999); M. D. Johnson, *Making Sense of the Bible: Literary Type As an Approach to Understanding* (Grand Rapids: Eerdmans, 2002); D. B. Sandy and R. L. Giese, Jr., ed., *Cracking Old Testament Codes: A Guide to Interpreting Literary Genres of the Old Testament* (Nashville: Broadman & Holman, 1995); D. A. Dorsey, *The Literary Structure of the Old Testament: A Commentary on Genesis – Malachi* (Grand Rapids: Baker, 1999); and J. L. Bailey and L. D. Vander Broek, *Literary Forms in the New Testament* (Louisville: Westminster John Knox, 1992).

13 On this see C. K. Barrett, *The Second Epistle to the Corinthians,* BNTC (London: Black, 1973; Peabody, MA: Hendrickson, 1993), 193–95; cf. 11–12. For an extensive discussion of the issues surrounding 6:14–7:1 in the context of 2 Corinthians, see V. P. Furnish, *II Corinthians,* AB (Garden City, NY: Doubleday, 1984), 359–83. For an alternative appraisal that proposes a chiastic structure see C. L. Blomberg, "The Structure of 2 Corinthians 1–7," *CTR* 4 (1989): 3–20.

14 Such an announced transition occurs at 1 Cor 7:1 where Paul moves specifically to answer questions his readers had raised. In the OT editors may announce to readers their intentions as sections develop, e.g., Gen 22:1; and 1 Sam 23:1, 8.

warning.[15] In interpreting a passage in manner that is consistent with its context, interpreters must recognize the possibility of an abrupt transition either before or after the text. This protects the interpreter from creating forced contextual insights where the writer intended none.

Literary Context of the Entire Book

The book in which the Bible passage occurs is the second most important literary context in determining the author's intended meaning. To understand a passage correctly means to understand it in terms of the whole book in which it occurs.[16] Read shorter books carefully and repeatedly. Try to read through longer books in one sitting, more than once if possible. Work out a tentative outline of the book's structure and then make use of reference works that summarize or outline their message.[17] Three kinds of information about the entire book are significant for proper understanding of any given passage within that book:

1. The book's purpose(s) or controlling theme(s)
2. The basic outline of the book
3. Parallel passages within the book that deal with the same subject

It is helpful, first, to understand the *book's purpose(s) or controlling theme(s)*. Knowing why the writer composed the book sets limits on the meaning for its individual parts. We assume that individual statements or sections contribute in some way to the writer's goal. Sometimes the writer makes it easier for interpreters by explicitly stating the purpose for the book. For example, at the beginning of his Gospel, Luke precisely states his aim:

> Seeing that many others have undertaken to draw up accounts of the events that have reached their fulfilment among us, as these were handed down to us by those who from the outset were eyewitnesses and ministers of the word, I in my turn, after carefully going over the whole story from the beginning, have decided to write an ordered account for you, Theophilus, so that your Excellency may learn how well founded the teaching is that you have received. (Lk 1:1–4; NJB).

---

15 To return to 1 Cor for examples, no transition normally occurs between the various topics Paul sequentially considers (see e.g., 5:1; 6:1; and 6:12). To come back to the OT, after listing David's final words (2 Sam 23:1–7) and David's mighty men (23:8–39), the writer resumes the narrative with a simple, "Again the anger of the Lord . . ." (24:1). At first glance the Judah-Tamar episode (Gen 38) seems to disrupt the narrative, but recently scholars have recognized, among other things, its anticipation of Judah's crucial, leading role later (e.g., 43:3, 8; 44:14, 16, 18; 46:28).

16 Long before compilers of our canon divided them into the books familiar to us, Joshua to 2 Kings probably comprised a major Israelite historical work, the so-called "Deuteronomic History" (DtH), with Deuteronomy as its introduction. Thus, for purposes of interpretation, both the individual canonical books and Deuteronomy—2 Kings as a whole constitute a "book" circle of context. Also, students may interpret Deuteronomy—2 Kings as a whole as the work of a single author (commonly called "the Deuteronomic Historian" or "DtH") or the individual books as his works just as one would handle, say, Luke-Acts or the Pauline Epistles.

17 The chief helps on this score come from so-called introductions. See the bibliography for suggestions for both Testaments.

Luke lived in a day when multiple written records and oral reports were creating confusion about the details of Jesus' life. Thus, he purposed to confirm for Theophilus the credibility of the information about Jesus' life by providing a carefully investigated and orderly record. In contrast to Luke, the author of the Fourth Gospel waited until near the end of his book to indicate that his purpose was to promote eternal life by generating and sustaining belief in Jesus (Jn 20:30–31). Other books like Romans and 1 Corinthians have multiple purpose statements at various places in the book.

For OT books, explicit purpose statements are more difficult to discover (if we can discover them at all). The first two verses of Joshua probably encapsulate the subject matter of the book: the crossing of the Jordan River and the conquest of "the land I am about to give to them—to the Israelites" (Josh 1:2). But if we inquire *why* the writer composed the book, that is more difficult to answer. Perhaps we discover the answer in the book's conclusion with all its warnings and reminders to be faithful in serving the Lord—to follow the example of Joshua and Israel during his life. That is, the writer's purpose could well be to encourage a later generation of Israelites to "Be very strong; be careful to obey all that is written in the Book of the Law of Moses, without turning aside to the right or to the left" (23:6). They needed to affirm along with Joshua's contemporaries, "We will serve the Lord our God and obey him" (24:24).

So when books lack formal purpose statements, interpreters must infer them from the contents. They must observe what the author or editor accomplishes in the book, and then deduce the purpose from that information. While this approach may prove reasonably accurate in finding the writer's goal, it remains conjectural. Rather than speculate about questionable, inferred purposes, we suggest that in such cases interpreters identify the dominant themes of the books. The end product will not differ much on either approach. Interpreters can discover the controlling themes by noting those topics the author emphasizes in the book. For example, in a short book like Obadiah, the dominant theme of God's judgment against Edom and his vindication and blessing of the house of Jacob is readily discernible. For the longer book of Galatians, Paul clearly seeks to champion the principle of justification by faith in Christ alone, against the teachings of some "Judaizers" who apparently insisted that the converting Gentiles must follow the Jewish Law to attain salvation. Then each passage is interpreted according to its contribution to one or more of those subjects.

The *basic plan* of the book is another important part of the literary context of the book. The contribution an individual passage makes to the total message of a book depends primarily on its location. For longer books this involves two main elements: the *general* train-of-thought of the entire book and the *specific* train-of-thought of the section of the book where the passage occurs. By discovering the theme of each of the main divisions of the book, the interpreter can determine whether there is any significance in their order. Once an interpreter understands how the theme of each major division fits into the book's overall flow of thought, the focus narrows to a closer look at the specific section containing the passage for study. To summarize: an interpretation is more likely to be the correct one when it explains the passage in a way that is consistent with the theme of the section in which the passage occurs. Then the likely interpretation shows how that section contributes to the overall progress of the book itself.

The final item considered in studying the literary context of the whole book concerns *parallel passages* in the book that deal with the same subject as the specific passage under study. When a writer refers to a subject more than once in a book, one or more of the passages may clarify vague aspects in another. The procedure for this study is straightforward. Skim or quickly read the book to locate other passages that deal with the same subject and then study them to discover what they contribute to the understanding of the passage.[18]

So, for example, to understand the Day of the Lord in Joel 2:31 (part of the section that Peter quotes on the day of pentecost in Acts 2:20), the student must investigate what else Joel says about the Day of the Lord in his prophecy (e.g., 1:15; 2:1, 11; 3:14), or other places where that theme emerges even when the specific vocabulary does not occur.[19] Likewise, for insight into what James means by saving faith in the section that starts with 2:14, the student must gain insight from other references to faith in the letter (1:3, 5–8; 2:1; 5:15).

But a word of caution is in order. We must always make sure that the passages are truly parallel before we allow them to inform each other. Sometimes passages use identical words but with different meanings for those words. This would be only an *apparent* parallel. Even when both passages are true parallels, one cannot simply read the ideas of one passage into the other without proper justification. We must keep ever before us the goal of interpretation: the author's intention as reflected in the text at hand. We become liable to serious errors when we interpret a passage in light of another while ignoring the immediate context of each passage. As a precaution, always interpret each parallel passage according to its own immediate context and the entire book context before comparing the passages. Once we know the contextually valid meaning for each parallel passage, we can compare the passages to see if any of them sheds light on specific details in the passage under study.

So for both the examples cited above—from Joel and James—the interpreter would need to be sure that the authors were using the concepts in truly parallel ways before simply imposing the other texts' features onto the passages under study. Do Joel's other references to the Day of the Lord have historical (for Joel's time) or eschatological (some time in the future) significance? We need to be sure of the answer before simply forcing their meanings on his use at 2:31. Does James use "faith" uniformly in his letter? Students must investigate each passage individually to determine whether the definition of faith in 2:14–26 is the sense that James employs elsewhere.

Context of the Entire Bible

This final element is more controversial and more difficult to control. As we observed earlier, the Bible possesses an overall unity despite its diversity of human authors. Scripture's divine inspiration gives continuity of thought to books written over a 1500–year period. As Vanhoozer succinctly puts it, "taken together, the various books of the Bible constitute the Word of God."[20] Furthermore, the Bible's human authors

---

18 Often a concordance helps in this task, though students must be careful not to trust merely the co-occurrence of common words to locate parallel passages, much less theological matches. This would be a grave error, as we will discover later in the discussion of words. See the bibliography chapter for suggestions on concordances.

19 Israel's prophets shared a common tradition of themes, language, and an understanding of history. So, after studying one prophet's wording or development of a theme, one may also check its occurrence in other prophets, especially ones who ministered in the same century.

20 K. J. Vanhoozer, *Is There a Meaning in This Text?* (Grand Rapids: Zondervan, 1998), 349.

participated in the same ongoing Judeo-Christian religious tradition. Some later writers knew books written previously and drew heavily upon them. In 2 Pet 3:15–16 the author refers to letters written by Paul, even implying their status on a par with other Scriptures (i.e., the OT). The OT book of Chronicles probably drew upon Samuel and Kings to some extent. Pss 105–106 appear to depend upon sections from the Pentateuch.[21] The most popular theories of Gospel composition suggest that one or more depended upon others. Luke's prologue (1:1–4) cited above implies that very fact.

Because of this unity, the entire Bible provides a literary context for all passages in it. But here comes the controversy and the difficulty. How do we allow individual authors their unique perspectives—the Bible's diversity—and yet affirm the Bible's unity?

We do not expect that all biblical writers on an issue will have the same perspective or present their views in the same ways. They will have different slants and distinct emphases, depending upon their purposes for writing. But due to the Holy Spirit's inspiration of the entire Bible, we posit that the correct meaning of every portion of Scripture will be *consistent* with the rest of the teaching of the Bible on that subject. One passage will not contradict the clear teaching of the rest of the Bible on that subject.[22]

Three groupings of biblical books should be consulted in interpreting a passage according to the context of the entire Bible: (1) parallel passages in other books by the same author (for Paul's view of the Law in Romans, also consult other Pauline books); (2) passages in books by other authors in the same Testament (see what other writers in the NT say about the Law); and finally, (3) passages in books by authors in the other Testament (study the Law in the OT).

First, we study parallels in other books attributed to the *same author*. These writings come from the same mind energized by the Holy Spirit, thus promising the highest level of linguistic and conceptual continuity. There is the highest degree of probability that the same person talking about the same subject in a similar way means the same thing. Furthermore, each biblical writer has a personal understanding of and fairly consistent pattern for articulating an aspect of God's truth. Thus, to comprehend Paul's understanding of faith in Rom 3:22 the interpreter is wiser to consult passages in Galatians (e.g. 2:16; 3:8, 11, 24) than passages in James. This applies not merely to the words used but even more to the ideas they represent.[23]

Parallels in books by different writers in the *same Testament* rank second in significance. Writers from the same Testament have the most in common with others writing from or about the same phase of God's redemptive program. OT writers used the

---

21 In the last two decades, this assumption has opened up a fruitful area of inquiry in OT studies called "inner-biblical exegesis," the study of the various ways later biblical writers utilize earlier biblical texts (e.g., see what Joel 3:10 does with Isa 2:4 / Mic 4:3).

22 A challenge constantly facing the interpreter who shares this presupposition of unity, however, is to interpret each text on its own terms, especially when distinct texts seem to conflict with each other. We must avoid glossing over these places in our attempts to preserve *what we view* as biblical consistency. We must let the texts speak for themselves even if the results are not as harmonious as we would prefer.

23 Of course, we must employ the same guidelines and cautions about using parallel passages we noted above. While we are dealing with the same author, we are now in different books. We must assure ourselves that the passages are truly parallel before simply imposing meaning from one place to another. In addition, an author's ideas may progress over the years.

Hebrew (or Aramaic) language and reflected a Semitic culture in a primarily Israelite setting. They shared a focus on the nation of Israel as God's special people, on exclusive loyalty to Yahweh as an expression of that relationship, and on the prophetic promises of future blessings. That gave them, diverse as they were, a unique camaraderie.[24] NT writers, by contrast, employed the Greek language and resided in the predominantly Hellenistic culture of the Roman Empire. They lived in the age of messianic fulfillment and proclaimed the good news of God's grace made available through the death and resurrection of Jesus.[25] Antecedent writings i the same Testament likely known by a later author take precedence over later writings not yet known to that author.

Since the writing of the OT covers at least a thousand years, interpersonal relationships were rare among its writers. So the help that other writers or books can provide for interpreting individual passages might appear to be considerably diminished from what we can discover in the NT. Yet a common religious legacy, shared convictions, and a reverence for the Mosaic tradition or the Davidic monarchy on the one hand and the writings of earlier prophets on the other, provided some unity and sense of continuity.[26] Studying OT parallels requires paying close attention to the time when the writers lived and when the OT books became complete. For example, since the ministries of Hosea, Amos, Isaiah, and Micah overlapped (eighth century B.C.), the interpreter can learn about the religious apostasy of Israel and Judah at the time by comparing parallel passages. They provide helpful commentaries on each other at certain points.

The writers of the NT experienced a different situation. Joining as members of the Church that included believers from many nationalities, they composed the NT books over a brief period of fifty or so years. The authors, a select group of apostles and their close associates, often had contact with each other. Of course, this does not mean they always agreed with each other, as Gal 2:11–14 shows. However, even allowing for diverse expressions of Christianity within the NT, interpreters can expect a high degree of continuity in the way these early Christians communicated their faith.

The final type of parallel passages consists of those from the *other Testament*. OT parallels for NT studies prove highly valuable. Because most NT writers knew the OT well, they borrowed theological language and categories from it. After all, the Bible of the early church was the OT, most often its Greek translation (LXX). Just as the English language

---

24 On the harmony of OT theology see W. C. Kaiser, Jr., *Toward an Old Testament Theology* (Grand Rapids: Zondervan, 1978).

25 On the unity of NT theology see esp. G. E. Ladd, *A Theology of the New Testament,* rev. by D. A. Hagner (Grand Rapids: Eerdmans, 1993); G. B. Caird (completed and edited by L. D. Hurst), *New Testament Theology* (Oxford, UK: Clarendon, 1994); and D. Guthrie, *New Testament Theology* (Leicester, UK and Downers Grove, IL: InterVarsity, 1981).

26 The unique nature of the OT requires us to nuance this point slightly. According to Jer 18:18, the OT has three main schools of thought or "traditions" whose influences we see evident both in single books and across several books: "instruction" (or "law") as the province of priests (e.g., the Pentateuch), the "word" as the province of the prophets (e.g., the prophetic books), and "wisdom" as the province of the wise teachers (e.g., Job, Proverbs, Ecclesiastes). Further, the OT evidences other historical and theological "traditions"—e.g., creation, the ancestral promise, the Exodus, the Sinai events, God as warrior, etc.—that also reappear in many OT (and NT) books. Both these "traditions" comprise part of the *same Testament* circle of context when interpreting the OT.

shows the influence of the Bible,[27] so the NT language reflects Greek Septuagintal expressions.[28] In fact, some of the arguments in the book of Hebrews depend upon the formulation of the OT in the LXX version (e.g., 1:6 cf. Deut 32:43; 10:5–7 cf. Psa 40:6–8). Furthermore, their entire thought-world, especially the religious concepts in which they formulated their belief system—monotheism, covenant, election, people of God, atonement, and sin, to name a few—derived from OT theological convictions.

Obviously, in the other direction, the NT did not influence the writing of the OT, but NT parallels to OT texts help readers find the total teaching of the Bible on a subject and may draw out further implications.[29] This demonstrates the relevance of the OT teaching as it unfolds, for example, in Jesus' ministry where he fulfills OT texts.[30] In Lk 4:18–21 Jesus explicitly identifies his ministry as the fulfillment of Isa 61:1–2. In Mt 11:4–5, however, when Jesus says, "Go back and report to John what you hear and see: The blind receive sight, the lame walk, those who have leprosy are cured, the deaf hear, the dead are raised, and the good news is preached to the poor," his answer more implicitly expands Isa 35:4–6 and 61:1.

At the same time, interpreters must exercise extreme caution to avoid an undue Christianizing of the OT. Parallel NT passages should not be used to make OT passages teach NT truth. The early church had the tendency—one continued by Protestants after the Reformation—to read NT theological concepts back into OT passages. We must avoid this error; our first task is always to understand each text on its own terms—as its writer and readers would have understood it. Only after we understand the meaning of the OT text can we address the canonical issue of how the two Testaments complement each other to fill out the entire biblical teaching.

We heard of an incident that shows how tempting and prevalent this error is among Christians. After a visiting speaker preached a sermon on Jeremiah's call in which he stressed insights for responding to God's leading today, a parishioner bluntly admonished him at the door, "Young man [a clear sign of trouble], preach Christ!" The confident, "But I did, sir!" did not reassure the indignant parishioner who felt that every OT passage had to serve as a springboard for a Christ-centered gospel message. Unfortunately, he, and many others like him, have failed to realize that God's message in the OT for the Church today must grow out of the intended meaning of the text itself. Its

---

27 For example, even completely secular people refer to their "thorn in the flesh," "going the extra mile," or being a "good Samaritan."

28 Carson, Moo, and Morris say of the author of the third Gospel, "He starts with a paragraph in classical style (1:1–4). The remainder of his first two chapters has a strongly Hebraic strain, while the remainder of the book is in a good Hellenistic Greek that constantly reminds the reader of the Septuagint" (*An Introduction to the New Testament* [Grand Rapids: Zondervan, 1992], 115). On the influence of the LXX on the language of the NT, see K. H. Jobes and M. Silva, *Invitation to the Septuagint* (Grand Rapids: Baker; Carlisle, UK: Paternoster, 2000), 193–205. In various places readers will encounter the term "Semitisms" to describe possible Semitic influences or elements in the NT. Semitisms may come from the Hebrew OT, the LXX, or the infusion of Aramaic and possibly Hebrew terms or constructions, say, from everyday life in first-century Palestine.

29 As noted above, when one interprets Joel 2:28–32, it helps to read Acts 2:14–36 to see what Peter did with the Joel text.

30 Like the modern "colorizing" of old black and white movies, fulfillment in this messianic age adds depth and new perspectives to OT passages. Christians cannot read OT messianic passages apart from their understanding of the texts' fuller revelation in Christ.

significance for our lives may differ greatly from its significance to its original readers, but *not its essential meaning.* Many people fail to discover the great truths about God's character and His relationship with His people in the OT because of their well-intentioned but misguided belief that every part of the Bible must convey NT truth. Primarily, the OT must stand on its own merits. We must interpret its passages in keeping with the intention of its texts; that constitutes the essential goal of OT interpretation.[31]

Interpreting passages in light of the context of the entire Bible has a limited scope. Check parallels to see if they contribute to the understanding of the meaning of the passage. The careful use of parallels gives the Bible student an ability to appreciate the contribution that the text under consideration makes to the total teaching of the entire Bible on a given theme.

HISTORICAL-CULTURAL BACKGROUND

Biblical passages not only express a writer's train of thought but also reflect a way of life—one that in most ways differs radically from that of present-day readers. The literature and events recorded in the Bible originated thousands of years ago. Beyond reflecting ancient languages, cultures, and lifestyles, the biblical writers wrote their messages for people different from us. Consequently, every time we study a Scripture text, we must be aware of these cross-cultural and epoch-spanning dimensions. Each passage was God's Word to other people before it became God's Word to us. In a sense, the Bible always comes to us secondhand, through others who lived at different times and in different places. This is the basis of an important principle of hermeneutics: *The correct interpretation of a biblical passage will be consistent with the historical-cultural background of the passage.* There are three reasons why this principle is important: perspective, mindset, and contextualization.

The Significance of the Historical-Cultural Background
Perspective

First, the circumstances in which communication occurs substantially affect, if not determine, meaning. We need to comprehend the *perspective* of the original communicators—initiator and receptor—to understand the correct meaning. Because both the writer and the recipients shared the same cultural background and information and lived at the same time in history, they never make explicit their perspective. This tendency is true even today. If someone shows us a personal letter, even if the letter comes from a mutual friend, some things may need explanation because they refer to an experience known only by the writer and recipient. Lacking this information—this perspective on the situation—another reader has difficulty making sense out of these references.[32]

Such "over-the-shoulder" reading describes the situation of present-day readers of the NT Epistles. Apostles or others sent these first-century letters to specific people living in certain places concerning particular circumstances in their lives. In most instances the writer and recipients had shared familiar experiences; they spoke the same

---

31 W. C. Kaiser, Jr., *Toward An Exegetical Theology* (Grand Rapids: Baker, 1981), rightly propounds the principle that he calls the "analogy of [antecedent] Scripture"—that one may deduce the original *meaning* of a passage only on the basis of what it says or on the basis of texts that *preceded* it in time, even if later scripture may expand or extend its *significance* (136–37).

32 Alternatively, read a political cartoon in a newspaper or magazine from another city or, better, a different country. Unless one comprehends the issues or persons in view, the cartoon remains a mystery.

Greek language and possessed common information about each other and their world. To interpret correctly these books today, the reader needs to understand as much as possible about the details of this historical and cultural background.

The same applies equally to the majority of biblical books that are not letters. Many of the psalms of ancient Israel reflected experiences of worshipers living in a monarchy in a world replete with kingdoms and empires. The writer of Judges characterizes the days prior to the monarchy in a closing statement: "In those days Israel had no king; everyone did as he saw fit" (Judg 21:25). They were "wild and woolly" times to be sure—unquestionably and literally worlds apart from the modern era. Likewise, the apocalyptic prophecies grow out of a world-view and use literary techniques largely foreign to our experience.[33]

Our life setting differs so radically from virtually every biblical situation it is no wonder that at first glance many Bible statements make a different impact on us than that intended by the original writer.[34] Present-day Bible interpreters need to put themselves in the sandals of the writer and initial recipients, that is, they need to understand a passage from their perspective. Biblical writers did not have our situation in mind. They wrote from the perspective of their own circumstances, and we must understand their writings from that vantage point.

Mindset

The second reason why we must interpret a passage consistent with its historical-cultural setting grows out of the possibly subtle factor of *mindset*. A mindset describes a mental attitude or inclination. Speech acts not only communicate content; they do it in certain ways, for specific purposes, and with certain intended *emotional impact*. Each culture manifests a system of values and a way of looking at the world that regulates this affective or feeling dimension of discourse. The effect of a statement may vary from culture to culture, depending on each culture's standards of right and wrong or scale of values.[35] For example, when Jesus called Herod Antipas a fox (Lk 13:32), his hearers understood "fox" to represent a certain value.[36] To call someone a fox today would have different meanings or values, depending upon the culture (or subculture) involved.[37] If a reader simply imposed a current value for "fox," the original intent would be obscured or even lost. In some cultures, fox might have no connotative value, and the meaning would simply be opaque.[38] Biblical revelation was communicated within cultures. It could not be otherwise, for all human language is culturally conditioned.

---

33 Of course, we provide specific help in understanding these and other various genres in following sections.

34 Speaking in terms of locutions, we can miss their energy and intended effects even if we get the content.

35 We here limit the discussion to values at this point. Obviously, a culture's mindset may include other dimensions. Individuals also have unique mindsets that we can learn something about if we know them well enough, or read enough of their writing. Otherwise, this is somewhat elusive.

36 According to I. H. Marshall, in rabbinic literature a fox typified low cunning, but it was also an insignificant creature in comparison to a lion (*Commentary on Luke*, NIGTC [Exeter: Paternoster; Grand Rapids: Eerdmans, 1978], 571). Most commentaries on Luke point to either cunning or insignificance as the point of the "fox" reference.

37 Connotations today might include clever, crafty, sly, and sexually attractive.

38 Bible translators need to discover such things and make appropriate adjustments.

To develop an awareness of the mindset of people in biblical times, we need to study the historical-cultural background of their world, because an interpretation must make sense for the people "back then," even if it remains strange to us. We have to resist the temptation to "sanitize" the Bible so it conforms to our values and mindset.[39] Once we understand what a passage *meant*, we can apply that meaning in light of today's cultural values so that it can have the appropriate impact and emotional effect on us.

Contextualization

The third reason why we must interpret a passage consistent with its historical-cultural background goes to the very heart of the interpretive task. While the first two reasons, perspective and mindset, stress the importance of knowing the historical-cultural background for discovering the meaning intended for the original recipients, this reason focuses on expressing that message accurately in today's world. The word *contextualization* helps capture this perspective.[40] Contextualizing biblical truth requires interpretive bifocals. First, we need a lens to look back into the background of the biblical world to learn the intended meaning. Then, we need another lens to see the foreground to determine how to best express—contextualize—that sense for today's world. We stress this dimension given our conviction that biblical interpretation must never remain an exercise in the ancient world. The Bible is God's Word to us.

The astute interpreter lives in two worlds: the ancient biblical world and modern society.[41] The Bible was fashioned within specific ancient cultures; in contrast, we are the products of our modern and increasingly postmodern cultures. These two horizons comprise the alternating foci of the perceptive interpreter.[42] Effective exegesis not only perceives what the message meant originally but also determines how best to express

---

39 A comparison between English word usage in the 17th and 21st centuries illustrates the point about mindsets. The KJV translators did not hesitate to use the word "piss" (e.g., 2 Kgs 18:27; Isa 36:12), while most modern versions find this term offensive and beyond the bounds of acceptable contemporary diction. Words have "affective" values that grow out of a culture's mindset. Mention the words "evolution" or "abortion" in certain conservative Christian subcultures, and its mindset will emerge.

40 Arising in missiological circles, the term *contextualization* describes the process of "packaging" biblical truth in ways that are relevant to the diversity of current cultures. Missiologists, in general, welcome the insights of anthropology and sociology in their quest to impact cultures with the gospel. For further insight and analyses see B. J. Nicholls, *Contextualization: A Theology of Gospel and Culture* (Downers Grove, IL: InterVarsity, 1979); B. C. Fleming, *Contextualization of Theology; An Evangelical Assessment* (Pasadena: William Carey, 1980); and H. M. Conn, "Contextualization: Where Do We Begin?" in *Evangelicals and Liberation*, ed. C. E. Armerding (Nutley, NJ: Presbyterian & Reformed, 1977), 90–119. In a similar vein, the gospel must be presented and shown to be good news in a postmodern context. On this see, e.g., B. D. McLaren, *A New Kind of Christian* (San Francisco: Jossey-Bass, 2001) and D. Tomlinson, *The Post-Evangelical* (Grand Rapids: Zondervan, 2003).

41 From the preacher's perspective this concept is foundational. See J. R. W. Stott, *Between Two Worlds: The Art of Preaching in the Twentieth Century* (Grand Rapids: Eerdmans, 1978); R. C. Chisholm, *From Exegesis to Exposition: A Practical Guide to Using Biblical Hebrew* (Grand Rapids: Baker, 1999); S. D. Mathewson, *The Art of Preaching Old Testament Narrative* (Grand Rapids: Baker, 2002); S. Greidanus, *The Modern Preacher and the Ancient Text* (Grand Rapids: Eerdmans, 1988); and P. S. Wilson, *The Practice of Preaching* (Nashville: Abingdon, 1999), 125–94. For a specific example using African historical, cultural and traditional imagery in order to communicate the gospel more effectively see J. W. Z. Kurewa, *Preaching & Culture Identity: Proclaiming the Gospel in Africa* (Nashville: Abingdon, 2000).

42 Recall A. C. Thiselton, *The Two Horizons* (Grand Rapids: Eerdmans, 1980).

and apply that meaning to one's contemporaries. The process of contextualization expresses anew the ideas presented in a biblical passage in the language of today so that they convey the same impact to modern hearers.

The interpreter must be conscious of the nature of this task. We have to know both the biblical and the modern worlds in order to bridge their differences. Because our present culture has molded how we understand things (our preunderstanding), we risk fashioning our perception of the biblical message in terms of our way of life without first understanding it according to its own historical-cultural setting. If we succumb, the message we hear from Scripture may not correspond to what the text in fact means; we may simply have recast it according to *our* meanings. Our task must lead to application, but not before we have understood clearly the text's meaning.

Principles for Historical-Cultural Interpretation
The Original Historical-Cultural Background

Several principles guide the interpreter in taking proper account of the historical-cultural backgrounds of the biblical worlds. First, *we must understand each passage consistent with its historical and cultural background.* For any interpretation to qualify as the intended meaning of a text, it must be the most likely meaning given the circumstances of the original writing and reading of the passage. Any suggested explanation of a passage that would have been inconsistent with or inconceivable in the historical or cultural setting of the author and recipients cannot be valid. One must ask, given the original circumstances, what interpretation fits most naturally? This principle means that an interpreter must understand the historical and cultural setting as accurately as possible and must interpret the biblical message consistent with that picture.

Fortunately, archaeological findings, historical research, and sociological and cultural studies have provided a vast reservoir of information for this task.[43] So impressive is the material available that Russell Spittler boasted, "Advances in lexicography and archaeology have put us in a place to know more about the ancient world than it knew about itself."[44] While there is much truth in this statement, we must take care not to overestimate our knowledge of the biblical world. We must now analyze and classify by such highly developed academic disciplines as anthropology, sociology, linguistics, history, and psychology the routine experiences of daily existence in the ancient world. Despite of all the detailed insights gained by these studies, our knowledge of some of the details of the interrelated components of each Bible story remains extremely limited.[45] What we do not know and cannot find out far exceeds the valuable information available to us; consequently, we must always make modest and realistic claims for any of our historical-cultural reconstructions—and the interpretations that depend on them.

Understanding each passage according to its background involves determining how the biblical setting was like ours and how it differed from ours. There will always

---

43 The bibliography provides a list of helpful resources.

44 R. Spittler, "Scripture and the Theological Enterprise: View from a Big Canoe," in *The Use of the Bible in Theology / Evangelical Options,* ed. R. K. Johnston (Atlanta: John Knox, 1985), 56–77; quote on 75.

45 See E. M. Yamauchi, *The Stones and the Scriptures,* 2d ed. (Grand Rapids: Baker, 1981), for a good discussion of how limited this knowledge can be.

be some similarity between our lives and theirs. These common elements provide reference points that help present-day audiences understand the meaning. Differences, on the other hand, must be studied carefully to provide the interpreter with information that can remove historical-cultural ambiguities.

The letter to the church at Laodicea (Rev 3:14–22) provides an intriguing example. In the Lord's description of this church, he condemns it for being "neither cold nor hot." He goes on to state, "I wish you were either one or the other!" (v. 15). He finds no reason to commend the people of this church; they are completely useless—neither like hot water (as in a comfortable bath) nor like cold water (as in a refreshing drink). Apart from insight growing out of archaeological studies, interpreters might seriously misconstrue the point. That is, we must interpret "hot" and "cold" in light of the historical context of Laodicea, which was located close to both hot springs (by Hierapolis) and a cold stream (by Colossae). Now both hot and cold water are desirable; both are useful for distinct purposes. But the spiritual state of this church more closely resembled the tepid lukewarm water that eventually flowed into Laodicean pipes. Neither hot nor cold, it was putrid and emetic. Jesus is *not* saying that active opposition to him (an incorrect interpretation of "cold") is better than being a lukewarm Christian.[46]

The Original Impact

The second principle moves from the factual information about the biblical setting to the emotional dimension: *We must determine the impact that the biblical message would have had in its original setting.* This principle involves the factor of mindset. Interpreters should seek to know, where possible, how the original recipients would have reacted to what was written. Clearly, we are not always in a position to know this with any degree of certainty, nevertheless, to the extent that we are able (through our historical research), we seek to discover if a text would conflict or agree with the readers' value systems and to identify whether their feelings about it would resemble or differ from ours.

The book of Amos can illustrate this point. As "the Lord roars from Zion" (1:2), he pronounces judgment against Israel's (the Northern Kingdom's) neighbors (1:3–2:5). One can sense the people of Israel gloating in self-satisfaction and complacency. No doubt those other nations deserved God's judgment, they thought. But then the ax falls and Amos pronounces God's final judgment—against Israel! Israel will not escape, and the book proceeds to detail God's case against her. Equally, modern readers can sense the emotional impact of 4:1 where Amos calls the self-indulgent women of Israel "cows of Bashan."[47] Modern readers who live in urban areas must strain to feel the urgency of a prophecy that pronounces plagues and blights upon fields and gardens in that agrarian culture, which was totally dependent upon what the people could produce in their fields (5:16–17). Sometimes we get a hint when we experience or read about drought conditions in Africa. Or, can we feel with the original readers what it would be like to hear God's assessment: "I hate, I despise your religious feasts; I cannot stand your assemblies" (5:21)? Imagine how we would feel if the Lord pronounced these words on our church worship. The parable of

---

46 A succinct analysis of the latest evidence occurs in C. J. Hemer, *The Letters to the Seven Churches of Asia in Their Local Setting,* JSNTSup 11 (Sheffield, UK: JSOT, 1986), 186–91. Cf. M. J. S. Rudwick and E. M. B. Green, "The Laodicean Lukewarmness," *ExpT* 69 (1957–58): 176–78. Also see recent commentaries on Revelation.

47 Bashan was famous for its fine cattle (cf. Psa 22:12; Ezek 39:18).

the *good* Samaritan provides another example. We have "Good Samaritan" hospitals; the phrase strikes us positively. To Jesus' Jewish listeners, however, Samaritans were anything but good; they were despised. Yet Jesus makes a despised enemy the hero of his story about true neighborliness—in contrast to the religious leaders whom the Jews respected. Can we feel the discomfort of the audience?

This emotive angle of interpretation fosters a fuller appreciation of a passage's intended meaning. It supplies insight into the effect of the message as well as a comprehension of its concepts or ideas. It gives us a "feel" for the ideas and an "understanding" of them.

The Correct Expression

The third principle relates to the contextualization aspect of historical-cultural interpretation: *We must express biblical truth in our language in ways that most closely correspond to the ideas in the biblical culture.* The challenge for the interpreter is to find adequate contemporary idioms to articulate the intention of the passage so that people today will sense the meaning and impact that the original readers sensed. Certainly the NIV does a commendable job of capturing the thought of Rom 12:2: "Do not conform any longer to the pattern of this world." But readers have continued to appreciate J. B. Phillips' rendition: "Don't let the world around you squeeze you into its own mould."[48] These words express Paul's concept in a memorable idiom that a contemporary English speaker can easily understand. E. H. Peterson puts it this way: "Don't become so well-adjusted to your culture that you fit into it without even thinking."[49] Again, the paraphrase expresses the meaning more clearly for us. This principle naturally applies to the work of translators, but no less to interpreters who desire to understand and communicate the Bible's meaning to contemporary audiences or readers.

Those wishing to interface the biblical message with our contemporary culture face significant challenges and risks. One perennial danger concerns syncretism. Generally, "the combination of different forms of belief or practice,"[50] it comes to have a subjective and more pejorative sense: "The subjective meaning includes an evaluation of such intermingling from the point of view of one of the religions involved."[51] So, for Christians syncretism denotes the merger of biblical and nonbiblical beliefs to form a hybrid, and thus unacceptable, religion. Most Christians view syncretism negatively, for the mixing of Christian beliefs with tenets of other belief systems results in an amalgam that is non-Christian.

---

48 J. B. Phillips, *The New Testament in Modern English,* 2d ed. (London and Glasgow: Bles and Collins, 1960), 332.

49 E. H. Peterson, *The Message: The Bible in Contemporary Language* (Colorado Springs: NavPress, 2002).

50 *Merriam-Webster's Tenth New Collegiate Dictionary* (Springfield, MA: Merriam-Webster, 1998), 1192.

51 A. Droogers, "Syncretism: The Problem of Definition, the Definition of the Problem," in *Dialogue and Syncretism: An Interdisciplinary Approach,* ed. J. Gort, et al. (Grand Rapids: Eerdmans; Amsterdam: Editions Rodopi, 1989), 7. For further insight into this issue see E. S. Heideman, "Syncretism, Contextualization, Orthodoxy, and Heresy," *Missiology* 25 (1997): 37–49; M. J. Oleska, "Evangelism and Culture," *International Review of Mission* 84 (1995): 387–393; L. Newbigin, *Foolishness to the Greeks: The Gospel and Western Culture* (Geneva: WCC, 1986); H. G. Coward, *Pluralism: Challenge to World Religions* (Maryknoll, NY: Orbis, 1985); and P. G. Hiebert, "Critical Contextualization," *Missiology* 12 (1984): 287–296.

In 1 Kgs 12:25—13:34, we find that Jeroboam committed this error. He served as the first monarch of the Northern Kingdom of Israel after the ten tribes seceded from the Southern Kingdom of Judah. Fearing that his subjects' religious pilgrimages to Jerusalem to offer sacrifices would cause their loyalty to revert to King Rehoboam of Judah, Jeroboam established an alternate religion with worship centers within his own country. While preserving many of the features of the Mosaic beliefs and worship, his new religion, which focused worship on two golden calves, also embraced idolatrous elements from neighboring religions. While the new hybrid may have been more attractive to the king and his subjects, the Lord forcefully condemned this syncretistic religion by sending a prophet to denounce it on the very day the king attempted to offer sacrifices at the new shrine at Bethel (13:1–4).

Like Jeroboam of old, many today blend their understanding of the Christian faith with the best elements of the "religions" in their contemporary culture. Describing this approach W. Larkin says: "Though the Bible still has a role to play, it is now placed in dialectical relationship with the contemporary context."[52] Evangelicals reject this approach to contextualization because it contradicts the gospel's claim to be the one and only saving faith.[53] We believe that proper contextualization uses concepts from the contemporary culture to communicate the *Bible's own message* effectively in a way that avoids syncretism.[54] When seeking to convey the Bible's message, interpreters must take care not to choose words or other features from the culture that would involve the assimilation of elements incompatible with the Christian faith. Indeed, they may need to apply the biblical message in a cogent way to correct the thought-forms of a culture.

Proper contextualization requires that the interpreter be sensitive to both the biblical and the current cultures. The ultimate goal of good interpretation is a clear, accurate, and relevant explanation of the text's intended meaning in language that is meaningful to one's contemporaries. Bridging the gap between the biblical culture and modern culture requires knowing the language, values, and significant symbols of modern society. While all translation involves interpretation, interpretation goes beyond good translation. Traditionally, biblical interpreters have been better trained and skilled in exegeting Scripture than in exegeting contemporary culture. Since the agenda of hermeneutics includes developing principles for discovering the text's meaning and its relevance of the Bible for today's world, that must include guidelines for exegeting culture.

The Priority of the Plain Sense

The ever-present need for balance and perspective alerts us to the "cart-before-the-horse" syndrome. A final word of counsel for historical-cultural exegesis is a negative

---

52 W. J. Larkin, *Culture and Biblical Hermeneutics* (Grand Rapids: Baker, 1988), 140.

53 Indeed, the Lausanne Covenant of 1974 states, "We also reject as derogatory to Christ and the Gospel every kind of syncretism and dialogue which implies that Christ speaks equally through all religions and ideologies" ("The Lausanne Covenant," in *Let The Earth Hear His Voice,* ed. J. D. Douglas [Minneapolis: World Wide Publications, 1975]), 4.

54 This challenge confronts evangelists and church leaders who look for ways to make Christianity "seeker-friendly." In the process they must avoid truncating the message so it becomes sub-Christian.

warning: *Do not allow features of the historical-cultural background to sabotage the main task of understanding the point of the text.* Sometimes interpreters become so preoccupied with the historical-cultural insights that they identify the main point of a passage as something that is inconsistent with the textual wording. This requires caution for there is an inevitable circularity involved. The historical and cultural details enable us to understand the text, but the words of the text point to the historical issues at stake. A good illustration is the interpretation of the parable of the unjust steward (Lk 16:1–13). This passage has troubled many Christians because Jesus appears to compliment a dishonest action. Some interpreters unravel the historical situation to suggest that the businessman for whom the steward worked probably charged his creditors exorbitant and illegal interest rates. The steward's reducing the creditors' bills simply eliminated the unethical padding of the original bills.[55] So when this boss commends his fired employee for cutting in half all his creditors' debts, he admits the justice of this action. For such interpreters, the lesson of the parable becomes one of justice, the righting of wrongs when that is in one's power. While this explanation has the advantage of reversing the troublesome impression of Jesus' compliment—he's commending justice, not dishonesty—is this correct?

Actually, the owner compliments his former manager for his shrewdness, not his justice. Nothing in the context or in Jesus' application of the parable suggests the theme of justice. Nowhere does the passage state or imply that the owner had charged excessive interest. Whether he did or did not is not part of Jesus' story, and we cannot be sure the original readers or audience would have understood that background. Yet the circumstances surrounding the parable and the lessons Jesus drew from it provide the two clues to the meaning of parables. Furthermore, the surprise element, now recognized as a major characteristic and indicator of meaning in many of the parables of Jesus,[56] supports a focus on shrewdness, not justice. Receiving notice of his impending termination, the steward used the occasion to prepare for his long-range needs.[57]

Jesus' first application to the disciples underscores this point. Like the clever, dismissed bookkeeper, they too should act shrewdly in using present financial resources to make friends for eternity. The historical information about ancient loan practices

---

55 Defenders of this basic explanation include J. A. Fitzmyer, "The Story of the Dishonest Manager (Lk 16:1–13)," *Theological Studies* 25 (1964): 23–42; and K. E. Bailey, *Poet and Peasant* (Grand Rapids: Eerdmans, 1976), 86–110.

56 F. H. Borsch, *Many Things in Parables: Extravagant Stories of New Community* (Philadelphia: Fortress, 1988), uses the terms "exaggeration" and "extravagance," 14–15. Cf. B. B. Scott, *Hear Then The Parable* (Minneapolis: Fortress, 1989); and J. D. Crossan, *In Parables* (San Francisco; Harper & Row, 1973). E. Linnemann puts it in terms of *unusual features* "which do not result from a natural context in the representation in the parable narrative, [but] take their origin from the reality of which the narrator wishes to speak" (*Parables of Jesus* [London; SPCK, 1966], 28). See also A. J. Hultgren, *The Parables of Jesus: A Commentary* (Grand Rapids: Eerdmans, 2000) and our fuller discussion of the genre of parables below.

57 The definitive defense of this view appears in D. J. Ireland, *Stewardship and the Kingdom of God: An Historical, Exegetical, and Contextual Study of the Parable of the Unjust Steward in Luke 16:1–13* (Leiden: Brill, 1992). D. L. Mathewson, "The Parable of the Unjust Steward (Luke 16:1–13): A Reexamination of the Traditional View in Light of Recent Challenges," JETS 38 (1995): 29–40, defends this same perspective against several more recent, and odder, alternatives.

proves valuable for understanding the parable. Indeed, it may explain one facet of the fired employee's shrewdness. He may have known that the boss did not dare take him to court for canceling half of the debts owed him because he had given tacit agreement to the unethical charges.

Thus, while knowledge of the historical-cultural setting is important for discovering the intended meaning, it should always serve the supportive role of aiding one's understanding of the text itself. It must never supplant the plain meaning of the text. Authors communicate messages through the words of the text. Background material should help us understand the meaning of the text; it must not become an additional message that contravenes that meaning.

Retrieving the Historical-Cultural Background

Exploring the world of the biblical setting involves two distinct studies: (1) studying the background of a biblical book and (2) studying the background of specific passages in the book. Background information learned about the entire book gives insight into its overall setting and provides a general perspective for each passage. It becomes a historical-cultural "backdrop" for understanding the individual sections within the book. But each individual passage also requires special analysis to explain the historical-cultural factors that are pertinent to it.

Exploring the General Background of the Book

Before studying a particular biblical passage, the Bible student should become familiar with the historical-cultural background of the book in which it occurs. This includes pertinent facts about the writer/editor, recipients, date, and purpose of the book. Detailed personal research will probably not be necessary every time the student begins analyzing passages in a given book. Undoubtedly the student will already be familiar with much of the historical-cultural background through information received at church, college, or seminary. The student may need only to review (or perhaps, supplement) what he or she already knows about the book. Those students who have not had the opportunity of prior studies should consult sources such as Bible-survey and introduction books, commentaries, Bible dictionaries, and encyclopedias.[58] At times even the brief introductions in many recent study Bibles can provide a helpful start.

When relying on these secondary sources, students should look up the biblical references to acquaint themselves with the specific evidence in the book itself and in other parts of the Bible, both for better understanding, and to confirm the validity of others' claims. Besides insight about its authorship, destination, date, and purpose, good reference works also include valuable facts drawn from ancient, nonbiblical literary sources and archaeology.

When time permits, the following supplemental strategy to studying a book's background will pay rich dividends. Students should read through the book at one sitting (perhaps several times) and record everything they find about the writer, recipients, date, and purpose of the book on separate sheets of paper. After they analyze and review this material (preferably prior to consulting other sources), the articles in the reference works will become more meaningful.

---

58 For a list and description of the best resources for this study, see the bibliography.

Concerning the *author, editor,* or *writer,* the student will want to research matters of identity, characteristics, position among God's people, relationship with the recipients, and circumstances at the time of writing. This information will help the student understand the book from the perspective of the writer. Of course, such material may be more accessible for some books than for others. We cannot obtain information about who wrote many books of the Bible for they are anonymous; for others the authorship is uncertain. In such cases, the inductive insight we gain from reading the book itself may be all we can say about the writer.

Where possible, knowing about the *recipients*—their characteristics, circumstances, and community—sheds light on a passage, in particular on how and why the writer develops specific subjects. For many books in both Testaments, we have little information available about the recipients. In some prophetic books the situation is complex in that the audience addressed by the prophet may differ from the city or nation about whom the prophecy is made. For example, Obadiah prophesied about God's judgment against Edom though he addressed the book to Israel to provide encouragement.

Date is another key historical-cultural factor. Knowing when a book was written enables the student to include in the analysis historical information from other sources for that period. For some biblical books there is not enough evidence to determine a precise or reliable date. The historical facts included in the book may fit several periods equally well. Or we may be able to set a book only within a given century at best. In such situations the main emphasis should be on the general circumstances in that period of time in that part of the world. For example, Jonah's prophecy is set in the eighth century B.C. during the reign of the violent Assyrians. Thus, the brutal militarism of these hated pagans explains Jonah's reluctance to go to Nineveh to prophesy. For interpretive purposes, knowing the characteristics of a given period of time provides more insight than knowing a specific date.

For many NT books we can be fairly confident about locating their time of composition, at least within five to ten years. So, knowing that Paul exhorted the Romans to submit to the governing authorities during the early part of Nero's reign sheds light on his words (Rom 13:1–5). When Paul wrote (ca. A.D. 56), that infamous emperor had not yet exhibited the cruelty he demonstrated in later years. We might even speculate whether Paul would have framed his instructions differently were he writing during Nero's atrocious pogroms against Christians in the middle 60s. In historical books, Psalms, Proverbs, and some prophecies, interpreters may need to distinguish, if possible, between the time when the material was composed and the time when a writer or final editor organized the book into its final shape.

Examining the Historical-Cultural Factors of a Specific Passage

Discovering the historical-cultural background of a biblical book provides the initial framework for understanding specific passages within that book. Determining the meaning of a passage requires interpreting each paragraph consistent with its natural meaning in its specific, original situation, that is, what the writer most likely meant by these words to these recipients in this set of circumstances. To understand correctly each literary unit within the book, one must first determine whether historical information learned about the book as a whole applies in a particular way to the specific passage under scrutiny. A proposed interpretation of a passage must fit the historical-cultural background of the whole book.

Beyond this, individual passages within the book may contain special historical-cultural features that are pertinent to the meaning of that passage. While this background information may not be included in the description of the setting of the whole book, it is absolutely essential for the meaning of this text. Though a student may learn much about the background to the book of Amos, all that insight will not help interpret the meaning of the words in Amos 5:26, "Kaiwan your star-god" (NRSV) or "star of your God, Kaiwan" (NJB).[59] The student may understand the background for the writing of Matthew's Gospel without having a clue about the wide phylacteries worn by the Pharisees (Mt 23:5).[60] Thus, the student of Scripture also must research the specific historical and cultural details mentioned in the passage. On the cultural side, the student should identify and seek to understand features reflected in the text. These include such things as:

- worldview: values, mindset, or outlook of the writer/editor, recipients, other people mentioned in the text, or in society at large

- societal structures: marriage and family patterns, roles of men and women, or racial issues

- physical features: climate and weather, structures, implements, or ease and means of transportation

- economic structures: means of making a living, issues of wealth and poverty, slavery, or economic mobility

- political climate: structures, or loyalties, including actual personnel

- behavior patterns, dress, or customs

- religious practices, power centers, convictions, rituals, or affiliations.

After identifying these items in the text, the student must attempt to discover additional information that could shed light on them. The first resource to consult is the Bible itself. It contains valuable data concerning many historical-cultural phenomena. Materials in other parts of the specific Bible book, in other writings by the same author or to the same audience, in other parts of the Bible in general, or in specific parallel accounts of the same event often help to reconstruct the original situation. Beyond the Bible, other sources provide the principal and necessary means to secure background

---

59 All standard commentaries wrestle with the meaning of this reference. The NIV translates it as "the star of your god." For further help consult S. Paul, *Amos,* Hermeneia (Philadelphia: Fortress, 1991). Other useful tools include J. Jeremias, *The Book of Amos: A Commentary,* OTL (Louisville: Westminster John Knox, 1998); F. I. Andersen and D. N. Freedman, *Amos,* Anchor Bible (Garden City, NY: Doubleday, 1989); and J. L. Mays, *Amos: A Commentary* (Louisville: Westminster John Knox, 1969). M. D. Carroll R., *Amos—The Prophet and His Oracles: Research on the Book of Amos* (Louisville: Westminster John Knox, 2002) provides a compendium of research on issues in Amos.

60 For further insight on this issue consult J. Bowman, "Phylacteries," *Studia Evangelica* 1, ed F. L. Cross, TU 73 (Berlin: Akademie-Verlag, 1959), 523–38 and standard biblical dictionaries or encyclopedias (see bibliography). Wearing phylacteries (Hebrew *tefillin*) began at least by the first century (Josephus, *Ant.* 4. 8.13 mentions them). Black boxes containing Scripture texts, they are fastened to the left arm and forehead during prayer (Deut 6:4–9).

information. Many specialized works, not to mention introductions, Bible dictionaries, encyclopedias, and commentaries contain helpful material for clarifying historical or cultural references.[61]

The goal of historical-cultural research is to *reconstruct,* or at least to comprehend, the historical setting and cultural features of the specific passage as clearly as possible. Unfortunately, we are not always in a position to discover all we would like to know about certain features. But where feasible, this task involves explaining:

1. the situation of the writer, especially anything that helps explain why he or she wrote this passage;
2. the situation of the people involved in the text and/or the recipients of the book that can help explain why the writer penned this material to them;
3. the relationship between the writer and audience or the people involved in the text;
4. the cultural or historical features mentioned in the text.

Then we seek to explain the meaning and importance of the text in light of this historical-cultural reconstruction of the original setting. To the extent that we enter the world of the biblical setting, we can grasp the meaning of the passage. An interpretation that accurately reflects the original setting has a better claim to validity than one that does not.

WORD MEANINGS

By its very nature language communication employs words. People transmit ideas by combining words together into larger units of thought. Without words people would be limited in their ability to express their thoughts precisely. They would be restricted to nonverbal sounds, symbols, and pictures. The centrality of words in language communication underscores the importance of the lexical principle of hermeneutics: *The correct interpretation of Scripture is the meaning required by the normal meaning of the words in the context in which they occur.*

On the surface words seem so simple. They make up such a routine part of our lives that we seldom stop to think about their complexity. To appreciate fully what is involved in the "normal" meaning of words, we must first understand several characteristics of words: nature, range of meaning, semantic fields, change of meaning, and nuances of meaning.

---

61 See the bibliography—especially the sections "History of the Ancient World" and "Customs, Culture, Society"—for further help in locating useful sources. Other sections list dictionaries, encyclopedias, and commentaries. For those able to search the Bible electronically, searches of terms, people, places, or short phrases—e.g., "altar," "Moab," "Caiaphas," "shepherd's rod," etc.—often yield much useful information.

Crucial Issues about the Nature of Words
Words Are Arbitrary Signs

To study words we must understand their characteristics. First, words are usually *arbitrary signs*.[62] Simply stated, a word is a combination of sounds or letters that is meaningful in a language. A more precise definition is that a word is a semantic sign—a combination of symbols or sounds that represents an idea.[63] Spoken words are a combination of sounds that stand for a specific idea; written words combine letters representing those sounds to symbolize a concept. The idea designated by any given word can be communicated either orally or visually. But why a word means what it does is mostly a matter of convention. That's just the way it is!

How do words become signs indicating a specific idea? Suppose someone were to ask the question, "How is your 'kebof'?" Probably all English speakers would be puzzled. "What on earth is my 'kebof'?" they would ask. Why? Is there something wrong with the word "kebof?" It sounds like a perfectly good word. It combines consonants and vowels in proper syllables. It is easily pronounceable. It has all the attributes of a good word, except for one—it conveys no meaning, at least not in English! On the other hand, another five-letter word, "maple," immediately brings to mind a type of tree. While several English-speaking people may envision different shapes of trees, depending upon their experience with maples, if any, they all acknowledge that "maple" refers to a type of tree, or to the wood that comes from a maple tree.[64]

What makes "maple" different from "kebof"? Throughout the development of a language, users of that language arbitrarily assign meanings to the words they use. By common practice English speakers associate "maple" with a certain meaning. When English speakers hear the word "maple," their minds automatically identify one member of the kind of plants commonly known as trees. But since English speakers have not assigned a meaning to "kebof," it represents nothing and thus calls nothing to mind.

This illustrates the most foundational fact about words: each word comes to represent a given idea (or ideas) only by its repeated *use* within a common language group. Thus, if two people wish to communicate, they both must use words in a similar way. From the standpoint of hermeneutics, accurate interpretation requires that we understand a word in the same way the writer used it. To illustrate, American English makes

---

62 M. Silva puts it this way, "Little genuine progress can be made in language study unless we recognize that, as a rule, the association of a particular word with a particular meaning is *largely* a matter of convention" (*Biblical Words and their Meaning: An Introduction to Lexical Semantics*, rev. ed. [Grand Rapids: Zondervan, 1995], 103–4; emphasis his). We say that words are usually arbitrary signs because in some instances where words sound like sounds (a dog's bark, "woof, woof"), the association between word and meaning is not simply arbitrary.

63 The reader who wishes more detailed help into the intricacies of the modern study of words, especially in light of linguistic studies, should consult: P. Cotterell and M. Turner, *Linguistics and Biblical Interpretation* (Downers Grove: InterVarsity, 1989); Silva, *Biblical Words and Their Meaning*; J. P. Louw, *Semantics of New Testament Greek* (Philadelphia: Fortress, 1982); J. F. A. Sawyer, *Semantics in Biblical Research: New Methods of Defining Hebrew Words For Salvation* (London SCM, 1972); and E. A. Nida and J. P. Louw, *Lexical Semantics of the Greek New Testament* (Atlanta: Scholars, 1992).

64 For the sake of simplicity we will avoid other senses of "maple" such as someone's last name or a flavor of syrup or ice cream.

only a minor distinction between "pants" and "trousers." However, in British English these two words refer to two entirely different garments. Trousers indicate their American counterpart while pants denote "underpants."[65] To secure a "two-legged outer garment that extends from waist to ankle" in Aberdeen, Scotland, a wise American purchaser would ask the clerk for trousers, not pants. Understanding and using words the way other speakers of the language use them is critical for effective communication.

Needless to say, this complicates the task for Bible students. Since the original writers wrote in ancient languages that are foreign to us, we do not know intrinsically the meanings of the terms they used. We need translators to render the meaning of the biblical texts into English. Fortunately, scholars carefully study the biblical languages and do their best to convey the precise meaning of the biblical words in English. A hermeneutical point clearly emerges from this information. *Interpreters must deliberately pursue what the original words of a passage meant at the time they were written in the context in which they occur.* The correct meaning of the words, not what ideas may occur to us when we read the passage, is the objective for word studies. We must always remember that the biblical writer selected certain words to express specific thoughts. Our aim is to recover the ideas that the writer sought to communicate by means of those words.

Words Have a Range of Meanings

To complicate matters further, a word may have more than one meaning. In fact, most words have a *range of meanings.*[66] The very same word, spelled identically, may have several vastly different meanings.[67] Take for example the English word "hand." The "hand" that is a part of the human body is not at all like the "hand" on a clock, the "hand" held by a card player, a unit of measurement for horses, a worker as in "All 'hands' on deck," or the idea expressed by the request to "Give them a 'hand'!"[68] In each case the word remains the same, but the meaning changes. These different meanings constitute at least part of the range of meanings of the word "hand." Normally such multiple meanings of a word do not cause any confusion or misunderstanding. Aided by the context, native speakers usually pick the right meaning without any trouble. The ideas expressed in the larger message of the literary context usually clarify the intended meaning.

These facts also hold true for the ancient biblical languages. Both the Hebrew word *shālôm* and the Greek *eirēnē*, often translated "peace" in English, have several meanings. For the Hebrew *shālôm* the range includes "absence of strife" in the sense of prosperity, completeness, wholeness, harmony, and fulfillment. So it denotes a sense of well-being

---

65 British friends tell us this distinction is now breaking down due to the pervasive influence of television and American tourists.

66 We saw that the range of meaning of "pants" is broader in American English (able to denote trousers and underpants) than in British English (only denotes underpants). Consider English words like "run" or "ball" to get a feel for how wide a range some words can have. Some dictionaries have dozens of meanings for "run."

67 Recall our previous example of the word "trunk."

68 Interestingly, note how even this sentence is ambiguous. It could mean, "Give them applause," or "Help them." In addition, in using "hand," we introduce only instances where it functions as a noun. "Hand" also occurs as a verb ("*Hand* me a book.").

where relationships are unimpaired. In addition, it means the state of fulfillment that results from God's presence and righteousness; its source is God and comes as his gift. Finally, *shālôm* can mean the eschatological state of eternal peace.[69] The range of meaning for the Greek *eirēnē* includes an external absence of hostility, an internal tranquility, and the first Hebrew sense of well-being.[70] To understand what a biblical author means by "peace" in a specific text in a given Testament, one must determine which of these potential meanings best fits the context. A reader can neither pick a meaning arbitrarily, one he or she prefers, nor collect several. One has only to return to the word "hand" to see how silly it would be to assign the wrong meaning in a specific context. No less is true in our study of biblical words.

Several times during the "Upper Room Discourse" (Jn 13–17) Jesus promised "peace" to the apostles. Certainly Jesus did not mean "absence of hostility." He was not promising them trouble-free lives, for he ended this discourse with the statement, "I have told you these things, so that in me you have peace. *In this world you will have trouble.* But take heart! I have overcome the world" (Jn 16:33, emphasis added). In fact, though they would encounter considerable hostility, Jesus' command to "take heart" makes it clear that he was promising the apostles inward tranquility or an ultimate sense of their own well-being. So, the fact that many words have a range of meaning complicates language communication. To know the message intended by a speaker or writer, interpreters must discern which meaning makes the best sense in its context.

Word Meanings Overlap

The third factor to know about the nature of words is that *each meaning of a word exists as part of a distinct semantic field or domain.*[71] One meaning of "hand," we will call it "hand$_1$," resides in the domain of "parts of the human body." Another meaning, "hand$_2$," fits in the domain of "ways to show appreciation in a public setting" (along with "applause," "cheers," "clapping," and "ovation"). Put simply, a number of words in the same language include meanings similar to or closely related to other words. Often we call these words synonyms. Clearly, "hand$_2$" is closer in meaning to "ovation" than it is to "hand$_1$."

Two (or more) words are synonyms when, out of their total range of meanings at least one of the meanings of one word overlaps with one of the other. "Run" is synonymous with "unravel" in the sentence, "These stockings are guaranteed not to _____,"

---

69 See P. J. Nel, "שָׁלוֹם" *NIDOTTE*, 4:130–35; and G. von Rad, "*shālôm* in the OT," *TDNT*, 2:402–406.

70 While these three meaning categories are not all listed as such in any one of the major Greek lexicons, a comparison of W. Bauer, F. Danker, W. F. Arndt, and F. W. Gingrich, *A Greek-English Lexicon of the New Testament and Other Early Christian Literature*, 3d ed. (Chicago: Univ. of Chicago Press, 2000), 287–88, with J. P. Louw and E. A. Nida, *A Greek-English Lexicon of the New Testament Based on Semantic Domains*, 2 vols. (New York, et al.: United Bible Societies, 1988), 1:22.42, 25.248, suggests this range of meanings.

71 Silva, *Biblical Words,* has a brief treatment of the basic concepts (161–63). For more technical introductions see J. Lyons, *Semantics,* 2 vols. (Cambridge: Cambridge University Press, 1977), 1:250 ff.; and W. W. Klein, "A Semantic Analysis of Paul's Election Vocabulary" (Ph. D. dissertation, University of Aberdeen, 1977), 127–147. A language divides the total conceptual sphere at a given synchronous state into fields, as a kind of mosaic. Within each semantic field words have meaning in relationship to the other words in that field.

but not (usually) in "She is ready to _____ the race."[72] Note, only one meaning of "hand" overlaps with "ovation." They are synonyms in only a portion of their ranges of meaning. Consider these two sentences: "The audience gave her a hand," and "The audience gave her an ovation." Though the two words are synonymous in these uses, they do not convey exactly the same meaning.[73] "Hand$_2$" is probably less formal than "ovation." The comedian gets a rousing hand from the audience while the soprano merits a standing ovation. Most English speakers probably use "ovation" less frequently and usually only with "standing." They reserve it for specific occasions. By seeing which part of a semantic field a specific word occupies, one is able to define the meaning of each term used within that field more precisely. This helps the interpreter to recognize the specific nuances of a word that distinguish it from other terms.

In studying the Greek word for "peace" (*eirēnē*), Louw and Nida say that it belongs to two different semantic fields: first, domain 22 containing words used to express trouble, hardship, relief, or favorable circumstances;[74] and second, domain 25 listing terms for attitudes and emotions.[75] These two fields of meaning differ greatly. In the first category "peace" is one of six words in the subdomain indicating "favorable circumstances or state" (22:42–22:47), whereas the other uses of the word belong to the subdomain including "worry, anxiety, distress, peace" (25:223–25:250). The same word may refer to external circumstances free from hostility or to a psychological state of inward tranquility. Knowing this distinction enables the interpreter to watch for clues in the context to decide between the two.[76]

Word Meanings Change Over Time

Word meanings do not remain fixed: they change over time. New meanings develop through usage, and old ones become obsolete.[77] The KJV readily illustrates this phenomenon. Revered for numerous qualities, including its poetic beauty and its familiarity, the venerable translation frequently shows how English words no longer mean what they did when it emerged in 1611. In some places the wording merely causes confusion; in others, the present meaning differs drastically from that of the original Elizabethan English. Look at the KJV's uses of the word "conversation" (2 Cor 1:12; Gal 1:13; Eph 2:3; 4:22; Phil 1:27). These texts have little to do with what we think of when we use the word "conversation"; so modern versions replace "conversation" with "conduct" or "way of life" to convey the Greek texts' original intent, because the meaning of the English word has changed over time.

---

72 We say *usually* here, because one could always envision a setting when even an "odd" word could be made to fit. We are discussing normal usage.

73 We will take up this element of connotation later.

74 Louw and Nida, *A Greek-English Lexicon,* 1:242–248.

75 Louw and Nida, *A Greek-English Lexicon,* 1:288–320.

76 Interestingly, the student who only used the Bauer lexicon would not be aware of the use of *eirēnē* meaning freedom from worry and anxiety, because this meaning is not listed. The closest they come is the sense of "a state of well-being, peace" (BDAG, 287–88).

77 E. Weiner and J. Simpson, eds., *Oxford English Dictionary,* 2d ed., 20 vols. (Oxford: Oxford University Press, 1990), is the standard and monumental tool for tracing the changes of the meaning of English words over time.

Then again, consider the passage promising the rapture of saints to meet Christ at his second coming. The KJV renders 1 Thes 4:15, "We which are alive and remain unto the coming of the Lord shall not *prevent* them which are asleep" (emphasis added). In 1611 "prevent" more closely followed its Latin derivation and conveyed the idea "to go before." Today it means "to stop" or "to hinder." Because the meaning of the English word has changed, what served as a good translation in the seventeenth century no longer communicates Paul's original meaning. Hence, most modern versions substitute the word "precede" for the KJV's "prevent."

The same principle holds true for the biblical languages. Words changed their meanings over the centuries. The original meaning of a word or the meaning derived from a word's etymology or root may be of no more than historical interest to the interpreter.[78] Past meanings may be interesting and even colorful, but we must always resist the temptation to believe that past meanings exert some residual influence on current usage. One may not simply discover a meaning for a word that existed in classical Greek, for example, and assume that meaning could occur at the time of the NT.[79] Many would argue that Classical Greek made a distinction between two words for knowing: *oida* and *ginōskō*.[80] The first denoted an acquired knowledge of facts or people; it had a kind of certainty about it. The second referred to the procurement of knowledge, an experiential knowledge often with the sense of "come to know." However, in the Hellenistic period during which the NT came into existence, Greek speakers did not always comply with the classical distinctions. Indeed, in their lexicon, Moulton and Milligan confidently assert, "The distinction between *oida,* 'to know' absolutely, and *ginōskō,* 'come to know' cannot be pressed in Hellenistic Greek."[81] Burdick believes that Paul normally followed the classical distinctions, though not always. But, he wisely observes, "Each occurrence must be evaluated on its own merits."[82] Silva's analysis is considerably more linguistically nuanced.[83] He rightly concludes that Paul's uses of these verbs may be heavily influenced by stylistic as well as semantic factors.

---

78 An array of scholars has repeated this point. The earliest voice was probably J. Barr, *Semantics of Biblical Language* (Oxford: Oxford University Press, 1961), 107, 109.

79 This would be as inappropriate as for a modern male to call a woman a "hussy" with the defense that its original meaning was positive—a diminutive for "housewife." Today it conveys a lewd and derogatory message. Original meanings may have no significance for current usage. The same applies to biblical studies.

80 See H. Seesemann, "oida," *TDNT* 5: 116–19; and R. Bultmann, "γινω,σκω, ετ αλ." *TDNT* 1: 689–719, esp. 689–92. The former, *oida*, had more the sense of "to have experienced, learned to know." On the second, Bultmann stresses that in Greek usage the sense was the intelligent comprehension of an object or matter: "to experience, to perceive" (689). This sense of the act of comprehension may fade into the background so the sense is merely: "to know or understand." Both authors recognize that these distinctions were not hard and fast, and that often the words appear to occur synonymously.

81 J. H. Moulton and G. Milligan, *The Vocabulary of the Greek New Testament* (Grand Rapids: Eerdmans, 1930), 439. See the careful, sober analysis in D. W. Burdick, "*Oida* and *Ginōskō* in the Pauline Epistles," in *New Directions in New Testament Study,* ed. R. N. Longenecker and M. C. Tenney (Grand Rapids: Zondervan, 1974), 344–56.

82 Burdick, "*Oida*," 354.

83 Silva, *Biblical Words*, 164–69.

That is, not only were the distinctions of meaning from the classical period in the process of breaking down, but certain constructions sounded or worked better than others. For example, the phrase "standing ovation" works better in English than "standing hand." If we want to indicate that an audience demonstrated its approval by clapping while standing on its feet, we are virtually locked into using "ovation" rather than "hand," semantic considerations aside. In the same way Bible students must determine the range of meanings that was in common use at *the time a book was written.* Interpreters err in attempting to retain the distinctions of classical Greek as if the NT writers were obligated to observe them (or even knew them). They must scrupulously avoid the archaic meanings of an earlier phase of the language.

Conversely, they must avoid anachronism—reading in meanings of later periods after the NT. The fallacy of anachronism occurs even more blatantly when we read later meanings *in English* into an earlier use of a biblical word. A serious contemporary example of this abuse occurs when a preacher defines the first century Greek word for power, *dynamis,* using a commodity invented in the nineteenth century, namely dynamite, simply because the words look and sound similar and because the English word derived from the Greek![84]

Words Have Connotative and Denotative Meanings

A fifth characteristic of words is that they may convey significance in addition to their explicit denotative reference.[85] This may include a *connotative* or a figurative meaning. While the word "dog" *denotes* a four-legged, hairy animal, when used of a person in the statement, "You dog!" it usually communicates an emotive sense of disapproval. In this specific use, "dog" figuratively stands for a person, and it has a connotation it does not have in the use, "Harley is our family dog." When Paul warns the Christians at Philippi, "Watch out for those *dogs,* those men who do evil, those mutilators of the flesh" (Phil 3:2, emphasis added), the word carries a noticeable derogatory force. First-century Jews considered dogs despicable creatures (as do some cultures today). Thus they expressed their dislike of the Gentiles by calling them "dogs." Paul criticizes certain Jewish troublemakers by throwing back at them their own contemptuous use of the term "dog." This connotation is not necessarily present in other uses of "dog" in the NT. A good example occurs in Jesus' parable of the rich man and Lazarus in which "dog" has its more common and neutral meaning (Lk 16:21). Interpreters, therefore, must study words carefully to discern not only their denotative meaning but also any connotative subtlety that the original recipients would have sensed.

---

84 D. A. Carson, *Exegetical Fallacies,* 2d ed. (Grand Rapids: Baker, 1996), 33–34, cites this fallacy in addition to a number of others interpreters commit in their well-intentioned attempts to interpret Scripture. We highly commend Carson's little volume. Every interpreter needs to heed his cautions.

85 D. A. Black observes, "Linguists distinguish between *denotation,* or the meaning a word has for all who hear it, and *connotation,* or the special meaning the same word may have for a limited group of speakers" (*Linguistics for Students of New Testament Greek* [Grand Rapids: Baker, 1988], 131). To illustrate he contrasts the denotation of "children," persons between infancy and adulthood, and its connotation, which might range from awkward, immature, obstinate, to impulsive.

Steps for Performing Word Studies

Determining the meaning of any given biblical word is a multifaceted task. Because of the complex nature of words, we must examine several types of information to discover a word's contextually appropriate meaning. The steps outlined below are a useful guide to follow in this process.

1. Select Words that Require Detailed Analysis

We cannot understand a passage without knowing what the words in it mean. Now not all of the words in a passage will require intricate study, for the meanings of most terms will be clear when the student compares a good sample of modern translations. Those students who have facility in the biblical languages will have even more insight into the meanings of the words. However, some words do require more careful analysis.

How does the student choose words for further study? One category includes words the student does not understand in English. If the student does not have a church background, many words may fit this category. Even for the majority of readers, some words will be puzzling at first. So these words, like covenant, Jubilee, ephod, redeemer, justify, or yokefellow, need to be studied in more detail. And all interpreters must be careful not to neglect pivotal terms simply because they assume they know their meaning. Words that are crucial for a passage, that are theologically significant, or upon whose meaning the entire sense of a passage rests, warrant careful study. It is better to do a preliminary study of a term and then rule out more exhaustive study than to overlook a term whose meaning makes a crucial impact upon a passage. Study rare words—particularly those that occur only once[86]—especially if they might have a major impact on the meaning of a passage. Then, too, a word that a writer repeats in a passage is usually significant and worth further study, especially to clarify its function in the passage.[87] The student should take particular care to investigate terms that are figures of speech in order to understand the sense implied. If English translations diverge on the meaning of a word, the interpreter should investigate to discover the most accurate sense of the word.

2. Determine the Range of Meaning for the Word

The first part of this step involves research in *lexicons* to determine the range of meaning the word had at the time of the author.[88] Weighing these possible meanings of the word in light of the train of thought in the immediate context and the historical background enables the interpreter to make a preliminary selection of the best English translation. While many lexicons assist in making this choice by listing biblical references under the various meanings of a specific word, the interpreter should always weigh the contextual evidence for him or herself rather than simply accept this opinion.

---

86 Technically, we call a word that occurs only once in the Bible a *hapax legomenon*, from the Greek meaning "being said once."

87 The use of "head" in 1 Cor 11:2–16 is an example. It occurs with different meanings here.

88 In semantics this is called "synchronic analysis." Though words may have an interesting array of meanings over their history (thus "diachronic analysis"), interpreters must discover what words mean at the time in question.

Simply put, the interpreter seeks to get into the shoes of the original readers to sense how they would hear the words of the passage. This involves securing as much information as possible about the words and concepts of the time. Lexicons serve students well at this point, for they provide information about the possible meanings of words throughout the history of time the lexicon covers.

But where do lexicons get their information? Various kinds of lexicons research one or more fields of study and catalog their findings. Typically, they investigate various ancient literary sources—documents, published works, and letters, for example. Beyond that, some lexicons include nonliterary materials like epitaphs on tombs, receipts, or inscriptions on buildings, and other places. Often parallel or cognate languages are compared, as well as findings in those languages that parallel biblical languages. Of course, previous Scripture provides a prime source for discovering meanings of words, so lexicons may survey the Septuagint (LXX—the OT translated into Greek in the second century B.C.). This provides help, at times, since it shows how the Jews at that time rendered the Hebrew into Greek.[89] Lexicons do not neglect current Scripture. That is, they also seek to understand the meanings of words by evaluating the uses they discover either in the OT or the NT. Searching the lexicons is a fact-finding mission. What options exist for the crucial words in a passage? We only know the options by surveying actual uses.

At this juncture we must allow for two kinds of students: those who do not or cannot have facility in the biblical languages and those who do—at least to some degree. For the first group of interpreters several works provide access to the meanings of words: R. F. Youngblood, and F. F. Bruce, eds. *Nelson's New Illustrated Bible Dictionary: An Authoritative One-Volume Reference Work on the Bible, with Full-Color Illustrations;*[90] M. C. Tenney, ed., *Zondervan Pictorial Encyclopedia of the Bible,* 5 vols.;[91] P. J. Achtemeier, ed., *HarperCollins Bible Dictionary;*[92] G. W. Bromiley, ed., *International Standard Bible Encyclopedia Revised,* 4 vols.;[93] D. N. Freedman, ed., *The Anchor Bible Dictionary,* 6 vols.;[94] T. C. Butler, ed., *Holman Bible Dictionary;*[95] and D. N. Freedman, ed., *Eerdmans Dictionary of the Bible.*[96] These comprise a fine range of sources in which students who do not work in Hebrew and/or Greek (and those who do) can learn valuable insights into words in both Testaments.[97]

---

89 This does not mean, however, that if we seek to know what a Greek word meant, we can simply see what Hebrew word it translated in the LXX and then find the meaning of the Hebrew word. As we have seen, the specific Hebrew and Greek words could have more than one meaning. Which translated which? In addition, there never is a one-to-one overlap between languages; often the LXX paraphrases rather than translates, and frequently the LXX is motivated by theological or practical concerns in how it renders the OT.

90 Rev. and updated ed. (Nashville: Nelson, 1995).

91 (Grand Rapids: Zondervan, 1975).

92 Rev. ed. (San Francisco: Harper, 1996).

93 Rev. ed. (Grand Rapids: Eerdmans, 1979–86).

94 (New York: Doubleday, 1992).

95 (Nashville: Broadman, 1991).

96 Grand Rapids: Eerdmans, 2000).

97 See the bibliography for further discussion and information about these sources.

Students who know the biblical languages to some degree have the distinct advantage of access to further important resources. At the same time, even students with limited knowledge of Hebrew or Greek might want to make use of these more "advanced" resources from time to time. Particularly with the use of interlinear Bibles, computer programs, and other "helps," many fine insights are accessible to those willing to do some hunting. How would this work in practice? The following examples will illustrate the procedure and clarify the types of information we are seeking.

For OT studies L. Koehler and W. Baumgartner, *The Hebrew and Aramaic Lexicon of the Old Testament* [abbreviated *HALOT*] surveys the range of meanings for words in light of the most recent scholarship for those able to find the appropriate Hebrew word.[98] F. Brown, S. R. Driver, and C. A. Briggs, *A Hebrew and English Lexicon of the Old Testament* [BDB] also provides help for studying the range of meanings for words, though again one must be able to find the appropriate Hebrew term.[99] Though less up-to-date than *HALOT*, the entries in BDB tend to be a little more complete, many listing every occurrence of a word. Another source, more convenient to use, provides a compact discussion of key Hebrew words: R. L. Harris, et al., eds., *Theological Wordbook of the Old Testament,* 2 vols. [*TWOT*].[100] Even better is W. A. VanGemeren, *New International Dictionary of Old Testament Theology and Exegesis,* 5 vols. [*NIDOTTE*]. One advantage of *NIDOTTE* is its combination of articles about individual Hebrew words and various topical articles that include comments on the appropriate Hebrew words.[101]

As a beginning, these sources help students discover the basic range of meaning for a word through its history. This often includes a word's etymology, but students must recall that a word's history may offer little or no clues to its current meanings. For example, in Gen 9 or 15 the word "covenant" figures prominently. A quick check in Einspahr's *Index* shows that "covenant" is the translation of the Hebrew word *bᵉrîth* and that BDB discusses the word on p. 136.[102] Turning to BDB we find the basic meaning

---

98 (Leiden: Brill; Grand Rapids: Eerdmans, 1994–2000). When its projected eight volumes are completed, D. J. A. Clines, *Dictionary of Classical Hebrew* (Sheffield: Sheffield Academic Press/Continuum, 1993–), will offer the most definitive Hebrew lexicon to date.

99 (Peabody, MA: Hendrickson, repr. 1996). It codes words to *Strong's Exhaustive Concordance* (New York: Hunt Eaton; Cincinnati: Cranston Curts, 1894; and subsequently reprinted by Hendrickson, Zondervan, and most recently with revisions and significant improvements by Nelson as *The New Strong's Expanded Exhaustive Concordance of the Bible,* 2001), which lists the English words of the KJV. In addition, B. Einspahr compiled an *Index to Brown, Driver and Briggs Hebrew Lexicon* (Chicago: Moody, 1976), employing the New American Standard Bible (La Habra, CA: The Lockman Foundation, 1972, 1995) in its references. Using this *Index* one can locate where a Hebrew word occurs in the OT, discover its meaning, and locate the page and section in BDB where it is discussed. The older BDBs remain serviceable; they merely lack the correlation to Strong's.

100 (Chicago: Moody, 1980).

101 (Grand Rapids: Zondervan, 1997). Each article has a number, and those without Hebrew knowledge may access its contents in two ways: by finding the word's number under its English equivalent in E. W. Goodrick and J. R. Kohlenberger, *Exhaustive Concordance of the NIV* (Grand Rapids: Zondervan, 1990), or by converting a Strong's number to a *NIDOTTE* number through the conversion chart in Goodrick-Kohlenberger.

102 Cf. *HALOT,* no. 1454. Alternatively, one would discover *bᵉrîth* from reading a tool such as *The NIV Interlinear Hebrew-English Old Testament,* ed. J. R. Kohlenberger, III (Grand Rapids: Zondervan, 1987); or J. J. Owens, *Analytical Key to the Old Testament.,* 4 vols. (Grand Rapids: Baker, 1990–93).

for *bᵉrîth:* pact, compact, covenant. The lexicon subdivides this basic meaning into three categories: I. between men; II. between God and man; and III. phrases (as in covenant making, covenant keeping, and covenant violation). If we further scrutinize the first category, we find a variety of nuances of covenants between people: (1) treaty or alliance, as in Abram's alliance with the Amorites (Gen 14:13); (2) a constitution or ordinance between a monarch and subjects (2 Sam 5:3); (3) a pledge (2 Kgs 11:4); (4) alliance or friendship, as between David and Jonathan (1 Sam 18:3; 23:18); and (5) a marriage alliance (Prov 2:17; Mal 2:14). BDB delineates the other two categories with equal thoroughness.

It appears that *bᵉrîth* can have the sense of a bilateral arrangement in which two parties draw up a mutually agreeable pact or relationship. But it can also denote a more unilateral arrangement that God (or a victorious monarch) determines and imposes. For example, God unilaterally established a covenant with Abraham (Gen 17:3–10; Exod 6:4), though Israel was required to keep its terms to enjoy God's promised blessings.

Surveying *TWOT*[103] students will find definitions similar to those in BDB but also a more elaborate discussion of the various uses and extensive bibliographic helps for further insight or study. The author assesses the possible etymology of *bᵉrîth* along with possible connections to Akkadian words. He adds a crucial element to the discussion: uses of *bᵉrîth* need to be understood based on whether the two parties to the covenant are equals or whether one is superior to the other. So the covenant between Abram and the Amorites is between equals (Gen 14:13), but not so between Israel and the Gibeonites (Josh 9).

The discussion in *NIDOTTE* rounds out these findings.[104] McConville gives some attention to the relationship of *bᵉrîth* to Akkadian, and while the term occurs only in Hebrew, the ANE provides many examples of treaties and law codes that help fill out the background for the concept. This background identifies six elements of Hittite vassal-treaties that help us understand those in Deuteronomy: titulary (the parties to the covenant), historical prologue (their past relations), stipulations, document clause (requirements for preserving the document), god list (witnesses to the treaty), and blessings and curses (invoked for keeping or breaking the treaty). Thus for Israel we see that Israel's suzerain Yahweh has invoked a treaty that demands certain commitments from the people for it to be preserved. Importantly, McConville observes, "The historical prologue is relevant here, because it puts the treaty/covenant into the context of a continuous relationship."[105] He also spells out in more detail the kinds of covenants between God and his people in the OT, e.g., the Noachic covenant, the Abrahamic covenant, the Mosaic covenant, and the Davidic covenant. He includes a section surveying the concept of covenants in the prophets observing that, though they use it rarely, they often substitute different ideas to capture the essence of God's relationship with his people, as in marriage in Hosea or election in Amos. In the prophets we also encounter the question of whether the covenant ceased at the exile, though ultimately they deny that possibility but present a renewed vision of God's restoration and the

---

103 E. B. Smick, "ברה" *TWOT* 1:128–30.

104 J. G. McConville, "ברית" *NIDOTTE* 1: 747–55.

105 *NIDOTTE* 1: 747.

promise of the new covenant (see Jer 31:31–34). The article concludes with a short section on post-OT uses, as at Qumran, a short trajectory of the idea into the NT, and an extensive bibliography.[106]

At this point the student has a good grasp of the range of meaning of *bᵉrîth*. In places it may overlap with the meaning of the modern word "contract," into which two parties enter and agree to certain obligations and benefits. But it also may mean a "treaty" that a victorious king imposes on a vanquished foe. It refers, too, to a pact or arrangement that God decides upon in order to provide for and bless people. In this instance he requires their obedience and trust in response, or he may cancel the covenant. The distinctly biblical idea that emerges is one of a personal God who freely enters into a gracious relationship with his people. Even though his people fail, he will ultimately accomplish his purposes for them.

Students who know Greek will find two lexicons most valuable for studying NT words: *A Greek-English Lexicon of the New Testament and Other Early Christian Literature*, 3d ed., by W. Bauer, F. Danker, W. F. Arndt, and F. W. Gingrich, [abbreviated BDAG],[107] and *A Greek-English Lexicon of the New Testament Based on Semantic Domains*, 2 vols., by J. P. Louw and E. A. Nida.[108] While both provide excellent help in finding the range of meaning for Greek words, the Bauer lexicon provides the more extensive references for each entry, often including every NT occurrence of a word. Louw and Nida, on the other hand, provide essential definitions and insight about a word's field of meaning that is lacking in other lexicons.

The Greek word *kyrios* (lord) can serve as a comparative example of the two lexicons. In surveying the uses of this word during the Hellenistic period, BDAG divides the range of meaning into two main categories. The general designation includes: (1) owner: "one who is in charge by virtue of possession, owner"—master or lord; and (2) one who is in a position of authority, "Lord" or the title of respect, "sir." Religious usage indicated Lord used of God, of deified kings, Jesus, and other supernatural beings like angels.[109]

Louw and Nida conveniently list the range of meaning in the index volume (II) under the entry of *kyrios*: Lord, owner, ruler, and sir.[110] The domain reference numbers listed indicate that each meaning comes from a different domain. "Lord" belongs to the domain of words indicating supernatural beings and powers (12.9). The definition in Vol. 1 identifies this as a title for God or Christ, indicating "one who exercises supernatural authority over mankind."[111] The second meaning, "owner," occurs in the

---

106 More thorough still is the discussion in *TDOT*, 2:253–78, which supplies the fullest discussion in English. The main entries for this 25–page essay include: I. etymology; II. meaning; III. semantic range; IV. covenantal ceremony; V. covenant and law; et al. The bibliography is more extensive, yet heavily leaning to German scholarship.

107 (Chicago: Univ. of Chicago Press, 2000). See the more extensive comments about these excellent sources in the bibliography. We also provide additional help in utilizing the wealth of information they provide.

108 (New York, et al.: United Bible Societies, 1988).

109 BDAG, 576–9.

110 Louw and Nida, *A Greek-English Lexicon*, 2:149.

111 Louw and Nida, *A Greek-English Lexicon*, 1:139.

domain of words that express ownership or possession (57.12). Here the definition of *kyrios* is "one who owns and controls property, including especially servants and slaves, with important supplementary semantic components of high status and respect"; "owner," "master," and "lord" are good glosses.[112] *Kyrios,* meaning "ruler," occurs in the group of words used to indicate control or rule and in the subdomain focusing on ruling or governing other people (37.51). The proposed translations, "ruler," "master," "lord" communicate its meaning as "one who rules or exercises authority over others."[113] When *kyrios* means "sir" (87.53), it belongs to the domain of words indicating status and the subdomain of words expressing high status or rank. Thus, it was "a title of respect used in addressing or speaking of a man—sir, mister."[114] Looking these up in Vol. 1 discloses both the specific domain to which each of these meanings belongs, and a precise definition of each meaning.

Having this canvass of the lexicons, the student next attempts to identify the semantic domain to which a specific use of the word most likely belongs. In the case of a "covenant," does the occurrence of *bᵉrîth* fall into the domain of "imposed, unilateral arrangements" or "mutually negotiated treaties"—if we may describe them in such stark terms? How are we to understand the use in Job 31:1, "I made a *covenant* with my eyes not to look lustfully at a girl" (emphasis added)? Though the use is figurative, did not the speaker impose, by means of personal discipline, a restriction on his eyes?

Or what does the following text imply in speaking about the Servant of the Lord: "I will keep you and will make you to be a *covenant* for the people and a light for the Gentiles" (Isa 42:6, emphasis added)? Is this the "new covenant" that God promises to provide (see Jer 31:31–34; cf. Heb 8:8–12)? Is it an imposed arrangement or one mutually enacted? Might God cancel its benefits as he did with Israel and the first covenant? These may be difficult decisions but these questions demonstrate the issues the interpreter must investigate.

Using the NT example of *kyrios,* in Acts 9:5 Paul addresses the voice he hears with the question, "Who are you, *Lord?*" (emphasis added). Here the interpreter must decide whether this use is a title of respect (i.e., "sir" indicating high status), whether Paul (or the writer) intends a higher sense ("Lord," perhaps even with a supernatural connotation), or whether the writer has in mind a double entendre.

In addition to understanding a word's range of meaning, the interpreter needs to know how the specific meaning of the word in the passage relates to the other words in its field of meaning. By discovering the particular meaning of a word within its field of meaning, the interpreter learns the general sphere of ideas to which this meaning of the word belongs; the relationship that exists between this word and the other words used in this semantic field; and perhaps what distinguishes this word from the others in its semantic field.

One aspect of word studies brings the two Testaments together. Since Greek had replaced Hebrew as the spoken language of the Jewish community in Alexandria in the second century B.C., Jews there produced the Septuagint.[115] Subsequently, the Jews living in

---

112 Louw and Nida, *A Greek-English Lexicon,* 1:559.

113 Louw and Nida, *A Greek-English Lexicon,* 1:478.

114 Louw and Nida, *A Greek-English Lexicon,* 1:739.

115 The title Septuagint (from the Latin for seventy), thus abbreviated LXX, originates in the legend that seventy (or seventy-two) Jewish scholars produced the translation. For accounts see Philo, *Vita Mosis* 2. 5.-7.25–44; Josephus, *Ant.* 12.2.1–15; Justin, *Apology* 1.31; and Irenaeus, *Against Heresies* 3.21.2.

the Roman world used the LXX translation. In fact, it became the Bible of most of the early Christians during the writing of the NT. Because of their experience of the OT through this Greek translation, the NT writers used many Greek words with meanings not normally found in the everyday use of the same terms, much like Christians today might use terms like "fellowship" or "redemption" with meanings not normally understood by secular people.[116] Religious and theological ideas developed in the OT became attached to the words, adding new nuances to their meanings.

The Septuagint use of *kyrios* (lord) is one of many examples of this kind of influence on NT words. This word appears over 9000 times in the LXX with the majority—6,156 to be exact—translating the divine name "Yahweh."[117] The use of *kyrios* to translate the Hebrew term for Lord, *'adōnāi,* which the OT sometimes used as a title for God, was quite natural. However, the translation of God's sacred name "Yahweh" by this word reflects the Jewish aversion to uttering the divine name lest they be guilty of desecrating it. Given how consistently the LXX translated the Hebrew "Yahweh" as "Lord," many scholars affirm the high probability that references to Jesus as "Lord" in the NT carry strong connotations of deity.[118]

Another example of the insights gained from a study of the Septuagint influence can be seen in the NT use of the word "firstborn." When the title "firstborn" is used concerning Jesus, it may carry merely the literal meaning of the first child born to his mother as in Lk 2:7, "She gave birth to her firstborn, a son." But this literal sense does not *fit* the two theological uses of the word in the titles for Christ in Colossians, "the firstborn of all creation" (1:15 NRSV) and "the firstborn from the dead" (1:18 NRSV). While some have suggested that "firstborn of all creation" means that Jesus was the first

---

116 E. Ferguson gives other common examples when he writes, "The distinctive religious meaning of many New Testament words (e.g., *ekklēsia, baptisma, presbyteros, psallō, cheirotonia*) is to be found not from etymology or classical usage but from the adaptations already made by Greek-speaking Jews" (*Backgrounds of Early Christianity* [Grand Rapids: Eerdmans, 1987], 346–47). The Greek words he cites mean, respectively, church (assembly), baptism (immersion), elder, sing psalms, and lifting up of one's hand.

117 The KJV rendered this Hebrew word "Jehovah," another interesting story.

118 C. E. B. Cranfield says concerning Paul's use of *kyrios* at Rom 10:9, "Paul applies to Christ, without—apparently—the least sense of inappropriateness, the *kyrios* of LXX passages in which it is perfectly clear that the *kyrios* referred to is God Himself." He goes on, "We take it that, for Paul, the confession that Jesus is Lord meant the acknowledgment that Jesus shares the name and the nature, the holiness, the authority, power, majesty and eternity of the one and only true God" (*The Epistle to the Romans,* 2 vols. ICC [Edinburgh: T. & T. Clark, 1979], 2:529). Confirming this conclusion in commenting on the use of *kyrios* at Acts 2:36, F. F. Bruce notes, "To a Jew, there was only one name 'above every name'—the Ineffable Name of the God of Israel, represented in synagogue reading and in the LXX text by the Title 'Lord.' And that the apostles meant to give Jesus the title 'Lord' in this highest sense of all is indicated by the way in which they do not hesitate on occasion to apply to Him passages of OT scripture referring to Jehovah" (*The Book of Acts,* NICNT [Grand Rapids: Eerdmans, 1954], 74). Finally, speaking of Paul's use of "Lord" in 1 Cor 12:1–3, G. D. Fee observes, "The use of 'Lord' in such a context meant absolute allegiance to Jesus as one's deity and set believers apart from both Jews, for whom such a confession was blasphemy, and pagans, especially those in the cults, whose deities were called 'lords'" (*The First Epistle to the Corinthians,* NICNT [Grand Rapids: Eerdmans, 1987], 581–82).

created being and, therefore, is not God,[119] strong evidence from Septuagint usage suggests an entirely different meaning that fits the context more naturally. In their discussion of the word *prōtotokos* (firstborn) Louw and Nida argue,

> In Jewish society the rights and responsibilities of being a firstborn son resulted in considerable prestige and status. The firstborn son, for example, received twice as much in inheritance as any other offspring.[120]

This prestige associated with being the firstborn in the Jewish culture gave rise to a figurative meaning for firstborn indicating superiority or higher status. This meaning of the Greek "firstborn" belongs to the semantic domain indicating status and to the subcategory of words expressing high status or rank. Thus, Louw and Nida translate Col 1:15, "existing superior to all creation."[121] The NIV seeks to capture this connotation by the phrase "firstborn *over* all creation." This finding gains further support from the LXX use of "firstborn" as a messianic title in Psa 89:27, defined by Hebrew parallelism in precise superiority language,

> I will appoint him my firstborn,
> the most exalted of the kings of the earth.

Contextual information in Col 1 confirms that Paul used firstborn as a title to stress Jesus' superiority over all creation. The references to his kingdom and the purpose statement in verse 18, "so that in everything he might have the supremacy," corroborate that the superiority of Christ over creation is the meaning of firstborn in this passage. These contextual factors make it clear that the phrase "firstborn from among the dead" (Col 1:18), the second occurrence of firstborn in this passage, also communicates this idea of superiority. Clearly, the Septuagint usage of the word "firstborn" has influenced Paul's choice of this messianic title to show Christ's primacy over both creation and those who will experience resurrection from the dead.

Thus, the serious student of the NT must ask whether a given word's meaning reflects Septuagint influence that shifted its meaning beyond what was current among Greek speakers at the time. To discover any such influences, note the main meanings of the Hebrew words that the Greek word used to translate in the Septuagint. The final step always requires studying the specific NT context to test any potential Septuagint influence. The best help for evaluating Septuagintal usage and potential influence on the NT comes primarily from two sources: C. Brown, ed., *New International Dictionary*

---

119 This is a standard explanation propounded today by the Jehovah's Witnesses, for example. They say, "Being God's first creation, he was with the Father in heaven from the beginning of all creation. Jehovah God used him in the creating of all other things that have been created" (*From Paradise Lost to Paradise Regained* [Brooklyn: Watchtower Bible & Tract Society, 1958], 126–27). "The Bible shows that there is only one God . . . 'greater than His son,' . . . And that the Son, as the First-born, Only-begotten and 'the creation by God,' had a beginning" (164). Among many refutations of their use of "firstborn," see B. M. Metzger, "The Jehovah's Witnesses and Jesus Christ: a Biblical and Theological Appraisal," *Theology Today* 10 (1953): 65–85. Reprinted in pamphlet form (Lancaster, PA: Lancaster Press, 1953), Metzger's article evaluates the Witnesses' doctrine of Christ and their *New World Translation*.

120 Louw and Nida, *A Greek-English Lexicon*, 1: 117.

121 Louw and Nida, *A Greek-English Lexicon*, 1: 117, 738.

of New Testament Theology, 4 volumes [*NIDNTT*],[122] and G. Kittel and G. Friedrich, *Theological Dictionary of the New Testament,* 10 volumes [*TDNT*].[123]

The final area that we need to explore to determine the potential meaning of a word is its *nonbiblical* use in the everyday speech, literature, and inscriptions at the time the biblical book was written. Knowing the popular meaning of a word in the daily life of the people often gives insight into the frame of reference by which both writer and recipients understood the term.

For such insights into the language of the OT one should consult R. L. Harris, et al., eds., *TWOT,* and G. J. Botterweck and H. Ringgren, eds., *Theological Dictionary of the Old Testament* [*TDOT*].[124] Returning to our discussion of *bᵉrîth,* both *TWOT* and *TDOT* mention that the appearance of G. Mendenhall's article, "Covenant Forms in Israelite Tradition," led to a rash of further studies on treaties in the ancient Near East.[125] These show the close relationship between the treaties of fourteenth and thirteenth century B.C. Hittite kings with their vassal rulers and the covenants enacted by Joshua during the conquest and settlement of Israel (and especially Josh 24:1 ff.). These findings, reported in *TWOT* 1:129 and *TDOT* 2:266–69, shed great light on the biblical records and may help us understand both the religious and political ramifications of the covenantal idea in the OT. The elements of the Hittite treaties also seem to be reflected in the organization of Exod 19–24 and perhaps the book of Deuteronomy.[126]

While students can find specific examples of everyday use of Hellenistic Greek for NT studies in J. H. Moulton and G. Milligan, *The Vocabulary of the Greek New Testament,*[127] the work is dated and sketchy, and now its most valuable insights are incorporated into *NIDNTT* and *TDNT*.[128] As an example, from *NIDNTT* one learns that the Greek word for "lord" (*kyrios*) was not a title Greeks used for their gods in the early classical period of their language. The servile relation of the slave to his or her master [*doulos* (slave) to *kyrios* (master)] was so repulsive to the early Greeks that they did not consider "lord" a suitable divine title. However, by NT times the oriental practice of calling both gods and kings

---

122 (Grand Rapids: Zondervan, 1975–78).

123 (Grand Rapids: Eerdmans, 1964–78). A one-volume abridgment, sometimes called "little Kittel" makes the essentials available in a more compact form: G. Kittel and G. Friedrich, *Theological Dictionary of the New Testament* (Grand Rapids: Eerdmans, 1986). Again, see the bibliography for further insight on these and other tools.

124 Twelve volumes (Grand Rapids: Eerdmans, 1974–2002).

125 *Biblical Archaeologist* 17 (1954): 50–76.

126 Beyond that, Weinfeld notes, "Deuteronomy abounds with terms originating in the diplomatic vocabulary of the ancient Near East. Such expressions as 'hearken to the voice of,' 'be perfect with,' 'go after,' 'serve,' 'fear' (revere), 'put the words on one's heart,' 'not turn to the right hand or to the left,' etc., are found in the diplomatic letters and state treaties of the second and first millenniums B.C., are especially prominent in the vassal treaties of Esarhaddon, which are contemporaneous with Deuteronomy" (*TDOT,* 2:268f.). Smick adds insight about the complexity of the background to covenant in the OT citing influences from religious practices, family structures, and the marriage relationship *(TWOT* 1:129). See J. G. McConville, *Deuteronomy: Apollos Old Testament Commentary* (Downers Grove: InterVarsity, 2002), and P. C. Craigie, *The Book of Deuteronomy,* NICOT (Grand Rapids: Eerdmans, 1972).

127 (Grand Rapids: Eerdmans, 1930).

128 Also, consult H. Balz and G. Schneider, eds., *Exegetical Dictionary of the New Testament* [*EDNT*], 3 vols. (Grand Rapids: Eerdmans, 1990–92).

"Lord" (because kings were viewed as representatives of the gods) began to penetrate the Mediterranean world. While early emperors like Augustus (31 B.C.—A.D. 14) and Tiberius (A.D. 14–37) discouraged the practice of attributing deity to them by the title "Lord," their successors Caligula (A.D. 37–41) and Nero (A.D. 54–68) promoted it and encouraged the imperial title "Lord and God." With Domitian (A.D. 81–96), claiming divine imperial status by the title, "Lord and God" reached a climax.[129] At the same time, the prevailing first-century Christians' attitude of submission expressed by calling themselves "slaves" of the "Lord" Jesus Christ conflicted with the traditional Greek religious mindset and put these believers on a direct collision course with the growing trend toward emperor worship.

An intriguing development for NT studies appears in the use of the Greek word for *covenant (diathēkē)*. In Rom 11:27 Paul uses covenant of God's unilateral commitment to establish a relation with people (cf. Acts 3:25; Heb 8:10). *Diathēkē* also means the agreement or pact between people that carries benefits and obligations (Gal 3:15). However, the range of the Greek *diathēkē* went beyond the Hebrew *bᵉrîth* and included the sense of "to make a will or testament."[130] The writer of Hebrews employs *diathēkē* in this sense of "will" in 9:16–17, creating a fascinating play on the same word used to mean "covenant" in the immediate context of 9:15 and 18.

In addition to lexicons the student should consult *concordances*. These alter the focus from word meanings and definitions in a range of sources to actual usage in the Bible, and from the range of possibilities to specific biblical contexts.[131] This may seem to duplicate the work of the lexicographers, but a brief review in a concordance will provide the student with an important firsthand sense of the range of meaning and uses. Having said this, students may decide to consult concordances even prior to their investigations of the dictionaries and lexicons. Such a search will provide an inductive appreciation of the apparent alternatives. Since we can determine the intended meaning only from assessing the related ideas within the text, we need to check an author's use of a given word in other places in the same writing and in other works. We can obtain further insight by reviewing how other authors use a word in the Bible. One author may use a word in a distinctive way that sets his use apart from that of other authors. For OT words, we should especially observe whether a word's usage seems concentrated in certain books with unique content (e.g., Leviticus, Lamentations), in books of prose or poetry (e.g., Judges or Song of Songs, respectively), or in books associated with the priestly, prophetic, or wisdom traditions. Sometimes a distinct pattern of usage is discernible that gives the interpreter evidence that clarifies the meaning in the passage under consideration. At other times one discovers wide variety in its usage by an author or OT tradition. But even this has value because it helps to inform the interpreter concerning the types of contexts in which certain meanings of the word occur.

Interpreters must remember that the concept of contextual circles of meaning applies here, too. That is, word-uses closer to the passage under study have greater

---

129 H. Bietenhard, "Lord, master," *NIDNTT*, 2:510–11.

130 This appears to be its primary sense in classical Greek. See H. G. Liddell and R. Scott, *A Greek-English Lexicon*, 9th ed (Oxford: Clarendon, 1940; supplement 1996), 394–95.

131 Students able to search biblical words electronically in essence can assemble concordance information in a few seconds. We will forbear here to illustrate with our examples *bᵉrîth* and *kyrios*. See the bibliography for helps in selecting appropriate concordances.

weight than word-uses at the periphery. So how the author uses words in the same book has more relevance than how that author uses the same words in other books. From there we would consider how other authors in the same Testament use the words, then how another author uses these words elsewhere in the Bible, and finally how nonbiblical writers use the words.

3. Select the Meaning that Best Fits the Context

Once students have a good feel for the possible meanings of a word, they must select the one that fits best in the passage under study. They must exercise care to avoid simply (and illegitimately) imposing one of the possible senses onto a specific use. This temptation is especially great where one meaning fits the interpreter's theology or preferred position. Though novices must be wary of over-confidence, within reason students may probe the lexicons, and be willing even to call into question the category of meaning in which the experts have located a specific text. Though students are wise to trust the best resources, at least this tactic will assure that interpreters have wrestled with the issues. Because of the complexity of word meanings, the interpreter should seek to discover all the information about a word that may help in determining its meaning in a specific passage. The best alternative makes best sense in the context.

Once the student knows the potential meanings of the word, *contextual factors* become the supreme arbitrator for selecting the most probable meaning. Often the general subject of the passage will strongly favor one semantic domain of the word. This marks the key principle: *The use of a word in a specific context constitutes the single most crucial criterion for the meaning of a word.* Thus the interpreter must scrupulously evaluate the total context to decide which of the possible meanings fits best in the passage under study. The elements we have discussed up to this point become crucial determiners. Which meaning fits best given the historical-cultural background of the passage? Which best fits the literary context? Which fits the argument of the narrative or the poetic structure (e.g., its parallel words), et al., in the most appropriate manner? Remember, though words have a range of possible meanings through their history, individual speakers or writers decide how they will use words in specific contexts. Writers may modify meanings or employ words in unique ways. In fact, writers may deliberately use words ambiguously or with double meanings, as occurs with the Greek word *anōthen* ("again" and/or "from above") in Jn 3:3, 7. Did Jesus mean that people needed to be born again, born from above, or both? To repeat, *context is the single most significant determiner of the meaning of a word or phrase.*

GRAMMATICAL-STRUCTURAL RELATIONSHIPS

As important as it is to know the meanings of words, our task is not yet complete. Indeed, as we just asserted, apart from larger contexts we cannot be completely certain about what words mean. People communicate by combining words together in larger units. The grammatical and structural relationships of words and word-groups make up the final component of language communication we must assess to understand a writer's meaning. How are words combined so that people can communicate? Before we proceed to explain in subsequent chapters how the various genres of literature function, we must explore the topics of grammar and structure, at least in a general way.

Technically speaking, grammar consists of two elements: morphology and syntax.[132] *Morphology* concerns the forms of individual words—typically how words are inflected (manipulated) to indicate their function in a language. To take only one simple example, in English we may put an -s on the end of some nouns to indicate "more than one." The -s is a morpheme designating "plural" in English. So, we say, "She ate one apple, but I ate two apple*s*."[133] Functioning like the English -s, Hebrew employs *îm, ê,* or *ôt* at the end of its words to make plurals. Greek is more complex yet, with different plural morphemes (these formal indicators) often associated with each case (nominative, genitive, etc.). On another level, we put -ed at the end of some verbs to mark past time: "Today I will pick a red apple, though I pick*ed* a green one yesterday."

In addition to morphology, *syntax* describes the system each language has for combining its various constituents in order to communicate. Word order is a crucial element of syntax for the English language. "John hit the ball" means something quite different from "The ball hit John." Because the words "John" and "ball" are not marked in any other way, English indicates their functions in this example by word order.[134] Word order is less fixed for languages like Hebrew and Greek. Some conventions apply, but the languages exhibit more variety than English permits. For some languages like Greek, case markings (back to morphology—the forms of words) on nouns, pronouns, adjectives, etc., indicate functions to show whether a word serves as the agent or the recipient of an action. Students who have studied German (to cite another highly inflected language) know the importance of word endings to indicate whether a noun functions as subject, object, or indirect object. Thus, syntax expresses the way a language arranges words to form a meaningful phrase, sentence, or larger unit.

Most guides to exegesis and analysis tend to work on the level of the sentence, and that remains an essential task for all interpreters. More recently, however, linguists have stressed the need for analysis of larger units—paragraphs and entire discourses. Communication rarely occurs simply in isolated sentences. Often called discourse

---

132 Two fine introductions to a modern understanding of language, especially in its application to biblical studies, are Cotterell and Turner, *Linguistics*; and S. E. Porter and D. A. Carson, eds., *Linguistics and the New Testament: Critical Junctures*, JSNTSup 168 (Sheffield, UK: Sheffield Academic Press, 1999). A seminal article on the topic is E. A. Nida, "Implications of Contemporary Linguistics for Biblical Scholarship," *JBL* 91 (1972): 73–89. For more general introductions to grammar as understood by modern linguists, see J. Lyons, *Introduction to Theoretical Linguistics* (Cambridge: Cambridge University Press, 1977); and id., *Language and Linguistics* (Cambridge: Cambridge University Press, 1981). Perhaps this is the place to remind readers that grammar only *describes* how languages function. That is, the modern study of grammar is descriptive, not prescriptive.

133 Rules for English are so difficult since it has shamelessly assimilated words from so many other languages. While we put an -s on apple to indicate plural, it takes -es for box, -en for ox, -ies and the removal of y for sky, -i after removing -us for cactus, -a in place of -um for stadium, a change of the final -i to -e for crisis, the replacement of -f by -ves for hoof, but not a thing for sheep or deer.

134 Of course, in poetry some of these "rules" for word order may change, showing they are not really rules at all—only conventions. Thus, when one enters a different genre one expects new criteria for combining elements. We discuss poetry in the next chapter.

analysis or text linguistics, this program is bearing good fruit.[135] In one sense language consists of combining various elements, as building blocks, to construct meaningful communication. In simple terms, combining morphemes (minimal elements of meaning, like the plural marker -s in English) produces words; putting words together produces phrases, clauses, and sentences; and combining sentences results in paragraphs, passages, or discourses.

This process of putting words together to communicate successfully involves many factors. The relationship that exists between the multiple words that make up a sentence and the sentences that constitute an entire passage may be indicated by word order, the forms of words, and the use of connecting words (conjunctions, prepositions, etc.). This underscores the absolute necessity of interpreting every biblical passage consistent with its grammar. Since grammar is a basic component in how writers organize words to express their thoughts and how audiences decipher the meaning from the words, grammatical analysis is an essential aspect of correct interpretation.

The Importance of Grammatical Relationships

To understand the meaning of any statement one must understand how words, phrases, sentences, and larger units interact (or are interrelated). Each word's contribution to the thought expressed stems from its relationship with the rest of the words in the sentence. Returning to our simple statement above, a minor rearrangement of the words, "John hit the ball," to "The ball hit John," changes the meaning drastically. Both sentences use the identical words, but they communicate different meanings depending upon whether "John" or "ball" functions as the subject or object.[136] If these two short sentences involved a fastball thrown by a major league baseball pitcher, the consequences for the batter would differ radically! In other words—grammar matters.

Grammatical study is strategic for correct interpretation because the biblical languages sometimes convey nuances that are hard to capture in an English translation. The First Epistle of John begins with an explicit assertion of the reality of Christ's physical body. Attempting to counteract a docetic Gnostic teaching that claimed Jesus only appeared to have a physical body, the author affirms that his message about Jesus is based upon that "which we *have heard*, which we *have seen* with our eyes" (1:1, emphasis added). Both verbs occur in the Greek perfect tense, which expresses a resulting state of affairs that is ongoing. Blass, DeBrunner, and Funk [BDF] call it "the continuance

---

135 See S. E. Porter and J. T. Reed, eds., *Discourse Analysis and the New Testament*, JSNTSup 170 (Sheffield, UK: Sheffield Academic Press, 1999); D. A. Carson and S. E. Porter, ed., *Discourse Analysis and Other Topics in Biblical Greek*, JSNTSup 113 (Sheffield: Academic Press, 1995); R. D. Bergen, ed., *Biblical Hebrew and Discourse Linguistics* (Dallas: Summer Institute of Linguistics; Winona Lake, IN: Eisenbrauns, 1994); E. A. Nida, et al., *Style and Discourse* (Capetown: Bible Society, 1983); A. B. de Toit, "The Significance of Discourse Analysis for New Testament Interpretation and Translation," *Neotestamentica* 8 (1974): 54–79; and E. Talstra, "Text Grammar and Hebrew Bible. I. Elements of a Theory," *Bibliotheca Orientalis* 35 (1978): 169–74. Outside of strictly biblical usage see J. P. Gee, *An Introduction to Discourse Analysis: Theory and Method* (London and New York: Routledge, 1999).

136 Obviously, other combinations prove unacceptable in English. "Hit John ball the" conveys no message despite clear meanings for the individual words. With some flexibility English grammar prescribes acceptable word order—in essence substituting word order for the case endings typical of other languages.

of completed action."[137] By using the perfect tenses, the author relates that his experience of Jesus was vivid and personal. What he had heard and seen produced a new state of affairs in which he now lives. This is no mere historical reporting of past events.

In similar fashion the command in 1 Jn 4:1, "Dear friends, *do not believe* every spirit, but test the spirits to see whether they are from God" (emphasis added), uses a present imperative of prohibition, a grammatical construction often employed to forbid the continuation of something already happening.[138] In this context, "Stop believing every spirit" might well express the grammar more precisely. The grammatical construction used here may suggest that the Christians gullibly accepted some allegedly spirit-induced utterances.[139] The negative command in 1 Jn 3:13, "*Do not be surprised,* my brothers and sisters, if the world hates you" (TNIV) might well carry the same force, suggesting that confusion troubled some believers and needed to stop. Taking up another matter, the "if" clause does not mean, "maybe the world hates you and maybe it doesn't." In using this type of conditional Greek clause, the writer does not question that the believers were experiencing hatred; for the sake of his argument, he assumes the existence of that hatred.[140] On the other hand, an "if" whose premise is uncertain (as in "If it rains, we will get wet") occurs in Mt 5:13. Jesus tells his followers, "You are the salt of the earth. But *if* the salt loses its saltiness, how can it be made salty again?" (emphasis added). Jesus does not assume "salt" (the disciples) will lose its saltiness or

---

137 F. Blass and A. DeBrunner, *A Greek Grammar of the New Testament and Other Early Christian Literature,* trans. and rev. R. W. Funk (Chicago and London: University of Chicago Press, 1961), 175. On the "perfective/stative" aspect, which describes the significance of the perfect tense, S. E. Porter says, "the action is conceived of by the language user as reflecting a given (often complex) state of affairs" (*Idioms of the Greek New Testament* [Sheffield, UK: Sheffield Academic Press, 1992], 21–22).

138 BDF § 336 (3), 172. Cf. H. E. Dana and J. R. Mantey, *A Manual Grammar of the Greek New Testament* (Toronto: Macmillan, 1927, 1955), 301–2; and N. Turner, *Syntax,* vol. 3 of *A Grammar of New Testament Greek,* by J. H. Moulton, 4 vols. (Edinburgh: T. & T. Clark, 1963), 74–76. On the other hand we must be alert to the fact that this grammatical construction does not always forbid an action in progress; it may do so in less than half of its occurrences in the NT as J. L Boyer, "A Classification of Imperatives: A Statistical Study," *GTJ* 8 (1987): 40–45, has shown. He found that in only 74 of the 174 instances of the negated present imperative in the NT did the writer call for the termination of ongoing activity. Porter, *Idioms,* 224–26; D. B. Wallace, *Greek Grammar Beyond the Basics* (Grand Rapids: Zondervan, 1996), 724–25; and many other grammarians affirm this conclusion.

139 At the same time, grammatical analysis must always take care not to "overexegete" such fine points. It would be inappropriate apart from further contextual evidence to posit too confidently its existence or how pervasive was the problem to be stopped. Clearly, the prohibition seeks to prevent and, if necessary, stop false beliefs. Again, the grammar allows for or opens up the potential for this nuance. Context determines its presence or absence.

140 At the risk of oversimplification, we note here that some older grammarians of Greek mistook the meaning of the "first class condition." That is, this Greek usage does not necessarily mean that the premise (if-clause) is actually true. It merely indicates that the writer/speaker assumes its truth for the sake of the argument. It may or may not be factually true; the context rules again. In his research Boyer discovered that the "if" in such first class conditions could be accurately translated "since" (indicating its obvious truthfulness) in only 37 percent of its NT uses. Another 12 percent are false premises, while the remaining 51 percent are indeterminate. See J. L. Boyer, "First Class Conditions: What Do They Mean?" *GTJ* 2 (1981): 75–114; cf. Porter, *Idioms,* 255–59; and Wallace, *Greek Grammar,* 690–94.

that it will not. This remains an open issue. These differences in the significance of the conditional conjunction "if" go back to different Greek conjunctions or adverbs (*ei*, *ean*), but will not be readily apparent in translations.

If we consider Hebrew, we encounter a language whose verbs function quite differently from English: in certain contexts imperfect (incomplete action) and perfect (completed action) may indicate past, present, or future actions. Hebrew does not use a negative particle with the imperative as we just saw in Greek; however, it does employ features that appear similar to those we find in Greek or English—nouns, adjectives, participles, prepositions, and infinitives, to name a few. One feature of Hebrew employs an infinitive before a finite verb. For example, "hear (infinitive) and hear (finite verb)" and "see and see" literally render the words in Isa 6:9, as in the RSV: "Hear and hear, but do not understand; see and see, but do not perceive." However, this feature of Hebrew grammar is a way to indicate "surely, indeed, certainly." Thus, "hear and hear" may be a direct translation,[141] but it obscures the meaning. Better is the NIV: "Be ever hearing . . . be ever seeing" or "Keep listening . . . keep looking" (NRSV).

As with Greek, Hebrew also has the capacity to use different kinds of conditions whose nuances students must study carefully. Conditions may be assumed fulfilled, contrary to fact, or more or less probable.[142] Another common Hebrew grammatical feature, the "construct state," consists of one word—noun or adjective—occurring with another noun, adjective, pronoun, or clause. The result appears as "X of Y." The relation between the two is a matter of the interpreter's understanding of the context since the construction may indicate various ideas. The English reader may not always realize that the translator made the decision how to render the construct. For example, the phrase "wisdom of Solomon" (1 Kgs 4:30) stands for the wisdom that Solomon displays.[143] On the other hand, "mourning of an only son" (Amos 8:10) in context clearly means *not* the mourning that the son does, but that others mourn *for* an only son.[144] Or the construct state may be descriptive: "scales of righteousness" (Lev 19:36) must mean "honest scales" as the NIV translates.[145] Psa 23:2 literally reads, "He makes me lie down in pastures of grass." "Grass" or "grassiness" somehow characterizes the pastures. Most English versions translate this as "green pastures." At other times the relationship is one of apposition—where the second term in effect renames or defines the first—as in "the land of Canaan" (Num 34:2) or "daughter of Zion" (Isa 1:8).

These limited examples illustrate that English versions do not always clarify certain nuances in the biblical languages or how much translations result from interpretive decisions by translators. They illustrate, as well, that when translations differ, an English reader may be at a loss to understand why. One may be more direct in the sense of closely paralleling the original's words, but another may better capture an original

---

141 We use the word "direct" instead of the more common but tricky term "literal" since linguists and translators prefer it and it avoids confusion. A truly literal translation of one language into another would be largely unreadable. The more direct translations seek to remain closer to the structure and wording of the source. Recall our prior discussion in chapter 4.

142 For a more complete discussion see B. K. Waltke and M. O'Connor, *An Introduction to Biblical Hebrew Syntax* (Winona Lake, IN: Eisenbrauns, 1990), 636–38.

143 This is analogous to the Greek subjective genitive.

144 This parallels the Greek objective genitive.

145 This parallels the Greek descriptive genitive.

nuance. Moreover, as we saw, "direct" may or may not be more accurate. A better goal may be equivalent effect or, in terms we used before, a faithful replica of the speech act. Therefore, reliable biblical interpretation requires careful evaluation of the grammatical nuances of the biblical languages. It follows also that accurate interpretation must be based on the original language texts of the Hebrew and Aramaic OT and the Greek NT. Ideally, every interpreter should know these biblical languages. Many grammatical features are apparent only in the original languages. Even the best of translations do not and probably should not bring them out. Where good modern translations do express clearly some grammatical nuances, they involve a greater or lesser degree of interpretation, for scholars do not always agree on the significance of certain grammatical constructions in a given passage. Knowing the biblical languages equips the interpreter to weigh the contextual evidence to identify the grammatical explanation that fits the text best. People who do not know Hebrew or Greek must always remember that they work at a disadvantage. Every reader who aspires to become a biblical scholar must become competent in the biblical languages.

However, we are realistic enough to admit that it is impractical to expect all interpreters to know the biblical languages. Stage of life, the pressures and responsibilities of living, language aptitude, access to a program of instruction—all these and more make this ideal impossible for many Bible students. Yet we sincerely believe that *all believers are competent to study the Bible.* They must compensate for their limitation of not knowing the biblical languages by having a good grasp of English grammar, by using the best direct English translations of the Bible, and by using reliable commentaries and other resources written by scholars who can explain the grammar. On the last point, by comparing several sources on a specific passage, one can determine whether an alleged grammatical analysis has general consensus. Further, the contextual evidence cited in support of a suggested grammatical point will enable the reader to understand the issues involved better.[146]

Accurately understanding a passage requires analyzing its structure and the significance of important grammatical constructions. While some grammatical insights cannot be discovered apart from the original language texts, the willing student can uncover a surprising amount of important grammatical information by carefully analyzing the English text. This is especially true of the structure. Analyzing the structure for meaningful grammatical insights requires an English translation that carefully preserves the original language sentence pattern. Many find the New American Standard Bible (NASB),[147] the Revised Standard Version (RSV), the New Revised Standard Version (NRSV),[148] or the English Standard Version (ESV), most valuable for this type of study. While many modern translations break up longer, complex sentences in the original

---

146 Again we draw our readers' attention to Carson, *Exegetical Fallacies*, which contains a short but helpful section on "Grammatical Fallacies" (65–86). Though focusing on the Greek NT, Carson raises numerous cautions that could well apply to the OT. For example, all interpreters should heed his warning about reading more into tenses than is there.

147 NASB updated ed. (La Habra, CA: The Lockman Foundation, 1995).

148 NRSV, copyright 1989, Division of Christian Education of the National Council of the Churches of Christ in the USA. This is the revision of the previous RSV, 1946–52, whose language was more in the KJV tradition. The NRSV, however, does seek to use the modern idiom and to be more inclusive in its use of language.

languages into several brief sentences in English, the nasb and RSV often keep the long involved sentences with their many subordinate clauses.

Obviously, the modern trend to shorter sentences contributes to smoother reading and higher comprehension. We highly recommend the versions that seek better ways to communicate the Bible's message. For example, a dynamic equivalent translation seeks to convey in English what a biblical writer would have said were he speaking English in *his own time*. The *Good News Bible* is a prime example of this tactic.[149] Another highly recommended version of this type is the *New Living Translation* (NLT). For the NT, J. B. Phillips takes another approach.[150] He seeks to say in modern (British) English what the biblical writer would say were he writing *today*. So looking at Lk 13:11, where the GNB has "a woman who had an evil spirit" (how a modern English-speaker would have phrased this idea in Jesus' time), Phillips has "a woman who had been ill from some psychological cause" (how Phillips imagines the author would express the idea were he alive today). E. Peterson's *The Message*[151] takes an even more paraphrastic approach than Phillips. Whereas the NIV renders Lk 13:19, "It is like a mustard seed, which a man took and planted in his garden. It grew and became a tree, and the birds of the air perched in its branches," *The Message* has, "It's like a pine nut that a man plants in his front yard. It grows into a huge pine tree with thick branches and eagles build nests in it." Both seek to recast the literal words and structures of the Hebrew and Greek languages into modern idioms and ways of expression, though their translation theory governs how they do it.[152]

However, the gain in readability in some modern translations comes with price tags: some original meaning, not to mention nuances, is lost (an evil spirit differs from a psychological malady, and a mustard seed is not a pine nut), and one may fail to appreciate the text's original structural relationships. Most often and for most people, paraphrases are worth the price. But for serious study, more direct versions have their evident value. Studying biblical passages in the original languages forces the interpreter to interact with the text's own meanings and its sentence structures to determine how subordinate clauses and phrases relate to the main statement of the sentence and/or to each other. For this dimension of study, the more direct the English translation, the better. Different kinds of translations have their place in other phases of one's study.[153]

---

149 2d ed. (New York: American Bible Society, 2001); also called *Today's English Version*. The American Bible Society also publishes the *Contemporary English Version* (1995), also not a paraphrase but a translation of the original manuscripts.

150 *The New Testament in Modern English* (London: Bles, 1960).

151 E. H. Peterson, *The Message: The Bible in Contemporary Language* (Colorado Springs: NavPress, 2002), 1886.

152 For superb introductions to these issues consult J. Beekman and J. Callow, *Translating the Word of God* (Grand Rapids: Zondervan, 1974); E. A. Nida and C. R. Taber, *The Theory and Practice of Translation* (Leiden: E. J. Brill, 1974); and J. de Waard and E. A. Nida, *From One Language to Another: Functional Equivalence in Bible Translating* (Nashville: Thomas Nelson, 1986). The journal *Bible Translator* consistently addresses issues of interest to those involved in this task. Apropos our discussion see J. Beekman, " 'Literalism' a Hindrance to Understanding," *BT* 17 (1966): 178–89. Also consult the various essays in G. G. Scorgie, M. L. Strauss, and S. M. Voth, eds., *The Challenge of Bible Translation* (Grand Rapids, Zondervan, 2003).

153 This is a brief summary of what we said about these issues in our section on texts and translations in chapter 4.

Steps for Discovering Structural Relationships

Structural analysis involves several simple steps—simple, that is, if one understands basic English grammar. Unfortunately, we cannot make that assumption. We often do things in our own language without understanding why or what we have done. We can also unknowingly commit grammatical errors. People express ideas in language in the ways they learned. So even studying an English text requires conscious effort.[154] To explain the thought flow of a given passage often requires paying attention to and thinking carefully about the significance of the obvious. Sometimes the relationships that exist in a passage are so obvious that we ignore their contribution to its total meaning.

Natural Divisions

First the interpreter must *discover the natural divisions* of the section for study. The direction this takes will depend upon the kind of literature, and we provide specific help for various genres in the chapters that follow. But to illustrate, in historical narratives major sections may encompass many chapters in our current Bibles (for example, the story of Joseph encompasses Gen 37–50), and the interpreter needs to divide the section into its smaller elements. The same holds true for NT Gospels or Epistles. Each section will require analysis to discern the writer's flow of thought. In poetry, of course, the individual poem constitutes the unit for analysis—some shorter, others longer. Wisdom literature requires more care, for the units may be more difficult to classify. A segment may consist of one proverb, an isolated psalm (e.g., Psa 37), a speech (e.g., Job 23:1–24:25), an entire book, or our Lord's Sermon on the Mount. Apocalyptic is the most troublesome; it puts modern readers in the most unfamiliar territory. But the dream of Dan 7:1–14 is one unit; its interpretation in 7:15–28 is another.

Flow of Thought

Usually the interpreter seeks to understand one passage, at least one at a time. So the next step involves tracing the flow of thought in the passage for study.[155] How does the writer's logic develop in the passage?[156] First, one must isolate, where appropriate,

---

154 One fine source of help is M. Kolln, *Understanding English Grammar*, 6th ed. (Harlow, UK: Longman, 2001). Not designed for English majors or specialists, the book seeks to explain standard English grammar to speakers, writers, and readers. A briefer summary of basic English grammatical categories—preparing students to undertake Greek, though it would help anyone review grammar— is found in the initial chapter of J. Wenham, *Elements of New Testament Greek*, 2d ed. (Cambridge: Cambridge University Press, 2002).

155 Many books present methods of structural analysis to represent visually the configuration of a passage. W. C. Kaiser calls his approach a syntactical display or block diagram and illustrates his method using English, Hebrew, and Greek (*Toward An Exegetical Theology* [Grand Rapids: Baker, 1981] 99–104; 166–81). See also G. D. Fee, *New Testament Exegesis*, 3d ed. (Philadelphia: Westminster John Knox, 2002), 41–58; and Osborne, *The Hermeneutical Spiral*, 96–98. Students must determine which method suits their individual needs. The objective is to understand the thought-flow or argument of a passage, however one can attain it. Often structural visualization provides useful insights.

156 This is an overview of steps that we develop later specifically for individual genres. Hence, each step will not necessarily be applicable for each genre. Clearly, what we next say about paragraphs does not apply to a proverb.

the individual paragraphs.[157] Paragraphs typically develop a unit of thought, often incorporating a topic sentence that the paragraph develops. Then the interpreter proceeds to analyze the building blocks of paragraphs—sentences—and how their assertions or propositions develop the writer's argument or narration.[158] Placing proper proportionate weight on each element in a sentence involves distinguishing the main statement (independent clause) or statements from any subordinate (dependent) clause or clauses that qualify it.

One helpful approach to understanding the basic structure of a passage involves a method for identifying the main statement(s) in each sentence, then identifying the subordinate clause or clauses in each sentence, and determining how each modifies or qualifies the ideas expressed in the main statement(s). The following limited analysis of a paragraph of Jas 1 illustrates this procedure. We underline each main clause with a solid line. Those not underlined are subordinate clauses or phrases. The functions of some clauses or phrases are given in italics above each.

command　　　　　*addressees*　　　　　*temporal clause*
(2) <u>Consider it pure joy</u>, my brothers and sisters,[159] whenever you face trials of many kinds,

　　　　　reason clause
(3) because you know that the testing of your faith produces perseverance.

　　command　　　　　　　　　　*purpose clause*
(4) <u>Let perseverance finish its work</u> so that you may be mature and complete,

　　description　　　*conditional clause*　　　　　　*command*
not lacking anything. (5) If any of you lacks wisdom, <u>you should ask God</u>,

　　description　　　　　　　　　　　　　　　　*assertion*
who gives generously to all without finding fault, <u>and it will be given to you</u>.

　temporal clause　　　　*command*　　　　　　　　　*reason clause*
(6) But when you ask, <u>you must believe and not doubt</u>, because the one who doubts is like

　　　　　　　　　　　　　　　　　　　　　　　command
a wave of the sea, blown and tossed by the wind. (7) <u>Those who doubt should not</u>

　　　　　　　　　　　　　　　　　　　　　assertion
<u>think they will receive anything from the Lord;</u> (8) <u>they are double-minded and unstable in all they do</u>.[160]

---

157 For specific help on locating paragraphs see Beekman and Callow, *Translating*, 279–81. In his discussion of discourse analysis, Porter lists several features that signal the boundaries between individual units of a discourse: shifts in grammatical person (e.g., first to third) and shifts in verb tenses (*Idioms*, 301–2).

158 A guide to understanding Hebrew sentences is F. I. Andersen, *The Sentence in Biblical Hebrew* (The Hague/Paris: Mouton; Berlin/New York: Walter de Gruyter, 1974); cf. also the appropriate sections of C. L. Seow, *A Grammar for Biblical Hebrew: Revised Edition* (Nashville: Abingdon, 1995).

159 Literally, the Greek word is *adelphoi*, "brothers," which, of course, refers to all the Christian readers of the letter, not males exclusively. Many recent versions now account for this kind of language throughout the Bible. The NCV and NRSV, for example, translate *adelphoi* in Jas 1:2 as "brothers and sisters." The rest of the translation also reflects the concern for using inclusive language where it is clearly the intent of the text (author).

160 Jas 1:2–8; TNIV.

The main clause of the first sentence is "Consider it pure joy." Three subordinate elements then qualify this statement. For each subordinate (dependent) clause or phrase the student must determine: (1) what word it modifies, (2) what type of clause or phrase it is (a chart showing possible types follows below), and (3) how this affects the meaning of the sentence. Most clause types answer one of the six well-known journalistic questions: *who, what, why, when, where,* or *how.* In the first sentence the first subordinate phrase "my brothers and sisters" qualifies the understood subject "you" of the verb "consider," while the remaining two clauses modify the verb. The first subordinate element, the phrase "my brothers and sisters," indicates *who* is to count it all joy; the second, the clause "whenever you face trials of many kinds," shows *when* this is to be done; and the final one answers the question *why?* giving the reason for "considering it all joy."

To discover how each element influences the meaning of the sentence the student should ask, "What would this statement mean without each subordinate clause or phrase?" Without the phrase "my brothers and sisters," in Jas 1:2 the recipient might not know who were to respond to trials with an attitude of joy. The second clause identifies the specific occasion when joy must be exhibited. Without the last clause a reader would be thoroughly perplexed since joy is not an attitude normally associated with trials. This clause argues for a genuine reason for joy even in experiences of adversity that do not automatically stimulate that response.[161] The knowledge that difficult experiences contribute to the development of perseverance provides legitimate grounds for joy. This passage does not advocate some sadistic enjoyment of hardship.

In the second sentence of this passage, verse 4, two subordinate clauses follow the main statement, "Let perseverance finish its work." The first clause, introduced with "so that . . ." modifies the verb, "let finish," and expresses the purpose (why?) for allowing perseverance to finish its work. The sentence ends with the phrase, "not lacking anything," which modifies the words "mature and complete" at the end of the subordinate clause. Answering the question, "What?" this phrase further explains the meaning of being mature and complete by describing it negatively.

The third sentence in v. 5 presents a more complicated structure. It begins with a subordinate clause followed by a compound main clause that is broken up by another subordinate clause. The compound main clause reads, "you should ask God [for wisdom] . . . and it [wisdom] will be given to you." The opening subordinate clause, "If any of you lacks wisdom," is a conditional clause that qualifies the verb "should ask." It indicates the specific condition in which one should offer this prayer. The subordinate clause that divides the main clause, "who gives generously to all without finding fault," is a descriptive (adjectival in the chart below) clause that modifies "God." This reminder of God's benevolent character encourages the reader to pray for wisdom in times of trial.

While an analysis of the structure of the remaining sentences in this paragraph would further illustrate the process and value of this approach, we leave that for the reader. The chart below provides a full list of the types of subordinate clauses that may occur. They indicate the kinds of logical relations possible in the structures of sentences.

---

161 In Greek, joy (*chara*) expresses a positive subjective feeling, a sense of well-being that normally comes from a positive objective cause (E. Beyreuther, "Joy, Rejoice," *NIDNTT* 2:352–4).

TYPE[162]	JOURNALISTIC QUESTION	SAMPLE CONSTRUCTIONS
Adverbial[163]		
temporal	when?	when, after, before
local	where?	beside, above, below
causal	why?	because, for, since
purpose	why?	that, so that, in order that
result	why?	so, so that, hence
conditional	when?	if, provided, unless
concessive	how?	although, in spite of the fact
comparative	how?	as, just as, likewise
Noun[164]		
subject	who or what?	who, which, that
object	who or what?	whom, what, that
apposition	who or what?	
direct address	who?	(identifies persons, objects)
Adjectival[165]		
modifier	who or what?	who, which, that

Is all this analysis worth the trouble? We sincerely believe so, for asking such structural questions enables the interpreter to identify the flow of the text's argument or narration, the associations, and the inter-relationships not otherwise evident. The interpreter is able to perceive the logic of a writer's flow of thought, breaks in thought, unusual features, and directions that readers easily miss without the time and effort spent to analyze the structure in these ways.

Verbs

The next step in the grammatical study of a passage focuses on the *impact of the verbs*. The complex verb systems of the biblical languages influence the meaning of sentences in several different ways. Understood in conjunction with their contexts, verbs

---

162 Here we provide classifications mainly in relationship to English. Were students to conduct their analyses in the original language texts, certain of these categories would look different in places, as each language has unique ways to communicate. A worthy analysis of Hebrew grammar is Waltke and O'Connor, *Introduction*. The best comparable source for Greek is D. B. Wallace, *Greek Grammar*. For other standard Greek grammars consult: Blass, Debrunner, and Funk, *Grammar*; N. Turner, *Syntax*, vol. 3 of *A Grammar of New Testament Greek*; S. E. Porter, *Idioms*, and Dana and Mantey, *Grammar*.

163 Adverbial clauses modify or qualify verbs, or occasionally adjectives, in the ways listed. For example, the first shows *when* the action of the verb occurs, the second *where*, the seventh shows the circumstances despite which the action occurs, etc.

164 Noun clauses, as the name suggests, function as nouns. In the sentence, "Professors who love to ski seek teaching posts in Colorado," the entire clause "professors who love to ski" functions as the subject of the verb "seek." It operates like a noun in the sentence structure.

165 In similar fashion adjectival clauses or phrases modify or describe nouns or pronouns.

designate the mood, aspect, time, kind, and voice of the action expressed.[166] The *mood* of the verb in each main clause indicates whether the writer was making a statement, asking a question, giving a command, expressing a possibility, or making a wish. The interpreter must understand each sentence consistent with the mood expressed. It makes a big difference whether a sentence asserts a fact, merely expresses a possibility, or asks a question.[167] Interestingly, in James' paragraph above the predominant mood is the imperative. Each of the five sentences contains a command. The only assertions come in verses 5 and 8. After commanding the person who lacks wisdom to pray, James asserts in 1:5, "and it will be given to him"—a statement that carries the force of a promise. Verse 8 certifies the nature of the person who doubts God. While a careful reading of the English text makes most of these mood-uses clear, students should verify their observations with good commentaries.

Influenced by the field of linguistics, an increasing number of biblical interpreters recognize the need to classify verbs according to their *aspect*.[168] Although tense in English mainly concerns *time,* in other languages—Hebrew and Greek are examples— the tense of a verb primarily indicates aspect (or "kind of action").[169] That is, in the biblical languages tense specifies the kind of action from the *perspective of the writer.* It indicates whether the writer or speaker conceives of the action of the verb as a completed state (perfective or stative), still in process (imperfective or progressive), or an unspecified whole—an occurrence (aoristic). English typically employs perfect or simple past tenses to convey perfective / stative action: She *has read* that book; or She *read* that book. English marks a continuous (progressive / imperfective) action with present

---

166 Waltke and O'Connor (*Introduction,* 344) provide an illuminating look at the Hebrew verbal system in their analysis of the form *wayakûhā,* conventionally translated "And they smote it" (Judg 1:8). They note that this one form, the combination of a conjunction and a verb, expresses: (1) the action of smiting; (2) the subject of the action; (3) the object; (4) active voice; (5) case frame (verb is transitive); (6) type of action (Hebrew *hiphil*)—causative rather than simple action; (7) time of action—smiting already past; (8) quality of action—it has an endpoint; and (9) mood—action is an independent assertion.

167 Compare these: "This dog bites"; "This dog may bite"; and "Will this dog bite?"

168 For elaborate assessments of aspect in the Greek language of the NT see S. E. Porter, *Verbal Aspect in the Greek of the New Testament with Reference to Tense and Mood* (New York: Peter Lang, 1989); B. M. Fanning, *Verbal Aspect in New Testament Greek* (Oxford: Clarendon, 1990); and K. L. McKay, *A New Syntax of the Verb in New Testament Greek: An Aspectual Approach* (Bern et al.: Peter Lang, 1994). A briefer analysis occurs in Porter, *Idioms,* 20–45, the first intermediate Greek grammar that incorporated verbal aspect as a major ingredient in its analysis of NT Greek. Subsequent grammars have followed suit, e.g., Wallace, *Greek Grammar,* see 499–504 and the pages on which he discusses each specific tense. Inevitably minor disagreements remain among these grammarians concerning the specific applications of aspect theory.

169 More technically, grammarians divide the topic of tense into aspect, *Aktionsart,* and to a much lesser extent, time. Both aspect and *Aktionsart* pertain to the nature of the verbal action— whether it is ongoing, completed with results, or a simple occurrence. Aspect designates the author or speaker's actual presentation of the action in a linguistic context. It defines how the speaker or author conceives of the action. *Aktionsart* refers more to the actual, objective nature of a verbal action (see Fanning, *Verbal Aspect,* 31, 85; Porter, *Verbal Aspect,* 88; Wallace, *Greek Grammar,* 499). Strictly speaking, Hebrew does not have tenses in the English language sense of categories for specifying the time of the action of a verb. But the language does employ forms for perfect and imperfect action. In specific contexts both may denote past, present, or future time. See Waltke and O'Connor, *Introduction,* 347–350, 461–66, 481–95.

or past progressive forms: She *is reading/was reading* that book. An unspecified (aoristic) kind of action might be expressed by: She *reads* a book. How the writer actually frames the action (aspect) may or not conform to reality, but that is not the issue. The Greek tense specifies how the writer presents the nature of the action.[170] For example, note John's words in Jn 1:29: "On the next day, he *sees* Jesus coming to him, and he *says* . . ." This is our direct translation where the italicized words highlight what grammarians call the "historical present." For his desired effect of creating a sense of vividness for his readers, John presents past actions as now happening (continuous action).[171]

Hebrew verbal systems also allow for another phenomenon under the category of aspect: causative constructions. At times a writer depicts an agent not simply as performing an action; the agent actually causes the action to occur. In English we employ additional verbal forms to convey causation: "They *make* me eat spinach." Or we may add a prefix to a verb. Compare "They closed the door" to "They *en*closed the yard" (They caused the yard to be closed in). The Hebrew language has special adjustments to the *verb* form to alter "They eat spinach" to "They cause to eat spinach." In Greenberg's words, "The *hif'il* is commonly causative: the subject makes the object do the action or be in the state expressed by the *qal* verb; *qal* 'he remembered,' *hif'il* 'he reminded' (lit., 'made remember')."[172]

Besides aspect and kind of action, verb forms indicate other details that contribute to correct interpretation. In places, verbs (or various other syntactical techniques) mark the *time* of action (past, present, or future). And a verb's *voice* shows whether its subject performs the action (active voice: "Mary *cut* the pie"), is acted upon (passive voice: "The pie *was cut* by Mary"), or acts in reference to itself (middle voice in Greek often indicated by reflexive pronouns in English: "Mary *cut herself* a piece of pie").[173] Or the verb may have no voice but merely specify a state of being, as in, "That cat *is* very large." Because verbs convey all of these types of information, the careful interpreter must evaluate each one closely in light of the context and weigh all the nuances the verbal form indicates. For those who do not know the biblical languages, there is no substitute, again, for multiple translations and reliable commentaries that evaluate the verbal elements.

Connectives

The discussion of important grammatical elements must include *connectives*. Connectives (usually conjunctions, but also relative pronouns) occur at the beginning of sentences to link them with what precedes and within sentences to indicate the relationship between the words, phrases, and clauses through which ideas are

---

170 For example, we may say, "It has been raining all day." We specify an imperfective kind of action (continuous), even though in reality it has rained only off and on during the day—with long spells of no rain at all.

171 Most English versions obscure this effect. The NIV has, "John saw Jesus coming toward him and *said* . . ." To conform to modern English the NASB has a similar translation, but it indicates such instances of the historical present by appending an asterisk to the verb.

172 M. Greenberg, *Introduction to Hebrew* (Englewood Cliffs, NJ: Prentice-Hall, 1965), 43. *Qal* and *hif'il* refer to different Hebrew verbal stems. Their meaning need not detain us at this point.

173 The Greek language has "voices" similar to English. Hebrew employs "binyans," similar to conjugations, which also indicate voice. The three voices in Hebrew correspond to active, passive, and reflexive. See Waltke and O'Connor, *Introduction*, 354–55.

conveyed.[174] The previous discussion of the relationship between main and subordinate clauses already underscored the significance of connectives as indicators of how the different parts of a sentence fit together. Although connectives are often small and seemingly insignificant, they exert an influence on meaning that far exceeds their size. Like joints and junctions in a plumbing system of pipes, they regulate the flow of a text's argument. The following chart presents the vast scope of connectives that the interpreter must note in order to understand precisely the meaning of a passage.[175]

TYPES		SAMPLE CONNECTIVES
Temporal or Chronological	Time:	after, as long as, before, now, meanwhile, since, then, until, when, whenever, while
Local or Geographical	Place:	where, beside, upon, above, under, below, on, over, at
	Direction:	to, toward, from
Logical	Continuative:	and, also, besides, both . . . and, furthermore, moreover, likewise, not only . . . but also, whereupon
	Contrast:	although, but, however, much more, nevertheless, not only . . . but also, yet, otherwise, still, whereas
	Purpose:	in order that, that, so that
	Result:	so that, as a result, hence, consequently, so, then
	Inference:	therefore, thus, then, wherefore
	Reason:	as, because, for, inasmuch as, since, whereas, why
	Condition:	as if, as though, if, lest, provided, providing, unless
	Concession:	although, yet, in spite of, though, unless, while
Modal	Agency/Means:	by, through, by means of
	Manner:	as
	Comparison:	also, as, as . . . so, just as . . . so, indeed, in fact, likewise, so also, so as, moreover, than
	Example:	for, for example, indeed, in fact, namely
Emphatic	Emphasis:	indeed, only, finally

---

174 English, Hebrew, and Greek use a variety of connectives to indicate subordination. Hebrew often coordinates items by using *waws*. (Readers without Hebrew can ignore that comment.) For those wanting further insight see R. J. Williams, *Hebrew Syntax: An Outline*, 2d ed. (Toronto: University of Toronto, 1976), 70–79; and Waltke and O'Connor, *Introduction*, 632–55.

175 For particles and conjunctions in Greek see BDF §§ 438–57; Porter, *Idioms*, 204–17; and Dana and Mantey, *Grammar*, 239–67. Andersen (*Sentence*) and Seow (*Grammar*) survey the various ways Hebrew accomplishes connections.

Adjectives and Adverbs

Several remaining grammatical items require the attention of the careful interpreter, namely *adjectives and adverbs.* These modifiers adjust the sense of a noun or verb in some significant way. Waltke and O'Connor cite Hos 1:6 to display a wide use of adverbs in Hebrew.[176] They translate: "Call her name *Not*-Pitied, *for indeed* I will *not* continue *any longer* to have pity on the House of Israel." Each italicized word represents a Hebrew adverb, one giving time, several negating, and one providing emphasis. That is, "any longer" suggests that God had shown compassion on Israel, but would "not" do so "any longer." Thus one may now characterize the nation as those "Not-pitied *any longer.*" The termination of God's pity merits an emphatic "indeed." Another example illustrates several adjectives: "They will hear of your *great* name and your *strong* hand and your *outstretched* arm" (1 Kgs 8:42). Each provides additional color to the noun it modifies. These Hebrew adjectives are similar to those used in English and Greek. Often, though, Hebrew performs the function of description through "construct" phrases to which we referred earlier [as in "the royal seed" (lit. seed of royalty; 2 Kgs 25:25), the "royal throne" (lit. throne of royalty; 1 Kgs 1:46)], or even through apposition ["the deceitful tongue" (lit. tongue of deceit; Psa 120:2)].[177]

In Jas 1:2 discussed above, the writer significantly strengthens the initial command by the inclusion of the Greek adjective "all," translated "pure" in the TNIV.[178] To "Consider it *pure* joy whenever you face trials of many kinds" is far more demanding than just to "Consider it joy." Without the adjective "pure" this command would be unclear about the quality or amount of obligatory joy. Similarly, the adverb "generously" in verse 5 adds a vital dimension to God's giving. He does not simply give, James avers; God gives *generously* to all who ask him for wisdom.

Pronouns

Students must not underestimate the significance of several other seemingly routine grammatical items: the *use of pronouns* and whether nouns and pronouns are *singular or plural.* It is important to determine the antecedents of all pronouns to ascertain to whom or to what they refer. The marking of pronouns, both their case usage and whether singular or plural, is often clearer in Hebrew and Greek than in English. Hebrew marks personal pronouns as to number, person, and gender. In addition, Hebrew employs demonstrative pronouns (this, that), interrogatives and indefinites (who, what, whoever, how, why, where), and relative pronouns (who, whom, which). Greek, likewise, employs a wide array of pronoun types: personal, relative, demonstrative, intensive (as in the *same* man or the man *himself*), possessive (his, her, my), reflexive (yourself), reciprocal (love *one another*), interrogative, and indefinite.

Whereas the pronoun "you" may be either singular or plural in English, Greek (as well as Hebrew) makes a clear distinction. Twice in 1 Corinthians Paul identifies believers as the temple of the Holy Spirit. Warning against the serious dangers of sexual

---

176 Waltke and O'Connor, *Introduction,* 657.

177 Waltke and O'Connor, *Introduction,* 255–256.

178 The TNIV "pure" here is preferable to the potentially ambiguous "all" where "all" may appear to be a direct object of the verb consider. The point is not to "consider all [things] as joy"; rather, "consider [it] pure joy when . . ."

immorality in 6:18–19, he reminds them that each Christian's physical body is a temple of God indwelt by the Holy Spirit. However, Paul's reference to God's temple in 3:16–17 pictures the corporate group of believers—namely, the entire Church—as God's temple indwelt by the Spirit. Second-person plural pronouns make this distinction clear. Paul uses the same temple analogy in two distinct ways: to refer both to individuals and to the entire Church. Unfortunately, many sincere believers have missed the point of Paul's warning in chapter three not to destroy God's temple. Thinking of their individual body as God's temple, they understand Paul's admonition as a call to personal piety; they do not perceive Paul's true intent—a plea not to allow divisions to destroy the Church.[179] At the conclusion of both letters to Timothy the writer says, "Grace be with *you*" (emphasis added). We might mistakenly think these are Paul's concluding benedictions to an individual, Timothy. Actually, the Greek pronouns are plural, so in fact, he invokes God's blessing upon the entire church.[180]

The specific distinctions that Greek relative pronouns make between singular and plural, as well as between masculine, feminine, and neuter, provide a precision not available in our generic English "who" and "what."[181] Direct English translations of Jesus' genealogy in Matthew do not clarify that Jesus is the child of only Mary, not of both Joseph and Mary. Mt 1:16 reads, "and Jacob the father of Joseph, the husband of Mary, of *whom* was born Jesus, who is called Christ." Yet, the Greek text uses a feminine singular relative pronoun that restricts "whom" to Mary alone.[182]

Many such grammatical details that exist in the biblical languages do not always appear in English translations—even the so-called "literal" ones (what we have called "direct" translations). By their very nature translations are limited in their ability to bring out all nuances. After all, no two languages ever mirror each other. Hence, accuracy and thorough understanding demand that students check all interpretations against the original languages to be certain they are consistent with the grammar of the text. As we have repeatedly urged, students must surround themselves with a range of good translations and key biblical commentaries that provide insight into the nuances of grammar.[183]

---

179 Cf. Fee, *1 Corinthians*, 146–50; 260–66.

180 Southern American English has a colloquial mechanism for plural you: "y'all." "Ye" served as the plural pronoun of the second person in the subjective case in Old English (ca. A.D. 1000). Other languages today can also distinguish between singular and plural "you."

181 So the one pronoun "who" can serve in all these ways: "Who is my neighbor?" (singular); "Who are those children?" (plural); "She is the woman who taught me Greek" (feminine singular); "The men who race cars live down the street" (masculine plural). Like English, Hebrew also employs undeclined relative pronouns, e.g., 'ăšr and š.

182 The TNIV avoids the ambiguity by saying, " . . . the husband of Mary, and Mary was the mother of Jesus who is called the Messiah."

183 The bibliography lists the best resources.

8

GENERAL RULES OF HERMENEUTICS: BIBLICAL POETRY

Comprising about one-third of the entire Bible, poetry is its second most common literary feature.[1] Poetry abounds even outside the so-called poetical books like Psalms, Job, Song of Songs, and Lamentations. Old Testament narrative books periodically present long sections of poetry, and most prophetic oracles take poetic form.[2] Also, contrary to a common impression, poetry dots the pages of the NT, in original forms as well as in quotations of the OT.[3] Indeed, against present practice, the printing of more of those texts as poetry rather than as prose in modern Bibles would enable readers better to appreciate their poetic nature.[4] Small wonder that Ryken warns, "There is *no* book in the Bible that does not require the ability to interpret poetry to some degree, because every book includes some figurative language."[5]

The purpose of this section is to prepare interpreters to enjoy and to know how to interpret the Bible's poetic literature. As Longman notes, since "the Bible is an affective book that communicates much of its meaning by moving the feelings and the will of its readers," readers must be careful not to "depoeticize its form" by ignoring its literary conventions.[6] An understanding of its unique literary dynamics will not only

---

1 J. B. Gabel, C. B. Wheeler, and A. D. York, *The Bible as Literature*, 4th ed. (New York/Oxford: Oxford University Press, 2000) 37, 129–31; and L. Ryken, *How to Read the Bible As Literature* (Grand Rapids: Zondervan, 1984), 87.

2 For examples of poetry amid narratives, see Exod 15:1–18; Judg 5; 1 Sam 2:1–10; 2 Sam 22; 23:1–7. For the most definitive study of the phenomenon thus far, see J. W. Watts, *Psalm and Story: Inset Hymns in Hebrew Narrative*, JSOTSup 139 (Sheffield: Sheffield Academic Press, 1992).

3 Though some are questionable, likely sections include Mt 11:17; 13:13; Lk 1:46–55, 67–79; 2:29–32; 6:20–26; 7:32; Jn 1:1–18; Rom 11:33, 36; Eph 5:14; Phil 2:6–11; Col 1:15–20; 1 Tim 3:16; 2 Tim 2:11–13; 1 Jn 2:12–14; Rev 4:11; 5:9–10; 7:15–17; 11:17–18; 12:10–12; 13:10; 15:3–4; 16:5–7; 18; 19:1–8; cf. C. F. Burney, *The Poetry of Our Lord* (Oxford: Clarendon, 1925).

4 So L. Ryken, *Words of Life: A Literary Introduction to the New Testament* (Grand Rapids: Baker, 1987), 101–102.

5 Ryken, *How to Read*, 87. According to N. K. Gottwald ("Poetry, Hebrew," *IDB*, K-Q: 829), only seven OT books—Leviticus, Ruth, Ezra, Nehemiah, Esther, Haggai, and Malachi—seem to lack any poetic lines.

6 T. Longman, III, "Biblical Poetry," in L. Ryken and T. Longman, III, eds., *A Complete Literary Guide to the Bible* (Grand Rapids: Zondervan, 1993), 81.

heighten the enjoyment but will also enable interpreters to "hear" the poets' thoughts more clearly.[7] Fortunately, as we shall see, though scholars still debate many important issues, recent scholarly study of Hebrew poetry has uncovered for us a rich lode of insights to mine in studying the poetry of both Testaments.

THE DYNAMICS OF POETRY

What is poetry? Poetry consists of written compositions typified by terseness, vivid words, and a high degree of structure.[8] Put differently, poetry displays a higher degree of structure, sound, and language than prose. We say to a "higher degree" because many prose texts also have poetic elements. Indeed, one should not think of poetry and prose as completely distinct, unrelated categories; rather, they represent the ends of a literary continuum. The more intense, dense, and compact a literary piece is, the closer it approaches the poetry side of the continuum.[9]

The opening lines of the poem "The Eve of St. Agnes" by John Keats illustrate the basic elements of poetry:[10]

> St. Agnes' Eve—Ah, bitter chill it was!
> The owl, for all his feathers, was a-cold;
> The hare limp'd trembling through the frozen grass,
> And silent was the flock in woolly fold.

Structurally, what dominates the piece is not a grammatical sentence or paragraph but the poetic line. Each line is terse—so terse, in fact, that none fills out a full line of the printed page. Read aloud, each shows a natural rhythm of accented and unaccented syllables (and SI-lent WAS the FLOCK in WOOL-ly FOLD).

In turn, the rhythmic structure dictates an economy of language. The poet has carefully carved his thoughts into a few precise words that fit the rhythmic scheme; there are no "wasted words"—words just thrown in to fill blank space or to impress the reader. As for sound, the most obvious feature is the poem's rhyme. The final words of every other line rhyme ("was"/"grass"; "a-cold"/"fold").[11] More subtly, observe the repetition of the sound "f" in the words "for," "feathers," "frozen," "flock," and "fold." The

---

7 Occasionally, that understanding may also help us solve thorny textual problems or interpret difficult verses. See the example from Amos 6:12 in W. S. LaSor, D. A. Hubbard, and F. W. Bush, *Old Testament Survey*, 2d ed. (Grand Rapids: Eerdmans, 1996), 231.

8 Cf. R. Alter, *The Art of Biblical Poetry* (New York: Basic Books. 1985), x ("the best words in the best order"); A. Berlin, *The Dynamics of Biblical Parallelism* (Bloomington: Indiana University Press, 1985), 5, 16 (a high degree of "terseness and parallelism"); cf. also the detailed discussion of criteria in W. G. E. Watson, *Classical Hebrew Poetry*, JSOTSup 26 (Sheffield: JSOT, 1984), 46–62.

9 Cf. D. L. Petersen and K. H. Richards, *Interpreting Hebrew Poetry* (Minneapolis: Fortress, 1992), 13–14. Of course, the border between poetry and prose can often be difficult to pinpoint; cf. the illuminating treatment of the problem in S. E. Gillingham, *The Poems and Psalms of the Hebrew Bible*, Oxford Bible Series (Oxford: Oxford University Press, 1994), 18–43.

10 For the full text, see O. Williams, ed., *Immortal Poems of the English Language* (New York: Washington Square Press, 1952), 333–43. What follows draws its inspiration and content from C. S. Lewis, *Christian Reflections* (Grand Rapids: Eerdmans, 1967), 129–35.

11 In describing poetry, the / sign means "parallels" or "corresponds to." Later we will use // to signal the end of a poetic unit of parallel lines (e.g., two or more such lines joined by /).

poet has crafted rhyme and repetition into his lines so they sound pleasant when read aloud.

Finally, several things are striking about the poem's language. First, the poet offers concrete images to convey an abstract idea. He could have simply stated his main idea like "It was very cold on St. Agnes' Eve." Instead, he described the cold through three images—an owl, a hare (a rabbit), and a flock of sheep. How cold was it? It was so cold that the owl's feathers could not keep him warm, the rabbit could barely hop, and the flock could not even bleat a "baah." Now, that's cold![12]

Indeed, this leads us to a second observation. Through vivid language ("bitter chill," "limp'd," "frozen grass," "woolly fold"), the poet wants us to experience his topic—to *feel* the cold of that particular night. So his words appeal not so much to our reason as to our imagination. They paint imaginary pictures that allow us to experience the topic—its feel, sights, smells, touch, or taste. Our imagination sees the freezing owl, the limping rabbit, and the silent sheep; we feel that evening's "bitter chill." In sum, "poetry is a language of images that the reader must experience as a series of imagined sensory situations."[13]

But some may object that prose often betrays an underlying rhythm and employs similarly vivid language. They may ask, then, how poetry differs from prose. At this point it is best to distinguish between poetic language (i.e., rhythmic sentences and concrete imagery) and poetry. Prose does make use of poetic language, particularly prose that is written for public presentation. The distinct attributes of poetry, however, are its sparseness and its restricted structure; these are not intrinsic to prose. Though prose may be compact and carefully structured, its structure is formed of sentences and paragraphs. The structure of poetry, by contrast, consists of tightly arranged lines and compact language.[14] Further, compared to prose, poetry features a higher degree of metaphors and images—what we often call "poetic language."

How does biblical poetry compare to the poetry most familiar to us? Consider the overview of Hebrew poetry that this clever limerick offers:

> Hebrew poems are not just a mess,
> nor is this, we hope, a mere guess.
> They may not have rhyme,
> but you'll find every time
> that the poets composed under stress.[15]

---

12 Cf. the observation by Lewis (*Christian Reflections*, 131) that adjectives dominate poetic language.

13 Ryken, *How to Read*, 91 (his italics omitted).

14 So Berlin, *Dynamics*, 16, with reference to the constitutive structure of biblical poetry, parallelism (to be discussed later); cf. Petersen and Richards, *Interpreting Hebrew Poetry*, 14 ("parallelism, rhythm, and style"). Against J. L. Kugel (*The Idea of Biblical Poetry* [Baltimore: Johns Hopkins, 1981], 85, 94–95), who wrongly denies the idea of "biblical poetry." Kugel mistakenly equates "poetry" with "meter," overlooking the former's more typical feature, mimesis; cf. R. Raphael, "That's No Literature, That's My Bible: On James Kugel's Objections to the Idea of Biblical Poetry," *JSOT* 27 (2002): 37–45.

15 Watson, *Classical Hebrew Poetry*, 100. For a useful survey of the poetic devices used by Jesus, see R. H. Stein, *The Method and Message of Jesus' Teachings*, rev. ed. (Philadelphia: Westminster, 1994), 7–32. The classic catalog of biblical poetic techniques remains E. W. Bullinger, *Figures of Speech Used in the Bible* (Grand Rapids: Baker, 1968 [orig. 1898]).

As was true of the Keats poem explored above, the Bible's poetry is "not just a mess" but has sound (but not rhyme), structure, and language. The interpreter's task is to understand each of these three features and, hence, to be able to interpret biblical poems with insight and understanding.

THE SOUNDS OF HEBREW POETRY

Rhyme and Meter

First we will consider the feature of *sound*.[16] Traditional English poetry uses two aspects of sound: rhyme and meter. *Rhyme* occurs when a poet pairs at least two words with identical sounds at the end of successive or alternating lines (e.g., "The owl, for all his feathers, was *a-cold* / And silent was the flock in woolly *fold*" [italics added]). *Meter* involves the rhythmic alternation between accented and unaccented syllables within each poetic line. By printing the accented syllables in capital letters, we can readily see the accentual alternation of the line just quoted from Keats:

> The OWL, for ALL his FEA-thers, WAS a-COLD
> And SI-lent WAS the FLOCK in WOOL-ly FOLD.

Observe that in this example an accent falls specifically on every other syllable, and that each line has a total of five accents.[17]

Hebrew poetry differs from English poetry in its uses of sound. For example, it lacks the rhyme that English speakers deem so basic to poetry. That is, Hebrew poets did not normally structure poetic lines so that their final words rhymed. On the other hand, they occasionally used rhyming sounds with great effect.[18] The most common use is end-rhyme in which the poet rhymes the final sounds of successive lines using suffixes or endings. For example, all four lines of Isa 33:22 end with the same sound, the suffix *–nû/-enû* ("our" or "us"). The other use is word-pair rhyme in which the poet rhymes two or more words in a row. Observe the three rhymed words that conclude this example from Isa 22:5:

kî yôm	*mehûmâ*	*umebûsâ*	*umebûkâ*
For it is a day	of tumult,	trampling,	turmoil.[19]

---

16 Obviously, this subject relates primarily to readers who can access the original Hebrew and Greek texts. Nevertheless, an awareness of these additional dimensions of OT poetry will enable Bible students to benefit from the occasional comments on the original languages in major reference books. For an example of where sound also figures in NT poetry, see below.

17 Drawing on analogies from ancient Greek poetry, scholars have assigned technical labels to kinds of poetic meter. They call the alternation of unaccented and accented syllables ("in WOOL-ly FOLD") *iambic*; its opposite (i.e., accented followed by unaccented syllables) *trochee*. With five accents in each line, the Keats poem follows a common meter called *iambic pentameter*.

18 Cf. the discussion in Watson, *Classical Hebrew Poetry*, 229–34. See also our discussion below of the related phenomena, assonance and alliteration.

19 Watson, *Classical Hebrew Poetry*, 232, who provides other examples of both types of rhyme (231–32).

Does Hebrew poetry have regular meter? For the last three decades, a lively discussion, spurred in part by studies of extra-biblical Semitic poetry, has produced a divided scholarly house on the question. On one extreme, some scholars virtually deny that biblical poetry has any meter at all.[20] Others argue that it does indeed have meter and explain it by counting letters or syllables, by alleging uses of stressed syllables, or by analyzing syntax.[21] The problem is that, thus far, no system adequately explains all the poetic phenomena available. At one point or another each has to squeeze or stretch the poetry to fit its preconceived systematic mold.[22]

In our view, Hebrew poetry follows neither lock-step, sing-song meter nor an unanchored free verse. Instead, it follows what Hrushovski calls a *free rhythm,* that is, the flexible use of accented syllables within certain broad limits.[23] It shows such flexibility in several respects. First, a given poetic line may have two, three, or four words with accented syllables. Second, its parallel line(s) may or may not have the same number of such words. Scholars commonly use numbers to describe the accented syllables in a poetic couplet. For example, they would call a couplet in which each line has three stresses 3:3. If the second line had two or four stresses, it would be 3:2 or 3:4, respectively. Third, the number of unaccented syllables between accented ones varies, although at least one must intervene. Fourth, the number of parallel lines forming a poetic unit may vary from two to four but normally not more than four. Finally, unlike European metrical poetry, a given Hebrew poem need not consistently follow one rhythmical pattern throughout.

---

20 Most recently, D. R. Vance, *The Question of Meter in Biblical Hebrew Poetry* (Lewiston, NY: Edwin Mellen Press, 2001), 496 ("one may safely conclude that the poetry of the Hebrew Bible does not contain meter"); Kugel, *The Idea of Biblical Poetry,* 301 ("no meter has been found because none exists"); cf. also Berlin, *Dynamics,* 4 ("biblical poetry lacks any easily discernible meter"). While conceding the periodic presence of poetic stress, Alter believes "the term meter should probably be abandoned for biblical verse" (*The Art of Biblical Poetry,* 9).

21 The latest defense of the syllable-counting approach is J. P. Fokkelman, *Major Poems of the Hebrew Bible: At the Interface of Hermeneutics and Structural Analysis,* vol. 2 (Assen: Van Gorcum, 2000); cf. D. N. Freedman and J. C. Geoghegan, "Quantitative Measurement in Biblical Hebrew Poetry," in R. Chazan, W. W. Hallo, and L. Schiffman, eds., *Ki Baruch Hu: Ancient Near Eastern, Biblical, and Judaic Studies in Honor of Baruch A. Levine* (Winona Lake, IN: Eisenbrauns, 1999), 229–49. Vance (*The Question of Meter,* 41–222) offers an exhaustive discussion and critique of all ancient and modern theories; cf. more briefly, Watson (*Classical Hebrew Poetry,* 97–110) and Berlin (*Dynamics,* 18–30). The writings of O. Loretz argue for a letter-counting method (for bibliography, see Watson, *Classical Hebrew Poetry,* 105–106). Appealing to syntactical analysis are M. O'Connor, *Hebrew Verse Structure* (Winona Lake, IN: Eisenbrauns, 1980) and T. Collins, *Line-Forms in Hebrew Poetry* (Rome: Biblical Institute Press, 1978).

22 Even Fokkelman, who claims that ancient poets counted syllables and used such counts to shape their poems, deems it "highly unlikely that the debate will ever reach a consensus"; cf. J. P. Fokkelman, *Reading Biblical Poetry* (Louisville: Westminster John Knox, 2001), 23. But he also proposes two "escape routes" around the impasse (23–24).

23 B. Hrushovski, "Prosody, Hebrew," *Encyclopaedia Judaica,* 18 vols. (Jerusalem: Keter Pub.; New York: Macmillan, 1972), 13: 1201; followed by Alter, *The Art of Biblical Poetry,* 8; similarly Longman, "Biblical Poetry," 83; Gillingham, *Poems and Psalms,* 67–68; Petersen and Richards, *Interpreting Hebrew Poetry,* 43–47 ("rhythmic patterns" of regularity, variation, grouping, and hierarchy). We owe much of what follows to the discussions in Hrushovski (cols. 1200–1203) and Watson, *Classical Hebrew Poetry,* 97–103.

On the other hand, biblical poetry does operate within certain assumed poetic limitations—that is, within its own "poetics." First, regardless of how many accents it has, each line or pair of lines constitutes either a phrase, or a syntactical or logical unit. In other words, each will express either one complete thought or two related ones.[24] Second, couplets are either of equal or similar length (i.e., 3:3; 3:2; 3:4). Hebrew poetry avoids overly long or short line-pairs (e.g., 5:1; 4:1, etc.). Third, as noted above, two accented syllables never occur in a row; at least one unaccented syllable intervenes. Fourth, also as noted above, normally the number of parallel lines never exceeds four. Finally, Hebrew poetry seems to have certain fixed patterns that occur in certain literature. For example, the 3:2 pattern is typical of funeral dirges (see further development in chapter 9).[25]

Does knowledge of Hebrew rhythm help us interpret OT poetry more accurately? The answer is a qualified yes. First, it should make us cautious about adopting alterations in the present Hebrew text because of meter. Since the nineteenth century, it has been common practice for scholars to suggest such minor changes by tailoring the Hebrew to fit an alleged, expected metrical pattern. Their goal is a good one—to recover the wording of (or, at least, that closest to) the original Hebrew text (i.e., the method called textual criticism). Though less popular than before, the practice still appears in commentaries and other books.[26] Given the flexibility of Hebrew meter, however, Bible students should carefully evaluate such textual suggestions before adopting them outright.

Second, an awareness of Hebrew rhythm allows us to capture additional dimensions of a text.[27] Indeed, even students without knowledge of Hebrew can sense those added dimensions. Granted, as a translation, an English Bible provides no glimpse of the accents of the actual Hebrew words, but a relatively literal, word-for-word English translation (e.g., KJV, NASB, ESV) does reveal the relative lengths of the Hebrew poetic lines. In turn, line lengths may point to one aspect of a poem's rhythm, namely, its tempo (the speed at which one should read it). Again, that tempo may say something about the speed of the actions that the words portray.

For example, long lines or several long words convey the idea of slowness (cf. Psa 19:7–9 [Heb. 8–10];[28] Lam 3:6a, 15), while short lines or series of short words suggest

---

24 The Hebrew texts signal the end of the line by a grammatical stop (a phenomenon called "end-stopping"; cf. Watson, *Classical Hebrew Poetry*, 332–33). The commas or semicolons in English translations commonly indicate such stops.

25 For those who know Hebrew, Watson (*Classical Hebrew Poetry*, 99–103) provides details about how to identify stresses and meter. Recently, several scholars have argued strongly against the assumption that dirges have a unique meter; cf. Vance, *The Question of Meter*, 485–87; R. de Hoop, "Lamentations: the Qinah-Meter Questioned," in M. Korpel and J. Oesch, eds., *Delimitation Criticism: A New Tool of in Biblical Scholarship* (Assen: Van Gorcum, 2000), 80–104. The metrical study of Lamentations by Freedman and Geoghegan ("Quantitative Measurement," 238–39) confirms the presence of the 3:2 "falling rhythm" but argues that its parallelism with "rising rhythm" and "balanced lines" suggest that "Qina content and falling rhythm should not be tied together too closely."

26 Cf. the occasional appeal to "m cs" (i.e., *metri causa*, "because of meter") in the textual notes of the current Hebrew text, *Biblia Hebraica Stuttgartensia*. Of course, if Hebrew poetry lacks meter (so Vance, *The Question of Meter*, and Kugel, *The Idea of Biblical Poetry*) such appeals plainly err.

27 We are indebted for most of what follows to the fine discussion in Watson, *Classical Hebrew Poetry*, 111–113.

28 The abbreviation "Heb." in brackets identifies the Hebrew verse numbers whenever they differ from the numbers in our English Bibles.

staccato-like rapidity (cf. Judg 5:22; Jer 46:3–4). At the same time, a sudden, surprising change in line length alters the tempo of reading from fast to slow or vice versa, casting the spotlight on those lines—a kind of poetic "special effects." The shift compels the reader to pay special attention.

Consider an example from the prophet Nahum. He describes the fall of Nineveh, capital of Israel's hated enemy, Assyria:

> The crack of whips
>   the clatter of wheels,
> galloping horses
>   and jolting chariots!
> Charging cavalry,
>   flashing swords
>   and glittering spears!
> Many casualties,
>   piles of dead,
> bodies without number,
>   people stumbling over the corpses—
> all because of the wanton lust of a harlot,
>   alluring, the mistress of sorceries,
> who enslaved nations by her prostitution
>   and peoples by her witchcraft. (Nah 3:2–4)[29]

The short, compact lines convey both rapid action and quick close-ups of specific aspects of a broad scene. They create a vivid sense of action happening in all directions. But by elongating the concluding lines, the writer suddenly slows down the action to a complete halt. The sudden stop in the action directs the reader's focus to one thing: Nineveh's lust. The last lines hammer home the point: Nineveh dies because of her prostitution (i.e., her political seduction of other nations).

In sum, careful study of a good literal English translation gives even the nonspecialized student a partial glimpse of the Hebrew original. That glimpse provides clues to a poem's tempo and to its meaning.

The Sounds of Poetic Words

Besides rhythm, biblical poets also used the sounds of words to create poetic effects. Knowing these various uses is an extremely helpful aid to proper interpretation of biblical poems.[30]

---

29 Occasionally, the translation in a commentary captures the rhythm of the Hebrew. For a good example see the rendering of Nahum and Habakkuk in O. P. Robertson, *The Books of Nahum, Habakkuk, and Zephaniah*, NICOT (Grand Rapids: Eerdmans, 1990).

30 For a full discussion, see Watson, *Classical Hebrew Poetry*, 222–50, on whom much of what follows depends; cf. also Berlin, *Dynamics*, 103–26. As we said earlier, full appreciation of word sounds requires knowledge of Hebrew and Greek. We include treatment here, however, to prepare readers for comments about words in standard reference books on the Bible. To hear the full effect of the examples below, readers would need to pronounce the transliterated Hebrew texts.

Assonance is the repetition of the same or closely similar vowel sounds in a series of words. Its primary purpose is to give a feeling of unity to a poetic unit, whether a single phrase, a single line, or a series of parallel lines. By calling attention to itself, assonance also serves a secondary purpose—to give special emphasis to the words that use it. It does so by linking the sounds of the words with their meaning in the same poetic unit. To use a contemporary example, in the days of the Soviet Union one might have said, "I would rather live under communism than die in a nuclear war." But the simple alliterative phrase "Better Red than dead" is far more striking and memorable. The repeated "eh" sound (b*e*tter, r*e*d, d*e*ad) provides unity, emphasis, and memorability.

In its simplest form assonance features the recurrence of a single vowel sound. For example, observe the heavy use of -a- sounds in this couplet:

Transliteration	*maddûaʿ yārash malkām ʾet-gād*
	wᵉʿammô bᵉʿārāyw yāshāb[31]
Translation	Why then has Molech taken possession of Gad?
	Why do his people live in its towns? (Jer 49:1)

The Bible also offers more complex uses of assonance that combine several sounds in the same unit. A good example is the repetition of the sound-sequence *a-a-i* in this line:

Transliteration	*lō-ʾaᵘmîn kî-yaᵘzîn qôlî*[32]
Translation	I do not believe he would give me a hearing. (Job 9:16b)

Alliteration offers a similar use of sounds: the repetition of the same or similar-sounding consonants within a poetic unit. Alliteration serves purposes similar to those of assonance—to give its poetic unit (usually a line) a sense of wholeness as well as special emphasis. Also, it is common for a key word to be dominant in biblical poems, and alliteration around that word also serves to highlight it.[33] Finally, by linking sound with sense, alliteration makes the words more memorable. That is why even children can remember the line "Peter Piper picked a peck of pickled peppers."

Hebrew poets use this word device in various ways. Sometimes they alliterate the first letter of each word of a phrase or line ("word-initial alliteration"). Notice, for example, the repetition of initial sh- sounds in the second line of this couplet:

---

31 Cf. the use of "e" (Jer 49:8), "i" (Psa 113:8), "o" (Isa 58:12; Job 5:21), "u" (Lam 4:15).

32 One word of clarification about assonance: as Petersen and Richards point out (*Interpreting Hebrew Poetry*, 5–6, 34), the sounds of the present Hebrew text may not correspond exactly to those of the original. The reason is that originally the Hebrew text had only consonants; later scribes called "Masoretes" added the vowels so that future generations would not forget the language. Thus, our perception of assonance assumes a close similarity, if not identity, between the present Hebrew text and its original; cf. Berlin, *Dynamics*, 104, who limited her treatment of sound play to consonants.

33 For examples and discussion of other functions, see Watson, *Classical Hebrew Poetry*, 228. In a prose text, observe the repetition of the key thematic word *šûb* ("to return") throughout Ruth 1.

Transliteration	*'im-yhwh lō'-yishmār-'îr* *shāwᵉ' shāqad shômēr*[34]
Translation	Unless the Lord watches over the city, the *watchmen stand guard in vain.* (Psa 127:1b, our italics)

The most common form of alliteration is the repetition of similar sounds over parallel lines. Notice the recurrence of the -k- and -ts- sounds in this example:

Transliteration	*kᵉtsîts yātsā' wayyimmāl* *wayyibrach katstsēl wᵉlō' yaᵃmôd*
Translation	Like a *blossom* he *blooms,* but withers; he is fleet as *a shadow* and does not stay. (Job 14:2)[35]

In the first line the -ts- sound occurs twice in the first word (*kᵉtsîts*), then reappears a third time in the second word (*yātsā*). This repetition gives the line a unity of sound. Further, in the second line the consonantal combination -k-ts- of *kᵉtsîts* ("like a blossom") recurs in the phrase *katstsēl* ("like a shadow"), thereby giving the entire poetic pair a cohesive sound. In other cases, the alliteration appears over a series of lines. For example, in Joel 2:15–16a the letter -q- appears eight times in eight lines, four times as the initial letter of a line.[36]

Frequently, poets employ both assonance and alliteration in the same series of words. For example, consider the word pair *lintôsh wᵉlintôts* ("to destroy and demolish"), a pleasing phrase in Jeremiah's prophetic commission (Jer 1:10). Except for the final letters, the two words sound exactly alike (*wᵉ* is the conjunction "and"). Similarly, the phrase *bᵉqeren ben-shāmen* concludes the introduction to Isaiah's memorable "Song of the Vineyard" (Isa 5:1). All three words end with the same sound (*-en*), making the phrase almost rhyme.[37]

The opening line of the book of Hebrews also combines assonance and alliteration to great effect:

Polumerōs kai polutropōs palai ho theos lalēsas tois patrasin en tois prophētais.

---

34 Notice also that the repetition builds on the line's key word *šmr*. Cf. the repetition of initial "b" sounds in the line's preceding parallel.

35 Watson's translation (*Classical Hebrew Poetry*, 227).

36 Watson, *Classical Hebrew Poetry*, 227. Cf. Nah 1:10 where a series of initial "s" sounds "may actually parody the lisp of a drunk"; cf. T. Longman, III, "Biblical Poetry," 87. A common, extended form of alliteration is the "alphabetic acrostic" in which each verse begins with succeeding letters of the alphabet. Cf. Pss 9; 10; 25; 111; 119; Prov 31:10–31; Lam 1–4; Nah 1:2–8; etc.; H. Minkoff, "As Simple as ABC: What Acrostics in the Bible Can Demonstrate," *Bible Review* 13 (1997): 27–31, 46–47; K. C. Hanson, *Alphabetic Acrostics: A Form Critical Study* (Unpubl. Ph.D. diss., Claremont Graduate School, 1984); and the recent treatment of acrostic psalms in D. N. Freedman, *Psalm 119* (Winona Lake, IN: Eisenbrauns, 1999), 1–23.

37 In a prose context, a similar combination gives the last line of Ruth 1:6 (*lātēt lāhem lehem,* "giving them food") added emphasis and memorability.

"Many times and in many ways, long ago God spoke to our ancestors by the prophets" (Heb. 1:1, our translation).

Besides the repetition of initial "p" sounds (see the bold letters), the first two
adverbs ("many times," "in many ways") both begin and end with the sounds *polu-* and
-ōs. The cluster of sounds subtly enhances the line's rhetorical power and sets a poetic
tone for the book's opening paragraph (vv. 1–4).[38]

Some years ago, we heard a preacher contrast the views of self-esteem of Norman
Vincent Peale and the apostle Paul. After arguing that Paul's view was the superior one,
he commented, "That's what makes Paul so appealing and Peale so appalling." That
delightful line employed *word play* (also called paronomasia, or more commonly, a
"pun"). Hebrew poetry also uses the familiar sound device of word-play.[39] In the most
common form, a poet pairs up two or more words that differ in one of their three consonants. For example, observe how Isaiah concluded his song about Israel as a vineyard
that Yahweh planted to produce good fruit (Isa 5:7):

> And he [Yahweh] looked for justice (*mishpāṭ*),
> > but saw bloodshed (*mishpāch*);
> > for righteousness (*tsᵉdāqâ*),
> > but heard cries of distress (*tsᵉʿāqâ*).

Slightly more sophisticated is the "root-play," a pun in which one word's consonants reappear in later words but in a different order. Consider the clever play on the
reversible roots *b-w-sh* and *sh-w-b* in Psa 6:10 [Heb. 11] (our translation):

> May all my enemies be ashamed (*yēbōshû*) and dismayed;
> > may they turn back (*yāshubû*),
> > may they be suddenly disgraced (*yēbōshû*).

Coming in the psalm's final verse, the pun gives the text's conclusion a special rhetorical flourish.

Sometimes the pun plays on changes in vowels between words of the same consonants (i.e., the same root). For example, when Jeremiah told God, "I see the branch of
an almond tree (*shāqēd*)," Yahweh's reply picked up on the root (*sh-q-d*): "I am watching (*shōqēd*) to see that my word is fulfilled" (Jer 1:11–12).[40] At other times poets

---

38 This example slightly adapted from D.A. Black, "Translating New Testament Poetry," in
D.A. Black, ed., *Scribes and Scripture: New Testament Essays in Honor of J. Harold Greenlee* (Winona
Lake, IN: Eisenbrauns, 1992), 120–21. For a larger poetic treatment of vv. 1–4, see his "Hebrews
1:1–4: A Study in Discourse Analysis," *WTJ* 49 (1987): 175–94.

39 The classic study remains I. M. Casanowicz, *Paronomasia in the Old Testament* (Boston: J. S.
Gushing et al., 1894); but cf. more conveniently, E.L. Greenstein, "Wordplay, Hebrew," *ABD*,
6:968–72; J. M. Sasson, "Wordplay in the OT," *IDBS*, 968–70, and Watson, *Classical Hebrew Poetry*,
237–50.

40 Cf. Isaiah's play on the root *'kl*, i.e., *tōkēlû* "you shall eat," *tᵉukkᵉlû* "you shall be eaten" (Isa
1:19–20).

employ a double meaning or "double entendre" wordplay. This involves the repetition of the same word but with a different meaning in each case. Observe how the Preacher repeated the same formula (*'ēn lāhem mᵉnahēm,* "there was no one to . . . ") but with a different meaning for *mᵉnahēm:*

> I saw the tears of the oppressed,
> > and I saw that there was no one to *comfort* them.
> Strength was on the side of their oppressors,
> > and there was no one to *avenge* them. (Eccl 4:1, NEB, our italics)

The NT also provides a ready example of play on similar-sounding words in Jesus' statement to Peter: "And I tell you, you are Peter (*petros*), and on this rock (*petra*) I will build my church" (Mt 16:18 NRSV). The similar sounds leads the hearer to compare the two words, while their differences in sound and sense serve to convey Jesus' meaning. "Peter" translates (actually transliterates) the Greek word *petros* ("stone") and "rock" translates *petra* ("fixed rock, rock shelf"), the wordplay on Peter's name suggesting that Christ will found his Church on Peter (as the early chapters of Acts then play out).[41]

Word repetition is another common type of wordplay. In this case the poet simply repeats a word or words, perhaps in slightly different forms, throughout a series of poetic lines. The prophet Isaiah skillfully used this device in the opening lines of his "Song of the Vineyard" (Isa 5:1). Observe the recurrence of the words "sing" / "song" (*shîr*), "lover" (*lîdîdî, dôdî*), and "vineyard" (*kerem*):

> I will *sing* (*shîr*) for the one I love (*lîdîdî*)
> > a *song* (*shîr*) of my *lover* (*dôdî*) about his vineyard (*kerem*):
> My loved one (*lîdîdî*) had a vineyard (*kerem*)
> > on a fertile hillside. (Isa 5:1)[42]

Finally, poets sometimes use *onomatopoeia,* that is, words whose own sounds imitate the actual sounds of the actions they portray. The English language has many onomatopoetic words. So we say that a bee "buzzed" around our head, that a baby "babbled," or that a drainpipe "gurgled." Each word imitates the sound made by a bee, baby, or drainpipe. Similarly, one can almost hear the sounds of galloping horses in the second line of this battle scene (Judg 5:22):

> Then thundered the horses' hoofs—
> > galloping,   galloping go   his mighty steeds.
> > *middharôt*   *daharôt*   *'abbîrāw*[43]

To cite an example from the NT, in Jas 5:1 the author invites the rich to "weep and wail." The first word (*klausate*) may describe audible weeping, but the second term

---

41 D. A. Hagner, *Matthew 14–28*, WBC, Vol. 33B (Dallas: Word, 1995), says, "Peter is also the 'rock' upon which Jesus the Messiah will build his community" (469).

42 After Berlin, *Dynamics*, 113.

43 Cf. Isaiah's imitation of birds chirping (Isa 10:14) and gibberish language (28:10, 13).

(*ololyzontes*) is certainly an onomatopoeic word that sounds like howling. Some suggest that the verb *battalogeō* ("keep on babbling") in Mt 6:7 is also onomatopoetic for it sounds like babbling.

Now the use of such literary devices is valid and valuable in and of itself for it highlights the beauty and creativity both of human language and of the poets who skillfully shape it into poetry to entice and delight readers. But how does a knowledge of Hebrew sounds contribute to proper interpretation? Consider that by the clever use of sounds, biblical poets called special attention to their words. While amusing and pleasurable in itself, such showcasing of sounds also signals the poets' intentions. It casts a spotlight on the words that the writer sought to emphasize, and, thus, may point to the poem's meaning. In some cases, wordplay underscores the poem's theme. Certainly, the repetition of "Praise him" (*hallelûhû*) in some psalms shows their theme to be the praise of Yahweh (see Psa 148:3–5; 150; cf. Rev 19:1, 3, 4, 6). In other cases, wordplay highlights a strategic contrast. To retrieve an earlier example, by reversing the letters *b-w-sh* and *sh-w-b*, the psalmist stressed the reversal of fortune for which his prayer pled (Psa 6:10 [Heb. 11]). Hearing the sound of the poet's words is indeed a useful tool in interpreting biblical poetry.

THE STRUCTURE OF HEBREW POETRY

Parallelism

Scholars refer to the structure of Hebrew poetry as *parallelism of members,* a phenomenon that also shaped the writings of NT writers.[44] The term has, unfortunately, spawned a common misunderstanding.[45] Many people understand "parallelism" to mean that a second poetic line merely restates or contrasts the point of the previous line in different words. They assume that an equal sign (=) links the lines together. Actually, parallelism is that phenomenon whereby two or more successive poetic lines dynamically strengthen, reinforce, and develop each other's thought. As a kind of emphatic additional thought, the follow-up lines further define, specify, expand, intensify, or contrast the first. As Berlin puts it,

> Parallelism focuses the message on itself but its vision is binocular. Like human vision it superimposes two slightly different views of the same object and from their convergence it produces a sense of depth.[46]

Concerning the effect of the movement from line to line, Alter adds insightfully:

---

44 Cf. J. L. Bailey and L. D. Vander Broek, *Literary Forms in the New Testament: A Handbook* (Louisville: Westminster John Knox, 1992), 77 ("[t]he use of parallelism in the New Testament most certainly has its origin in Hebrew poetry").

45 Historically, this discovery goes back to R. Lowth's inaugural lectures as professor of poetry at Oxford (cf. R. Lowth, *De Sacra Poesi Hebraeorum* [Oxford: Clarendon, 1753]; ET: *Lectures on the Sacred Poetry of the Hebrews* [London: S. Chadwick & Co., 1847]). For a critical reassessment of Lowth's work, however, see Kugel, *The Idea of Biblical Poetry*, 204–86. Later discoveries showed the practice of parallelism to be widespread among Semitic poets. For Ugaritic examples, see M. S. Smith, *Ugaritic Narrative Poetry*, Writings from the Ancient World 9 (Atlanta: Scholars Press, 1997).

46 Berlin, *Dynamics*, 99; cf. her "Parallelism," *ABD*, 5:155–62. In our view, our discussion reflects an emerging consensus evident in Kugel, *The Idea of Biblical Poetry*, 8; Alter, *The Art of Biblical Poetry*, 10–26; and Berlin, *Dynamics*, 140–41.

> In the abundant instances, . . . the characteristic movement of mean-
> ing is one of heightening or intensification . . . of focusing, specifica-
> tion, concretization, even what could be called dramatization.[47]

In other words, succeeding parallel lines do not simply restate the opening line; rather, they add to or expand its thought. Isa 1:10 illustrates this dynamic:

> Hear the word of the Lord, you rulers of Sodom;
> listen to the instruction of our God, you people of Gomorrah!

The correspondences between these two lines are obvious. Their grammatical structures are exactly alike—imperative + direct object and a vocative. Individual words also correspond to each other in meaning: "hear" / "listen to"; "word of the Lord" / "instruction of our God"; and "rulers of Sodom" / "people of Gomorrah."

As we said above, however, the second line is not simply a restatement of the first in different words; both lines betray subtle differences. For example, though some words overlap in meaning, they are not actually synonyms. "Instruction" (Heb. *tôrâ*) is not really another way of saying "word" (*dābār*) nor is "people" (*'am*) the exact counterpart of "rulers" (*qātsîn*). The Bible associates "word" with the message of a prophet and "instruction" with the teaching about the Law by a priest (see Jer 18:18). Similarly, "Sodom" and "Gomorrah" are not simply two names for the same town; they designate separate, though proximate, cities (cf. Gen 10:19; 14; 18). At the same time, when mentioned together (usually the case) they designate "twin cities of sin."

In our view, this combination of similarity and difference serves Isaiah's rhetorical purpose. On the one hand, it stresses that he wants to talk to everyone—both "rulers" and "people"—and cleverly implies that all are sinful (like residents of Sodom and Gomorrah). On the other hand, the change from "word" to "instruction" indicates a subtle but significant development in Isaiah's train of thought. "Word" signals that what follows is a divine revelation, while "instruction" tells the hearers to accept Isaiah's message as they would teaching by a priest.

This well-known saying of Jesus likewise combines similarity and difference rhetorically:

> Love your enemies,
> do good to those who hate you,
> bless those who curse you,
> pray for those who abuse you. (Lk 6:27b NRSV)[48]

Both grammatically and semantically, the four lines at first glance seem parallel. Each comprises an imperative and its direct object whose meanings apparently overlap (e.g., "love"//"do good," "enemies"//"those who hate you," etc.). A closer look, however, reveals subtle nuances in succeeding lines. The latter further clarify the meaning of the first: "enemies" are not military invaders but "those who hate you"; they are people who "curse" and

---

47 Alter, *The Art of Biblical Poetry*, 19.

48 This example comes from Gillingham, *Poems and Psalms*, 84. We commend her excellent discussion of parallelism in Jesus' poetic aphorisms (82–88).

"abuse" believers. To "love" them means to "do good" to them (i.e., to do whatever benefits them), to "bless" them (i.e., to wish them God's blessing), and to "pray" on their behalf.

These examples underscore what Kugel emphasizes: the relationships between lines of biblical poetry are amazingly complex.[49] The careful Bible student will determine what relationship exists between the poetic lines in each text taking care not to assume a simplistic notion that their unity boils down to one or two main principles. Rather, one must reckon the double logic of parallelism—that it simultaneously invokes the "logic of synonymity and the logic of progression."[50]

Basic Units of Parallelism

Traditionally, scholars subdivided parallelism into three types—synonymous, antithetical, and synthetic—depending on whether the succeeding line restated, contrasted, or developed the first, respectively.[51] Recent study, however, has tended to avoid those categories as overly simplistic and misleading.

So, below we will follow a recently proposed, useful scheme simply to suggest a few ways in which parallelism works. Our purpose is two-fold: (1) to sensitize students to the potential communicative power of parallelism, and (2) to help them thread their way through what otherwise might seem an impenetrable thicket of complexity. To do this we will first need to consider how scholars describe poetic lines. With this knowledge we will be able to describe poetic lines precisely and, more importantly, to visualize the similarities and differences between them. In turn, these preliminary steps will enable us to understand how the lines interrelate.

The technical term for a single line of poetry is *stich* (pronounced "stick").[52] Two parallel lines form a unit that scholars designate either as a *couplet* or a *distich*. Three parallel lines form a triplet or *tristich*. Just as the Bible's subdivision into chapters and verses allows us to identify its subparts, so scholars commonly assign a capital letter to each stich deemed parallel to the next line(s). Thus, the first line of a tristich would be "A" and the next two lines "B" and C," respectively. They also use small letters for the subparts within a single stich. Consider this example in which two stichs, designated A and B, are fairly synonymous (Psa 77:1):

	a	*b*	*c*
A	I cried out	to God	for help;
	a'	*b'*	*c'*
B	I cried out	to God	to hear me.

Both stichs have three parts labeled *a, b,* and *c* in A, and *a', b',* and *c'* in B. Two schematic principles are at work here. First, in each stich the same letter designates

---

49 Kugel, *The Idea of Biblical Poetry*, 2–7, provides an illustrative sample. As Alter warns (*The Art of Biblical Poetry*, 18), "the evidence of line after line of biblical verse suggests that we are too quick to infer automatic and formulaic rhetorical gesture of repetition when more than that is going on."

50 Longman, "Biblical Poetry," 84.

51 Cf. conveniently Petersen and Richards, *Interpreting Hebrew Poetry*, 24–27. As they point out, the traditional definition of synthetic parallelism has proved to be very problematic.

52 From Gk. *stichos* "row, line (of writing)"; plural *stichoi* (pronounced "STICK-oy"). Other scholars prefer the term "colon" (plural "cola"); Alter (*The Art of Biblical Poetry*, 9) opts for "verset," while Petersen and Richards favor "colon" or "line" (*Interpreting Hebrew Poetry*, 23).

elements that have the same meaning (are semantically parallel) or that play the same grammatical role in the sentence (are syntactically parallel). Second, the addition of ' to a letter (e.g., *a'*, called *"a prime"*) shows that it belongs to the second stich.[53] Thus, one would describe the structure of stich A as *a b c*, stich B as *a' b' c'*, and that of the whole verse as *a b c / a' b' c'*.

As a second example consider this verse in which the stichs express a contrast (Prov 14:34):

	a	*b*	*c*
A	Righteousness	exalts	a nation,
	-a	*-b*	*-c*
B	but sin	is a disgrace	to any people.

Syntactically, the two lines are parallel, but semantically they express opposite meanings. To indicate that contrast, we prefix the letters describing stich B with a minus sign (-). Hence, we describe its structure as *-a -b -c* and that of the entire verse as *a b c / -a -b -c*.

Frequently, however, a second (or third) stich may omit items found in the first, a phenomenon called *ellipsis*. For example, it is common for the second stich (B) to assume the presence of the verb from the first stich but not to repeat it. This omission leaves the second stich without a verb. Study this example (Amos 8:10):[54]

	a	*b*	*c*
A	I will turn	your religious feasts	into mourning
		B'	*c'*
B	and	all your singing	into weeping.

The second stich (B) assumes but omits a verb such as "I will turn" in the first stich (A). Presumably, the wording chosen for the second stich dictated the omission of the verb. That omission does not mean, however, that the second stich is shorter than the first. It may, in fact, be about the same length or even longer. When a succeeding element is longer than its parallel, we signal this with a capital letter (e.g., *B'* [B heavy prime] on line B above).[55]

In other cases, the second stich (B) may omit the verb and add elements unparalleled in the first:

---

53 Were there a third parallel line, each of its components would bear a double prime (e.g., *a"* called "a double prime"). Those of a fourth parallel line (a rare but possible occurrence) would have "*a* triple prime" (e.g., *a'''*).

54 We owe the first example to LaSor, et al., *Old Testament Survey*, 233, the second to Kugel, *The Idea of Biblical Poetry*, 6. For "ellipsis" Alter prefers the term "hidden repetition" (*The Art of Biblical Poetry*, 23; cf. his illuminating discussion of the phenomenon, 24–26).

55 In Mary's Magnificat (Lk 1:52 NRSV), though A ends with a prepositional phrase, B omits it: "He [God] has brought down the powerful from their thrones, / and lifted up the lowly (...)." The parallelism is *a b c d / a' b' c'*; cf. Bailey and Vander Broek, *Literary Forms*, 163–64.

	a	*b*	
A	He summons	the heavens above,	
		b'	*c*
B	and	the earth,	that he may judge his people.
			(Psa 50:4; cf. Amos 9:10)

The second stich omits (but assumes) the verb "he summons" but also adds a phrase (*c*) that, quite significantly, specifies the purpose of that summons. In other words, rather than simply restate the point of A, here the second one further *develops* it by stating its purpose.[56] This example has the structure *a b / b' c.*

How Parallelism Works

The relationships that bind parallel stichs range across a continuum of increasing complexity—a complexity that is not adequately described by the traditional categories of parallelism (i.e., synonymous, antithetical, synthetic). At one end of the continuum are the rare cases of synonymous parallelism in which the second stich simply restates the first in different words (Prov 19:5):

> A false witness will not go unpunished,
> and he who pours out lies will not go free.[57]

The parallels are obvious: "false witness"/"he who pours out lies" and "will not go unpunished"/"will not go free." There is no perceptible development from the first line to the second. At the other end of the continuum are cases in which line B shows no similarity at all to the first (Psa 115:18):

> It is we who extol the Lord,
> both now and forevermore.

In this case, B completes the first grammatically; the two stichs form a single sentence.[58] As we shall see, most biblical poetry falls somewhere between these two extremes. In order to determine where a stich should be placed on the continuum we need to understand the dynamics of parallelism—how it works. This understanding is crucial for an accurate analysis of poetry.

As Berlin has shown, parallel lines may interrelate grammatically, lexically and semantically, and phonologically.[59] Some parallels are interrelated by only one of these

---

56 Because *c* does not repeat anything from line A, it is not called "*c* prime." Notice also the development from "heavens" to "earth," that is, from the upper extreme of the created cosmos to the lower one. Such paired extremes (heaven and earth) are called *merismus* (see below).

57 Cf. Alter, *The Art of Biblical Poetry*, 22; Job 27:4. Here belong also the even more extreme, rare exact parallelisms, that is, repeated refrains like "for his loyalty is forever" (Psa 136) or "praise him" (Psa 150); cf. Berlin, *Dynamics*, 130.

58 Cf. Berlin, *Dynamics*, 90, n. 42.

59 Here we offer a simplified overview of Berlin's excellent, detailed treatment (*Dynamics*, 31–126; cf. also the summary paradigm, 29).

factors, others by all three. The *grammatical factor* is the structural skeleton of parallelism. It concerns the elements of grammar (tense, mood, case, number, etc.) that appear in each line of a parallel pair. For example, in comparing stichs, one might observe a change in nouns from singular to plural or in verbs from present to future tense. Stich A might make a statement while its parallel (stich B) asks a question; another stich might state something positively, while its parallel states it negatively.[60]

If grammar provides the skeleton, the *lexical-semantic factor* provides the flesh and blood.[61] This aspect focuses on the relationship between the specific words in each parallel line. For example, like their linguistic kinsfolk at ancient Ugarit, Hebrew poets often built their poetry around "word pairs," sets of words commonly associated together.[62] This explains why parallel lines commonly develop around pairs of synonyms (eat/drink, earth/dust) or antonyms (right/left, there is/there are not).[63] At the same time, it also permits a poet to juxtapose two nonassociated words creatively for poetic effect (for examples, see below).

The *phonologic factor* refers to the use of words of similar sounds (e.g., word-play or paronomasia) either within a single stich or in parallel ones. English speakers commonly use this delightful device for rhetorical effect. One popular joke, for example, tells of a man condemned to hang for continuously making puns. As he stood on the scaffold, the merciful crowd commuted his sentence, to which he replied, "No noose is good news!" Of course, to access this aspect in the OT the student must read the Hebrew aloud, listening for similar sounds. Nevertheless, English Bible readers need to understand this phenomenon because biblical commentators often refer to it. Occasionally, footnotes in English translations point out puns on Hebrew names (in NIV, e.g., Jer 1:12; 19:7; Mic 1:10–15; etc.).

Types of Parallelism

How do parallel lines of Hebrew poetry interrelate? Here we follow the three main "variations" of parallelism proposed by Gillingham to express further nuances of Kugel's basic definition "A, then B."[64] We have gleaned some examples from recent studies and arranged them systematically within Gillingham's categories. Our purpose is to train the reader's eye to identify parallelism and to provide some terms to describe how the lines function—key elements in interpreting poetry.

---

60 Cf. the examples provided by Berlin, *Dynamics*, 56–57, 59: "For in Death there is no mention of you / In Sheol who can acclaim you?" (Psa 6:5 [Heb. 6]). "My son, do not forget my teaching / And let your heart guard my commandments" (Prov 3:1).

61 Berlin, *Dynamics*, 64.

62 Cf. Y. Avishur, *Stylistic Studies of Word-Pairs in Biblical and Ancient Semitic Literatures* (Neukirchener-Vluyn: Neukirchener, 1984). For catalogs of this phenomenon, see M. Dahood, "Ugaritic-Hebrew Parallel Pairs," *Ras Shamra Parallels* [=*RSP*] (Rome: Biblical Institute Press, 1972), 1:71–382 (ed. L. R. Fisher); *RSP* (1975), 2:1–39 (ed. L. R. Fisher); *RSP* (1981), 3:1–206 (ed. S. Rummel). For its interpretation, see Berlin, *Dynamics*, 65–102.

63 Watson, *Classical Hebrew Poetry*, 131–32 (cf. also his fine overview, 128–44).

64 Gillingham, *Poems and Psalms*, 78–82. The subcategories below, however, are our own, based on examples gleaned from Berlin, Alter, and Kugel. We are grateful to our colleague, Professor D. Carroll R., for supplying examples used below from the book of Amos.

1. The first variation of parallelism (A = B) occurs when A and B are interchangeable in some fashion—i.e., B either echoes or contrasts A.[65] In Jesus' famous words, for example, B simply echoes A (i.e., *a b c / a' b' c'*):

		a	*b*	*c*
A	For	my yoke	is	easy
		a'	*b'*	*c'*
B	and	my burden	is	light	(Mt 11:30)

On the other hand, Prov 11:20 (NCV) illustrates how A=B also may signal a contrast:

		a	*b*	*c*
A		The LORD	hates	those with evil hearts
			-b	*-c*
B	but		is pleased with	those who are innocent.

The ellipsis of the subject ("the Lord") and the contrast in B produces the parallelism *a b c / -b -c*. The verse sharply contrasts Yahweh's response to two kinds of people. He "hates" the wicked but "is pleased with" the righteous. This comprises an "antithetical" contrast because it speaks of opposites that share no common ground. In the Bible, good and evil are opposites engaged in deadly combat. Because of his nature, Yahweh cannot delight in the wicked nor detest the righteous. In passing, one should notice the double-edge this proverb wields—it both encourages and warns. On the one hand, it encourages the righteous to keep up their blameless lives. On the other, it warns the wicked to abandon their hateful conduct.

Occasionally, parallel lines may convey a contrast that is not antithetical. For this reason we define this category as one of "contrast," not "antithesis."[66] Consider Judg 5:25:

		a	*b*		*c*
A		He	asked for		water,
		a'	*b'*	*d*	*c'*
B	and	she	gave	him	milk.

The line contrasts the water, which the Canaanite general Sisera sought, and the milk, which the Kenite woman, Jael, served him. Unlike the previous example, there is no antithesis here, for water and milk are acceptable alternatives, not direct opposites. In sum, parallelism of contrast involves both simple contrast and actual antithesis.

2. In the second variation of parallelism (A > B), A states the main idea while B qualifies it, thus more fully bringing the thought of A to completion. For example, biblical poetry often displays a parallelism of *subordination* in which the second stich is

---

65 This "variation" combines the older categories of synonymous and antithetical parallelism. As examples, Gillingham cites Job 10:12; Psa 33:6–7; Isa 62:1; Amos 9:2; Mt 5:42//Lk 6:30; Mk 10:38//Mt 20:22; Lk 11:17 (in our view, wrongly); Mk 13:24–25//Mt 24:29; Lk 6:27, 37–38//Mt 7:1–2; Lk 15:32; 16:10; cf. Gillingham, *Poems and Psalms*, 78–80, 84–85. For other examples of contrast, see Amos 6:3, 6; 8:8.

66 So Berlin, *Dynamics*, 95.

grammatically subordinate to its parallel. In Psa 111:6, for example, stich B describes the *means* by which Yahweh accomplished what stich A stated:[67]

A   He has shown his people the power of his works,
B   giving them the lands of other nations.

In other words, A leaves the reader with a question: how did Yahweh show his people his power? The B stich answers it: he displayed it by taking territory owned by other nations and giving it to his people.

It is also common for one stich to state the *reason* for the claims of the other, as Exod 15:21 shows:

A   Sing to the LORD,   (statement)
B   for he is highly exalted.   (reason)
C   The horse and its rider   (example)
D   he has hurled into the sea.

Correct interpretation requires the reader carefully to follow the logic of each line. "Sing to the Lord" states the main idea, demanding that one burst into song. But why should one sing Yahweh's praise? Because he is a "highly exalted" God (cf. also Psa 13:6). That is, he is the cosmic ruler of heaven and earth. But the verse answers one last question: What evidence confirms his exalted position? The answer follows: "The horse and its rider he has hurled into the sea"—an allusion to Yahweh's stunning defeat of Pharaoh at the Red Sea. In sum, in this case the poet qualifies the command with a reason, then supports the reason with an example (see also Psa 106:1; 107:1). To understand the poet's meaning properly, one must walk through the lines, sorting out each one as we did above.

In other cases, one stich specifies the *time* of its parallel:

A   By the rivers of Babylon
         we sat and wept   (statement)
B   when we remembered Zion. (Psa 137:1)   (temporal clause)[68]

Here the poet describes how exiled Israelites sat down and wept in Babylon. The temporal clause defines the time when they wept—when they remembered Zion, the holy mountain in their homeland. Implicitly, however, the temporal clause also reveals the reason for the people's grief—memory of beloved Zion.[69]

---

67 So Berlin, *Dynamics*, 81; cf. Amos 4:1b-c; 5:15a; Gillingham, *Poems and Psalms*, 80–81 and 85–86, who offers other examples (Gen 4:24; Prov 30:8; Isa 45:12; Jer 2:15; Mt 6:12//Lk 11:4; Mt 7:7–8//Lk 11:9–10; Mt 7:17; Mk 2:27; Lk 12:48, 49–50; 18:14).

68 Cf. Psa 14:7b, "When the Lord restores the fortunes of his people [temporal clause] / let Jacob rejoice and (let) Israel be glad!" [call to rejoice]. In this case, the statement also expresses the *result* of the temporal clause.

69 Cf. also cases where one stich is a prepositional phrase subordinate to the other: "There on the poplars / we hung our harps" (Psa 137:2; so Alter, *The Art of Biblical Poetry*, 19). Cf. Judg 5:25b.

The careful student must learn to distinguish both types and to interpret such cases accordingly.

3. The third variation of parallelism (A < B) occurs when A states the introductory idea on which B expands to complement or complete A. In cases of parallelism of *continuation,* for example, succeeding parallel lines present a progression of thought. For example, observe how Isa 40:9 creates the illusion of simple repetition but actually portrays progress:[70]

A	You who bring good tidings to Zion,
B	go up on a high mountain.
C	You who bring good tidings to Jerusalem,
D	lift up your voice with a shout,
E	lift it up, do not be afraid;
F	say to the towns of Judah,
G	"Here is your God!"

At first glance, repeated phrases and parallel words create the impression that succeeding lines restate the first in other words.[71] Actually, the text paints the actions of the messenger in the order in which they would normally occur. First, he would ascend a high mountain to address a large area, and then he would shout out his message. Only then would he say, "Here is your God!"—reserved here for the climactic last line. Hence, to understand such examples, the reader must look past the illusion of repetition and think through the logic of each line to discover how each interacts with its predecessor. Failure to work through this process will result in a misreading of the text.

In a parallelism of *comparison,* parallel lines form a simile, that is, a comparison. (For similes, see below; Amos 2:13). Psa 103:13 illustrates this common parallelism:

A	As a father has compassion on his children,
B	so the LORD has compassion on those who fear him.

Here the psalmist describes the Lord's compassion by comparing it to that of a father toward his children. He explains the unknown (or lesser known)—the Lord's compassion—by appeal to something well (or at least better) known—the compassion of a father. Through the comparison, the poet puts flesh on what otherwise would remain an abstract idea ("the Lord has compassion"). Implicitly, he recalls the reader's own childhood experiences—how mercifully his or her father had glossed over glaring goofs with a smile and a hug. The reader now visualizes the Lord's mercy along similar lines. And that is the point—"the Lord has compassion." But this couplet also subtly explains who are the Lord's children—not just ethnic Israelites, but "those who fear him."

Sometimes, however, the comparison is implicit rather than explicit. We say "implicit" because in these cases the Hebrew text lacks the explicit signals of the simile—the words

---

70 Cf. Berlin, *Dynamics,* 90–91, who, however, offers a more technical linguistic discussion; cf. also Isa 16:5; Amos 1:5, 8; Eph 5:14; 2 Tim 2:11–13. Gillingham's examples of the A < B variation (*Poems and Psalms,* 81–82 and 86–87) include Judg 5:4–5, 26–27; Psa 29:1, 10; 77:17; Isa 40:3; Jer 31:21; Mt 7:11//Lk 11:13; Mt 8:20//Lk 9:58; Mt 10:32–33//Lk 12:8–9; Mt 15:11; Lk 9:24//Mt 16:25//Mk 8:35. Cf. also Amos 1:4–5; 5:5–6, 15.

71 I.e., "you who bring good tidings," / "lift up (your voice)," "Zion" / "Jerusalem."

"like" or "as." Instead, it simply aligns two stichs side-by-side without clarifying their connection (i.e., a metaphor). Consider how Psa 125:2 reads literally:

A   Jerusalem—mountains surround it;
B   And YHWH surrounds his people.[72]

Why did the psalmist arrange these two stichs together? How do they interrelate? Obviously, he juxtaposed "mountains" and "YHWH" (Yahweh) because they somehow compare. What do they have in common? Both protect Jerusalem from the attacks of her enemies. Hence, the couplet compares the protection both offer. As before, the poet speaks of an abstract idea in a concrete way. The line about Jerusalem's mountains serves as a simile for the protection given by Yahweh. Recognizing this, the NIV rightly makes the implicit simile explicit by using the English grammatical marker "as":

> As the mountains surround Jerusalem
> so the LORD surrounds his people. [73]

Pondering Yahweh's protection, one imagines it to be a huge, towering wall of solid rock—something impossible for enemies to penetrate. To understand the poet's meaning, the reader must determine how mountains and the Lord compare, and whether the psalmist's real focus is on the mountains or on the Lord (obviously, the latter). When interpreting comparisons, the student must take care to avoid being preoccupied with the simile distinction (the meaning of "mountains" or "father"), as if that were the poet's meaning. Rather, the student must seek to understand the main point (the Lord's compassion or protection) in light of the simile's portrait.

A comparison also underlies examples where poets invoke the traditional argument "from the lesser to the greater." Jesus' saying in Mt 7:11 (NRSV) exemplifies this:[74]

A   If you then, who are evil, know how to give good gifts to your children,
B   how much more will your Father in heaven give good things to those who ask him!

The lines compare the generosity of earthly fathers, who are "evil," with that of "your Father in heaven," who presumably is "righteous." The comparison argues that if the former (the "lesser") give their children gifts, the latter ("the greater") will do so even more generously if asked. Clearly, B gives the main point after the introduction by A.

In the parallelism of *specification,* each succeeding stich makes more specific what the opening stich states in general terms. In other words, the movement is from general to specific.[75] There are various forms of specification. Sometimes it has to do with spatial or geographic entities. Isa 45:12 illustrates this type (NRSV, our italics):

---

72 The example and translation come from Berlin, *Dynamics*, 101 (cf. the entire discussion and other examples, 100–101).

73 Cf. also Prov 26:9.

74 Cf. Gillingham, *Poems and Psalms*, 86.

75 We owe much of what follows to Alter, *The Art of Biblical Poetry*, 9–26; cf. his comment (19): "The rule of thumb . . . is that the general term occurs in the first verset [i.e., stich] and a more specific instance of the general category in the second verset." Cf. Amos 5:15a.

A	I made the *earth,*	(general)
B	and created *humankind upon it;*	(specific)
C	it was my hands that stretched out the *heavens,*	(general)
D	and I commanded all their *host.*	(specific)

In these two distichs, Yahweh affirms that he created the universe.[76] Observe how each first line (A, C) concerns a general geographical realm (the earth, the heavens) while the second (B, D) focuses in on something more specific within that realm, namely, its inhabitants. This movement, from general to specific, narrows the reader's attention to a smaller perspective. At the same time, lines CD continue the thought of AB concerning the theme "Yahweh is sovereign creator." They do so by shifting the site of that sovereignty from earth (AB) to the heavens where he "commanded" (and "commands") their mighty army ("their host")—the means through which God can rescue Israel.

In other cases of this type, succeeding stichs provide an explanation of the opening line. Consider, for example, how the lines in Isa 48:20b-21 explain the opening line by giving specifics:

A	Say, "The LORD *has redeemed* his servant Jacob.
B	And they *did not thirst* in the deserts where he led them;
C	water from a rock he *made flow* for them.
D	He *split* a rock and *water gushed out.*"[77]

The first line (A) offers the general statement "the Lord has redeemed Israel"; those that follow (B, C, D) explain that redemption. Further, the following lines become increasingly more specific, each implicitly answering a question arising from its immediate parallel. Alter describes this technique as an "explanatory chain":

> What does it mean that God "redeemed" Israel (first verset [i.e., line])? They were not thirsty in the desert (second verset). How could they not have been thirsty?—because He made water flow from a rock (third verset). How did He make water flow from a rock?—by splitting it so the water gushed (fourth verset).[78]

The poet might have taken the subject of Israel's redemption in many directions. His comments might have recalled, for example, the defeat of Pharaoh at the Red Sea, the wondrous provision of manna, Israel's freedom from slavery, or the meeting with God at Mt. Sinai. Instead, he focused on one episode—the day Yahweh split a rock to give Israel water (cf. Num 20:11). Again, proper interpretation carefully considers the development of thought between the opening and subsequent lines.

In another variety of the parallelism of specification, the second stich specifies the first in a dramatic fashion; the general terms of stich A are followed by striking language in B. Notice, for example, the dramatic effect achieved by a simple change in a verb:

---

76 In context, the strophe provides evidence to banish his people's doubt about his ability to bring them home from exile (see vv. 11–13). The argument (technically, "from the greater to the lesser") runs: "If my power made the whole massive cosmos, it can certainly redeem Israel from human hands."

77 Our translation; italics as in Alter, *The Art of Biblical Poetry*, 20.

78 Alter, *The Art of Biblical Poetry*, 20.

A   The desert tribes will *bow before him*
B   and his enemies will *lick the dust.*. (Psa 72:9, our italics)

The context is prayer for a successful reign by Israel's king, perhaps on the occasion of his coronation.[79] The speaker (possibly a priest) affirms one aspect of that hoped-for success: the king's wide dominion. Typically, stich A makes a general statement that desert tribes will submit to the king's rule. In ancient custom to "bow before" someone was to show that person great honor. Stich B, however, gives two specifics: it details that these tribes are not royal friends but "enemies," and it graphically portrays their bowing—they "lick the dust." The startling language dramatically states the completeness of their surrender.

In yet another variety, the second stich may specify the purpose of the first. Consider Prov 4:1, for example:

	a	*b*
A	Listen, my sons,	to a father's instruction;
	a'	*c*
B	pay attention	[to a father's instruction] and gain understanding.

The parallelism between "listen" (a) and "pay attention" (a') creates the impression that B (*a' c*) simply restates A. The ellipsis of *b* ("to a father's instruction"), however, permits the poet some rhythmic space to add a purpose clause (*c,* "and gain understanding"). Thus, *a' c* goes beyond a mere restatement of *a b*—it specifies the latter's purpose (Why should a son listen to his father's teaching? To gain understanding). The complementary nature of the second stich must be recognized for a proper interpretation. A correct paraphrase of the proverb would be: a wise son listens to his father's teaching so that he may gain understanding.

The last major use of the A < B variation of parallelism is the parallelism of *intensification.* Intensification occurs when the second stich of a couplet restates the first in a more pointed, extreme, or forceful way. To paraphrase the dynamics, we might say the second develops the first by saying, "Not only that but more so!"[80] The effect of this intensified language is to heighten the poetic power of the entire distich. The most obvious example of intensification is the use of numbers in parallelism. Consider this verse from Moses' farewell address to Israel shortly before his death:

A   How could *one* man chase a *thousand,*
B   or *two* put *ten thousand* to flight? (Deut 32:30, italics ours)

Obviously, the numbers "one" and "two" or "thousand" and "ten thousand" are not synonyms but paired lesser-to-greater amounts. Moses' question invokes two hypothetical military manpower ratios, the second greater than the first, to highlight the great odds against victory. Now, after the 1:1000 ratio in A, the word "two" in B primes the reader to expect a doubled ratio of 2:2000. Instead, "ten thousand" unexpectedly

---

79 Cf. E. S. Gerstenberger, *Psalms 1*, FOTL 14 (Grand Rapids: Eerdmans, 1988) 19; Pss 2; 110.

80 Alter, *The Art of Biblical Poetry*, 11, who compares it to the *a fortiori* logical argument; cf. Kugel's summary formula "A is so, *what's more,* B is so" (*The Idea of Biblical Poetry*, 8). This compares to what some scholars call "climactic parallelism"; so L. Ryken, *Words of Delight* (Grand Rapids: Baker, 1987), 181–82. For other examples, see Amos 1:11; 2:2b; 2:14–16; 5:16b–17; 9:2–4.

increases the odds ten times to achieve a climatic poetic effect: to heighten the image of the stunning military rout to which Moses refers.[81]

Intensification occurs in other ways as well. Observe, for example, the contrast of intensity between the verbs in this verse:

A   Your granaries *will be filled* with abundance,
B   with new wine your vats will *burst*. (Prov 3:10, Alter's translation, our italics)

In content, the lines supplement each other: A is about grain, B is about wine. Taken together, they make the single point that God will amply provide for those who honor him (i.e., both food and drink). There is an emotive contrast, however, between the verbs "be filled" and "burst." The former describes a passive state; the latter paints a dramatic picture of action with a touch of hyperbole. That is, Israel will have so much wine that her vats will burst! Other poets achieve the same effect by stringing together parallel nouns. Consider, for example, these lines:

A   Is your love declared in the grave,
B   your faithfulness in Destruction (*ᵃbaddôn*)?
C   Are your wonders known in the place of darkness,
D   or your righteous deeds in the land of oblivion?
     (Psa 88:11–12 [Heb. 12–13]; cf. Isa 59:9–10)

In context, the psalmist presses Yahweh to save him from death. Surprisingly, he argues that God should do so because only the living, not the dead, are able to praise Yahweh. As Alter notes, however, the language combines two sets of parallel words, one fairly synonymous, the other signaling development. The near synonyms are "love" / "faithfulness" and "wonders" / "righteous deeds." The other set, however, "carries forward a progressive imaginative realization of death."[82] The poet first pairs the common term "grave" with the poetic synonym "Destruction" (*ᵃbaddôn*). The latter steps up the emotive intensity slightly by pointing out the grim fate—extinction—that the grave cruelly imposes.

Then, he parallels another everyday word (darkness) with a second poetic expression for the underworld (the land of oblivion). "Darkness" goes beyond "grave," however, because it introduces the sensory experience of death, thereby making the fate more personal. Finally, "land of oblivion" both summarizes the previous lines and brings them to an emphatic close. It implies that "death is a realm where human beings are utterly forgotten and extinct, and where there can be no question of God's greatness being recalled."[83]

Now, in some texts, the student may have difficulty distinguishing the dimension of intensification from that of specification since the two overlap somewhat. We must also allow the possibility that both phenomena may be present in a single passage. This may be the case, for example, in this well-known line from Paul's short hymn to Christ (Phil 2:6–11): "he humbled himself and became obedient to the point of death—even death on

---

81 Cf. also "seven" / "seventy-seven" in Lamech's boast (Gen 4:24). A more common phenomenon is to parallel a number with a number larger by one (e.g., "three" / "four," Prov 30:15, 18; Amos 1:3, 6, 9; etc.; "seven"/ "eight," Eccl 11:2; Mic 5:5 [Heb 4]). Scholars describe this device with the formula "n / n + 1." For a full discussion of numerical parallelism, see Watson, *Classical Hebrew Poetry*, 144–49.

82 Alter, *The Art of Biblical Poetry*, 14.

83 Alter, *The Art of Biblical Poetry*, 14.

a cross" (v. 8b NRSV).[84] Paul affirms that Jesus' humble obedience to God led him voluntarily to accept death, but the last line ("even death on a cross") offers both specification of *how* he died (i.e., by execution as a criminal, not of natural causes) and emotional intensification in "cross" (i.e., an image of "the ultimate in human degradation").[85]

With any poem the student must scrutinize succeeding poetic lines to define precisely what relationship links them. As Petersen and Richards point out, "The juxtaposition of an A and B provides the opportunity for an almost infinite number of correspondences."[86]

By way of summary, parallelism presents readers a wide range of colorful and creative ways of expression. In our analysis, we have detected numerous ways parallelism works. Perhaps it would help, at the conclusion of this section, to display these ways in outline form. We have described three major ways that parallelism works (A = B, A > B, and A < B), which can be further delineated into seven categories. Then, we suggested subdivisions for two of the categories.

Types of Hebrew parallelism.

A = B	1.	Echo
	2.	Contrast
A > B	3.	Subordination
		Means
		Reason
		Time
A < B	4.	Continuation
	5.	Comparison
	6.	Specification
		Spatial
		Explanation
		Dramatic effect
		Purpose
	7.	Intensification

Other Poetic Structures

To conclude our survey of Hebrew poetic structure, we introduce the reader to other distinct structural devices that are common among biblical poets. As its name implies, *staircase (or stairstep) parallelism* is a couplet (or tristich) in which the succeeding lines

---

84 There is general agreement that these verses comprise an early Christian hymn, but there is no consensus as to its strophic structure and its authorship (the possibilities: Paul, another early Christian, a borrowing from non-Christian sources); for full discussion, see R. P. Martin, *A Hymn of Christ: Philippians 2:5–11 in Recent Interpretation and In the Setting of Early Christian Worship* (Downers Grove: InterVarsity Press, 1997); and G. F. Hawthorne, *Philippians*, WBC 43 (Waco, TX: Word, 1983), 76–79. For a theological exposition of the hymn in the context of Paul's understanding of the cross, see G. B. Caird, *Paul: An Introduction to His Thought*, Outstanding Christian Thinkers Series (London: Geoffrey Chapman, 1994), 105–109.

85 Hawthorne, *Philippians*, 90, who also observes (89) how grammatically the "intensive or explicative [Greek] conjunction *de* ("even") . . . calls special attention to this most striking element in the humiliation of Christ"; cf. Martin, *Hymn of Christ*, 228 ("the lowest point in the dramatic parabola").

86 Petersen and Richards, *Interpreting Hebrew Poetry*, 35.

develop in steps.[87] That is, they add things not found in the opening couplet, frequently with the use of ellipsis. Observe the stairstep structure of these three examples:

A   Return, O Virgin Israel,

B   return   to your towns. (Jer 31:21b)

A   Awake, my soul!

B   Awake,   harp and lyre!

C   I will awaken   the dawn. (Psa 57:8 [Heb. 9])[88]

A   What has come into being in him was *life*,

B   and   the *life* was the *light* of all people.

C   The *light* shines in the *darkness*,

D   and   the *darkness* did not overcome it.

          (John 1:4–6 NRSV, our italics)[89]

In the example from John 1 "life" marks A as the first staircase step and becomes the initial key word in the next step (B). To "life" B adds "light" which then becomes the initial key word in the third step (C), while C concludes with "darkness" which provides the initial key word for the final step (D). Paired words link pairs of lines (i.e., "life" [A // B], "light" [B // C], "darkness" [C // D]) and lay out a stairstep development of thought through the addition of new key words in succeeding lines. In short, by combining repetition and variation, follow-up lines extend the thought of the first forming a verbal "staircase." The concluding element actually completes the thought. The poetic effect is for each line to build on its predecessor, the last line serving as a kind of climax.

Chiasm (or chiasmus) is another common structural device in which the word order of a parallel line is the reverse of its predecessor (*a b / b' a*). Lines drawn between the parallel elements would form an X—the Greek letter *chi* from which the device draws its name. Generally the chiasm can be observed only in the Hebrew text (cf. Job 6:15; Psa 137:5–6a; Amos 5:7, 14–15, 24), but occasionally it is reflected in the English translation. Observe this example from Lk 1:71–74. Note how the lines hinge on the central affirmation of God's covenant. The words "enemies" and "father(s)" indicate the parallels.

a   salvation from our *enemies*

          and from the hand of all who hate us—

b   to show mercy to our *fathers*

c   and to remember his holy covenant,

b'   the oath he swore to our *father* Abraham:

a'   to rescue us from the hand of our *enemies*,

          and to enable us to serve him without fear.

---

87 Cf. Watson, *Classical Hebrew Poetry*, 150–56.

88 These examples (but not their translation) come from Watson, *Classical Hebrew Poetry*, 151.

89 Expanded and adapted from Ryken, *Words of Life*, 101, who observes how "the last key word in a line becomes the first main word in the next line."

Study the word order reversal and X pattern (*a b c* / *b 'c' a'* and *a b c* / *c' b' a*) of these examples:

a	*b*	*c*	
In Judah	God	is known;	
	b'	*c'*	*a'*
	his name	is great	in Israel. (Psa 76:1)

a	*b*	*c*
The sabbath	was made	for humankind,
c'		*a'*
and not *humankind* ( )		for the *Sabbath*. (Mark 2:27 NRSV, our italics)[90]

The chiasm in the first example hinges on the reversal of the parallel elements "in Judah"/ "in Israel" and "is known" / "is great." In the second, the words "sabbath" and "humankind" exchange places. Usually, chiasm is more than just a decorative device. Poets use it to convey something about the meaning of the lines concerned. For example, a poet might use chiasm to underscore the contrast between the content of two stichs (to show a reversal of fate or to stress their antithesis [cf. antithetical proverbs]). The Bible student, thus, must analyze how each case of chiasm affects the meaning of the biblical text.[91]

The use of chiasm is not limited to individual parallel lines. We also find examples of *extended chiasm* in the Bible, that is, chiastic structures that underlie entire passages and even entire books.[92] When extended chiasm occurs, the second half of a text or book corresponds to its first half except in reverse order. Each corresponding section has parallel content, and in the case of single texts, often the very same or similar words.

Further, the climax of an extended chiasm falls in the structural center of the text, the one section that lacks a parallel. The climax constitutes the structural hinge or turning point that joins the text's two halves. This is precisely where we find the main point of the passage. Finally, a text's secondary emphasis appears in its frames, that is, in the sections at the beginning and the end (i.e., A and A').

---

90 Adapted from Bailey and Vander Broek, *Literary Forms*, 178.

91 For further discussion with examples, see Gillingham, *The Poems and Psalms*, 78–82; Watson, *Classical Hebrew Poetry*, 201–208. Chiasm also occurs in lines of prose texts (e.g., Gen 4:4–5; Ruth 1:14; et al). On chiasm in the NT see J. L. Bailey and L. D. Vander Broek, *Literary Forms*, 49–54, 178–83.

92 Cf. Amos 2:11–12; 5:1–17. Extended chiasm was a common literary technique in the ancient Near East. J. W. Welch, ed., *Chiasmus in Antiquity: Structures, Analyses, Exegesis* (Hildesheim: Gerstenberg, 1981; repr. Provo: Research Press, 1998 with updated bibliography) provides the best critical collection of suggested biblical and extra-biblical examples. J. Lundbom, *Jeremiah: A Study in Hebrew Rhetoric*, 2d ed. (Winona Lake, IN: Eisenbrauns, 1997), 82–146, explores the topic in Jeremiah, and I. H. Thomson, *Chiasmus in the Pauline Letters*, JSNTSup 111 (Sheffield: Sheffield Academic Press, 1995) does the same for the Pauline epistles. For other NT examples, see N. W. Lund, *Chiasmus in the New Testament* (Peabody, MA: Hendrickson, 1992; repr.); J. A. Draper, "Genesis and Narrative Thrust of the Paraenesis in the Sermon on the Mount," *JSNT* 75 (1999) 25–48; and C. L. Blomberg, "The Structure of 2 Corinthians 1–7," *Criswell Theological Review* 4 (1989): 7–8 (with bibliography).

Jer 2:5–9 offers an example of extended chiasm in a single text. Observe the correspondence between parallel parts (e.g., A / A', B / B', etc.), the inverse order of the second half, and the turning point (E in all caps).[93] To highlight the links between sections, we have set key words in italics:

This Yahweh has said:

A	What did your *fathers* find wrong with me,	2:5
	to keep their distance from me?	
B	Chasing "Delusion" and being deluded,	
C	*Never saying:*	:6
	"Where is Yahweh?"	
D	who brought us from the *land,* Egypt,	
	steered us through the desert,	:7
	through the *land* of steppe and chasm,	
	through the *land* both hot and dark,	
	through the *land* no one crosses,	
	where no man lives.	
E	I BROUGHT YOU TO AN ORCHARD LAND, TO EAT ITS LOVELY FRUIT.	
D'	But, on arrival you fouled my *land,*	
	my bequest you made disgusting.	
C'	The priests *never said:*	:8
	"Where is Yahweh?"	
	Law-experts did not know me,	
	pastors rebelled against me;	
B'	prophets prophesied by Baal,	
	and after "no-go(o)ds" ran.	
A'	So, my case against you rests,	:9
	Yahweh's word,	
	against your *grandchildren* is my case.	

The parallels between most of the corresponding sections are evident. C' repeats the wording of C while D' recalls the emphasis on land in D. B' clarifies the word "delusion" in B as a reference to idolatry, while the familial terms "fathers" (A) and "grandchildren" (A') parallel each other. Without a parallel, E forms the structural hinge and states the text's main point: that Yahweh (vice Baal) brought Israel to a fruitful (vice barren) land. The frames A / A' state that Yahweh condemns all Israel, both ancestors and descendants. Obviously, an understanding of the structure provides a key starting point for interpreting passages such as this. It helps readers to isolate the text's main point, and that in turn enables them to interpret the whole text—i.e., to study how the surrounding content supports that point.

---

93 The example (slightly modified) comes from W. G. E. Watson, "Chiastic Patterns in Biblical Hebrew Poetry," in Welch, ed., *Chiasmus in Antiquity,* 141.

Extended chiasm may also underlie the overall structure of a biblical book. For example, study the detailed, parallel structure proposed by Alden for the Song of Songs:[94]

A 1:1–4a "Take me away"
  B 1:4b Friends speak
    C 1:5–7 "My own vineyard"
      D 1:8–14 "Breasts," "silver," "we will make"
        E 1:15–2:2 "House"
          F 2:3–7 "His left arm" "daughters of Jerusalem … so desires," "apple," "love"
            G 2:8–13 "Fragrance," "come my darling," "blossoming"
              H 2:14–15 "Vineyards," "show me"
                I 2:16–17 "My lover is mine"
                  Ja 3:1–5 "The watchmen found me"
                    Jb 3:6–11 Description of carriage, "gold," "Lebanon," "daughters of Jerusalem"
                  Jc 4:1–7 Description of girl, "Your eyes … hair … teeth"
                K 4:8–15 "Myrrh," "spice," "honey," "honeycomb," "wine," "milk"
                  L 4:16 "Into his garden"
                  L' 5:1a "Into my garden"
                K' 5:1bc "Myrrh," "spice," "honey," "honeycomb," "wine," "milk"
                  J'c 6:4–11 Description of girl, "Your eyes, … hair … teeth"
                    J'b 5:10–6:1 "Gold," "Lebanon," "daughters of Jerusalem"
                  J'a 5:2–9 "The watchmen found me"
                I' 6:2–3 "My lover is mine"
              H' 6:13–7:9a [10a] "Vines," "wine," "that we may gaze on you"
            G' 7:9b-13 [10b-14] "Fragrance," "come my darling," "blossom"
          F' 8:1–5 "His left arm," "daughters of Jerusalem … so desires," "apple," "love
        E' 8:6–7 "House"
      D' 8:8–9 "Breasts," "silver," "we will build"
    C' 8:10–12 "My own vineyard"
  B' 8:13 "Friends"
A' 8:14 "Come away"

According to this structure the book's main focus is on *L // L'* and the motif of intimate human love ("Into his/my garden"). This glimpse of the book's overall structure

---

94 Reproduced with the permission of R. L. Alden in D. E. Garrett, *Proverbs, Ecclesiastes, Song of Songs,* NAC 14 (Nashville: Broadman, 1993), 376. For a suggested, simple chiasm underlying the Book of Revelation, see Lund, *Chiasmus in the New Testament,* 325–26, and his discussion (326–30); for a suggested chiastic structure underlying the book of Kings, see Y. T. Radday, "Chiasmus in Hebrew Biblical Narrative," in Welch, ed., *Chiasmus in Antiquity,* 62 (cf. his discussion of chiasm in Kings, 61–67). Cf. also recently D. S. Williams, "Once Again: The Structure of the Narrative of Solomon's Reign" *JSOT* 86 (1999): 49–66.

provides a starting point for further interpretation of the Song of Songs.[95] A closer look at what its center (*L // L*) says about human physical love becomes the key to understanding the main themes of the entire book since they presumably support or expand on it. Finally, knowledge of the central motif and main themes in turn would help illumine interpretation of individual sections within the book as a whole.[96]

Merismus is another literary device that appears in both prose and poetry. Merismus occurs when a writer mentions the extremes of some category in order to portray it as a totality—that is, those opposites and everything in between them.[97] One common form of merismus is the use of polar word pairs in a single phrase. In some cases the phrase's wording expressly states a continuum. For example, consider these lines from the prophet Jeremiah:

> No longer will a man teach his neighbor . . . saying, "Know the
> LORD," because they will all know me, from the *least* of them to
> the *greatest*. (Jer 31:34a, our italics)

The prophet wanted to stress that under the new covenant everyone would know the Lord. To reinforce his point he invoked the extremes of the category "important people" through the merismus "from the least [important] . . . to the greatest." Paraphrased, the latter means, "from unimportant to important people—and everyone in between." In other cases, only the word "and" joins the two extremes. For example, the Bible's familiar opening line uses merismus: "In the beginning God created the *heavens* and the *earth*" (Gen 1:1, our italics). The phrase "heavens and earth" invokes the extremes of the category "universe" to affirm that God created them and everything in between.[98]

A second common merismus employs polar word pairs in parallel stichs. Study how the psalmist displayed God's greatness in this double merismus:

> In his hands are the *depths of the earth,*
> and the *mountain peaks* belong to him.
> The *sea* is his, for he made it,
> and his hands formed the *dry land*. (Psa 95:4–5, our italics)

To achieve a comprehensive effect, the psalmist portrays two pairs of extremes of the category "earth," each in a parallel stich. The first pair describes earth's vertical extremes ("depths" / "peaks"), the other its horizontal ends ("sea" / "dry land"). The

---

95 We deeply regret that our beloved colleague, Professor Robert L. Alden, did not live to provide us his own exposition of this structure.

96 For suggested chiastic structures in shorter NT texts, see N. T. Wright, "Poetry and Theology in Colossians 1.15–20," *NTS* 36 (1990): 449; Bailey and Vander Broek, *Literary Forms*, 49–54 (Pauline letters), 178–83 (the Gospels and Acts).

97 Watson, *Classical Hebrew Poetry*, 321–24; cf. Amos 9:2–4.

98 This phenomenon closely resembles another device called hendiadys (Gk. *hen dia dys*, "one through two"). Hendiadys joins two words by "and" to convey a single idea; cf. Isa 51:19 ("ruin and destruction" meaning "destructive ruin"). More precisely, the two nouns mutually define each other; hence, one serves as an adjective modifying the other. For discussion, see Watson, *Classical Hebrew Poetry*, 324–28.

total effect is to affirm forcefully that God owns everything on earth, and in context, this offers evidence of his greatness.

The final structural device we mention also occurs in both prose and poetry: *inclusio*— framing a poem by repeating words or phrases from its opening lines at its conclusion.[99] This repetition provides a unity and finality the poem would not have otherwise.[100] For example, Psalm 8 opens and closes with these lines that form an inclusio:

> O LORD, our Lord,
> how majestic is your name in all the earth! (Psa 8:la, 9)[101]

The observation of this inclusio is important for two reasons: it signals that the psalm's main theme is the majesty of Yahweh on earth, and it suggests that one must understand all remaining verses (1b-8) in light of that theme. In other words, they illustrate or amplify it. Take, for example, the lengthy section about humanity (vv. 3–8). It marvels at a strange mystery—that God cared enough about puny humans to appoint them as rulers over his own created works. The thematic inclusio indicates, however, that humanity's elevation to greatness is simply an expression—perhaps even a reflection— of God's greater majesty. In other words, God displayed his own greatness by condescending to raise insignificant mortals to a position of great importance.[102] Or notice how Mt 19:30 (NRSV) includes the words, "But many who are first will be last, and the last will be first," virtually repeated, though reversed in a kind of chiasm, in Mt 20:16 (NRSV): "So the last will be first, and the first will be last." By employing this inclusio Matthew intends readers to understand the intervening parable of the landowner who hired workers for his field throughout the day in light of this principle—the reversal of values in the kingdom of God.

THE LANGUAGE OF POETRY

In addition to unique structure and sound, biblical poetry also uses distinct *language*. Unfortunately, a preoccupation with the phenomenon of parallelism too often creates the impression that parallelism alone is the essence of biblical poetry. But as Ryken observes,

---

99 For prose examples, see 1 Sam 3:1 and 21; Ruth 1:6 and 22; Mt 4:23–25 and 9:35. Poets invoke inclusios in both longer and shorter poems; cf. the extensive treatment of them in Lundbom, *Jeremiah*, 36–81. In Amos 7:9–17 the word "sword" limits the context and encourages the reader to trace the thematic development within those limits.

100 Watson calls this the envelope figure (*Classical Hebrew Poetry*, 282–87); cf. E. S. Gerstenberger, "The Lyrical Literature," in D. A. Knight and G. M. Tucker, eds., *The Hebrew Bible and Its Modern Interpreters* (Philadelphia: Fortress/Chico, CA: Scholars Press, 1985), 423; Berlin, *Dynamics*, 130.

101 Observe also the operation of parallelism here, i.e., how the distich conveys a single sentence composed of *a* as a vocative, *b* as an exclamation. Cf. Pss 103:la, 2a, 22b; 118:1, 29; 146–150.

102 Closely akin to the inclusio is the use of refrains, that is, the repetition of a phrase within a poem, e.g., Psa 136 ("his love endures forever"); Song 2:7; 3:5; 8:4 ("Do not arouse or awaken love until it so desires"); Amos 4:6, 8, 9, 10, 11 ("yet you have not returned to me"); cf. Watson, *Classical Hebrew Poetry*, 295–99.

> Parallelism . . . is not the most essential thing that a reader needs to know about biblical poetry. Much more crucial . . . is the ability to identify and interpret the devices of poetic language.[103]

We hope to prepare the reader to do just that—"to identify and interpret the devices of poetic language." We will treat two aspects of poetic language: imagery and poetic devices.

Imagery

Initially, we must understand the nature of poetic language. Poets are essentially artists who paint pictures with words. From their poetic palette they draw *images*—"words that evoke a sensory experience in our imagination."[104] If well chosen, those words conjure up vivid mental pictures and stir up powerful emotions. By appealing to our senses and emotions, they compel us to see and experience their word-pictures. Thus, to be effective an image must be concrete, not abstract. For the abstraction, "The Lord takes good care of me," the biblical poet substitutes, "The Lord is my shepherd, I shall not be in want" (Psa 23:1). He paints a simple but warm picture of care at its best: a shepherd who ensures that his sheep get everything they need. Further, effective images also have an element of surprise, either by introducing a new, unknown image or by giving an old one a new twist. Certainly, Jeremiah startled his hearers when he described the state funeral that God had planned for King Jehoiakim:

> He will have the burial of a donkey
> —dragged away and thrown
> outside the gates of Jerusalem. (Jer 22:19)[105]

Normally, respectful Hebrews did not speak of their kings with such disgust! And no doubt the disciples warmed when Jesus applied the caring shepherd image to himself ("I am the good shepherd"). But then he surprised them by adding, "The good shepherd lays down his life for the sheep" (John 10:11), affirming a stunning self-sacrifice not typical of most shepherds. In both examples, the surprise element is what makes the use of images so effective. Poets constantly speak in the concrete, familiar terms of daily life—of clouds and rain, rocks and rivers, flowers and grass, lions and lambs, mothers and fathers. It is that familiarity and vividness that makes their words so appealing and so memorable.

Devices of Poetic Language
Similes and Metaphors

Similes and metaphors are two poetic devices that are significant in biblical poetry.[106] A *simile* is a figure of speech that compares two things using the words "like" or

---

103 Ryken, *How to Read*, 90, who commends the essay by C. S. Lewis ("The Language of Religion," in *Christian Reflections* [Grand Rapids: Eerdmans, 1967], 129–41) as a good introduction to poetic language.

104 Ryken, *How To Read*, 90.

105 Watson, *Classical Hebrew Poetry*, 252; cf. Jer 9:21; 17:11.

106 Composers of biblical prose also use poetic devices. For example, Luke uses similes to report how the Holy Spirit came upon Jesus "in bodily form *like* a dove" (Lk 3:22, italics ours) and that the crowd at Pentecost heard "a sound *like* the blowing of a violent wind" (Acts 2:2, italics ours).

"as."[107] OT poetry uses several kinds of simile. A simple simile draws a single correspondence between two items in a single sentence. Consider these three examples:

> Now then, I will crush you
> *as a cart* crushes
> when loaded with grain. (Amos 2:13, italics ours; cf. 3:12; 5:24)

> *Like a lily* among thorns
> is my darling among the maidens. (Song 2:2, italics ours)

> To what should I compare the kingdom of God?
> It is *like yeast* that a woman took and mixed in with three measures of
> flour until all of it was leavened.
> (Luke 13:20–21 NRSV, italics ours)

In the first case, Yahweh compares his imminent crushing judgment to the ground being crushed by the wheels of a heavily loaded cart. He will roll over Israel, crushing her into the dust. In the second case, the lover brags about how much prettier his girlfriend is than other girls; she stands out in a crowd—like a solitary lily in a field of thorns. Finally, Jesus compares the kingdom to yeast that leavens bread—a subtle, invisible force that transforms everything.

The parallelism typical of biblical poetry easily lends itself to the use of paired similes. These are similes that are part of parallel lines. Study these examples:

> The mountains melt beneath him,
> and the valleys split apart,
> *like wax* before the fire,
> *like water* rushing down a slope. (Mic 1:4, italics ours)

> He [the righteous king] is *like the light* of morning at sunrise
> on a cloudless morning,
> *like the brightness* after rain
> that brings the grass from the earth.
> (2 Sam 23:4, italics ours; cf. Amos 3:12; 5:24)

Micah's two similes graphically display what horrible devastation God's arrival will wreak on mountains and valleys: first they disintegrate from solids into liquids ("like wax"), then they quickly cascade away into oblivion ("like water"). More positively, David's pair of similes compares the blessings of a righteous king to the "light" of a cloudless dawn and the "brightness after rain," both symbols of relief and renewed hope after darkness and storms; his righteousness guarantees that good days lie ahead ("that brings the grass").

---

107 Hebrew forms similes with the preposition *kᵉ / kᵉmô*, the conjunction *ka'ᵃšer*, the verb *mašal* ("to be like"), and the formula *kᵉ . . . kēn* ("like . . . so [is]"); cf. Watson, *Classical Hebrew Poetry*, 257–62, from whom some of what follows derives; and Petersen and Richards, *Interpreting Hebrew Poetry*, 50–60. Greek forms similes with *hōs* (Mt 28:3; 1 Thes 2:7; Rev 1:14, 15) *hōsei* (Mt 3:16; Acts 6:15; Heb 1:12), and *homoios* (Lk 12:36; Gal 5:21; Rev 18:18), all meaning "like" or "as."

Frequently, biblical poets string together series of three or more similes to heighten the effect. Examine the four-item series of similes in this description of Yahweh's future judgment of Israel:

> So I will come upon them *like a lion,*
> *like a leopard* I will lurk by the path.
> *Like a bear* robbed of her cubs,
> I will attack them and rip them open.
> *Like a lion* I will devour them;
> a wild animal will tear them apart. (Hos 13:7–8)

Pairing similes or stringing them together in series is an extremely effective poetic device. Each simile compares to the brush strokes of a painter on a canvas: the more there are, the richer the portrait. Observe the progression of thought and increasing terror effected by the simile series.[108] The first mention of the lion sparks instinctive human fear but does not specify the animal's actions. With the lurking leopard, however, the prophet clarifies the danger and increases the reader's feelings of fear: at any moment Yahweh can spring upon Israel from his hiding place. The bear adds even more clarity and more terror: Yahweh is driven by outrage, so he will rip Israel to pieces, killing her. The lion delivers the final blow—Yahweh will devour Israel's national carcass, leaving only useless carrion behind. In sum, the string of similes forecasts terrible judgment for Israel. Yahweh will pounce on her (lion), taking her by surprise (leopard), killing her for personal injury (bear), and eating her bloody remains (lion). Hosea certainly demonstrates how powerful similes can be. "Like a lion" also functions as an inclusio.

That same power flows from a series of vivid similes in Matthew's report of Jesus' resurrection:

> [The angel's] appearance was *like lightning,* and his clothing white *as snow.*
> For fear of him the guards shook and became *like dead men.*
> (Mt 28:3–4 NRSV, our italics)

The evangelist's simile series creates a clear mental image of the scene: the bright, angelic sight froze normally brave guards into terrified corpses. Similarly, a chain of two similes enables Jesus' listeners better to ponder what the kingdom of God is like (Lk 13:18–21).

Finally, biblical poets often developed an extended simile, making a simple comparison, then amplifying it with a lengthy commentary on the poetic image invoked. For example, review how Jeremiah compared an Israelite who depends on Yahweh to a fruitful tree:

> Blessed are those who trust in the Lord,
> whose trust is in the Lord.

---

108 Here we follow the insights of Petersen and Richards, *Interpreting Hebrew Poetry,* 55–57. Cf. T. L. Brensinger, *Simile and Prophetic Language in the Old Testament* (Lewiston: Mellen Biblical Press, 1996); J. C. Exum, "Of Broken Pots, Fluttering Birds, and Visions in the Night: Extended Simile and Poetic Technique in Isaiah," in P. R. House, ed., *Beyond Form Criticism: Essays in Old Testament Literary Criticism* (Winona Lake, IN: Eisenbrauns, 1992), 349–72.

Simile:	They will be *like a tree* planted by water, sending out its roots by the stream.
Comment:	It shall not fear when heat comes, and its leaves shall stay green; in the year of drought it is not anxious, and it does not cease to bear fruit. (Jer 17:7–8 NRSV, our italics)[109]

To interpret such examples properly, the student must first define the image invoked (e.g., a tree rooted by a stream) and then observe what the writer says about that image. In this case, Jeremiah stresses how, rooted beside a reliable water source, the tree calmly faces deprivations and thrives. The point is that the believer's trust gives him or her a calm confidence of thriving amid turmoil. Though not stated explicitly, the text implies that Yahweh will surely meet the believer's needs.

In these instances, students must be careful to interpret the image in light of the commentary. Here the student might ask how the tree's being rooted by a stream illustrates the nature and benefits of trusting in Yahweh: why do the "roots" create such fearless confidence in the face of daunting circumstances?

Like a simile, *a metaphor* also draws a comparison between two things;[110] however, the metaphor draws the correspondence more bluntly. Omitting the words "like" or "as," it states straightforwardly "A *is* B."[111] So, the psalmist solemnly affirms:

> Your word is a *lamp* to my feet
> and a *light* for my path. (Psa 119:105, our italics)

The writer compares God's Word to a lamp illuminating a dark path. As a lamp helps a traveler stay safely on the path, so the Word illuminates believers on what lifestyle pleases God. In another example, the prophet Zephaniah describes the civic leaders of Jerusalem:

---

109 Cf. also his comparison of someone who trusts in human strength to a bush in a desert (vv. 5–6); Psa 1:1–3; Ezek 31:2–9.

110 Recent movements in linguistic philosophy and literary criticism have engendered a lively, influential discussion on the subject and definition of metaphor. For overviews, see D. S. Miall, ed., *Metaphor: Problems and Perspectives* (Atlantic Highlands, NJ: Humanities Press, 1982); and M. Johnson, ed., *Philosophical Perspectives on Metaphor* (Minneapolis: University of Minnesota Press, 1981). C. L. Blomberg, *Interpreting the Parables* (Downers Grove: InterVarsity, 1990), 134–44, reviews and critiques the discussion's influence on recent interpretation of NT parables. Cf. more recently, I. Paul, "Metaphor and Exegesis," in C. Bartholomew, C. Greene, and K. Möller, eds., *After Pentecost: Language and Biblical Interpretation*, Scripture and Hermeneutics Series 2 (Carlisle, UK: Paternoster, 2001), 387–402.

111 Ryken, *How To Read*, 91. Much of what follows derives from Ryken, *Words of Delight*, 166–69; and Watson, *Classical Hebrew Poetry*, 263–72. For a slightly broader treatment, see B. Green, *Like A Tree Planted: An Exploration of Psalms and Parables through Metaphor* (Collegeville, MN: Liturgical Press, 1997). For NT metaphors, see the compendious treatment in A. Byatt, *New Testament Metaphors* (Edinburgh: Pentland Press, 1995).

> Her officials are *roaring lions,*
> her rulers are *evening wolves,*
> who leave nothing for the morning. (Zeph 3:3, our italics)

What a vivid picture of political tyrants! They are hungry animals recklessly roving Jerusalem day and night, terrifying her inhabitants, and preying on her weak. Their appetite so drives them that they never delay their destruction.[112] Finally, recall this psalmist's portrait of God:

> The *eyes* of the LORD are on the righteous
> and his *ears* are attentive to their cry;
> the *face* of the LORD is against those who do evil,
> to cut off the memory of them from the earth. (Psa 34:15–16, our
>   italics)

He pictures God as a human being with eyes, ears, and a face—a type of metaphor called an *anthropomorphism.*[113] The point is not that God has an actual body just like humans, but that God constantly tunes his senses to the needs of his people and will confront those who try to harm them.

How do metaphors work? Implicitly, metaphors compare two things that, although *different,* share something in common; in some way the two words or concepts overlap in meaning.[114] The comparison of two basically dissimilar things gives the metaphor its striking effect. For example, study the line "The eyes of the Lord are on the righteous" just cited from Psa 34:15. Here the comparison is between human eyes and the Lord. What do these have in common? They share the trait of focused attention. As human eyes "watch" things with keen interest, so Yahweh "watches"—pays close attention to—his beloved people.

Similarly, the line "Her officials are roaring lions" (Zeph 3:2) implicitly compares city officials with wild animals. In this case, the overlap between these two concepts is less obvious. Without exhausting the possibilities, we suggest that they share great hunger and humanly unstoppable power. The two traits of the animals are physical— a ravenous appetite for prey and overwhelming physical strength. The traits of the leaders are more abstract—a ravenous greed for financial gain and unlimited political power to obtain it.

Like similes, metaphors may also occur in series and in extended form. For example, Jacob's blessing of his children (Gen 49) strings together a series of metaphors, one for each son. Judah is a lion's cub (v. 9), Zebulun a safe harbor (v. 13), Issachar a donkey (v. 14), Dan a viper (v. 17), Naphtali a doe (v. 21), Joseph a fruitful vine (v. 22),

---

112 Cf. also Micah's graphic description of Israel's leaders as cannibals (Mic 3:1b–3) and Amos' sarcastic portrait of Israelite upper-class women as "cows of Bashan" (Amos 4:1). Along a slightly different line, cf. the stinging metaphor "You brood of vipers!" thrown on several occasions by both John the Baptist and Jesus at the Pharisees (Mt 3:7; 12:34; 23:33).

113 Psa 18:8–16 teems with anthropomorphisms. God has nostrils, a mouth (vv. 8, 15), feet (v. 9), and a voice (v. 13). Verse 16 also implies that he has hands. See also images of God as roaring lion (Amos 1:2; 3:8), water spring (Jer 2:13), rock (Psa 18:2), and mother hen (Psa 91:4).

114 Watson, *Classical Hebrew Poetry,* 263.

and Benjamin a ravenous wolf (v. 27). By painting each son metaphorically, the poet pictures their varied tribal destinies. As a whole, the series of metaphors also offers an impressive poetic collage of Israel's complex future as a nation.

In addition, the Bible teems with examples of extended metaphors. Consider this lengthy description of female beauty:

> Your lips drop sweetness as the honeycomb, my bride;
> milk and honey are under your tongue.
> The fragrance of your garments
> is like that of Lebanon.
> You are a garden locked up, my sister, my bride;
> you are a spring enclosed, a sealed fountain.
> Your plants are an orchard of pomegranates
> with choice fruits. (Song 4:11–13)

This lengthy description appeals to all the reader's senses. It enables one to taste, smell, and see this great beauty. Its effect is cumulative and comprehensive.[115]

Permit us, however, to warn readers against the "overinterpretation" of similes and metaphors. Overinterpretation occurs when the student draws meanings from an image that the poet never intended. For example, we once heard someone speak on Psa 92:12, "The righteous flourish like the palm tree" (NRSV). Ignoring the specific point made by the context, he expounded thirteen(!) ways the righteous resemble palm trees. Jesus' metaphorical statement "You are the salt of the earth" (Mt 5:13) frequently suffers from similar overinterpretation. One hears commentators interpret it in light of various modern uses of salt (as a seasoning) rather than in light of its surrounding context and use in Bible times (a preservative). Such "insights" owe more to the creativity of the interpreters than the meaning of the biblical text. In short, this is not interpretation at all but eisegesis—"reading in" a meaning not intended by the text.

The best guard against overinterpretation is to adhere to the rule of context. We must understand poetic images in light of their use in the immediate context and of what would have come to people's minds in *biblical* times. Since images commonly invoke only a few points of comparison, the proper interpretation requires that we understand them within this limited range rather than read in meanings not intended by the writer.

Other Poetic Language Devices

The devices of simile and metaphor certainly dominate biblical poetry, but readers must also be aware of several other common figures of speech. By *personification* a poet writes about something nonhuman—an inanimate object or abstract idea—as if it were human.[116] This figure of speech enables the poet to make the subject vivid and concrete. Biblical poets use it in several ways. Sometimes they employ personification to bring an abstract idea to life. Consider this example:

---

115 For other extended metaphors, see the descriptions of Jerusalem's judgment as a full cup (Ezek 23:32–34), Tyre as a shipwreck (Ezek 27:25–36); and Egypt as a crocodile (Ezek 29:3–5).

116 Ryken, *Words of Delight*, 178.

> Send forth your light and your truth,
> let them guide me;
> let them bring me to your holy mountain,
> to the place where you dwell. (Psa 43:3)

Here the poet portrays the abstract concepts "light" and "truth" as people—guides who will help him find the temple. Of course, the implication is that to find the temple is to meet God since he lives there. Similarly, Prov 8 presents the abstract idea "wisdom" as a woman calling out to passersby in the streets:

> To you, O people, I call,
> and my cry is to all that live. . . .
> Hear, for I will speak noble things,
> and from my lips will come what is right; . . .
> I walk in the way of righteousness,
> along the paths of justice,
> endowing with wealth those who love me,
> and filling their treasuries. (Prov 8:4, 6, 20–21 NRSV)[117]

The picture of a woman brings the abstract idea of wisdom to life. It enables us to understand it in "personal" terms and, hence, to relate to it more personally than we would otherwise.

Other personifications picture objects as people:

> Let the rivers clap their hands,
> let the mountains sing together for joy. (Psa 98:8)

Obviously, rivers do not have hands to clap nor mountains voices to lift in song. But the psalmist treats them as if they had those human traits to evoke the tumultuous joy that should greet the arrival of King Yahweh. Another form of personification is to portray a nation, tribe, or city as a person:

> Gilead stayed beyond the Jordan.
> And Dan, why did he linger by the ships?
> Asher remained on the coast
> and stayed in his coves. (Judg 5:17).[118]

In Rom 6:19 Paul counsels his readers to offer the members of their bodies "in slavery to righteousness leading to holiness." In this way he personifies the positive

---

117 Later, the "woman" gives her credentials—her participation in the creation of the universe (vv. 22–31). Cf. R. E. Murphy, "The Personification of Wisdom," in J. Day, R. P. Gordon, and H. G. M. Williamson, eds., *Wisdom in Ancient Israel: Essays in Honour of J. A. Emerton* (Cambridge: Cambridge University Press, 1995), 222–33.

118 The OT frequently personifies Jerusalem (often called "Zion") in various ways (e.g., Psa. 48:11 [Heb. 12]; 97:8; Isa. 12:6; 37:22; et al.); cf. K. M. Heim, "The Personification of Jerusalem and the Drama of Her Bereavement in Lamentations," in R. S. Hess and G. J. Wenham, eds., *Zion, City of Our God* (Grand Rapids: Eerdmans, 1999), 129–69.

traits of "righteousness" and "holiness" as the new benevolent master to whom they ought to enslave themselves (i.e., to render them complete devotion).

The device of *apostrophe* closely resembles that of personification. Indeed, poets frequently employ both in the same context (see the examples below). Apostrophe is "a direct address to someone or something absent as though it were present."[119] Typically, it appears suddenly in a context, as if the poet, overcome by emotions, blurts out his address. The thing addressed may be an abstract idea or an inanimate object. Apostrophe serves a twofold purpose: to give vent to strong feelings and to generate a sense of excitement.

We occasionally use apostrophe ourselves. For example, arriving home from work, parents discover that their kids have left the family kitchen a mess. As if the offenders were present, the parents say, "You kids are in big trouble now!" Again, safely out of earshot of the boss a frustrated employee might explode, "I'm going to get you for this, boss!" Examine the addressees and emotions evident in these three biblical examples:

> Therefore, you kings, be wise;
> be warned, you rulers of the earth. (Psa 2:10)

> Where, O death, is your victory?
> Where, O death, is your sting? (1 Cor 15:55; cf. Hos 13:14)

> Now listen, you rich people, weep and wail
> because of the misery that is coming upon you. (Jas 5:1)

In the first example, the psalmist addresses the kings of the earth, none of whom was probably present on the occasion of this psalm. Also, his address marks a noticeable literary shift in the context: it follows a report of God's decree establishing the Davidic monarchy (Psa 2:7–9). In the second, Paul breaks off his discourse on Christian hope to address "death"—presumably absent—as a mighty warrior. In the third, James comforts his poor, oppressed readers by condemning their (absent) oppressors. Appearing suddenly in the context, each conveys strong emotional feelings and generate a sense of excitement.[120]

Occasionally all of us resort to the common device of *hyperbole*. "I worked until I dropped," we say to describe our physical exhaustion. A frazzled parent might reprimand, "I've told you a *thousand times* to make your bed!" Hyperbole is "conscious exaggeration for the sake of effect."[121] Its purpose is to state something the poet feels strongly—the joy of salvation, the bitterness of death, the awfulness of judgment. Hence, as Ryken notes, it stretches the literal truth for the sake of emotional impact. Study these examples:

> At this my heart pounds
> and leaps from its place. (Job 37:1)[122]

---

119 We owe the definition and the discussion to Ryken, *Words of Delight*, 177–78.

120 Cf. the excitement generated by the catalog of apostrophes in Psa 148. For more examples, see Bullinger, *Figures of Speech*, 901–905.

121 Ryken, *Words of Delight*, 177; cf. Watson, *Classical Hebrew Poetry*, 316–21.

122 Job 37:1 exemplifies the parallelism of intensification that we discussed earlier; that is, the hyperbole of the second stich gives more intensity than the first.

I am poured out like water,
and all my bones are out of joint.
My heart has turned to wax;
it has melted away within me. (Psa 22:14)

Saul and Jonathan—in life they were loved and gracious,
and in death they were not parted.
They were swifter than eagles,
they were stronger than lions. (2 Sam 1:23)

"I wish those who unsettle you would castrate themselves!"
(Gal. 5:12 NRSV)

Obviously, the four speakers offer exaggerated descriptions of their situations. In the Job passage Elihu's heart did not literally jump out from his chest. He simply exaggerated—"It pounded so hard it popped out!"—to show his excitement at God's greatness. Similarly, the psalmist's entire skeleton did not really get out of joint nor did his heart suddenly become melted wax. Through exaggeration he emphasizes, "I've got no fight left in me." By the same token, David's exaggerated tribute to Saul and Jonathan underscored their great physical prowess. And Paul actually has no urgent desire that Jews in Galatia, who want new Christians there to undergo circumcision voluntarily, model even greater devotion by volunteering for castration. He's simply "had it" with their improper stance and the distraction it has created among sincere new believers.

Biblical poets also use numbers to express hyperbole:

The city that marches out a
thousand strong for Israel
will have only *a hundred* left;
the town that marches out a *hundred* strong
will have only *ten* left. (Amos 5:3, our italics; cf. Isa 4:1)

The prophet is not presenting precise statistics here. He is exaggerating the numbers, both high and low, to portray Israel's high casualty rate—that the coming divine judgment will be catastrophic for the nation. Nor does Jesus advocate mutilation in calling his disciples to gouge out their eyes or literally to cut off their hands (Mt 5:29–30; cf. Gal 5:12). He exaggerates to urge his disciples to take the dangers of sin so seriously that they avoid it at all costs.

The Bible abounds with examples of extended hyperbole in which the exaggeration continues at length (see Job 3:4–9; Jer 5:16–17; Nah 3:15b-17).[123] Similarly, the Evangelist clearly exaggerates the extent of the crowds coming to Jesus when he says, "Then the people of Jerusalem and all Judea were going out to him, and all the region along the Jordan, and they were baptized by him in the river Jordan, confessing their sins" (Mt 3:5–6 NRSV). His hyperbole aims to convey the excitement that Jesus' ministry generated at the time.

---

123 For an example that uses hyperbole, apostrophe, and personification, see Psa 114 and Ryken's comments (*Words of Delight*, 179–80).

The device called *metonymy* features the substitution of a word or idea for one closely associated with it. The substitute serves as a verbal stand-in representing the other. Note these examples of metonymy (cf. the metonymic word in italics):[124]

> You prepare a *table* before me
> in the presence of my enemies. (Psa 23:5a)

> The high places of *Isaac* will be destroyed
> and the sanctuaries of Israel will be ruined. (Amos 7:9)

> Truthful *lips* endure forever,
> but a lying *tongue* lasts only a moment. (Prov 12:19)

The psalm does not say that God will make the psalmist a brand new piece of furniture to impress his enemies; rather, "table" substitutes for the bountiful "meal" that a host spreads across it for a guest. Similarly, biblical history identifies Isaac as a patriarchal ancestor of Israel. So, Amos 7:9 "Isaac" rightly becomes another way of saying "Israel" (Isaac / Israel). Or Mt 23:37 reports that Jesus often longed to gather and shelter *Jerusalem* which, by metonymy, stands for all Jews. Again, Prov 12:19 does not teach that liars will suddenly lose their tongues. Instead, the physical organs of speech, "lips" and "tongue," represent the speakers who lie or tell the truth—and suffer the consequences each deserves. In sum, the device of metonymy represents something indirectly by substituting something else associated with it.

A similar principle underlies a related device called *synecdoche*. In synecdoche, a part of something serves to represent the whole idea or item. This device allows the writer to focus the reader's attention on something specific as a symbol of something larger. Study these examples with the synecdochal word in italics:[125]

> I will turn your religious feasts into mourning
> and all your *singing* into weeping. (Amos 8:10)

> I do not trust in my *bow*,
> my *sword* does not bring me victory. (Psa 44:6 [Heb. 7])

> And it shall come to pass afterward,
> that I will pour out my spirit on all *flesh* . . . (Joel 2:28 [Heb. 3:1] RSV)

> But when he saw the *wind*, he was afraid and, beginning to sink, cried
> out, "Lord, save me!" (Mt 14:30)

In Amos 8:10, "singing" parallels the word "feasts" in the preceding line. Singing constituted one important part of Israelite feasts, so "singing" rightly represents the whole series of festival activities. Along the same line, "bow" and "sword" (Psa 44:6 [7]) symbolize the larger category of weapons. Again, in Joel 2:28 [3:1] one constituent of human nature, "flesh," represents the whole person. Thus, "all flesh" really means "all people," a conclusion confirmed by the following verse ("my servants, both men and

---

124 We owe these examples to M. S. Terry, *Biblical Hermeneutics*, rev. ed. (New York: The Methodist Book Concern, 1911), 161–62. For more examples, see Bullinger, *Figures of Speech*, 538–612.

125 We have gleaned OT examples from Alter, *The Art of Biblical Poetry*, 73–74; and Bullinger, *Figures of Speech*, 614–56. Cf. also Terry, *Biblical Hermeneutics*, 162–63.

women"). Matthew writes that Peter's outlook changed when he saw the wind, a synecdoche for the storm, and with failing faith began to sink (Mt 14:29–30).

Besides identifying metonymy and synecdoche, the interpreter must consider the writer's purpose in using them. In other words, what effect does each example intend to convey? We suggest, for example, that the phrase "you prepare a table before me in the presence of my enemies" (Psa 23:5a) aims to conjure up more than the general idea of food. In context "table" portrays the idea of God's plenteous provision of food despite the enemies' attempts to cut off such supplies. Similarly, Amos 8:10 specifies "singing" rather than another festival activity like "praying" because the former symbolizes joy and celebration. Thus, "(joyous) singing" serves to contrast the "mourning" and "weeping" that the coming divine judgment will inflict.

Finally, we mention the device of *irony* in which a writer says the very opposite of what he means. In contemporary terms, he speaks tongue-in-cheek; a moment later the reader expects to hear an emphatic "Just kidding!" At times, irony becomes sarcasm whereby the speaker pokes fun at the object of his or her words. Though not all drawn from poetry, the following verses illustrate the use of irony:

> Go to Bethel and sin;
> go to Gilgal and sin yet more.
> Bring your sacrifices every morning,
> your tithes every three years. (Amos 4:4; cf. v. 5; 6:13)

> And the LORD said to me, "Throw it to the potter"
> —the handsome price at which they priced me! (Zech 11:13)

> At noon Elijah began to taunt them [i.e., the priests of Baal]. "Shout louder!" he said. "Surely he is a god! Perhaps he is deep in thought, or busy, or traveling. Maybe he is sleeping and must be awakened." (1 Kgs 18:27)[126]

Amos knew the city of Bethel as a center of Israelite pagan worship ("Go to Bethel and sin"). Hence, despite his command to "bring your sacrifices," he really wants Israel *not* to go, that is, to repent of its pagan practices. Similarly, the phrase "handsome price" intends to convey just the opposite meaning—the price asked is insultingly low. Further, Elijah does not believe that Baal is a god actually preoccupied with other activities. His words, in fact, sarcastically state the opposite: Baal has not answered the prayers of his priests because he does *not* exist; hence, he can *not* do anything.[127] Finally, a NT passage that drips with irony is 1 Cor 4:8–10 where Paul says,

> Already you have all you want! Already you have become rich! You have become kings—and that without us! How I wish that you really had

---

126 Two of the above examples (1Kgs 18:27; Zech 11:13) come from Terry, *Biblical Hermeneutics*, 165–66. For others, see Bullinger, *Figures of Speech*, 807–815.

127 Recent studies have explored the use of irony in whole books; cf. M. D. Nanos, *The Irony of Galatians: Paul's Letter in First-Century Context* (Minneapolis: Fortress Press, 2002); G. M. Feagin, *Irony and the Kingdom in Mark: A Literary-Critical Study* (Lewiston, NY: Mellen Biblical Press, 1997). For the OT, see L. R. Klein, *The Triumph of Irony in the Book of Judges*, JSOTSup 68 (Sheffield: Almond Press, 1988); E. M. Good, *Irony in the Old Testament*, 2d ed. (Sheffield: Almond Press, 1981 [1965]).

become kings so that we might be kings with you! For it seems to me that God has put us apostles on display at the end of the procession, like men condemned to die in the arena. We have been made a spectacle to the whole universe, to angels as well as to men. We are fools for Christ, but you are so wise in Christ! We are weak, but you are strong! You are honored, we are dishonored!

Certainly, such effective irony would have shamed the Corinthian Christians into repenting of their arrogance. At least that was Paul's desire.[128]

How to Interpret Poetic Language

To interpret the meaning conveyed through poetic devices, we suggest that the student take the following steps.[129] First, *identify* the kind of figure of speech present (i.e., simile, metaphor, personification, etc.). Remember that more than one device may be present in the same biblical text. For example, a verse may employ hyperbole through both a simile and a metaphor.

Second, *interpret* the figure of speech by distilling its figurative meaning from its literal meaning. By "literal meaning," we mean the actual physical object denoted, the ideas that object conjures up, and the emotional connotations the reader associates with it. By "figurative meaning," we mean the aspect of the literal meaning that the poet desires to highlight. The student will have to decide which of the literal meaning's many associated ideas and connotations best fit the emphasis of the context.

For example, one psalmist describes his enemies this way:

> I am in the midst of lions;
> I lie among ravenous beasts—
> men whose teeth are spears and arrows,
> whose tongues are sharp swords. (Psa 57:4)

From the first two lines, one might see the poet as literally cornered by terrible beasts. Men with "teeth" and "tongues" in the last two lines, however, indicate an allusion to verbal slander. Literally, the metaphors "spears and arrows" and "sharp swords" refer to common weapons of ancient warfare. The latter have three main features: (1) the enemy launches them from a distance (spears and arrows) or from close-by (sharp swords); (2) they inflict painful, if not fatal, wounds by piercing the body; (3) an ordinary person has no defense against them.

These observations point to the metaphor's figurative meaning, that is, what those weapons suggest about slander. They portray it as harsh, "pointed" words that wound their victim. They conjure up images of a victim flinching with continuous pain. The words also imply that slander sometimes strikes suddenly, "out of the blue"—probably an allusion to the secrecy of slander. Furthermore, by striking suddenly, slander leaves its victim defenseless; there is no way to protect against it. In sum, literal weapons figuratively illumine the psalmist's portrait of verbal slander.

---

128 Other examples where Paul famously employs irony include Rom 2:17–24 and 2 Cor 11:7–17.

129 Cf. Ryken, *How to Read,* 94–96; id., *Words of Delight,* 161–62, 177–78.

Finally, the student should determine the *function* of the figure in its context. In other words, why did the poet use this particular figure? What did it contribute to the meaning he desired to convey?

Let us apply these steps briefly to Psa 18:2 [Heb. 3] as an example:

> The LORD is my rock, my fortress and my deliverer;
> my God is my rock, in whom I take refuge.
> He is my shield and the horn of my salvation,
> my stronghold.

The kind of figure the psalmist used here is metaphor. As for the literal meaning, the verse pictures several common, concrete images: "rock," "fortress," "shield," "horn," and "stronghold." Together they suggest ideas of immovability, impenetrable protection, and great strength ("horn").[130] Emotionally, their connotations are positive; the reader would view them as "saviors" in a day of near-death.

This analysis helps us see the figurative meaning. What fortresses and shields have in common with Yahweh is great strength and protection. Thus, the figurative meaning is that Yahweh is the psalmist's protection, the one whose awesome strength surrounds him. Finally, we suggest that within Psa 18 the figures function to sound one of the psalm's main themes—God's protection—a theme the psalmist's own testimony (Psa 18:4–19) confirms.[131]

LARGER UNITS OF POETRY

Sense Units

Thus far, our discussion may have created the impression that all Hebrew poetry consists of only a few lines. Obviously, a glance at the psalms quickly confirms that this is not the case![132] The Bible's parallel lines actually form part of larger structural units we will call *sense units*.[133] A sense unit constitutes the major subdivision of an entire poem. Just as a house may have one or more rooms, so a poem has at least one sense unit but may have many more of varying sizes.

The key indicators of a poem's sense units are as follows: (1) changes in content, grammar, literary form, or speaker; (2) the concentration of keywords in a section; and (3) the appearance of refrains or repeated statements.[134] Psalm 32 provides an example of sense units and their indicators:[135]

---

130 Of course, this step requires the student to have a good understanding of the biblical world. For example, we must discover what "horn" connoted in Bible times, not today. We recommend the regular use of Bible dictionaries and encyclopedias as excellent sources of background on figures of speech. Recall our prior explanation of word studies and historical and cultural backgrounds.

131 Careful readers must also watch for poetic language in nonpoetic passages (e.g. Gen 4:7; Mt 23:37; Jas 1:15); cf. Ryken, *Words of Delight*, 180.

132 The NT writers do not include long poems such as we find in the OT psalms, but we do find examples of extended hymnic material such as Col 1:15–20 and Phil 2:6–11.

133 We borrow the term from Petersen and Richards (*Interpreting Hebrew Poetry*, 60–63) as an alternative to popular but ambiguous terms like "stanza" and "strophe" (against Watson, *Classical Hebrew Poetry*, 160–67). Fokkelman favors the term "stanza" (*Reading Biblical Poetry*, 117–40) and offers an illuminating discussion of this larger unit with examples.

134 These same indicators may also signal the main literary divisions of prose passages.

135 Cf. Gerstenberger, *Psalms 1*, 140–43. Having your Bible open here is crucial to see this point.

Sense Unit	Verses	Indicators
1	1–2	form: impersonal "blessed is the person" formula content: sin, forgiveness function: to provide general thematic introduction
2	3–5	transition: "for" change of speaker: "I" form: report of personal experience content: experience of forgiveness function: to illustrate the forgiveness theme
3	6–7	transition: "for" form: exhortation (v. 6), affirmation of confidence (v. 7) addressee: God ("you" singular) content: prayer, protection, deliverance function: to urge people to pray
4	8–10	form: instruction (cf. prohibition [v. 9], proverb [v. 10]) addressee: Israel ("you" singular) content: teaching about trust in Yahweh function: to teach the benefit of trust
5	11	form: call to rejoice addressee: righteous Israelites ("you" plural) content: rejoicing, gladness, singing function: to call for response to entire psalm

Sense units are basic to the structure of a poem, so if we want to decipher this structure we must first identify the poem's sense units. With a piece of notepaper in hand, read the poem watching for the key indicators mentioned above. When these indicators change significantly, indicating a break between sections, write the verses of the sense unit just concluded. Continue this analysis until the entire poem's sections are identified. After identifying the sense units, the student should isolate any subsections within those sense units. Read the poem a second time, identifying the subsections within each sense unit. Write the verses for each subsection under the verses for each sense unit.

Finally, beside the verses for each sense unit/subunit, write a short label that describes its literary form. Be sure that the label describes the literary *form* rather than the *content*. The difference is this: a content label describes *what* a sense unit says (its content); a literary label describes *how* it says what it says (its literary form). For example, Psa 73:1

("Surely God is good to Israel, / to those who are pure in heart") constitutes a sense unit whose content is about God's goodness to Israel. Its form, however, is that of an affirmation. By the same token, in content Amos 5:6a ("Seek the Lord and live") is about devotion to God, but its form is a call to worship.

To illustrate this procedure, consider how you would describe these three sections of Psa 32:

vv. 3, 5   When I kept silent, my bones wasted away
            through my groaning all day long . . .
        Then I acknowledged my sin to you
            and did not cover up my iniquity.
        I said, "I will confess my transgressions to the LORD"
            —and you forgave the guilt of my sin. . . .

v. 9   Do not be like the horse or the mule,
            which have no understanding
     but must be controlled by bit and bridle
            or they will not come to you. . . .

v. 11   Rejoice in the LORD and be glad, you righteous;
            sing, all you who are upright in heart!

Obviously, the excerpt of vv. 3 and 5 describes the ending of personal trouble through the confession and forgiveness of sin. One might depict the *content* as "The trouble and forgiveness of sin" or "Confession of sin ends trouble." Observe, however, that this is not an impersonal, abstract discussion of human suffering caused by sin. Rather, it offers a personal report given by an individual about a past experience of forgiven sin. The proper literary label (*form*) would be something like "Personal report: trouble and forgiveness."

Taken by itself, the content of v. 9 easily wins labels like "An appeal for self-control" or "An example of stubbornness." Since it follows up v. 8, however ("I will instruct you . . . in the way you should go"), one might describe its content more precisely as "Stubborn resistance to good teaching." Literarily, however, notice that v. 9 is not a description but a prohibition ("Do not be like the horse or the mule") that the speaker urges upon his audience. So, one should label it literarily as a "Prohibition." As for v. 11, its content readily calls to mind a label like "Rejoicing and singing." Again, however, observe the form: two commands with which the speaker exhorts the audience ("Rejoice . . . sing"). Literarily, then, one should describe it as an "Exhortation" or "Call to Worship."

After completing the descriptions of sense units and their subparts, we suggest two final steps. First, one should write a literary outline based on those descriptions. The purpose of such an outline is to present the poem's literary structure in visual form. The outline, then, can become the basis for analyzing the poem's literary and thematic development. A literary outline of Psa 32 might look like this:[136]

---

136 The following is a modification of Gerstenberger, *Psalms 1*, 140. For a fuller treatment of this method and its application to poetic and nonpoetic texts, see G. M. Tucker, *Form Criticism of the Old Testament* (Philadelphia: Fortress, 1971).

I.	Superscription	1a
II.	The Psalm	1b–11
	A. Declaration	1b–2
	B. Personal report: trouble and forgiveness	3–5
	1. Description: trouble	3–4
	2. Description: forgiveness	5
	C. Exhortation and confession	6–7
	1. Exhortation	6
	2. Confession	7
	D. Instruction	8–10
	1. Statement of intention	8
	2. Instruction itself	9–10
	a. Prohibition	9
	b. Proverb	10
	E. Closing exhortation	11

Notice the consistent use of literary terms rather than descriptions of content. As indicated, we describe vv. 3–5 as a "Personal report" because that is its form (the comment "trouble and forgiveness," however, adds some clarification). Because the exhortation of v. 11 concludes the psalm, we call it a "Closing exhortation." Our "Prohibition" (v. 9), however, forms only part of a larger section (vv. 8–10) along with a proverb (v.10) and a declaration of intention to give instruction (v. 8). Since v. 8 introduces what follows as instruction (vv. 9–10), we label the entire section as "Instruction."

Second, using the literary outline as a guide, the student should analyze the poem's structure. To do so, study the outline to answer questions like the following:

1. What comes first in the poem? What comes last? Why?

2. What comes in the middle of the poem? Why?

3. What organizing principle underlies its structure (e.g., liturgical practices, thematic development, etc.)?

4. What is (are) the poem's main theme(s)?

5. How does each sense unit contribute to its thematic development?

6. What is the poem's intention or purpose (i.e., What did the poet hope to accomplish?)?

7. What is its main point?

In sum, analysis of a poem's structure is more than an academic exercise. Applied carefully, it provides readers with a helpful tool of interpretation. In fact, one may also apply this same method—the preparation of a literary outline—to nonpoetic texts. In such cases, however, the outline would describe its subparts though not as poetic sense units. Our method provides a way for readers to break a text down into its constituent parts. Awareness of those parts gives readers the basis for tracing the thematic development of a passage.

PART IV—UNDERSTANDING BIBLE GENRES

9

GENRES OF THE OLD TESTAMENT

The challenges of reading and understanding literature came home to us recently when we heard our friend's story. His son was studying at a large public university in a neighboring state, and on schedule our friend had made two of three payments for his tuition and fees. But before the third payment came due the university sent him what looked like a statement of his son's account. We say "looked like" because he noticed that its format and ink color differed from those of earlier statements, the total amount of the semester's tuition and fees also was less, and it said nothing about his two previous payments. Without actually crunching the numbers, he decided that the latter must somehow account for the statement's smaller total.

The real surprise was that it listed an unexpected state "grant" that wiped out the remaining balance. The statement came with no cover letter of explanation, but the numbers were there in black and white. After pondering the matter, our friend accepted the text at face value (excuse the pun!), grateful that the mysterious grant had spared him the third payment. Naturally, when notice of the latter arrived, he ignored it, but two subsequent "overdue payment" notices led him to straighten the matter out by telephone.

"There must be some mistake," he explained. "We shouldn't owe anything because you sent me a statement that applied a state grant to my son's account to cover what we owed."

"Oh, that," the official replied. "That wasn't really a statement of account. It's just something the legislature requires us to send each student each semester to remind them how much the state pays toward their education. It's not really a 'grant' applied to someone's account. You still owe us the balance." Thus enlightened, our friend immediately paid it.

This episode illustrates how easily one can misread a simple text. On the surface, the above mailing read like the genre "statement of account" whose intention was to inform someone of the balance of an account. Its form convinced our friend to ignore the slightly different format and the numbers that did not quite jibe. Its life-setting in a large university also led him (wrongly, of course) unconsciously to accept the numbers as the result of bureaucratic errors. In this setting, however, the genre turned out to be subtle propaganda by the state legislature to remind students that they were not paying the entire cost of their education.

The potential for similar misreadings of the Bible lead us to offer readers two chapters introducing the Bible's major literary genres. The Bible is, in fact, written literature—

compositions of prose and poetry in various sizes and shapes written by human beings in human language. God chose to convey his revelation to humans in a way they could understand—by written literature. To interpret it properly, then, we must use literary tools for they alone enable us to understand the Bible holistically.[1] They sharpen our mind so we can discover its ideas; they tune our imagination so its truth can grip us emotionally.

Specifically, literary tools help Bible readers to develop what John Barton calls *literary competence*.[2] Like our friend, they may have "linguistic competence"—the ability to understand the words and numbers written on a page—but lack sufficient cultural familiarity to recognize the cues of a particular genre (so-called "genre recognition"). Each kind of literature has its own frame of reference, ground rules, strategy, and purpose. Literary competence is the ability to discern cues within the text that indicate the kind of literature present and, hence, what to expect or not to expect from it.[3]

In the above example, the incongruities should have alerted our friend that this was no ordinary "statement of account," but only direct contact with the text's setting clarified its background and intention. Similarly, the Bible student who knows the formation, function, and background of each literary type is in the best position to interpret correctly and to avoid serious misunderstandings.

As with the preceding chapter about poetry, the discussion below draws on the remarkable recent advances in our understanding of the Bible's rich and varied literary landscape. This chapter mines the insights of OT *form criticism* to illumine our understanding of the structure, literary type or genre, original life-setting, and intention of much OT literature.[4] It consults the study of *poetics* to help clarify *how* texts, especially OT narratives, work by identifying their devices and literary dynamics.[5] It also draws

---

1 Cf. L. Ryken, *How to Read the Bible As Literature* (Grand Rapids: Zondervan, 1984), 11–12: "[W]hen the Bible employs a literary method, it asks to be approached as literature and not as something else."

2 J. Barton, *Reading the Old Testament*, rev. ed. (Louisville: Westminster John Knox, 1996), 8–16. Cf. Annemarie Ohler, *Studying the Old Testament from Tradition to Canon* (Edinburgh: T. & T. Clark, 1985), 9: "The foundation of work with the Old Testament . . . is the art of reading texts in relation to their literary form." The same principle applies to the NT.

3 Ryken, *How to Read*, 25; and G. W. Coats, "Genres: Why Should They Be Important for Exegesis?" in G. W. Coats, ed., *Saga, Legend, Tale, Novella, Fable: Narrative Forms in the Old Testament*, JSOTSup 35 (Sheffield: JSOT, 1985), 8.

4 Two good introductions to OT form criticism are Barton, *Reading the Old Testament*, 30–44; and G. M. Tucker, *Form Criticism of the Old Testament* (Philadelphia: Fortress, 1971); cf. R. Knierim, "Criticism of Literary Features, Form, Tradition, and Redaction," in *Reading the Hebrew Bible for a New Millennium: Form, Concept, and Theological Perspective*, 2 vols., ed. W. Kim, D. Ellens, M. Floyd, and M. A. Sweeney, (Harrisburg, PA: Trinity Press International, 2000), 2:1–41. For a survey of major biblical genres, see M. D. Johnson, *Making Sense of the Bible: Literary Type as an Approach to Understanding* (Grand Rapids: Eerdmans, 2002). For major OT types, see D. B. Sandy and R. L. Giese, Jr., eds., *Cracking Old Testament Codes: A Guide to Interpreting the Literary Genres of the Old Testament* (Nashville: Broadman and Holman Publishers, 1995).

5 Such markers include, for example, plot, characterization, descriptions, style, narrative pacing, point of view, the use of word-plays or word-repetition, the inclusion / exclusion of key details, etc. For poetics, cf. the ground-breaking study of R. Alter, *The Art of Biblical Narrative* (New York: Basic Books, 1981); and M. Sternberg, *Poetics of Biblical Narrative: Ideological Literature and the Drama of Reading* (Bloomington: Indiana University Press, 1985).

on the methodological ally of poetics, the so-called *new literary criticism*, for further illumination.[6]

To enhance the reader's literary competence in both the OT and the NT, this chapter and the following one will survey briefly the Bible's main literary forms. Their purpose is threefold: (1) to provide reliable first steps in thinking "literarily" about the Bible; (2) to teach a preliminary literary vocabulary to aid in interpretation; and (3) to help readers both to enjoy the Bible's riches more and to understand it better. In so doing, we hope they will experience what Jasper describes:

> By concentrating on the literary qualities of the biblical texts, the reader encounters with new immediacy their power and mystery. Like all great texts of literature, they are seen as both historical *and* contemporary, as living with history.[7]

NARRATIVES

Everyone loves a good story. From the bedtime "Once upon a time . . . " of childhood to the newest Hollywood film, we enjoy losing ourselves in the imaginative worlds of books, plays, and the big screen. Bible writers love stories, too; that is why narratives are the most common literature found in the Bible—40 percent of the OT.[8] In reality, rather than a single type of "Old Testament narrative" the OT has narratives of many kinds.

Recall some memorable biblical scenes: the knife in Abraham's hand a frozen instant from slaying Isaac; the raging Red Sea waters pliantly obeying Moses' uplifted little rod; God's thunderous voice rolling down Mt. Sinai to Israel's frightened ears; deadeye David's shot that toppled Goliath like a tree. Recall some memorable biblical characters: clever Rebecca scheming to win young Jacob the firstborn's blessing; crafty Laban outfoxing love-struck Jacob on his wedding night; bold Moses telling God "no" when told of his destruction plans; grieving Rizpah shooing away buzzards from her two sons' corpses. For great stories and vivid characters, Hollywood has nothing on the Bible! More important, we often see ourselves in them.

---

6 For one view of the *new literary criticism*, see D. J. A. Clines and J. C. Exum, "The New Literary Criticism," in *The New Literary Criticism and the Hebrew Bible*, ed. J. C. Exum and D. J. A. Clines (Valley Forge, PA: Trinity Press International, 1993), 11–25. Instead of *poetics*, some scholars prefer the term "narrative criticism"; cf. P. E. Satterthwaite, "Narrative Criticism: The Theological Implications of Narrative Techniques," in *NIDOTTE*, ed. W. A. VanGemeren (Grand Rapids: Zondervan, 1997), 1:125–33. Other useful summaries of a literary approach include V. P. Long, "Reading the Old Testament as Literature," in *Interpreting the Old Testament: A Guide for Exegesis*, ed. C. C. Broyles (Grand Rapids: Baker, 2001), 85–123; J. P. Fokkelman, *Reading Biblical Narrative: An Introductory Guide* (Louisville: Westminster John Knox, 1999); S. Bar-Efrat, *Narrative Art in the Bible*, JSOTSup 70 (Sheffield: JSOT, 1989).

7 D. Jasper, "Literary Readings of the Bible," in *The Cambridge Companion to Biblical Interpretation*, ed. J. Barton (Cambridge: Cambridge University Press, 1998), 27. We gratefully acknowledge the helpful comments of our colleague, Professor D. Carroll R. concerning this chapter.

8 G. Fee and D. Stuart, *How to Read the Bible for All Its Worth*, 2d ed. (Thorndike, ME: G. K. Hall, 1993), 120. For a survey of the main narrative types, see J. B. Gabel, C. B. Wheeler, and A. D. York, *The Bible as Literature: An Introduction*, 4th ed. (New York/Oxford: Oxford University Press, 2000), 18–19; and Johnson, *Making Sense of the Bible*, 35–47. Cf. also Ryken, *How to Read*, 33–73. Though Bible readers commonly call OT narratives "history," we prefer the literary term "narrative" because we believe that "history" describes the content of the material; "narrative," its literary form.

To learn to read its stories clearly—i.e., to have the requisite literary competence—is the first step to hearing God's clear voice speaking through them.[9] After all, unlike historians, their purpose is more to instruct than to inform; more to teach later generations about God-honoring conduct than to make sure they have the facts straight. But two points of clarification seem in order here. First, though most narratives display some marks of the storyteller's craft, the amount of conscious literary art will vary from narrative to narrative. Some will display great literary art, while others will narrate the facts with little embellishment.[10] The writers include only what serves to communicate their key themes. Second, to speak of biblical narratives as "stories" does not by itself imply that they are not historical. As Goldingay rightly observed, "The historical 'having happened-ness' of the story matters."[11]

In our view, to speak of a biblical text as "story" means to highlight the literary form in which its implied historical claims address us. Further, despite some scholarly claims to the contrary, history-writing is not in and of itself a literary genre; rather, it has a concern with reporting history that may find expression in various genres, even fictional ones.[12] However superb their literary art, biblical narratives "are more than history, not less than history."[13] Proper literary competence requires readers to appreciate their historical content and literary form.

Old Testament Narrative Genres

Earlier we noted that the Old Testament has many different types of narratives, so what follows surveys those genres. Some of the descriptive categories below reflect standard scholarly terminology, some offer our own classifications, and some borrow descriptions used for comparable ancient and modern narratives.[14] Readers should regard these terms as descriptive, not technical. Further, genre categories describe two levels—both an individual biblical passage as well as the larger context it serves. The reason is that one genre

---

9 Cf. Ryken, *How to Read*, 33: "Narrative is the dominant form in the Bible . . . What this means to readers of the Bible is that the more they know about how stories work, the more they will enjoy and understand vast portions of the Bible."

10 Cf. Ryken's helpful distinction (*How to Read*, 33) between biblical stories that, like entries in a historical chronicle, simply tell *about* an event and full-fledged stories (e.g., David, Job) that *present* an event in full detail. For the thesis that the ethical intent of biblical narratives arises from their narrative art, see G. J. Wenham, *Story as Torah: Reading the Old Testament Ethically*, Old Testament Studies (Edinburgh: T. & T. Clark, 2000).

11 J. Goldingay, "How Far Do Readers Make Sense? Interpreting Biblical Narratives," *Themelios* 18/2 (1993): 5.

12 For full, balanced discussion of the relationship between "story" and "history," see V. Philips Long, *The Art of Biblical History*, Foundations of Contemporary Interpretation 5 (Grand Rapids: Zondervan, 1994), 56–119; and D. M. Howard, Jr., *An Introduction to the Old Testament Historical Books* (Chicago: Moody, 1993), 44–58; cf. also T. Butler, "Narrative Form Criticism," in *A Biblical Itinerary: In Search of Method, Form, and Content*, ed. E. E. Carpenter, JSOTSup 240 (Sheffield: Sheffield Academic Press, 1997), 57 ("Form criticism . . . does not place a historical judgment upon the materials"). We prefer this understanding to the distinction between "narrative" and "history" in Sandy and Giese, *Cracking Codes*, 69–112.

13 J. Goldingay, *Models for Interpretation of Scripture* (Grand Rapids: Eerdmans, 1995), 32.

14 For additional details, see the comprehensive surveys and concluding glossaries in G. W. Coats, *Genesis*, FOTL 1 (Grand Rapids: Eerdmans, 1983), 1–10 ("Introduction to Narrative Literature"); B. O. Long, *1 Kings*, FOTL 9 (Grand Rapids: Eerdmans, 1984), 1–8 ("Introduction to Historical Literature"), 243–65; and, less comprehensively, Ryken, *How to Read*, 75–85.

(e.g., a history) may contain several other specific genres within it (e.g., a historical story, an anecdote, a battle report, etc.). Similarly, one genre (e.g., a song) may be a component of a larger genre (e.g., a historical story).

Reports

The simplest biblical narrative, the basic building block of the Bible's narrative complexes, is the *report*: a "brief, self-contained narration, usually in third-person style, about a single event or situation in the past."[15] It narrates the facts of what happened in a straightforward style without literary embellishment. OT examples include reports about tribal settlements in Canaan (Judg 1:16–17), royal construction projects (1 Kgs 7:2–8; 12:25), and military campaigns (1 Kgs 14:25–26; 2 Kgs 24:20b-25:7). Occasionally, reports serve an aetiological purpose, explaining how a certain place acquired its name—i.e., how a certain oak tree came to be called the Oak of Weeping (Gen 35:8 [NRSV Allon-bacuth]) or a certain watering hole came to be known as Bitter (Exod 15:23 [NRSV Marah]; et al.).

The OT has several kinds of reports. An *anecdote* is a report that details an event or experience in the life of a person—in other words, more private biography rather than public history. It may report conversations as when Elijah symbolically summons Elisha to become his disciple (1 Kgs 19:19–21) and may use imaginative descriptions. Another example of an anecdote is the report of gift-cities that King Solomon gave to King Hiram of Tyre (1 Kgs 9:10–14), a report that ends by tracing the area's apparently derogatory name Cabul (perhaps "like nothing" or "bound") to the incident.[16]

A *battle report* recounts a military clash between opposing forces and its outcome, whether of victory or defeat. Among the Bible's many battle reports are defeats of the Amorites (Num 21:21–24), Moabites (Judg 3:26–30), Arameans (2 Sam 10:15–19), two Midianite kings (Judg 8:10–12), and the Canaanite city of Ai (Josh 7:2–5). A *construction report*, on the other hand, recounts the construction of important buildings or objects and describes their size, materials, and decoration in great detail (Exod 36:8–38:20 [the tabernacle]); 1 Kgs 6–7 [the Jerusalem temple]).

Told in first- or third-person, the *dream report* details an individual's experience of a dream. Two stylistic features help identify this genre: repetition of the verb "to dream" and use of the phrase "and behold" (Heb. *wᵉhinnēh)* to demarcate major changes in the dream's subject matter. Usually a separate, subsequent scene interprets the experience for the awakened dreamer. OT dream reports include those concerning Joseph (Gen 37:5–11), his two prisoner friends (40:9–11, 16–17), the Egyptian Pharaoh (41:1–8), and a Midianite soldier (Judg 7:13–14).[17]

---

15 Long, "Historical Literature," 5; cf. Coats, "Narrative Literature," 10. Long labels a short report a "notice," a longer one an "account." For ancient analogies, see the Siloam inscription and report of Egyptian expeditions in *ANET*, 227–28, 229–30, 321, etc. For more on reports discussed below, see Long, "Historical Literature," 244, 247, 248.

16 Coats, "Narrative Literature," 10; Long, "Historical Literature," 243–44. An *annal* is a report, often part of royal records, that details chronologically events concerning an institution like the monarchy or the temple. According to Long ("Historical Literature," 243), the OT has no annals, although some texts may be based on them (e.g., 1 Kgs 3:1; 9:15–23; 2 Chr 11:5–12).

17 Cf. also the dreams of Nebuchadnezzar in the narrative sections of the book of Daniel (Dan 2:1–11; 4:1–18). For a broad, comparative study of dream phenomena, see J.-M. Husser, *Dreams and Dream Narratives in the Biblical World*, The Biblical Seminar 63 (Sheffield: Sheffield Academic Press, 1999). Cf. also A. Ages, "Dreamer, Schemer, Slave, and Prince: Understanding Joseph's Dreams," *Bible Review* 14 (1998): 46–52.

An *epiphany report*, by contrast, reports an experience in which God or the angel of the Lord appears to someone, often to convey a message. Typically, the verb "to appear, become visible" (Heb. *rā'â*, niph.) signals the beginning of such epiphanies. They played an important role in the lives of Abraham (Gen 12:7; 17:1–22; 18:1–33), Isaac (26:2–5, 24), Moses (Exod 3:2–12), Samson's parents (Judg 13), and King Solomon (1 Kgs 3:5–15; 9:1–9).[18] The report of Jacob's experience at Bethel is a *dream epiphany* since it involves God's appearance in a dream (Gen 28:12–16; cf. 48:3–4; Mt 2:19–20).[19]

The genre *historical stories* are reports written with more literary elaboration than an ordinary report.[20] They develop a rudimentary plot (moving from tension to resolution), record dialogues and speeches by characters, and include dramatic literary touches. Like the simple report, they aim to recount an event, but they do so with an appealing written flair. Two excellent examples are the stories of Saul's emergence as king (1 Sam 11:1–11) and of Ahab's confrontation with the prophet Micaiah ben Imlah (1 Kgs 22:1–38; see also Judg 9:1–21; 1 Kgs 12:1–20; 20:1–43).

Authors or editors may compile a series of reports and consciously structure them to underscore connections between events and to sound certain themes. The result is a *history*, a lengthy document that focuses on a particular subject or historical era.[21] Explicitly or implicitly, the authors / editors convey their evaluation of the sequence of events reported in order to apply instruction or legitimation from the past to situations or institutions in the author / editor's own day. This genre includes the book of Kings, the book of Chronicles, and a hypothetical document called the "court history of David" (2 Sam 9–20; 1 Kgs 1–2).[22]

Finally, we mention a subtype of history, the *memoir*. Written in the first-person, a memoir reports incidents in an individual's life in order to portray the history, not of the writer, but of the era in which he or she lived. Scholars believe the memoirs of Ezra

---

18 For the suggestion that a ritual of royal induction inspired the report of Solomon's dream, see B. Lang, *The Hebrew God: Portrait of an Ancient Deity* (New Haven: Yale University Press, 2001), 8–11; cf. Husser, *Dreams and Dream Narratives*, 124–128.

19 Cf. Husser, *Dreams and Dream Narratives*, 128–132. Inexplicably, Long reckons all divine appearances as dream epiphanies even when the context either says nothing about a dream or, in the cases of Abraham (Gen 18) and Moses (Exod 3), actually specifies their non-dream circumstances ("Historical Literature," 248).

20 Long, "Historical Literature," 6–7.

21 Long, "Historical Literature," 7–8, who notes (8), "The OT is unrivaled in the ancient Near East for its use of this literary genre." Scholars commonly assume that palace scribes responsible for recording affairs of state prepared such histories.

22 Most scholars believe that the "court history" in Kings later formed part of a larger historical work, the "Deuteronomistic History," edited during Israel's exile in Babylon (sixth century B.C.) and encompassing the books from Deuteronomy to 2 Kings; cf. M. Noth, *The Deuteronomic History*, JSOTSup 15 (Sheffield: JSOT Press, 1981). For a recent treatment, see A. F. Campbell and M. A. O'Brien, *Unfolding the Deuteronomistic History: Origins, Upgrades, Present Text* (Minneapolis: Fortress, 2000). A popular introduction is available in T. E. Fretheim, *Deuteronomic History* (Nashville: Abingdon, 1983). The foundational study of the "court history" (formerly "the succession narrative") is L. Rost, *The Succession to the Throne of David* (Sheffield: Almond, 1982), 65–114. Concerning the compilation and purpose of Chronicles, see conveniently G. H. Jones, *1 & 2 Chronicles*, OT Guides (Sheffield: JSOT Press, 1993), 86–111.

(Ezra 7:27–9:15) and Nehemiah (Neh 1:1–7:73a; 12:27–13:31) comprise part of the books that bear their names.[23]

Principles of Interpretation—Reports

Note the following principles for interpreting reports:

1.In interpreting a simple report the reader should focus on its main subject and how it contributes to the themes of the larger context.

2. Since reports tend to stress factual matters (i.e., what happened, who did what, etc.), they tend not to provide obvious devotional content. Hence, readers must deduce their theological themes from the larger context that surrounds them. The exceptions to this rule are reports in which God participates (e.g., dream reports, epiphany reports). For example, Jacob's dream report (Gen 28) stressed God's personal relationship with Jacob and assured him of God's presence on his journey. Such themes certainly have implications for today.

3. Typical of narratives, reports make their points indirectly. The reader must ask: What is this text trying to say? What subtle signals has the writer woven into the account to convey the message? The student will probably find more interpretive clues in historical stories and histories than in simple reports. For example, 1 Kgs 22 obviously portrays the prophet Micaiah ben Imlah as the courageous hero persecuted by a corrupt Ahab. In so doing, it condemns Ahab's nominal Mosaic religion and, by implication, all other examples of less than fully committed faith.[24]

4. Histories are like choirs—a series of individual voices (i.e., reports) joined to sound common themes. To find those themes, the reader must analyze the emphases of the individual reports to see what they share in common. For example, compared to Kings, Chronicles focuses on Judah, David's patronage of Israel's worship, and the importance of the temple. Whereas Kings evaluates the Israelite monarchy as a spiritual disaster, Chronicles seeks to highlight its positive spiritual contribution, its establishment of proper temple worship. Written for post-exilic Judah, the book reviews Israel's history in order to urge its audience to worship Yahweh obediently.[25]

Heroic Narrative

A more common OT genre is the *heroic narrative*.[26] This comprises a series of episodes that focus on the life and exploits of a hero whom people later consider significant enough

---

23 See conveniently, R. W. Klein, "Ezra-Nehemiah, Books of," *ABD*, 2:733–734; H. G. M. Williamson, *Ezra, Nehemiah*, WBC 16 (Waco, TX: Word, 1985), xxiv–xxxii; but cf. R. North, "Nehemiah," *ABD*, 4:1070 ("hardly likelihood of any 'Ezra-Memoir' at all").

24 For discussion of this narrative with particular interest in its literary use of anonymity, see R. L. Hubbard, Jr., " 'Old What's His Name': Why the King in 1 Kings 22 Has No Name," in *God's Word for Our World*, ed. J. H. Ellens et al. (Sheffield: Sheffield-Continuum, 2003), forthcoming.

25 W. Riley, *King and Cultus in Chronicles*, JSOTSup 160 (Sheffield: JSOT Press, 1993), 202–204; conveniently, W. S. LaSor, D. A. Hubbard, and F. W. Bush, *Old Testament Survey*, 2d ed. (Grand Rapids: Eerdmans. 1996), 545–49.

26 Ryken, *How to Read*, 75–80. For this category, Coats ("Narrative Literature," 6) and Long ("Historical Literature," 250) prefer the term "heroic saga," but the definition and appropriateness of the term "saga" remains a matter of dispute; cf. the positive assessment in R. W. Neff, "Saga," in *Saga, Legend, Tale, Novella, Fable*, ed. G. W. Coats, JSOTSup 35 (Sheffield: JSOT Press, 1985), 18–32; and the negative assessment of J. Van Seters, *Abraham in History and Tradition* (New Haven: Yale University Press, 1975), 131–37. Cf. also the key question posed by Butler, "Narrative Form Criticism," 56: "If Israel told materials as family history or as promise narratives, why load ambiguous titles such as saga or legend to such materials?"

to remember. Typically, such heroic narratives include some account of the person's birth, marriage, life work, and death. They place particular emphasis on the hero's displays of virtue and extraordinary heroism. As Ryken observes,

> Such stories spring from one of the most universal impulses of literature—the desire to embody accepted norms of behavior or representative struggles in the story of a character whose experience is typical of people in general.[27]

Heroic narratives may seek to inculcate such behavioral norms by both positive and negative examples. A hero who failed offers as powerful a lesson about important life values as one who succeeded.

The life of Moses (Exodus-Deuteronomy) offers the best OT example of this genre.[28] At length, it depicts his birth, marriage, sense of vocation, exploits as leader and lawgiver, and his death.[29] Certainly, his life embodies both the struggles of Israel's national life during that period and the ideal of consummate loyalty to God. Again, one may consider the book of Judges as a collection of heroic narratives.[30] The stories of Deborah (Judg 4–5), Gideon (Judg 6–8), and Samson (Judg 13–16) particularly show traits of this genre. They symbolize Israel's dual struggles during that period: invasions from outside and idolatry inside. Their successes and failures embody Israel's own national struggles with political survival and faithfulness to God.[31]

The *epic* represents a subvariety of heroic narrative since it tells the heroic exploits of a virtuous hero.[32] Two unique traits set it apart: its greater length and its magnification of

---

27 Ryken, *How to Read*, 75.

28 Cf. F. F. Greenspahn, "From Egypt to Canaan: A Heroic Narrative," in *Israel's Apostasy and Restoration: Essays in Honor of Roland K. Harrison*, ed. A. Gileadi (Grand Rapids: Baker, 1988), 1–8; G. W. Coats, *Moses: Heroic Man, Man of God*, JSOTSup 57 (Sheffield: JSOT Press, 1987). In the NT, the Gospel accounts of the life of Jesus show traces of this genre, although they focus more on his teaching than on his biography. See our discussion of the Gospel genre in the following chapter.

29 Knierim even argues that the genre of the whole Pentateuch is the biography of Moses with particular emphasis on his unique role as mediator at Mt. Sinai; cf. R. P. Knierim, "The Composition of the Pentateuch," in *SBLSP* 24, ed. K. H. Richards (Atlanta: Scholars Press, 1985), 409–415. That the character of Moses still makes fascinating biography is evident in J. Kirsch, *Moses: A Life* (New York: Ballantine Books, 1998).

30 So Ryken, *How to Read*, 80, conceding, however, that "certain features of the book resemble epic" (on which, see below). Cf. the stimulating literary analysis by K. R. R. Gros Louis, "The Book of Judges," in *Literary Interpretations of Biblical Narratives* 1, ed. K. R. R. Gros Louis et al. (Nashville: Abingdon, 1974), 141–62.

31 Within the book of Judges, however, their lives contribute to its main theme, i.e., Israel's need for a king to stave off invasions, to end tribal rivalries, and to ensure religious fidelity (Judg 17:6; 18:1; 19:1; 21:25); cf. T. Schneider, *Judges*, Berit Olam (Collegeville, MN: Liturgical Press, 2000), 284–85; LaSor, Hubbard, Bush, *Old Testament Survey*, 164. Along with Schneider, M. Wilcock, *The Message of Judges: Grace Abounding* (Downers Grove: InterVarsity, 1992) offers an insightful treatment of Judges.

32 Ryken, *How to Read*, 78–81; cf. the typology of epics applied to Ancient Near Eastern examples in A. Berlin, "Ethnopoetry and the Enmerkar Epics," in *Studies in Literature from the Ancient Near East Dedicated to Samuel Noah Kramer*, ed. J. M. Sasson (New Haven: American Oriental Society, 1984), 17–24. For a broader literary study, see D. A. Miller, *The Epic Hero* (Baltimore: Johns Hopkins University Press, 2000). Admittedly, our treatment of epic applies to prose narratives a term normally associated with poetic ones.

the hero's exploits to a greater scale of importance. An epic displays a strong nationalistic interest with the hero representing the destiny, not just of a family, but of a whole nation. In other words, it narrates events that the entire nation admires in retrospect as epoch-making. Hence, its themes are large-scale ones—conquest, kingdom, warfare, and dominion. Since epics portray a nation's formative history, they abound with historical allusions.[33]

In addition, the epic involves supernatural settings, events, and characters. Events play themselves out in a cosmic arena, which includes both heaven and earth, and supernatural agents participate directly in human history on earth. Again, the plot of an epic is mildly episodic (it presents separate incidents rather than a chain of connected events) and often aims at a central feat or quest by the hero.

Gen 1–11 offers a *cosmic epic* because it narrates the formative story, not just of a nation, but of the cosmos and its human inhabitants.[34] Supernatural elements abound, for God participates directly with Adam and Eve in the garden (Gen 3) and with Noah in the great flood (Gen 6–9). Later, he scatters people across the earth and separates them into distinct language groups (Gen 11). The genealogies of Adam (Gen 5) and Noah (Gen 10) also evidence a variation of the nationalistic motif: interest in the origins of earth's major ethnic groups.[35]

Historical allusions include references to the beginning of human occupations (Gen 4:20–22), the giant race called the Nephilim (Gen 6:4; cf. Num 13:32–33), and the foundation of ancient cities (Gen 10:10–12; cf. 11:2–3).[36] In these texts the hero is not an individual but a series of individuals, yet, in context, they serve to represent early humanity as a whole. Again, recall that toward the end of this epic, the narrative focus narrows to the Semites, the racial ancestors of the Hebrews (Gen 11:10–32).

Gen 12–36 offers an *ancestral epic*.[37] It certainly shows nationalistic themes—the destiny of Israel and her ownership of the land of Canaan. Indeed, the programmatic promise to Abram (Gen 12:1–3) predicts Israel's destiny as the instrument of blessing for all other

---

33 For discussion of Ancient Near Eastern epics and their implications for biblical epics, see conveniently J. H. Walton, *Ancient Israelite Literature in Its Cultural Context: A Survey of Parallels Between Biblical and Ancient Near Eastern Texts* (Grand Rapids: Zondervan, 1989), 46–49, 58–65.

34 Cf. Coats, "Narrative Literature," 5–6 ("the primeval saga"). Since an ancient Near Eastern parallel, the "Epic of Atrahasis," follows a similar narrative structure, it lends some cultural support to our categorization of Gen 1–11 as epic; cf. A. R. Millard, "A New Babylonian 'Genesis' Story," in *"I Studied Inscriptions from Before the Flood": Ancient Near Eastern, Literary, and Linguistic Approaches to Genesis 1–11*, ed. R. S. Hess and D. T. Tsumura (Winona Lake, IN: Eisenbrauns, 1994), 114–128; I. M. Kikawada and A. Quinn, *Before Abraham Was* (Nashville: Abingdon, 1985). For a translation of the epic, see V. H. Mathews and D. C. Benjamin, *Old Testament Parallels: Laws and Stories from the Ancient Near East* (New York: Paulist Press, 1991), 16–27.

35 For the function of these genealogies within Genesis, see F. Crüsemann, "Human Solidarity and Ethnic Identity: Israel's Self-Definition in the Genealogical System of Genesis," in *Ethnicity and the Bible*, ed. M. G. Brett, Biblical Interpretation Series 19 (Leiden: E. J. Brill, 1996), 57–76. R. S. Hess, "The Genealogies of Genesis 1–11 and Comparative Literature," in Hess and Tsumura, "*I Studied Inscriptions*," 58–72, discusses the forms of biblical genealogies within their ancient context.

36 For the interpretation of Genesis 6:1–4, see B. K. Waltke (with C. J. Fredricks), *Genesis: A Commentary* (Grand Rapids: Zondervan, 2001), 115–117, who suggests that the Nephilim descend from demon-possessed ancient royal tyrants; cf. also Millard, "A New Babylonian 'Genesis Story,'" in Hess and Tsumura, eds., "*I Studied Inscriptions*," 122–123. Waltke (*Genesis*, 165–175) discusses the ethnographical information in Genesis 10.

37 Cf. Coats, "Narrative Literature," 6 ("family saga"); B. C. Birch, W. Brueggemann, T. E. Fretheim, and D. L. Petersen, *A Theological Introduction to the Old Testament* (Nashville: Abingdon, 1999), 68 ("The stories involve fathers and mothers, sons and daughters, aunts and uncles—simply put, families").

ethnic groups. Though not prominent, supernatural elements are nevertheless present. Yahweh actively participates, appearing to the patriarchs (Gen 17:1; 18:17–33; 26:2; 35:1, 7), raining down destruction on Sodom, and giving elderly Sarah a son (21:1–2; cf. also Lot's angelic rescuers [19:1, 15] and Jacob's mysterious wrestling match [32:22–32]).

As for historical allusions, in our view Abraham's defeat of Kedorlaomer's military coalition (Gen 14:1–16) recalls an ancient event long-remembered in the region.[38] Granted, the patriarchal narratives involve a sequence of four heroes rather than one. Nevertheless, their story traces Israel's national roots and defines her national destiny. Further, the idea of promise that drives the plot of Gen 12–36 (Gen 12:1–3; etc.) favorably compares to the motif of the typical epic quest (the quest for land and national destiny).[39]

Prophet Story

The *prophet story* recounts events in the life of a prophet, particularly those that demonstrate virtues worthy of emulation and, more importantly, that theologically critique the world in which the story's readers lived.[40] Its purpose, thus, is two-fold: to edify its audience by presenting the prophet as a model of proper conduct and to discredit the larger politico-religious system for its denial of Yahweh as sovereign Lord. They reflect the Bible's larger driving dynamic—a theological and ideological movement to reshape the readers' view of the world and radically to reform their values. The narratives about Elijah and Elisha (1 Kgs 17–2 Kgs 9; 2 Kgs 13:14–21) and Daniel (Dan 1–6) best illustrate prophet stories.[41] For example, Elijah and Elisha model perseverance in the

---

38 Cf. G. Wenham, *Genesis 1–15*, WBC 1 (Waco, TX: Word, 1987), 319 ("the evidence . . . suggests that this chapter is based on one of the oldest literary sources in Genesis"); Coats, "Narrative Literature," 317 (cf. also pp. 118–22), whose genre glossary lists Gen 14:1–24 under "annals" with the definition "a report from the archives of the royal court"; but cf. O Margalith, "The Riddle of Genesis 14 and Melchizedek," *ZAW* 112 (2000): 501–508 (a "para-myth" reflecting wars in the late 13th cent. B.C.); and C. Westermann, *Genesis 12–36: A Commentary* (Minneapolis: Augsburg, 1985), 193 ("It cannot be traced back to a definite historical event in the form in which it is preserved").

39 With good reason, Johnson (*Making Sense of the Bible*, 35) says the OT comprises "large epics" woven into "the grand narrative of the Bible"—the story from creation to the post-exilic period. He also calls Joshua to 2 Kings an "epic"; cf. Ryken, *How to Read,* 80 (the book of Joshua as "the conquest epic"; also the rise of King David [1 Sam 16–2 Sam 8]). For an insightful literary study of the story of David, see M. J. Steussy, *David: Biblical Portraits of Power* (Columbia, SC: University of South Carolina Press, 1999); cf. W. Brueggemann, *David's Truth In Israel's Imagination and Memory*, 2d ed. (Minneapolis: Fortress, 2002).

40 "Prophet story" replaces the often-used term "legend" after the suggestion of R. M. Hals, "Legend," in Coats, *Saga*, 55 (cf. also pp. 45–51); similarly, J. J. Scullion, "Märchen, Sage, Legend: Towards a Clarification of Some Literary Terms Used by Old Testament Scholars," *VT* 34 (1984): 334. But cf. M. A. Sweeney, *Isaiah 1–39*, FOTL 16 (Grand Rapids: Eerdmans, 1996), 20–21 ("Introduction to Prophetic Literature"), whose major types are "prophetic story" and "prophetic legend"; cf. his larger treatment of "Prophetic Narrative" (18–22). For possible subcategories of prophetic stories, see A. Rofé, *The Prophetical Stories* (Jerusalem: Magnes Press, 1988). We are particularly grateful to Professor Carroll for his helpful comments on this section.

41 Cf. the illuminating comparison of Elijah and Elisha to Shakespeare's Hamlet by K. R. R. Gros Louis, "Elijah and Elisha," in Gros Louis, et al., *Literary Interpretations* 1: 177–90. Cf. also U. Simon, *Reading Prophetic Narratives*, Indiana Studies in Biblical Literature (Bloomington, IN: Indiana University Press, 1997); J. Goldingay, "Story, Vision, Interpretation: Literary Approaches to Daniel," in *The Book of Daniel In the Light of New Findings*, ed. A. S. van der Woude (Leuven: Uitgeverij Peeters, 1993), 295–314; and D. Gunn and D. N. Fewell, *Narrative in the Hebrew Bible* (Oxford: Oxford University Press, 1993), 174–188 (an insightful literary treatment of Daniel 3).

face of royal political pressure and boldly challenge the tyranny and errors of state-spon-sored religious apostasy. In prophet stories about Elisha miracles sometimes play a promi-nent role (e.g., Elisha's healing of the Shunammite woman's son [2 Kgs 4:8–37] and his rescue of the sunken ax head [6:1–7]). The miracles display Yahweh's unchallenged omnipotence and by implication expose the impotence of the popular god, Baal.

Similarly, Daniel shows faithfulness in the face of pressures from foreign overlords like Nebuchadnezzar and models an unwavering confidence in God's sovereign protec-tion of his people. At the same time, the book of Daniel offers a powerful critique of the terrible oppressions of empires and of the dangerous self-delusions of emperors.[42] The book of Jonah also fits in this category, although it instructs through a negative example. In our view, its literary style intentionally imitates the prophetic stories about Elijah. Again, it clearly has a didactic aim—to teach the reader about God-honoring attitudes toward non-Israelites (see Jonah 4:10–11).[43]

Principles of Interpretation—Heroic Narratives and Prophet Stories

To interpret heroic narratives and prophet stories, we suggest the following principles:

1. Interpretation should focus on the life of the main character, whether an indi-vidual, a family, or a nation. The two questions to consider are: How does the hero's life model a relationship with God and with other people? And what aspects of the orig-inal reader's worldview does it seek to critique or discredit?

2. Since heroes portray values, the student must ask what values a given hero rep-resents. For example, several texts elevate Abraham as an example of dogged faith (cf. Gen 15:6; 22:12). Thus, he exhibits the kind of trust in God expected of ancient Israel and of modern Christians, too. The student should also ask, How do those values chal-lenge and seek to reshape the values dominant in the biblical and the modern worlds?

3. Besides the values presented, interpretive priority should be given to finding the large themes involved (election, conquest, religious apostasy, etc.). For example, the life of Elisha portrays Israel's disloyal rejection of Yahweh in favor of Baal. By implication, it underscores how important loyalty is to the covenant requirements for Israel to expe-rience God's blessing and how God's servants must sometimes challenge any leadership promoting other values.

4. Application of these narratives should focus on analogous situations between Israel and the Church. For example, one theme in the ancestral epic presents God miraculously overcoming infertility to keep the patriarchal line alive (cf. Gen 21; 29–30). But the appli-cation is not that God always provides believers with children. For reasons known only to him, God may choose *not* to give them children in some situations. A better analogy is that the epic reminds Christians of God's firm commitment to carry out his salvation plan today. It is better because it draws on a biblical truth that never changes rather than on one subject to God's mysterious will.

---

42 Cf. J. E. Goldingay, "The Stories in Daniel: A Narrative Politics," *JSOT* 37 (1987): 99–116. For the ideological critique in Amos, see M. D. Carroll R., *Contexts for Amos: Prophetic Poetics in Latin American Perspective*, JSOTSup 132 (Sheffield: Sheffield Academic Press, 1992).

43 L. C. Allen, *The Books of Joel, Obadiah, Jonah, and Micah*, NICOT (Grand Rapids: Eerdmans, 1976), 175, 190–91 ("the unwelcome truth of God's sovereign compassion for foreigners and beasts"). For literary treatments of Jonah, see Gunn and Fewell, *Narrative in the Hebrew Bible*, 129–146; and P. Trible, *Rhetorical Criticism: Context, Method, and the Book of Jonah*, Guides to Biblical Scholarship OT Series (Minneapolis: Fortress, 1994).

Comedy

To modern readers, the term *comedy* probably conjures up images of comic television shows. In literature, however, a comedy is a narrative whose plot has a happy ending, in some cases through a dramatic reversal. It often aims to amuse.[44] Typically, the following features play prominent roles in comedies: disguises, mistaken identity, providential coincidences, surprising turns-of-events, escapes from disaster, and the conquest of obstacles. Comedies often conclude with a marriage, a celebratory feast, reconciliation with opponents, or victory over enemies.

We classify the book of Esther as a comedy.[45] Its plot turns tragedy into triumph, involves the conquest of obstacles (Haman's treachery and King Ahasuerus' ignorant complicity; Esth 3:1–11); disguise (Esther's hidden Jewish identity; Esth 2:10, 20); providential coincidence (the timing of Ahasuerus' insomnia; 6:1–11); surprise (the unmasking of Haman's plot; 7:1–6); sudden reversal of fortune (chaps. 8–9); and a concluding feast (Purim; 9:18–19).[46] Thematically, it also critiques the self-deluded pretentions of empires and emperors, and perhaps gender bias as well.

The story of Joseph (Gen 37–50) offers a second example of OT comedy.[47] From the tragedy of Joseph's exile and imprisonment in Egypt (Gen 37, 39–40) the plot ends in triumph: Pharaoh elevates him to prime minister (41:39–40), Joseph rescues Egypt and his own family from famine (42–50), and Joseph is reconciled with his brothers (42–45, 50). In between, one reads of obstacles overcome, providential events (cf. 41:51–52; 45:7–8; 50:21), and Joseph's hidden identity (42–44). In sum, it is a fitting example of comedy.

Principles of Interpretation—Comedy

The following principles are useful for interpreting OT comedy:

1. Since plot drives a comedy, interpretation must trace how tragedy turns to triumph. So, the student would trace how Joseph and Esther save Israel from their respective crises.

---

44 W. Harmon and C. H. Holman, *A Handbook to Literature,* 7th ed. (Upper Saddle River, NJ: Prentice Hall, 1996), 105–109. For an insightful treatment of Job as comedy, see J. W. Whedbee, "The Comedy of Job," in *On Humour and the Comic in the Hebrew Bible*, ed. Y. T. Radday and A. Brenner, JSOTSup 92 (Sheffield: Sheffield Academic Press, 1990), 217–249. For OT tragedies, the negative counterpart of comedy, we suggest Gen 3 and the life of Saul (1 Sam 9–31).

45 For recent literary treatments of Esther, see A. Berlin, *Esther*, JPS Bible Commentary (Philadelphia: Jewish Publication Society, 2001); M. V. Fox, *Character and Ideology in the Book of Esther*, 2d ed. (Grand Rapids: Eerdmans, 2001); T. K. Beal, *Esther*, Berit Olam (Collegeville, MN: Liturgical Press, 1999); and K. M. Craig, Jr., *Reading Esther: A Case for the Literary Carnivalesque* (Louisville: Westminster John Knox, 1995). Cf. also H. Fisch, "Esther: Two Tales of One City," *Poetry With a Purpose: Biblical Poetics and Interpretation*, ed. H. Fisch, Indiana Studies in Biblical Literature (Bloomington, IN: Indiana University Press, 1988), 8–14.

46 The definitive literary treatment of Esther remains S. B. Berg, *The Book of Esther: Motifs, Themes, and Structure*, SBLDS 44 (Missoula, MI: Scholars, 1979), in addition to the more recent works of Fox, Beal, and Craig mentioned in the previous note. See also W. T. McBride, "Esther Passes: Chiasm, Lex Talio, and Money in the Book of Esther," in *"Not In Heaven": Coherence and Complexity in Biblical Narrative*, Indiana Studies in Biblical Literature, ed. J. P. Rosenblatt and J. C. Sitterson, Jr. (Bloomington: Indiana University Press, 1991), 211–223.

47 Cf. C. Westermann, *Joseph: Eleven Bible Studies on Genesis* (Minneapolis: Fortress, 1996); D. A. Seybold, "Paradox and Symmetry in the Joseph Narrative," and J. S. Ackerman, "Joseph, Judah, and Jacob," in Gros Louis, et al., *Literary Interpretations* 1: 59–73 and 85–113 (respectively). For possible literary connections between the Joseph story and the book of Esther, see Berg (*Esther*, 123–42, 173–87). For a reading of it as a novella, see W. L. Humphreys, "Novella," in Coats, *Saga*, 85–88.

In the process of tracing this development it is particularly important to define the story's crisis, the turning point, and the climax.

2. Character development merits some attention. Note the character traits of both heroes and villains and how they contribute to their respective success or demise. Also observe positive and negative developments in characters. For example, Esther seems to change from a reluctant intermediary to a bold, courageous leader (cf. Esth 4; 7). At the same time, Haman appears to degenerate from supreme self-confidence to childish self-pity (Esth 3; 6).

3. Discern what role God plays in the story: is it a direct or an indirect one? Ask whether or not the biblical writer views accidents and coincidences as acts of hidden divine providence.

4. Define the comedy's main theme(s). The Joseph story sends several clear thematic signals: God guided Joseph's ups and downs to preserve Israel's existence (Gen 45:7–9; 50:20). Esther sounds its themes more subtly, but certainly a major one would be God's preservation of his people before tyrants.

5. Application follows from the comedy's main theme(s). So, for example, Joseph and Esther echo a key biblical truth that God takes care of his people, whatever their hardships.

Farewell Speech

Finally, the *farewell speech* deserves mention because of the important role it plays at key junctures of OT narrative literature. The farewell speech is an address in the first-person voice reportedly given by someone shortly before his or her death.[48] Typically, the speaker refers to his or her old age or imminent death and exhorts the hearers to live along certain lines in the future.[49] The speakers are usually leaders of such great historical prominence that the speeches tend to mark momentous turning points in Israel's national life. Though expounding legal instructions, the series of speeches given by Moses in Deuteronomy represent an expanded form of the farewell speech.

Principles of Interpretation—Farewell Speech

The following principles will be helpful in interpreting the farewell speech:

1. The student must determine what makes the occasion of the speech historically pivotal. In other words, why did the speaker give the speech? What surrounding circumstances or pressing issues lie in the background?

2. Given the historical setting, the student must also summarize the speaker's main point in a brief sentence. What does the aging leader urge his audience to do about it?

---

48 Long, "Historical Literature," 249. The list of farewell speeches reads like an abbreviated outline of OT history: Jacob to his sons (Gen 49:29–30), Moses to Israel (Deut 29:2–30:20; 31:1–8), Joshua to Israel (Josh 23), Samuel to Israel (1 Sam 12), and David to Solomon (1 Kgs 2:1–9); cf. Paul in Acts 20:18–35; and Jesus in Jn 13:1–17:26. Cf. also the poetic "Last Words of David" (2 Sam 23:1–7).

49 Often a brief report of the speaker's death and burial follow the speech (Gen 49:33; Deut 34:5–6; 1 Kgs 2:10; cf. Josh 24:29–30). Though not speeches, NT epistles written late in an apostle's life seem to carry on the same tradition (e.g., 2 Tim 4:6–8; 2 Pet 1:12–15).

3. Decide what a given speech contributes to the themes of the larger context. For example, how does Samuel's speech (1 Sam 12) develop the themes of the book of 1 Samuel?

4. Look for application from the speech's momentous historical setting and its main point. The student should think of a contemporary situation that closely compares to the biblical one and then apply the speaker's main point to that situation. For example, Samuel's words would exhort us to serve God faithfully despite our fears of criticism from unbelievers.

A Sample Narrative: Judges 7:1–15

This episode, which weaves together several narrative genres and literary devices, offers a useful example to illustrate how to interpret a narrative.[50] It is set in the context of horrible oppression by marauding tribes—Midianites, Amalekites, and people of the east—whose seven-year hegemony reduced north-central Israel to near-starvation (see 6:2–6). Though suffering for unfaithfulness (6:1), Israel's ongoing distress-cry eventually moved God to send a deliverer, Gideon (6:14, later called Jerubbaal [6:32; 7:1]), who has assembled a huge army by the spring of Harod within striking distance of the enemy (7:1).

The narrative structure features two parts: two reports of God's command to reduce the force's numbers (vv. 2–3, 4–8) and a report of Gideon's secret visit to the Midianite camp (vv. 9–15). The former reduces the troop number from 20,000 to 300 by "sifting out" weak soldiers (Heb. *ṣrp* "to refine, test"), while the latter features a dream report by a Midianite soldier overhead by Gideon (vv. 13–14) that emboldens him to issue the battle order (v. 15).

Notice two key themes that emerge in the narration. The first concerns the lesson Israel is to learn from victory—that Yahweh's power, not huge troop strength, achieved it. The narrator sounds it in Yahweh's explanation of the reduction (v. 2), ironic in contradicting the preference of human commanders for overwhelming force. Gideon personifies the second theme—whether Gideon surrenders to his fears or boldly trusts Yahweh (vv. 10–11)—a widespread biblical theme of special relevance to an Israel wavering between reliance on Yahweh or on other gods.

The dream report (vv. 13–14) marks the episode's dramatic turning point, drama sharpened by the narrator's clever use (v. 13) of word repetition and a word play on a Hebrew root. He uses *hinnēh* ("Look!") to highlight the providential surprise that the Midianite began to speak just as Gideon passed his tent (i.e., "Gideon entered the camp, and—Shhhh! What's that guy saying?"). He hears (our paraphrase): "Look (*hinnēh*), here's my dream: See (*hinnēh*), this barley loaf was 'rolling' (*hpk* hith.) in the camp . . . . It struck the tent; it turned upside down (*hpk* qal) . . . . " His buddy then interprets its symbolism (v. 14): the barley cake is "Gideon's sword"; the tent's upset is Midian's defeat by God through Gideon (a cake normally would bounce off or crumble). Thus reassured, Gideon rallies his small band (v. 15) and routs the enemy (vv. 16–25).

The text underscores God's power to use crumbly barley cakes (i.e., frail humans) to overturn mighty armies. It reminds readers of the many biblical words of reassurance

---

50 For a more complete literary reading of this text and Judges as a book, see B. G. Webb, *The Book of Judges: An Integrated Reading*, JSOTSup 46 (Sheffield: Sheffield Academic Press, 1987).

(e.g., "I am with you," Isa 41:10; Mt 28:20) that dispel fears of inadequacy. Gideon models the proper response—trust in that power, not in other gods, and bold actions of faith.

Embedded Genres

Popular Proverb

Other kinds of literature are embedded within OT narratives. When we say, "That's the way the ball bounces," we invoke a *popular proverb* (Heb. *mašal*)—a pithy, well-known saying that comments on everyday people and events. Colorfully, it says, "That's life!" Ancient Israel had similar sayings, normally prefaced by the formula "so it became a saying" or "that is why they say. . . ." For example, 1 Samuel twice reports the popular proverb "Is Saul also among the prophets?" Apparently that Israelite expression highlighted someone's unexpected, uncharacteristic behavior (10:12; 19:24).[51] Popular proverbs always occur as quotations in a larger context, although the book of Proverbs may incorporate some in its collections (Prov 18:9; 24:26; 29:5). (For the interpretation of proverbs, see below under wisdom).

Israel also commonly invoked blessings and curses as part of her daily life. The formula "Blessed is/be [someone]" (Heb. *bārûk*) was the way Israelites wished others well (Gen 9:26; Deut 28:3; Ruth 2:19, 20). The opposite formulas, "cursed is/be [someone/thing]" (Heb. *'ārûr*) or "cursed is/be one who [is/does something]" (Heb. *'ārûr hā'îš 'ᵃšer*) seeks the opposite consequence for its object (see Gen 9:25; Deut 27:15; Judg 5:23; Jer 11:3).[52]

Riddles, Fables, and Parables

OT narratives also contain examples of riddles, fables, and parables.[53] A *riddle* (Heb. *ḥîdâ*) is a simple statement whose hidden meaning must be discovered. The classic example is the one Samson used to stump his Philistine companions: "Out of the eater, something to eat; out of the strong, something sweet" (Judg 14:14; see the answer [v. 18]). The posing of clever riddles was typical fare at wedding feasts, and Samson's verbal art in that context enabled him both to head off possible physical

---

51 Cf. R. P. Gordon, *I & II Samuel: A Commentary* (Grand Rapids: Zondervan, 1986), 119. Other examples: "Like Nimrod, a mighty hunter before the Lord" (Gen 10:9); "From evildoers come evil deeds" (1 Sam 24:13); "The 'blind and lame' will not enter the palace" (2 Sam 5:8); "The days go by and every vision comes to nothing" (Ezek 12:22); "Like mother, like daughter" (Ezek 16:44); "The fathers eat sour grapes, and the children's teeth are set on edge" (Ezek 18:2; cf. Jer 31:29).

52 For Israel's understanding of this practice, see the convenient summary of J. Scharbert, " '*ārar*," *TDOT* 1:408–12, 416–18; and id., "*bārak*," *TDOT* 2:302–308. The genre "imprecation" also wishes dire misfortune on someone but without invoking the curse formula and without addressing the person directly (e.g., Psa 109:6–20). Though resembling a blessing on the surface, a "beatitude" actually makes a declaration ("Blessed is the person who . . . ") rather than a wish (e.g.. Psa 1:1).

53 For a brief survey, see K. J. Cathcart, "The Trees, the Beasts, and the Birds: Fables, Parables and Allegories in the Old Testament," in *Wisdom in Ancient Israel: Essays in Honour of J. A. Emerton*, ed. J. Day, R. P. Gordon, and H. G. M. Williamson (Cambridge: Cambridge University Press, 1995), 212–221. Besides texts we introduce below, he treats three allegories from Ezekiel—the useless vine (Ezek 15), the lioness and the vine (19), and the great tree (31)—as well as the tale of Balaam's ass (Num 22:22–35) and the ravens feeding Elijah (1 Kgs 17:1–6).

violence by his Philistine hosts and to exert some control over a tricky political situation.[54]

By contrast, *fables* teach moral truths through brief stories in which plants and animals behave like people. Modern readers immediately recall Aesop's fables—for example, the famous race between the tortoise and the hare—and fables from ancient Egypt and Mesopotamia abound. The OT offers two fine examples, both of a political sort. In one, Jotham told how trees sought a king among various trees and vines but found only the thorn bush willing to serve (Judg 9:8–15).[55] His fable warned the people of Shechem to be wary of Abimelech's leadership as king. Then in 2 Kgs 14:9 King Jehoash responded to the challenge of Amaziah with a little fable of a thistle that sent a message to a cedar. Meanwhile, a wild animal trampled on the thistle. Jehoash's message to Amaziah was clear: do not think too highly of yourself and your strength![56]

A *parable* is a brief story with common human characters that illustrates an important truth. Though OT writers used this form much less than did the rabbis and Jesus, the OT has at least two good examples, one in a narrative context and the other in a wisdom book. The prophet Nathan told King David how a greedy rich man stole a poor man's only lamb to feed a visiting guest. The story, a judicial parable alluding to David's adultery and act of murder, caused him to face his sin (2 Sam 12:1–4).[57] Similarly, the Preacher told how the wisdom of a poor man had once saved a besieged town but that afterward no one remembered him (Eccl 9:13–15; cf. 4:13–16). The lesson was that wisdom is better than strength even if people disregard it (9:16).[58] As with the NT, OT parables always occur as part of a larger context.

Songs

Singing played a significant role in Israel's daily life, so it is not surprising that OT narratives quote several kinds of *songs*. The ancient "Song of the Well" (Num

---

54 So C. V. Camp and C. R. Fontaine, "The Words of the Wise and Their Riddles," in *Text and Tradition: The Hebrew Bible and Folklore*, ed. S. Niditch, Semeia Studies (Atlanta: Scholars Press, 1990), 127–151. They conclude (148–149) that riddles are the stock-in-trade of Israel's wisdom tradition for use in political diplomacy. Solomon and Daniel were renowned for their ability to solve riddles (1 Kgs 10:1; Dan 5:12). A. Wolters, "The Riddle of the Scales in Daniel 5," *HUCA* 62 (1991): 155–177, suggests that the famous wall inscription of Belshazzar has three levels of meaning, all adding up to God's sovereign toppling of the proud king.

55 For discussion see Cathcart, "Trees, Beasts, and Birds," in Day, et al., *Wisdom*, 215–216, who cites several ANE parallels; cf. also G. S. Ogden, "Jotham's Fable: Its Structure and Function in Judges 9," *BT* 46 (1995) 301–308.

56 Cf. A. M. Vater Solomon, "Jehoash's Fable of the Thistle and the Cedar," in Coats, *Saga*, 126–132 (cf. also her helpful introduction to the genre [114–25]); more briefly, Cathcart, "Trees, Beast, and Birds," in Day, et al., *Wisdom*, 217–218.

57 Cathcart, "Trees, Beasts, and Birds," in Day, et al., *Wisdom*, 216–217; U. Simon, "The Poor Man's Ewe Lamb: An Example of a Juridical Parable," *Bib* 48 (1967): 207–42; cf. also S. Lasine, "Melodrama as Parable: The Story of the Poor Man's Ewe-lamb and the Unmasking of David's Topsy-turvy Emotions," *Hebrew Annual Review* 8 (1984): 101–124.

58 Cf. Z. Weisman, "Elements of Political Satire in Koheleth 4:13–16; 9:13–16," *ZAW* 111 (1999): 554–560. He categorizes the text as a satirical, "quasi-historical anecdote" on the futility of political upheavals.

21:17–18) apparently was a work song sung during the digging of wells.[59] Israel also sang victory songs after winning great military battles. Hence, the "Song of the Sea" (Exod 15:1–18) celebrated Yahweh's victory over Pharaoh at the Red Sea, and the "Song of Deborah" (Judg 5) celebrated his conquest of Jabin the Canaanite king (cf. also Exod 15:21; Num 21:27–30; 2 Kgs 19:21–28). Jonah sang a song of thanksgiving from the belly of the great fish (Jon 2:1–9), and God rescued him (v. 10).[60]

On the other hand, the loss of loved ones, particularly fallen military comrades, was the occasion for the singing (or chanting) of a funeral *dirge* (Heb. *qînâ*). One key to recognizing such dirges is the opening word "How. . .!" (Heb. *'êk*). They also have a distinctive poetic meter—five stressed syllables per line—that scholars call the *qînâ* (i.e., "dirge") rhythm. The best-known examples are David's laments for Saul and Jonathan (2 Sam 1:19–27) and for Abner (2 Sam 3:33–34; cf. 2 Chr 35:25).[61] (Further information on dirges in the prophets follows.)

Lists

Finally, OT narratives also often incorporate ancient *lists*. A list is a recounting of names or items whose shared characteristics allow their logical categorization.[62] In the ancient world, compiling lists was a common practice. Sometimes these lists served as a means of accounting or inventory-control; at others they functioned as a primitive classification of observed phenomena.[63] OT narratives include lists reflective of similar activity in ancient Israel—e.g., lists of booty (Num 31:32–40), votive offerings (Exod 35:5b-9; cf. vv. 21–29), Israelite cities and towns (Josh 15–19), royal mercenaries (2 Sam 23:24–39), and royal officials (1 Kgs 4:2–6, 8–19).

Numbers 33 records an ancient itinerary, the list of places where Israel camped en route from Egypt to Mount Hor (see vv. 5–37).[64] The most common list, however, is the genealogy or list of ancestors (Gen 10; 22:20–24; 25:1–4; Ruth 4:18–22; 1 Chr 2–3).[65]

---

59 Other texts mention rejoicing and singing that celebrated other occasions; see Gen 31:27; Judg 9:27; 21:21; 1 Sam 18:6–7; Isa 16:10; and the convenient table of E. Werner, "Music," *IDB*, K-Q: 458. Cf. also V. H. Mathews, "Music in the Bible," *ABD*, 4: 930–934; I. H. Jones, "Musical Instruments," *ABD*, 4: 934–939. For other kinds of songs, see our discussion of poetry below.

60 His study of the song's metrical structure leads Christensen to suggest that its two stanzas may originally have been sung; cf. D. L. Christensen, "The Song of Jonah: A Metrical Analysis," *JBL* 104 (1985): 217–231.

61 Though technically not funeral dirges, Lam 1–2 and 4 offer a collection of dirges over the city of Jerusalem similar in content and rhythm to David's funeral laments. For recent scholarly doubts concerning whether the OT has the dirge genre, see our discussion in the chapter on biblical poetry.

62 Cf. B. E. Scolnic, *Theme and Context in Biblical Lists*, South Florida Studies in the History of Judaism 119 (Atlanta: Scholars Press, 1995), especially the "Master List of Lists Proper" and "Types of Lists in the Bible" (15–18); Long, "Historical Literature," 4–5.

63 For lists from Ugarit, see C. H. Gordon, *Ugaritic Textbook*, AnOr 38 (Rome: Pontifical Biblical Institute, 1965), 17.2 (290–91). For Egyptian examples, see the lists of Ramses III (12th century B.C.) in *ANET* 261–62.

64 Scolnic (*Lists*, 67–133) concludes that, unlike other pentateuchal narratives, Numbers 33 presents the wilderness period positively as "A March of Triumph" (his chapter title) —i.e., "a nation . . . presented with a view of a glorious past as an inspiration for the creation of a glorious future" (133).

65 The definitive study of genealogy, both biblical and extrabiblical, remains R. R. Wilson, *Genealogy and History in the Biblical World* (New Haven: Yale University Press, 1977); cf. also conveniently, his "Genealogy, Genealogies," *ABD*, 2: 929–932. Concerning genealogies and Genesis, see B. S. Childs, *Introduction to the Old Testament as Scripture* (Philadelphia: Fortress, 1979), 145–53.

This list traces the descent of an individual or tribe from antiquity down to a later time. Genealogies tend to bore the modern reader, but ancient peoples regarded them as crucial legal documents. They used genealogical records to establish their claims to be king or high priest, to possess certain property, and to marry into certain families.[66]

Principles of Interpretation—Embedded Genres

The following principles will help the student to interpret embedded genres:

1. Usually, an embedded genre forms a component of a larger context rather than an independent context itself.[67]

2. Thus, the goal of interpretation is to find what that component contributes to the message of the whole.

3. To attain that goal: (a) define the main point of the embedded genre (read by itself, what does it say?); (b) define the main idea(s) of its surrounding context (what subject does the context treat and what does it say about it?);[68] and (c) analyze the relationship between the point of the embedded genre and the idea(s) of its context (why does the compiler change genres in mid-context; how is the change supposed to affect the reader; what does it contribute to the message of the whole?).

To illustrate the application of these principles, let us briefly consider two examples. The first is the genealogy of Adam's descendants (Gen 5). Besides giving their names in order, the passage seems to focus on two key statistics for each descendant—his age when he fathered a son and his total lifespan. Its main point is that many generations and many years passed between Adam and Noah. As for the context, it apparently revolves around two ideas—the negative results of the fall of humankind (Abel's murder, Gen 4) and its numerical growth (Gen 6:1). In our view, the genealogy contributes two ideas to the context. By tracing many generations, it shows the proliferation of human life between Adam and Noah. It also serves as a literary bridge between them, as if to say simply, "Much time passed here."

The second example is the song Hannah sang after she gave birth to Samuel (1 Sam 2:1–10).[69] At first glance, the song seems slightly out of place in the context—an unexpected musical disruption in the narrative's flow. Its content soars far beyond the simple thanks of a once barren woman for her infant son. Rather, it praises God's great sovereign power over history in routing his enemies and in exalting his friends. Further, it falls between reports of Samuel's dedication to Yahweh (1:21–28) and the sinfulness of Israel's priesthood (2:12–17).

What does the song contribute to the context? In our view, it signals that the sovereign God of history stands behind the emergence of Samuel (and, later, of David,

---

66 The genealogy of Jesus (Mt 1:1–17) serves a similar purpose. By tracing Jesus' descent from David, it establishes his claim to David's royal throne, thus to his identity as Messiah; cf. J. C. Hutchison, "Women, Gentiles, and the Messianic Mission in Matthew's Genealogy," *BSac* 158 (2001): 152–164.

67 Some longer texts like songs or dirges represent exceptions to this principle. One may, in fact, study them both as independent contexts and as components of their surrounding context.

68 Here "context" actually means a series of contexts that surround the embedded genre as if the latter were the center of several concentric circles. The closest "circle" (the *immediate* context) probably will consist of a few verses before and after the genre. Succeeding circles (the *larger* context) may be a chapter, several chapters, or both.

69 Cf. Childs, *Introduction*, 272–73; also R. C. Bailey, "The Redemption of YHWH: A Literary Critical Function of the Songs of Hannah and David," *BibInt* 3 (1995): 213–31.

too). That he routs his enemies anticipates the prophecies of divine judgment on the priesthood that follow (2:27–36; 3:11–18).

LAW

Law probably strikes most readers as a rather dull subject. They may even wonder why we would treat it here as "literature."[70] Actually, the Pentateuch embeds Law within the context of narratives, thus giving it at least a narrative context if not a story-like "feel." That larger story is the setting for what scholars believe are four major collections of laws: the Covenant Code (Exod 20:22–23:33), the Deuteronomic Code (Deut 12–26), the Holiness Code (Lev 17–26), and the Priestly Code (Exod 25–31; 34:29; Lev 16; parts of Numbers).[71] With the oppressive, cruel social system of Egypt as background, these collections offer a comprehensive, radically different view of human community and the social values it promotes. Surely that amount of material driven by that sweeping, alternative vision of society merits some comment in an introduction to OT genres.[72]

Comparative study of large legal codes from the ancient Near East has considerably enriched our understanding of biblical Law.[73] In this brief survey of Law we will first discuss the OT's two main types of legal forms, and then we will discuss the genres of legal collections. Finally, we will suggest some principles for interpreting OT Law.

Types of Old Testament Legal Material

Casuistic Law

The first main type of legal form is *casuistic law* (or "case law").[74] Its distinctive "if . . . then" grammatical structure and impersonal third-person style make it easily recognizable.

---

70 In reality, Levinson makes an intriguing case for the literary nature of Law based on two literary phenomena, the adjustment by editors of conflicting laws within the Bible and their pseudonymity in doing so; cf. B. M. Levinson, "The Right Chorale: From the Poetics to the Hermeneutics of the Hebrew Bible," in Rosenblatt and Sitterson, "*Not in Heaven,*" 129–53.

71 For a convenient overview of the codes, see Johnson, *Making Sense of the Bible*, 66–72; cf. also R. Sonsino, "Forms of Biblical Law," *ABD*, 4: 252–254.

72 Excellent discussions of the codes underlying view of society are available in M. Douglas, *In the Wilderness: The Doctrine of Defilement in the Book of Numbers* (Oxford/New York: Oxford University Press, 2001); id., *Leviticus as Literature* (Oxford/New York: Oxford University Press, 1999). For their ethical implications, see J. G. Millar, *Now Choose Life: Theology and Ethics in Deuteronomy*, New Studies in Biblical Theology (Grand Rapids: Eerdmans, 1998); C. J. H. Wright, *Walking in the Ways of the Lord: The Ethical Authority of the Old Testament* (Downers Grove: InterVarsity, 1995); id., *God's People in God's Land: Family, Land, and Property in the Old Testament* (Grand Rapids: Eerdmans; Carlisle, UK: Paternoster, 1990); and D. Patrick, *Old Testament Law* (Atlanta: John Knox, 1985), 63–261.

73 A good introduction is S. Greengus, "Biblical and ANE Law," *ABD*, 4: 242–252. The major extrabiblical collections are the Laws of Ur-Nammu, the Lipit-Ishtar Law Code, the Laws of Eshnunna, the Code of Hammurabi, the Middle Assyrian Laws, the Hittite Laws, and the Neo-Babylonian Laws. For translations of the collections, see *ANET* 159–98; more conveniently, Mathews and Benjamin, *Old Testament Parallels*, 62–73. For a survey and critical assessment, see Walton, *Ancient Israelite Literature*, 69–92.

74 The classic study of the two basic forms is A. Alt, "The Origins of Israelite Law," in *Essays on Old Testament History and Religion* (Garden City, NY: Anchor Books, 1966), 101–71. For the larger discussion, see Sonsino, "Forms of Biblical Law," 252–53; and W. M. Clark, "Law," in *Old Testament Form Criticism*, ed. J. H. Hayes (San Antonio: Trinity University Press, 1977), 105–116.

The "if" clause describes the case concerned, the "then" clause describes the legal penalty for infractions (Exod 21:2, 32, 36; Deut 24:10). Consider this example:

condition If men quarrel and one hits the other with a stone or with his fist and he does not die but is confined to bed,

penalty the one who struck the blow will not be held responsible if the other gets up and walks around outside with his staff; however, he must pay the injured man for the loss of his time and see that he is completely healed. (Exod 21:18–19)

By stating both the condition and the penalty, legal precision carefully defines everything. That the form (and to some extent, the content) of Israelite casuistic law resembles ancient Near Eastern law suggests that the roots of this genre pre-date Israel's entrance into the arena of history.[75] With regard to content, OT casuistic law primarily treats civil or criminal cases rather than religious ones.[76]

Apodictic Law

The second major category is *apodictic law* (or "absolute law"), laws promulgated in unconditional, categorical directives such as commands and prohibitions.[77] Instead of finely tuned case descriptions, they issue absolute orders about right and wrong without considering any exceptions. They also feature personal direct address ("you shall / shall not") and primarily treat moral and religious matters.[78] The best-known form of apodictic law is the *prohibition* or negative command (e.g., "You shall not murder," Exod 20:13) that directly orders, "Don't do this!" Though less common, the *admonition* issues a positive command (Heb. imperative): "Honor your father and your mother . . ." (Exod 20:12; cf. v. 8). The admonition commands, "Do this!" without considering any exceptions (see a similar wisdom form below).

---

75 B. S. Jackson, *Studies in the Semiotics of Biblical Law*, JSOTSup 314 (Sheffield: Sheffield Academic Press, 2000), 63; cf. S. Paul, *Studies in the Book of the Covenant in Light of Cuneiform and Biblical Law*, VTSup 18 (Leiden: E. J. Brill, 1970), 112–18. Cf. this example from the Laws of Eshnunna (*ANET* 162, para. 30): "If a man hates his town and his lord and becomes a fugitive, (and if) another man takes his wife—when he returns, he shall have no right to claim his wife." For a comparative discussion of biblical and extrabiblical legal forms, see the essays in *Theory and Method in Biblical and Cuneiform Law: Revision, Interpolation and Development*, ed. B. M. Levinson, JSOTSup 181 (Sheffield: Sheffield Academic Press, 1994).

76 Patrick further subdivides casuistic law into *remedial law* (laws that prescribe a legal remedy for violations) and *primary law* (laws that prescribe the rights and duties of legal relationships; cf. Exod 22:25); cf. Patrick, *Old Testament Law*, 23; id., "Casuistic Law Governing Primary Rights and Duties," *JBL* 92 (1973): 180–84.

77 Alt, "The Origins of Israelite Law," 133–71. With Alt, we use this category to describe various formally non-conditional laws, but against him we make no assumption that they are either uniquely Israelite or originate in an early Israelite cultic setting. For a survey of the controversy concerning this category, see Sonsino, "Forms of Biblical Law," 252–53.

78 Only a few examples of apodictic law appear in ancient Near Eastern law codes; cf. the Code of Hammurabi (*ANET* 174, para. 187): "The (adopted) son of a chamberlain, a palace servant, or the (adopted) son of a votary, may never be reclaimed"; cf. also the Laws of Eshnunna, paragraphs 15–16 and 51–52 (*ANET* 162, 163).

Another apodictic subgenre draws its name from its grammatical form. The *participle law* deals with capital crimes: "Whoever strikes a person mortally shall be put to death." (Exod 21:12 NRSV).[79] The Hebrew participle ("Whoever strikes") describes the case while the main verb prescribes the penalty ("put to death"). Typical of apodictic law, the statement is categorical and considers no exceptions.

Last, we mention the well-known *law of retaliation* (or "lex talionis"):

> If there is serious injury, you are to take life for life, eye for eye, tooth for tooth, hand for hand, foot for foot, burn for burn, wound for wound, bruise for bruise. (Exod 21:23–25; cf. Gen 9:6; Lev 24:18–22; Deut 19:21)

Like other apodictic law, it addresses the audience personally ("you are to"). Its subject is premeditated crimes involving bodily harm (but see Deut 19:21). Strikingly, it articulates a broad legal principle—the equivalence of injury and penalty—rather than a specific action.[80] As with casuistic law, this genre goes back to pre-Israelite ancient legal practice.[81]

We may rightly lay to rest, however, the older view that the law of retaliation represented a "primitive" form of justice. On the contrary, it responds to a culture whose dominant legal principle was that of blood revenge—endless cycles of tit-for-tat violence (see Gen 4:23–24)—and marks "an effort to introduce the principle of proportionality into Israel's law."[82]

Legal Series

Laws rarely occur in isolation, so a consideration of legal literature must include types of legal collections. Scholars call a text with a small number of laws phrased in a similar style a *series* of laws. Apodictic laws typically occur in series and thereby take on an almost poetic quality when read.[83] Probably the best-known OT series is the Ten Commandments (Exod 20:2–17; Deut 5:6–21). They typify a unique ten-member

---

79 Grammatically, the participle is the subject of the verbal clause "must be put to death." Cf. also Gen 26:11; Exod 22:19; Lev 20:10; 24:16, 21; Num 35:21.

80 According to Ohler (*Studying the Old Testament,* 129), the point is "justice must be maintained."

81 E.g., the Code of Hammurabi, para. 196: "If a seignior has destroyed the eye of a member of the aristocracy, they shall destroy his eye" (*ANET* 175); cf. Greengus, "Biblical and ANE Law," 248–49. For recent discussion of the talion form, see Jackson, *Semiotics,* 271–97; J. Van Seters, "Some Observations on the lex talionis in Exod 21:23–25," in *Recht und Ethos im Alten Testament—Gestalt und Wirkung,* ed. S. Beyerle, G. Mayer, and H. Strauss (Neukirchen-Vluyn: Neukirchener, 1999), 27–37.

82 B. C. Birch, *Let Justice Roll Down: The Old Testament, Ethics, and Christian Life* (Louisville: Westminster John Knox, 1991), 163–64. In essence it says, "Only *one* eye for an eye, only *one* tooth for a tooth," etc. Another apodictic genre, the curse, occurs only in Deuteronomy as a legal form, e.g., "Cursed is the person who . . . " (Deut 27:15–26; cf. Gen 3:17) or "Cursed are you/is your . . . " (Deut 28:16–19; cf. Gen 3:14; 4:11). For discussion and bibliography, see J. Scharbert, "ʾārar," *TDOT* 1: 408–412; C. A. Keller, "ʾa-rar," *THAT* 1: 236–40.

83 Patrick, *Old Testament Law,* 20–22; cf. series of prohibitions (Exod 20:13–17; Lev 18:6–24; 19:11–18, 26–29; cf. Jer 7:9; Hos 4:2), participle laws (Exod 21:15–17; 31:14–15; Num 35:16–18), and curses (Deut 27:15–26; 28:16–19).

series or decalogue (cf. Deut 10:4) like the one Exodus 34 claims to have (see v. 28; one is hard pressed, however, to count exactly ten commandments). Though certainty eludes us, such texts may reflect an ancient practice that viewed such series as an ideal law code.[84]

Casuistic laws are grammatically more complex and wordy than apodictic laws. Hence, the OT organizes them, not in series, but in *topical groups*. A brief review of one context replete with casuistic laws, the so-called Covenant Book in Exodus, makes this evident. There we find sections of laws that prescribe policy for the treatment of servants (Exod 21:2–11), bodily injuries (21:18–32), and property losses (22:1–15).[85]

Legal Instruction

The Pentateuch has two lengthy instruction genres. As its name implies, *priestly instruction* aims to instruct priests in professional matters such as ritual procedures.[86] To recognize this genre the reader must determine from both the context (e.g., Lev 6:9) and the content that the text addresses the tasks of priests. Examples of priestly instruction include Lev 6–7 (about offerings) and Lev 21 (about priestly purity). Given their intended audience, it is best to interpret them as texts that concern the duties and expectations specifically of leaders.

The other instructional genre is *ritual* or instruction for laypeople about how to perform rituals properly—for example, how to bring offerings and what to offer (Lev 1–5). To recognize this genre the reader must determine from the context and content of the passage whether it addresses a lay audience.[87]

Principles of Interpretation—Law

OT Law poses an interpretive challenge for the Bible student, mainly because of a common misunderstanding of the nature of biblical Law. To the modern mind, the word "Law" conjures up images of massive, intricate legal codes and a spirit of "legalism." Yet in reality, for all its detail, the OT's legal sections do not constitute a comprehensive legal code. Many OT laws (e.g., the Ten Commandments) fail to specify a penalty for violations and to task an authority with enforcing compliance. They seem simply to assume an honor-system of self-enforcement by the Israelites themselves.

---

84 Concerning the significance of the Decalogue, see S. M. Hauerwas and W. H. Willimon, *The Truth About God: the Ten Commandments in Christian Life* (Nashville: Abingdon, 1999); M. Weinfeld, "The Decalogue: Its Significance, Uniqueness, and Place in Israel's Tradition," in *Religion and Law: Biblical-Judaic and Islamic Perspectives*, ed. E. B. Firmage, B. G. Weiss, and J. W. Welch (Winona Lake, IN: Eisenbrauns, 1990), 3–47.

85 For in-depth discussion, see F. Crüsemann, *The Torah: Theology and Social History of Old Testament Law* (Minneapolis: Fortress, 1996), 109–200; J. M. Sprinkle, *"The Book of the Covenant": A Literary Approach*, JSOTSup 174 (Sheffield: Sheffield Academic Press, 1994).

86 Begrich long ago called this genre *priestly da'at* (Heb. *da'at*, "knowledge"); cf. Hos 4:6; Mal 2:7; J. Begrich, "Die priesterliche Tora," *Gesammelte Studien zum Alten Testament,* TBü 21 (Munich: Chr. Kaiser, 1964), 251–58. To our knowledge, no sources in English treat this genre.

87 An earlier generation of scholars referred to such instructions for laity as *tôrâ* ("instruction"); cf. R. Rendtorff, *Studien zur Geschichte des Opfers im Alten Israel*, WMANT 23 (Neukirchen-Vluyn: Neukirchener, 1967), 7–10. While recognizing the lay orientation of Lev 1–5, Milgrom terms all of Lev 1–16 as *tôrôt* ("instructions, rituals"); cf. J. Milgrom, *Leviticus 1–16*, AB 3 (New York: Doubleday, 1991), 2.

Instead of a code in a modern sense, OT laws present a select sample of illustrative cases or topics whose legal principles were to guide Israelite individuals, the larger community, and lawmakers in making decisions and in living out Israel's worldview. Their purpose was to teach the Israelite fundamental values—what it means to live all of life in the presence of God—not to provide them with a handy legal reference tool.[88] In short, their aim was instructional rather than judicial. Further, OT Law is best understood in a covenant framework. It articulates the stipulations of the covenant made between God and Israel at Mt. Sinai; thus, OT Law represents the personal demands of Israel's sovereign Lord, not an abstract system of morality or a technical legal code.[89]

In light of this, readers must interpret Law relationally—as the guidelines that govern Israel's ongoing life with her gracious God. In return for his protection and blessing, God expects his people to obey what the Law commands—in short, to maintain their relationship with God on a healthy footing. The Ten Commandments (Exod 20; Deut 5) express the broad, overarching ethical principles whose details the subsequent legal codes flesh out.[90] Thus, Bible students must interpret them as foundational ethical principles to maintain relationship with a loving Lord and to cultivate a covenant community, not as a legal code.[91] Their complex contents aim to create a distinctive people of God, one whose community structure and ethics accurately mirror the nature of its Lord.

For modern Bible students the question is: *How does the Law apply to Christians today?* In reply, we affirm two fundamental interrelated assumptions about the nature of OT Law.[92] First, we believe that God intends it to serve as a paradigm of timeless ethical, moral, and theological principles. In other words, the Law is more than a temporary, dispensable cultural phenomenon. Actually, it plays a key role in Israel's priestly ministry as a "light to the nations" (Isa 49:6 NRSV; cf. Exod 19:5–6). Christians who dismiss it as outmoded and irrelevant deprive themselves of the teachings God conveyed through it. They miss an additional resource for understanding what it might mean to be "Christ-like."

---

88 Birch, *Justice*, 171–172; R. L. Hubbard, Jr., *The Book of Ruth*, NICOT (Grand Rapids: Eerdmans, 1988), 50. In fact, the nature of ancient law remains a matter of ongoing discussion; cf. the essays in Levinson, *Theory and Method*; and C. M. Carmichael, *The Origins of Biblical Law: The Decalogues and the Book of the Covenant* (Ithaca/London: Cornell University Press, 1992).

89 So R. E. Averbeck, "Law," in Sandy and Giese, *Cracking Codes*, 134–35; Birch, *Justice*, 145–46 (cf. also his discussion [146–57] of "The God Who Makes Covenant"); cf. also E. A. Martens, "How Is the Christian to Construe Old Testament Law?" *BBR* 12 (2002): 199–216. Here we accept ancient treaty-making as the background of the Mosaic covenant as in G. Wenham, "Grace and Law in the Old Testament," in *Law, Morality, and the Bible*, ed. B. Kaye and G. Wenham (Downers Grove: InterVarsity, 1978), 9–13.

90 Birch, *Justice*, 168; G. Wenham, "Law and the Legal System in the Old Testament," in Kaye and Wenham, *Law, Morality, and the Bible*, 28–29. For an excellent description of the community the Law intended to shape, see Birch, *Justice*, 172–84.

91 For a topical treatment of five types of law, see C. J. H. Wright, *An Eye for An Eye. The Place of Old Testament Ethics Today* (Downers Grove: InterVarsity, 1983), 153–59. We prefer his more sociologically based categories to the traditional division of OT Law into civil, ceremonial, and moral types. For a broader treatment of ethics, including discussion of crucial contemporary issues, see id., *Walking in the Ways of the Lord: The Ethical Authority of the Old Testament* (Downers Grove: InterVarsity, 1995); C. S. Rodd, *Glimpses of a Strange Land: Studies in Old Testament Ethics* (Edinburgh: T & T Clark, 2001).

92 Wright, *Eye*, 40–45, 156–57, 161–62, 170–71.

Second, to interpret Law properly the student must discover the timeless truth it conveys. In some cases, the truth lies right on the surface unobscured by culture. Prohibitions like "Do not murder" and "Do not steal" (Exod 20:13, 15; Deut 5:17, 19) need no cross-cultural translation; they clearly identify murder and stealing as wrong. Similarly, the timeless aspect of the instructions about equitable legal procedure (Exod 23:1–8) is fairly obvious: witnesses should tell the truth, not cater to the crowd (vv. 1–3); opponents at law should treat each other civilly (vv. 4–5); and judges should judge by evidence and refuse bribes (vv. 6–8).

In other instances, the underlying, universal truth may be difficult to perceive behind its present cultural form—ancient Israelite Law—so careful interpretation is necessary. Consider, for example, the perplexing laws that decree a woman's menstrual bleeding makes her and everything she touches unclean (Lev 15:19–30).[93] These laws seem rather harsh and unfair, in effect making women untouchable one week out of every four. We wonder what timeless principle could possibly underlie them.

To answer this question we need to consider the Israelite cultural background. Israelite women married early, had children early, weaned their children late (at ages two or three), and tended to have large families (cf. Psa 127:4–5). Thus, a monthly menses was much less common among Israelite women than it is today, especially among married women. In actuality, unmarried, adolescent women were those most directly and frequently affected by these laws. We suggest, then, that these laws, in effect, sought to regulate teenage passions and discourage sexual relations between young unmarried Israelites.[94] If so, the underlying truth appears to be that sexual relations outside of marriage displease God and may adversely affect the orderly relations between Israelite families.

From early on, Christians have often spoken of Christ as the key to interpreting the OT. Jesus himself established precedent for this view when he declared, "Do not think that I have come to abolish the Law or the Prophets; I have not come to abolish them but to fulfill them" (Mt 5:17). Clearly the Gospel writers believed that Christ fulfilled many prophecies; five such "fulfillment quotations" appear in Mt 1–2 alone. But here Jesus refers to "the Law" as well as to the Prophets, presumably meaning all the Hebrew Scriptures, and Matthew goes on to illustrate Jesus' code of ethics in contrast to the OT Law. Therefore, to fulfill a law must mean to bring to completion everything for which that law was originally intended (cf. v. 18: "until everything is accomplished").[95]

In some cases, as with sacrifices and various ceremonies (cf. Col 2:16–17), that point of completion was Christ's death and resurrection. Throughout his ministry, Jesus challenged fundamental principles of both oral and written *Torah,* especially those relating to Sabbath and dietary laws. At the same time, he never broke any of the written Law while

---

93 Here we draw on the comments of G. J. Wenham, *The Book of Leviticus,* NICOT (Grand Rapids: Eerdmans, 1979), 219–24. Anyone who was "unclean" could not, among other things, join the community in public worship.

94 So Wenham, *Leviticus,* 224. Conceivably, other factors also come into play in this instance (e.g., ritual taboos associated with bodily emissions).

95 For the thesis that Paul understood Christ as the "termination," not just the "goal," of the Law, see J. P. Heil, "Christ, the Termination of the Law (Romans 9:30–10:8)," *CBQ* 63 (2001): 484–98. On the wider topic of the Law in the Gospels and Paul, see conveniently R. S. Hendel, "The Law in the Gospel: The Law Is An Essential Precondition for the Gospel," *Bible Review* 14 (1998): 20, 52.

it remained God's will for his people (i.e., before the cross, resurrection, and sending of the Holy Spirit at Pentecost inaugurated the age of God's new covenant).[96] In other cases, as with many moral injunctions, the point of completion will not occur until Christ's return.

Mt 5:17, therefore, suggests the following hermeneutical principle for applying the OT in the NT age: *All of the OT applies to Christians, but none of it applies apart from its fulfillment in Christ.*[97] Thus, our view falls in the middle ground between the views of classic covenant theology (all the OT applies except what the NT repeals) and in classic dispensationalism (none of the OT applies except what the NT repeals). The former would logically lead to prohibitions against most modern farming practices and clothing fashions (Deut 22:9–12), while the latter would logically lead to the acceptance of sorcerers, mediums, and spiritists (despite Deut 18:9–13)! For in neither case does the NT say anything one way or the other about these specific practices. Instead, we suggest that all of the OT laws as "useful for teaching, rebuking, correcting and training in righteousness" (2 Tim 3:16), but only as one discovers how those laws are fulfilled in Christ.

How may we determine how Christ fulfills them? We suggest that where the NT specifically cites a particular law, the interpreter's task is eased considerably. We obey the laws of sacrifice by trusting in Christ as our once-for-all sacrifice (Heb 9:1–10:25), not by bringing sheep or goats to be slain each Sunday in church. The kosher laws were designed to set the Israelites apart from the other nations so we obey this principle as we pursue a Christ-like lifestyle that avoids sin (2 Cor 6:17), even though Christ declared that all foods are clean (Mk 7:19b). The symbol of baptism parallels the principle behind the law of circumcision (Col 2:11b-12a), though the rites are not identical in all aspects. For example, Christians baptize women as well as men, and most likely the NT envisioned only people old enough to repent from sin rather than infants as recipients (Col 2:11a-12b).

Where the NT does not address a particular law, we must discover if it fits a category of Law the NT does address. For example, orthodox Jews view the command "you shall not boil a kid in its mother's milk" (Exod 23:19 NRSV; 34:26; Deut 14:21) as a dietary law that prevents them from serving milk and meat dishes at the same meal. Even if this was the law's original intention, this command takes its place with the other kosher laws that no longer apply literally to Christians' diets since Jesus has declared all foods clean (Mk 7:19).[98] Alternately, it may have been a command meant to dissociate the Israelites from certain pagan, religious practices, much like the otherwise unrelated warnings, "Do not cut the hair at the sides of your head or clip off the edges of your

---

96 Cf. especially R. Banks, *Jesus and the Law in the Synoptic Tradition*, SNTSMS 28 (Cambridge, UK: Cambridge University Press, 1975); D. J. Moo, "Jesus and the Authority of the Mosaic Law," *JSNT* 20 (1984): 3–49. See also the recent, nuanced discussion in W. R. G. Loader, *Jesus' Attitude Toward the Law*, WUNT 97 (Tübingen: J. C. B. Mohr [Paul Siebeck], 1997).

97 Cf. esp. D. A. Dorsey, "The Law of Moses and the Christian: A Compromise," *JETS* 34 (1991): 321–34.

98 Though quoted three times (for texts, see above), the background of the prohibition against boiling a kid in its mother's milk remains uncertain. The best one can say is that it prohibits a practice thought to compromise Israel's exclusive relationship with Yahweh; so J. I. Durham, *Exodus*, WBC 3 (Waco, TX: Word, 1987) 462; cf. D. L. Christensen, *Deuteronomy 1:1–21:9*, rev. ed., WBC 6A (Nashville: Nelson, 2001), 289–90, 294–295.

beard. Do not cut your bodies for the dead or put tattoo marks on yourselves" (Lev 19:27–28).[99] Any practices, whether relating to diet or personal appearance, that represent pagan worship (as in the self-mutilation practices of several world religions and occult sects today) remain strictly forbidden for believers. But if Christians partake of goat's meat and milk or get tattooed for some nonreligious reason, they do not transgress God's commands.

To summarize, OT Law relates to Christians in light of the NT in the following ways:

- Some laws retain literal validity for Christians. For example, Jesus reaffirmed the OT injunctions to love the Lord wholeheartedly and to love one's neighbor (Mt 5:21–48; 22:40; cf. Deut 6:5; Lev 19:18). Similarly, Paul invoked the OT legal requirement of two or three witnesses to establish guilt in the case of accusations against Christian leaders (1 Tim 5:19; cf. Deut 17:6; 19:15; 2 Cor 13:1). Any other laws that the NT applies to Christians remain valid.

- In some cases, the NT actually makes the OT Law more strict. For example, in the case of marriage, the seventh commandment forbids adultery, and the OT permits divorce and remarriage (Exod 20:14; Deut 5:18; 24:1–4). But unlike the OT, the NT regards divorce and remarriage (and, by implication, polygamy) as adultery (Mt 19:3–12; Mk 10:2–12; Lk 16:18). Further, Jesus permitted divorce only when marital infidelity had occurred (Mt 19:9); Paul, only in the case of desertion by an unbeliever (1 Cor 7:15–16). The truth behind both OT and NT laws was the value of preserving stable marriages.[100]

- Some laws no longer have literal validity because of NT teachings (i.e., their fulfillment in Christ renders their literal practice obsolete).[101] Thus, Christians no longer need to follow literally the OT sacrificial system (Heb 10:1–10), to obey its food laws (Mk 7:19; cf. Acts 10:9–16), or to perform circumcision (Gal 5:2–6).

- Laws that no longer apply literally still teach important timeless truths. Thus, the OT sacrificial system graphically reminds Christians that God takes sin seriously, requires a severe penalty, yet graciously offers forgiveness. Similarly, the clean animals in OT food laws probably symbolized Israel as the chosen people, in contrast to her ritually "unclean" pagan neighbors. Hence, eating reminded Israelites (and, by implication, Christians) of their gracious election by God and their resulting duty to pursue God-like holiness.[102] Even

---

99 Association with pagan mourning rites seems the most likely rationale; cf. J. Milgrom, *Leviticus 17–22*, AB 3A (New York: Doubleday, 2000), 1690–93; E. S. Gerstenberger, *Leviticus: A Commentary*, OTL (Louisville: Westminster John Knox, 1996), 276–77.

100 Wenham, "Law and the Legal System," 36–37, who comments, however, "in practice the differences [between OT and NT teachings] were quite slight."

101 Cf. J. J. Davis, *Foundations of Evangelical Theology* (Grand Rapids: Baker, 1984), 257–58.

102 Wenham, "Law and the Legal System," 30.

the cultic law concerning the sabbatical fallow year (Lev 25; Deut 15) proves instructive, underscoring that compassionate humanitarian service ultimately represents service for God.[103]

Understanding Jesus as the fulfillment of the Law also has implications for interpreting NT ethics more generally. Kingdom demands, like the Mosaic Law, flow from and respond to the redemption of God's people but do not "earn" anyone's salvation. But failure to observe OT laws often led to specific sanctions and punishments; failure by the nation at large eventually led to loss of peace, prosperity, and land. Because Jesus' single sacrifice has fulfilled all of God's demands in Scripture for justice, few NT ethical texts ever suggest that keeping or transgressing God's commandments today lead to the identical material blessings or punishments.[104]

Although the story of the woman caught in adultery almost certainly was not in John's original text, a good case can be made for its authenticity as a true story about what Jesus did and said.[105] In it he establishes a precedent for forbidding the application of OT sanctions even for such a fundamental moral issue as adultery. A possible exception appears in the case of murder. Because what we would call "first-degree homicide" was the only sin for which a ransom could not be substituted for a sacrifice (Num 35:31),[106] some Christians believe capital punishment for murder remains appropriate in the Christian era. But many others point to Christ's once-for-all sacrifice as obliterating the need for further sanctions—whether physical or spiritual—for all sin.

As for specific *principles of interpretation,* we recommend the following:

1. Whatever its literary type, the collection or series in which an individual law appears serves as its literary context. Thus, the student should investigate surrounding laws for interpretive clues.

2. The student should endeavor to understand the original meaning of laws in light of their cultural background. Since many readers lack such knowledge, we recommend that they liberally consult Bible dictionaries, commentaries, and other background sources. See the bibliography at the end.

3. Apply laws primarily to the NT counterpart of the original audience. For example, laws aimed at Israel as a whole make proper application to Christians in general. Since the NT affirms the "priesthood of all believers," both priestly and ritual instructions would also apply to Christians in general, not just to clergy.

---

103 Wright, *Eye,* 156–57. Cf. also Paul's application of Deut 25:4 ("Do not muzzle an ox while it is treading out the grain") to the right of Christian leaders to earn their living by ministry (1 Cor 9:7–12); and his teaching that love underlies—and, thereby, its practice fulfills—the Law (Rom 13:8–10). For additional discussion of the application of Law, see J. D. Hays, "Applying the Old Testament Law Today," *BSac* 21 (2001): 21–35.

104 For a standard, full treatment of NT ethics, see G. H. Stassen and D. P. Gushee, *Kingdom Ethics: Following Jesus In Contemporary Context* (Downers Grove: InterVarsity Press, 2003).

105 See esp. G. M. Burge, "A Specific Problem in the New Testament Text and Canon: The Woman Caught in Adultery (John 7:53–8:11)," *JETS* 27 (1984): 141–48. For recent interpretation, see L. J. Kreitzer and D. W. Rooke, eds., *Ciphers in the Sand: Interpretations of the Woman Taken in Adultery (John 7:53–8:11),* Biblical Seminar Series (Sheffield: Sheffield Academic Press, 2000).

106 See esp. W. C. Kaiser, Jr., *Toward Old Testament Ethics* (Grand Rapids: Zondervan, 1983), 165–68.

4. Whether a given law applies literally, in principle, or both, depends upon how it compares to laws in the categories discussed above. The reader may use the latter as guidelines for making application.

A Sample Legal Text: Exodus 21:7–11

A brief study of this text—in form, casuistic law—permits us to apply the above discussion.[107] Set within a larger slave law (vv. 1–11), vv. 7–11 concern the redemption of an Israelite woman whose father, presumably driven by financial necessity, has sold her into a slave-marriage. Structurally, the text first defines the case (Heb. *kî*; "When . . . , she shall not . . . ," v. 7 NRSV), then details its subconditions (Heb. *'im*; "if . . . , then . . . ," vv. 8–11).

Now a male slave needs no redemption because he automatically goes free after six years of service (v. 2), so the instruction mandates the redemption of a female slave—the paying off of the debt to free her—under two conditions: 1) she no longer "pleases" the man; 2) he has given her legal status as a wife (v. 8). On the other hand she enjoys standing as a "daughter" if the man has given her to his son as wife (v. 9).

Two things are striking about this law. First, it gives the woman remarkable protection against abuse by her displeased husband. It forbids him from selling her to a foreigner or from denying her spousal rights to food, clothing, and sexual relations (vv. 8–11). Second, the reason for her right to redemption is his breach of faith (i.e., "since he has dealt unfairly [Heb. *bgd*] with her"; v. 8b). The law makes the loss of favor his responsibility; indeed, the root *bgd* ("to deal treacherously") seems to imply a breach of faith on his part that opens the possibility of her freedom.

Several implications flow from this legal instruction. First, the law bases marriage in understandings and commitments inherent in the relationship rather than in one member's "likes" or "dislikes." Second, in protecting a socially vulnerable woman, it implies God's commitment to protect the vulnerable from abuse. Now, the NT shares that commitment to the lowly, so to apply the OT Law today would entail two things: on the one hand, an honest examination of one's relationships for possible abuse of people, and, on the other, a look-around for any abused or vulnerable near us whom one might offer protection.

Deuteronomy

In a sense, the book of *Deuteronomy* represents a collection of laws, yet as a unique literary genre, it requires special consideration. Deuteronomy offers a comprehensive restatement of the Mosaic Law. Excluding the brief narrative opening (1:1–5) and lengthy conclusion (31–34), the book consists of Moses' farewell speeches to the Israelites while they were camped east of the Jordan River (1:6–4:40; 5–26; 27:11–28:68; 29:2–30).[108] Scholars commonly describe the rhetoric of these speeches

---

107 For further discussion and bibliography, see R. L. Hubbard, Jr., "The Divine Redeemer: Toward a Biblical Theology of Redemption," in *Reading the Hebrew Bible for A New Millennium: Form, Concept, and Theological Perspective*, ed. W. Kim, et al., Studies in Antiquity and Christianity (Harrisburg, PA: Trinity Press International, 2000), 1: 189–91.

108 Useful introductions to the book are available in M. Weinfeld, "Deuteronomy, Book of," *ABD*, 2: 168–83; R. E. Clements, *Deuteronomy*, OT Guides (Sheffield: JSOT Press, 1989); and Christensen, *Deuteronomy 1:1–21:9*, lvii-lxxix.

as *parenesis*—a style of speech that intends to persuade the audience to adopt a certain course of action.[109]

Further, the structure of the book closely resembles that of suzerain-vassal treaties like those of the Hittites and Assyrians (second and first millennia B.C., respectively).[110] Such treaties dictated the relationship between a major power (the suzerain) and its subject nation (the vassal). Like the latter, Deuteronomy has a historical prologue (1:6–4:43), a list of stipulations (chaps. 5–26), mention of witnesses to the agreement ("heaven and earth," 4:26; 30:19; 31:28), and blessings and curses (chaps. 27–28).

On the other hand, in one significant respect Deuteronomy differs from ancient treaties: in the latter, the Hittite or Assyrian king addresses the subject nation; in the former Moses, not King Yahweh, addresses Yahweh's subject, Israel. Thus, though "treaty-like" in form, Deuteronomy is best read as the "testament" of Moses—a series of exhortations that articulate his ethical "will" as if he were addressing his successor, whether Israel as a whole, a later king, or both.[111]

Principles of Interpretation: Deuteronomy

We suggest that readers interpret Deuteronomy according to these guidelines:

1. Deuteronomy is best heard as Moses' impassioned speeches to God's people threatened by temptations to compromise their exclusive commitment to God.

2. Its crucial historical background is the potential, corrupting influence of the Canaanite religion on Israel. The foreboding shadow of Baal worship haunts much of its content, a fact that should shape our interpretation of it.

3. Approach the laws of Deuteronomy as Moses' passionate exhortations—i.e., a series of farewell speeches just prior to his death and Israel's entry into Canaan—rather than as abstract, technical legal instruction. At its heart lies the theological issue of religious accommodation to idolatry, an issue still relevant today.

4. The literary nature of each section should dictate the interpretive approach to it. For example, poetic sections (chaps. 32–33) require treatment appropriate to poetry; laws, those proper for legal materials, etc. Similarly, application should follow guidelines for each genre.

POETRY

After narratives, poetry is the most common literary form in the Bible. Virtually all biblical books, even those not traditionally called "poetical," contain some poetry.[112]

---

109 So Long, "Historical Literature," 255, citing Deut 6–11; Zech 1:3–6; Josh 24:2–15; 1 Kgs 8:56–61.

110 See the helpful summary with bibliography in D. J. McCarthy, *Old Testament Covenant* (Richmond, VA: John Knox, 1972), 10–34; more recently, J. J. M. Roberts, "The Ancient Near Eastern Environment," in Knight and Tucker, *The Hebrew Bible*, 93–94. For translations of Egyptian and Hittite treaties, see *ANET* 199–206.

111 Of course, Moses' exhortations restate the covenant just before Israel enters the Promised Land. In passing, we observe that a few OT narratives report ancient Israelite legal processes. Awareness of their legal nature will enable the reader to understand them better. These include an investigative procedure called an ordeal (Num 5:11–31), several criminal trials (Gen 31:25–42; 2 Sam 1:1–16; 4:5–12), and a civil process about prior rights (Ruth 4:1–12).

112 Gabel and Wheeler, *The Bible as Literature*, 37. For example, Exodus and Judges each have a lengthy victory song, the "Song of Moses" (Exod 15:1–18; cf. v. 21) and the "Song of Deborah" (Judg 5; see also 1 Sam 2:1–10; 2 Sam 23:1–7; Jonah 2).

Now poetry is not a genre per se but a literary style—the alternative to prose. So to study poetry we will survey the major literary types of OT poetry and conclude with suggested principles of interpretation.

Types of Old Testament Poetry

Prayers

Prayers are specially worded, extended statements spoken (not sung) to God by individuals or groups. The *complaint* constitutes the most common genre of prayer in the psalms.[113] Whether prayed by an individual or the corporate worshiping community, a complaint is a heart-felt petition for Yahweh to deliver from some humanly unsolvable crisis. For an individual the crisis might be severe illness, misfortune, or false accusations; for the community, it might be a drought, plagues, or invasions by enemies.[114] Most scholars assume that complaints were prayed at a sanctuary, such as the temple in Jerusalem, as part of a larger ritual process. Unlike dirges or laments, in which speakers vent deep grief and hopeless despair, complaints voice deep suffering but assume that the crisis can be resolved by God's intervention.[115]

Psalm 22 provides an excellent example of the typical complaint psalm.[116] It opens with an invocation of God's name(s) as a way of making contact with Yahweh (vv. 1–2). It includes an affirmation of confidence (vv. 3–5) by which the petitioner affirms trust in God. The complaint element (vv. 6–18) describes in general terms the affliction threatening the individual or community. In the petition (vv. 19–21) the worshiper specifically asks for God's help in resolving the problem. Finally, complaints often close with a thanksgiving element—in this case, a hymn of thanksgiving (vv. 22–26)—in which the petitioner offers thanks in advance of receiving his petition.[117] When the

---

113 Cf. R. E. Murphy, *The Gift of the Psalms* (Peabody, MA: Hendrickson, 2000), 11–14; B. W. Anderson (with S. Bishop), *Out of the Depths: The Psalms Speak for Us Today*, 3d ed. (Louisville: Westminster John Knox, 2000); E. S. Gerstenberger, *Psalms 1*, FOTL 14 (Grand Rapids: Eerdmans, 1988), 11–14 ("Introduction to Cultic Poetry"), 108; id., "Psalms," in Hayes, *Old Testament Form Criticism*, 198–205; and H. Gunkel and J. Begrich, *Introduction to the Psalms* (Macon, GA: Mercer University Press, 1998 [Ger orig. 1933]), 82–98, 121–98.

114 For the communal complaints, see the fine study by P. W. Ferris, Jr., *The Genre of Communal Lament in the Bible and the Ancient Near East*, SBLDS 127 (Atlanta: Scholars Press, 1992).

115 With great insight, W. Brueggemann (*The Message of the Psalms* [Minneapolis: Augsburg, 1984], 18–23) calls the complaints psalms of disorientation because the psalmist's experience of suffering seems to imply a disturbed relationship with God. These disorientation psalms contrast the psalms of orientation (i.e., songs of praise) and of new orientation (i.e., thanksgiving songs after restoration from suffering). For an insightful treatment of the psalms from a multicultural perspective, see S. B. Reid, *Listening in: A Multicultural Reading of the Psalms* (Nashville: Abingdon, 1997).

116 Cf. T. Longman, III, "Lament," in Sandy and Giese, *Cracking Codes*, 199–201 (discussion of features) and 210–12 (treatment of Psalm 77 as an example). For an illuminating, in-depth study of complaints, see also D. Dombkowski Hopkins, *Journey Through the Psalms*, rev. ed. (St. Louis: Chalice Press, 2002), 77–132. For an introduction to the psalms with an eye toward prayer, see S. L. Jaki, *Praying the Psalms: A Commentary* (Grand Rapids: Eerdmans, 2001).

117 Other common elements include a confession of sin or assertion of innocence (e.g., Psa 7:3–5; 51:3–5) and an imprecation against enemies (e.g., Psa 5:10; 109:6–20); cf. the list of these psalms in Gerstenberger, *Psalms 1*, 14. C. Mandolfo, *God in the Dock: Dialogic Tension in the Psalms of Lament*, JSOTSup 357 (Sheffield: Sheffield Academic Press, 2002), studies another phenomenon, the transition from first and second to third person speakers within the same complaints, and concludes (197–206) that they reflect actual dialogues in cultic settings.

king either speaks or is spoken of, we designate that psalm a *royal complaint* (see Psa 89; 144).[118]

A few complaint psalms include an imprecation as part of the petition. Hence, such texts are sometimes called *imprecatory psalms*.[119] The horrible things that the imprecations request from God trouble some readers (e.g., "For the curses and lies they utter, consume them in wrath, consume them till they are no more," Psa 59:12b-13; cf. 10:15; 109:6–15; 137:7–9; 139:19–22). We suggest, however, that students should understand their extreme language as hyperbole—emotional exaggerations by which the psalmist hopes to persuade Yahweh to act. In other words, the psalmist wants God to know how strongly he feels about the matter.

They, thus, serve an important two-fold function: to expose the world's violence and oppression lest it be ignored, and to give its victims the words in which to express their legitimate outrage. Further, as prayers they occur within an ongoing relationship with God; they direct their fury to the right person, the God of justice and vengeance whom their pain touches and who will meet their needs and respond according to his will. At the same time, one must read imprecatory psalms in light of the Bible's criticism of blind vengeance (e.g., Rom 12:9, 21) and, hence, not appeal to them to justify revenge.[120]

A *dirge* is a funeral lamentation spoken as part of ancient mourning rites. Its main components are expressions of moaning or wailing, a description of some disaster, and a call for others to weep and wail.[121] Obviously, the emotional mood is one of utter despair over an irreversible loss. Though dirges are absent from the Hebrew Psalter, their influence is evident on several psalms (Psa 35:13–14; 44; 74). Parts of the book of Lamentations, however, have dirges that lament, not the loss of a person, but the destruction of a city and its population (see chaps. 1–2, 4). Indeed, the book may reflect an ancient custom of mourning the loss of a city.[122]

---

118 Complaints also occur in Jer 10–20 and in Job; cf. K. M. O'Connor, *The Confessions of Jeremiah: Their Interpretation and Role in Chapters 1–25*, SBLDS 97 (Atlanta: Scholars Press, 1988); R. E. Murphy, *Job: A Short Reading* (New York: Paulist Press, 1999). For a recent reassessment of the nature and canonical function of royal psalms, see S. R. A. Starbuck, *Court Oracles in the Psalms: The So-Called Royal Psalms in their Ancient Near Eastern Context*, SBLDS 172 (Atlanta: SBL, 1999).

119 Cf. recently the treatment of Psalm 137 by P. D. Miller, "The Hermeneutics of Imprecation," in *Theology in the Service of the Church: Essays in Honor of Thomas W. Gillespie*, ed. W. M. Alston, Jr. (Grand Rapids: Eerdmans, 2000), 153–63; and the insightful chapter in H. C. Bullock, *Encountering the Psalms* (Grand Rapids: Baker, 2001), 227–38.

120 Cf. Miller, "Imprecation," 158–62; Bullock, *Psalms*, 237–38. For further suggestions concerning their liturgical use, see Miller, "Imprecation," 162–63.

121 Gerstenberger, *Psalms 1*, 10–11. For the best examples, see our comments about genres embedded in OT narratives. For doubts concerning this genre, see the chapter on poetry above.

122 See S. N. Kramer, *Lamentation over the Destruction of Ur*, Assyriological Studies 12 (Chicago: Oriental Institute, 1940); *ANET* 455–63; Mathews and Benjamin, *Old Testament Parallels*, 169–75. For a discussion of the relationship between Sumerian antecedents and Lamentations, see Walton, *Ancient Israelite Literature in Its Cultural Context*, 160–63. Recent larger treatments of Lamentations are available in K. M. O'Connor, *Lamentations and the Tears of the World* (Maryknoll, NY: Orbis, 2002); and T. Linafelt, *Surviving Lamentations: Catastrophe, Lament, and Protest in the Afterlife of a Biblical Book* (Chicago: University of Chicago Press, 2000).

Recognition of the Bible's dirges is beneficial in several ways. First, it enables the interpreter to read the text with a specific scenario in mind: wailing mourners bitterly rending their clothes or donning sackcloth. Second, it underscores the hopelessness of the situation that the text describes. Death remains a tragedy with no conceivable human remedy. The reader, thus, must sense the emotional despair in Lamentations, even though the author's appeal to God for rescue does offer hope (cf. 1 Thes 4:13). Third, it legitimizes the expression of human grief among Christians today. By honoring grief practices of old, the Bible stamps them as "normal" for God's people who suffer similar losses today.[123]

Songs

The singing of songs—especially those sung in worship at the temple—played a prominent role in the life of God's people. Apparently, even Israel's neighbors highly valued her musical expertise, for the Assyrian king Sennacherib proudly listed male and female musicians among the items of tribute given to him by king Hezekiah of Jerusalem (eighth century B.C.).[124]

The *thanksgiving song* (Heb. *tôdâ*) is closely associated with the complaint. Through such songs, the individual or community voiced joyful gratitude to God for deliverance from previous misery. They, as it were, made good on their previous promises of thanks.[125] Significantly, speakers directly address their remarks both to Yahweh and to others participating in the ceremony.

Psalm 30 illustrates the two elements at the heart of this song: the praise of Yahweh for his help (vv. 1, 12b) and the invitation for others to join in thanking and praising Yahweh (vv. 4–5). A third key element is an account of salvation that reports what Yahweh has done to merit praise (vv. 2–3, 6–12a). As with complaints, when the king either speaks or is spoken of, we designate such a text as a *royal thanksgiving song* (see Pss 18; 21).

The *hymn* (or song of praise) closely resembles the thanksgiving song and comprises a major genre in the Psalter. Originally part of a large, colorful Israelite festivity, a hymn is a song that praises Yahweh.[126] (For hymns in prophets and Job, see below.) Psalm 96 exemplifies the two main structural components of a hymn: the summons to praise, addressed to other worshipers and probably sung by a song leader or choir (vv. 1–3; cf. vv. 7–13); and the actual praise of Yahweh (vv. 4–6).[127] In some cases, an individual offers praise for

---

123 Hopkins (*Journey*, 105–132) offers an insightful, pastoral treatment of the process of lament with examples of ways in which congregations might incorporate it in worship today.

124 See the Prism of Sennacherib, *ANET*, 287–88. Further, Psa 137:3 ("Sing us one of the songs of Zion!") may imply that the Babylonians found Israelite music appealing, just as many people find delight in modern Hebrew music.

125 Murphy, *Psalms*, 10–11; Hopkins, *Journey*, 133–40, who also cites Psalm 30 as an example; cf. Gunkel, *Psalms*, 199–221. According to Gerstenberger (*Psalms 1*, 15) the offertory formula "I give you thanks" means "I am handing over to you my thank offering" (Psa 118:21; 138:1–2; cf. Isa 12:1).

126 Cf. Murphy, *Psalms*, 9–10; Hopkins, *Journey*, 32–58; Gunkel, *Psalms*, 22–65. According to the book of Chronicles, families of temple singers, not the congregation, sang such hymns (1 Chr 15:16–22; 16:5–7; 2 Chr 5:12).

127 For other examples of hymns, see Pss 8; 19; 65; 66; 67; 68; 95; 96; 100; 104; 105; et al. According to Wolters, Proverbs 31's many hymnic characteristics commends it as a heroic hymn; cf. A. Wolters, "Proverbs 31:10–31 as Heroic Hymn: A Form-critical Analysis," in *Poetry in the Hebrew Bible: Selected Studies from Vetus Testamentum*, ed. D. E. Orton (Leiden/Boston: E. J. Brill, 2000), 186–97.

some personal experience of Yahweh's greatness, so we call that a *personal hymn* (see Pss 8; 77; 103–104; 139; et al.).[128]

Several other hymns were limited to ceremonies that either involved the king or celebrated the uniqueness of Jerusalem. Indeed, for that very reason, many scholars have called them "royal psalms" (occasionally, "messianic psalms"). For example, Pss 2 and 110 (and possibly 72) are *coronation hymns* sung or read during ceremonies at the accession of a new king to power (see 2 Kgs 11:4–12).[129] A *Zion hymn* is one that praises Mount Zion as the residence of Yahweh, the main site of Israelite worship, and Jerusalem as a royal city (see Pss 46; 48; 76; 84; 122; 132). Presumably, on various festive occasions Israel commemorated such divinely sanctioned truths about Jerusalem. Also at home in such liturgical festivities was the *Yahweh-kingship hymn* that extols his supreme rulership as well as his association with the Davidic dynasty (Pss 47; 93; 96–99).[130]

Finally, the OT contains a few *love songs*. For example, Psa 45 is a royal *wedding song* that was probably sung at royal marriage ceremonies.[131] Verse 2 eulogizes the king's beauty (cf. 1 Sam 9:2; 16:12) while vv. 10–12 address the bride. Recognition of this genre enables the reader to understand references to the ceremony's participants and proceedings (vv. 9, 14, 15). The reader can imagine a splendid scene—one not unlike modern royal weddings—repeated over the centuries when monarchs ruled Israel. More important, it helps the reader learn something of the behavior and policy God expected of those rulers.

The Song of Songs offers the Bible's best-known love songs.[132] Though its origin is a matter of dispute, the book probably is a collection of love poetry some of which may have been used at weddings (see 3:6–11). Recognizing this aspect of the literary style enhances proper interpretation. It allows the book to be read as an anthology united around common themes, not as a narrative with plot and development. It also allows the interpreter to take the book's eroticism with full seriousness—as glorification of human sexual love within the context of marriage.[133]

---

128 Hymns were also common elsewhere in the ANE; cf. J. L Foster (translator) and S. T. Hollis (editor), *Hymns, Prayers, and Songs: An Anthology of Ancient Egyptian Lyric Poetry*, Writings from the Ancient World 8 (Atlanta: Scholars Press, 1995); Mathews and Benjamin, *Old Testament Parallels*, 153–56.

129 For discussion, see Starbuck, *Court Oracles*, 122–68; Gunkel, *Psalms*, 99–120.

130 Gerstenberger, "Psalms," 216–18: cf. Ryken, *How to Read*, 117, who uses the term "Worship psalms" for "Zion songs." What we call "Yahweh-kingship-hymns" Gunkel (*Psalms*, 66–81) and Hopkins (*Journey*, 140–147) designate as "enthronement psalms." For the larger theme, see M. Z. Brettler, *God Is King: Understanding an Israelite Metaphor*, JSOTSup 76 (Sheffield: JSOT Press, 1989).

131 Starbuck, *Court Oracles*, 114 ("written for a royal wedding, but its historical specificities have been leveled without a trace"); Gerstenberger, *Psalms 1*, 186–90, with additional bibliography and discussion of alternate views.

132 Song of Songs renders the book's Hebrew title (lit., "the best song"; cf. "Song of Solomon" in many older Bible versions). For recent treatments, see T. Longman, III, *Song of Songs*, NICOT (Grand Rapids: Eerdmans, 2001); R. E. Murphy, *Wisdom Literature*, FOTL 13 (Grand Rapids: Eerdmans, 1981), 98–104. For extra-biblical parallels, see W. G. E. Watson, "Some Ancient Near Eastern Parallels to the Song of Songs," in *Words Remembered, Texts Renewed: Essays in Honour of John F. A. Sawyer*, ed. J. Davies, G. Harvey, and W. G. E. Watson (Sheffield: Sheffield Academic Press, 1995), 253–71; M. V. Fox, *The Song of Songs And the Ancient Egyptian Love Songs* (Madison, WI: University of Wisconsin Press, 1985); J. B. White, *A Study of the Language of Love in the Song of Songs and Ancient Egyptian Poetry*, SBLDS 38 (Missoula, MT: Scholars, 1978).

133 Cf. C. E. Walsh, *Exquisite Desire: Religion, the Erotic, and the Song of Songs* (Minneapolis: Fortress, 2000), who explores the erotic aspects of the OT and how they relate to Israel's experience of God. For a topical treatment, see T. Gledhill, *The Message of the Song of Songs*, The Bible Speaks Today (Downers Grove: InterVarsity, 1994).

Liturgies

Israel worshiped together as a community in the temple in Jerusalem, and undoubtedly it used *liturgy* psalms on such occasions. A liturgy is a text used in worship in which two or more speakers participate in response to each other. The most common speakers include priests as worship leaders and the whole congregation speaking as "we" or "us." Less frequently, individual laypersons speak as "I" and prophets give messages from Yahweh. For instance, observe the different participants evident in the following excerpt from Psa 118, a "thanksgiving liturgy" that celebrates a great national victory:[134]

Call to praise (*priests*)	Give thanks to the LORD, for he is good; his love endures forever. Let Israel say:
Response (*congregation*)	"His love endures forever."
Call (*priests*)	Let the house of Aaron say:
Response (*congregation*)	"His love endures forever . . . ."
Testimony (*an individual*)	In my anguish I cried to the LORD, and he answered by setting me free. . . . All the nations surrounded me, but in the name of the LORD I cut them off. . . .
Petition/Thanks (*congregation*)	O LORD, save us; O LORD, grant us success. . . . The LORD is God, and he has made his light shine upon us. . . .
Thanksgiving (*an individual*)	You are my God, and I will give you thanks; you are my God, and I will exalt you.
Call to praise (*priests*)	Give thanks to the LORD, for he is good; his love endures forever. (Psa 118:1–3, 5,10, 25–26, 28–29; cf. Pss 66; 75; 136)[135]

---

134 Cf. E. S. Gerstenberger, *Psalms, Part 2 and Lamentations*, FOTL 15 (Grand Rapids: Eerdmans, 2001), 300–308, who categorizes the psalm a "Thanksgiving of the Individual." Israel might originally have recited this liturgy during a procession that ended at the temple gate (see vv. 19–21). If so, the phrase "from the house of the Lord we bless you" (v. 26) and the reference to the "horns of the altar" (v. 27) suggest that the procession was at that point inside the temple grounds. But Gerstenberger (*Psalms 2*, 307) understands the psalm's present setting to be the "exilic and postexilic thanksgiving rites within Jewish congregations of 'righteous' Yahweh believers" led by an "officiant" instead of a "priest" (301).

135 Pss 15 and 24:3–6 may reflect an ancient "entrance liturgy," a ceremony with a question-and-answer format performed originally at the temple gate where worshipers affirmed their readiness to enter into the sanctuary; cf. Gerstenberger, *Psalms 1*, 89. The worshipers ask a series of questions that the priest answers from inside the gate with a *torah* instruction; cf. Isa 33:14–16; Mic 6:6–8. Psa 95 features a congregational processional (vv. 1–7a) followed by an exhortation (vv. 7b-11), perhaps by a prophet or priest (but cf. Gerstenberger, *Psalms 2*, 182 ("Yahweh-Kingship Hymn; Sermon"); see Psa 12 with an oracle of salvation in vv. 5–6 and the sermon in Psa 50:7–23.

Wisdom Psalms

Long ago scholars recognized that certain psalms seemed to belong not to Israel's public worship life but to the private educational sphere of her wisdom teachers (see Jer 18:18).[136] Their language, style, and themes more closely resemble the books of Proverbs and Ecclesiastes than the Psalter's woeful complaints and joyous thanksgivings. More meditative in mood and didactic in intention, they focus on ethical issues such as the justice of human suffering and God's apparent injustice in tolerating it. Theologically, their interest lies more in God as Creator and cosmic Ruler than as Israel's Redeemer and Lord.

Hence, we call such psalms *wisdom psalms*. Uncertainty over what literary elements constitute such a genre, however, has produced scholarly disagreement as to which psalms fit it. The strongest case can be made for Pss 1, 19, 33, 39, 49, 127.[137] Psa 1, for example, shows the common wisdom theme of the contrasting fates of the wicked and the righteous. The comparison of the righteous to a tree planted by flowing streams also has a parallel in Egyptian wisdom literature, which suggests that it is a common wisdom motif. When the psalmist beholds God's glory in the heavens (Psa 19), he reflects wisdom's love of creation and its empirical approach to discovering truth. By including a lengthy section of instruction (vv. 12–19), Psa 33 betrays the priority of wisdom, which is to teach a God-pleasing lifestyle, and Psa 127 sounds like Ecclesiastes when it stresses the vanity of human efforts.

Principles of Interpretation—Poetry

From this survey of poetic genres we can suggest the following interpretive principles:

1. Poems originated as complete units, so the student should interpret them in their entirety rather than as isolated verses. They should be read as poetry skillfully crafted by poets who "speak" by creating images in our imagination and by evoking emotional responses.[138]

---

136 Gerstenberger, *Psalms 1*, 19–21. Concerning the "wisdom school" and its literature, see K. Dell, "Wisdom in Israel," in *Text in Context*, ed. A. D. H. Mayes (New York; Oxford: Oxford University Press, 2000), 348–75; B. K. Waltke and D. Diewert, "Wisdom Literature," in *The Face of OT Studies*, ed. D. W. Baker and B. T. Arnold (Grand Rapids: Baker; Leicester: InterVarsity, 1999), 295–332; J. L. Crenshaw, *Old Testament Wisdom: An Introduction*, rev. ed. (Louisville: Westminster John Knox, 1998).

137 J. L. Crenshaw, "Wisdom," in Hayes, *Old Testament Form Criticism*, 250–52, who also sees wisdom influence in Psa 32:8–9; 94:8–11; and possibly 104:13–18. To our list Murphy would add Pss 32, 34, 37, 112, and 128 and affirm "wisdom influence" in Pss 25:8–10, 12–14; 31:23–24; 39:5–7; 40:5–6; 62:9–11; 92:6–8; 94:8–15; cf. R. Murphy, "A Consideration of the Classification of 'Wisdom Psalms'," in *Congress Volume Bonn, 1962*, VTSup 9 (Leiden: Brill, 1962), 156–67 (reprinted in *Studies in Ancient Israelite Wisdom*, ed. J. L. Crenshaw [New York: KTAV, 1976], 456–67). For additional discussion of background and of several illustrative psalms, see Hopkins, *Journey*, 59–76.

138 To understand their poetry, see our chapter on biblical poetry. For the relationship between poetic imagery and theology, see W. P. Brown, *Seeing the Psalms: A Theology of Metaphor* (Louisville: Westminster John Knox, 2002). For how the psalms assess and imagine life and politics, see W. Brueggemann, *Israel's Praise: Doxology Against Idolatry and Ideology* (Philadelphia: Fortress, 1988); and id., *The Message of the Psalms: A Theological Commentary*, Augsburg Old Testament Studies (Minneapolis: Augsburg, 1984).

2. For purposes of interpretation, each psalm serves as its own literary context because the psalm and the psalms that surround it undoubtedly originated independently of each other rather than as a single piece of literature. On the other hand, we may use psalms of the same genre to interpret each other since they share a common literary form, setting, and purpose. But in so doing we must treat them as representatives of a common literary type with a shared background, not as literature composed by the same person.[139]

3. The occasion on which ancient Israel used a psalm constitutes its historical context. For example, a liturgy, wedding song, or dirge must be interpreted as if it was used at a worship, wedding, or funeral service, respectively. If a poem implies the presence of several speakers (pronouns "I," "we," "you," etc.), our interpretation must incorporate that fact together with knowledge of its underlying setting. In interpreting wisdom psalms, the reader must determine from each case whether its content reflects original use in public or private prayer, liturgical instruction in worship, or private instruction by wisdom teachers.[140]

4. The unique features of each literary type determine how we should interpret it. For example, we must interpret corporately any psalms spoken by the community rather than individuals (communal complaints, liturgies, songs, etc.). They voice the petitions and praise of Israel as a nation, not those of an individual Israelite. Similarly, we should interpret the hyperbole of love songs ("there is no flaw in you," Song 4:7) as language exaggerated for effect rather than literal application.

5. The student must take into account the structure of a poetic genre and the development of its thought. The student will need to determine its major sections, the main point each makes, and the contribution of each to the message of the whole. (For an example, see our earlier discussion of the nature of poetry.)

6. Application must conform to the situation behind each genre. In other words, apply corporate texts to the Christian community and individual texts to the Christian individual. Individual complaint psalms speak to situations of individual suffering. Royal psalms relate best to the modern counterparts of Israel's kings: the leaders of the Christian community. At least initially, the student should resist the temptation to extract devotional content in violation of the text's original context.

7. Contemporary use should coincide with the poem's original purpose, occasion, and speakers. So, for example, the student should reserve wedding songs for weddings and complaints for times of extreme hardship. Similarly, communal poems (communal thanksgiving songs, liturgies, etc.) are best used in corporate worship. (Of course it is permissible to appropriate principles and lessons from them that may apply to individuals, say, in private worship, while recognizing the distinction.) We also advise that texts with several

---

139 Recent studies have asked whether the Psalter might comprise a "book" rather than just a "collection," most notably G. H. Wilson, *The Editing of the Hebrew Psalter*, SBLDS 76 (Missoula, MT: Scholars 1985). Until a firmer consensus emerges, we recommend that students limit considerations of context only to certain sections—i.e., Pss 1 and 2 as an introduction, the "Songs of Ascent" (Pss 121–134), and the concluding doxology (Pss 146–150).

140 This caveat concerning wisdom psalms follows Gerstenberger ("Psalms," 221; *Psalms 1*, 20–21) who, observing that some are prayers, rightly questions whether one should relegate them exclusively to the private, educational sphere of wisdom teachers. He argues that priests may have penned some wisdom psalms as liturgical compositions as a kind of pastoral counseling for public use. Cf. Crenshaw ("Wisdom," 252) who senses a close connection between wisdom psalms and prayer, though not a literary genre of wisdom prayer.

speakers be read along that line. Again, the creative use of the processions and rituals implied by some texts might enrich a worship service.[141]

8. Christians believe that Christ is the new David who fulfills the latter's kingship. Thus, we may apply the royal psalms typologically to the kingly role that the NT gives to Jesus as Lord. The OT kings, thus, serve as types that anticipate the reign of their greatest Descendant. Secondarily, and more tentatively, we might also apply appropriate principles of leadership from the royal psalms to church leaders today while recognizing, we insist, the crucial inherent differences between monarchs and church leaders.[142]

PROPHECY

When Israel grievously strayed into idolatry, God sent prophets to announce his plans for his people. Though their proclamation often produced "foretelling" (i.e., predictions about the future), its main staple was "forthtelling" (i.e., announcements of imminent divine judgment in the present or near future). Today we read their proclamations in the books of the OT Prophets, the written record of their words and deeds, a record that reflects the great rhetorical and literary creativity of both the prophets themselves and the disciples who compiled them.

Thus, to understand the prophets will require us to reckon both with the completed books that bear their names and with individual passages—narratives and poetry—to determine *what* they say, *how* they say it, and *why* they say it that way.[143] We will need to apply insights gained in the earlier chapters on prose and poetry.

Basic Types of Prophecy
Prophecy of Disaster

The most common genre among the prophets is the *prophecy of disaster*, an announcement of imminent or future disaster either to an individual or to an entire nation.[144] Typically, its structure includes an indication of the situation, a messenger formula ("Thus says the Lord"), and a prediction of disaster. The "indication of the situation" states the

---

141 Excellent resources are available to foster the use of the psalms in private and corporate worship; e.g., S. B. Reid, ed., *Psalms and Practice: Worship, Virtue, and Authority* (Collegeville, MN: Liturgical Press, 2001); and J. C. Holbert, S. T. Kimbrough, Jr., and C. R. Young, eds., *Psalms for Praise and Worship* (Nashville: Abingdon, 1992).

142 For a sample treatment of a poem, see our discussion of Isa 5 below and of Psa 32 in the earlier chapter on poetry.

143 Two recent introductions to prophecy are D. B. Sandy, *Plowshares and Pruning Hooks: Rethinking the Language of Biblical Prophecy and Apocalyptic* (Downers Grove: InterVarsity, 2002); and D. L. Petersen, *The Prophetic Literature: An Introduction* (Louisville: Westminster John Knox, 2002). Our approach accepts the literary fact that we access the prophets only through the present biblical books bearing their names, books probably edited by others. But we assume that, just as the Gospels convey the *ipsissima vox* ("the very voice") of Jesus, so the prophetic books still convey the "the very voice" of the prophets. We, thus, bypass the major literary genre of "prophetic book" to focus a select sample of subgenres among what Sweeney ("Prophetic Literature," 22) calls "prophetic speech." For further discussion of the interpretive issues surrounding prophetic books and the original words of prophets, see conveniently Sweeney, "Prophetic Literature," 10–15 and (concerning the "book" genre) 16–18.

144 Sweeney, "Prophetic Literature," 23–24, who prefers the term "prophetic judgment speech" and who distinguishes (23–25) other subgenres of "prophetic announcement"; cf. also the classic study of C. Westermann, *Basic Forms of Prophetic Speech* (Louisville: Westminster John Knox, 1991); and the critique of Westermann in W. E. March, "Prophecy," in Hayes, *Old Testament Form Criticism,* 153–54.

problem(s) that occasion the message, the prediction details the disaster to come, and the messenger formula authenticates the word as coming from God.[145] A "therefore" (Heb. *lākēn*) commonly introduces the prediction section.

Often prophecies of disaster have other elements: at the beginning they may include a prophetic *commission* ("Go and say," etc.) and a call to hear ("Hear this word!" etc.); they may also give reasons for the disaster introduced by "because of this" (Heb. *'al-'ašer)* or "for" (Heb. *kî*). An oracle given by Elijah to King Ahaziah and reported within a prophetic story offers a simple illustration of this genre:

Prophetic commission	Go up and meet the messengers of the king of Samaria and ask them,
Indication of the situation	"Is it because there is no God in Israel that you are going off to consult Baal-Zebub, the god of Ekron?"
Messenger formula	Therefore this is what the LORD says:
Prediction	"You will not leave the bed you are lying on. You will certainly die!"
	(2 Kgs 1:3–4; cf. Jer 28:12–14, 15–16; Mic 1:2–7)

In this example, the indication of the situation subtly suggests the reason for the disaster. By consulting Baal-Zebub instead of Yahweh, Ahaziah implied that Israel had no god or at least that Yahweh was unable to heal his injury. The prediction announces that Ahaziah would pay for that insult with his life. Many prophecies of disaster, however, are structurally more complex than this simple example. Most lack the prophetic commission, while many have other elements: descriptions, commands to invading armies to attack, calls for their victims to mourn, etc. Also, most disaster prophecies are longer, and the order of their component parts may vary considerably.

Nevertheless, the careful student, familiar with the form's essential elements, will clearly recognize the additional elements and varying structure. The important thing is to determine the disaster announced and the reason(s) for it. Notice, for example, the similarities and variations in the following example:

Messenger formula	This is what the Sovereign LORD, the Holy One of Israel, says:
Indication of the situation	"In repentance and rest is your salvation, in quietness and trust is your strength, but you would have none of it.
Prediction	You said, 'No, we will flee on horses.' Therefore you will flee! You said, 'We will ride off on swift horses.' Therefore your pursuers will be swift! A thousand will flee at the threat of one; at the threat of five you will all flee away,

---

145 The messenger formula was the standard phrase that identified the source of a message given by a messenger on behalf of someone (Gen 32:4; Exod 5:10; Judg 11:15; 1 Kgs 2:30; et al). It functioned much like a signature or official stamp does today.

> till you are left like a flagstaff on a mountaintop,
> like a banner on a hill." (Isa 30:15–17)

Unlike the earlier example, here the indication of the situation comes between the messenger formula and the prediction. Also, compare the twofold repetition of the "therefore" to its single use in the first example. Again, the key is to find the prediction and the indications of the situation, and to observe other significant elements.

Prophecy of Salvation

Prophets also announced restoration for individuals and nations. So the prophecy of disaster has a positive counterpart—to announce hope for the future. In structure, the *prophecy of salvation* resembles the disaster prophecy, but its content is as positive as the latter's is negative.[146] A prophetic narrative in Jer 28 provides a simple example of this form given by the prophet Hananiah. (Though he proved to be a false prophet, he followed the typical ancient form.)

Messenger formula	This is what the LORD Almighty, the God of Israel, says:
Prediction	
Basic statement	"I will break the yoke of the king of Babylon.
Amplification	Within two years I will bring back to this place all the articles of the LORD'S house that Nebuchadnezzar king of Babylon removed from here and took to Babylon. I will also bring back to this place Jehoiachin son of Jehoiakim king of Judah and all the other exiles from Judah who went to Babylon," declares the LORD,
Emphatic restatement	"for I will break the yoke of the king of Babylon." (Jer 28:2–4; cf. Isa 2:1–5; Amos 9:11–15 etc.)

As indicated, the structure exactly parallels that of the prophecy of disaster. Similarly, the salvation prophecy may include additional elements, may continue for great length, and may show a variable order of components. As was true of the negative counterpart, the basic goal is to identify the future hope announced, in this case, the return of Judah's king and the temple's articles from Babylon.

Woe Speech

The prophets also announced doom through the *woe speech*.[147] Its distinguishing feature is the opening interjection "Woe to those who/you who" followed by participles

---

146 Sweeney, "Prophetic Literature," 25–27 ("prophecy of salvation") with various subgenres.

147 Sweeney, "Prophetic Literature," 28 (with bibliography); cf. W. Janzen, *Mourning Cry and Woe Oracle*, BZAW 125 (Berlin: deGruyter, 1972); Westermann, *Basic Forms*, 190–94. For examples, see Isa 5:8–10, 11–14, 18–19, 20, 21, 22–25; 10:1–3; 28:1–4; 29:1–4, 15; 30:1–5; 31:1–5; Amos 5:18–20; 6:1–7.

describing those addressed. The description details the evil deeds that make them worthy of woe. The woe speech concludes with a prediction of divine punishment, usually without the "therefore, thus says the Lord" introductory formula.

The form's opening interjection (Heb. *Hôy*, "woe!") and description have raised the question about where it originated in Israelite society. Did the prophets invent it or borrow some pre-existing form? Probably, the woe speech represents the prophets' adaptation of the ancient funeral lament.[148] But these speeches are more than just an ordinary lament for the dead. Rather, they resemble the lament for a murder victim in which the lament condemns the killers for the outrage. If so, one must hear the woe speeches as expressions of prophetic outrage at the sinful behavior they condemn.

In the following example of the woe speech, notice the opening interjection, the description of the doomed addressees and their crimes, and the disaster predicted (our translation):

Declaration of woe	Alas [Woe] for those who devise wickedness and evil deeds on their beds!
Explanation: offenses	
Basic statement	When morning dawns, they perform it, because it is in their power.
Amplification	They covet fields, and seize them; houses, and take them away; they oppress householder and house, people and their inheritance.
Messenger formula	Therefore thus says the LORD:
Prediction	"Now, I am devising against this family an evil from which you cannot remove your necks; and you shall not walk haughtily, for it will be an evil time. On that day they shall take up a taunt song against you, and wail with bitter lamentation, and say: 'We are utterly ruined; the LORD alters the inheritance of my people; how he removes it from me! Among our captors he parcels out our fields.' Therefore you will have no one to cast the line by lot in the assembly of the LORD." (Mic 2:1–5 NRSV)

Given this genre's likely cultural background, the opening "Woe!" might imply that Micah "mourns" the people he has in mind. But his sharp indictment of their greedy schemes quickly dispels any impression of sympathy. In fact, according to his prediction, the opposite lies in store after disaster strikes: yes, people will "mourn"

---

148 Janzen, *Mourning Cry*; G. M. Tucker, "Prophecy and the Prophetic Literature," in Knight and Tucker, *Hebrew Bible*, 340; contra Westermann, *Basic Forms*, 194–99 (woes derived from ceremonies of curses against enemies); E. Gerstenberger, "The Woe-Oracles of the Prophets," *JBL* 81 (1962): 249–63; and J. W. Whedbee, *Isaiah and Wisdom* (Nashville: Abingdon, 1971), 80–110, who both argued that the woe was the negative counterpart of the blessing saying ("Happy is the person who. . . .").

them—but in ridicule, faking phony lamentation as a gleeful taunt whose true message is "Good riddance!" The genre's literary effect is to underscore the judgment as a "done deal" and (by sarcasm) to undercut audience sympathy.

Prophetic Dirge

Along similar lines, the prophets occasionally recited a *dirge* or funeral lament over Israel (for this form, see above under poetry).[149] They addressed the nation as if she were a corpse ready for burial. In other words, the literary effect of using the dirge here is to portray her awful future as a *fait accompli*. Amos provides a sample of these potent passages:

Call to hear	Hear this word, O house of Israel, this lament I take up concerning you:
The Dirge	Fallen is Virgin Israel, never to rise again, deserted in her own land, with no one to lift her up.
Messenger formula	This is what the Sovereign Lord says:
Prediction	"The city that marches out a thousand strong for Israel will have only a hundred left; the town that marches out a hundred strong will have only ten left." (Amos 5:1–3; cf. Isa 14:4–23; Ezek 19; 26:17–18; 27)

Amos sees Israel as a tragic figure, a virgin who dies unmarried and alone. The prediction says that forces defending Israel will suffer ninety percent casualties. Through the dirge Amos speaks as if this had already happened. What a powerful way to announce the certainty and horror of Israel's imminent national demise!

Prophetic Hymn

Occasionally, the prophets used genres drawn from Israel's worship practices. Examples of the *hymn* appear occasionally in the prophetic books (for hymns, see above under poetry; for hymns in Job, see below).[150] The following short example illustrates how Amos includes brief hymnic pieces that extol Yahweh:

> For lo, the one who forms the mountains,
> creates the wind,
> reveals his thoughts to mortals,
> makes the morning darkness,
> and treads on the heights of the earth—
> the LORD, the God of hosts, is his name!
>
> (Amos 4:13 NRSV; cf. 5:8–9; 9:5–6)

---

149 Cf. Sweeney, "Prophetic Literature," 518–19.

150 Some prefer the term "doxology"; so Sweeney, "Prophetic Literature," 29, 519, 521; cf. J. L. Crenshaw, *Hymnic Affirmations of Divine Justice: The Doxologies of Amos and Related Texts in the Old Testament*, SBLDS 24 (Missoula, MT: Scholars Press, 1975).

Amos ended the previous section (vv. 6–12) by announcing that Israel should "prepare to meet your God" in judgment (v. 12) since she had turned a deaf ear to Yahweh's earlier efforts to confront her. The hymnic lines quoted above give the announcement a climactic rhetorical flourish, painting a vivid picture of Yahweh's majesty to underscore the certainty of judgment.[151]

On the other hand, Isaiah used longer hymn pieces to illustrate the song of praise Israel would sing when Yahweh finally brought her exiled citizens home:

Introduction	In that day you will say:
The hymn	"Give thanks to the LORD, call on his name;
	make known among the nations what he has done,
	and proclaim that his name is exalted.
	Sing to the LORD, for he has done glorious things;
	let this be known to all the world.
	Shout aloud and sing for joy, people of Zion, for great is the Holy One of Israel among you." (Isa 12:4–6; cf. vv. 1–3; 25:1–8, 9–12; 26:1–19; 42:10–13; 49:13)

By citing a praise hymn to be sung upon return from exile, the prophet not only finds words worthy of their awesome divine subject but also taps into the joy his audience would associate with such songs. In short, after dreary exile, this will be a day for singing!

Prophetic Liturgy

The prophets also used various kinds of *liturgies* as part of their message (for liturgy, see poetry above).[152] As noted previously, a liturgy is a text used in worship in which two or more speakers participate in response to each other. Isa 63:7–64:12, for example, contains a lengthy, sad liturgy that asks Yahweh finally to end his angry punishment of exiled Israel. It involves two speakers: the prophet reminiscing about Yahweh's great past deeds (63:7–14) and a communal complaint pleading for God's mercy (63:15–64:12).

Jer 14 offers a second example of a communal complaint set in a time of severe national drought. Given the background of communal complaints, the text takes an unexpected turn. Normally, when Israel prayed for help during similar national disasters, she expected Yahweh to answer positively—usually through a prophet—with a prophecy of salvation. In the following excerpts, observe Israel's complaint and how Yahweh answers it:

Introduction	This is the word of the LORD to Jeremiah concerning the drought:

---

151 As Carroll R. points out (*Contexts for Amos*, 206–21), the irony of this imminent "meeting" with Yahweh the awesome Creator is that Israel had sought to meet him and to gain his blessing at the sanctuaries of the Northern Kingdom (vv. 4–5) but had missed meeting him in the series of disasters (vv. 6–11).

152 Cf. Isa 12; Joel 1–2; Habakkuk; and Nahum. Sweeney, "Prophetic Literature," 29–30, notes that the prophets "employ standard liturgical genres" and that prophetic liturgies "apparently reflect the cultic setting in which prophetic literature was performed and perhaps produced."

Description	"Judah mourns, her cities languish;
	    they wail for the land, and a cry goes up from Jerusalem.
	The nobles send their servants for water;
	    they go to the cisterns but find no water. . . ."

Complaint	Although our sins testify against us,
	    O LORD, do something for the sake of your name. . . .
	You are among us, O Lord, and we bear your name;
	    do not forsake us!

Messenger formula	This is what the Lord says about this people:

Message	"They greatly love to wander;
	    they do not restrain their feet.
	So the LORD does not accept them;
	    he will now remember their wickedness
	    and punish them for their sins." (Jer 14:1–3, 7, 9, 10, 19–22; cf. Joel 1–2)

There are two things to highlight here. First, notice Yahweh's answer: he flatly denied Israel's petition for relief. Israel expected a prophecy of salvation but received one of disaster instead. The reversal of expectation has the literary effect of heightening the shock (and the horror) of God's reply. Second, unlike Isa 63–64, here the liturgy and divine response serve as a prophecy of disaster. They function as an announcement ("the word of the Lord") about the drought—it will continue as Israel's punishment.

This example reinforces a point we made earlier about interpreting a genre: one must interpret both what it says by itself as well as how it functions in the context. Here the liturgy and response say that Israel prayed and Yahweh answered. Introduced by "this is the word of the Lord," it *functions* as a prophecy of disaster.

The book of Habakkuk offers another variety of liturgy, a "dialogue of complaint" (for complaints, see poetry above). By way of background, scholars believe that normally God answered individual complaints with a prophecy of salvation promising relief from the distress. That same complaint-answer structure underlies the opening section of Habakkuk (1:2–2:4) with two significant differences.

Psalmic complaints have a single complaint without any recorded answer from Yahweh, but Habakkuk has two complaints (1:2–4; 1:12–2:1) and an answer reported for each (1:5–11; 2:2–4). For that reason we call this subgenre a dialogue of complaint.[153] Jeremiah also lifted complaints to God, in his case, in response to persecution for his preaching. The "confessions of Jeremiah" record his intensely personal pleas for protection from enemies and vindication of his prophetic ministry. Like Habakkuk, he received direct divine answers to his complaints (Jer 11:18–23; 12:1–6; 15:10–11, 15–21).[154]

---

153 Cf. Sweeney, "Prophetic Literature," 30. The interpretive difficulty as to whether the second answer ends at 2:4 or 2:5 does not affect our point here.

154 For other "confessions" without divine answers, see Jer 17:14–18; 18:18–23; 20:7–13; cf. the lament in 20:14–18 and its parallel genre in Job 3. For recent discussion of the "confessions," see C. Bultmann, "A Prophet in Desperation? The Confessions of Jeremiah," in *The Elusive Prophet: The Prophet as a Historical Person, Literary Character and Anonymous Artist,* ed. J. C. de Moor, Oudtestamentische Studiën 45 (Leiden: Brill, 2001), 83–93; O'Connor, *The Confessions of Jeremiah.*

Prophetic Disputation

Occasionally, the prophets employed a rhetorical form called the *disputation* that apparently originated in Israel's wisdom tradition (for its importance in Job, see below). In a disputation, the speaker tries to persuade the audience to accept the validity of some truth.[155] Disputations comprise most of the book of Malachi, but the prophet Amos provides an apt, short illustration:

Series of Questions	Do two walk together
	unless they have agreed to do so?
	Does a lion roar in the thicket
	when he has no prey? . . .
	Does a bird fall into a trap on the ground
	where no snare has been set? . . .
	When a trumpet sounds in a city,
	do not the people tremble?
	When disaster comes to a city,
	has not the LORD caused it?
Conclusion	Surely the Sovereign LORD does nothing
	without revealing his plan
	to his servants the prophets.
Lesson	The lion has roared—who will not fear?
	The Sovereign LORD has spoken—
	who can but prophesy? (Amos 3:3–4a, 5a, 6–8; cf. 9:7)

This example highlights several features that distinguish the disputation from the prophecy of disaster. First, here the prophet himself speaks as a fellow-Israelite, not in the first person as the direct voice of Yahweh. Second, the speaker does not announce new revelation; he simply argues for a point, in this case, that nothing happens without a cause. Third, disputations commonly use rhetorical questions to involve the audience and conclude with a lesson.[156]

In this case, Amos draws his audience into discussion with three initial, non-threatening questions about daily life all with the same obvious answer ("Of course not!"). But the next two suddenly threaten the hearer with a frightening invasion sent by Yahweh, and they require an affirmative answer ("Of course!"). Now alert and anxious, the audience receives the lesson: "I [Amos] prophesy because I've heard God's voice of

---

155 The major study remains A. Graffy, *A Prophet Confronts his People*, AnBib 104 (Rome: Biblical Institute Press, 1984); but cf. also D. F. Murray, "The Rhetoric of Disputation: Re-examination of a Prophetic Genre," *JSOT* 38 (1987): 15–121. Sweeney ("Prophetic Literature," 28, 519) offers a convenient summary and list of texts. Typical prophetic disputations have three parts: statement of the thesis under dispute, statement of the proposed counterthesis, and the actual argumentation in its favor.

156 For other disputations, see Isa 10:8–11; 28:23–28; Jer 2:23–28; 3:1–5; 8:1, 8–9; Mic 2:6–11; and most of the book of Malachi. For an illuminating exposition of the disputation in Isa 28, see Whedbee, *Isaiah and Wisdom*, 51–68. For the disputation in Nahum, see M. A. Sweeney, "Concerning the Structure and Generic Character of the Book of Nahum," *ZAW* 104 (1992): 364–77.

judgment."[157] Its guilt and spiritual blindness exposed, Israel must confront the horrible consequences before Israel's holy God in the rest of the book of Amos.

Prophetic Lawsuit

Some prophetic speeches draw on ancient Israel's legal practices. In the *lawsuit speech* (Heb. *rib)*, for example, a prophet speaks as if Israel were on trial accused of a crime.[158] Hence, one finds references to trial procedures—calls to plead a case, appeals to witnesses, the hearing of testimony, etc.—and legal terms like "case," "accusation," and "indictment." Yahweh seems to play the dual role of both prosecutor and judge. Often, such speeches charge Israel with breach of covenant, e.g., with violating the agreement she entered with Yahweh at Mt. Sinai (Exod 24). For that reason, some scholars have called this form the "covenant lawsuit speech."[159] Consider this example from the prophet Micah:

Call to hear	Listen to what the LORD says:
Summons to trial	"Stand up, plead your case before the mountains;
	let the hills hear what you have to say.
	Hear, O mountains, the Lord's accusation;
	listen, you everlasting foundations of the earth.
Reason	For the LORD has a case against his people;
	he is lodging a charge against Israel."
Yahweh's testimony	
Question	"My people, what have I done to you?
	How have I burdened you? Answer me.
Testimony proper	I brought you up out of Egypt
	and redeemed you from the land of slavery.
	I sent Moses to lead you, also Aaron and Miriam.
	My people, remember what Balak king of Moab
	counseled and what Balaam son of Beor answered.
	Remember your journey from Shittim to Gilgal,
	that you may know the righteous acts of the
	LORD." (Mic 6:1–5; cf. Psa 50; Isa 1:2–3; 3:13–15;
	Jer 2:4–13; Hos 4:1–3)

---

157 Literally, the metaphor of the roaring lion connects the disputation with 1:2 and 3:12, and thus underscores its importance for the message. Carroll R. (*Contexts for Amos*, 182–92) discusses other literary features.

158 Sweeney, "Prophetic Literature," 27–28 (with bibliography); cf. K. Nielsen, *Yahweh as Prosecutor and Judge: An Investigation of the Prophetic Lawsuit (Rib Pattern)*, JSOTSup 9 (Sheffield: JSOT, 1979). For the influence of this form on the Gospel of John's presentation of Jesus' life, see recently A. T. Lincoln, *Truth on Trial: The Lawsuit Motif in the Fourth Gospel* (Peabody, MA: Hendrickson, 2000).

159 The original setting from which the prophets adapted this form remains disputed (e.g., treaty formulas, international law, the covenant between Yahweh and Israel, ordinary law courts, etc.). But a recent consensus seems to favor the latter background (so Tucker, "Prophecy and the Prophetic Literature," 338).

Obviously, careful interpretation of the lawsuit speech requires that we take the legal metaphor seriously. The student must closely observe what roles Yahweh, the prophet, and Israel play in each of the metaphorical legal processes. One might also imagine the dramatic, public scene that the prophet "acts out" and review the past relationship of the parties at trial. One might reflect on the legal basis for the charges in light of Yahweh's testimony, and what the prophet might imply by omitting testimony from Israel. Finally, the student must decide what purpose each lawsuit serves: does it serve to level charges, to provide evidence to prove guilt, to announce a verdict, or to impose a sentence? In the above case, the speech merely aims to establish Israel's guilt and worthiness of punishment.

Prophecy Against Foreign Nations

Many prophetic books have lengthy collections of *prophecies against foreign nations*.[160] Technically, these do not constitute a separate literary genre but employ genres of various kinds. Prominent among them is the "war oracle," a genre that probably goes back to Israel's ancient tradition of holy war where it aimed to curse her enemies.[161] Originally, God gave military leaders the go-ahead for their operations and assured them of victory through a war oracle. For example, in 1 Kgs 20:28 God spoke to Ahab during an Aramean attack against Israel:

> This is what the LORD says: "Because the Arameans think the LORD
> is a god of the hills and not a god of the valleys, I will deliver this vast
> army into your hands, and you will know that I am the LORD."

The prophets, however, press war oracles into service as prophecies of disaster against foreign nations. Their twofold purpose is to announce the enemy's defeat and to reassure Israel that God protects her security. After observing the presence of war oracle motifs in a text, the student must determine how the prophet is using them.

For example, the war oracle in Zech 9:1–8 announces doom for Israel's historic enemies. In succession, the prophet describes awful destruction for Damascus, Tyre, and the Philistine cities (vv. 1–7). It concludes, however, with a promise concerning Jerusalem (v. 8):

> "But I will defend my house against marauding forces.
> Never again will an oppressor overrun my people,
> for now I am keeping watch."

---

160 See Isa 13–21, 23, 34; Jer 46–51; Ezek 25–32, 35, 38–39; Joel 3:1–16; Amos 1–2; Obad; et al. For recent studies, see P. R. Raabe, "Why Prophetic Oracles Against the Nations," in *Fortunate the Eyes that See: Essays in Honor of David Noel Freedman*, ed. A. Beck, et al. (Grand Rapids: Eerdmans, 1995), 236–57; D. H. Ryou, *Zephaniah's Oracles Against the Nations*, Biblical Interpretation Series 13 (Leiden: E. J. Brill, 1995); J. Barton, *Amos's Oracles Against the Nations: A Study of Amos 1:3–2:5* (Cambridge: Cambridge University Press, 1980); and cf. D. L. Christensen, *Prophecy and War in Ancient Israel: Studies in the Oracles Against the Nations in Old Testament Prophecy* (Berkeley: BIBAL, 1989).

161 Cf. Deut 20:1–4; 1 Kgs 22:1–40; Christensen, *Prophecy and War*, 18–72, 281; Sweeney, "Prophetic Literature," 26–27. This tradition taught that Yahweh, the divine warrior, went out in battle to defeat his (and Israel's) enemies (Exod 15:3; Num 10:35; Josh 10:42; etc.). In addition, the war oracle includes the following subgenres: summons to battle, summons to flight, summons to mourn, battle curses, announcements of victory or defeat, and victory and taunt songs (cf. Christensen, *Prophecy and War*, 15). T. Longman, III and D. G. Reid, *God Is a Warrior* (Grand Rapids: Zondervan, 1995) conveniently survey the biblical tradition of Yahweh at war.

The defeat of her enemies frees Jerusalem from threats, and God's promise of protection guarantees her security. Here the function of the war oracle is to reassure Jerusalem of a secure future. That, in turn, lays the groundwork for the following prophecy (vv. 9–13) about the advent of a great king. It ultimately functions, however, to support the appeal for exiled Judeans to return (v. 12). In sum, the war oracle reassures them that a God-given peace has replaced Jerusalem's violent past so they may come home without fear.[162]

Prophetic Vision Report

OT prophets were also known as "seers," probably because they sometimes saw visions (1 Sam 9:9; Amos 1:1; 7:12; Mic 3:6–7; cf. Num 23–24). Thus, some prophetic books include *prophetic vision reports.*[163] These are autobiographical reports of things the prophet saw or heard in a vision that convey God's message. The following features make this genre readily recognizable: the words "see" or "made to see" (Heb. *rā'â*, qal and hiph., respectively) and the phrase "and behold" (*uᵉhinnēh*) followed by a description of the vision.

Based on variations in content and style, we can distinguish three types of vision reports. The "oracle-vision" features a question-and-answer dialogue between Yahweh and the prophet about something the latter sees that provides the occasion for an oracle. For example, Jeremiah's glimpse of two baskets of figs—one with good figs, the other with bad ones—becomes the occasion for God to contrast the good and bad future fates, respectively, of Israelites exiled in Babylon and those surviving in Jerusalem (Jer 24; cf. 1:11–14; Gen 15; Amos 7:7–8; 8:1–2; Zech 5:1–4). The "dramatic word vision" depicts a scene in heaven that portends some future event on earth that the prophet presumably is to announce. It closely resembles the vocation reports (on which see below) of Isaiah (Isa 6) and Ezekiel (Ezek 1–3).

For example, the Lord showed Amos the locusts and fiery disaster he was preparing for Israel's imminent judgment (Amos 7:1–6; cf. 1 Kgs 22:17–22; Jer 38:21–22). In the "revelatory-mystery vision," an angelic guide dialogues with the prophet about the bizarre symbolic imagery he sees. The purpose of the conversation is to reveal the veiled secrets of God's future plans. So Zechariah conversed with an angel about his vision of a man with a measuring line and learned about plans for Jerusalem to be rebuilt (Zech 2:1–4; cf. 4:1–6; Dan 8; 10–12).

Prophetic Narratives

Two narrative literary types commonly appear in the prophetic books. Best known, the *vocation reports* narrate the personal experience by which God called and commissioned someone as a prophet (Isa 6; Jer 1; Ezek 1–3; cf. Amos 7:14–15; Hos 1:2).[164]

---

162 To good rhetorical effect, the prophets occasionally turn this genre against Israel or Judah, addressing them among doomed nations (see Isa 13–23; Amos 1–2).

163 Sweeney, "Prophetic Literature," 18–19; cf. B. O. Long, "Reports of Visions Among the Prophets," *JBL* 95 (1976): 353–65; id., *1 Kings*, 263–64; Tucker, "Prophecy and the Prophetic Literature," 341–42.

164 Sweeney, "Prophetic Literature," 20 ("Vocation Account"); cf. the still foundational study of N. Habel, "The Form and Significance of the Call Narratives," *ZAW* 77 (1965): 297–323; B. O. Long, "Prophetic Call Traditions and Reports of Visions," *ZAW* 84 (1972): 494–500. "Vocation Reports" replaces the older, now discarded term "call narratives" (cf. March, "Prophecy," 170–72, 176). Concerning their purpose, see B. O. Long, "Prophetic Authority as Social Reality," in *Canon and Authority: Essays in Old Testament Religion and Theology*, ed. B. O. Long and G. W. Coats (Philadelphia: Fortress, 1977), 3–20.

Structurally, they share the following features: a confrontation with God, a commissioning, an objection by the prophet, God's reassurance, and a sign. This genre may have derived from the ancient requirement for ambassadors or messengers to present their credentials to the party to whom they had been sent (see Gen 24:35–48).

In the prophetic books, vocation reports serve a similar purpose: they authenticate the prophet's authority and message by showing that God had indeed sent him. Literarily, they also serve to underscore the theological themes central to a given prophet's message. The OT shows two types of vocation reports. Some report a vision of God's court like other vision reports (Isa 6; Ezek 1–3; 1 Kgs 22:19–23). The other type details how someone heard the coming of the word (Jer 1:4–10; Exod 3–4; Judg 6:11–14).

The second narrative genre in prophetic books is divine *instruction about symbolic actions* that the prophet is to perform.[165] Typically, such narratives include: a command to perform an action, a report of the performance, and its interpretation through a follow-up prophetic word or vision (2 Kgs 13:14–19; Hos 1:2–9).[166] Jer 19 provides an excellent example. The Lord commissioned Jeremiah to take a pottery jug, smash it before Jerusalem's leaders in the Hinnom Valley, and proclaim a message. That action symbolized the crushing disaster that God would soon send against the city. The sight of such symbolic gestures would undoubtedly unsettle its witnesses because they assumed that, like the prophet's words, the actions set Yahweh's future plans in motion (cf. 2 Kgs 13:14–19).[167] Within a prophetic book they literarily illustrate its main message and give it added rhetorical force.

General Principles for Interpreting Old Testament Prophecy

Most Bible readers would agree with the great reformer Martin Luther who said of the prophets: "They have a queer way of talking, like people who, instead of proceeding in an orderly manner, ramble off from one thing to the next, so that you cannot make head or tail of them or see what they are getting at."[168] Several aspects of the prophetic books probably mystify and frustrate readers. As Rofé observed, "Readers are held back by what at first glance seems disorder within the books."[169] They may find it difficult to decide when one message ends and the next begins, and the books create

---

165 See Hos 1, 3; Isa 7:3; 8:1–4; 20; Jer 13:1–11; 16:1–4, 5–7, 8–9; 32:1–15; Zech 11:4–16. Cf. Sweeney, "Prophetic Literature," 19–20; K. G. Friebel, *Jeremiah's and Ezekiel's Sign-Acts*, JSOTSup 283 (Sheffield: Sheffield Academic Press, 1999). The older, classic study remains useful; cf. G. Fohrer, *Die symbolischen Handlungen der Propheten*, ATANT 25 (Zurich: Zwingli, 1953).

166 There is also a simpler form that has only a command and the interpretation (Isa 8:1–4; Jer 16:2–4) or report and interpretation (1 Kgs 11:29–31; Jer 28:10–11). For even simpler examples, see 1 Kgs 19:19–21; Isa 7:3; 20.

167 Tucker, "Prophecy and the Prophetic Literature," 342; but cf. W. D. Stacey, *Prophetic Drama in the Old Testament* (London: Epworth, 1990), who argues that these reports exemplify and enhance the effect of the prophet's message but do not cause events; and K. Friebel, "A Hermeneutical Paradigm for Interpreting Prophetic Sign-Acts," *Didaskalia* 12 (2001): 24–45 (they comprise "rhetorical nonverbal communication"). The symbolic action of Jesus in cursing the figless tree parallels the example of Jer 19 (Mk 11:12–14, 20–21, par.).

168 Quoted by G. von Rad, *Old Testament Theology*, 2 vols. (New York: Harper & Row, 1965), 2: 33, n. 1.

169 A. Rofé, *Introduction to the Prophetic Literature*, The Biblical Seminar 31 (Sheffield: Sheffield Academic Press, 1997), 7.

the impression of repetition with little evident thematic development. Many prophetic messages also strike them as hopelessly obscure. What is one to make, they wonder, of all those spooky creatures flying or crawling over the earth?[170]

To overcome such obstacles, a good starting point is to understand the nature of prophecy and of prophetic books. Fundamentally, prophecy is a biblical phenomenon by which God conveyed messages to his people through human speakers or writers. It assumes that God has something important he wants people to understand—that he wishes to communicate not obfuscate—whether spoken orally by a living prophet or by a finished prophetic book. The books of the prophets not only preserved their legacy—their original words and deeds—but also rhetorically ordered their messages to address later generations, including us.

Thus, to grasp the relevance of their "forthtelling" (i.e., announcements about the present) and "foretelling" (i.e., future predictions), the reader must reckon with the rhetorical strategies that shaped the books and their contents. What follows suggests some principles to help readers savor spiritual benefits from the rich feast of OT prophecy.[171]

Interpreting Prophetic "Forthtelling"

To defend his own preaching, Jeremiah reminded his opponent, Hananiah, that all the prophets who preceded them announced imminent doom rather than hope just as he did (Jer 28:8–9). In other words, most prophecy involves *forthtelling*—messages for a prophet's own audience about their own day or the near future. To understand those messages, we suggest the following interpretive considerations.[172]

First, the reader must understand the historical situation in which a given prophet spoke. One needs to review the events and the state of Israel's religious life during his lifetime by consulting a book on the history of Israel.[173] Besides an assessment of the period, such books also point the reader to crucial biblical texts to be read as well. In a historical review, important questions to answer include: What were Israel's relations

---

170 At the same time, there is no shortage of recent writers who confidently cross-reference current events (especially those in the Middle East) with, say, the goat's fourth horn of Daniel (Dan 8) or Ezekiel's Gog (Ezek 38–39). Such identifications, of course, do enjoy one distinct advantage: the more obscure the prophet, the less ground modern readers have to dispute the interpreter's views! But to date all such depictions have proved false in some respect, which should warn us against imitating them or following them very closely.

171 Some scholars have suggested that a few prophetic books (e.g., Isaiah) were originally compiled to be read aloud to audiences as a kind of "oral performance." Students would do well to keep that possible background scenario in mind as they interpret them. For insights into prophetic rhetoric, see Z. Weisman, *Political Satire in the Bible*, SBLDS 32 (Atlanta: Scholars Press, 1998); Walter Brueggemann, *The Prophetic Imagination*, 2d ed. (Minneapolis: Fortress, 2001); id, *Hopeful Imagination: Prophetic Voices in Exile* (Philadelphia: Fortress, 1986); cf. M. D. Carroll R., "Living Between the Lines: A Reading of Amos 9:11–15 in Postwar Guatemala," *Religion & Theology* 6 / 1 (1999): 50–64.

172 Cf. the useful guidelines for interpretation in T. C. Butler, "Announcements of Judgment," in Sandy and Giese, *Cracking Codes*, 166–68, and their illustration in a brief study of Jer 8 (168–73).

173 Excellent resources for history include I. Provan, V. P. Long, and T. Longman, III, *A Biblical History of Israel* (Louisville: Westminster John Knox, 2003); and J. Bright, *A History of Israel*, 4th ed. (Louisville: Westminster, John Knox, 2000). For Israel's religion, see P. D. Miller, *The Religion of Ancient Israel* (Louisville: Westminster John Knox, 2000). See the bibliography at the end for more resources.

with surrounding nations like at the time? How good was its economy, and who were benefiting and / or not benefiting from it? What was the quality of Israel's religious life? This step is essential in two respects: first, it frames the background for interpretation of prophetic texts; and second, it provides the historical basis for contemporary application (see below).

Second, the reader needs to determine the kind of judgment announced by a prophetic text. For example, the immediacy and urgency of this message must have scared Jeremiah's audience:

> Raise the signal to go to Zion!
>   Flee for safety without delay!
> For I [Yahweh] am bringing disaster from the north,
>   even terrible destruction. (Jer 4:6)

His proclamation concerns the coming of a terrifying military invasion, and it is important to identify the army (if possible) to which the prophet alludes (in this case, probably Babylon). But other prophecies announce future exile from Israel's homeland (e.g., Isa 5:13; Amos 4:2–3; 5:27; Mic 1:16) and horrible natural disasters as the list of past judgments sent by Yahweh in Amos 4:6–10 illustrates (i.e., famine, drought, blight and mildew on crops, and a plague of locusts).

Normally, the syntactical marker "therefore" (Heb. *lākēn*) introduces descriptions of judgment as a distinct section toward the end of an announcement (e.g., Isa 5:5–6; Jer 7:12–15; Amos 2:13–16), but they may occur earlier (e.g., Amos 4:2–3, 12–13). Consideration of the means, both natural and historical, through which God has sent judgment in the past confronts the reader with the theological reality that God treats his people's sin with deadly seriousness, and sometimes God judges them for it.

Third, the reader must pay close attention to the reasons given for the judgment announcement. Usually, words like "for," "because," and "since" grammatically mark what follows as a statement of God's reason(s) for his actions, and such statements may precede, follow, or be interwoven within messages. Consider the preexilic prophet Hosea's explication of Yahweh's indictment against Israel:

> There is no faithfulness, no love,
>   no acknowledgement of God in the land.
> There is only cursing, lying and murder,
>   stealing and adultery;
> they break all bounds,
>   and bloodshed follows bloodshed. (Hos 4:1b-2)

This description, which explicitly cites violations of at least three of the Ten Commandments (cf. Exod 20:13–15; Deut 5:17–19), contextually serves to indict the priests for failing to instruct Israel in what Yahweh expects (Hos 4:4–8). Statements that explain the rationale for judgment may occur in a distinct section (e.g., Amos 2:6–12), be interspersed throughout a passage (e.g., Hos 4:6, 8), or appear in direct address or descriptions without the explicit markers noted above (e.g. Amos 4:1; Mic 3:2–3). If not based on specific OT laws, the rationales for judgment rest on expected standards of conduct deeply rooted in Israel's covenant with Yahweh. Careful definition of the reasons within the covenant's relational framework is important because it forms the basis for the application of the passage to contemporary Christian life. Indeed, sometimes they sound so painfully contemporary that readers may wish they did *not* understand them!

In application, the principle of analogy provides the bridge from Israel in the past to Christians in the present. Having carefully defined Israel's sin(s), the reader now may seek analogies to them in modern life. To use the above example from Hos 4, one might ask in what ways contemporary Christians show "no faithfulness, no love, no acknowledgment of God" (v. 1b). In what ways might cursing, lying, murder, stealing, murder, and bloodshed typify our lives—and how might we change our ways?[174]

Two words of caution merit mention, however. First, since Israel was a nation, it is tempting to apply the messages of the prophets to the situations of modern nations. Since the prophets reflect what God values and hates, certainly some application of those values to nations in general is permissible. But, unlike other nations, Israel was specifically a *covenant* people bound by a relationship with God that entailed a lifestyle aligned with his will. Thus, for Christians the most proper application of the prophets is not to modern nations but to the modern covenant people, the Christian Church, a collective, spiritual people bound to Israel's God through Christ and committed to a God-pleasing lifestyle.

A second caution: some readers may wrongly infer from OT prophecy that divine judgment might follow their individual sins. Instead, one must remember that divine judgment fell on Israel, not for a few sins, but after a long history of their sinfulness, rebellion, and resistance to repentance (see Jer 7:12–15). Thus, the implication of prophetic announcements of judgment is not that God will punish *every* sin but that he may intervene against a persistent, proud, sinful lifestyle.

Though less numerous, OT prophets also proclaimed prophecies of salvation, primarily about return from exile and restoration to the land after judgment.[175] For example, some prophecies of salvation spoke comfort to Israel during its painful exile in Babylon:

> Why do you say, O Jacob, and speak, O Israel,
> "My way is hidden from the LORD,
> and my right is disregarded by my God"?
> Have you not known? Have you not heard?
> The LORD is the everlasting God,
> the Creator of the ends of the earth. . . .
> He gives power to the faint,
> and strengthens the powerless. (Isa 40:27–29 NRSV)

---

174 Butler ("Announcements of Judgment," 167) rightly clarifies that OT announcements of judgment should not be used as "bribes" to benefit a given preacher or congregation, nor do they in any way limit God's freedom to judge or not to judge according to his own will.

175 The foundational treatment of these prophecies remains C. Westermann, *Prophetic Oracles of Salvation in the Old Testament* (Louisville: Westminster John Knox, 1991). But cf. also Sweeney, "Prophetic Literature," 25–26; W. A. Van Gemeren, "Oracles of Salvation," in Sandy and Giese, *Cracking Codes*, 131–55.

Addressing the exiles' fear that God has abandoned them, the prophet reassures them that God's strength will sustain them even where they are.

But most oracles of salvation proclaim God's promise that exiled Israel will one day return home, as Jer 30:10–11a (NRSV) illustrates:

> But as for you, have no fear, my servant Jacob, says the LORD,
> and do not be dismayed, O Israel;
> for I am going to save you from far away,
> and your offspring from the land of their captivity.
> Jacob shall return and have quiet and ease,
> and no one shall make him afraid.
> For I am with you, says the LORD, to save you. (cf. 24:5–7; 29:10–14;
> 32:1–15)

The prophet's message, poignantly addressing the exiles by the revered ancestral name "Jacob," is two-fold: it comforts God's discouraged people ("have no fear") and promises them divine deliverance from captivity and a return home ("I am going to save you"; "Jacob shall return").[176] Both Isa 40 and Jer 30 aim to promote the exiles' perseverance through despair until the return occurs, as it in fact did a few decades later in 538 B.C.

The application of such messages builds on the principle of analogy noted above.[177] The reader, first, needs to understand Israel's exile—its causes, its purposes, its events, and its results—then ask what modern experiences of "exile" compare to it. Finally, a review of the text's specific words of encouragement opens the way to reflections on how those words encourage Christian perseverance in our exile experiences.[178]

Interpreting Prophetic "Foretelling"

The above discussion concerned messages that either addressed Israel in the past or reached their fulfillment in the OT era. The former indicted God's people for rebellious idolatry and cruel injustices, while the latter concerned exilic and postexilic issues. But consider the implications of prophecies like these:

---

176 So Van Gemeren, "Oracles," in Sandy and Giese, *Cracking Codes*, 153, who observes that, by addressing Israel as "Jacob," Jeremiah roots the promise in the ancient promises to the patriarchs (e.g., Gen 35:9–12).

177 The fact that the texts' historical fulfillment clearly occurred in the 6th century B.C. permits our interpreting them in such a spiritual sense. With any prophecy of salvation, however, the possibility remains of another fulfillment later, provided—and this is the crucial point—later Scriptures either so interpret it or support such an interpretation (on this see below).

178 For other principles of interpretation, see Van Gemeren, "Oracles," in Sandy and Giese, *Cracking Codes*, 146–152. As one might expect, the "forthtelling" of the postexilic prophets spoke to the crucial issues of their day, especially the need to rebuild the temple in Jerusalem (Haggai and Zechariah, late 6th cent. B.C.) or to repent of lackadaisical religious life (Malachi, 5th cent. B.C.). Their interpretation applies the same approach as discussed concerning the preexilic and exilic periods. For an introduction to their books, background, and message, see conveniently R. J. Coggins, *Haggai, Zechariah, Malachi*, OT Guides (Sheffield: Sheffield Academic Press, 1996). For a recent commentary, see P. L. Redditt, *Haggai, Zechariah, and Malachi*, NCB (Grand Rapids: Eerdmans, 1995).

On this mountain [Zion] the Lord of hosts will make for all peoples a feast of rich food, a feast of well-aged wines, of rich food filled with marrow, of well-aged wines strained clear. And he will destroy on this mountain the shroud that is cast over all peoples, the sheet that is spread over all nations; he will swallow up death forever. Then the Lord GOD will wipe away the tears from all faces, and the disgrace of his people he will take away from all the earth, for the LORD has spoken. (Isa 25:6–8 NRSV)

I will save my flock, and they shall no longer be ravaged; and I will judge between sheep and sheep.
I will set up over them one shepherd, my servant David, and he shall feed them: he shall feed them and be their shepherd.
(Ezek 34:22–23 NRSV)

Isa 25 announces a future banquet, not for Israel but for "all peoples"; it also foresees the final end of death and human grief. It clearly anticipates events that far exceed anything seen by Israel during the OT period. Ezek 34 promises that David will "shepherd" and "feed" God's flock (i.e., rule as king). Now, the last surviving king of Israel was Jehoiachin who was exiled to Babylon where he probably died (see 2 Kgs 24:12, 15; 25:27–30), although those who returned from exile may have regarded Zerubbabel as one sent to restore the Davidic kingship.[179] Even if the latter is true, subsequent OT books show little interest in the matter.[180] If it is to find any fulfillment, the restoration of the Davidic monarchy must find it after the OT closes.

How, then, do we interpret "foretelling" prophecies that apparently go beyond the OT period? The simple answer is that we must interpret them in light of the NT. On that premise, students need to bear in mind several *general characteristics* of biblical

---

179 Two matters are at issue: first, whether messages given Zerubbabel by Haggai and Zechariah (e.g., Hag 2:20–23; Zech 4:6–10) view him as a royal figure; and, second, whether at the time local populations might legitimately regard as "king" someone whom the Persian empire recognized by the title "governor" (Hag 1:1, 14; 2:2, 21). For recent discussion and bibliography on the issue, see conveniently H. G. M. Williamson, "Exile and After: Historical Study," in Baker and Arnold, *Face*, 253–54. According to M. J. Boda, *Haggai, Zechariah*, NIVAC (Grand Rapids: Zondervan, forthcoming), Zech 6 views Zerubbabel as a royal figure who will restore the Davidic monarchy.

180 E.g., G. H. Jones, *1 and 2 Chronicles*, OT Guides (Sheffield: Sheffield Academic Press, 1993), 109 ("there was no king in the post-exilic community known to the Chronicler"). Ezra and Nehemiah invoke David retrospectively as patron of the temple and its personnel (Ezra 3:10; 8:20; Neh 12:24, 36, 45, 46), record his descendants (Ezra 8:2), use his name in geographical locations (Neh 3:15, 16; 12:37), but say nothing about a contemporary royal figure. Only Zech 12 assumes the presence of the "house of David" (but never "King David") in Jerusalem when a future international attack against the city happens (vv. 7, 8, 10, 12; cf. also 13:1; 9:9), but the date of Zech 9–14 is problematic (for a balanced discussion, see Boda, *Haggai, Zechariah*, forthcoming; cf. Coggins, *Haggai, Zechariah, Malachi*, 60–71). It is striking, however, that Zech 9–14 exalts only one king, Yahweh (Zech 14:9, 16, 17; cf. Mal 1:14). The mention of David in Isa 55:3 is probably not postexilic.

prophecy.[181] First, the OT prophets understood that history has two major periods—the present age and the age to come—although they did not always make a hard-and-fast distinction between the two. Most OT prophecies concern the present age, even those that predict events in the distant future. But introductory phrases like "in the latter days," "in that day," or "days are coming" often signal a prophecy about the age to come (e.g., Isa 2:2; 11:10, 11; 24:21; Jer 23:5; 31:31; Zech 14:1; etc.). There are exceptions to this general rule, however (e.g., Jer 30:3; Amos 4:2; etc.), so only the content of a text can determine which prophetic age it concerns.

Second, it is helpful to understand that the OT prophets have a telescopic view of the future. From Denver, Colorado, the Rocky Mountains appear as a series of distant peaks close together, though in reality the peaks are many miles from each other. Similarly, the prophets saw the future as a single succession of events (i.e., the view of distant "peaks" from Denver), but the NT shows that, in fact, large time gaps intervene between them (i.e., distance between "peaks" when viewed from above).[182] Isaiah 9:6–7 (Heb. 5–6) provides a good example:

> For to us a child is born,
> > to us a son is given . . .
> He will reign on David's throne . . .
> > from that time on and forever.[183]

Isaiah foresees the birth of a royal son who will reign on David's throne forever. The text assumes that the birth and reign occur during the son's lifetime—that he will succeed his father closely. Christians read "forever" as a clue that, besides an immediate fulfillment in Isaiah's time (cf. chaps. 7–8), this text anticipates the birth and reign of David's greatest son, Jesus Christ the Messiah, the one whose coming inaugurates the "last days." Unlike Isaiah, who sees the birth and reign of this future Davidic ruler as telescoped (i.e., chronologically close rather than separated), the NT teaches that the present so-called church age comes between Christ's birth and his future earthly reign.

The point is that, because the prophets viewed the age to come telescopically as a whole scene without obvious time gaps, our interpretive task is to align the content of OT prophecies with the NT's perspective. According to the NT, the first coming of Jesus introduced the future age to come into the present age. The work of Christ and the Church represents an invasion of that future age of judgment and salvation into the present one.[184] Hence, we must interpret OT prophecies about the age to come in terms of the historical turning point that Jesus initiated.

---

181 Here we draw on the illuminating discussion in T. N. Sterrett, *How To Understand Your Bible* (Downers Grove: InterVarsity, 1974), 140–42.

182 Fee and Stuart (*How to Read the Bible,* 292) provide a good visual illustration of this telescopic concept.

183 Concerning the birth announcement formula ("to X is born a son"), see R. L. Hubbard, "Ruth iv 17: A New Solution," *VT* 38 (1988): 295–98; S. B. Parker, "The Birth Announcement," in *Ascribe to the Lord: Biblical and Other Essays in Memory of Peter C. Craigie,* ed. L. Eslinger and G. Taylor, JSOTSup 67 (Sheffield: JSOT Press, 1988), 133–49.

184 On this subject, see G. E. Ladd, *A Theology of the New Testament,* rev. ed. by D. A. Hagner (Grand Rapids: Eerdmans, 1993), 60–67, including several useful diagrams (66–67); id., *The Presence of the Future* (Grand Rapids: Eerdmans, 1974). Cf. also N. T. Wright, *Jesus and the Victory of God* (Minneapolis: Fortress, 1996), 467–74.

To be specific, while OT prophets saw the coming age as a whole, the NT presents it as having several major phases. Opinions among Christians may differ as to the number and definition of such phases, but it has at least two periods, the present church age and the period initiated by Christ's second coming.[185] Hence, when plotting the fulfillment of OT prophecies about the future, we must carefully analyze their content to see where they fit in this larger schema.

A third characteristic of biblical prophecy is that an OT prophecy may have two fulfillments, one near the prophet's lifetime, and one long past it.[186] We know of these multiple fulfillments because the NT itself reapplies already-fulfilled prophecy to a later event. For example, God promises David that his son, Solomon, will succeed him as king (2 Sam 7:12–16). In v. 14, God even promises David that "I will be his father, and he will be my son." When Solomon later became king (1 Kgs 1–2), this prophecy found its fulfillment. But Heb 1:5 also applies 2 Sam 7:14 to Jesus, not just as son of David, but as Son of God. Sound theology undergirds the idea of such multiple fulfillments—belief that God rules all human history and can bring about both "sons."[187]

Fourth, NT teaching associates all prophetic fulfillments with Christ's first and second comings. That teaching leads us *not* to expect fulfillments in between those two events. Thus, one should not suggest that a certain contemporary event "fulfills biblical prophecy" unless one can also demonstrate that current events also imply the imminent return of Jesus. Lacking the latter, Bible students should treat such alleged fulfillments as speculations, not biblical interpretation.

Finally, one must remember that many prophecies are conditional not absolute.[188] By this we mean that their fulfillment hangs on two crucial factors, the sovereignty of God (i.e., his freedom to do or not do as he wishes) and the status of the relationship between the people and God (i.e., their rebellion or repentance). In Jer 18, God articulated the principle that underlies all of his prophetic dealings:

> If at any time I announce that a nation or kingdom is to be uprooted,
> torn down and destroyed, and if that nation I warned repents of its evil,
> then I will relent and not inflict on it the disaster I had planned. And if
> at another time I announce that a nation or kingdom is to be built up
> and planted, and if it does evil in my sight and does not obey me, then
> I will reconsider the good I had intended to do for it. (vv. 7–10)

---

185 So-called premillennialists also regard a third major historical period, the thousand-year reign of Christ (or millennium) inaugurated by his second coming, as part of the age to come. For a summary of this view, see R. G. Clouse, R. N. Hosack, and R. V. Pierard, *The New Millennium Manual: A Once and Future Guide* (Grand Rapids: Baker, 1999), 46–49.

186 In most cases, it seems likely that the original prophets were unaware of a future fulfillment, but using Matthew's citations of Isaiah, Blomberg argues that Isaiah actually foresaw both an immediate and a future fulfillment; cf. C. L. Blomberg, "Interpreting Old Testament Prophetic Literature in Matthew: Double Fulfillment," *TrinJ* 23 (2002): 17–33.

187 The same principle may help us explain Matthew's application (Mt 1:22–23) of Isaiah's prophecy about Immanuel's virgin birth (Isa 7:14). For discussion of the Matthew text, see D. A. Hagner, *Matthew 1–13*, WBC 33A (Dallas: Word, 1993), 1: 15–16, 20–22; and C. L. Blomberg, *Matthew*, NAC 22 (Nashville: Broadman Press, 1992), 59–61. For the Isaiah text, see conveniently J. N. Oswalt, *The Book of Isaiah, Chapters 1–39*, NICOT (Grand Rapids: Eerdmans, 1986), 207–13.

188 Cf. the helpful discussion in Sandy, *Plowshares and Pruning Hooks*; and J. B. Green, *How to Read Prophecy* (Downers Grove: InterVarsity, 1984), 100–103.

God says that an evil nation may escape judgment already announced against it by sincerely repenting, and that by rebelling a nation on whom he has already announced blessing may receive judgment instead.

The case of Jerusalem in Jeremiah's day illustrates the second scenario (i.e., blessing to judgment). Jeremiah announced the condition of the city's survival—repentance (Jer 26:1–6; cf. 7:1–15; 36:1–7)—but Jerusalem rejected the offer, and God destroyed the capital two decades later (Jer 52). The fate of Jonah and the city of Nineveh illustrates the first scenario (i.e., judgment to blessing). Jonah's message seemed straightforward and unconditional: "Forty more days and Nineveh will be overturned" (Jonah 3:4). But the forty days came and went without destruction falling on the city because the people repented and received God's mercy (3:5–10). In both cases, though he had already announced his plans, God exercised his sovereignty by altering them because of the status of the relationship with the humans concerned.[189]

The Many Ways of Fulfillment

Given the discussion above, it is not surprising that biblical prophecy finds fulfillment in many ways.[190] As we shall argue, that larger pattern provides us with useful options to apply to our interpretation of prophecy.

(1) As we might expect, some prophecies commonly find *historical fulfillment* in subsequent events. We might also call this a literal fulfillment. In some cases, the fulfillment follows a short time later. For example, Elisha predicted that, though cut off from outside supplies by a Syrian siege, Samaria would have inexpensive food by the next day (2 Kgs 7:1–2; cf. 19:20–36). Other prophecies find historical fulfillment within their respective biblical periods. Thus, an unnamed prophet prophesied that Josiah would desecrate the idolatrous altar at Bethel (1 Kgs 13:1–3), and three hundred years later he did (2 Kgs 23:15–16).

Similarly, Jesus successfully predicted his own death (Mt 16:21; 27) and the destruction of Jerusalem (Lk 19:41–44).[191] Then, too, some OT prophecies reach historical fulfillment in the NT period. So the preaching of John the Baptist prepared the way for Jesus just as Isaiah had said (Isa 40:3–5; Lk 3:3–6), and Jesus announced that his ministry fulfilled the messianic mission foreseen by Isaiah (Isa 61:1–2; Lk 4:16–21).[192]

(2) At the same time, the rhetorical structure of some OT prophetic books reflects what one might call *frustrated or suspended fulfillment*. In other words, their present form leads readers through a series of surprising, incomplete fulfillments that, in the

---

189 Similarly, G. V. Smith, "Prophet; Prophecy," *ISBE*, rev. ed., 3: 1002. Green (*How to Read Prophecy*, 100–102) even believes—rightly, in our view—that the same condition applies to the promises to Abraham (Gen 12:1–3; 15; 17). Contrast Sterrett (*How to Understand Your Bible*, 144) who accepts some prophecies as unconditional.

190 Here we build on the insights of Sterrett, *How to Understand*, 139–40; 142–43. Cf. also the more complete discussion in Green, *How to Read Prophecy*, 83–108.

191 Here we assume with the many scholars that the synoptic gospels were written prior to A.D. 70 and, thus, record genuine predictive prophecies. For further defense see, inter alia, D. A. Carson, et al., *An Introduction to the New Testament* (Grand Rapids: Zondervan, 1992), 76–79, 96–99, 116–117; and D. Guthrie, *New Testament Introduction*, 4th ed. (Downers Grove/Leicester, UK: InterVarsity, 1990), 53–56, 84–89, 125–131. For an alternative evangelical view, see P. J. Achtemeier, J. B. Green, and M. Meye Thompson, *Introducing the New Testament* (Grand Rapids: Eerdmans, 2001), 69–74.

192 Cf. also Mic 5:2 and Mt 2:4–b. For other prophecies fulfilled literally, see the selective list in Sterrett, *How to Understand Your Bible*, 142–43.

end, rhetorically point to a fulfillment beyond the book's own historical perspective. The present books of Isaiah and Amos exemplify this rhetorical strategy, addressing the prophet's original message to a much later audience.[193]

(3) The NT also indicates that OT prophecies may reach historical fulfillment in unique, less-than-literal, ways. They may, for example, find a *historical / figurative fulfillment*. Given our discussion of typology above, consider Jesus' application of Zech 13:7b ("Strike the shepherd, and the sheep will be scattered") to the flight of his disciples after his arrest (Mt 26:31). According to Zechariah (Zech 13:7–9), God would severely judge Israel by killing both the shepherd (her leader) and his scattered sheep (the people of Israel). Two-thirds of them will die, but God will refine the remaining third and enter into a covenant with them (v. 9). Obviously, for Jesus this involves no precise historical fulfillment. Granted, one may rightly regard Jesus as the shepherd (cf. Jn 10), and one might even say that God did "judge" him. The problem is that, according to Zechariah, God judged the shepherd for his own sins, while Jesus, completely sinless, suffered God's judgment for the world's sin (cf. Gal 3:13; 1 Pet 2:24–25). Further, when the disciples scattered, God did not kill eight of them and bless the remaining four. Thus, Zech 13:7 apparently found its fulfillment historically in the death of Jesus and the flight of the disciples, but only in a figurative sense.

(4) Other OT prophecies reach what we call a *historical / spiritual fulfillment*. For example, Amos 9:11–12 prophesied about the restoration of the Davidic monarchy and its rule over Edom and other nations. The context gives the reader no reason to expect anything but a historical fulfillment, but in Acts 15:16–17 James says the fulfillment of Amos 9 is the admission of non-Jewish believers to the company of Jesus' followers.[194] He does so by interpreting Amos' prediction of David's future political rule as representing Christ's spiritual rule over non-Jewish Christians. In sum, James sees the prophecy fulfilled in a historical/spiritual way—historical in that it happened in history to God's people and spiritual in that it also involves Gentiles.[195]

---

193 For further discussion of Isaiah, see E. W. Conrad, *Reading Isaiah*, Overtures in Biblical Theology (Minneapolis: Fortress, 1991); and for Isaiah and Amos, see M. D. Carroll R., "The Power of the Future in the Present: Eschatology and Ethics in O'Donovan and Beyond," in *A Royal Priesthood: The Use of the Bible Ethically and Politically*, ed. C. Bartholomew, A. Wolters, and J. Chaplin (Grand Rapids: Zondervan, 2002), 116–43.

194 For the textual problems, see the NIV footnote and the thorough discussions in C. K. Barrett, *A Critical and Exegetical Commentary on Acts of the Apostles*, ICC (Edinburgh: T & T Clark, 1998), 2: 724–29. For recent discussion of the Amos text, see J. Jeremias, *The Book of Amos: A Commentary*, OTL (Louisville: Westminster John Knox, 1998), 161–70.

195 Similarly, since OT history records no fulfillment of Jeremiah's prophecy about the new covenant (Jer 31:31–34), one might expect its fulfillment in the last days. But Hebrews rightly interprets its fulfillment in the Church and sealed by Jesus' atoning death (see 8:8–12; 10:15–17; cf. 1 Cor 11:25)— i.e., a historical / spiritual fulfillment. From Rom 11 one might argue that prophecies like Amos 9 and Jer 31 might still have a future *historical* fulfillment involving Israel, but we contend that the NT seems to assume that such prophecies have already been fulfilled through Christ and the Church—the latter, a single people composed of Jews and Gentiles (cf. Isa 19:19–25; Rom 2:28–29; Gal. 6:16; Eph 2; 1 Pet 2:9–10). On the other hand, Rom 11 does foresee future Israel's being grafted back into God's olive tree— in our view, a future outpouring of faith among *ethnic* Jews, not *national* Israel. Also, we deny that it says anything about its unique rights to particular geography; cf. C. E. B. Cranfield, *A Critical and Exegetical Commentary on the Epistle to the Romans*, 2 vols., ICC 32 (Edinburgh: T & T Clark, 1980–1983), 2: 576–79. For a similar view that leaves open the possibility of future fulfillments, see D. L. Bock, "The Reign of the Lord Christ," in *Dispensationalism, Israel and the Church: The Search for Definition*, ed. C. A. Blaising and D. L. Bock (Grand Rapids: Zondervan, 1992), 36–67.

(5) Some OT prophecies receive *unexpected / historical fulfillment* in the NT.[196] They may take on new meaning in time and their fulfillment may also involve a surprise—something that goes beyond the original prophecy. Jesus himself best illustrates this element of surprise. Though some significant pre-Christian interpreters understood the suffering servant of Isa 52–53 to refer to an eschatological figure, the rejection of Jesus' predictions of his death by the disciples (e.g., Mk 8:27–33) suggests that most of Jesus' Jewish contemporaries probably did not and, hence, OT prophecy did not prepare them for his crucifixion.[197] They expected a conquering Messiah (cf. Isa 9; 11), not a suffering one. So they stumbled over the cross of Christ; meant to be a bridge, it became a barrier to their belief (1 Cor 1:23).[198] Does this mean that God is unpredictable? Not at all. Enough continuity exists between the original prophecy and its unexpected fulfillment for readers to recognize their connection, as did the disciples after Easter vis-à-vis the crucifixion. Instead, such surprises suggest that God has the right to exceed the expectations of his ancient words in light of the new historical situation and in line with his redemptive purposes for his creation.

Stephen Travis offers a helpful human illustration of this point. He compares God to a loving parent who, knowing his children's expectations, delights in outdoing them. A little girl may expect a doll for Christmas, but the doll she receives—one that walks, talks, weeps, and wets—far exceeds her expectations. She gets what she wanted—a new doll—so continuity connects her expectations with their fulfillment. She does not feel deceived by the difference between them but happily surprised.[199] Likewise, God's fulfillment of some prophecies may exceed the expectations his people have of them.

An important implication flows from this illustration, one not always heeded in popular writings: readers must interpret predictive prophecy tentatively rather than dogmatically. We should not approach prophecy as if it were a script written for God by someone else from which God could not deviate. As sovereign Lord, God has the freedom to bring about the fulfillment or non-fulfillment of OT prophecies as he wishes. This does not imply divine unpredictability, as if God arbitrarily changes his mind simply because he "feels like it." Certainly, God's sovereign purposes do not change, and we may expect him to adhere to much of the prophetic design. We still regard the prophecies that involve the major milestones in God's plan for history—e.g., the return of Christ, God's final triumph over his enemies, and the creation of a new heavens and a new earth—as unconditional and therefore unaffected by any Christian apostasy. Their grounding rests solidly upon God's sovereign, unchangeable, larger will for his creation, not upon an exact course of events en route to its realization.

---

196 Green, *How to Read Prophecy*, 103–105.

197 For convincing evidence that some pre-Christian writings interpreted the servant of Isa 53 as a suffering eschatological figure, see M. Hengel, "Zur Wirkungsgeschichte von Jes 53 in vorchristlicher Zeit," in *Der Leidende Gottesknecht: Jesaja 53 und Seine Wirkungsgeschichte*, ed. B. Janowski and P. Stuhlmacher, Forschungen zum Alten Testament 14 (Tübingen: J. C. B. Mohr, 1996), 49–91. That the idea may also go back to Jewish ideas of the martyrdom of the righteous, see C. A. Evans, "Messianism," in *Dictionary of New Testament Background*, ed. C. A. Evans and S. E. Porter (Downers Grove: InterVarsity, 2000), 700; and R. L. Hubbard, Jr., "Redemption," in *New Dictionary of Biblical Theology*, ed. T. D. Alexander and B. Rosner (Leicester: InterVarsity, 2000), 719, 720.

198 Similarly, in the NT the OT promise of land to Abraham takes on new meaning. For Christians the promised land is not earthly Palestine but "a better country—a heavenly one" (Heb 11:16; cf. vv. 8–15).

199 S. H. Travis, *I Believe in the Second Coming of Jesus* (Grand Rapids: Eerdmans, 1982), 140.

So, as the apostle Paul wrote, we live "by faith, not by sight" (2 Cor 5:7). With complete confidence Christians may rightly anticipate the future advent of these great events. But as he has in the past, he may delight to ad-lib some unexpected lines, so Bible students should interpret prophecy tentatively rather than dogmatically. Our God is a God of surprises, and he may still have some left!

Now, some readers may wonder how NT writers can interpret apparently literal OT prophecies so nonliterally (2 through 5 above). In our view, they make a fundamental theological assumption, one that also frames the way readers should interpret prophecy today. Put simply, NT writers believed that Jesus Christ and the Christian Church represent the fulfillment of Israel's God-given mission in history.

The NT writers regard Jesus as the new David (cf. Isa 11:1–5; Jer 23:5–6) and the Church as the new Israel. They do not deny that Israel still exists, nor do they say it has no prophetic future (e.g., Rom 10:1–4; 11). But they stand convinced that Jesus and the Church—with both Jewish and Gentile members—fulfill Israel's prophetic hopes and, hence, constitute God's one, true elect people (see Eph 1–2).[200] That explains why their term for "church" is *ekklēsia* ("assembly"), the same word the Septuagint used to describe Israel as a spiritual community. That also explains why Paul called believers of all ethnic backgrounds the children of Abraham (Rom 4:11–12; Gal 3:6–9).[201]

(6) Finally, some OT and NT prophecies remain *unfulfilled*. In our view these pertain to the Second Coming of Christ and the events at the end of the age. The world, for example, still awaits the idyllic state of perfect harmony that Isaiah foresaw. Nations have not yet given up warfare (Isa 2:4), and lambs still wisely avoid lying beside wolves (11:6). We do not believe these have been "spiritually" fulfilled in the Church. Christians have yet to hear the sound of archangel and trumpet signaling the return of Christ (1 Thes 4:13–18), and they still anticipate the great wedding supper of the Lamb (Rev 21:1–11). In our view, the presence and ministry of the Church does not sufficiently account for the diversity of prophecies given to Israel according to the OT. Surely some are realized spiritually in the Church, but others seem more concretely and ethnically tied to historical, physical Israel. Thus history awaits the day when the people of ethnic Israel will receive God's mercy and the full realization of all their ancient hopes (Rom 11). Unfulfilled prophecy offers believers great things to anticipate—to borrow a phrase from Jeremiah, "a future with hope" (Jer 29:11 NRSV; cf. Rom 15:4).

Specific Principles for Interpretation—Prophecy

In summary we suggest several basic principles for the proper interpretation of prophecy:

1. The best starting point for interpretation is to read a whole prophetic book at one or two sittings in order to become familiar with its contents, especially its main

---

200 For one perspective on God's true elect people, see W. W. Klein, *The New Chosen People: A Corporate View of Election* (Eugene, OR: Wipf & Stock, 2001). Paul understood the Church as the body of Christ (e.g., 1 Cor 10:16; 12:27; Eph 4:12).

201 Green (*How to Read Prophecy*, 116–20) further develops these ideas. For details on this key word, see J. Roloff, "*ekklēsia*," *EDNT*, 1: 410–15; and V. Verbrugge, *The Theological Dictionary of New Testament Words* (Grand Rapids: Zondervan, 2000), 388–96; cf. its OT background in G. Carpenter, "*qāhāl*," *NIDOTTE*, 3: 888–92. An excellent treatment of the theme of Christianity's connections with ancient Judaism is M. R. Wilson, *Abraham Our Father: Jewish Roots of the Christian Faith* (Grand Rapids: Eerdmans, 1989).

themes, and to begin to sense its rhetorical strategy. For example, a careful reading of Isaiah might reveal the importance of the prophet's visions (Isa 2:1–4; chaps. 6–39) and the calls for later readers to respond with action (2:5) or to draw encouragement from them (chaps. 40–66). One might also notice that the vineyard metaphor, a symbol of Israel, recurs (e.g., 1:8; 3:14; 5:1–7; 27:2–6) and may suggest possible links to the NT (e.g., Jn 15).

2. After these readings (or during subsequent readings), it is a good discipline to write down one's observations (with sample references) concerning the book's recurring themes, prominent metaphors, probable intention or purpose, possible audience, and overall rhetorical strategy. The key question is: Why does the book develop the way it does? Further study may lead one to refine or supplement these observations, but they provide a good starting point.

3. After some reflection, list ways in which the book's worldview may differ, if not challenge, the ways Christians see the world today. Here the key question is: In what ways might the book wish to transform, perhaps even radically, our worldview today?

4. In light of the book context, the reader may then focus on smaller contexts (i.e., a section of verses, a whole chapter, or several chapters, etc.). Notice *what* it says (i.e., its themes), *how* it says it (i.e., its metaphors, thought development, etc.), and what it is about the "how" that gives the "what" its rhetorical power. The ultimate goal should be to understand the major point(s) that each section stresses, what it contributes to the whole book, and what transformations it seeks to make in readers.

5. Concerning fulfillments of prophecy, the Bible itself offers the best guide to determining which prophecies were fulfilled during the OT and NT periods, and suggests patterns for interpreting OT prophecies today. The question is: Given its nature, when did / will a given prophecy most likely reach fulfillment—in the OT, NT periods, or in the future?

6. In most cases, OT prophecies about Israel and Zion find their fulfillment spiritually in the Church. But those that seem to pertain more to a physical nation of Israel may anticipate a historical fulfillment.

7. With a highly symbolic apocalyptic text, the student should, first, strive to understand the meaning of its main symbols and, then, to decide on the whole text's major thematic points. Ask, for example, what light does the use of a given symbol in the OT or in extra-biblical literature cast on its possible meaning in this prophecy? What is the purpose of the prophecy as a whole (i.e., to condemn empire-builders, to encourage perseverance by God's people, to warn of coming accountability, etc.)? Also, what does it say about the nature of God or about Israel's sin?

8. As for application, we suggest that the student find a situation in modern life that seems analogous to the situation addressed either by a whole book or by at least one section. To be "analogous," at least several key characteristics of the modern situation must closely compare with those of the biblical one. For example, it should: 1) concern the same kinds of people (e.g., political or religious leaders, the people as a whole, merchants, average laborers, foreigners, etc.); and 2) involve the same problematic issue (e.g., power or powerlessness, idolatry, greed, callousness to need, lack of faith, selfishness, etc.). After confirming the validity of a proposed analogy, the question to ask is: What does this prophetic section say about that analogous situation?

A Sample Prophetic Text: Isaiah 5:1–7

A close reading of this text, often called Isaiah's "Song of the Vineyard," allows us to apply the above principles to an example of prophetic "forthtelling." Cleverly, the prophet weaves together a love song (vv. 1–2), two direct addresses by Yahweh (vv. 3–6), and the prophet's concluding explanation (v. 7) to form a judicial allegory (vv. 1–7).[202] As allegory, elements of its story symbolize historical parties, and the whole serves to make a point; the language of "judge between" (Heb. *špt bᵉ*, "to judge between"; cf. Deut 25:1; Isa 2:4) signals its judicial subject matter.

Rhetorically, the prophet plays on two possible senses of the vineyard metaphor—the warm memories of a lovely bride in the song (e.g., Song 2:15; 4:16–17) and of Israel as Yahweh's own personal "vine" in the addresses (e.g., Psa 80:8–16). The love song so lures the audience into the prophet's rhetorical hand that they cannot escape hearing the aggrieved landowner, whose actual identity Isaiah hides until near the end (v. 6). As we will see, Isaiah also musters parallelism and aural poetic devices to give his words added power.

The love song warmly lauds the landowner's devotion and generosity (vv. 1–2): his selection of a fertile hill, his labors clearing away its stones, his planting of choice vines, his construction of a protective watchtower, his expectant digging of a wine vat. But the song suddenly stops after reporting the resulting crop—useless "wild grapes." Confused and uneasy, the audience now hears the vineyard owner, as if just barging in unannounced, ask them to "judge between me and my vineyard" (vv. 3–4 NRSV)—to decide the "innocent" and "guilty" parties in the dispute. His first rhetorical question (v. 4) defends his innocence, and his second ("Why . . . wild grapes?") implies a guilty vineyard.

By now, the audience probably realizes that the metaphorical vineyard is not a bride but Israel and Judah. But before the listeners can say a word, the owner—still unidentified, though they probably suspect Yahweh—announces his own intention to remove its protection, leaving it vulnerable to attack (v. 5). Notice how the virtually synonymous parallelism makes the announcement sound all the more emphatic and the vineyard owner all the more determined (v. 5b, our translation): "I'll remove its hedge, and it'll burn // "I'll tear down its wall, and it'll be trampled."

V. 6 skillfully wields Hebrew poetics to detail the future scenario (our translation):

Summary	I will make it a waste;
Amplification: A Contrast	it shall not be pruned or hoed, but briers and thorns will overgrow it;[203]
Intensification	I will also command the clouds not to rain any rain upon it.[204]

To loss of owner protection against outsiders (v. 5) the prophet adds loss of owner care against overgrowth (v. 6a)—in sum, total abandonment. Now, briers and thorns

---

202 Cf. Sweeney, "Prophetic Literature," 121–24.

203 Notice that the poet combines alliteration and assonance both to unify individual stichs and to highlight their contrasting content. Assonance in the first line (*lō' yizzāmēr uᵉlō yēʿādēr* "not pruned or hoed") plays on the repetition of *lō'* ("not") and "a" and "e" sounds, while alliteration plays on the initial "y" and final "r" sounds. In its parallel (*uᵉʿālâ šāmîr wāšāyît* "but briers and thorns will overgrow") assonance puns on first-syllable "a" and final-syllable "i" sounds, while alliteration repeats "sh" sounds.

204 Again, notice how the prophet puns aurally on two words from the Heb. root *mṭr* ("to rain"): *mēhamṭîr* ("[not] to cause rain") and *māṭār* ("rain"), in sum, "to not cause *rain* to *rain* on it."

can survive with minimal moisture, but v. 6b intensifies the "waste" motif with a final, fatal step of abandonment: the owner will prohibit rainfall on it. A vineyard that cannot even grow weeds is truly abandoned! More importantly, this line immediately confirms listener suspicions that the owner is Yahweh since Israelites knew that rain clouds did his bidding (e.g., Psa 104:3, 13–15; Zech 10:1). The point of the allegory is now clear: outraged at his "wild grapes," Yahweh will leave Israel to destruction.

Now Isaiah himself speaks a concluding word of explanation (v. 7). By synonymous parallelism and chiasm, he identifies the vineyard ("the vineyard is Israel" // "and Judah is Yahweh's pleasant planting"), then climatically wields ellipsis, word plays, and two contrasting parallelisms to distinguish Yahweh's expectations from his people's "wild grapes" (our translation):

he [Yahweh] hoped for	justice	(*mišpāṭ*),
but	look—bloodshed	(*mišpāḥ*)!
	righteousness	(*ṣᵉdāqâ*),
but	look—a cry!	(*ṣᵉ`āqâ*)

Notice how, though synonymous in meaning, the second contrast ("righteousness" / "cry [of distress]") actually is sequential to the first ("justice" / "bloodshed"); the victim of injustice responds by crying out for divine justice and rescue. In short, Yahweh will leave Israel to destruction because they preferred injustice (forbidden to God's people) to justice (modeled by God, expected of his people).

Certainly, this text reminds modern Christians how deadly seriously God regards the pursuit of justice by his people. Notice that God "planted" Israel and expected a harvest of "justice," but when the harvest produced "wild grapes," he destroyed it. This seems to imply that God views our doing of justice as the proper fruit (i.e., one purpose) of our salvation; in other words, God transforms us in Christ not just to spare us eternal damnation but that we might work for justice. Also, Jesus clearly echoes Isa 5 in the parable of the wicked tenants (Mt 21:33–46; Mk 12:1–12): the vineyard metaphor and the owner's actions (i.e., "planted, dug, built a watch tower") clearly recall wording from Isaiah 5:2.[205] Rhetorically, Jesus compares his opponents to rebellious ancient Israel and, thus, implicitly confronts them (and us) with the hazards of not accepting Jesus as God's Messiah and not living their (and our) lives in complete obedience to his will.

Apocalyptic Prophecy

Thus far we have presented the genres of what we might call "prophecy proper." Though formally diverse, prophecy proper shares two features in common. First, it communicates the "word" of God directly, as if God himself were speaking. The so-called messenger formula, "Thus says the Lord," introduces Yahweh's own speeches to his people (given, of course, by the human prophet). Second, it presupposes that God works within ordinary human history. So, prophecy proper announces the coming of God's judgment or salvation through the actions of human armies (e.g., the Assyrians,

---

205 For detailed discussion of the connections, see W. J. C. Weren, "The Use of Isaiah 5, 1–7 in the Parable of the Tenants," *Bib* 79 (1998): 1–26; and C. A. Evans, "On the Vineyard Parables of Isaiah 5 and Mark 12," *BZ* 28 (1984): 82–86.

Babylonians, or Persians). Statistically, prophecy proper encompasses most of the OT prophetic material.

But the OT also includes a second major type of prophecy called *apocalyptic* (Gk. *apokalypsis,* "revelation"; cf. Rev 1:1). Though the line between prophecy proper and apocalyptic often blurs, the following comparative chart highlights the features that set the latter apart.[206]

Prophecy vs. Apocalyptic

Prophecy	*Apocalyptic*
Repentance from sin	Sin too great, destruction inevitable
God's displeasure with his evil people	People's displeasure with evil, desire for God's intervention
Call for God's people to repent	Call for a faithful remnant to persevere
Divine intervention by natural or human means	Direct divine intervention by supernatural means
Direct speech by God	Mysterious, symbolic, indirect speech by intermediary
Prediction of imminent and future events	Prediction of cosmic, final solutions

Apocalyptic describes prophecies in which God "reveals" his hidden future plans, usually through dreams or visions with elaborate and at times strange symbolism or numbers. The form of apocalyptic (i.e., dreams, visions, symbols) makes its communication less direct than the spoken "word" of prophecy proper. This explains in part why it poses such an interpretive challenge.

More important, apocalyptic has a unique view of God's relationship to human history. Rather than work within it, the apocalyptic God radically intervenes from outside it. Behind this lay a profound religious crisis among the Israelites. The events of human history had plunged them into such despair that they doubted whether God still controlled it. In reply, apocalyptic held out hope of God's sovereign intervention beyond history, an intervention so radical as to usher in an utterly new era. Dan 7–12 and Revelation offer the best biblical examples of apocalyptic, but apocalyptic influence is also evident in the "Little Apocalypse" (Isa 24–27), Ezek 38–39, Joel 2:28–3:21, and Zech 1–6 and 9–14 (cf. Mt 24–25).[207]

---

206 Simplified from D. B. Sandy and M. G. Abegg, Jr., "Apocalyptic," in Sandy and Giese, *Cracking Codes,* 178–179; cf. also their helpful discussion (179–81). For additional discussion, see Green, *How to Read Prophecy,* 31, 49–67; J. J. Collins, "Apocalyptic Literature," in Evans and Porter, *Dictionary of New Testament Background,* 40–45; and id., *The Apocalyptic Imagination: An Introduction to Jewish Apocalyptic Literature,* 2d ed. (Grand Rapids: Eerdmans, 1998). See also "Revelation as Apocalyptic" in the next chapter.

207 Technically, the term apocalyptic denotes a type of literature, a historical movement, and a view of history. For a convenient survey of genres unique to apocalyptic literature, including apocryphal apocalypses, see J. J. Collins, *Daniel with an Introduction to Apocalyptic Literature,* FOTL 20 (Grand Rapids: Eerdmans, 1984), 2–24. For a discussion of apocalypticism as a movement, see P. D. Hanson, "Apocalyptic Literature," in Knight and Tucker, eds., *Hebrew Bible,* 465–88.

Principles of Interpretation—Old Testament Apocalyptic.

The apocalyptic genre presents unique challenges to the interpreter. The following principles of interpretation will help readers meet those challenges.[208]

1. Set a modest goal: rather than trying to understand everything, try simply to grasp as much as possible about what a text says. Apocalyptic probably presents some of the Bible's most difficult passages to interpret. Even Daniel himself found one such vision "beyond understanding" (Dan 8:27; cf. 12:8).

2. It is best to take the symbolism and numbers seriously but not literally. Symbolism and imagination fascinated ancient peoples more than did statistical accuracy. For example, it is significant that Daniel sees four *beasts* rather than, say, four *grapes* in Dan 7. They symbolize four kingdoms that threaten to ravage the world (v. 17), and the beast metaphor (imagine its connotations!) shows how the book "thinks" and "feels" about empires. But we need not make anything out of the fact that the first one is a lion, the second a bear, and so on. For the same reason, the various groups of "sevens" in Dan 9:24–27 probably represent complete periods of time—whether long or short—rather than groups of actual seven-year periods. We recommend that readers consult a Bible dictionary or encyclopedia about biblical symbols and numbers to understand their symbolic significance.[209] Above all, ponder the metaphorical and emotional connotations of the symbols. For example, contrast the rhetorical world created by portraying empires as beasts with that portraying "one like a human being coming with the clouds of heaven" (7:13 NRSV).

3. Read OT apocalyptic in connection with NT apocalyptic like Mt 24 (pars.) and Revelation. The latter either will indicate the fulfillment of the former prophecies or will supplement their predictions.[210]

4. Observe the prophet's pastoral concern for his audience. As we noted above, the roots of apocalyptic lie in a crisis of Israel's faith in God's control over history. Its primary purpose, therefore, is to encourage suffering saints. For example, Daniel repeatedly stresses that the "saints" (i.e., Israelite believers) will survive their present hardships to enjoy ruling history's final kingdom (see 7:18, 21–22, 27; 8:25; cf. 12:1–4). He does so to encourage Jews suffering under foreign domination.

5. Ultimately, the student needs to move beyond the details to determine the main points. The key question is: What is the text about as a whole? What does it say about temples, empires and their victims? So, whatever one makes of Daniel's beasts and weeks, his point is that God abhors oppressive empires, has planned their demise, and will end the agony of his people. Similarly, Zechariah stresses the vindication of Jerusalem and Judah before all her historical enemies (e.g., Zech 12–14).

---

208 Cf. Sandy and Abegg, "Apocalyptic," in Sandy and Giese, *Cracking Codes*, 187–190; for the principles for interpreting symbolism and numbers, see Green, *How to Read Prophecy*, 74–81.

209 For example, articles like "Biblical Numbers." One may also consult L. Ryken, et al., eds., *Dictionary of Biblical Imagery* (Downers Grove: InterVarsity, 1998), and commentaries on Daniel; cf. J. Goldingay, *Daniel*, WBC 30 (Dallas: Word, 1989); and J. G. Baldwin, *Daniel*, TOTC (Downers Grove: InterVarsity, 1978). On numbers in Revelation, see esp. F. J. Murphy, *Fallen is Babylon: The Revelation to John*, The New Testament in Context (Harrisburg: Trinity Press International, 1998), 24–27.

210 For help, see G. K. Beale, *The Use of Daniel in Jewish Apocalyptic Literature and in the Revelation of St. John* (Lanham, MD: University Press of America, 1984); and A. B. Mickelsen, *Daniel and Revelation* (Nashville: Thomas Nelson, 1984).

6. Applications should derive from the text's main points. Implicitly, Daniel and Zechariah call their readers to persevere through lengthy persecution. So they also call Christians today to the same faithfulness to God in the face of social opposition if not outright oppression.

7. Above all, learn to enjoy reading this imaginative and uplifting literature. As Sandy and Abegg note, "like cliffs for the climber and caviar for the connoisseur, apocalyptic can provide special delights for those who learn to appreciate it."[211]

WISDOM

Our earlier discussion of the wisdom psalms introduced ancient Israel's educators, the so-called wisdom teachers. Here we survey the many genres of the OT "Wisdom Literature," the larger category that includes the books of Proverbs, Job, and Ecclesiastes.[212] Readers must remember that the roots of wisdom thought lie in creation theology. A person acquires wisdom not by receiving divine revelation but by recording observations about what works or fails to work in daily life in the world created by God. Based on creation, wisdom provides an indirect, limited form of revelation. Its principles are tentative because they may be overridden by the mysterious freedom of God (e.g., Job) or by the teaching of other direct revelation.

Further, OT wisdom offers sharply different perspectives on life—e.g., the calm certainty of Proverbs versus the dogged skepticism of Ecclesiastes—so its books are best read canonically. One glimpses the full rainbow of biblical wisdom only by reckoning with its several perspectives. Finally, its literary nature also requires readers to apply principles for interpreting both poetry and narratives treated earlier. To understand it one must carefully tease out the dynamics of its parallelisms, the meanings of its metaphors, and its subtle use of drama, characterization, and plot. As Alter rightly warns, the subtle literary craft of wisdom literature insures that "if we are not good readers we will not get the point of the sayings of the wise."[213]

Types of Wisdom Literature

Proverbs

Probably the best-known form of Wisdom Literature is the *proverb*: "a concise, memorable statement of truth" learned over extended human experience.[214] Grammatically, a proverb occurs in the indicative mood and thus makes a simple declaration about life as it is. Imagine, for example, the many cases observed over centuries that produced this proverb:

---

211 Sandy and Abegg, "Apocalyptic," 177.

212 In the Apocrypha, the wisdom books are Ben Sira and the Wisdom of Solomon. For an overview of wisdom, see R. E. Murphy, *The Tree of Life: An Exploration of Biblical Wisdom Literature*, 2d ed. (Grand Rapids: Eerdmans, 1996); and J. L. Crenshaw, *Old Testament Wisdom: An Introduction*, rev. ed. (Louisville: Westminster John Knox, 1998). Cf. also W. P. Brown, *Character in Crisis: A Fresh Approach to the Wisdom Literature of the Old Testament* (Grand Rapids: Eerdmans, 1996); and G. von Rad, *Wisdom in Israel* (Nashville: Abingdon, 1972).

213 R. Alter, *The Art of Biblical Poetry* (New York: Basic Books, 1985), 168.

214 Ryken, *How to Read*, 121. Cf. Murphy, *Wisdom Literature*, 4, who classifies the proverb as a subtype of "saying."

> One who is quick-tempered acts foolishly,
>> and the schemer is hated. (Prov 14:17 NRSV)

Proverbs show great variety in form and content. "Descriptive proverbs" state a simple observation about life without reckoning with exceptions or applications:

> Some give freely, yet grow all the richer;
>> Others withhold what is due, and only suffer want.
>>> (Prov 11:24 NRSV; cf. also 15:23; 17:27–28; 18:16)

On the other hand, a "prescriptive proverb" does more than observe something significant about life. It states its truth with a specific aim to influence human behavior. For example, Prov 19:17 surely invites obedience when it says,

> Whoever is kind to the poor lends to the Lord,
>> and will be repaid in full. (NRSV; cf. Prov 14:31; 15:33;
>> 22:22–23)[215]

It is the specific promise of benefit, often by God's intervention, that distinguishes the prescriptive proverb from its descriptive counterpart. By extending that promise, it subtly appeals for reader obedience.

Some proverbs make their point by using comparisons. "Better is a dinner of vegetables where love is than a fatted ox and hatred with it" (Prov 15:17 NRSV) lauds the importance of love in the home (cf. 16:8, 16, 19; 17:1; 21:9; etc.). Such comparisons seek to underscore the superiority of certain character traits or personal conduct over others. Numerical proverbs, by contrast, cleverly drive their truths home by using the formula x / x + 1 in the title. For example:

> There are three things that are too amazing for me,
> four that I do not understand:
> the way of an eagle in the sky,
> the way of a snake on a rock,
> the way of a ship on the high seas,
> and the way of a man with a maiden. (Prov 30:18–19)

In this case, "x" is three and "x + 1" is four.[216] The title introduces the subject—things too amazing to understand—while the subsequent list enumerates four examples. The greatest emphasis, however—the *truly* amazing thing—falls on the last item ("the way of a man with a maiden"). The previous ones merely serve to heighten the wonder or disgust

---

215 Our "descriptive" and "prescriptive" proverbs correspond to Murphy's "experiential (or observational) saying" and "didactic saying," respectively (*Wisdom Literature*, 4–6).

216 This formula occurs in texts both within and outside of the Wisdom Literature (Prov 30:15b–16, 21–23, 29–31; Amos 1:3–2:8). Also, other schemas occur: one / two (Job 33:14–15; cf. Psa 62:11–12); two / three (Sir 26:28; 50:25–26); six / seven (Job 5:19–22; Prov 6:16–19); and nine / ten (Sir 25:7–11). For an Akkadian example of six / seven, see the "Dispute between the Tamarisk and the Date Palm," *ANET* 593 (lines 17–18).

over it. In such cases, proper interpretation must focus, not on the entire list, but on the final element and how it differs from or even surpasses the others.[217]

The most common proverb is the "antithetical proverb," the form that dominates the large collection in Prov 10–15. By painting a stark contrast, such proverbs attempt to commend wise conduct highly and to make foolishness completely unappealing. Since antithesis is the key to this form, proper interpretation requires the reader to focus on the contrast presented. One must isolate the two traits or types of people that the proverb sets side-by-side and then decide which of the opposites the proverb commends and why.

For instance, note these two examples:

> Those who are hot-tempered stir up strife,
> but those who are slow to anger calm contention. (Prov 15:18 NRSV)

> Anxiety weighs down the human heart,
> but a kind word cheers it up. (Prov 12:25 NRSV)

The first example compares quick-tempered and patient people; it commends patience over an ill temper. The reason, of course, is that fiery people cause dissension while patient ones bring calm. The second example contrasts an anxious heart with a kind word. It commends the latter as the soothing antidote for the former.[218]

Principles of Interpretation—Proverbs

An initial, general word of clarification about how to apply proverbs properly is in order.[219] Put simply, proverbs teach probable truth, not absolute truth. By nature, proverbs are not absolute promises from God that guarantee the promised outcome if one follows them. Rather, they point out patterns of conduct that, if followed, give one the best chance of success, all things being equal. In other words, they offer general principles for successful living rather than a comprehensive "legal code for life." Further, proverbs place a higher premium on etching themselves on one's memory than on theoretical accuracy. That is, their primary goal is to state an important, simple truth about life in easy-to-remember terms. Hence, they do not intend to cover every imaginable circumstance. Readers must decide which proverbs apply to specific contemporary situations.

Consider this example: "All hard work brings a profit, but mere talk leads only to poverty" (Prov 14:23). This proverb teaches that success always hinges on good effort, not on good promises. But the principle does not include other factors that might hinder success, despite one's best efforts—economic recessions, company bankruptcies, or

---

217 There are several lists of two (Job 13:20–22; Prov 30:7–8) and four items (Prov 30:24–28; Sir 25:1–2) that share the feature(s) stated in the title. Evidently, this form aims to treat the title's subject comprehensively by giving several illustrations of it. Cf. Murphy, *Wisdom Literature*, 180.

218 Lest we leave the mistaken impression that proverbs only occur in Proverbs, we note in passing that they also appear in sections of Ecclesiastes (4:6, 13; 5:10–12; 7:1–12; 9:11–12, 17–18; 10:1–2, 6, 8–9; 11:4; et al). For NT examples, see Mt 11:30; Gal 6:7; Jas 3:6 (so Ryken, *How to Read*, 121–22).

219 Cf. Fee and Stuart, *How to Read the Bible*, 353–63.

hailstorms, for example. As a result, to interpret proverbs properly, we must balance our understanding of each one, first, in light of other proverbs in the Bible, and, second, in light of other scriptural teachings.

But what do we do with those proverbs that our own experience seems to contradict? For example, Prov 13:4 promises:

> The appetite of the lazy craves, and gets nothing,
> while the appetite of the diligent is richly supplied. (NRSV)

Obviously, the proverb commends diligent work over lazy daydreaming. But how does it square with reality today? Hardworking Christian farmers in places like the Philippines and Peru barely eke out a living, much less find their "appetite . . . richly supplied." Poor soil, inhospitable climate, and political conflict all conspire against them. Has God failed to keep his "promise" in their case? In response, we must highlight several factors that readily apply to other proverbs as well.

First, as we noted above, a proverb expresses a truth observed to work in most cases. It may be limited to the sage's personal experience and certain specific contexts. It does not deny that exceptions occur; it merely omits them from consideration. Thus, in application, we cannot simply pick and choose proverbs that "sound good"; rather, we must carefully ensure that their original context and our proposed application context closely match up. Second, we must take care not to interpret a proverb by modern Western standards of desires. The proverb does not refer to nice homes, new cars, ski trips, and ocean cruises. Probably, it envisions rather simple desires—a small house, enough food (by ancient standards!), and a happy family. Third, the reality of a fallen world must factor into our interpretation (cf. Gen 3:17–19). Sadly, the world struggles with the results in nature and history of Adam's rebellion. Poor soil, poor climate, and poor politics are some of its symptoms. Thus, though the proverb may be true in most cases ("all things being equal"), our fallen world may prevent its full realization—all things are not equal.

Further, the starting point for understanding any proverb is its literary traits—its parallelism, metaphors, word plays, and even its narrative features. Analysis of its careful literary formulation opens the doorway to our understanding of its contents. Finally, the wide-ranging content of biblical proverbs may be best studied through topical surveys (e.g., family relations, business dealings, etc.) or character studies (e.g., the fool, the lazy person, the wicked, etc.).

Instruction

Israel's wisdom sages also spoke in the imperative mood in the genre *instruction*.[220] Instruction may be simply a brief exhortation such as Prov 8:33: "Listen to my instruction and be wise; do not ignore it." The "sayings of the wise" (Prov 22:17–24:22) contain another variety of the short instruction in which a prohibition ("Do not") is supported by a motive clause ("for" or "because"). Sometimes this shorter type makes explicit the truth urged indirectly by other proverbs:

> Do not exploit the poor because they are poor
> and do not crush the needy in court,

---

220 Murphy, *Wisdom Literature*, 6, 50–51.

for the LORD will take up their case
and will plunder those who plunder them.
    (Prov 22:22–23, directly prohibiting what 14:31 implies; cf. 16:3
    and 20)

As this example illustrates, the purpose of instruction is to persuade the hearer to adopt or abandon certain conduct or attitudes. The frequent motive clauses (e.g., "for the Lord will take up their case") give the reasons for compliance, making the teaching all the more persuasive.[221]

On the other hand, instruction may take a longer form, for example, the series of lengthy instructions that constitute the heart of Prov 1–9.[222] The wisdom teacher urges his "child(ren)" at length (e.g., 1:8; 2:1; 4:1; 7:1; etc.) to follow the way of wisdom. An unusual feature of these instructions is that they occasionally include a unique subgenre called the *wisdom speech*.[223] Here they personify wisdom as a woman who openly proclaims her message in the public streets and squares (1:20–33; 8; 9:1–6; cf. folly as a woman [9:13–17]).

Principles of Interpretation—Instruction

The following principles of interpretation are based on the literary format of the instruction genre:

1. The student should carefully observe that this literary form's commands or prohibitions present absolute demands for obedience not tentative suggestions for consideration. Readers must respond to them with seriousness.

2. The student must approach wisdom speeches as if listening to a woman passionately pleading with passing crowds to follow her advice. That very passion underscores the seriousness of her advice—how crucial for people to obey it, and how menacing is the danger that stalks those who do not. One should hear the passage as the urgent plea of a concerned friend, not as an abstract treatise.

3. The student should pay special attention to any motive clauses present for they offer the rationale for the instruction given.

4. Having read the passage, the student might capture its form and content by completing this sentence: "This shouting woman urges me to . . ."

Example Story and Reflection

The wisdom books also contain two somewhat autobiographical genres. In an *example story*, the writer narrates a personal experience or other illustration from which

---

221 Crenshaw, "Wisdom," 235. Commands and prohibitions (i.e., instruction) also appear in Ecclesiastes (cf. 5:1–2; 7:16–17, 21–22; 8:1–4; 9:7–10; 10:20; 11:1–2, 6, 8–10).

222 For structural details, see Murphy, *Wisdom Literature*, 49; for additional background on Prov 1–9, including the possible influence of Egyptian wisdom and Israelite prophecy on the collection, see pp. 50–52. Cf. also the recent treatments by C. E. Yoder, *Wisdom as a Woman of Substance: A Socioeconomic Reading of Proverbs 1–9 and 31:10–31*, BZAW 304 (Berlin/New York: de Gruyter, 2001); S. L. Harris, *Proverbs 1–9: A Study of Inner-Biblical Interpretation*, SBLDS 150 (Atlanta: Scholars Press, 1995).

223 Appealing to Egyptian parallels, Crenshaw ("Wisdom," 248–49) classifies these as hymns in praise of wisdom, but in our view they are best seen as speeches since, Egyptian analogies notwithstanding, they lack the obvious traits of hymns.

he has distilled an important truth to pass on.[224] Formally, example stories often open with formulas like "I saw and considered" or "I passed by," followed by the story proper. They conclude with a statement concerning the moral to be drawn. Prov 24:30–34 illustrates this genre:

Opening	I passed by the field of one who was lazy,
	by the vineyard of a stupid person;
Example Story	and see, it was all overgrown with thorns;
	the ground was covered with nettles,
	and its stone wall was broken down.
	Then I saw and considered it;
	I looked and received instruction.
The Moral	A little sleep, a little slumber,
	a little folding of the hands to rest,
	and poverty will come upon you like a robber,
	and want, like an armed warrior.[225] (NRSV)

This example story begins with observations about the terrible disrepair of a certain lazy person's field and vineyard. From reflections ("I saw and considered") flow the moral, i.e., that laziness ends in the cruel surprise of irresistible poverty. For the reader the obvious implication is that hard work is better than sloth regardless of how alluring long naps might be.

The second autobiographical genre is the *reflection*.[226] In a reflection, the writer reports personal musings and conclusions about a truth, often citing firsthand observations, example stories, and lengthy thought. Though loosely structured, reflections have the following formal features: (1) opening formulas like "I saw and considered" or "I passed by"; (2) the quotation of proverbs, use of rhetorical questions, or citation of example stories; and (3) a concluding moral.

The reflection dominates the book of Ecclesiastes (e.g., 1:12–2:26) though with a less obvious structure than the above example.[227] Section after section opens with "I have seen" or "I looked and saw" (1:14; 3:16; 4:1; 5:13; 6:1; et al). Then, mixing prose and poetic musings, example stories, and proverbial quotations, the writer wrestles with the futility of life. The book's literary tone is realistic, sober, and disarmingly honest—a tone that readily draws readers into its world because of its freshness and integrity. Finally, at intervals, he draws the morals from his observations (2:24–25; 3:22; 5:18–20).

---

224 Murphy, *Wisdom Literature*, 176. For the use of this genre in the NT, see J. T. Tucker, *Example Stories: Perspectives on Four Parables in the Gospel of Luke*, JSNTSup 162 (Sheffield: Sheffield Academic Press, 1998).

225 Cf. Murphy, *Wisdom Literature*, 130, 176. For other examples, see Prov 4:3–9; 7:6–27; Eccl 4:13–16; 9:13–16; cf. Psa 37:25, 35–36.

226 The term "reflection" follows Murphy, *Wisdom Literature*, 130, 181; but Crenshaw ("Wisdom," 256–58) prefers the term "confession" or "autobiographical narrative." Scholars generally believe this autobiographical style originated in Egypt, where examples abound (so Crenshaw, "Wisdom," 256).

227 For recent discussion of this intriguing book, see Dell, "Wisdom in Israel," in Mayes, *Text and Context*, 364–67; cf. also the introduction in T. Longman, III, *Ecclesiastes*, NICOT (Grand Rapids: Eerdmans, 1998).

Principles of Interpretation—Example Story and Reflection

Based on the format of the example story and reflection we suggest the following guidelines for interpretation:

1. The key is to determine how their components support the concluding moral. For example, the reflection in Eccl 4:7–12 extols the value of human companionship. The example story of a rich but lonely single person (v. 8) poses the problem—how miserable to be alone. The lengthy discourse (vv. 9–12) illustrates the moral—that life is better when two people share it than when one lives alone.

2. Longer texts or series of texts (e.g., Prov 1, 5, 7–9) offer a special opportunity to consider their narrative aspects—their development of plot, themes, and character. Such narrative qualities allows readers to understand the text through both mind and imagination.

3. Readers should observe how each text works literarily, considering its structure, thematic development, mood, and theological assumptions.

4. The concluding morals merit particular attention because they express the writer's main point. The example from Prov 24 above, for example, concluded that laziness ends in economic disaster. The writer warns of the dangers of laziness and, by implication, praises hard work.

5. Applications of an example story or reflection need to flow from the concluding moral. So Eccl 4 challenges believers to cultivate friendships, for God has ordained them to make human life less miserable. For Christians, a local church community provides one good opportunity for this.

6. Ultimately, in reading Ecclesiastes students should, on the one hand, fully appreciate its unique literary style and grapple with its realistic perspective, and, on the other, interpret its teaching canonically in light of other biblical revelation.

Disputation Speeches

A massive literary masterpiece, the book of Job incorporates many genres.[228] Setting aside Job's narrative framework (Job 1–2; 42:7–17), the rest of the book consists of the genre *disputation*. As we noted above, in a disputation a speaker seeks to persuade the audience of some truth. In contrast to prophetic examples (see above) that report only the prophet's side, Job reports the arguments of both Job and his friends. [229] Specifically, we hear the lengthy

---

228 So far, attempts to define the genre of the book as a whole have not won a consensus. Among the options are the following: a frame tale (M. Cheney), dramatization of a lament (C. Westermann), a judicial process (H. Richter), paradigm of the answered lament (H. Gese), comedy (J. W. Whedbee), and *sui generis* (D. Wolfers); cf. Dell, "Wisdom in Israel," in Mayes, *Text and Context*, 361–62; Murphy, *Wisdom Literature*, 16–19. Among possible ANE parallels, Job most closely resembles a work called the *Babylonian Theodicy* (so Crenshaw, "Wisdom," 253–54; Murphy, *Wisdom Literature*, 10). For the text, see *ANET* 601–604; for a careful comparative analysis, see Walton, *Ancient Israelite Literature in Its Cultural Context*, 184–87.

229 After Job's opening soliloquy (chap. 3), we hear Eliphaz (chaps. 4–5, 15, 22), Bildad (chaps. 8, 18, 25), Zophar (chaps. 11, 20), and the latecomer Elihu (chaps. 32–37). In between, Job offers his rebuttals (chaps. 6–7, 9–10, 12–14, 16–17, 19, 21, 23–24, 26, 27–28), closing with a climactic soliloquy (chaps. 29–31). Crenshaw ("Wisdom," 253–54) prefers the term "dialogue" (Germ. *Streitgespräch*), but we believe "disputation" better captures the argumentative nature of the book's dialogue (so Murphy, *Wisdom Literature*, 175–76). For cultural background, see K. van der Toorn, "The Ancient Near Eastern Literary Dialogue as a Vehicle of Critical Reflection," in *Dispute Poems and Dialogues in the Ancient and Mediaeval Near East*, ed. G. J. Reinink and H. L. J. Vanstiphout (Louvain: Departement Oriëntalistick [Peeters], 1991), 59–75.

disputation speeches in which the speakers debate the cause of Job's suffering. In the end, however, the Lord's dramatic, irrefutable speeches (chaps. 38–39, 40–41) reduce Job to humble acquiescence (42:1–6).

Occasionally, the book's disputation speeches incorporate into their argument literary forms from Israel's worship. In Job 16, for example, Job sounds like a psalmist when he voices a *complaint* or passionate cry of despair (for this see above under poetry). He describes the attack of his enemy—God himself—and affirms his innocence:

> Surely, O God, you have worn me out;
>> you have devastated my entire household . . . .
> My face is red with weeping,
>> deep shadows ring my eyes;
> yet my hands have been free of violence,
>> and my prayer is pure. (Job 16:7, 16–17)

Then Job lifts a petition—a pained cry for justice through an advocate pleading his case in heaven:

> O earth, do not cover my blood;
>> let my outcry find no resting place.
> Even now, in fact, my witness is in heaven,
>> and he that vouches for me is on high.
> My friends scorn me;
>> my eye pours out tears to God,
>> that he would maintain the right of a mortal with God,
>> as one does for a neighbor. (Job 16:18–21 NRSV)

In the end, however, Job despairs that, barring an answer from God, death is his only future:

> If I look for Sheol as my house,
>> if I spread my couch in darkness, . . . where then is my hope?
>> Who will see my hope?
> Will it go down to the bars of Sheol? (Job 17:13, 15–16a NRSV; cf. 30)

In terms of interpretation, complaints remind the reader of the speaker's frame of reference: acute affliction suffered unjustly and the assumption that an appeal to God might bring rescue. This background helps underscore why Job's fate is especially bitter: God himself, not his human peers, is Job's implacable enemy; and, rather than rescue Job, God remains silent.

Also, disputations include a *hymn* or *hymnic elements*. We can recognize them by their lengthy description of things that the Lord does on an ongoing basis (in Hebrew, primarily participles). Observe this psalmic song of praise to Yahweh's greatness:

> He who removes mountains, and they do not know it,
> when he overturns them in his anger; . . .
> who alone stretched out the heavens
> and trampled the waves of the Sea;
> who made the Bear and Orion,

the Pleiades and the chambers of the south;
Who does great things beyond understanding,
and marvelous things without number. (Job 9:5, 8–10 NRSV; cf. also
5:9–16; 11:7–12; 12:13–25; 25:2–6; 26:5–14; cf. 38:31; Amos
5:8.)

From Israel's worship practices also comes the *avowal of innocence*, a statement by which an individual attempts to prove his or her innocence. For example, one may voluntarily take on an oath of horrible consequences to be suffered if guilty.[230] Job does this as the capstone of his impassioned, closing soliloquy (Job 31):[231]

If I have walked with falsehood,
and my foot has hurried to deceit— . . .
then let me sow, and another eat;
and let what grows for me be rooted out. . . .
If I have withheld anything that the poor desired,
or have caused the eyes of the widow to fail,
or have eaten my morsel alone,
and the orphan has not eaten from it— . . .
if I have seen anyone perish for lack of clothing,
or a poor person without covering, . . .
if I have raised my hand against the orphan,
because I saw I had supporters at the gate;
then let my shoulder blade fall from my shoulder,
and let my arm be broken from its socket. (Job 31:5, 8, 16–17, 19,
21–22 NRSV)

Job lists the conditions ("If I")—the alleged guilt—then the dire punishment to follow if those conditions apply. His willingness to risk disaster argues for his innocence since no guilty person who takes God's vengeance seriously would dare do so.

Principles of Interpretation—Job

The following principles for interpretation apply to the various genres found in the book of Job:

1. Since disputation speeches dominate the book, the student should determine what truth(s) dominates each speaker's attempts at persuasion.[232]

---

230 Cf. Psa 7:3–5. Alternatively, the speaker may simply deny any guilt through a series of "I did" or "I did not" statements (see Psa 17:3–5; 26:4–6; Jer 15:16–17). The repetition of emphatic denials gives the avowal its persuasive power. We do not encounter this type of avowal in Job (but see 9:29–31). For oaths, see T. W. Cartledge, *Vows in the Hebrew Bible and the Ancient Near East*, JSOTSup 147 (Sheffield: Sheffield Academic Press, 1994).

231 Murphy (*Wisdom Literature*, 38) compares it to "a final statement before a judge"; cf. M. B. Dick, "Job 31, the Oath of Innocence, and the Sage," *ZAW* 95 (1983): 31–53. S. C. Mott, "The Ideal Righteous Person in the Hebrew Bible," *Christian Social Action* 9 (1996): 35, offers insightful reflections on Job 31.

232 The size of Job commends the excellent overviews of its contents available in Alter, *Biblical Poetry*, 85–110; Murphy, *Job*; and R. N. Whybray, *Job* (Sheffield: Sheffield Academic Press, 1998).

2. The book's narrative framework identifies Job as the hero. He is the most right-eous person alive (1:8); in the end God sides with Job against his opponents (42:7–9) and doubly restores his losses (42:10–17). Thus, the student should pay particular attention to Job's self-defense and beware that the seemingly good advice of his companions often reflects a position diametrically opposite from God's.

3. When other genres support the disputation speeches, we need to analyze how they work, why the poet included them, and what they contribute thematically. For example, from the occasional use of hymns it would be misleading to read Job as a kind of musi-cal play in which the debaters periodically break into song! In the above example, by por-traying God's irresistible power, the hymnic section provides evidence—evidence made more powerful by its musical form—to support the preceding line, "who has resisted him, and succeeded?" (9:4b). In the end, Job drew the obvious inference: such power threat-ens to overwhelm any human who attempts to argue with it (vv. 14–20).

4. Job's avowal of innocence (chap. 31) provides a crucial interpretive clue to understand the book. By forcefully affirming his innocence, Job denies that his own guilt has caused his suffering. Chaps. 1–2 seem to confirm this claim by portraying Job's righteousness and God's recognition of it. In the psalms, avowals of innocence support the psalmist's plea for God to issue a legal verdict in his favor. Thus, the form also implies that the goal of Job's avowal is to receive legal vindication from God.[233]

5. In light of the above, the student must decide from careful consideration of God's long, poetic soliloquy—the only presentation of his point of view—what his main point is and to what degree it "answers" Job's disputations. From Job's responses (chap. 42:1–6) one must ponder whether Job is truly innocent and what the book teaches about the cause and purpose of his (and our) suffering.[234] Consequently, we suggest that the book's lesson is that the ultimate root of *some* (not all) human suffer-ing lies in the mysterious, hidden purposes of God for his people.[235]

6. The book's ending provides a crucial clue to the interpretation of the whole book. God vindicates and rewards Job and criticizes the arrogance of his friends. Job encourages believers to trust God for similar, ultimate vindication from unjust suffer-ing, whether it comes in this life or the next.

7. As with Ecclesiastes and Proverbs, whatever main theme one concludes from Job must be understood alongside the perspectives of the other wisdom books and in light of later revelation.

---

233 Job frequently uses motifs drawn from Israel's legal system (e.g., Job 9:14–16; 9:29–10:1; 13:18–21; etc.), though not major legal genres. Hence, it pays to read such sections in light of that legal background. Psa 7:3–5 provides another excellent example. For a discussion of Psa 7 and its legal background, see R. L. Hubbard, Jr., "Dynamistic and Legal Processes in Psalm 7," *ZAW* 94 (1982): 267–80.

234 Cf. the insightful treatment of the whirlwind scene in Alter, *Biblical Poetry*, 94–110. Several earlier passages may anticipate God's soliloquy from the whirlwind (e.g., Job 9:5–10; 12:7–25; 28; 11:7–9 [Zophar]; 15:7–8 [Eliphaz]; 37:14–24 [Elihu]). We are grateful to Professor Carroll R. for this suggestion.

235 Cf. LaSor, et al., *Old Testament Survey*, 493–94. Dell, "Wisdom in Israel," in Mayes, ed., *Text and Context*, 363–64, surveys alternative views on Job's theological themes.

A Sample Wisdom Text—Proverbs 30:24–28

Close consideration of the following wisdom text will help illustrate the proper application of the above principles:[236]

> Four things on earth are small, yet they are exceedingly wise:
> the ants are a people without strength, so they provide their food in
>   the summer;
> the badgers are a people without power, so they make their homes in
>   the rocks;
> the locusts have no king, yet all of them march in rank;
> the lizard can be grasped in the hand, yet it is found in kings' palaces.

Literarily, these lines string together four proverbs (vv. 25–28) under an introduction (v. 24) to form a parable within the "words of Agur" (Prov 30). The proverbs run through four small but very wise non-human creatures to teach humans how to behave properly. The first three model cardinal virtues extolled by wisdom (vv. 25–27), while the last underscores the surprising rewards their quiet adaptation to the created order reaps (v. 28). Contextually, their quiet adaptation sharply contrasts the four upstarts whose conduct disrupts the social order (vv. 21–23).

Strikingly, the first two lines each boldly invoke people as a metaphor (e.g., people symbolize ant conduct rather than the reverse). Ants are "people" who lack brute physical strength (Heb. *'āz*) so they show the virtue of wisely timed hard work, storing food to survive the usual winter shortage (v. 25). Badgers are "people" who lack the ant's army-like numerical strength (Heb. *'āṣûm*) so they reside in rocks to protect their small, more defenseless numbers behind inaccessible terrain (v. 26). They show the virtue of seeking appropriate shelter.

Locusts lack a king, but they still stay in step together, thereby modeling the virtue of self-disciplined community (v. 27). Finally, the lizard illustrates how wisdom rewards its practitioners: though easily controllable by size, his wise adaptation gains him unexpected eminence in society's highest levels—free run of the palace.

Agur draws no explicit moral, but in context the parable seems to promote the theme of the wisdom of adaptability to creation—of accepting the "givens" of one's limitations and adjusting one's life accordingly. Applications of this text would pursue our present limitations—the world as it is—and ways in which we might adapt to it by living out wisdom's virtues (timely hard work, proper shelter, community) today. We might also ask how what is it about those virtues that serve to please God and bring him glory. Finally, applications might describe some of the rewards or benefits for such God-pleasing adaptability. Along such lines we implement wisdom's foundational theme, the "fear of the Lord."

CONCLUSION

This survey shows that the OT is a fertile literary garden. Its major species are narrative, law, poetry, prophecy, and wisdom, and everywhere varieties of literary devices

---

236 Translation and comment below draws on B. K. Waltke, *The Book of Proverbs*, NICOT (Grand Rapids: Eerdmans, forthcoming)

flourish within them. Some texts reflect the rich inheritance the people of Israel received from their cultural ancestors in the ancient Near East, while others derive from Israel's own creative cultural life. Our goal has been to cultivate in our readers "literary competence"—the ability to read a text in light of its own background and purpose—by suggesting principles of interpretation keyed to the diverse nature of OT literature. We hope that they provide a helpful map to walk readers through its wonderful literary terrain and to enhance both their understanding of the OT's ideas and their sheer pleasure in meandering through its fascinating world.

10

GENRES OF THE NEW TESTAMENT

The NT is not nearly as long as the OT, so it does not contain as many literary genres or forms. Still, four major genres appear with various subforms embedded in them. As in the OT, principles of interpretation may vary according to genre or form.

THE GENRE OF THE GOSPELS

The Greek word *euangelion* (gospel) means "good news." Before the NT was written, the term often referred to news such as the announcement of a military victory. In the NT the term refers to the good news of the message proclaimed by Jesus. Mark may well have been the first person to use the term in this way (cf. Mk 1:1, 14–15; 8:35; 10:29; 14:9). After Matthew, Mark, Luke, and John had all written their accounts of the life of Jesus, Christians came to refer also to those narratives as Gospels. But the older sense still lingered on so the people who first began to collect the four Gospels together entitled them "The Gospel according to so-and-so." Each document reflected the one unified message from Jesus, which was now also about him and witnessed in four different accounts.[1]

Noncanonical documents also came to have the label "gospel" attached to them. But none of these followed the same genre as the four canonical Gospels. Some, like the Coptic Gospel of Thomas, were not narratives but collections of numerous sayings allegedly from Jesus, loosely strung together with almost no connections between them. Others took narrative form but focused only on one small portion of Jesus' life, such as his childhood (e.g., The Infancy Gospel of Thomas) or his death and resurrection (e.g., the Gospels of Peter and Nicodemus). Still others resembled extended treatises on Jesus' postresurrection teaching for his disciples (e.g., the Gospels of Philip and Mary). Most of these documents clearly came from unorthodox factions of early Christianity, usually related to Gnosticism. They contain various teachings or beliefs that are legendary and / or incompatible with the claims of the canonical Gospels.[2]

---

1 Cf. e.g. R. H. Gundry, "ΕΥΑΓΓΕΛΙΟΝ: How Soon a Book?" *JBL* 115 (1996): 321–25. M. Hengel (*The Four Gospels and the One Gospel of Jesus Christ* [Harrisburg: Trinity Press International, 2000]: 48–53), however, suggests that Mark himself called his document a Gospel and that the other Evangelists imitated him.

2 The two main collections of noncanonical works in which these various gospels appear are E. Hennecke, *New Testament Apocrypha*, vol. 1, rev. and ed. W. Schneemelcher, 2d ed. (Philadelphia: Westminster, 1990); and J. M. Robinson, ed., *The Nag Hammadi Library*, 3d ed. (Leiden: Brill, 1996).

So in the earliest centuries of Christianity the word "gospel" did not refer primarily to a literary genre in any formal sense. It is obvious, however, from even a cursory study of the four Gospels that these books all have much in common both in form and in content. Therefore, we will classify them together and seek to identify their genre more closely.

Throughout most of the Church's history, Christians have thought of the Gospels as *biographies* of Jesus. But in the modern era this identification has been widely rejected. After all, Mark and John say nothing about Jesus' birth, childhood, or young adult years. Luke and Matthew include selected incidents related to his birth and one episode about his teachings in the temple at age twelve, but otherwise they too are silent. On the other hand, all four Gospels devote a disproportionately large space to the last few weeks and days of Christ's life. What is more, the main events of Jesus' ministry appear in different order in the different Gospels, and rarely are we told how much time elapsed between any two events.

As a result, modern scholars have looked for other generic labels to apply to the Gospels. A few have identified them with well-known genres of Greco-Roman fiction. Some have called the Gospels *aretalogies*: accounts of episodes from the life of a "divine man," usually embellishing and exaggerating the feats of a famous hero or warrior of the past. Some have applied the language of playwrights to them, associating the Gospels with *comedies* (stories with a triumphant ending) or *tragedies* (stories in which the protagonist is defeated, despite having shown signs of greatness). A few link these books with *parables,* seeing an entire Gospel as a metaphorical discourse designed both to reveal and to conceal. And occasionally, despite their similarities, one or more Gospels are treated as representing a different genre from the others. Matthew, for example, has been viewed as a *midrash* of Mark and Q (material common to Matthew and Luke not found in Mark): an interpretive retelling of sacred tradition in which straightforward history is elaborated and embellished with various fictitious additions in order to communicate important theological beliefs. More commonly, John is set apart from the three "Synoptic" Gospels as more *drama* than history or biography.[3] More conservatively, it has been analyzed as a Hebrew trial (*ribh*) in which God brings a lawsuit against his people.[4]

Problems exist with each of these suggestions, however, so that none has commanded a consensus. A common view in modern scholarship suggests that the four Evangelists in essence created a new genre when they composed their Gospels. But a substantial number of studies are again linking the Gospels with Hellenistic *biography*. Earlier readers were thrown off track because conventions for writing biography in the ancient Greco-Roman world did not always correspond to modern standards. Hellenistic biographers did not feel compelled to present all periods of an individual's life or to narrate everything in chronological order. They selected events carefully in order to teach certain moral lessons

---

3 For a more detailed description and critique of each of these views, with bibliographic references to representative advocates, see C. L. Blomberg, *The Historical Reliability of the Gospels* (Leicester and Downers Grove: InterVarsity, 1987), 44–49, 235–40; on John, cf. id., *The Historical Reliability of John's Gospel* (Leicester and Downers Grove: InterVarsity, 2001).

4 A. E. Harvey, *Jesus on Trial: A Study in the Fourth Gospel* (London: SPCK; Atlanta: John Knox, 1977); A. T. Lincoln, *Truth on Trial: The Lawsuit Motif in the Fourth Gospel* (Peabody: Hendrickson, 2000).

or promote a particular ideology, and they frequently focused on a person's death because they believed the way people died revealed much about their character. Luke's prologue (Lk 1:1–4), in fact, closely resembles the introductions to the historical writings of ancient Jews, Greeks, and Romans such as Josephus, Herodotus, Tacitus, Arrian, Dio Cassius, and Sallust.[5]

Of course, if a gospel is about Jesus, by that criterion it will differ from other Hellenistic biographies. Robert Guelich offers a judicious survey of modern proposals concerning gospel genre and concludes with his own:

> *Formally,* a gospel is a narrative account concerning the public life and teaching of a significant person that is composed of discreet [sic] traditional units placed in the context of Scriptures . . . . *Materially,* the genre consists of the message that God was at work in Jesus' life, death, and resurrection effecting his promises found in the Scriptures.[6]

This seems best to us, too. "Formally," then the Gospels have parallels in other literature; "materially" they prove uniquely Christian. Perhaps it is best, therefore, to call them *theological biographies.*[7]

Implications for Interpretation

Historical Trustworthiness

There is a widespread belief that only a small portion of the canonical Gospels preserves accurate historical information about the words and deeds of Jesus and his companions. This has led to the development of *tradition criticism* and its "criteria of authenticity" for tracing the growth of the Jesus-tradition. In this view the tradition ranges from fairly authentic sayings and factual narratives to the more complex combinations of history and legend or myth found in the final form of the canonical Gospels. For many scholars, only (what they deem to be) the earliest stage or most authentic material is normative for Christians today.[8] Others postulate varying degrees of normativeness based on the layer and the tradition to which a given verse or text can be assigned.[9] The Jesus Seminar gained notoriety in the 1990s for its two books that color-coded all of the sayings and narratives of Jesus in the *five* Gospels (including the Gnostic Gospel of Thomas) and concluded that

---

5 On the Gospels as biographies, see esp. R. A. Burridge, *What Are the Gospels?* SNTSMS 70 (Cambridge: Cambridge University Press, 1992). On Lk 1:1–4, see L. Alexander, *The Preface to Luke's Gospel* (Cambridge: Cambridge University Press, 1993).

6 R. Guelich, "The Gospel Genre," in *The Gospel and the Gospels,* ed. P. Stuhlmacher (Grand Rapids: Eerdmans, 1991), 206.

7 Cf. I. H. Marshall, "Luke and His 'Gospel,' " in *Gospel and Gospels,* ed. Stuhlmacher, 273–82.

8 The classic and perhaps most skeptical 20th-century work that sought to trace *The History of the Synoptic Tradition* was the book by R. Bultmann with that title (New York: Harper & Row, 1963 [Ger. orig. 1921]). The best example of a work treating the earliest stages of the tradition as most normative is the far less skeptical book by J. Jeremias, *New Testament Theology,* vol. 1 (London: SCM; Philadelphia: Westminster, 1971).

9 E.g., J. D. Crossan (*The Historical Jesus* [San Francisco: Harper Collins, 1991]) parcels out the Gospel traditions into four strata. The later the stratum, the less likely he believes it to be historical and the less significant for determining the permanent relevance of Jesus for Christians (see esp. 426).

only 18 percent of the sayings and 16 percent of the narratives of Jesus actually reflected something he said or did in reasonably accurate form.[10]

Now to be sure, we must not force the Gospels, anachronistically, to measure up to modern conventions for writing history or biography. Instead, they must be evaluated according to the standards of their day.[11] They employ frequent paraphrase rather than direct quotation (neither Greek nor Aramaic used quotation marks or felt a need for them). Readers today encounter much interpretation, abbreviation and digests of long speeches and narratives, topical as well as chronological arrangement of accounts, and careful selection of material to fit a writer's particular theological emphasis. But once all this is recognized, the Gospel materials actually measure up quite well by the most valid criteria of authenticity.

So, for example, we should not be surprised when Mark and Luke report that the voice from heaven at Jesus' baptism declared, "You are my Son, whom I love" (Mk 1:11; Lk 3:22), while Matthew's account has "This is my Son, whom I love" (Mt 3:17). Matthew has probably reworded Mark to emphasize that the heavenly voice spoke not only for Jesus' benefit but also for the crowd's. Or again, Matthew and Luke differ as to which of Satan's temptations of Jesus they place second and which third—jumping off the temple to be rescued by the angels or worshipping Satan to receive all the kingdoms of the earth (cf. Mt 4:1–11 with Lk 4:1–13). But Luke does not use any chronological connectives in his account, only the Greek words *de* (but) and *kai* (and). Luke has probably placed what occurs as Matthew's second temptation last so that the climax of Jesus' temptations, as with his ministry overall, would end with Jesus at the temple in Jerusalem, a motif that Luke stresses.

Sometimes the differences between parallels prove more substantial. At first sight, Mt 10:37 appears to tone down Lk 14:26 drastically. Luke writes, "If anyone comes to me and does not hate father and mother . . . such a person cannot be my disciple" (TNIV). But Matthew has, "Anyone who loves their father or mother more than me is not worthy of me" (TNIV). Matthew accurately paraphrases what Luke reports more literally. In Semitic language and thought "hate" had a broader range of meanings than it does in English, including the sense of "leaving aside," "renunciation," or "abandonment." "I prefer this to that" was often stated as "I like this and hate that."

Another famous "alleged" contradiction between Gospels involves the story of raising Jairus' daughter. In Mk 5:21–43 Jesus is summoned to Jairus' home twice, once before and once after the child has died. Mt 9:18–26 reports only one summons—at the beginning of the passage in which Jairus says the child has already died. By contemporary standards of reporting this would be an inaccuracy, but in light of ancient tendencies to abbreviate and "telescope" such reports significantly (combining separate stages of an episode into one), no one would likely have charged Matthew with falsifying his report.

We could offer many other illustrations.[12] All of these types of changes are natural and common in ancient biographies and should cause no concern. But it is quite a dif-

---

10 R. W. Funk, R. W. Hoover, and the Jesus Seminar, *The Five Gospels: The Search for the Authentic Words of Jesus* (New York and London: Macmillan, 1993); R. W. Funk and the Jesus Seminar, *The Acts of Jesus: The Search for the Authentic Deeds of Jesus* (San Francisco: HarperSanFrancisco, 1998).

11 On which, see esp. C. Hemer, *The Book of Acts in the Setting of Hellenistic History*, WUNT 49, ed. C. H. Gempf (Tübingen: Mohr, 1989), 63–91. Cf. S. Byrskog, *Story as History—History as Story*, WUNT 123 (Tübingen: Mohr, 2000).

12 On the general historical trustworthiness of the Gospels, with these and numerous additional examples of resolutions of alleged contradictions among parallels, see Blomberg, *Historical Reliability*, esp. 113–89.

ferent matter to allege that entire sayings or narratives in the Gospels were created out of whole cloth and do not correspond in any recognizable fashion to what Jesus said and did. Such claims go far beyond what the evidence actually suggests.[13]

Reading Horizontally and Vertically

Gordon Fee and Douglas Stuart helpfully summarize the task of interpreting the Gospels' unique blend of history and theology with the concepts of thinking horizontally and vertically.[14] Because many narratives of the teachings and actions of Jesus occur in more than one Gospel, the serious student should consult a synopsis or harmony of the Gospels that prints parallel accounts in parallel columns.[15] Then the student can *read and think horizontally*—across the page—and compare the ways in which the different Gospel writers treat a certain passage. Often the distinctive emphases of a given Evangelist appear most clearly in those portions of an episode that he alone has chosen to record. The student should apply this procedure to individual passages, to major sections of narrative, and to the Gospels as complete units. Thus, for example, the reader will discover that Matthew's version of the parable of the wicked tenants uniquely stresses the transfer of God's kingdom from Israel to the Church (Mt 21:43), a theme that reappears throughout his Gospel (e.g., 8:10–12; 11:20–30; 13:10–12; 22:1–14; 25:31–46; and 10:5–6 vs. 28:18–20). In the resurrection narratives, only Mark highlights the fear and misunderstanding of Jesus' followers (Mk 16:8), a motif he, too, distinctively underlines elsewhere (e.g., 4:13, 40; 6:52; 8:21, 33; 9:14–29; 10:35–45). And a reading of all of Luke discloses his particular interest in showing Jesus as the friend of sinners and outcasts in Jewish society—most notably Samaritans, Gentiles, tax collectors, prostitutes, poor people, and women. See, for example, the otherwise unparalleled stories of the good Samaritan (Lk 10:25–37), Mary and Martha (10:38–42), the prodigal son (15:11–32), the rich man and Lazarus (16:19–31), the nine Jewish and one Samaritan lepers (17:11–19), and the Pharisee and tax-collector (18:9–14). Interpretation and application of a given passage in the Gospels should stress the particular emphases of the Gospel in which the passage occurs, rather than blurring its distinctives by immediately combining it with other parallels. God chose to inspire not a harmony of the Gospels but four distinct ones, and we should respect his choice rather than undermine it by our interpretation.[16]

---

13 Cf. R. T. France, *The Evidence for Jesus* (Downers Grove: InterVarsity, 1986); I. H. Marshall, *I Believe in the Historical Jesus* (Grand Rapids: Eerdmans, 1977).

14 G. D. Fee and D. Stuart, *How to Read the Bible for All Its Worth*, 2d ed. (Grand Rapids: Zondervan, 1993), 121–26.

15 The most complete edition with perhaps the most attractive layout, yet remarkably affordable, remains K. Aland, ed., *Synopsis of the Four Gospels* (New York: UBS, 1982). It is also available in Greek / English and Greek only editions. See, further, the bibliography in the appendix.

16 It is still widely believed that Mark was the first Gospel written, that Matthew and Luke both relied on Mark as well as other sources including "Q" (other material common to Matthew and Luke), and that John was not as directly dependent on any of the other canonical writings. This approach to "source criticism" means that Matthew's and Luke's differences from Mark and from each other are more likely to be significant than Mark's or John's differences from either Matthew or Luke or each other. But these views have been challenged, and the methods we encourage here do not depend on any one particular source-critical hypothesis. Readers interested in pursuing the debate should consult D. A. Black and D. R. Beck, eds., *Rethinking the Synoptic Problem* (Grand Rapids: Baker, 2001).

← H O R I Z O N T A L L Y →				
Matthew	**Mark**	**Luke**	**John**	
1	1	1	1	
			6:1–15 5000 fed	
	6:32–44 5000 fed	9:10–17 5000 fed		
14:13–21 5000 fed				
28	16	24	21	

(Left and right margins read vertically: V E R T I C A L L Y)

May we assume the first readers of an individual Gospel would recognize these distinctives before they had the other written Gospels with which to compare them? Yes, we may, because a common body of information about Jesus circulated by word of mouth (often called the *kerygma,* from the Greek for "proclamation"). Thus, Christians among one Gospel's readers would have easily recognized some of the ways in which that Gospel differed from the "standard" kerygma. This also means that the Gospel writers could assume that the people to whom they wrote already had a fair amount of prior knowledge about Jesus and the Christian faith (cf. also Lk 1:4).[17] So it is appropriate in thinking horizontally to use one Gospel to interpret another, so long as one does not mask the distinctives of each. For example, by comparing Mt 27:56, Mk 15:40, and Jn 19:25, it is reasonable to deduce that Zebedee's wife's name was Salome and that she and Jesus' mother, Mary, were sisters. Jesus would then have been cousins with his two disciples John and James. This information, if true, might well have been widely known in early Christianity so that no one Gospel writer felt a need to spell it out. But we cannot prove any of this. Any application of the stories of Jesus' death that focused more on these possible relationships than on the actual information in the Gospels would be misguided.

Thinking vertically, therefore, should take priority over thinking horizontally. By this we mean that any passage in the Gospels should be interpreted in light of the overall structure and themes of that Gospel despite the nature of any parallel accounts that appear in other Gospels. In other words, it is more important to read down the columns of a synopsis than across them. Frequently the Gospel writers group passages topically or thematically rather than chronologically. If we overlook these connections, we risk reading in a false interpretation. For example, Luke places the story of Jesus' preaching in the Nazareth synagogue at the beginning of his description of the Galilean ministry (Lk 4:16–30), even though chronologically it happened much later (cf. where the story occurs in Mk 6:1–6a; Mt 13:53–58). This is probably because he sees the episode as programmatic of the nature of Jesus' ministry and the response it would receive. Lk 4:14b-15 makes it clear that much time

---

17 This is true even for John, as stressed recently by R. Bauckham, "John for Readers of Mark," in *The Gospels for All Christians,* ed. R. Bauckham (Grand Rapids: Eerdmans, 1998), 147–71.

had already elapsed since Jesus began preaching in Galilee. Lk 5:1–11 moves (backward in time) to the calling of some of the disciples (cf. Mt 4:18–22; Mk 1:16–20) with the temporally indefinite introduction "while the people pressed upon him to hear the word of God" (Lk 5:1 RSV). But the modern reader, accustomed to strict chronology in biographies, could easily make the mistake of assuming 4:16–30 took place before 5:1–11 and conclude that Jesus called his disciples as a result of his rejection in Nazareth![18]

Similar examples occur throughout the Gospels. Matthew 8–9 present ten of Jesus' miracles from various stages in his ministry. Luke 9:51–18:14 is probably not the "travel narrative" or "Perean ministry" it is so often labeled; rather, it is a thematically structured collection of Jesus' teachings all spoken "under the shadow of the cross," which he knew would soon end his life (9:51).[19] Mk 2:1–3:6 groups together a series of pronouncement and conflict stories (on which, see below). In fact, thematic groupings in the Gospels are so common that it is best not to assume that two episodes that appear next to each other are in chronological order unless the text actually says so (by specifying, e.g., "After this"). And English Bibles may not always help because they sometimes translate Greek words for "and" or "therefore" as "then" or "now."

In other instances, even when passages occur in chronological order, the Gospel writers seem likely to have included and omitted material because of thematic parallels or contrasts. Thus Mk 8:31–9:32 presents, in turn, Jesus' predictions of his coming suffering, his transfiguration, and the failure of his disciples to exorcise a demon. In so doing Mark appears to juxtapose the theme of Jesus' imminent death with a foretaste of his coming glory and to contrast Jesus' sovereignty and authority with the disciples' weakness and misunderstanding. Or again, the sequence of three parables in Mt 24:43–25:13 graphically illustrates the point of 24:36 that no one can know when Christ will return. He may come back entirely unexpectedly (24:44), or sooner than people think (24:48), or much later (25:5). Even as straightforward a chronological account as Matthew's infancy narrative (Mt 1–2) seems more interested in excerpting those events that show Jesus as the fulfillment of Scripture (1:23; 2:6, 15, 18, 23) and as the true King of Israel (as against Herod the usurper) than in presenting anything like a comprehensive survey of the events surrounding Jesus' birth.[20]

Thinking horizontally and thinking vertically amounts to studying the Gospels along the lines of modern *redaction criticism*. Redaction criticism is best defined as the attempt "to lay bare the theological perspectives of a biblical writer by analyzing the editorial (redactional) and compositional techniques and interpretations employed in shaping and framing the written and / or oral traditions at hand (see Luke 1:1–4)."[21] When we compare parallel accounts and find a particular Evangelist's distinctives and then see those same themes emphasized throughout that

---

18 On Luke 4:16–30, see esp. W. W. Klein, "The Sermon at Nazareth (Luke 4:14–22)," in *Christian Freedom*, ed. K. W. M. Wozniak and S. J. Grenz (Lanham: University Press of America, 1986), 153–72.

19 Cf. esp. C. L. Blomberg, "Midrash, Chiasmus and the Outline of Luke's Central Section," in *Gospel Perspectives III*, ed. R. T. France and D. Wenham (Sheffield: JSOT, 1983), 217–61.

20 Cf. esp. C. L. Blomberg, "The Liberation of Illegitimacy: Women and Rulers in Matthew 1–2," *BTB* 21 (1991): 145–50.

21 R. Soulen, *Handbook of Biblical Criticism*, 3d ed. (Louisville: Westminster John Knox, 2001), 158.

Gospel, we may feel rather confident that we have discovered a key point the Gospel writer wished to make. To be sure, redaction criticism has been widely abused, turning "distinctives" into "contradictions," but this is a problem with its practitioners not with the method itself.[22]

The Gospels' First Audiences

Thinking about the theological emphases and distinctives of each Gospel leads naturally to a consideration of their original readers or audiences. Presumably, Matthew, Mark, Luke, and John each highlighted different aspects of the life of Christ mainly because those aspects were particularly relevant to the individuals and congregations to whom they were writing. Redaction criticism has expended much effort in trying to reconstruct the situations of these early Christian communities. This enterprise is by nature more speculative than that of comparing parallels to determine theological distinctives. Probably, certain parts of each Gospel were included simply because they formed part of the common kerygma or because they were important for all Christians (or interested "inquirers") irrespective of their specific circumstances at the moment.[23]

Nevertheless, numerous proposals about the Evangelists' original audiences seem probable. For example, in his emphasis on the disciples' fear and misunderstanding Mark most likely intended to reassure and encourage a Gentile-Christian audience, possibly in Rome, as imperial persecution against Christians intensified. This hypothesis dovetails with the meager external evidence we have concerning the composition of Mark. If Jesus' disciples were prone to failure, yet God was still able mightily to use them, Christians feeling weak and inadequate in another time and place could take heart, too. Preachers and teachers today may thus choose to focus particularly on Mark as they seek to encourage beleaguered Christian communities.[24]

Similarly, John uniquely plays down the status of John the Baptist (1:19–28, 29–34; 3:22–36). Now Acts 19:1–7 describes a strange group of "disciples" in Ephesus, the traditional location of the churches to whom the apostle John later wrote, who knew only of John the Baptist and not of Jesus. Later Christian writings (most notably the third-century Pseudo-Clementine Recognitions) speak of a second-century sect in the same area that worshipped John. Quite plausibly, the Fourth Gospel's information about the Baptist was designed to temper any improper exaltation of John, at the

---

22 See esp. D. A. Carson, "Redaction Criticism: On the Legitimacy and Illegitimacy of a Literary Tool," in *Scripture and Truth,* ed. D. A. Carson and J. D. Woodbridge (Grand Rapids: Zondervan, 1983), 119–42. For a brief overview of the distinctive theologies of each of the four Evangelists, see C. L. Blomberg, *Jesus and the Gospels: An Introduction and Survey* (Nashville: Broadman and Holman; Leicester: InterVarsity, 1997), 117–20; 129–32; 145–50; 162–67. For outlines sensitive to thematic patterns, cf. pp. 115–17; 126–29; 140–45; 159–61.

23 For a brief survey of the most plausible proposals, see Blomberg, *Jesus and the Gospels,* 121–23; 133–35; 150–52; 167–70. *The Gospels for All Christians* (ed. Bauckham) argues that all of the Gospels were initially intended to address the Church in general. There is some plausibility to this, but it does not require jettisoning the notion that specific congregations were particularly in view, as the initial or primary recipients. See D. C. Sim, "The Gospels for All Christians? A Response to Richard Bauckham," *JSNT* 84 (2001): 3–27.

24 See especially E. Best, *Disciples and Discipleship: Studies in the Gospel according to Mark* (Edinburgh: T. & T. Clark, 1986).

expense of worshipping Christ, which might have crept into Ephesian churches. And if it was wrong to glorify the human leader of whom Jesus had said, "Among those born of women there is no one greater than John" (Lk 7:28), then surely it is inappropriate to exalt human leaders of God's people in any age. Contemporary Christians might choose, therefore, to highlight the Fourth Gospel's portrait of John the Baptist when struggling against church leaders who direct too much attention to themselves and too little to Christ.[25]

Recognizing that the disciples in the Gospels represent believers in any age also helps us avoid certain hermeneutical errors of the past. For example, medieval Catholicism sometimes argued that Jesus taught a two-tiered ethic. His more stringent demands, such as vows of poverty, were reserved for full-time Christian workers like priests, nuns, or monks—the religious elite. The contemporary Russian Church has sometimes struggled with the view, made understandable by decades of persecution, that Jesus intended the Great Commission (Mt 28:18–20) only for the apostles and not for all believers. Dispensationalists, particularly in the U.S., have sometimes maintained that because Jesus' disciples were Jewish one cannot assume his instructions to them also apply to Gentile Christians. But Scripture provides no support for any of these contentions, and the vast majority of Christian interpreters of all theological traditions down through the centuries have rightly rejected them.

Key Theological Issues

As discussed earlier, students must interpret every text in light of its historical background and literary context. Students need to interpret those parts of Scripture that contain numerous writings by the same author (notably with the epistles of Paul) or multiple accounts of the teaching of one individual (as with the Gospels) in light of larger theological contexts. To interpret the Gospels correctly in view of the basic message of Jesus' teaching, we must correctly understand two theological issues: Jesus' views on the kingdom and the nature of his ethic.

The Kingdom of God

The central theme of Jesus' teaching is the announcement of the arrival of the kingdom of God. This kingdom refers more to a power than to a place, more to a reign than to a realm. "Kingship" perhaps better captures this sense of "authority to rule." But interpreters continue to debate to what extent Jesus believed that God's kingship had actually arrived during his lifetime and to what extent he saw it as still future. Others differ over whether God's rule concentrates on empowering his people or on redeeming the cosmos. A related question asks whether the Christian's primary task is to encourage personal transformation or social reform. A correct understanding of the relationship of the kingdom to the Church and to Israel also seems vital.

Space prevents consideration of the strengths and weaknesses of each major position adopted on these questions. Suffice it to say we agree with a fair consensus of interpreters who believe that the kingdom of God arrived in part at Christ's First Coming but awaits its full consummation at his return (cf., e.g., Mk 1:15; Mt 12:28; Lk 17:20–21 with Mt 6:10; 25:1–13; and Acts 1:6–8). This is the view often known as

---

25 Cf. further R. E. Brown, *The Community of the Beloved Disciple* (New York: Paulist, 1979), 69–71.

inaugurated eschatology.[26] Like an inauguration at the beginning of a president's term of office, Jesus inaugurated God's kingdom at the beginning of his reign, even though much more awaits fulfillment. Because he could personally preach to only a handful of the world's population, Jesus' priority during his lifetime was to gather around himself a community of followers who would live out the principles of God's kingdom. These followers, as they made new disciples, could eventually demonstrate God's will for all the world concerning human life in community and society.

Personal conversion—repentance from sin and faith in Jesus Christ as Savior and Lord—alone secures eternal life and prevents eternal punishment and separation from God; so it must take priority over social transformation (Mk 1:15; Mt 9:2; Lk 9:23–27; Jn 3:16). But challenging sinful, systemic structures forms a crucial part of God's purposes for his world as well and must not be neglected (Mt 8:17; Lk 4:18–19; 7:22–23). The kingdom does not equal the Church. The Church is the group of believers in all ages over whom God reigns, who demonstrate to the world the presence of his kingdom. Nor was the kingdom something offered exclusively to Israel, rejected, and then replaced by the Church. What Jesus referred to as the mystery of the kingdom was not a shift from Israel to the Church but the surprising fact that the kingdom of God had arrived without applying the irresistible power many had expected.[27]

Andrew Kirk ties together these strands of thought with a comprehensive formulation of Jesus' kingdom priorities:

> The Kingdom sums up God's plan to create a new human life by making possible a new kind of community among people, families, and groups. [It combines] the possibility of a personal relationship to Jesus with man's responsibility to manage wisely the whole of nature; the expectation that real change is possible here and now; a realistic assessment of the strength of opposition to God's intentions; the creation of new human relationships and the eventual liberation by God of the whole of nature from corruption.[28]

Students need to keep in mind all these aspects when they interpret Jesus' teaching and actions, including those in which Jesus does not necessarily mention the kingdom explicitly.

Consider, for example, the Beatitudes of Mt 5:3–12 and Lk 6:20–23. It is probably significant that both versions begin and end with present tense blessings ("theirs / yours *is* the kingdom of heaven / God" [Mt 5:3; Lk 6:20 RSV]), but sandwich between these present promises future tense promises ("they / you *shall* be satisfied"[Mt 5:6; Lk 6:21 RSV, italics ours]). People who live in the way Jesus describes in the beatitudes (poor, mourning, meek . . .) are spiritually blessed in the present through life in Christ

---

26 This term is associated especially with the numerous writings of G. E. Ladd. Perhaps his best work on the Kingdom is *The Presence of the Future* (Grand Rapids: Eerdmans, 1974). The issue has been comprehensively surveyed again in J. P. Meier, *A Marginal Jew*, 4 vols. (New York: Doubleday, 1991), 2: 237–506.

27 In addition to Ladd, cf. esp. B. Chilton, *Pure Kingdom: Jesus' Vision of God* (London: SPCK; Grand Rapids: Eerdmans, 1996); S. McKnight, *A New Vision for Israel* (Grand Rapids and Cambridge: Eerdmans, 1999), 70–155.

28 A. Kirk, *The Good News of the Kingdom Coming* (Downers Grove: InterVarsity, 1983), 47.

and his Church, but they can expect full compensation for their suffering only in the life to come. Again, a correct understanding of kingdom theology prevents driving an improper wedge between Mt 5:3 ("Blessed are the poor in spirit") and Lk 6:20 ("Blessed are you poor"). Those who are blessed are both the materially and the spiritually poor. The probable Hebrew concept underlying the Greek term used here is that of the *'anawim*—the pious poor "who stand without pretense before God as their only hope."[29]

So, too, when we read in Mt 6:33 (cf. Lk 12:30) to "seek first [God's] kingdom and his righteousness and all these things [adequate food, drink, and clothing] shall be yours as well" (RSV), we must avoid two opposite misinterpretations. One error assumes that Jesus has guaranteed health and wealth (or even a minimally decent standard of living) for all who put him first in their lives. Many faithful believers throughout church history and particularly in the Two-thirds World today simply do not experience these blessings. And it is almost diabolical to accuse all such believers of having insufficient faith. On the other hand, we dare not so spiritualize the text that it no longer makes any demands on God's children to help their destitute brothers and sisters in material ways. In Mk 10:29–30 (RSV) Jesus promises his followers who give up their homes for the sake of discipleship that they will receive "houses" and "lands" "a hundredfold now in this time" as well as eternal life in the age to come. In other words, Jesus anticipated that his followers would share material possessions with each other![30]

Perhaps the simplest summary of Jesus' theology of the kingdom is the slogan "already but not yet." Christians struggling with faltering ministries or difficult personal circumstances, as well as those currently experiencing many victories and triumphs, need consistently to temper their despair or enthusiasm by reminding themselves of both halves of this slogan. Does Jesus' perspective suggest that some Christians should go into politics to help change the world? Yes, and he promises they can often expect to have a positive effect, although they may never know to what extent. Should a believer pray for healing from illness? Of course, and sometimes God will answer positively but always on his terms, though often he chooses to work through human frailty instead (2 Cor 12:8–9). Can Christians expect victory over sins that keep plaguing them? Yes—at least in some measure, usually over a substantial period of time, but painful relapses may recur, and God guarantees ultimate victory only on the other side of eternity.

The Ethics of Jesus

Understanding Jesus' kingdom theology enables interpreters to make good sense of his ethical demands. Interpreters have regularly puzzled over their stringency. Nowhere is this more obvious than in the Sermon on the Mount. Did Jesus seriously expect his followers to view hatred as murder, to view lust as adultery, never to retaliate when abused, and actually to love their enemies (Mt 5:21–48)? We have already noted the *traditional Catholic* response: only select disciples are expected to follow these more austere rules. *Lutherans* often viewed Jesus' ethics as "law" (rather than "gospel") meant to

---

29 R. A. Guelich, *The Sermon on the Mount* (Waco: Word, 1982), 75.

30 Cf. C. L. Blomberg, "On Wealth and Worry: Matthew 6:19–34—Meaning and Significance," *CTR* 6 (1992): 73–89; D. M. May, "Mark 3:20–35 from the Perspective of Shame/Honor," *BTB* 17 (1987): 83–87.

point out the hopelessness of our sinful condition and drive us to our knees in repentance and faith in Christ. Against both these views note that Jesus addressed his words to all his disciples, as well as to the crowds of would-be followers who flocked to hear him (Mt 5:1). *Anabaptists* frequently took these commands as seriously applying to public life and to all people on earth, so they renounced all violence and became pacifists. Tolstoy adopted a similar response on a personal level, as do many Mennonites and others today. But Jesus nowhere teaches that his kingdom principles should form the basis for civil law. *Nineteenth-century liberals* often preached a "social gospel" of human progress and moral evolution apart from the personal transformation of conversion to Christ, but twentieth-century worldwide warfare squelched much of their optimism. *Existentialists* see in Jesus' teaching precedent for decisive calls to ethical action without viewing any of his teaching as absolute. *Dispensationalists* have traditionally reserved Jesus' kingdom ethic for the millennial age and have not found it directly relevant for Christians now. But this requires a greater disjunction between Israel and the Church than Scripture allows. Jesus' choice of twelve disciples, for example, almost certainly was deliberate—to match the twelve tribes of Israel and portray the community of his followers as the new locus of God's saving activity.[31]

None of these approaches, furthermore, does justice to the interpretive framework of Jesus' inaugurated eschatology. Most of Jesus' teachings apply to all believers in all situations, unless Scripture itself clearly imposes certain limitations. When Jesus concludes the section of the Sermon on the Mount alluded to above, he declares: "Be perfect [whole, mature; Greek *teleios*], therefore, as your heavenly Father is perfect [whole, mature]" (Mt 5:48). This remains the standard or ideal of discipleship for all Christians. We will not attain wholeness in this life, but we can arrive at a measure of maturity. Jesus' standards should be our constant goal ("already but not yet"). He intended his ethic for *all* believers, not just a select few. But inasmuch as his ethic is primarily for *believers,* we dare not impose it on those outside the faith. We cannot expect unbelievers to follow or appreciate God's will, though (through common grace) we are sometimes pleasantly surprised when they do. We must not try to coerce an unregenerate world to conform to his standards, though surely believers ought to use all legal measures available to foster an ethical society.[32]

Occasionally, however, contextual material in the Gospels themselves clearly limits the application of certain teachings of Jesus. For example, some of the severe restrictions Jesus placed on the Twelve when he sent them out on their first mission (Lk 9:3–5) were later rescinded (22:35–38). Jesus did not intend his command to the rich young ruler to sell all he had and give the proceeds to the poor (Lk 18:22) to apply to all disciples because shortly afterwards Jesus praises Zacchaeus for giving (only!) half of

---

31 The fullest survey of interpretations of the Sermon on the Mount is C. Baumann, *The Sermon on the Mount: The Modern Quest for Its Meaning* (Macon: Mercer, 1985). A briefer sketch, but with very helpful perspectives on Jesus' ethics more broadly, is R. H. Stein, *The Method and Message of Jesus' Teachings*, 2d ed. (Philadelphia: Westminster, 1994), 90–114. Contemporary "progressive dispensationalism" is distancing itself from many of its traditional tenets such as this.

32 The best detailed unfolding of Jesus' ethics from the perspective of inaugurated eschatology is A. Verhey, *The Great Reversal: Ethics and the New Testament* (Grand Rapids: Eerdmans, 1984). From this perspective, elaborating on Christian ethics more generally, see esp. G. H. Stassen and D. P. Gushee, *Kingdom Ethics: Following Jesus in Contemporary Context* (Downers Grove: InterVarsity, 2003).

his possessions to the poor (19:8–9). Then he tells a parable praising two servants who wisely invested their master's money for his benefit rather than giving it away (19:11–27). Likewise, the statement about divorce and remarriage in Mt 19:9 could not have had every possible exception in view when Jesus declared that all who divorce "except for marital unfaithfulness" and marry another commit adultery. Later Paul felt free to add a second exception based on a new situation Jesus did not face in his lifetime—an unbelieving spouse wishing to leave a Christian partner (1 Cor 7:15–16).[33] But apart from a definable hermeneutical principle, it is irresponsible for interpreters to assume that a certain teaching of Jesus does not apply to us in our current circumstances.

The Forms Within the Gospels

As already noted for the OT, different literary genres (entire works) have different interpretive principles, and we must often treat individual forms (smaller self-contained units of material) in unique ways. In the Gospels, the three most prevalent and distinctive forms that merit special attention are the parable, the miracle story, and the pronouncement story.[34]

Parables

The stories Jesus told, such as the good samaritan, the prodigal son, and the sower, rank among the most famous and popular parts of all Scripture. Modern readers often express surprise to learn how differently these parables have been interpreted in the history of the Church. Until this century, most interpreters treated the parables as detailed allegories, assuming that most or all of the individual characters or objects in a parable stood for something other than themselves, namely, spiritual counterparts that enabled the story to be read at two levels. So, for example, in the story of the prodigal son (Lk 15:11–32), the ring that the father gave the prodigal might represent Christian baptism; and the banquet, the Lord's Supper. The robe could reflect immortality; and the shoes, God's preparation for journeying to heaven.[35]

Seldom, however, did two allegorical interpretations of the same parable agree, and what a particular detail was said to represent often seemed arbitrary and even anachronistic (neither Christian baptism nor the Lord's Supper had yet been instituted when Jesus

---

33 The last of these examples is the most controversial. But see C. L. Blomberg, "Marriage, Divorce, Remarriage and Celibacy: An Exegesis of Matthew 19:3–12, *TrinJ* n.s. 11 (1990): 161–96.

34 Form criticism has, of course, attempted to do much more than simply analyze constituent literary forms within the Gospels to interpret them rightly. E.g., it has often attempted to reconstruct the oral history of those forms. See esp. E. V. McKnight, *What Is Form Criticism?* (Philadelphia: Fortress, 1969). But the analysis of forms has been its most objective and successful enterprise, and the only one that concerns us here. For a more up-to-date survey and critique of the method, see C. L. Blomberg, "Form Criticism," in *Dictionary of Jesus and the Gospels,* 243–50. For further on the variety of forms in the Gospels see J. L. Bailey and L. D. Vander Broek, *Literary Forms in the New Testament* (Louisville, KY: Westminster John Knox, 1992), 91–183.

35 The fullest history of interpretation, including these examples, is W. S. Kissinger, *The Parables of Jesus: A History of Interpretation and Bibliography* (Metuchen, NJ: Scarecrow, 1979). For more recent research, see C. L. Blomberg, "The Parables of Jesus: Recent Trends and Needs in Research," in *Studying the Historical Jesus: Evaluations of the State of Current Research,* ed. C. A. Evans and B. D. Chilton (Leiden: Brill, 1994), 231–54; id., "Poetic Fiction, Subversive Speech, and Proportional Analogy in the Parables," *HBT* 18 (1996): 115–32.

told the parable of the prodigal). At the end of the nineteenth century, the German liberal Adolf Jülicher wrote a massive exposé of these inconsistencies and proposed a diametrically opposite alternative. He argued that parables are in no way allegories, and no detail "stands for" anything else. Rather, they make only one point apiece, as they teach rather general truths about spiritual realities. Thus the entire story of the prodigal can be reduced to the lesson of "the boundless joy of God's forgiveness." The richness of detail merely adds realism, vividness, and local color.[36]

Twentieth-century interpreters have increasingly sought ways to swing the pendulum back from Jülicher without returning to the allegorical excesses of his predecessors.[37] Most rejected his rather bland moralizations and tied the central truths of the parables more directly to Jesus' proclamation of God's kingdom. Many recognized that the parables often break the bounds of realism and shockingly subvert conventional expectation. Thus, no ancient, Oriental, well-to-do head of household would have run to greet a wayward son (a most undignified action) or interrupted him before he completed his speech of repentance, but God goes to greater extents than human fathers in trying to seek and save the lost. Because the majority of the parable (like parables more generally) draws on ordinary experiences of life to illustrate analogous truths about spiritual life, the unrealistic portion stands out all the more in comparison.

A growing minority of interpreters once again regards as appropriate a limited amount of allegorical interpretation. It is hard to make any sense of Jesus' story of the prodigal without assuming that the father in some sense represents God (or even Christ); that the prodigal stands for all the wayward and rebellious (like the tax-collectors and "sinners" of 15:1); and that the older brother represents the self-righteous hypocrite (like the Pharisees and scribes of 15:2). The literary context of a parable must be consulted, *contra* Jülicher and many contemporary existentialists, as a reliable guide to the meaning of the parable itself. At the same time, few have been willing to abandon the quest for one central truth per passage. But with respect to that issue, we return to the prodigal son. Is the main point the possibility of repentance for even the most rebellious? Or is it an emphasis on the lavish forgiveness God offers all his children? Or is it perhaps a warning against imitating the hard-heartedness of the older brother?[38]

---

36 A. Jülicher, *Die Gleichnisreden Jesu,* 2 vols. (Freiburg: Mohr, 1899), 2: 362. That no one has published a translation of Jülicher in English is one of the strangest omissions of modern biblical scholarship.

37 The two most significant 20th-century studies of the parables were C. H. Dodd, *The Parables of the Kingdom* (London: Nisbet, 1935); and J. Jeremias, *The Parables of Jesus,* 3d ed. (London: SCM; Philadelphia: Westminster, 1972 [Ger. orig. 1947]). Dodd's definition of a parable became a classic: "a metaphor or simile drawn from nature or common life, arresting the hearer by its vividness or strangeness, and leaving the mind in sufficient doubt about its precise application to tease it into active thought" (p. 16). But Jeremias reminded us that underneath the Greek *parabolē* lay the Hebrew *māshāl,* which had a very broad semantic range including "figurative forms of speech of every kind: parable, similitude, allegory, fable, proverb, apocalyptic revelation, riddle, symbol, pseudonym, fictitious person, example, theme, argument, apology, refutation, jest" (20).

38 Two important evangelical literary critics who have recognized allegory and multiple points in the parables are Ryken (see esp. his *How to Read,* 139–53, 199–203) and J. Sider, *Interpreting the Parables* (Grand Rapids: Zondervan, 1995). Particularly helpful in distinguishing the realistic from the surprise elements in parables is K. Bailey (see esp. his *Poet and Peasant* and *Through Peasant Eyes* [Grand Rapids: Eerdmans, 1983]—2 vols. bound as one).

We find the way forward through an appreciation of the parables as narrative fiction. Longer examples of this genre (novels or short stories) regularly communicate meaning through their main characters. They encourage readers to identify with one or more of these characters and experience the plot of the story from their various points of view. When we analyze the parables in terms of main characters, we discover that approximately two-thirds of Jesus' stories are *triadic* in structure. That is, they present three main characters (or groups of characters). More often than not, one is a master figure (king, master, father, shepherd) and two are contrasting subordinates (servants, sons, sheep). Consider, for example, the bridegroom with his two quite different groups of bridesmaids (Mt 25:1–13), the shepherd with his one lost and ninety-nine safe sheep (Lk 15:3–7), or the sower with his three portions of unfruitful seeds / soil versus his one fruitful section (Mk 4:3–9). In other cases the characters or groups of characters relate differently, but still there are three (the man who was robbed and beaten, the pair of clerics who ignore him, and the Samaritan who helps him, Lk 10:29–37). Or we may consider the king, the servant for whom he forgives an enormous debt, and that servant's underling who does not receive cancellation of even a paltry sum (Mt 18:23–35).

In about one-third of the parables, the narrative proves shorter and the structure simpler. Sometimes they contrast two characters without a master figure—wise and foolish builders (Mt 7:24–27), Pharisee and tax-collector (Lk 18:9–14). Or a master and one subordinate may appear, as with the parable of the unprofitable servant (Lk 17:7–10). In still other instances, we find a monadic structure. Here only one character appears—as in the parables of the mustard seed and leaven (Lk 13:18–21), the tower-builder and the warring king (Lk 14:28–33), and the hidden treasure and the pearl of great price (Mt 13:44–46).

In light of our illustrations of the problems of interpreting the prodigal son, it seems reasonable to suggest that readers should consider each parable from the perspective of each of the main characters. The three major suggestions for the "one point" of Lk 15:11–32, in fact, result from doing precisely this. A focus on the prodigal teaches about repentance; following the father's actions reveals God's lavish love and forgiveness; and attending to the older brother warns against hardheartedness. All three of these points reflect part of the parable's meaning.[39]

It seems that many interpreters have already unconsciously adopted this approach. Robert Stein, for example, sums up the "one" point of the parable of the great supper (Lk 14:16–24) as follows:

> It is impossible in reading this parable not to interpret the guests and their replacements as representing the attitudes of the Pharisees / scribes / religious leaders and the outcasts of Israel . . . the parable was not allegorical, because it posits only one main point of comparison. The point is that the kingdom of God has come and that those who would have been expected to receive it (the religious elite) did not do so, whereas the ones least likely to receive it (the publicans, poor, harlots, etc.) have.[40]

---

39 For all the details of the approach we are suggesting here, see C. L. Blomberg, *Interpreting the Parables* (Downers Grove and Leicester: InterVarsity, 1990).

40 R. H. Stein, *An Introduction to the Parables of Jesus* (Philadelphia: Westminster, 1981), 89; cf. S. Kistemaker, *The Parables: Understanding the Stories Jesus Told,* 2d ed. (Grand Rapids: Baker, 2002), 40, on the sower. Both texts nevertheless remain excellent introductory works for studying parables.

But this "point" is actually articulated in three independent clauses. Stein's interpretation seems perfectly correct, but it is inaccurate to call it one point and thereby to deny a certain allegorical nature to the parable.

Of course, there may be ways of combining the two or three points of dyadic and triadic parables into one simple sentence. Where this works, it is probably desirable to do so, in order to illustrate the thematic unity of the passage and the relationship between the various lessons learned from reading the story through the eyes of its different characters. Thus, from the parable of the two sons (Mt 21:28–32) we might deduce three lessons from the three characters: (1) like the father sending his sons to work, God commands all people to carry out his will; (2) like the son who ultimately disobeyed, some promise but do not perform rightly and so are rejected by God; and (3) like the son who ultimately obeyed, some rebel but later submit and so are accepted. Then a possible way of combining these three points emerges: "Performance takes priority over promise." This formulation helps preachers and teachers communicate the message of the parable in a much more memorable form! One might harmonize this short proposition with the longer series of three points by speaking of one main point with three subpoints or by equating the short summary with the parable's "plot" and the longer sentences with its various "points of view."

Not all of the parables, especially some of the longer more complex narratives, yield a simple, unified lesson so easily. It is arguably better, then, to preserve a more detailed and possibly cumbersome formulation than to compose a pithy summary that risks losing some of the message of the text. So, for example, with the good samaritan, interpreters should strive to preserve all three strands of meaning that have often been perceived. From the example of the priest and Levite comes the principle that religious status or legalistic casuistry does not excuse lovelessness; from the Samaritan we learn that we must show compassion to those in need; from the man in the ditch emerges the lesson that even an enemy is a neighbor. Or, in the case of the parable of the wicked tenants, four key characters or groups of characters teach us: (1) God is extremely patient in waiting for his rebellious people to do his will; (2) a day will come, however, when that patience is exhausted and he will destroy those who remain rebellious; (3) his purposes will not then be thwarted for he will raise up new, obedient followers; and (4) this turning point will occur at the time of the Jews' rejection and crucifixion of Christ (Mk 12:1–11).

Although there are other important things we could say about parables, one point is crucial. As metaphorical discourse, parables create an impact through their choice of imagery and narrative form, which is largely lost when one tries to communicate their meaning with one or more propositions. Yet against the so-called new hermeneutic (see chapter 2), it is both possible and important to "translate" parables into propositional language. Otherwise, modern readers may not understand their meaning at all![41] But with the new hermeneutic, it is equally appropriate and helpful to consider retelling a parable in modern garb to recreate the effect it would have had on its original audience. After two millennia of domestication, these texts sometimes convey to modern readers the exact opposite of what Jesus originally intended. Today even the most biblically

---

41 The best and fullest exposition of the parables from this perspective of the new hermeneutic is B. B. Scott, *Hear Then the Parable* (Minneapolis: Fortress, 1989). But it needs to be read in light of the massive methodological critique by A. C. Thiselton, *The Two Horizons* (Grand Rapids: Eerdmans, 1980).

illiterate Westerner "knows" that a Samaritan is compassionate and that Pharisees are "bad-guys." But this is precisely *not* what any first-century Jew would have thought—Samaritans were the hated half-breeds and Pharisees the most popular of the religious leaders. To have the proper impact on a typical conservative American congregation in the twenty-first century, a preacher ought to consider retelling the story with the man in the ditch as a white Anglo-Saxon Protestant, the priest and Levite as two upstanding local pastors, and the Samaritan as a fundamentalist Arab Muslim (or perhaps an atheist black feminist!). Such preachers who have particularly racist, sexist, or nationalist congregations ought also to consider if faithfulness to the Bible in this fashion might cost them their jobs and whether they are prepared to pay this price![42]

Miracle Stories

Another unique "form" in the Gospels is the miracle story. A biblical miracle "is a strikingly surprising event, beyond what is regarded as humanly possible, in which God is believed to act, either directly or through an intermediary."[43] Common motifs include the description of someone's distress, a cry for help, the response of the miracle worker, the miracle itself, the reaction of the crowd and the response of the miracle worker to that reaction. Numerous other features, with many variations, also frequently appear.[44]

Since the Enlightenment, all but the most conservative of interpreters have tried either to rationalize or to demythologize these stories. The older, rationalist approach sought to explain the apparently supernatural events of the Gospels as scientifically natural ones. The feeding of the 5,000 involved the large crowd sharing small crumbs of bread in anticipation of Jesus' institution of the Eucharist. Jesus appeared to walk on the water because he was wading out on a sandbar just beneath the water's surface.

By the mid-nineteenth century this approach was generally rejected as misguided. Scholars viewed the miracle stories as myths—fictitious accounts designed to glorify and exalt Jesus and promote his divinity. In the twentieth century, form critics and existential theologians developed the idea of demythologizing—seeking the theological message of a miracle-story that people could still believe and apply in a scientific age that had discarded the supernatural. In other words, they looked for what remained after they peeled away the "myth." Thus, while Jesus may not have miraculously healed people of illnesses or exorcised demons, nevertheless he did enable people to embrace psychosomatic wholeness and to reject all manifestations of evil that threatened their personal well-being.[45]

---

42 The inspiration for the "contemporization" of the good samaritan comes from Fee and Stuart's similar example (*How to Read*, 147). Bailey *(Peasant Eyes,* 48) comments from the perspective of a Western missionary in the Middle East that in twenty years he did not have "the courage to tell to the Palestinians a story about a noble Israeli, nor a story about the noble Turk to the Armenians."

43 E. Eve, *The Jewish Context of Jesus' Miracles* (New York and London: Sheffield Academic Press, 2002), 1.

44 For the fullest analysis, see G. Theissen, *The Miracle Stories of the Early Christian Tradition* (Edinburgh: T. &T. Clark, 1983).

45 For a survey and critique of various approaches to the miracles in view of the Enlightenment, see esp. C. Brown, *Miracles and the Critical Mind* (Exeter: Paternoster; Grand Rapids; Eerdmans, 1984). H. E. G. Paulus and D. F. Strauss were two of the nineteenth-century giants of the rationalistic and mythological schools of interpretation. In the twentieth century, R. Bultmann's program of dcmythologizing stands out above all others.

Science, of course, has never disproved the supernatural. Because of the uncertainties inherent in Einstein's theory of relativity and Heisenberg's indeterminacy principle, quantum physics has left contemporary scientists far more cautious in pronouncing the impossibility of God's existence and direct intervention in human history. Meanwhile, evangelical Christians never abandoned their belief in biblical miracles as historical events.[46] Ironically, however, much conservative *application* of the Gospel miracles has differed little from more liberal demythologizing. Conservatives do not reject the miraculous; they merely consign it to Bible times! *Jesus* may have supernaturally stilled the storm, but *we* would be foolish to expect him to intervene in the affairs of weather today. When in the mid-1980s evangelist and politician Pat Robertson claimed he helped veer a hurricane away from the Eastern seaboard of the U.S. through prayer, he was ridiculed by at least as many fellow evangelicals as by others. Instead, we are told, the correct application of this miracle-story is that Jesus "stills the storms of our lives," enabling us to be at peace in the midst of crises. With such an interpretation the distinctively supernatural element of the account remains irrelevant!

Interpreters from numerous theological traditions increasingly recognize a better approach.[47] The miracle-stories in the Gospels function first *christologically* to demonstrate who Jesus was, and then *salvation-historically* to corroborate his claims that the kingship of God was breaking into human history. Thus, when Jesus exorcised one demoniac, he declared, "If I drive out demons by the Spirit of God, then the kingdom of God has come upon you" (Mt 12:28). When John the Baptist sent messengers from prison to ask Jesus if he really was the Messiah who was to come, he told them to tell their master, "The blind receive sight, the lame walk, those who have leprosy are cured, the deaf hear, the dead are raised," and "blessed is the person who does not fall away on account of me" (11:5–6 TNIV). The storm-stilling miracle, therefore, shows Jesus as exercising divine prerogatives. Like Yahweh himself in the OT, Jesus is Lord of wind and waves (cf. Jonah 1–2 and Psa 107:23–32). The Gospel accounts agree that this miracle forced Jesus' disciples to raise the question of his identity (Mt 8:27; Mk 4:41; Lk 8:25). And while this particular miracle does not occur in John, the Fourth Gospel consistently affirms miracles to be "signs" (evidences of Jesus as Son of God) meant to bring people to belief in Christ (e.g., Jn 2:11; 7:31; 10:25; 20:31).[48]

Some of the more unusual miracle stories suddenly make sense when interpreted in light of the rule of God that Jesus' person and work introduced. Turning water into wine symbolized the joyful newness of the kingdom against the old constraints of Judaism (Jn 2:1–11); cursing the fig tree provided a vivid object lesson of the destruction of Israel if she persisted in rejecting her Messiah (Mk 11:12–14, 20–25); and Jesus' walking on the water disclosed his identity to his disciples—Yahweh himself (Mk 6:45–52 par.). We should probably understand Mark's enigmatic words, "He was about to pass by them," to mean, "He was about to reveal himself to them" (6:48; cf. God's

---

46 Some of the best recent scholarly defense appears in R. D. Geivett and G. R. Habermas, eds., *In Defense of Miracles* (Downers Grove: InterVarsity, 1997).

47 Cf. esp. G. H. Twelftree, *Jesus the Miracle Worker* (Downers Grove: InterVarsity, 1999); Meier, *A Marginal Jew*, 2: 509–1038; and R. Latourelle, *The Miracles of Jesus and the Theology of Miracle* (New York: Paulist, 1988).

48 At the same time, John is quick to point out that people should not have to have signs in order to believe. Cf. esp. 4:48 and 20:29.

self-revelation to Moses in Exod 33:22; 34:6). Then Jesus' subsequent announcement, "It is I" (more literally "I am"—Greek *egō eimi*—v. 50), forms an allusion to the divine name revealed to Moses in Exod 3:14.[49]

Contemporary application of Gospel miracles should thus be more evangelistic than pietistic. Jesus' stilling of the storm should provoke people to ask who such a man was and is—with the correct answer being the divine Messiah. And in an age when reports of apparently supernatural healings, exorcisms, and even occasional "nature" miracles are increasingly common, we may risk quenching the Spirit by refusing to pray for the risen Christ to repeat the miraculous in our day—not primarily to benefit believers but to help in converting the unsaved. Not surprisingly, many of the most dramatic modern-day miracles occur precisely in those parts of the world long dominated by non-Christian and even occult beliefs and practices (and sadly, more and more parts of the Western world are lapsing back into such paganism). Although the kingdom arrived decisively in first-century Israel, the process of establishing God's rule in the entire world has been a gradual, intermittent one that remains incomplete. We must always guard against counterfeit miracles, to be sure. But Christians today can expect to apply the Gospel miracle stories in valid ways by praying for similar manifestations of God's power in Jesus' name to demonstrate his deity and his superiority over all other objects of worship.[50]

Pronouncement Stories

A third important and distinctive Gospel form receives various labels: apophthegm, paradigm, pronouncement story, conflict story, and chreia. All of these terms have their own history and refer to slightly differing groups of texts. But "pronouncement story" is the most common and self-explanatory term.

Common in the Gospels, it designates a short, self-contained narrative that functions primarily to introduce a key climactic saying (or pronouncement) of Jesus. These pronouncements are usually proverbial in nature. As proverbs (see above), they inculcate wise generalizations in the form of concise memorable phrases and should not be interpreted as absolute truths. Most of them highlight the radical newness of Jesus' message and ministry that quickly aroused the opposition of Jewish readers; hence, they are also called "conflict stories." Some resemble the Greco-Roman literary form "chreia": "a brief statement or action with pointedness attributed to a definite person" designed to epitomize a key aspect of that individual's life or teaching."[51]

Mk 2:13–17 offers a classic example of a pronouncement story. The call of Levi builds to a climax with Jesus' final pronouncement against his Pharisaic critics: "It is not the healthy who need a doctor, but the sick. I have not come to call the righteous, but

---

49 For these three examples and related ones, see esp. C. L. Blomberg, "The Miracles as Parables," in *Gospel Perspectives VI, The Miracles of Jesus* (Sheffield: JSOT, 1986), 327–59.

50 A well-balanced statement of contemporary application of the miracles appears in L. B. Smedes, ed., *Ministry and the Miraculous: A Case Study at Fuller Theological Seminary* (Waco: Word, 1987). Also helpful at a slightly more popular level is J. Deere, *Surprised by the Power of the Spirit* (Grand Rapids: Zondervan, 1993).

51 Cf. esp. A. J. Hultgren, *Jesus and His Adversaries: The Form and Function of the Conflict Stories in the Synoptic Tradition* (Minneapolis: Augsburg, 1979); B. L. Mack and V. K. Robbins, *Patterns of Persuasion in the Gospels* (Sonoma: Polebridge, 1989), in which see p. 11 for the quotation; and M. C. Moeser, *The Anecdote in Mark, the Classical World and The Rabbis*, JSNTSup 227 (London and New York: Continuum/Sheffield Academic Press, 2002).

sinners" (v. 17). Obviously these are generalizations; healthy people did at times need physicians for preventative medicine, and Jesus did occasionally minister among those who considered themselves righteous, which is probably what the Greek *dikaioi* here means (cf. Lk 14:1–24). But both of these situations were exceptions and not the rule. At the same time, Jesus' claims challenged (and still challenge) conventional ideas of ministry. Neither in Jesus' day nor in ours do most religious people consider preaching and healing among the outcasts of society to be priorities. Not surprisingly, Mark includes this pronouncement / conflict story in a series of five (Mk 2:1–12, 13–17, 18–22, 23–28; 3:1–6) that concludes with the ominous note, "then the Pharisees went out and began to plot with the Herodians how they might kill Jesus" (3:6). This story, finally, captures concisely the heart of Jesus' mission and message—seeking and saving the lost despite increasing opposition. Another series of pronouncement stories appears in Mk 11:27–33; 12:13–17, 18–27, 28–34, and 35–37. In each case we should focus on the climactic saying, avoid turning it into a timeless truth, and recognize its radical challenge to the religious status quo.

Other Forms

Scholars have identified numerous other forms in the Gospels. Many of these have OT parallels—legal maxims, beatitudes and woes, announcement and nativity stories, calling and recognition scenes, farewell discourses, and so on.[52] Most figures of speech are prevalent in the Gospels. In fact, some estimate that Jesus couched over 90 percent of his teaching in poetic or figurative language. This would appeal to the crowds and prove easy to remember.[53] Although we cannot go into more detail here, the student who masters the principles we have outlined can proceed with confidence to interpret the majority of the accounts and passages in the Gospels.[54]

THE GENRE OF ACTS

As might be expected, Acts—the second volume of Luke's two-part work— bears a strong resemblance to the Gospel genre. Acts 1:1 harks back to the Gospel of Luke in a way that suggests its prologue (Lk 1:1–4) applies to both parts. If theological biographies best captures the essence of the Gospels, then *theological history*—a narrative of interrelated events from a given place and time, chosen to communicate theological truths—best characterizes Acts.[55] Instead of focusing on one main character as in a

---

52 The most useful treatments of all the constituent literary forms in the Gospels are Bailey and Vander Broek, *Literary Forms*, 89–188; and K. Berger, *Formgeschichte des Neuen Testaments* (Heidelberg: Quelle und Meyer, 1984). Berger covers all NT forms and genres with a comprehensive categorization of individual texts.

53 Cf. the helpful survey in Stein, *Method and Message*, 7–32.

54 Of more detailed studies, perhaps the most helpful for beginning students are S. McKnight, *Interpreting the Synoptic Gospels* (Grand Rapids: Baker, 1989); and G. M. Burge, *Interpreting the Gospel of John* (Grand Rapids: Baker, 1992). Cf. also M. A. Powell, *Fortress Introduction to the Gospels* (Minneapolis: Fortress, 1998).

55 R. Maddox, *The Purpose of Luke-Acts* (Edinburgh: T. & T. Clark, 1982), 16, W. C. van Unnik, "Luke's Second Book and the Rules of Hellenistic Historiography," in *Les Actes des Apôtres: traditions, redaction, theologie*, ed. J. Kremer (Gembloux: Duculot, 1979), 37–60. For three other complementary genre identifications indicated by their article titles, see D. W. Palmer, "Acts and the Ancient Historical Monograph" (1–29); L. C. A. Alexander, "Acts and Ancient Intellectual Biography" (31–63); and B. S. Rosner, "Acts and Biblical History" (65–82)—all in *The Book of Acts in Its Ancient Literary Setting*, ed. B. W. Winter and A. D. Clarke (Grand Rapids: Eerdmans, 1993).

biography, Acts broadens its scope to present key episodes in the lives of several early church leaders. Still, the title "Acts of the Apostles" is misleading because eleven of the Twelve disappear soon after the opening chapters. Most of Luke's narrative centers on Peter and Paul; subordinate characters such as the deacons, Stephen and Philip, garner the next greatest amount of attention. The "Acts of the Holy Spirit" might be a more descriptive title inasmuch as Luke sees the coming of the Spirit at Pentecost and his subsequent filling of believers as the key to the birth and growth of the fledgling Christian community.

As they do with the Gospels, many interpreters of Acts succumb to false dichotomies between theology and history. On the one end of the spectrum, conservative scholars of Acts have been preoccupied with archaeology and other kinds of research, hoping to substantiate the historical trustworthiness of Acts. But in successfully doing so, they have often lost sight of the theological emphasis foremost in Luke's mind.[56] Liberal scholars have often proved more sensitive to Luke's theological insights, but in so doing they have unnecessarily alleged that he contradicts the other Evangelists, the epistles of Paul, and historical facts.[57] A third approach plays down both Luke's theology and historical accuracy in favor of emphasizing those features of Acts that would have proved entertaining and adventuresome for ancient audiences. This approach views Acts akin to a popular novel or historical romance that includes many details simply to enhance its readers' enjoyment and delight.[58]

Implications for Interpretation

We believe that it is possible (and desirable) to embrace all three of these perspectives as part of the genre of Acts without pitting any one against the others. The cumulative evidence for the historicity of Acts—its wealth of detail about people, places and customs—is too overwhelming to be ignored.[59] But, as in his Gospel, Luke did not compile history for history's sake; rather, he compiled it to teach his readers what he believed God was accomplishing in the world and what God was commanding believers to do in and through the events he narrated. Like the authors of the other "acts" (*praxeis*) of the Greco-Roman world (including later apocryphal "acts" of various apostles of more dubious historical worth),[60] Luke wrote in a lively and entertaining way. So we must not assume that every minor detail necessarily conveys theological import. For example, the story of Paul's sea journey and shipwreck in Acts 27 is rich in nautical detail and high adventure that seems primarily designed to heighten the drama and suspense while also highlighting God's sovereign protection of Paul to enable him to fulfill his calling—cf. 23:11.

---

56 The classic example is W. Ramsay, *St. Paul the Traveller and Roman Citizen* (London: Hodder and Stoughton, 1895; rev. and upd. M. Wilson [Grand Rapids: Kregel, 2001]); cf. Hemer, *Acts*.

57 The classic example is E. Haenchen, *The Acts of the Apostles* (Oxford: Blackwell, 1971). More recently, cf. J. D. Crossan, *The Birth of Christianity* (Harper: San Francisco, 1999).

58 See esp. R. I. Pervo, *Profit with Delight. The Literary Genre of the Acts of the Apostles* (Philadelphia: Fortress, 1987). For evangelical appropriation, see Ryken, *Words of Life*, 77–87.

59 See esp. the massive presentation of the supportive data throughout Hemer, *Acts*. Cf. also information scattered about the five volumes in the series, "The Book of Acts in Its First Century Setting," ed. B. W. Winter (Carlisle: Paternoster; Grand Rapids: Eerdmans, 1993–96).

60 The collection of apocryphal "acts" appears in E. Hennecke, *New Testament Apocrypha*, vol. 2, 2d ed. (Cambridge: Clarke; Louisville: Westminster John Knox, 1992).

Thinking Vertically

It is likely that Luke composed Acts much as he did his Gospel: by combining information from shorter written accounts of various events with what he had learned by word of mouth, often from eyewitnesses. In addition, in several places his writing shifts from third- to first-person plural narrative (from "he" or "they" to "we" did such-and-such), which suggests that on those occasions he was personally present for the events he described.[61] But Luke has thoroughly reworked and integrated his material into a coherent whole. Thus, it is highly speculative in Acts to undertake either source criticism or that brand of redaction criticism that requires comparison between the canonical form and earlier sources.[62] If we had parallel books of Acts as we have parallel Gospels, it might well be a different matter, but we do not. So we cannot create a synopsis to enable us to *think horizontally.*

On the other hand, we have a wealth of data to enable us to *think vertically.* The overall outline of Acts is clearer than the outline of any of the four Gospels. We see Acts 1:8 as theologically programmatic for Luke's purposes. He wishes to narrate selected episodes related to the geographical and cultural expansion of Christianity in order to present the gospel as a message for all peoples. Thus, he begins his story by describing virtually all of the first followers of Jesus as Jews who lived in Jerusalem, the political and cultural capital of Israel. But the story ends a mere thirty or so years later with the gospel firmly planted in Rome, the political and cultural center of the empire that dominated Europe and the Middle East in the first century. Within that short span of time Christianity had been transformed from an almost exclusively Jewish sect to a predominantly Gentile, empire-wide religion.

In six instances, Luke marks off what appear to be major divisions in his narrative that punctuate this expansion of Christianity (6:7; 9:31; 12:24; 16:5; 19:20; 28:31). Each of these summary statements refers to the word of the Lord as growing and spreading. So a very plausible outline of Acts might well look like this:

I. The Christian Mission to Jews (1:1–12:24)
    A. The Church in Jerusalem (1:1–6:7)
    B. The Church in Judea, Samaria, and Galilee (6:8–9:31)
    C. Further Advances in Palestine and Syria (9:32–12:24)
II. The Christian Mission to Gentiles (12:25–28:31)
    A. First Missionary Journey of Paul and the Jerusalem Council (12:25–16:5)
    B. Wide Outreach through Paul's Two Other Missionary Journeys (16:6–19:20)
    C. To Jerusalem and then to Rome (19:21–28:31)[63]

---

61 See esp. C. Hemer, "First Person Narrative in Acts 27–28," *TynB* 36 (1985): 79–109, against the view that this is merely a fictitious device.

62 Scholarly speculations nevertheless abound. See the survey in J. A. Fitzmyer, *The Acts of the Apostles* (New York and London: Doubleday, 1998), 80–89.

63 R. N. Longenecker, "Acts," in *Expositor's Bible Commentary*, ed. F. E. Gaebelein, 12 vols. (Grand Rapids: Zondervan, 1981), 9: 234, with a few modifications.

To interpret correctly a particular episode in Acts, therefore, we should first correlate it to its place in Luke's unfolding outline and developing themes. This will help us to perceive Luke's primary purposes and to pass up secondary elements in the episode that he did not intend to resolve. Two excellent examples appear in chap. 8. The two main episodes of this chapter involve: (1) the conversion and baptism of the Samaritans, with their ringleader Simon Magus (8:5–25); and (2) the conversion and baptism of the Ethiopian eunuch on the road to Gaza (8:26–39). In light of modern debates about water baptism, baptism in the Spirit, and eternal security, readers of Acts today usually raise such questions as: Why didn't the Spirit come immediately when the Samaritans believed Philip's preaching? Was Simon Magus ever really saved, and, if so, did he lose his salvation? Is it significant that Philip baptized the Ethiopian eunuch as soon as they come upon a sufficiently large body of water?

Although all of these are legitimate questions, they are *our* questions. Probably none was in Luke's mind as he penned this chapter of Acts. This passage occurs in the section of his outline that concentrates on how the gospel began to leave exclusively Jewish territory. Thus, the two most striking features of Acts 8 become the reception of Philip's message first by *Samaritans* and then by a *eunuch,* both considered ritually unclean by orthodox Jews. The main applications of Acts 8 for Christian living today, therefore, should not center on the timing of the arrival of the Holy Spirit and its effects, nor on debates about how much water one needs for baptism, or how quickly it should follow on conversion. Rather, these texts should call all Christians today to determine who the Samaritans and eunuchs are in our world. Christian ministry must not neglect today's "untouchables" or outcasts—AIDS victims, the homeless, unwed mothers, drug addicts, gang members, and the like.[64]

Thinking vertically also involves treating *Luke-Acts* as one unit. Identifiable redactional or theological emphases in Luke's Gospel will probably recur in Acts, so students should give these special attention.[65] The theme of Jesus' compassion for outcasts identified above certainly fits in this category. So, too, does Luke's emphasis on the role of the Holy Spirit and of prayer in believers' lives. Thus, we should not pass lightly over those texts in which the church in a given community gathers and prays for God's guidance, seeking to be "of one accord" (1:14; 2:46; 4:24; 5:12). In an age when many Christians strongly voice their desire to imitate the "New Testament church," very few follow a process of decision-making that seeks unanimity or near-unanimity through prolonged prayer meetings of an entire body of believers. Yet that is the consistent pattern of Acts!

By comparing Luke and Acts we may discern structural or thematic parallels even apart from any comparison of Luke with the other Gospels. Frequently, the disciples in Acts closely imitate some facet of our Lord's life as described in Luke. Consider, for example, some of the first Christian miracles. The story of Aeneas (9:32–35) very closely resembles Jesus' healing of the paralytic in Lk 5:17–26, right down to the very wording, "get up and take your mat." Peter raising Tabitha from the dead (Acts 9:36–43) uncannily parallels Jesus raising Jairus' daughter (Lk 8:40–42, 49–56). In fact, the

---

64 See, e.g., B. Witherington, III, *The Acts of the Apostles; A Socio-Rhetorical Commentary* (Grand Rapids: Eerdmans; Carlisle: Paternoster, 1998), 279–301.

65 W. L. Liefeld, *Interpreting the Book of Acts* (Grand Rapids: Baker, 1996), identifies ten key theological themes (79–98).

Aramaic commands to the two dead women probably varied by only one letter—*Talitha cum* ("little girl, arise") and *Tabitha cum* ("Tabitha, get up")![66]

Or compare the endings of Luke and Acts. The Gospel ends with a long and detailed focus on Jesus' passion and death. In fact, Lk 9:51 introduces the theme of Jesus journeying toward Jerusalem and the cross earlier than does any other Gospel. Acts, too, slows down its narrative substantially to focus on Paul's final, fateful journey to Jerusalem and the sufferings and imprisonments that await him there, in Caesarea and in Rome. Luke may or may not have written his account after Paul's eventual death, but he certainly sees parallels in the closing stages of the lives of both Jesus and Paul. These kinds of similarities between Luke and Acts suggest that Luke saw the life of a faithful disciple as often imitating that of Christ, both in its spiritual power and in the necessity of suffering. What was true for Paul should therefore be true for us. Unfortunately, we rarely find the combination of the themes "power" and "suffering" in contemporary Christianity; those who successfully emphasize the one usually tend to play down the other.[67]

The Significance of Pentecost

Proper interpretation of Acts also requires an appreciation of the significance of the events of Acts 2. This marks the crucial turning point between the age of the Mosaic covenant and the age of the new covenant that was made possible by Jesus' atoning death, vindicating resurrection, and exaltation to the right hand of the Father (Acts 1:1–11). Careful exegesis necessitates a mediating view between, say, the extremes of traditional dispensationalism and unqualified covenant theology. In other words, the student must avoid interpretations that exaggerate either the continuity or the discontinuity between the two ages.[68] Luke's understanding of Peter's speech concerning the fulfillment of Joel's prophecy (Acts 2:14–21; cf. Joel 2:28–32) strongly suggests that a new, previously unavailable spiritual empowerment will henceforth characterize the lives of Jesus' followers. For example, the baptism and indwelling of all believers by the Spirit (2:38–39; cf. 1 Cor 12:13) and the phenomenon of tongues (2:5–12; 10:44–46; 19:4–7) mark a significant break from OT times. Though they do not recognize it immediately or without conflict, these first Christians come to believe that Jewish and Gentile believers alike no longer need observe laws of the OT apart from their fulfillment in Christ (10:1–11:18; 15:1–29). Thus, one must be careful, for example, not to assume that Acts 1:22–26 offers a model for how Christians should make decisions. Although "casting lots" was a common and proper practice in the OT era (cf. Lev 16:8; Num 26:55; Neh 10:34), it never reappears in the NT. Indeed, the giving of the Spirit that immediately follows

---

66 Cf. C. K. Barrett, *Acts: A Shorter Commentary* (Edinburgh: T. & T. Clark, 2002), 148.

67 For excellent evangelical summaries of Acts' major theological contributions, see I. H. Marshall and B. Peterson, eds., *Witness to the Gospel: The Theology of Acts* (Grand Rapids and Cambridge: Eerdmans, 1998).

68 Dispensationalism has taken great strides away from the excesses of past generations toward a more "centrist" position. Covenant theology, too, has made similar though often not as significant overtures. A helpful volume contrasting contemporary perspectives in both camps is *Continuity and Discontinuity: Perspectives on the Relationship between the Old and New Testaments*, ed. J. S. Feinberg (Westchester: Crossway, 1988).

this episode probably is meant to replace methods such as lots for Christian decision-making.[69]

On the other hand, interpreters must guard against driving too great a wedge between the days before and after Pentecost. Though we may not cast lots today, we should not accuse the first disciples of having erred when they practiced this method. The notion that Paul was God's true choice for Judas' replacement rather than Matthias finds no exegetical support in any NT text.[70] And the concern for prayer and unity that preceded the use of lots clearly continues on beyond Pentecost.

In not exaggerating the discontinuity between old and new ages, the student must also beware of minimizing the positive value of Acts on the grounds that it reflects a transitional period between covenants.[71] Of course, Acts does describe transitions. Where the disciples had not yet fully come to appreciate their freedom in Christ, we must be cautious about imitating their behavior, as, for example, when the Hebraic Jews in Jerusalem insist that Paul continue to support the sacrificial cult (Acts 21:17–26).[72] But such caution comes from sensitivity to Luke's own clues as a narrator as to what God approved and what he did not. As with many sections of OT historical narrative, students need to look for hints in the text itself concerning what it presents as a good, bad, or neutral example. Narrative often teaches more indirectly than didactic literature, but that makes it no less normative, once we correctly discern the text's original intent.[73] At the very least, then, the reader must guard against seeing Acts 21:17–26 as too positive a model inasmuch as the whole plot backfires (vv. 27–36).

But this does not hold true for Luke's descriptions of early Christian "communism." Though some argue (usually staunch capitalists!) that the experiments in communal sharing of 2:44–45 and 4:32–37 were misguided failures, Luke appears instead to present them as positive models. He words the results as follows: "And the Lord added to their number daily those who were being saved" (2:47), and "much grace was upon them all. There were no needy persons among them" (4:33b-34a).[74]

It is equally misguided to identify turning points within the book to show that the message of salvation should be offered to Jews no longer. Of course, on several occasions Paul turns from Jews to Gentiles because of the repeated rejection and hostility he receives from the Jewish people (13:46–48; 18:5–7; 19:8–10; 28:23–28). But the very fact that he repeats this pattern several times, as he moves from city to city, prevents us from alleging that any given episode indicates a more general strategy of abandoning the Jews in favor of an exclusively Gentile mission. Even the final turning from

---

69 A. Fernando, *Acts*, NIVAC (Grand Rapids: Zondervan, 1998), 79.

70 Rightly, W. J. Larkin, *Acts*, IVP NTC (Leicester and Downers Grove: InterVarsity, 1995), 47. *Contra*, e.g., G. C. Morgan, *The Acts of the Apostles* (NY: Revell, 1924), 19–20.

71 As classically in an older dispensationalism (see, e.g., M. R. de Haan, *Pentecost and After* [Grand Rapids: Zondervan, 1964], 8), but as widely practiced by others, too.

72 On the whole theme of "The Law in Acts," see C. L. Blomberg, "The Christian and the Law of Moses," in *Witness to the Gospels*, 397–416.

73 See esp. L. Ryken, *The Literature of the Bible* (Grand Rapids: Zondervan, 1974), 45–106. On the topic of what is normative versus descriptive in applying Acts, see Liefeld, *Interpreting Acts*, 113–28.

74 On this theme, cf. esp. R. J. Cassidy, *Society and Politics in the Acts of the Apostles* (Maryknoll: Orbis, 1987).

Jews to Gentiles in Rome that concludes Acts (28:23–38) does not justify any inferences about appropriate evangelistic strategy elsewhere. After all, in his farewell speech to the Ephesian elders—which he presents as a model for the ministry of subsequent Christian leaders (20:18–35)—Paul emphasizes proclamation "to both Jews and Greeks" (v. 21). And 19:10, 17–18 make clear that even after Paul shifted preaching venues in Ephesus, Jews continued to hear the gospel and to believe.[75] These observations thus rule out all of the older, more extreme forms of dispensationalism that viewed as normative for Gentile Christians only those parts of the NT that occurred after one of the alleged turning points in Acts.

Acts as Narrative

We have already stated that narrative often teaches more indirectly than didactic literature without becoming any less normative. Fee and Stuart correctly added to their older maxim that "unless Scripture explicitly tells us we must do something, what is only narrated or described does not function in a normative way," the additional clarification, "unless it can be demonstrated on other grounds that the author intended it to function in this way."[76] We wish to put it even more strongly: 2 Tim 3:16 provides the grounds to assume students can learn some kind of lesson from every passage, even in narrative literature. We have already illustrated in some detail how parables, for example, often contrast characters whose behavior is meant to be imitated or avoided. Sometimes a parable's context makes that point clear (e.g., Lk 10:37; 13:3–5; 18:1). This suggests that in other cases we should draw similar conclusions. Nevertheless, one must proceed much more cautiously when direct commands are absent. How then should we proceed to interpret Acts? Primarily, we need to study the entire book to determine if specific events form a consistent pattern throughout or if the positive models Luke presents vary from one situation to another. The former will suggest that Luke was emphasizing a normative, consistent principle; the latter, that applications *may* change from one time and place to the next.[77]

Examples abound. Gamaliel's advice to the Sanhedrin concerning the Twelve ("Leave these men alone! Let them go! For if their purpose or activity is of human origin, it will fail. But if it is from God, you will not be able to stop these men; you will only find yourselves fighting against God.") fortunately secured the disciples' freedom (Acts 5:38–39). But when Paul encountered "magical" religion in Ephesus (comparable to what we would call the "occult"), he employed a different strategy: strongly exhorting people to abandon such practices and to burn the scrolls containing incantations (19:17–20). Today, Islam is the largest and most powerful non-Christian religion in the world. Historically, Christians have largely ignored it, but after 1,500 years it has hardly gone away. So while God in his sovereignty graciously used Gamaliel's "logic" to help the disciples, we dare not imitate it in every instance. In other words, Acts' inclusion of Gamaliel's advice does not make it normative.

---

75 J. A. Weatherly, *Jewish Responsibility for the Death of Jesus in Luke-Acts*, JSNTSup 106 (Sheffield: Sheffield Academic Press, 1994).

76 Fee and Stuart, *How to Read,* 106. Cf. their first edition (1984, p. 97), where the additional clarification did not appear.

77 Particularly helpful in discerning timeless from situation-specific principles in Acts is Liefeld, *Interpreting Acts*, 113–27, though readers may dispute one or two of his conclusions.

Models of church government and organization in Acts disclose an even more bewildering variety of forms. Congregationalists, Presbyterians, and Episcopalians all legitimately point to passages in Acts to support their views of church structure and leadership. In 6:1–6 the entire congregation chooses the apostles' helpers. In 13:1–3 a select group of church leaders chooses Barnabas and Saul for their missionary ministry. And in Acts 20:17–38 Paul resembles a "bishop" who convenes all the Ephesian "elders" for instruction. Each of these models in turn draws on various Jewish or Greco-Roman precedents. Luke views all of these models as appropriate applications of leadership principles under various circumstances in various cultures. To apply them today, one needs to look for analogous circumstances in our cultures.[78] It is probably not mere coincidence that: a decision affecting everyone in a local congregation was discussed by all; that one limited to the personal ministries of church leaders was dealt with by that smaller group; and that general instruction for people in several congregations came from one who had authority over all of them.

On the other hand, sometimes patterns of ministry and mission remain constant throughout Acts. A good example is how Luke understands the filling of the Holy Spirit. Every time believers are filled with the Spirit—and this happens repeatedly to the same person or group (2:4; 4:8, 31; 9:17; 13:9)—they are enabled to proclaim the Word of God boldly or to do mighty works in Jesus' name. In his letter to the Ephesians, Paul describes different results of the Spirit's filling: praising, worshipping, and thanking God, and submitting to other believers (Eph 5:18–21). But these descriptions are complementary rather than contradictory. A proper doctrine of Scripture will not subordinate Acts to Paul simply because the one is narrative and the other didactic literature. Neither will it subordinate Paul to Acts because of an inherent preference by some for the phenomena of Acts (such as speaking in tongues).[79] The Spirit inspired *all* of Scripture; no one genre trumps the others.

The phrase "baptism in [or "of"] the Spirit" occurs only twice in Acts, but its seven uses in the NT are likewise all consistent. In every instance but one, it refers to the initiating experience of the Spirit creating the Church at Pentecost (Mt 3:11; Mk 1:8; Lk 3:16; Jn 1:33; Ac 1:5, 11:16), and the other usage declares that *all* the Corinthian Christians (and many of them were quite immature) had received this experience (1 Cor 12:13; cf. 1:7). On the other hand, only three times in all of the NT do tongues appear at someone's conversion or baptism (Ac 2:4, 10:46, 19:6). Therefore, while tongues remain a gift for God's Spirit to give as *he* chooses (1 Cor 12:11), speaking in tongues cannot serve as a criterion of salvation or even of Christian maturity. If we are to use the expression as does the NT, baptism in or of the Spirit cannot be equated with receiving any specific gift or post-conversion blessing (legitimate as those experiences may be), but should signify the Spirit's coming to live in a new believer at conversion.[80]

Probably the most important examples of consistent patterns within Acts relate to Luke's main theme—the expansion of the gospel from Jewish to Gentile territory. Amid the great diversity of sermons that Peter and Paul preach throughout the pages

---

78 E.g., the Greek *ekklēsia* ("assembly" of citizens), the Jewish synagogue elders, and the Roman territorial magistrates.

79 Generally well-balanced throughout is M. M. B. Turner, *The Holy Spirit and Spiritual Gifts: In the New Testament Church and Today*, rev. ed. (Peabody: Hendrickson, 1998).

80 See esp. James D. G. Dunn, *Baptism in the Holy Spirit* (Philadelphia: Westminster, 1970).

of Acts, we can discern a common kerygma (proclamation of salvation). The first Christians consistently focus on the death, resurrection, and exaltation of Jesus as the core of their message. Because of who Jesus was and what he did, all people must now repent in order to receive forgiveness of sins. To be sure, this message occurs elsewhere in the NT but, even if it did not, its consistent appearance in Acts would make it normative.[81]

Even the diversity within the sermons in which this kerygma appears points to another consistent feature of early Christian preaching: concern for contextualizing the gospel. When preaching to Jews, Peter and Paul appeal to the fulfillment of Scripture (2:14–39; 3:12–26; 13:16–41). When addressing the Stoics and Epicureans, Paul explains to them their "unknown god" (17:22–31). When he speaks to the superstitious believers in mythology in Lystra, Paul appeals to the testimony of the creator as found in rain and harvest (14:14–18). In each case these preachers sought to establish common ground with their audiences in order to gain the greatest possible acceptance of their message. In each case, too, they made sure to include a distinctive witness to the true and living God, usually explicitly in terms of the person and work of Christ. Christians in all ages can learn much about cross-cultural ministry from these models and would do well to emulate them.[82]

THE GENRE OF THE EPISTLES

Implications for Interpretation
General Considerations

At first glance, genre criticism of the Epistles might seem to have little to say. An epistle is a letter. The NT letters are less literary, formal, and artistic than many classical Greek treatises but still generally longer, more carefully structured, and more didactic than typical personal correspondence.[83] As writings from apostles and other early church leaders to various Christian communities and individuals, the Epistles primarily teach theology and offer ethical instruction. From one point of view, then, the interpreter's task is easier here than anywhere else in Scripture. For, presumably, the writers

---

81 The classic study of the core kerygma is C. H. Dodd, *The Apostolic Preaching and Its Developments* (New York: Harper and Row, 1951). Cf. the discussion in G. E. Ladd, *A Theology of the New Testament*, rev. and ed. D. A. Hagner (Grand Rapids: Eerdmans, 1993), 364–78.

82 A particularly helpful study of the patterns of ministry and preaching throughout Acts is M. Green, *Evangelism in the Early Church* (London: Hodder and Stoughton, 1970). The issue of the historicity of the speeches of Acts has generated extensive scholarly debate. Some rather uncritically cite the ancient Greek historian, Thucydides, as Luke's exemplar to prove both substantial trustworthiness and substantial fabrication! It is *not* clear, however, that there is only one Thucydidean view of reporting speeches. He apparently followed memory and eyewitness sources carefully at times and on other occasions made up speeches while striving for historical verisimilitude. See S. E. Porter, "Thucydides 1.22.1 and Speeches in Acts: Is There a Thucydidean View?" *NovT* 32 (1990): 121–42. On the speeches of Acts the most thorough and balanced study is C. H. Gempf, "Historical and Literary Appropriateness in the Mission Speeches of Paul in Acts" (Ph.D. thesis, University of Aberdeen, 1988). But for those who subscribe to the authority of the final form of Scripture, not considering its prehistory or tradition criticism, few hermeneutical issues hinge on the solution to this debate.

83 For details of ancient letter writing, cf. J. L. White, *Light from Ancient Letters* (Philadelphia: Fortress, 1986); S. K. Stowers, *Letter Writing in Greco-Roman Antiquity* (Philadelphia: Westminster, 1986); A. J. Malherbe, *Ancient Epistolary Theorists* (Atlanta: Scholars, 1988); M. L. Stirewalt, Jr., *Studies in Ancient Greek Epistolography* (Atlanta: Scholars, 1993); and id., *Paul the Letter Writer* (Grand Rapids and Cambridge: Eerdmans, 2003).

of the Epistles believed the doctrines they promulgated and obeyed the instructions they promoted. For example, a survey of Romans reveals Paul's concern to teach God's plan of salvation—from humanity's universal sinfulness (1:18–3:20), to justification in Christ (3:21–5:21), to sanctification by the Spirit and glorification in the future (Rom 6–8). Key ethical topics include holistic transformation of body and mind (12:1–2), faithful use of spiritual gifts (12:3–8), Christian love and submission (12:9–13:14), and exercising or restraining one's freedom (14:1–15:13). Little wonder many people have come to faith in Christ and grown in their walk with him simply by reading Romans— without a hermeneutics textbook!

A more careful analysis, however, reveals complexities in the Epistles. Though the most deliberately and directly didactic of all the NT genres, Epistles are also the most "occasional." In other words, the authors wrote the Epistles for specific occasions to address individual audiences who were facing unique problems. Interpreters must reconstruct those original "occasions" and purposes as precisely as possible in order to separate timeless principles from situation-specific applications. The same readers who found Romans so straightforward may puzzle quite a bit more when they come to 1 Cor 11 regarding Paul's instructions about men's and women's head coverings and the proper observance of the Lord's Supper. In many cultures Christians today seem to pay little attention to what people do or do not wear on their heads in church or to how long their hair is (there are exceptions here!), and few churches, if any, offer their communicants enough wine for anyone to worry about getting drunk. In fact, many prefer to substitute nonfermented juice for wine.[84]

While we discuss this problem of separating universal principles from context-bound or culturally limited applications more thoroughly in chapter 12, it is particularly acute for the interpretation of Epistles. Sometimes the historical context enables the interpreter to determine how to proceed; sometimes the text of the epistle itself offers clues. For example, the text on the Lord's Supper (1 Cor 11:27–29) permits Christians to draw general principles applicable to situations in which drunkenness poses no danger. Whenever one eats or drinks "in an unworthy manner" (v. 27), one profanes the body and blood of Christ. The problem with the Corinthians' gluttony and drunkenness was, foremost, that it undermined the theological truth of the unity of the body of Christ when it deprived others of getting enough to eat and drink (v. 21). So whenever members of a Christian congregation disregard each other's needs (and so subvert the body of Christ), they are not prepared to partake of the Lord's Table worthily. Notice that this application differs considerably from the common but mistaken notion that people should refrain from communion when they personally feel "unworthy." The Greek term is an adverb, not an adjective—we must not eat "unworthily."[85]

These last examples illustrate one further general hermeneutical consideration for the Epistles: interpreters must locate them as specifically as possible in a particular historical context. Fortunately, at least with the Pauline epistles, a close reading of a given

---

84 C. Kraft recounts the provocative story of his missionary work in Nigeria in which new believers could not understand why Western Christians "obeyed the Biblical commands against stealing but not those about head-coverings" (*Christianity in Culture* [Maryknoll: Orbis, 1979], 138).

85 See, e.g., A. C. Thiselton, *The First Epistle to the Corinthians*, NIGNT (Carlisle: Paternoster; Grand Rapids: Eerdmans, 2000), 890.

letter from start to finish usually discloses specific details about that letter's audience and relevant circumstances.[86] Comparison with information in Acts often yields additional data,[87] and the study of other ancient writers' descriptions of the various cities in which the apostolic churches were situated may help to round out the picture.[88] Thus, we can learn much about Paul's opponents in Philippi from references in the letter itself (Phil 1:15–18; 3:2–11). We may appreciate the superstitious, pagan attitudes Paul encountered in Galatia by reading background material in Acts (cf. Acts 14:11–13 with Gal 3:1). And we can understand why Paul wrote extensively about sexual morality in 1 Corinthians (5; 6:12–20;7) when we learn from other historical sources that the massive temple to Aphrodite, which towered over the city of Corinth from a nearby clifftop, had at one time employed over 1000 "sacred prostitutes"—male and female!

Of course, not all of the Epistles can be so easily set in their historical contexts. Galatians, for instance, polarizes interpreters who debate whether it was written to North or South Galatia, and whether it is to be dated "early" or "late" (i.e., before or after the apostolic council of Acts 15). The comparison between Acts 14 and Gal 3 made above works only if one adopts an early date and Southern provenance.[89] Hebrews (written anonymously) and most of the so-called General Epistles (James, 1 and 2 Peter, 1, 2, and 3 John, and Jude) tell us very little about their destinations or dates. And many scholars view as pseudonymous (i.e., written in the name of an apostle or other leading Christian figure by someone else) several of the letters ascribed to Paul (most notably Ephesians, Colossians, 1, 2 Timothy and Titus), as well as those of James, Peter, and Jude , perhaps dating from a generation or more after the lifetime of that individual.[90] Such a view relegates any discussion of provenance to enlightened speculation at best.

This issue of *pseudonymity,* therefore, deserves a few comments here. Authorship may make quite a difference in how one interprets, say, 1 Tim 2:8–15. For various reasons many scholars deny that Paul could have written the Pastorals (1, 2 Timothy and Titus). Instead, they view these three letters as the product of a disciple of Paul a generation later who wrote when the Church was becoming more institutionalized and chauvinistic. By that time, Christians had allegedly lost sight of the totally egalitarian positions of Jesus and Paul (cf. esp. Gal 3:28) and were lapsing back into the bad habits of the surrounding culture. Such a view, then, allows Christians to disregard the prohibitions in 1 Tim 2:12 against women teaching or having authority over men in church.

Some scholars have freely embraced pseudonymity when they perceived "contradictions" between the theologies of various epistles attributed to the same writer or noted marked changes in style or ethos. On the other hand, scholars who are more conservative have rejected pseudonymity as incompatible with the inspiration or authority

---

86 Recall our detailed instructions above for researching historical background issues.

87 Once the general trustworthiness of Acts is shown to be probable (on which see above).

88 Cf. esp. S. F. Johnson, *Paul: the Apostle and His Cities* (Wilmington: Glazier, 1987); and R. Brownrigg, *Pauline Places: In the Footsteps of Paul Through Turkey and Greece* (London: Hodder and Stoughton, 1989).

89 For details and a defense of this position, see R. N. Longenecker, *Galatians,* WBC 41 (Dallas: Word, 1990), lxi–lxxxviii.

90 As in most standard critical introductions to the NT, e.g., H. C. Kee, *Understanding the New Testament,* 5th ed. (Englewood Cliffs: Prentice-Hall, 1993).

of Scripture. If an epistle begins, "Paul, an apostle," they argue no one but Paul could have written it.

Neither of these approaches, however, can withstand close scrutiny. The linguistic and theological differences among the Epistles have been overblown. Given the limited amount of material we have from any one Scripture writer, and given the different styles authors will adopt for different circumstances, we doubt that a modern reader could ever conclusively say that the person whose name appears in the opening verse could not have written a given epistle.[91]

But neither must we read such texts uncritically. No one today protests that the *Congressional Record* errs when it attributes to a particular senator a speech that was written by an aide and possibly was never even delivered on the Senate floor. We understand the literary convention. Nor do readers of an autobiography of a famous public figure accuse its publishers of fraud when they discover in the preface that a ghostwriter actually made the celebrity's memoirs legible. Many books written by preachers today fit this category. In many instances "authors" do not even identify their ghostwriters, nor is the convention made explicit in any place in the book. The crucial question to ask, therefore, is whether or not pseudonymity would have been an accepted literary convention within first-century Christianity. The proliferation of popular intertestamental Jewish writings suggests that pre-Christian Judaism may have come to accept this device. Yet the battle with Gnostic and other heretical Christian writings, from the mid-second century on, demonstrates that later Christians regularly rejected it. But what of the first century? The jury is still out; the evidence is meager on both sides.[92]

One likely way to advance the discussion would occur if one could show that a particular epistle conforms to a demonstrably pseudonymous genre. Of several hypotheses, perhaps the most persuasive comes from Richard Bauckham, who relates 2 Peter to the consistently pseudonymous *testamentary* genre.[93] To Bauckham, 2 Pet 1:15 presents this epistle as "Peter's" final instructions to his followers shortly before his death. But, he observes, this is precisely the function of testaments written a generation or more later by a follower of a great individual, telling readers of that day what he believed the person would say if he were present. On this view, Peter's audience, knowing full well that Peter was long dead, would not have accused the epistle's author of any deception but would have recognized the attribution of authorship as a key to the letter's genre. Even as late as A.D. 200, Tertullian explained that "it is allowable that that which pupils

---

91 With respect to the Pastorals see esp. L. T. Johnson, *The First and Second Letters to Timothy*, AB (New York and London: Doubleday, 2001), 55–99.

92 For opposing evangelical perspectives, cf. D. Guthrie, *New Testament Introduction,* 4th ed. (Downers Grove: InterVarsity, 1990), 1011–28 (against pseudonymity); with D. G. Meade, *Pseudonymity and Canon* (Grand Rapids: Eerdmans, 1986) (for it). The further work of T. L. Wilder may, however, be tipping the scales against pseudonymity. See a convenient summary of his approach in his "Pseudonymity and the New Testament," in *Interpreting the New Testament*, ed. D. A. Black and D. S. Dockery (Nashville: Broadman and Holman, 2001), 296–335. For greater detail, see T. L. Wilder, "New Testament Pseudonymity and Deception" (Unpublished Ph.D. thesis, University of Aberdeen, 1998); J. Duff, "A Reconsideration of Pseudepigraphy in Early Christianity" (Unpublished D.Phil. thesis, Oxford University, 1998); and C. K. Horn, "Pseudonymity in Early Christianity: An Inquiry into the Theory of Innocent Deutero-Pauline Pseudonymity" (Unpublished Ph.D. diss., Southwestern Baptist Theological Seminary, 1996).

93 R. J. Bauckham, *Jude, 2 Peter*, WBC 50 (Waco: Word, 1983), 131–63.

publish should be regarded as their master's work" (*Against Marcion* 4:5). But, of course, testaments could be written by people in their own names as well, and not every feature of 2 Peter conforms to the genre; so even Bauckham's case must be declared only "possible" rather than conclusive. More importantly, this type of theory of pseudonymity does not diminish in any way the authority of the epistle; it remains just as normative for believers irrespective of authorship.

Specific Considerations

To interpret the NT Epistles correctly we need to compare them with other Greco-Roman letters of antiquity. A fairly typical structure, which even first-century students were exhorted to follow, began with a salutation (identification of author, recipients, and some kind of greeting) and a prayer or expression of thanks for the well-being of the recipients. Then one proceeded to the body of the epistle, which set forth the major reason(s) for writing. If the writer had advice or exhortation to give, this came after the body. A closing farewell rounded out the document.[94]

Understanding these conventions enables the interpreter to recognize what is typical and atypical in the NT Epistles. The opening prayers and thanksgivings, while certainly more theological than an average "secular" letter, in fact performed what all writers considered a common courtesy. On the other hand, when Galatians has no thanksgiving (had Paul written one, it would have come between 1:5 and 6), and when 1 Thessalonians has two (1 Thes 1:2–10; 2:13–16), readers should sit up and take notice. Paul stresses the severity of the Galatians' lapse into legalism by ignoring standard conventions and plunging directly into the heart of his complaint against them. Conversely, Paul has more words of sustained praise for the Thessalonians than for any other apostolic congregation. So it is not surprising that he should include an unconventional, added section of thanksgiving.

Scholars also divide Greco-Roman letters into various subgenres. An epistle like 1 Thessalonians illustrates the "parenetic" or *exhortational letter*. All the praise that Paul lavishes on the Thessalonians fits the strategy of this kind of writing. He gives them some very pointed moral instruction in 4:1–12 (particularly on sexual and business ethics), and he corrects crucial points of theology in 4:13–5:11 (regarding Christ's Second Coming). But he tactfully prepares his readers for this exhortation by establishing his friendship with them and by emphasizing how well they are progressing and how little they really need any further instruction.[95]

A second subgenre is the *diatribe*: a conversational method of instruction in which the writer considers and answers hypothetical objections from opponents. Most of Rom 1–11 fits reasonably well into this classification. So when Paul frequently tackles objections to his presentation of the gospel (Rom 3:1, 9; 4:1; 6:1, 15; 7:7), readers need not assume that such objectors were actually present in the Roman church. More likely, Paul was anticipating the types of questions his letter might elicit and answering them before they ever arose.[96]

---

94 For a helpful discussion see C. J. Roetzel, *The Letters of Paul*, 4th ed. (Louisville: Westminster John Knox, 1998), 51–66.

95 Cf. A. J. Malherbe, *The Letters to the Thessalonians* (New York and London: Doubleday, 2000).

96 S. K. Stowers, *The Diatribe and Paul's Letter to the Romans* (Chico, CA: Scholars, 1981).

Still another subgenre of epistle is the *letter of introduction or recommendation,* designed to introduce the bearer of the letter to its recipients before requesting a certain favor. Often the writer of the letter was a close friend or relative of the recipient(s) who was promising to return the favor in some way. Philemon exemplifies this genre. Paul asks Philemon to welcome home his runaway slave Onesimus without punishing him, promises to pay any damages Philemon incurred, and reminds Onesimus of the debts he owes Paul. The entire epistle is a masterpiece of tact and persuasion as Paul steers a delicate course between pleading and demanding. Since the letter of recommendation was a well-established genre of writing, Paul could expect Philemon to comply with his requests.[97]

Not every proposed subgenre in the criticism of the Epistles is as clear-cut as the examples of 1 Thessalonians, Romans, and Philemon. Nevertheless, a number of other suggestions possess value for honing our hermeneutical approach. Most of 2 Cor 1–7 likely forms an *apologetic letter of self-commendation,* a well-known Greco-Roman form of rhetorical self-defense. Although Paul recoils at the vacuous rhetoric of his opponents in Corinth, he, nevertheless, crafts a carefully structured and highly rhetorical response.[98] Chaps. 10–13 are particularly steeped in irony and a kind of legitimate boasting of which rhetoricians particularly approved.[99] Recognizing Paul's strategy prevents a misreading of 1 Cor 2:1–5. Paul does not reject all the standards of "secular" wisdom of his day; he merely rejects anything that intractably opposes the gospel of the cross of Christ. With the Spirit's guidance he happily employs effective rhetorical devices to persuade his audiences of his views. Good Christian communication in any age should do the same.

Some have tended to view Philippians as disjointed, even as a composite product of several epistles gathered haphazardly into one scroll. But more likely, this epistle illustrates the structure of the *family letter,* combining, in sequence: an address and greeting (1:1–2), a prayer for the recipients (1:3–11), reassurance about the sender (1:12–26), a request for reassurance about the recipients (1:27–2:18), information about the movement of intermediaries (2:19–30), an exchange of greetings with third parties (4:2–22), and a closing wish for health (4:23). Paul then departs from convention and adds a polemic against false teachers (3:1–4:1) and various other exhortations and thank-yous (4:2–20). The Philippians have recently sent him money, for which he expresses his gratitude, but they have also come under attack, which causes him distress. Because these two sections deviate from the norm, they would have stood out and received the most attention. Paul probably departed from the standard form of a family letter precisely to highlight these two special concerns.[100]

Another way of categorizing Epistles considers the kinds of rhetoric they employ. The ancient Greeks and Romans distinguished three major types: *judicial* (seeking to

97 D. E. Aune, *The New Testament in Its Literary Environment* (Philadelphia: Westminster, 1987), 211–12; Stowers, *Letter Writing,* 155.

98 L. L. Belleville, "A Letter of Apologetic Self-Commendation: 2 Cor. 1:8–7:16," *NovT* 31 (1989): 142–63.

99 Cf. esp. C. Forbes, "Comparison, Self-Praise and Irony: Paul's Boasting and the Conventions of Hellenistic Rhetoric," *NTS* 32 (1986): 1–30.

100 Cf. further L. Alexander, "Hellenistic Letter-Forms and the Structure of Philippians," *JSNT* 37 (1989): 87–101.

convince an audience of the rightness or wrongness of a past action), *deliberative* (trying to persuade or dissuade certain individuals concerning the expediency of a future action), and *epideictic* (using praise or blame to urge people to affirm a point of view or set of values in the present). A full-blown rhetorical address would contain all of the following features, though often one or more sections might be missing:

exordium	stated the cause and gained the audience's attention and sympathy
narratio	related the background and facts of the case
propositio	stated what was agreed upon and what was contested
probatio	contained the proofs based on the credibility of the speaker; appealed to the hearers' feelings and / or logical argument
refutatio	refuted opponents' arguments
peroratio	summarized argument and sought to arouse hearers' emotions.[101]

Many of the NT Epistles reasonably approximate this structure. As a basis for outlining NT Epistles, it can help the student understand how each part of a letter is functioning. For example, 2 Thes 2:1–2 forms the thesis or *propositio(n)* around which all of the letter is built—the day of the Lord is not as immediately at hand as some in the Church have been led to think.[102] Gal 3—4 gathers together the proofs *(probatio)* for Paul's proposition concerning justification by faith in 2:15–21. These reveal the diversity of arguments an ancient writer or speaker might employ to try to persuade. They also suggest strategies that we may still use effectively today. These include arguments from undeniable personal experience (the Galatians' reception of the Spirit, 3:1–5 vs. their previous non-Christian lives, 4:8–11); from Scripture (Gen 15:6; Gen. 12:3; Deut 27:26; Hab 2:4; Lev 18:5; and Deut 21:23 in Gal 3:6–14); from common human practice (in making covenants, guarding prisoners, and granting inheritances, 3:15–18, 21–22; 4:1–7); from Christian tradition (particularly in baptism, 3:26–29); from friendship (4:12–20); and from an analogy (with the establishment of the Abrahamic covenant, 4:21–31).[103]

Determining the rhetoric of an epistle often proves more difficult when authors mix two or three kinds together. Almost all NT letters function deliberatively because a primary purpose was to tell believers how to act or how not to act. Still, one may be able to distinguish an emphasis, say, between 2 and 3 John.[104] Third John seems primarily epideictic—"the elder" praises Gaius for his Christian lifestyle and hospitality. Although he encourages him to continue faithfully, Gaius does not need to be persuaded of the correctness of his behavior. But in 2 John, the elder employs primarily deliberative rhetoric, advising "the elect lady" (NRSV) on the correct course of action in light

---

101 G. A. Kennedy, *New Testament Interpretation through Rhetorical Criticism* (Chapel Hill: University of North Carolina Press, 1984), 24.

102 F. W. Hughes, *Early Christian Rhetoric and 2 Thessalonians,* JSNTSup 30 (Sheffield: JSOT, 1989), 56–57.

103 H.-D. Betz, *Galatians,* Hermeneia (Philadelphia: Fortress, 1989), 19–22; we have modified some of his labels.

104 Cf. D. F. Watson, "A Rhetorical Analysis of 2 John according to Greco-Roman Convention," *NTS* 35 (1989): 104–30; with id., "A Rhetorical Analysis of 3 John: A Study in Epistolary Rhetoric," *CBQ* 51 (1989): 479–501.

of the heretics who have seceded from the community. We, too, do well to know our audiences—when to praise and when to persuade. Faithful Christians do not need more sermons that tell them why they should do what they already know they ought to do. In an age of abundant motivation by guilt, we could do with a little more praise! Conversely, in evangelistic contexts and in an increasingly secularized, paganized, and postmodern world (or Church), we dare not assume that people comprehend or accept the logic and content of basic Christian beliefs or morals. We need to contend for them with carefully thought-out strategies.

Rhetorical analysis also demonstrates the unity of epistles previously thought to be composites. We have already observed this with Philippians and 2 Cor 1–7 above. A third example is Romans. Some scholars identify the long list of greetings in chap. 16 as a misplaced appendix, perhaps belonging instead at the end of the letter to the Ephesians. More plausibly, Paul concludes his Roman letter with epideictic rhetoric and the subgenre of an *ambassadorial letter*.[105] That is to say, Paul paves the way for an anticipated visit to Rome by commending his understanding of the gospel to the church there and by explaining the purposes of his travels. It is in his best interests to establish a good hearing for his message by referring to individuals in the Roman church with whom he is acquainted. As with Priscilla and Aquila, this probably took place when they had met or worked together elsewhere in the empire.

Distinctives of Hebrews and the "General Epistles"

Hebrews and three of the General Epistles—James, 1 John, and Jude—vary from traditional letter genres: Hebrews does not begin like a letter, James does not end like one, and 1 John has neither a salutation nor a closing. Hebrews describes itself as "a word of exhortation (or encouragement)" (Heb 13:22). Since this phrase occurs elsewhere in the NT only in Acts 13:15 where it designates a sermon, its author may well have designed Hebrews as a written sermon or homily. Among other things, this means that the numerous warnings against apostasy (2:1–4; 3:7–4:11; 6:4–12; 10:19–39; 12:14–29) are most likely not hypothetical. The writer of Hebrews seriously believed that some in his congregation were in danger of abandoning their profession of Christian faith, and he wanted to warn them against it.[106]

Perhaps the most significant study of the genre of a non-Pauline epistle is Peter Davids' analysis of James as a complex *chiasmus* (for this device, see above). Three themes stand out: trials and temptations, wisdom and speech, and wealth and poverty. Jas 1 introduces each of these themes twice, while chaps. 2–5 present them in greater detail in inverse order.[107] Even if this outline requires modification at points, it refutes two widely held notions about the letter. First, James is not simply a collection of teachings loosely strung together, like the book of Proverbs or other ancient wisdom literature. Second, James' main concern is not faith versus works (though that has been the primary preoccupation of commentators ever since Martin Luther). Though this concern is significant, James' indictment of a faith that produces no works (2:18–26) is

---

105 R. Jewett, "Romans as an Ambassadorial Letter," *Int* 36 (1982): 5–20.

106 On the genre and exegesis of Hebrews, see esp. W. L. Lane, *Hebrews*, WBC 47A & B (Dallas: Word, 1991).

107 P. H. Davids, *The Epistle of James*, NIGTC (Exeter: Paternoster; Grand Rapids: Eerdmans, 1982).

actually subordinate to the larger and more crucial topic: the appropriate use of one's material resources (see 2:14–17). Opponents of "lordship salvation" and promoters of "the American way of life" would do well to ponder at greater length the implications of 2:15–16 in the context of the rhetorical question of v. 14 (which anticipates the answer, no).[108]

First John neither begins nor ends like a letter. Out of several proposals, perhaps the best designates this document a *deliberative homily*.[109] Like Hebrews, it resembles a sermon more than a letter. Like other forms of deliberative rhetoric, it was designed to persuade. In this case, John calls the Ephesian churches to side with him and embrace true Christian doctrine and practice over against the false teachers who promoted heresy and ungodliness, and who had begun to split the church (2:19). If John had any outline in mind as he wrote, it has defied the best attempts of commentators to discover it. But perhaps he was composing instead a series of meditations around the themes of "the tests of life"—Jesus as fully human and fully divine, obedience to God's commandments, and love for one another—so that we should not try to impose more structure than was ever intended.[110]

Jude may well illustrate the more distinctively Jewish genre and interpretive techniques of *midrash* (see chapter 2),[111] though without introducing any fictitious details. Verses 3–4 state Jude's purpose in a nutshell: "I felt compelled to write and urge you to contend for the faith that the Lord has once for all entrusted to us, his people. For certain individuals whose condemnation was written about long ago have secretly slipped in among you" (TNIV). Verses 5–19 do not argue the case but merely present a series of illustrations of what this condemnation will be like. Here Jude draws heavily on Jewish Scripture and tradition. He likens the false teachers to three OT exemplars and then interprets these comparisons (vv. 5–10). Then he repeats the process with three more OT types (vv. 11–13). Turning to intertestamental sources, he cites and interprets the "prophecy" of 1 Enoch (vv. 14–16). Arriving finally at the NT age, Jude recalls and comments on the prophecies of the apostles (vv. 17–19). The effect was powerful, rhetorically, even if it seems troublesome to the modern reader. The harshness of Jude's polemic was actually mild by the standards of his day.

A fuller overview of recent proposals concerning the genres and rhetoric of various epistles could multiply our examples. The Eerdmans Socio-Rhetorical Commentary series develops these kinds of outlines in considerable detail.[112] Students should nevertheless proceed cautiously, because many of the proposals are quite recent and comparatively

---

108 According to James, those who profess to be Christians but continue to ignore fellow believers living in abject poverty around the world (to say nothing of the rest of the poor!), when they have the ability to share with them, prove thereby that their professions are vacuous. To James, such people are not saved and remain in danger of eternal damnation if they do not change their ways. On lordship salvation, cf. the brief but helpful study by J. F. MacArthur, Jr., "Faith according to the Apostle James," *JETS* 33 (1990): 13–34. On James and material possessions see esp. E. Tamez, *The Scandalous Message of James*, 2d ed. (New York: Crossroad, 2002).

109 Aune, *The New Testament in Its Literary Environment*, 218.

110 R. Law, *The Tests of Life* (Edinburgh: T. & T. Clark, 1909).

111 Bauckham *Jude, 2 Peter*, 3–6.

112 Most of which have been written by Ben Witherington, III (on Mark, Acts, 1 and 2 Corinthians and Galatians), but also by David DeSilva (on Hebrews).

untested. Several scholars have pointed out that one cannot automatically move from forms of oral speechmaking to written letters, and that we cannot be sure Paul and the other NT Epistle writers would have even known of all these forms.[113] Nevertheless, the letters were all originally written to be read aloud, and early Christian preachers like Chrysostom recognized some of these rhetorical forms in the NT.[114] So where there seems to be a particularly apt fit between form and contents, we may proceed with a given proposal with some confidence.

Individual Forms in the Epistles

Form criticism of the Epistles is not nearly as common as that of the Gospels. For the most part, NT letter writers did not rely on existent materials nor did they use self-contained forms. But important exceptions do occur. Perhaps the four most significant "forms" for a study of hermeneutics are creeds or hymns, domestic codes, slogans, and virtue and vice lists.

Creeds or Hymns

In several places in the Epistles, short, paragraph-length sections of a letter present key summaries of doctrine, usually of christology, in a fashion that resembles ancient poetry, hymnody, and confessions of faith. Scholars generally agree, therefore, that the epistle writers borrowed and/or modified units of material that were already well known and valued in the worship of the early Church. Commonly cited examples in Paul include Phil 2:6–11; Col 1:15–20; and 1 Tim 3:16. Peter perhaps used confessional forms in at least three instances: 1 Pet 1:18–21; 2:21–25; and 3:18–22. Criteria for recognizing these creeds include the presence of a carefully structured poetic style (rhythm and parallelism) that suddenly intrudes into ordinary prose; a self-contained unit of thought introduced with a relative pronoun as a rationale for various instructions; unusual language and vocabulary; and concise statements of doctrine listed sequentially.[115]

Of course, all this involves a substantial measure of speculation, but where proposals of hymns or creeds seem reasonable, several implications follow. We may discern information that reflects what the Church over a wide area deemed important in some of its earliest years. We may acknowledge liturgical aspects of early Christian worship, possibly including the discovery of baptismal liturgies.[116] And at times we may make educated guesses about distinctions between tradition and redaction. For example, Phil 2:6–11 falls relatively neatly into two stanzas that portray the condescension (vv. 6–8)

---

113 Cf. S. E. Porter, "The Theoretical Justification for Application of Rhetorical Categories to Pauline Epistolary Literature," in *Rhetoric and the New Testament*, ed. S. E. Porter and T. H. Olbricht (Sheffield: JSOT, 1993), 100–22; and J. A. D. Weima, "What Does Aristotle Have to do With Paul? An Evaluation of Rhetorical Criticism," *CTJ* 32 (1997): 458–68.

114 J. Fairweather, "The Epistle to the Galatians and Classical Rhetoric," *TynB* 45 (1994): 1–38, 213–43.

115 For an even more detailed list, see M. Barth, *Ephesians*, 2 vols., AB (Garden City: Doubleday, 1974), 1: 7–8.

116 A good introduction to the topic of pre-Pauline tradition in the Epistles appears in R. P. Martin, *New Testament Foundations*, 2 vols. (Exeter: Paternoster; Grand Rapids: Eerdmans, 1978), 2: 248–75. On pre-Petrine material, see especially J. N. D. Kelly, *The Epistles of Peter and Jude,* BNTC (London: A & C Black, 1969), 11–26, and ad loc. for passages cited.

and exaltation (vv. 9–11) of Jesus. Each of these in turn may subdivide into three strophes of three lines each, each line containing three stressed syllables. But one phrase breaks this symmetry: "even death on a cross" (end of v. 8). When we recognize that the cross occupied the center of Paul's preaching (1 Cor 2:2), it seems plausible that Paul incorporated into his letter a preexistent Christian hymn or creed to which he added one crucial line[117]—the line he wanted to stress.

The Domestic Code

Numerous ancient Jewish and Greco-Roman sources contain sections of instruction for individuals in a relationship of authority or submission. Often these instructions focused on relationships within the extended household: husbands and wives, parents and children, masters and slaves. Scholars thus refer to these materials as "domestic" or "household" codes, following Luther's use of the German term *Haustafeln*. Eph 5:22–6:9, Col 3:18–41, and 1 Pet 2:13–3:7 form three clear examples of this form. Probably the most significant discovery that emerges from a comparison of canonical and extra-canonical *Haustafeln* concerns the radical nature of the value the Christians placed on the subordinate partner in each relationship. Modern readers debate at great length to what extent Christian wives, children, slaves, and even citizens should still submit to those people and institutions traditionally seen as authorities over them. But few if any ancient readers would have concentrated on this. They took submission for granted but were probably shocked to read of the strict limitations imposed on the authority of husbands, parents, and masters. Perhaps if the Church today paid more attention to obeying these latter commands, the former ones would not seem so oppressive.[118]

Slogans

First Corinthians offers interpreters a relatively unique challenge. In this NT epistle Paul states that he is responding to a specific set of questions and controversies (posed both orally and in writing) from the church (1:11; 7:1). Hence, the outline of 1 Corinthians reads like a checklist of Paul's answers to these various problems: for example, on incest (5), lawsuits (6:1–11), sexual immorality more generally (6:12–20), marriage and divorce (7), and so on. In the process, Paul quotes views held by some at Corinth that he wishes to dispute. He can endorse these "slogans" up to a point but substantially qualifies them. We may refer to this as Paul's "yes-but" logic. In several instances these slogans are clear enough that recent NT translations employ quotation

---

117 E. Lohmeyer, *Kyrios Jesus: Eine Untersuchung zu Phil. 2,5–11* (Heidelberg: Winter, 1928). Numerous other analyses of Phil 2:6–11 caution against valuing this one too highly, but it still seems to us quite plausible. The most influential English language study of this passage, which agrees that the end of v. 8 is Paul's key addition to an existing hymn, is R. P. Martin, *A Hymn of Christ: Philippians 2:5–11 in Recent Interpretation and in the Setting of Early Christian Worship* (Downers Grove: InterVarsity, 1997).

118 On NT *Haustafeln,* see esp. D. Balch, *Let Wives Be Submissive: The Domestic Code in 1 Peter* (Chico, CA: Scholars, 1981); J. E. Crouch, *The Origin and Intention of the Colossian Haustafeln* (Göttingen: Vandenhoeck and Ruprecht, 1972); and E. Best, "The Haustafel in Ephesians," *IrishBS* 16 (1994): 146–60. For extensive bibliographies on this topic see id., *Ephesians*, ICC (Edinburgh: T. & T. Clark, 1998), 519–20; and W. W. Klein, *The Book of Ephesians: An Annotated Bibliography* (New York and London: Garland, 1996), 268–77.

marks (6:12; 6:13; and 10:23). Obviously, Paul himself could not have taught that "everything is permissible for me" (6:12) without substantial qualification!

In other instances we may not feel quite so confident, but the hypothesis of a Corinthian slogan remains probable. Given the likely influence of a quasi- or proto-Gnostic influence at Corinth, it is reasonable to interpret 8:1 with the NIV margin as "We all possess knowledge, 'as you say.'" Also 7:1 likely introduces a slogan, again as in the NIV margin: "It is good for a man not to have sexual relations with a woman."[119] Origen (ca. A.D. 200), for example, already considered this a slogan. In fact, all of chap. 7 falls into place once one recognizes that Paul is responding to an ascetic wing of the church that was overly zealous about celibacy. Paul's main point throughout, then, becomes: "Don't change your state in life or be too eager to preserve it just to avoid having sex." Notwithstanding various exceptions that he discusses, Paul tells the Corinthians that: married couples should not deprive each other of sex (vv. 2–7); widows and widowers should consider remaining unmarried only if they can do so without self-destructive lusting (vv. 8–9); divorce is not a legitimate way to avoid sex (vv. 10–16); and it is good for those who have never married to consider celibacy though marriage is not a sinful option (vv. 25–38). Personally, Paul clearly prefers celibacy, but he also recognizes that God has gifted only a limited number of believers for this lifestyle. So he acknowledges some validity to the pro-celibacy advocates in Corinth but substantially qualifies their enthusiasm. The "occasional" setting of 1 Corinthians accounts for Paul's tone and emphases, and helps readers to understand better how the same apostle could sound so enthusiastic about marriage in Ephesians (5:25–33), a letter, interestingly, that was likely intended for a much wider audience.[120]

These various Corinthian slogans share several common features: they are short and concisely worded (as slogans typically are); they reflect views with which Paul can agree in part, but which prove significantly misleading if interpreted without qualification; and they represent a common perspective found in the form of ancient Greek philosophy that eventually developed into Gnosticism. Recognition of these common features may enable interpreters to evaluate other proposals for slogans in 1 Corinthians. One of the most popular in recent decades, though apparently never seriously advocated before the last century, involves 14:33b–35. Proponents of this view understand Paul's comments about women being silent and in submission as another aberrant Corinthian view, which vv. 36–38 then reject. But vv. 33b–35 satisfy none of the criteria just noted. They are not concise or proverbial. If vv. 36–38 form Paul's response, then he does not endorse vv. 33b–35 even in part. And the perspective attributed to the Corinthians would be the opposite of the more egalitarian thrust of proto-Gnosticism. Numerous other options may account for vv. 33b–35, including some that support a modern egalitarian agenda, but the proposal that these verses form a slogan is one of the least likely of all.[121]

---

119 Again TNIV, NRSV, ESV, and HCSB all now put these statements in quotation marks.

120 This assessment of 1 Cor 7 and of slogans elsewhere in the epistle is heavily indebted to G. D. Fee, *The First Epistle to the Corinthians*, NICNT (Grand Rapids: Eerdmans, 1987), 266–357.

121 In our opinion the most convincing exegesis is that of Thiselton, *The First Epistle to the Corinthians*, 1150–61.

Vice and Virtue Lists

A final example of common forms within the NT Epistles consists of lists of qualities or actions that typify morality or immorality from a Christian perspective. Jews and pagans often compiled similar lists. Examples from the NT include Rom 1:29–31; 1 Cor 6:9–10; Gal 5:19–23; Jas 3:17–18; and 2 Pet 1:5–7. Comparison with extrabiblical parallels again reveals the NT distinctives as well as one or two principles of hermeneutics. For example, the ancient Greek world regularly condoned homosexual acts. Paul's uniform condemnation of them (cf. Rom 1:24–32; 1 Cor 6:9; 1 Tim 1:10) would have stood out and caused offense then as it does increasingly today. But faithfulness to the gospel requires that these sins be labeled as such in any age. First and last items on a list often prove the most important, but the subsequent order of items probably indicates no particular hierarchy.[122] So we should probably take "love" as the preeminent fruit of the Spirit and the highest goal of the life of faith (Gal 5:22; 2 Pet 1:7; cf. 1 Cor 13) and recognize that "wisdom" must be morally pure above all else (Jas 3:17).

Key Theological Issues for the Pauline Epistles

As noted above, when an author writes as many different books over a period of time as did Paul, distinctive theological questions arise. The two most pressing are: (1) Is there a unifying center of Pauline theology? and (2) Does Paul's theology "develop" from one period of time to another so that he changes his mind on any significant issue(s)?

The Center of Pauline Theology

Because of Luther's influence, most Protestants assumed that Paul's foremost concern was to stress "justification by faith" over all forms of "works-righteousness." Over time, however, certain planks in Luther's platform eroded. For example, there is no evidence that Paul struggled as a Jew with a guilty conscience, increasingly more frustrated with his inability to please God through good works. Quite the contrary, he thought that he was "blameless" under the Law (Phil 3:6 NRSV) and "advancing in Judaism beyond many" of his age (Gal 1:14).[123] The debate over Rom 7:14–25 continues to rage, but one conclusion seems clear: Paul does not there describe a personal battle he waged before his conversion. Either this details his post-conversion perception of what had previously occurred, or more likely, describes the struggle between his old and new natures that he continued to experience as a Christian.

Luther's "center," however, generally held firm though an occasional voice would propose a different, though often complementary, unifying theme (reconciliation or being "in Christ").[124] Sometimes a scholar or two would question whether Paul's theology was even consistent enough to have a unifying center.[125] But largely through the writings of E. P. Sanders and his followers since 1977, a quite new look on Pauline theology

---

122 Bauckham, *Jude, 2 Peter*, 172–93.

123 See esp. K. Stendahl, "The Apostle Paul and the Introspective Conscience of the West," *HTR* 56 (1963): 199–215.

124 Cf., respectively, R. P. Martin, *Reconciliation: A Study of Paul's Theology* (Atlanta: Knox, 1981); and W. D. Davies, *Paul and Rabbinic Judaism,* 4th ed. (Philadelphia: Fortress, 1980), 221–22.

125 E.g., H. Lüdemann, *Die Anthropologie des Apostels Paulus und ihre Stellung innerhalb seiner Heilslehre* (Kiel: Universitäts Buchhandlung, 1872). Among current scholars, see esp. H. Räisänen, *Paul and the Law* (Philadelphia: Fortress, 1986).

has taken center stage.[126] Many scholars today contend that "merit theology" or works-righteousness did not characterize first-century Judaism, so that Paul's main contrast with Judaism cannot be faith (or grace) versus works. Rather, Jews believed in "covenantal nomism." That is, obeying the Law saved no one, but obedience kept one within the exclusive covenant community God had established with Israel. Accordingly, Paul's radical challenge to Judaism was his (to the Jews) radical universalism: the message that one could come to God in Christ apart from the Torah. In this view, Paul's complaint with Jewish practices such as circumcision, the dietary laws, or the Sabbath ordinances was that most Jews had turned them into "badges" of national pride and identity. They were not trying to save themselves by performing these rituals. In this view the incorporation of Gentiles into the Church on equal terms with Jews thus replaces "justification by faith" as a unifying core of Paul's thought.

Obviously, the way one interprets much of what Paul wrote will depend on how one assesses this kind of debate over his theological center. For example, the two most recent commentaries in English on the Greek text of Romans by J. D. G. Dunn and T. R. Schreiner consistently come to quite different conclusions: Schreiner goes with the older consensus, while Dunn enthusiastically advocates the "new look."[127] Probably the truth lies somewhere between the two.[128] We introduce the debate here primarily to remind interpreters again that much depends on the theological grids they presuppose when they approach a text. While we have made this point more generally elsewhere, it is acute for the epistles of Paul, since nowhere else in Scripture do so many different documents come from the same writer. If a minor point of one document develops into a major point for all, or vice-versa, interpretation will be skewed.

Is There Development in Paul's Writings?

The proliferation of Pauline epistles leads to the second theological problem. Did Paul ever change his mind or "progress" in understanding on a particular issue? Evangelicals have typically rejected this idea where it implied contradiction within the NT even while regularly appealing to "progressive revelation" to account for God's clear policy changes between the old and new covenants. But what of Paul's harsh words against Peter and the Judaizers in Gal 2:11–21 when compared with his policy of bending over backwards to be "all things to all people" in 1 Cor 9:19–23 (NRSV)? And doesn't he believe in 1 Thes 4:13–18 that he will live to see Christ's return, whereas later he recognizes he might die first (2 Cor 1:8–11)?

One cannot exclude the possibility of development in Paul simply by an appeal to a high view of Scripture. Not only does revelation progress between the Testaments, but a prophet of the Lord may reverse his message completely in a matter of minutes based on a new word from God (cf., e.g., 2 Kgs 20:1–6). But having said this, we believe the case for development in Paul remains unproven. In each case better explanations account for the data than do hypotheses of development. For example, Gal 2 and 1 Cor 9 differ because at

---

126 See esp. E. P. Sanders, *Paul and Palestinian Judaism* (Philadelphia: Fortress, 1977). For a brief treatment of subsequent developments, see N. T. Wright, *What Saint Paul Really Said* (Grand Rapids: Eerdmans, 1997).

127 J. D. G. Dunn, *Romans,* WBC 38A & B (Waco: Word, 1988); and T. R. Schreiner, *Romans,* BECNT (Grand Rapids: Baker, 1998).

128 D. A. Carson, P. T. O'Brien, and M. A. Seifrid, eds., *Justification and Variegated Nomism,* 2 vols. (Tübingen: Mohr; Grand Rapids: Baker, 2001–).

Galatia the eternal lives of Paul's hearers were at stake. Any attempt to earn salvation through works only damns a person, so Paul resists the idea adamantly. To the Corinthians, however, he talks about morally neutral practices that establish common ground in order to win the gospel a good hearing. Actually, a unity underlies the two passages: Paul will do whatever it takes, without being immoral or unethical, to bring people to saving faith through the grace of Jesus Christ. In the case of 1 Thes 4 and 2 Cor 1, interpreters have probably misunderstood Paul's earlier comments. The "we" of 1 Thes 4:15 does not necessarily include Paul. Grammatically, the phrase "we who are still alive, who are left till the coming of the Lord" may simply mean, "whichever Christians are still alive."[129]

On the other hand, one may fairly speak of a development in Paul between 1 and 2 Thessalonians. In 1 Thes 4:13–5:11 Paul warns the Thessalonians against fearing that Christ's return would be overly delayed. In 2 Thes 2:1–12 he cautions them not to think that it has already taken place. Quite possibly, 2:2 indicates that they had overreacted to his first letter.[130] But no contradiction divides these two epistles; he simply affirms that one must maintain a crucial balance between assuming the Second Coming is too near or that it is too distant. We must evaluate each proposal concerning "development" in Paul, therefore, on its own merits. Can we articulate the alleged development without it resulting in a necessary contradiction in Paul's thought? Does it fit the best interpretation of each of the key texts involved? Does it make best sense of the historical contexts in which the various documents were written? Only after we answer these questions can we make confident pronouncements.

THE GENRE OF REVELATION

Even the great Reformer, John Calvin, admitted his uncertainty about what to do with the book of Revelation. He did not write a commentary on it even though he completed volumes on almost all the rest of the NT. Interpreters through the ages have shared Calvin's perplexity, and many of the writers of popular commentaries and guides to its prophecies might have done better to follow in his footsteps! Still, genre criticism can help the careful student sift the more likely from the less likely interpretations among the maze of opinions that compete for attention. Perhaps the most important key is to recognize that Revelation combines parts of three distinct genres: epistle, prophecy, and apocalyptic.[131]

Revelation as an Epistle

Revelation 1:4 states clearly that the author wrote this book to seven churches in Asia Minor. Chaps. 2–3 contain seven mini-letters with commendation and/or condemnation for each church. Thus, Revelation includes various characteristics of Epistles. For example, interpreters will need to try to reconstruct as accurately as possible the historical circumstances of each church.[132] Most of the details of the letters to the seven churches

---

129 On the issue of development as well as on other major hermeneutical issues for Paul's writings, see esp. T. R. Schreiner, *Interpreting the Pauline Epistles* (Grand Rapids: Baker, 1990).

130 I. H. Marshall, *1 and 2 Thessalonians,* NCB (Grand Rapids: Eerdmans, 1983), 24, 187.

131 On which, see esp. D. E. Aune, *Revelation 1–5,* WBC 52A (Dallas: Word, 1997), lxx–xc.

132 The two best resources for this enterprise, the first a classic and the second an important modern update, are W. M. Ramsay, *The Letters to the Seven Churches of Asia* (London: Hodder and Stoughton, 1904); and C. J. Hemer, *The Letters to the Seven Churches of Asia in their Local Setting,* JSNTSup 11 (Sheffield: JSOT, 1986; Grand Rapids: Eerdmans, 2000). On a more popular level see J. R. Michaels, *Interpreting the Book of Revelation* (Grand Rapids: Baker, 1992), 35–50.

make better sense when read against this background. For example, ancient Laodicea was well-known for its material wealth, the medicinal ointment it produced, and its woolen industry. But the pathetic state of its church led John to encourage believers there to purchase spiritual wealth, "white clothes to wear . . . and salve to put on your eyes, so you can see" (3:18). As was mentioned briefly in an earlier chapter, archaeology has shed light on the water supply of Laodicea. The city depended on water that came through aqueducts from either the cold mountain streams near Colossae or the natural hot springs near Hierapolis. Either way, the water was notorious for being disgustingly lukewarm by the time it arrived in town. So John calls the church there not to resemble its water supply but to be either refreshingly cold or therapeutically hot. The common view that "cold" here means "clearly opposed to the gospel" or "completely insensitive" is almost certainly the exact opposite of what John meant![133]

Sometimes we are not able to determine the original meaning of John's allusions so easily. The white stone of 2:17 might have been an admission ticket, a jury's vote of "not guilty," or an amulet with a divine name. "Satan's throne" in Pergamum (2:13 NRSV) might have referred to a temple of the Greek god Zeus, or to the imperial center for emperor worship, or to the shrine of Asklepios, the Greek god of healing. But in both instances the general sense of something highly desirable or undesirable is clear enough.

Studying Revelation as an epistle written to identifiable believers under specific circumstances is also appropriate for material outside chapters 2 and 3. Primarily, the book purposes to encourage Christians undergoing persecution, *not* to confuse or divide its readers over fine points of eschatology. In fact, many of John's visions of the future called to mind contemporary events in the Roman Empire near the end of the first century. The judgment of the third seal in 6:6 closely resembles the famine of A.D. 92. A day's supply of wheat and barley became so scarce as to consume an entire day's wage. But the olive trees and grapevines, whose roots grew deeper, were not as affected by the relatively short-lived drought. So it seems that God wanted the readers of Revelation to envision the coming judgment as similar to the famine they had recently experienced.[134]

Or again in 9:7–11, the bizarre description of the locusts of the fifth trumpet probably called to mind the distinctive appearance of the Parthian hordes that periodically attacked Rome in its northeastern-most outposts. Unlike the Romans, the Parthians relied heavily on a

> corps of mounted archers, whose tactics were to shoot one volley as they charged and another over their horses "tails". There was therefore some factual basis for John's surrealist pictures of "horses able to wound with their mouths and their tails."[135]

---

133 Cf. further M. J. S. Rudwick and E. M. B. Green, "The Laodicean Lukewarmness," *ExpT* 69 (1957–58): 176–78.

134 Cf. G. E. Ladd, *A Commentary on the Revelation of John* (Grand Rapids: Eerdmans, 1972), 101: "these words place a limitation on the degree of scarcity."

135 G. B. Caird, *The Revelation of St. John the Divine*, BNTC (London: Black; New York: Harper & Row, 1966), 122.

Just as the Parthians offered the severest threat known in first-century times to the seeming invincibility of the Roman empire, so Satan's endtime armies will prepare for the greatest battle ever conceived in human history (though chap. 19 describes how this "battle" ends before it is scarcely begun!).

Interpreting Revelation in light of the events of its day should caution overly zealous interpreters against looking for detailed correspondence between the events predicted and contemporary news items in the twenty-first (or any other) century. Many items familiar to first-century audiences contribute to the overall imagery without necessarily corresponding to any specific "endtimes" referent. Christian scholars generally agree that the writers of the popular endtime paperbacks in the local Christian bookstore have missed the message! A perennially best-selling work of nonfiction, Christian or otherwise, in the United States has been Hal Lindsey's *The Late Great Planet Earth*, yet over and over again he violates fundamental hermeneutical principles.[136] He asserts that in Rev 9:7–11 John was describing armed helicopters and their tailgunners! Now to be sure, Lindsey draws some striking parallels between John's locusts and modern-day flying machines, but in so doing he ignores the meaning that would have occurred to John's original readers in favor of one that could never have been imagined until a few decades ago. This violates the most basic principle of hermeneutics: seek the meaning of the text. What is more, his interpretation unwittingly "demythologizes" the text. Instead of depicting supernatural, demonic creatures coming out of the Abyss (vv. 2–3) ruled by Satan their king (v. 11), Lindsey reduces John's vision to one about mere human warfare.

Lindsey and many others would avoid such errors by observing a basic rule of hermeneutics that interpreters are prone to abandon when studying Revelation: *the text cannot mean something that would have been completely incomprehensible to its original audience*.[137] Nor may an interpreter appeal to Dan 12:9 in support of a different view. True, Daniel did not understand everything he prophesied (v. 8), and God did reply through an angel, "the words are closed up and sealed until the time of the end." But we must register three crucial observations. First, the only thing Daniel did not explicitly understand was "the outcome of all this" (v. 8). He did not ask for an explanation of what he had been told, but for further information about what had not been revealed. Second, concerning what had been revealed, he was told only that "none of the wicked will understand," but "those who are wise [i.e., not wicked] will understand" (v. 10). Third, Revelation differs from Daniel in that, as the completion of new covenant revelation, God brings his plan of salvation-history to the threshold of the end. All stands ready for Christ to return. So John is told exactly the opposite from what Daniel was instructed: "Do not seal up the words of the prophecy of this book, because the time is near" (Rev 22:10).

Revelation as Prophecy

Frederick Mazzaferri has shown how the closest generic parallels to Revelation appear in Isaiah, Jeremiah, and particularly Ezekiel. John stands in the tradition of the

---

136 (Grand Rapids: Zondervan, 1970). A similar approach is now popularized by the extraordinarily best selling *Left Behind* novels by T. LaHaye and J. Jenkins. For a powerful critique of this approach, see C. Hill, *In God's Time: The Bible and the Future* (Grand Rapids: Eerdmans, 2002).

137 Fee and Stuart (*How to Read*, 235) put it this way: "The primary meaning of the Revelation is what John intended it to mean, which in turn must also have been something his readers could have understood it to mean."

major prophets of the OT—foretelling as well as forthtelling.[138] Scholars have long debated four major interpretations of the time-orientation of Revelation. The *preterist* approach sees all events through chap. 19 as past; the *futurist,* as all still future (at least from chap. 6 on); the *historicist,* as tracing the development of the entire church age; and the *idealist,* as a symbolic presentation of the timeless struggle between good and evil.[139] When Revelation, with its liberal dose of symbolism appearing throughout, is viewed as similar to OT prophecy, a combination of preterist and futurist interpretations emerges as best. The climactic manifestation of the events that usher in Christ's return (chaps. 6–19) remains yet future, but the events will nevertheless resemble (even if on a larger scale) the victories and judgments that God's people and the world have experienced many times since creation. John's words proclaimed a message of comfort and urged his first-century readers to endure hardship (preterist). His prophecy also shows how God's people will need to persevere throughout this age as God brings it to its climactic end (futurist).

Not surprisingly, then, the seven seals closely resemble the signs that Jesus said must occur even though "the end is not yet" (Mt 24:6 NRSV): warfare, murder, famine, and earthquakes—disasters that have afflicted people through most ages of human history. The seven trumpets and bowls call to mind the plagues of God against the Egyptians in Moses' day (hail and fire, water turning to blood, darkness, and sores or boils on people; cf. Exod 7–11). Clearly, God is more concerned to warn his people with imagery familiar to them than with literal photographs of what everything will look like. So we cannot be certain how these prophecies of judgment will be fulfilled. But as prophecy they point to real events at the end of the church age that have not yet occurred. *The prophecies predict literal events, though the descriptions do not portray the events literally.*

Thus, we may not know exactly who the two witnesses of 11:3–6 are, but we know that God's Word will continue to be proclaimed with great power in the last days. If we should happen to be living in the final generation, this should encourage us to continue witnessing boldly for Christ. Again, we probably should not waste too much time trying to guess what great world figure or empire will play the role of the beast of 13:1–4. Numerous guesses have littered the pages of church history, and all of them so far have proved wrong.[140] But in the end we can expect some ruler and/or government to usurp the prerogatives of God and persecute his people, even as others have so many times throughout history.

If Revelation is prophecy, then only an antisupernatural bias will permit one to agree with Adela Yarbro Collins when she writes, "A hermeneutic which takes historical criticism seriously can no longer work with an interventionist notion of God."[141] In

---

138 F. D. Mazzaferri, *The Genre of the Book of Revelation from a Source-Critical Perspective* (Berlin: de Gruyter, 1989).

139 For further delineations of these various options see the introductions to most standard commentaries on the Apocalypse. Some of the best include: R. Mounce, *The Book of Revelation,* 2d ed., NICNT (Grand Rapids: Eerdmans, 1998); C. S. Keener, *Revelation,* NIVAC (Grand Rapids: Zondervan, 2000); and S. Kistemaker, *Exposition of the Book of Revelation,* NTC (Grand Rapids: Baker, 2001).

140 See the fascinating survey in B. McGinn, *Anti-Christ* (San Francisco: HarperSanFrancisco, 1994).

141 A. Y. Collins, "Reading the Book of Revelation in the Twentieth Century," *Int* 40 (1986): 242.

other words, she believes that modern readers cannot seriously expect the world to end with God's supernatural intervention by means of the various plagues and the tribulation described in Revelation. Certainly, we do not expect the universally visible and bodily return of Jesus Christ from heaven, she says. Yet an understanding of Revelation as prophecy must affirm precisely this, however much different schools of interpretation disagree concerning other details (most notably concerning the millennium and the rapture).[142]

Revelation as Apocalyptic

Probably the most significant of the three genres in Revelation is the last one. The title of the book, derived from its first line, designates the document as the *apokalypsis*: "the *revelation* of Jesus Christ, which God gave him to show his servants what must soon take place" (1:1, italics ours). Apocalyptic literature was prevalent in the world of the NT (cf. the earlier discussion of OT apocalyptic). Contemporary Jewish writings like 4 Ezra and 2 Baruch, and to a lesser extent 1 Enoch, exemplified this genre. Dan 7–12 and Zech 9–14 provide the closest OT parallels. Later Christian writings like the Apocalypse of John the Theologian and the Apocalypse of Peter offer still further illustrations.[143]

Characteristics of apocalyptic literature include a description of the events surrounding the end of world history, often said to have come from God by means of angelic or otherworldly intermediaries. Visions and dreams appear regularly. God's supernatural intervention into this age at the end of time rescues a sinful world in a way that no human ideology or schemes can accomplish. Elaborate and sometimes bizarre symbolism depicts past, present, and future events in a way that requires a careful decoding of the elements of the text. Battles between the forces of good and evil often appear with the good eventually triumphing. One of the primary purposes of apocalypses, therefore, is to encourage a beleaguered religious community in times of oppression or persecution.

More formal definitions of apocalypses are not easy to agree on. One widely endorsed definition that is more technical comes from John Collins in conjunction with a "working group" of scholars from the Society of Biblical Literature:

> "Apocalypse" is a genre of revelatory literature with a narrative framework in which a revelation is mediated by an other worldly being to

---

142 The fullest recent survey of issues surrounding apocalyptic literature is J. J. Collins, ed., *The Encyclopedia of Apocalypticism*, 3 vols. (New York: Continuum, 1998). Two symposia helpfully lay out the major perspectives and give each contributor a chance to respond to each other. *The Meaning of the Millennium: Four Views*, ed. R. G. Clouse (Downers Grove: InterVarsity, 1977), presents advocates for *postmillennialism* (Christ returns after the 1000 years described in Rev 20:4), *amillennialism* (the millennium is symbolic for either the whole church age or the new heavens and earth of chaps. 21–22), and *premillennialism* (Christ returns before the millennium)—which then subdivides into *historic* and *dispensational* forms. In *The Rapture and the Tribulation: Pre-, Mid-, or Post- Tribulational?* (Grand Rapids: Zondervan, 1984), R. Reiter, P. D. Feinberg, G. L. Archer, and D. J. Moo debate whether Christians alive just prior to Christ's return are bodily removed (or "raptured") from the earth before, during, or after the judgments of God described in chaps. 6 (7)–16.

143 Good studies of apocalyptic literature include D. Hellholm, ed., *Apocalypticism in the Mediterranean World and the Near East* (Tübingen: Mohr, 1983); and C. Rowland, *The Open Heaven* (New York: Crossroad, 1982). The fullest collection of texts is J. H. Charlesworth, ed., *Old Testament Pseudepigrapha*, vol. 1 (Garden City: Doubleday, 1983).

> a human recipient, disclosing a transcendent reality which is both temporal insofar as it envisages eschatological salvation, and spatial insofar as it involves another, supernatural world.[144]

On the other hand, Leon Morris nicely summarizes eight key *differences* between Revelation and typical apocalypses:

1. regular references to the book as prophecy;
2. typically prophetic warnings and calls for repentance;
3. lack of pseudonymity;
4. an optimistic worldview;
5. no retracing of past history in the guise of prophecy;
6. realized eschatology (the end times have begun with the First Coming of Christ);
7. little interpretation by angels; and
8. belief that the Messiah has already come and made atonement.[145]

In large measure we may account for these differences by distinctives of Christian rather than Jewish theology and by the fact that Revelation is prophetic as well as apocalyptic.

To the extent that Revelation shares features of other apocalypses, however, several important interpretive implications follow.[146] Most importantly, we must recognize that Revelation employs highly symbolic and figurative imagery that we dare not interpret too literally. Virtually every reader recognizes this in the most obvious instances: as when John specifically explains that the seven stars are angels (or messengers) and that the seven lampstands are churches (1:20); that the bowls of incense are the prayers of the saints (5:8); that the dragon is the devil (12:9); that ten horns are ten kings (17:12); and that the great prostitute is a city that rules over the kings of the earth (17:18). Symbols are a stock in trade of the genre.

But it is amazing how often those same readers do not recognize that they should interpret the other images in the book as equally symbolic. Instead, many insist that references to a temple (e.g., 11:1) must refer to a literal, rebuilt temple in Jerusalem, that the battle of Armageddon (Hebrew for Mt. Megiddo, 16:16) must occur at that specific geographical site in northern Israel, or that the mark of the beast (13:16–17) has to be some actual visible sign that distinguishes unbelievers from believers.[147]

A far more legitimate approach is to study each scene and each image in light of what Revelation itself tells about them, in light of relevant OT backgrounds, and in view of other historical information of which John's first-century audience would have been aware. Knowing that John pictures the churches as lampstands (1:20) and understanding the

---

144 J. J. Collins, "Introduction: Morphology of a Genre," *Semeia* 14 (1979): 9. More recently, cf. his *The Apocalyptic Imagination: An Introduction to Jewish Apocalyptic Literature*, 2d ed. (Grand Rapids: Eerdmans, 1998), 5.

145 L. Morris, *The Book of Revelation*, TNTC, 2d ed. (Leicester: InterVarsity; Grand Rapids: Eerdmans, 1987), 25–27.

146 Perhaps the best introductory guide for interpreting Revelation is B. M. Metzger, *Breaking the Code: Understanding the Book of Revelation* (Nashville: Abingdon, 1993).

147 A good list of symbols explained by Revelation, by the OT, or left unexplained, appears in M. C. Tenney, *Interpreting Revelation* (Grand Rapids: Eerdmans, 1957), 186–93.

background of olive trees in such OT texts as Psa 52:8; Jer 11:16, and Zech 4:3, 11, provide the modern reader clues for how to understand the two witnesses in Rev 11:1–13—who are "the two olive trees and the two lampstands" (11:4). Perhaps they are not individuals at all, but the witnessing Church. Deciphering the imagery of Revelation then becomes much like interpreting an editorial cartoon in a newspaper. A reader of an American paper in 1989, for example, who saw a picture of a large bear extending an olive branch in his paw to a bald eagle, would recognize the portrait of Russian overtures of peace to the United States. Similarly, we may see the woman who flies to the desert to escape the attacks of the serpent (who is also a dragon making war on her offspring) as the Church being protected by God even as individual believers are persecuted and sometimes martyred by Satan and those on earth who serve him (12:13–17).

It is crucial, therefore, to discover the symbolic elements of Revelation and seek to determine what they stand for. We suggest no shortcuts or simplistic answers. Interpreters must become familiar with the relevant historical background and the most likely theological significance of various details. As with parables, certain parts of an apocalyptic vision may function only to add life, color, or drama to the picture. Here, if ever, students must consult a representative sampling of the better commentaries on Revelation, and, where these disagree, students must try to decide which approach is most self-consistent and most likely to have made sense to John's original audience.[148] The more time the student spends reading apocalyptic, the more confidence he or she will gain in the process. Though we give only a small sampling of illustrations here, we hope they will clarify the proper procedures.

One image for which OT background is helpful is the bittersweet scroll of 10:9–11, which closely resembles the scroll Ezekiel was commanded to eat (Ezek 2:9–3:9). There it clearly referred to the message of both judgment and hope that God commanded his prophet to speak to his people. This fits perfectly in Revelation as well.

Or consider those who had been redeemed from the earth "who did not defile themselves with women" (14:4). At best this sounds like the comment of someone who does not believe in sex; at worst like the comment of a misogynist (woman-hater). Actually the OT brims with imagery of sexual faithfulness and faithlessness as symbols of spiritual loyalty or idolatry (e.g., Jer 5:7; Ezek 16:32; Hos 2:4). Thus, we see John figuratively referring to those who remained spiritually pure.

A final, more controversial example involves the three and one-half years (alternately referred to as forty-two months or 1260 days) of great tribulation (Rev 11:2; 12:6, 14; 13:5). This figure seems to come straight out of the book of Daniel where it refers to the period between the end of sacrifice and desolation of God's temple and the end of the age (9:27; cf. 12:7 and 12:11–12, where the number of days is slightly augmented). In view of Jesus' use of this imagery in Mt 24:15–31, the "tribulation" may well have begun with the destruction of the temple in A.D. 70. If so, it refers to virtually the entire church age.[149] Alternately, it may refer to a still future event that will

---

148 To those mentioned in previous footnotes we add esp. G. K. Beale, *The Book of Revelation* NIGNT (Carlisle: Paternoster; Grand Rapids: Eerdmans, 1999); and G. R. Osborne, *Revelation,* BECNT (Grand Rapids: Baker, 2002). Incisive popular-level exposition appears in E. H. Peterson, *Reversed Thunder: The Revelation of John and the Praying Imagination* (San Francisco: Harper and Row, 1988).

149 Carson, "Matthew," *Expositor's Bible Commentary,* 8:499–505.

bring on the last and most horrible events before Christ returns. Most important either way, three and one-half is half of seven—the sacred, perfect, and complete number throughout Scripture (harking back to the seven days of creation). Merely three and one-half—the period of tribulation years—it is not perfect or good. It is not God's final word, but only an imperfect, incomplete parody of the perfection to come. Whether or not it spans a *literal* three and one-half year period is impossible to determine. And of course if the period refers to the entire church age, then it is much longer!

This last example brings up the complex topic of numerical symbolism in Revelation. Seven, twelve, and 1000, and other numbers related to them, play a prominent role in the book. The famous 144,000 of 7:4 and 14:1 offers a classic example. One hundred and forty-four thousand is 12 times 12 times 1,000—the number of the tribes of Israel raised to the second power (or times the number of apostles; cf. 21:12, 14) and multiplied by a large round number. So this great company of the redeemed may in fact picture the Church as the fulfillment of the promises to Israel in a grand and glorious way. The notorious 666—the number of the beast (13:18)—may well be significant because each digit is one less than seven. Seven hundred and seventy-seven would be a perfect number fit for Christ, which 666 tries hard to imitate but falls notably short at every point. This makes a crucial point: each member of the "Satanic Trinity" of chaps. 12–14 (the dragon and the two beasts) parodies but falls short of duplicating the characteristics of his counterpart in the "Holy Trinity" (e.g., by mimicking the crucifixion [13:3] or working signs and wonders [13:13]).[150]

In other cases, numbers function merely to indicate short or long units of measurement. One thousand years is a long and wonderful "golden age" (20:4). The armies of 200,000,000 (literally two myriads of myriads, with a myriad as 10,000 equaling the largest named number in the Greek language) comprise the largest conceivable gathering of people in John's day (9:16). And the five-month plague of the demonic "locusts" (9:5) amounts to a relatively limited time (also equivalent to the life cycle of the insect).

Even given all these guidelines, interpreters will still no doubt diverge greatly. So, the most crucial axiom is this: determine the major theological principles of Revelation and avoid getting bogged down in the details. Arguably, chaps. 4–5 form the doctrinal center of the book, and they prove easiest to interpret: hymns of praise and adoration to God and Christ in view of the splendors of heaven; the atonement won for humanity by Jesus; and the promises of God's sovereignty and triumph mediated to his people in spite of the horrors of the end. In fact, the whole book exudes teaching on all the major doctrines of the Christian faith, not just eschatology. Interpreters must watch for these and highlight them. Even with respect to eschatology, we may agree to disagree on many details and still affirm the reality of Christ's future, visible, and universal return to judge all humanity, and to assign to people one of the only two possible destinies awaiting them: the unspeakable agony of eternal punishment or the indescribable glory of eternal life, based on their acceptance or rejection of Jesus.[151] Above all, if we learn the lessons of Mt 24:36 and Acts 1:6–8 and stop trying to guess if we are living in the final generation or how the latest news might fit in with this or that verse, then

---

150 See, respectively, Mounce, *Revelation*, 158; G. R. Beasley-Murray, *The Book of Revelation*, NCB (London: Oliphants, 1974), 220.

151 A salutary example of this unity within interpretive diversity is S. Gregg, ed., *Revelation: Four Views—A Parallel Commentary* (Nashville: Nelson, 1997).

we can focus on the grand theological themes of the book and be encouraged about God's sovereignty, love, and justice even during our hardest times.[152]

CONCLUSION

When interpreting NT passages, then, readers must always take into account whether they are reading a Gospel, the Acts, an epistle, or the book of Revelation. Each of these genres in turn contains various forms or subgenres. While the principles discussed in earlier chapters ("general hermeneutics") apply to all of Scripture, each genre or form has unique features that interpreters need to take into account as well. We cannot treat parables in exactly the same way as pronouncement stories. Teaching in Acts is often more indirect than in the Epistles, and apocalyptic differs from straightforward historical narrative. Our discussion has not been exhaustive, merely illustrative. But we have set the stage for an appreciation of the multiple dimensions of Scripture that will help us understand its meaning.

---

152 Particularly helpful with respect to major themes are G. Goldsworthy, *The Gospel of Revelation* (Exeter: Paternoster, 1984); and R. Bauckham, *The Theology of the Book of Revelation* (Cambridge: Cambridge University Press, 1993).

PART V—THE FRUITS OF INTERPRETATION

11

USING THE BIBLE TODAY

Does the Bible have a legitimate function in this modern scientific (and increasingly postmodern) world? Can this ancient book speak in any relevant way to the issues of life in today's diverse settings? We answer, yes and yes, especially if we employ it according to the principles of sound and accurate biblical interpretation. God's message is timeless and consistently relevant as we understand it correctly. The Bible has a message that we need to know, a message that will transform our lives—and the world. But we cannot comprehend the message as fully without the proper tools of interpretation.

Therefore, we reiterate our claim in the initial pages of this book: when we interpret the Bible according to good hermeneutical principles, we will derive maximum benefit from our reading of the Bible. And in light of all the principles of interpretation we have offered, we hope readers will feel that in using these principles—these tools—they will be more likely to "get out" of the Bible what God and his spokespersons "put in" it.

But hermeneutics is not an end in itself. Having studied the principles of interpretation, the student might ask, "Is there a reason for understanding the Bible beyond the acquisition of knowledge? Is it worth going to all this effort?" Again we answer, yes and yes. The Scriptures constitute God's revelation to his people—his very Word in written form. So as God's people we eagerly strive to understand and respond to his message. It is a message to be used—to encourage, to motivate, to guide, and to instruct. If we know how to decipher the message, we will be able to understand it and to use it. Therefore, in the following pages we will consider some of the ways that Christians use the Bible.[1] Then in the succeeding chapter we present principles to guide us in applying the Bible's message to our lives.

TO GAIN INFORMATION AND UNDERSTANDING

As the foundational document of the Christian faith, the Bible functions as the primary source of data or information. Christians believe that the Bible is God's written

---

1 Certainly many people other than Christian believers read or study the Bible. Scholars in fields such as sociology, ancient history, or archaeology—to name a few—study it in a variety of ways. Literary critics explore the Bible as literature. Others may read it out of curiosity, or even antagonistically, in an attempt to refute its claims. We acknowledge, of course, that some of what we say will apply to Jews and their use of the Tanakh (Hebrew Bible)—what Christians call the Old Testament. Nevertheless, we focus in what follows on those uses to which Christian believers put the Bible.

revelation to humans.[2] Theologians say the Bible is *special* revelation not available from any other source. Thus, those who wish to learn about the Judeo-Christian faith read and study the Bible. Christians believe that through the Bible God has conveyed information to people—information about who God is, what he has done in history, what he wants people to know, how they should respond to God, and, most significantly, the story of God's relationship to people.

The Bible reports the history and religious faith of Israel, the life and teachings of Jesus, and the establishment and spread of the Christian Church. In it we discover how Israel worshipped, how the prophets took the nation to task for her idolatry, and what ancient Israelites believed about their national destiny and future glory. It recites how Christians like Peter and Paul came to apprehend salvation through faith in Jesus and to spread this "gospel" (good news) throughout the Roman world.

Christians begin with the presupposition that through the Bible God conveys reliable information.[3] In order to comprehend this revelation, we must interpret the biblical accounts accurately; so our approach to hermeneutics governs what we learn from the Bible. A proper hermeneutic promotes our understanding and helps us to interpret the Bible's content accurately and to see the facts correctly. It protects us, for example, from interpreting poetry or apocalyptic as if their authors intended them to convey history. This enables us to discover the knowledge and insight that God wanted us to have.

TO WORSHIP

Since the Bible derives from God himself and records his mighty deeds and glorious person, his people naturally discover in its pages motivation and opportunities for worship. Worship occurs when people respond to God's revelation of himself and how he has acted in Jesus Christ.[4] God's grace and love prompt his people to respond in various

---

2 The writer of Hebrews makes this point explicit in saying, "In the past God spoke to our forefathers through the prophets at many times and in various ways" (Heb 1:1). The prophets wrote not simply their own musings or observations but messages conveyed to them by God. Again, "Above all, you must understand that no prophecy of Scripture came about by the prophet's own interpretation of things. For prophecy never had its origin in the human will, but prophets, though human, spoke from God as they were carried along by the Holy Spirit" (2 Pet 1:20–21 TNIV). The creeds of the Church affirm, then, that the Bible owes its origin to divine revelation, not to human invention.

3 For a consideration of various aspects of the Bible's truthfulness readers might want to consult the two books of essays edited by D. A. Carson and J. D. Woodbridge, *Scripture and Truth* (Grand Rapids: Zondervan, 1983); and *Hermeneutics, Authority, and Canon* (Grand Rapids: Zondervan, 1986); plus J. I. Packer, *Truth & Power: The Place of Scripture in the Christian Life* (Downers Grove, IL: InterVarsity, 1999).

4 R. G. Rayburn defines worship in this expansive way: "Worship is the activity of the new life of a believer in which, recognizing the fullness of the Godhead as it is revealed in the person of Jesus Christ and His mighty redemptive acts, he seeks by the power of the Holy Spirit to render to the living God the glory, honor, and submission which are His due" (*O Come Let Us Worship* [Grand Rapids: Baker, 1980], 21). Excellent studies of the topic of worship include D. A. Carson, ed., *Worship by the Book* (Grand Rapids: Zondervan, 2002); D. Peterson, *Engaging With God: A Biblical Theology of Worship* (Downers Grove, IL: InterVarsity, 2002); and R. E. Webber, *The Biblical Foundations of Christian Worship* (Peabody, MA: Hendrickson, 1993). For key analyses of the worship in ancient Israel, see the classic H. H. Rowley, *Worship in Ancient Israel* (Philadelphia: Fortress, 1967), especially "Psalmody and Music," 176–212; and S. E. Balentine, *The Torah's Vision of Worship*, Overtures to Biblical Theology (Minneapolis: Augsburg Fortress, 1999). On the early Church's worship see L. W. Hurtado, *At the Origins of Christian Worship: The Context and Character of Earliest Christian Devotion* (Grand Rapids: Eerdmans, 2000).

appropriate ways. When believers learn from their study of the Bible who God is and what he has accomplished on their behalf, their hearts well up in praise and adoration. In places the poetry of the Psalms draws readers into such an experience. For example, one of the psalmists writes:

> The heavens declare the glory of God;
> the skies proclaim the work of his hands.
> Day after day they pour forth speech;
> night after night they display knowledge.
> There is no speech or language
> where their voice is not heard.
> Their voice goes out into all the earth,
> their words to the ends of the world. (Psa 19:1–4)

Again, another poet proclaims:

> The LORD is my light and my salvation—
> whom shall I fear?
> The LORD is the stronghold of my life—
> of whom shall I be afraid? . . .
> One thing I ask of the LORD,
> this is what I seek:
> that I may dwell in the house of the LORD
> all the days of my life,
> to gaze upon the beauty of the LORD
> and to seek him in his temple. (Psa 27:1, 4)

In places the biblical writers expressly seek to worship God and to elicit from the readers their own adoration of God.

> I will praise you, O LORD, with all my heart;
> before the "gods" I will sing your praise.
> I will bow down toward your holy temple
> and will praise your name
> for your love and your faithfulness,
> for you have exalted above all things
> your name and your word. . . .
> May all the kings of the earth praise you, O LORD,
>   when they hear the words of your mouth. (Psa 138:1, 2, 4)

> Praise the LORD, all you nations;
> extol him, all you peoples.
> For great is his love toward us,
> and the faithfulness of the LORD endures forever.
> Praise the LORD. (Psa 117)

The Israelites incorporated these hymns into their Scriptures, and since the beginning of the Church, Christians have joined them in praising God through these treasured lines.[5]

The NT authors included fewer explicit hymns in their accounts,[6] yet the pages of the NT demonstrate that singing and music played important roles in the worship of the emerging Church. Commenting on the early Church, G. Delling observes: "The Word of Christ is alive in the community in teaching and admonition and in the singing of songs for God, i.e., in these the community praises God from the heart on account of the salvation which He has given by what He has done in Christ."[7] Music, indeed, was a central focus of the Christians' communal life as K. H. Bartels emphasizes: "Next to the preaching of the word and participation in the sacrament, the heart of worship was this 'spiritual singing,' a festive recognition of God in Jesus Christ as the Lord of the congregation and of the world."[8] Using prayers or anthems—some even drawn directly from the OT—the early Christians sought to lift up their readers to praise and adore their God. Paul says,

> Praise be to the God and Father of our Lord Jesus Christ, who has blessed us in the heavenly realms with every spiritual blessing in Christ.
>
> Now to him who is able to do immeasurably more than all we ask or imagine, according to his power that is at work within us, to him be glory in the church and in Christ Jesus throughout all generations, for ever and ever! Amen. (Eph 1:3; 3:20–21)

At other times believers throughout church history have responded to what they read in unique spontaneous worship. Whether or not Paul intended to evoke worship from his readers when he penned Rom 8:38–39, those stunning verses certainly must have inspired them to proclaim the greatness of their God:

> For I am convinced that neither death nor life, neither angels nor demons, neither the present nor the future, nor any powers, neither height nor depth, nor anything else in all creation, will be able to separate us from the love of God that is in Christ Jesus our Lord.

What believer can read of Jesus' loving sacrifice for his people without crying out in worship and praise for God's immeasurable charity lavished upon his people, "while

---

5 A wise assessment of OT Israel's worship with a view to contemporary Christian worship is A. E. Hill, *Enter His Courts With Praise! Old Testament Worship for the New Testament Church*, 2d ed. (Grand Rapids: Baker, 1997).

6 The number and extent of hymns actually incorporated into the NT letters are issues of some debate among scholars. For further insight in addition to our comments about the genre of hymns / poetry above, see R. J. Karris, *A Symphony of New Testament Hymns: Commentary on Philippians 2:5–11, Colossians 1:15–20, Ephesians 2:14–16, 1 Timothy 3:16, Titus 3:4–7, 1 Peter 3:18* (Collegeville, MN: Liturgical Press, 1996); R. P. Martin, *Worship in the Early Church,* rev. ed. (Grand Rapids: Eerdmans, 1975); V. H. Neufeld, *The Earliest Christian Confessions* (Leiden: Brill, 1963); and J. T. Sanders, *The New Testament Christological Hymns: Their Historical and Religious Background,* SNTSMS 15 (Cambridge: Cambridge University Press, 1971).

7 G. Delling, "ὕμνὸ [*hymnos*], et al.," *TDNT* 8:498.

8 K. H. Bartels, "Song, Hymn, Psalm," *NIDNTT* 3:675.

we were still sinners" (Rom 5:8)? The Bible performs this major role for the Christian: to elicit and to shape the worship of God's people.

Hence, the Bible is used in worship both individually and corporately. In their *personal* use of the Bible, believers read, study, and seek to respond to what they find within its pages. The Bible directs believing readers to praise and adoration, to confession of sins, and to prayers of thanksgiving. In response to the God revealed in the pages of the Bible, Christians seek to conform all dimensions of their lives to his will. The Bible provides inspiration and challenge; it generates religious experiences; it provides hope and sustenance. In short, the Bible furnishes the medium for individual worship. God speaks through his living and active Word, and his people venerate him.

This Bible also provides the basis for *corporate* worship. As the people of Israel worshiped their God, so also the Church seeks to be a believing and worshiping community. Applying OT terminology to the Body of Christ, Peter proclaims:

> But you are a chosen people, a royal priesthood, a holy nation, a people belonging to God, that you may declare the praises of him who called you out of darkness into his wonderful light. Once you were not a people, but now you are the people of God; once you had not received mercy, but now you have received mercy (1 Pet 2:9–10; cf. Exod 19:5–6; Hos 2:23).

In one sense, believers function as a worshiping community to announce to the unbelieving world "How Great Thou Art." From what they discover in the Bible believers can obey the admonition: "Through Jesus, therefore, let us continually offer to God a sacrifice of praise—the fruit of lips that confess his name" (Heb 13:15). Though the term "word" has a wide semantic range, as we now read Paul's instructions, "word of Christ" embraces the Bible: "Let the word of Christ dwell in you richly as you teach and admonish one another with all wisdom, and as you sing psalms, hymns and spiritual songs with gratitude in your hearts to God" (Col 3:16). To believers the Scriptures attest God's presence, activity, and love, particularly as expressed in his Son, Jesus Christ. They bring to their attention, in a concrete and graphic manner, God's personal and loving commitment to his people. And as such, the Scriptures move them to worship—individually and corporately.

TO CREATE LITURGY

The liturgy of the Christian Church has always incorporated texts from the Bible.[9] Whether "high" or "low," the liturgy of the Church employs prayers, hymns, various readings (e.g., responsive readings), psalms, and the ordinances (sacraments).[10] The

---

9 The English word "liturgy" derives from the Greek term *leitourgia,* which meant some kind of service. In Christian literature it meant service to God. Today it usually refers to a rite or body of rituals used in public worship. In J. F. White's words, "Liturgy is a work performed by the people for the benefit of others . . . the essential outward form through which a community of faith expresses its public worship" (*Introduction to Christian Worship* [Nashville: Abingdon, 1980], 23–24). Cf. R. E. Webber, ed., *Twenty Centuries of Christian Worship* (Peabody, MA: Hendrickson, 1995).

10 For an extremely thorough discussion of the history and practice of liturgy in the main traditions from the beginning to the postmodern era, see F. C. Senn, *Christian Liturgy: Catholic and Evangelical* (Minneapolis: Augsburg Fortress, 1997). M. J. Hatchett, *Sanctifying Life, Time, and Space: An Introduction to Liturgical Study* (New York: Seabury Press, 1976) is also helpful.

Scriptures inform all these elements; indeed, many feature scriptural portions directly. An obvious example is the chorus to the French Christmas carol "Angels We Have Heard on High," which quotes, *Gloria in excelsis Deo,* based on Lk 2:14 in the Latin Bible. Many contemporary praise choruses take their words verbatim from the Psalms; for example, "Come let us worship and bow down," from Psa 95:6. The chorus to the hymn "I Know Whom I Have Believed" quotes the KJV of 2 Tim 1:12. *The Book of Common Prayer* of the Protestant Episcopal Church incorporates portions of the Bible extensively in guiding worshipers, both individually and corporately.[11] The prayer books of other Christian traditions do the same. One has only to visit churches of different denominations (e.g., Roman Catholic, Greek Orthodox, Presbyterian, Anglican, and Plymouth Brethren) to grasp how different can be their celebration of the Lord's Supper. Though all based on the pivotal passages in the Gospels and 1 Corinthians, their components, rhythm, duration, place in the overall worship of the church, et al., vary enormously—often as the result of their distinct historical developments and theology.

Unquestionably, then, the Scriptures aid our worship and perform an appropriate liturgy-forming function, in which worship is holistic—not merely a matter of the head. Liturgy enables worshipers to enact elements of the salvific drama and embody their responses to God's grace. At the same time, we believe it is important that worshipers comprehend the biblical passages or allusions.[12] In some uses of the Bible that we will shortly consider (preaching or teaching), the goal may well be to help hearers to discover the meaning of the texts and actions. In using the wealth of liturgical forms, those who lead must find ways to help participants understand what they are hearing or doing in following the prescribed rituals. The Bible contains no magic charms. People need to understand what it says to profit from its message.

TO FORMULATE THEOLOGY

All humans operate on the basis of a belief system or worldview. For "theists" (i.e., those who believe in a god or gods) belief systems can be termed "theologies" (from the Greek word for god, *theos*). To formulate a theology, one affirms in an orderly fashion his or her belief system with theism at the center. Obviously, a biblical theologian regards the Bible as the necessary basis for theology. At the same time, to produce or write a "theology" is a human endeavor; it articulates an individual's or a group's understanding of reality with God at the center. To answer the question "How does a Christian group understand and express its faith?" requires an explanation of its theology.[13]

Though delineating theology is an ongoing task in the life of the Church, theology acts as an anchor for the Church and for Christians who occasionally may feel battered and trembling in a sea of relativism or competing world-views. Theology offers the Church a secure understanding of itself and how it fits into God's overall purposes in history and eternity. Theology protects the Church against the changing

---

11 *The Book of Common Prayer* (New York: HarperCollins 1991).

12 P. H. Pfatteicher, *Liturgical Spirituality* (Harrisburg, PA: Trinity, 1997) stresses the need for the interior life of the spirit that is formed and nurtured by the church's liturgy.

13 For a helpful discussion of the nature of doing theology and locating "systematic theology" on the theological map, see M. J. Erickson, *Christian Theology,* 2d ed. (Grand Rapids: Baker, 1998), 22–37.

winds that have challenged its existence and claims of truth since the beginning. From first-century Gnostics to modern scientism, the Church has contended with manifold alternative explanations of reality and truth.[14] Its understanding of theology has established the boundaries of orthodoxy. And whenever the Church claims to be biblical in its understanding of theology, then the Bible must stand at the center and comprise the source and norm of its theological thought.[15]

Yet there is a crucial distinction between "biblical" and "systematic" theology. If what we have just said is true, then virtually all Christians would insist that any enterprise that purports to call itself "theology" must be biblical. Nevertheless, since the eighteenth century Christian theologians have followed two distinct theological approaches.[16] Biblical theology relates more closely to the development of theology within the historical development of the Bible itself. It presents the theology that the Bible itself contains. George Ladd provides a ready definition:

> Biblical theology is that discipline which sets forth the message of the books of the Bible in their historical setting. Biblical theology is primarily a descriptive discipline. . . . Biblical theology has the task of expounding the theology found in the Bible in its own historical setting, and its own terms, categories, and thought forms.[17]

Thus, in "biblical theology" one could speak, for example, of the theology of the postexilic prophets in contrast to that of earlier prophets. Or one might compare the theology of the Synoptic Gospels with that of the Gospel of John.

To illustrate, it is possible to discuss Paul's particular theology of *faith* and show how that compares to the notion of faith presented by James or the writer of Hebrews. In this restricted sense, biblical theologians focus upon how individual biblical writers, sections, or books framed their messages to meet the needs of their specific readers in their historical contexts. The biblical writers' theologies were both explicit and implicit. That is, at times they expressed clearly their understandings of

---

14 Our mention of these two competitors is merely representative and readily acknowledges the positive benefits of modern science in general. Full-fledged Gnosticism was a second-to-third-century A.D. phenomenon that arose out of a variety of religious and philosophical ancestors and became a leading competitor to Christianity. For further insight, consult R. McL. Wilson, *Gnosis and the New Testament* (Philadelphia: Fortress, 1968); E. Yamauchi, *Pre-Christian Gnosticism: A Survey of the Proposed Evidences* (Grand Rapids: Eerdmans, 1973); and R. Roukema, *Gnosis and Faith in Early Christianity: An Introduction to Gnosticism* (Harrisburg, PA: Trinity, 1999). P. A. Heelan expresses what we mean by scientism: "Analytical philosophy generally defends the fundamental position that science is a knowledge of a privileged kind, not deriving from and not responsible to the projects and values of the Western cultural world . . . ; rather, it constitutes a socially and historically independent account of reality, more reliable than any given so far" ("Hermeneutical Phenomenology and the Philosophy of Science," in *Gadamer and Hermeneutics*, ed. H. J. Silverman [New York/London: Routledge, 1991], 214).

15 S. J. Grenz and J. R. Franke put it well in seeing "Scripture as the 'Norming Norm' of Theology" (*Beyond Foundationalism* [Louisville, KY: Westminster John Knox, 2001], 63–75).

16 For a helpful discussion of this development see G. Hasel, *Old Testament Theology. Basic Issues,* rev. ed. (Grand Rapids: Eerdmans, 1991), 10–17.

17 G. E. Ladd, *A Theology of the New Testament,* 2d. ed. D. A. Hagner (Grand Rapids: Zondervan, 1993), 20.

God and his ways, but in other places their theology emerges more implicitly; we see how their theological convictions determine and shape their prescriptions for their readers. Thus, biblical theologians recognize in their formulations that much of the canon consists of "occasional" writings: writings for specific occasions. The designs of the original writers shape biblical theology.

Put starkly, we are indebted to the errors of the Judaizers for motivating Paul to explain to the Galatians his view of justification by faith apart from works.[18] For Paul, *faith* goes to the heart of how one attains salvation; salvation comes through faith in Jesus Christ alone, not by following Jewish rituals—i.e., "works." Yet James' dispersed readers had a different struggle with *faith,* and that situation moved James to insist that a truly living and genuine faith must be one that is lived out in the circumstances of life. Faith must produce "works." Thus, we can speak of the contrasting views of faith in Paul's theology and that of James.[19] This does not mean the two are contradictory; it simply means that the writers expressed their views out of concrete situations that were strikingly different. Paul and James framed their theological responses differently because each was replying to specific problems in specific churches.

Biblical theology, then, emerges from historical conditions. Its formulation depends upon the movements and circumstances of people and events—the interaction of author and recipients in the heat of fast-breaking developments.[20] As Berkeley Mickelsen puts it, "In this approach the biblical theologian must be constantly aware of the biblical languages, all known historical factors, and the freshness of the message of God through his servant to men involved in a life and death struggle with dread realities."[21]

All this presents a decidedly different picture from a "systematic" theology. Millard Erickson identifies systematic theology as "that discipline which strives to give a coherent statement of the doctrines of the Christian faith, based primarily on the Scriptures, placed in the context of culture in general, worded in a contemporary idiom, and related to the issues of life."[22] Though systematic theology also makes a

---

18 To "judaize" is the attempt to make Christianity more Jewish (a phenomenon that still exists in the 21st century). Judaizers in the first century insisted, "Unless you are circumcised, according to the custom taught by Moses, you cannot be saved" (Acts 15:2). The "Council at Jerusalem" refuted this error (Acts 15), which Paul also attempted to do in Galatians (e.g., 2:15–16; 5:2–6). For discussions of correlating Paul and James at this point, see most standard commentaries on James at 2:14–26, especially: P. Davids, *The Epistle of James*, NIGTC (Grand Rapids: Eerdmans, 1982); R. P. Martin, *James,* WBC 48 (Dallas: Word, 1988); and D. J. Moo, *The Letter of James*, PNTC (Grand Rapids: Eerdmans, 2000).

19 For analyses of Paul's and James' views of faith, see the standard commentaries on the relevant texts.

20 For a list of the best examples of biblical theologies, see the bibliography.

21 A. B. Mickelsen, *Interpreting the Bible* (Grand Rapids: Eerdmans, 1963), 344.

22 Erickson, *Christian Theology*, 23. For their part, Lewis and Demarest say, "Systematic theology . . . aims to produce normative guidelines to spiritual reality for the present generation; it organizes the material of divine revelation topically and logically, developing a coherent and comprehensive world view and way of life" (G. Lewis and B. Demarest, *Integrative Theology* [Grand Rapids: Zondervan, 1996], 23). Finally, D. A. Carson provides his working definition of systematic theology: "the branch of theology that seeks to elaborate the whole and the parts of Scripture, demonstrating their logical (rather than their merely historical) connections and taking full cognizance of the history of doctrine and the contemporary intellectual climate and categories and queries while finding its sole ultimate authority in the Scriptures themselves, rightly interpreted" ("Unity and Diversity in the New Testament: The Possibility of Systematic Theology," in Carson and Woodbridge, eds., *Scripture and Truth*, 69–70).

valid claim to being biblical (that is, its goal is to exhibit the theology of the Bible), its categories are not always those of the biblical writers, but those of the theologian. Traditional (and novel, at least at the time of formulation) categories comprise the doctrinal framework for the biblical material. Often the frameworks derive from the theologians' interactions with the ongoing theological traditions,[23] philosophers, the social context in which the theologian works, and other religions or belief systems. So, for example, one may read Catholic, Reformed, or Lutheran systematic theologies and encounter categories that reflect, in part, the special concerns and issues relevant to these traditions. In other words, the theologians systematize the Bible's total teaching in a framework that they feel best represents the Bible's emphases in light of their own study *and the issues with which they are currently struggling*. That is to say, inevitably, systematic theologies reflect the philosophical frameworks and interpretive agendas of the systematizers.[24]

We must consider another issue. Put in categories we have discussed above, the systematic theologians' own preunderstandings shape the categories and issues they use in their systems (though they may insist, with some justification, that their goal is to allow the Bible's own teaching to provide guidance). As well, the theologians' own perspectives will guide their selection process as they choose various texts within each category and as they determine the relative weight to give the Bible's various teachings on specific issues. This is readily apparent when one reads the theologies dealing with specific controversial issues, say election versus free will.[25] People come to different positions on the Bible's teaching on this matter because they bring different preunderstandings to their analyses of the relevant texts and they give different weight to the relevant texts.[26]

In a sense, then, each generation, and perhaps each culture, needs to update its formulations of Christian theology. This does not mean that God's truth keeps changing. Rather, it reflects the nature of the process of systematizing: it always exhibits the perspectives and concerns of those who do it. To illustrate, most

---

23 At times the attempt is to "fit in" with a tradition; at other times the theologian seeks to adjust, challenge, or even jettison a tradition. A current debate concerns the "orthodoxy" (for evangelicals) of the so-called "openness of God" theology. So theologians devise theologies to include or exclude various options based on what they believe the Bible teaches.

24 As we write this S. Coakley is "embarking on a four-volume systematic theology which will be the first major systematics attempted from a feminist perspective" (M. Oppenheimer, "Prayerful Vulnerability," *ChrCent* 120 [2003]: 25).

25 An instructive specimen is D. Basinger and R. Basinger, eds., *Predestination and Free Will* (Downers Grove: InterVarsity, 1986). In this work the reader can see how the four writers differ in their view of the nature of God's foreknowledge. Based on their view that God determines and controls events, several argue that God knows future events without limit. Others argue for particular limitations on God's foreknowledge on the basis that God has freely chosen to give humans genuine autonomy. So, one asks, how can God really know beforehand the free choices that independent creatures will make when there is yet nothing to know? If human choices are truly free, how could God possibly know the outcomes in advance? In other words, one's philosophical starting point determines one's conclusion.

26 See W. W. Klein, "Exegetical Rigor with Hermeneutical Humility: The Calvinist-Arminian Debate and the New Testament," in A. M. Donaldson and T. B. Sailors, eds., *New Testament Greek and Exegesis: Essays in Honor of Gerald F. Hawthorne* (Grand Rapids: Eerdmans, 2003), 23–36.

Protestants will agree that the "Westminster Confession of Faith" introduced a marvelous and singularly important understanding of Christian theology. But, for example, its discussion of the "covenants" reflects issues, concerns, and the preunderstandings—religious and political—of Christians in seventeenth century Scotland and England.[27] Civil war had broken out in England and the king, Charles I, was forced to initiate reform. An assembly was called at Westminster to devise a creed that both Scots and English could affirm. Speaking about the "federal theology" that the Westminster Confession embodied, Dillistone observes,

> [It] seemed to provide just the system or schema that men were seeking in the period of consolidation after the revolutionary changes of the sixteenth century. A dialectical interpretation of reality does not lend itself to an easy formalization whereas a succession of contracts can be systematized within a legal framework.
>
> Once a group is established and inspired with growing confidence, it tends to look for something more concrete, more definite, more constitutional and this is exactly what the developing Churches of the Reformation found in the doctrine of the Two Covenants. . . . Puritan and Calvinist alike found in this one idea the necessary framework for a new theological and ecclesiastical system.[28]

Thus, our point here is *not* that the authors of the Confession were "right" on some points and "wrong" on others (depending upon one's theological persuasion), or that the issues they struggled with no longer concern us, or that language of the document is archaic. Rather, history shows that they formulated their declarations and addressed their own concerns to counter opposing viewpoints prevalent at that time. Their affirmations were not simply "objective" statements of theology, or "what the Bible actually teaches." Nor, we aver, ought we naively consider that Confession (or any other one) to be a timeless statement of Christian theology. Though we can learn much from previous theologians and ancestors in the faith, contemporary Christians require theologians living now to express what the Christian faith means

---

27 For helpful discussions of the historical background of the Westminster Confession consult R. T. Kendall, *Calvin and English Calvinism to 1649* (Oxford: Oxford University Press, 1979); and W. M. Hetherington, *History of the Westminster Assembly of Divines* (New York: Anson D. F. Randolph & Co., 1890). "Federal theology" is the term used to describe the brand of Calvinism that developed in the late sixteenth and seventeenth centuries in England and Scotland that gave great prominence to the doctrine of the covenants (the English word "covenant" translates the Latin *foedus*, hence, federal). The concept of covenants was crucial in the socio-political world of the time—namely, what covenants protected the "rights" of the king versus those of the people. It was natural that theologians thought in terms of covenants, and the federal Calvinists came to distinguish between the covenants of grace and works. Important to our discussion is this point: neither Calvin nor the other Reformers made this distinction between a covenant of grace (a phrase used only twice in Calvin's *Institutes*) and a covenant of works (not used at all) in the manner used in the Westminster Confession. Later systematizers introduced it.

28 F. W. Dillistone, *The Structure of the Divine Society* (Philadelphia: Westminster Press, 1951), 132. Our intent here is not to open a lengthy historical discussion, nor to debate Calvinism or so-called federal theology.

today.[29] Indeed Grenz and Franke argue, "the truly Reformed tradition is by its very nature 'open.' And this 'openness,' in turn, preserves the dynamic nature of tradition."[30]

Are the two disciplines of biblical and systematic theology at odds? Must we insist upon one or the other? Evangelicals accept the unity as well as the diversity of the Scriptures, as we affirmed above.[31] The Bible's *diversity* reflects the variety of its numerous authors and the circumstances of their times, places, and situations. Its *unity* derives from its single divine Source and Author. These two truths suggest the foundations for both biblical and systematic theologies. The approach of biblical theology uniquely exposes and highlights the inherent diversity of the Bible. The lenses of biblical theology enable us to perceive each author's or text's unique perspectives, distinctives, and emphases and to see clearly how they can speak most sensitively and creatively to parallel or similar circumstances today. Biblical theologians feel more deeply the rough edges of the Bible's teachings, for they are not obligated (at this point in their study) to harmonize or explain difficult teachings by resorting to what the Bible says elsewhere about an issue.[32] This approach takes the Bible on its own terms at each point and with each author.[33]

At the same time, we cannot be content with a mere collection of theological truths espoused by the various biblical authors. We need the organization and structure of the whole. At their best the systematizers bring together all the bits and pieces of the Bible's teaching on an issue and present them logically so we see how they all fit together. Since we presume divine authorship of the entire canon and that God has a unified

---

29 A sample of noteworthy evangelical systematizers includes: Erickson, *Christian Theology*; S. J. Grenz, *Theology for the Community of God* (Grand Rapids: Eerdmans, 2002); A. E. McGrath, *Christian Theology: An Introduction*, 3d. ed. (Oxford, UK: Blackwell, 2001); Lewis and Demarest, *Integrative Theology*; and D. Bloesch, *Essentials of Evangelical Theology*, 2 vols. (New York: Harper & Row, 1978). Patently illustrating that systematics exhibits the perspectives of the theologians, we cite J. R. Williams, *Renewal Theology* (Grand Rapids: Zondervan, 1990); or S. M. Horton, ed., *Systematic Theology: A Pentecostal Perspective* (Springfield, MO: Logion Press, 1994). Beyond these, key influential works in the last century include K. Barth, *Church Dogmatics,* 12 vols., translated by G. T. Thomson, G. W. Bromiley, et al. (Edinburgh: T. & T. Clark; New York: Scribner, 1936–69); P. Tillich, *Systematic Theology*, 3 vols. (Chicago: University of Chicago Press, 1976); and W. Pannenberg, *Systematic Theology*, 3 vols. (Grand Rapids: Eerdmans, 1997).

30 Grenz and Franke, *Beyond Foundationalism*, 125.

31 See J. Goldingay, *Approaches to Old Testament Interpretation*, rev. ed. (Downers Grove: InterVarsity, 1990); D. A. Carson, "Unity and Diversity," 65–100; and C. L. Blomberg, "Unity and Diversity of Scripture," in *New Dictionary of Biblical Theology*, T. D. Alexander, and B. S. Rosner, ed. (Downers Grove: InterVarsity Press, 2000), 64–72.

32 The need to harmonize unique perspectives leads many theologians to favor one biblical author's formulation over another's. Returning to our example above, did not Luther's preoccupation with Paul's view of justification by faith lead him to question James' orthodoxy? That is, Luther believed (wrongly, we think) that James' statement in 2:24 was incompatible with Paul's theology. Perhaps in his concern to systematize, Luther felt he needed to have a precise understanding of *faith*; he preferred Paul's, not James'. The biblical theologian retains the unique emphases of both Paul and James. Of course, this does not mean that evangelical biblical theologians simply leave the matter there. They seek to show how diverse perspectives are compatible.

33 W. W. Klein, *The New Chosen People: A Corporate View of Election* (Grand Rapids: Zondervan, 1990; repr. Eugene, OR: Wipf & Stock, 2001) attempts to understand the important concept of God's choosing from a biblical theological perspective.

message to present, the discipline of systematic theology seeks to express this larger picture in a coherent fashion.

Yet this process faces some latent pitfalls. At their worst the systematizers reflect only their own preunderstandings, which they read into the biblical material; their work amounts to a reader-response "take" on the entire Bible. They may fall prey to the temptation to claim more precision than the actual details of the biblical texts warrant. They may build entire systems in which many of the elements derive only from their own inferences rather than on explicit evidence from the Scriptures. Or they may cling tenaciously to their own categories and defend their own theological structures at all costs.[34] These hazards are ever-present. But as we will explain below, when informed by the best work of biblical exegetes and theologians, systematic theology can organize the biblical data into meaningful systems that provide great help and assistance to the Church.[35]

So how does the Bible inform theology? Most theologians seek to express the teaching of the Bible in contemporary terms. But how do they formulate the Bible's theology? Whether it be biblical or systematic,[36] we cannot espouse a self-structured theology that promotes its own self-serving agenda. Therefore, (1) *valid theologizing must follow the sound exegesis of the appropriate biblical texts.* To use our earlier example, if theologians wish to formulate a theology of "faith," they must investigate all the passages that speak to that issue. To borrow terms from the scientific arena, theology ought to originate *inductively* out of a responsible analysis (as we have attempted to elucidate in the previous chapters) of the relevant passages of the Bible. It will not do merely to invent theology and seek *deductively* to defend it in various texts. Once a tenet has been established (or even posited), one can deduce implications and see their potential effects in other areas. Induction and deduction both have their place, but each must inform and correct the other so that in the end theologians extract the Bible's teaching rather than impose their own. Unless a system of responsible hermeneutics guides the process of exegesis and theological formulation, theology, at best, will not rise above human wisdom, and, at worst, will be false, misguided, tendentious, and even dangerous.

A second key point is implicit in these assumptions, but we must state it explicitly: (2) *theology must be based on the Bible's total teaching, not on selected or isolated texts.* For example, suppose we want to develop a theology of election and free will. We cannot

---

34 It is risky to suggest examples here, for we all see more clearly the rigidity and inadequacies of others' systems rather than our own. One helpful book noted earlier exposes the influences of theological systems pertaining to interpreting the millennium: S. J. Grenz, *The Millennial Maze* (Downers Grove: InterVarsity, 1992).

35 At this point we will not develop explicitly the other two components of the classical theological curriculum: historical and practical theology. The former traces the development of theological understanding throughout the history of the Church. Two examples are A. E. McGrath, *Historical Theology: An Introduction to the History of Christian Thought* (Oxford: Blackwell, 1998), and G. W. Bromiley, *Historical Theology* (Edinburgh: T. & T. Clark, 2000). So-called practical theology focuses attention on the application of theology to real life about which we will have more to say below. Highly recommended is R. S. Anderson, *The Shape of Practical Theology: Empowering Ministry With Theological Praxis* (Downers Grove: InterVarsity, 2001). For further insight see Erickson, *Christian Theology*, 22–28.

36 We will no longer employ these distinctions in what follows. Again, we assume that both approaches seek to explicate the meanings of the biblical texts regardless of how they use the results.

develop a faithful and honest statement of this doctrine if we deny or discount texts that conflict with our preferred theory. If God authored the entire Bible and if its parts do not hopelessly contradict (these hark back to our presuppositions), then a valid theological statement about an issue must take into account *all* that God has said concerning it.

Other factors enter into the process of "weighing" the Bible's various teachings on an issue of theology. For example, in considering some doctrines we discover that certain texts speak more clearly to the issues than do other more obscure texts. In addition, some details appear in a range of places in the Bible, whereas other points may occur in only isolated or even single references. Some teachings occur in direct and didactic passages. They may even be propositional in nature as in these: "I am the Lord your God; conse-crate yourselves and be holy, because I am holy" (Lev 11:44); or "God is love. This is how God showed his love among us: He sent his one and only Son into the world that we might live through him" (1 Jn 4:8b-9). The Bible presents other points by means of metaphor, "God is light; in him there is no darkness at all" (1 Jn 1:5b), or in narrative (see how many of God's attributes emerge from God's speech in Job 38–39).

One finds biblical teaching in "earlier" parts of the Bible that are developed and enlarged in later revelation. We do not mean here that later parts of the Bible contradict or in every case supersede earlier sections, but that in some instances God revealed his truth progressively. In other words, some earlier truths prepared the way for people to understand and accept what God said and did in subsequent events. For example, viewed from hindsight, the OT sacrificial system was never an end in itself; rather, it prepared the way for the Lamb of God who would eventually come to take away the sins of the world (Jn 1:29; cf. Heb 10:1–18). Correspondingly, the OT Law, important as it was for the nation of Israel, finds fulfillment in Christ and no longer serves as the undisputed rule for the Church as it defined itself in Jerusalem following Jesus' resurrection.[37]

Our point in listing these various factors should be obvious: we must "weigh" evidence to arrive at adequate conclusions. The student must be conscientious and prudent about the evidence adduced in favor of a theological judgment. Clearer teaching must carry more weight than obscure texts whose points may be ambiguous. An interpreter may have more conviction about a point oft repeated than one made only once (though this does not allow the interpreter to discard any clear point in Scripture, even if made only once). Where metaphors or narratives leave conclusions more ambiguous, we dare not force them to overrule texts that speak more clearly or didactically. Likewise, where earlier revelation has progressively prepared the way for later formulations of God's truth, we must give priori-ty to the later.[38]

---

37 Cf., e.g., Mk 7:19; Acts 15:7–11; Rom 10:4; Heb 8–10. At the same time, as we argued above, NT ethics do not completely jettison the Law. The standard for Gentiles in Acts 15 did have roots in OT Law. Jesus insisted that his program fulfilled the Law (Mt 5:17–20). For helpful perspec-tives see F. Thielman, *The Law and the New Testament: The Question of Continuity*, Companions to the New Testament (New York: Crossroad / Herder, 1999); W. G. Strickland et al., *Five Views on Law and Gospel* (Grand Rapids: Zondervan, 1996); and T. R. Schreiner, *The Law & Its Fulfillment: A Pauline Theology of Law*, 2d. ed. (Grand Rapids: Baker, 1998).

38 This principle causes uncomfortable encounters between Christians and Jews. There is a move-ment afoot to affirm that Jews do not need Christ, for they represent God's chosen people and their way of salvation is sufficient for them. Much NT revelation calls this into question—where Jews themselves (e.g., Peter and Paul) presented Jesus as the Savior for all people, Jews and Gentiles. Recall Acts 4:12.

Another point parallels this: (3) *legitimate theology respects and articulates the Bible's own emphases.* We have noted repeatedly the inevitable effect preunderstandings have on interpreting and theologizing. This colors the content and the organization of any theological formulation. So theologians ought to strive to "major on the majors" in their theologies—to stress what the Bible portrays as most important. Theology should grasp God's principal concerns in the Scriptures, rather than merely mirror contemporary agendas and priorities.[39] Contemporary issues may pose the questions; but the answers must be biblical. Theology always runs the risk of being faddish when other issues determine its outcomes.

Further, if theology is to have life and significance—and fulfill its design, we would argue—theologians must do more than understand clearly and precisely what the relevant biblical texts mean. (4) *They must state theological points in ways that explain and illuminate their significance for the life and ministry of the Church today.* If God's message is to be applicable to people today, theology must display the Bible's truth in ways that disclose its Spirit-energized ability to transform life. Theology must show how the Bible's meaning broadens to new situations, edifies believers, stimulates righteousness, and secures God's will "on earth as it is in heaven." Nothing is more boring and irrelevant than a cold and sterile statement of theology. No doubt, theology (or "doctrine" as some call it) suffers some of its current bad press because of the omissions of its practitioners. When detached from life and divorced from practical implementation, theology fails to achieve its central mission—to express God's truth to his creatures. Scripture says of itself, "All Scripture is God-breathed and is useful for teaching, rebuking, correcting and training in righteousness" (2 Tim 3:16). Like good exegesis, good theology must be practical, and both theologians and exegetes must demonstrate the concrete implications of God's Word.[40]

An additional point requires careful consideration, which we divide into two items: the Bible is the definitive source for theology; yet we must be ready to learn from our spiritual ancestors. So, for the first part, (5) *theology must be centered in what God has revealed in Scripture*, not in what people, however enlightened, devise in their own thinking. This is the Reformation rallying cry: *sola scriptura.* Though study in numerous fields—for example, archaeology, paleography, ancient history, philology and linguistics, comparative religion, anthropology, sociology, etc.— sheds significant light on the Bible, such study must never supplant what the Bible itself says. Unless theology rests upon solid biblical foundations, it exists, at best, only as a monument to human brilliance.

---

39 Many popular Christian self-help books in recent decades address pressing problems and issues Christians face. For example, one dominant theme concerns the family. Many theological discussions of the family grow out of legitimate fears in the face of societal breakdowns and upheavals. They seek to support the family and elevate its importance, almost above all else. Yet we wonder if, indeed, the Bible exhibits such an emphasis upon the "traditional family," as often understood by American evangelicals. See, esp., R. Clapp, *Families at the Crossroads: Beyond Traditional & Modern Options* (Downers Grove: InterVarsity, 1993). Cf. R. S Hess and M. D. Carroll R., eds., *Family in the Bible* (Grand Rapids: Baker, 2003), for a survey of various perspectives within the canon.

40 For further help on this issue see the next chapter.

Yet, the downside of this important Reformation principle was Protestantism's denigration of the Church's rich heritage and tradition.[41] Fortunately, many are now seeing the error of this over-reaction, for, as Ferguson puts it, "Christian theology should be done in dialogue with the creeds and traditions of the church."[42] So we insist that (6) *modern theologians cannot do their work as if in a vacuum, as if no Christians have ever considered these issues prior to their own time.* We have much to learn from our sisters and brothers who walked in the faith before us. For two thousand years, in their own times and circumstances, believers have sought to transmit faithfully and live out authentically the teachings, symbols, and practices of the Christian faith (not to mention pious Jews before them).[43] We are only the latest to attempt to do so. Of course, traditions, creeds, and church dogmas cut in two directions. On one hand, as we explained above, they can restrict interpreters and theologians severely by predetermining what is orthodox or heterodox. As the Pharisees and rabbis of Jesus' time were locked into their own comfortable traditional wines and wineskins (Lk 5:37–39), our "traditions" may equally restrict our ability to let the biblical texts and biblical theology speak for themselves. For example, contemporary Christians tend to see God as primarily loving. But what about the God who judges, who is "a consuming fire" (Heb 12:29)? Do we filter out the idea that God is a warrior because we are uncomfortable with a God who seems so bloodthirsty? Again, though we cannot avoid our preunderstandings and even our church traditions and commitments, we must be scrupulous in subjecting our theological formulations to the confirmation of the Bible. We must foster a constant dialogue between our doctrines and the biblical text.

On the other hand, the theological insights of our spiritual predecessors can open up our thinking to ideas, implications, and conclusions that would never have occurred to us. These mentors serve as teachers and advisers about the truth of Scripture. At their best, the Church's councils and creeds attempt to articulate God's truth. Though dogmas or traditions are not on the same level as passages from the Bible, they do incorporate what our finest and best spiritual forebears understood the Bible to teach. As we attempt to do the same in our era, it makes sense to listen to their voices. We may decide to reject their teaching as being wrong or prejudiced; we may modify or rearrange it; but we lose much by simply ignoring their input. And if we ignore them, we run the great risk of missing sterling insights, committing similar errors, or wasting time redoing or rethinking what they have accomplished already for us.

TO PREACH

Accurate interpretation informs and governs the public proclamation of God's message. G. Osborne makes a striking statement: "The hermeneutical process culminates not in the results of exegesis (centering on the original meaning of the text) but

---

41 Grenz and Franke speak perceptively about this loss of tradition in Protestantism, in modern theology, and in evangelicalism: *Beyond Foundationalism*, 102–113.

42 D. S. Ferguson, *Biblical Hermeneutics: An Introduction* (Louisville, KY: Westminster John Knox, 1986), 113.

43 See R. Olson, *The Story of Christian Theology: Twenty Centuries of Tradition and Reform* (Downers Grove, IL: InterVarsity Press, 1999).

in the homiletical process (centering on the significance of the Word for the life of the Christian today)."[44] Though significance goes beyond preaching, as we will show, we affirm this sentiment.

Christian preaching has always purported to be biblical. Believing that the Bible is God's revelation to his creatures, Christians seek to proclaim its message to all who will listen. By its very nature, preaching attempts to convey biblical information and to persuade people to respond to it in appropriate ways. The origins of preaching probably go back to the post-exilic period of Ezra and Nehemiah. In Neh 8 the narrator explains the occasion when Ezra the scribe stood on a high wooden platform (v. 4), opened and read from the Book of the Law (vv. 5, 8), and proceeded to explain what he had read so the people could understand its meaning (v. 8). The result was an occasion of great rejoicing "because they now understood the words that had been made known to them" (v. 12). Jesus followed a similar tack when he read from the scroll of Isa 61 and proceeded to explain its significance to his hearers in the synagogue of Nazareth (Lk 4:16–30).[45] Accounts in the book of Acts provide additional examples of early Christian preaching (e.g., 2:14–41; 13:16–41).

Nevertheless, if preaching is to be more than just religious public speaking and if it is to convey more than the wisdom of the ages or of the preacher, it must be biblically informed. *Any claim to biblical preaching must rest on what the Bible actually teaches or clearly implies.* If preachers seek to inform people of God's ways and his will, they must be sure that sound hermeneutical principles guide the process, i.e., that they are preaching the intent of the biblical texts. If preachers say to their listeners, "God wants you to . . . ," they are bound ethically (and to their God-given function) to interpret God's will accurately.

We cannot stress too strongly, then, what a critical function sound hermeneutics performs. When people listen to preaching they want to "hear a word from God." When they cry out to know if there really is a God or how they may know him personally—when questions of ultimate destiny demand answers—mere human opinions fail to satisfy or convince. And if they receive erroneous answers, they will be misled, with possibly tragic and even eternal consequences. As people seek to find guidance and courage to live responsibly as Christians—or merely to survive in a crisis—they want

---

44 G. R. Osborne, *The Hermeneutical Spiral* (Downers Grove: InterVarsity, 1991), 343. H. W. Robinson, *Biblical Preaching: The Development and Delivery of Expository Messages*, 2d ed. (Grand Rapids: Baker, 2001), makes a strong case for the centrality of biblical exegesis in the task of sermon preparation and delivery. Likewise we highly recommend S. Greidanus, *The Modern Preacher and The Ancient Text: Interpreting and Preaching Biblical Literature* (Grand Rapids: Eerdmans, 1994); W. L. Liefeld, *New Testament Exposition. From Text to Sermon* (Grand Rapids: Zondervan, 1984); and J. R. W. Stott, *Between Two Worlds: The Challenge of Preaching Today* (Grand Rapids: Eerdmans, 1978). In an important reminder C. R. Wells, "New Testament Interpretation and Preaching," in *Interpreting the New Testament: Essays on Methods and Issues*, ed. D. A. Black and D. S. Dockery (Nashville: Broadman and Holman, 2001), 506–23, argue for critical thinking and methodology as essential friends, not enemies, of good preaching. An important collection of essays on biblical preaching is K. Willhite and S. M. Gibson, eds., *The Big Idea of Biblical Preaching* (Grand Rapids: Baker, 1998).

45 Cf. W. W. Klein, "The Sermon at Nazareth (Luke 4:14–22)," in *Christian Freedom: Essays in Honor of Vernon C. Grounds*, ed. K. W. M. Wozniak and S. J. Grenz (Lanham: University Press of America, 1986), 153–72.

to know how God can help or what he thinks about their situation. At such points no self-help or human wisdom suffices.

Preachers find their role at this very point. When true to their calling, preachers possess the great privilege and awesome responsibility of comprehending the ancient text, arriving at its correct meaning, and, most importantly, conveying its significance to people in their own time and culture so they may apply it to their lives. Thus, preachers serve as intermediaries who take the truth of God revealed in the Bible and transmit it to their hearers today. The sermon itself may stick close to the actual structure of a biblical text (sometimes called expository preaching) or it may gather biblical truth from various places in a topical arrangement—or numerous other formulae. The point is that biblical sermons seek their essence from the revelation in Scripture.

Of course much else than what we have just described alleges to be "preaching." Sadly, loyal parishioners will regularly hear all kinds of topical sermons or political orations that have little to do with the Bible. Or perhaps they will encounter addresses that start with a biblical quotation but then proceed to range far and wide with the Bible only a distant memory. They may receive only psychological prescriptions, a handy list of "how to's," or other human wisdom. These kinds of preaching fail to take seriously the message contained in the Bible and thus, in our estimation, seriously violate the preacher's assignment. To use the Bible for the preacher's own agenda constitutes a reprehensible abuse of both the preaching office and the Bible. Biblical preaching invites people to hear God's voice, to obey his will, and to respond to his redemptive acts on their behalf. Since the Bible reliably records that voice, that will, and those redemptive acts, only a faithful proclamation of the Bible's message fulfills the preacher's calling.[46]

TO TEACH

Much that we have asserted about preaching applies also to a parallel use of the Bible—teaching. Indeed, we cannot press too strict a distinction between preaching and teaching, for good teaching always calls those taught to some response.[47] But for our purposes let us refer to teaching as specific training or instruction in matters of Christian beliefs and practice. Since in some sense the Bible functions as the Christians'

---

46 Much excellent material elucidates the task of preaching. In addition to works cited earlier we also recommend R. J. Allen, *Why Preach from Passages in the Bible?* (Louisville: Westminster John Knox, 1996); T. R. Schreiner, "Biblical Preaching," *SBJT* 3 (1999): 1–96; G. Goldsworthy, *Preaching the Whole Bible as Christian Scripture: The Application of Biblical Theology to Expository Preaching* (Grand Rapids: Eerdmans, 2000); E. R. Achtemeier, *Preaching from the Minor Prophets* (Grand Rapids: Eerdmans, 1998); S. D. Mathewson, *The Art of Preaching Old Testament Narrative* (Grand Rapids: Baker, 2002); and D. S. Jacobsen, *Preaching Luke-Acts* (Nashville: Abingdon, 2001).

47 The NT itself employs various terms that mark these activities. One term, *kērygma*, meant proclamation or announcement and could be understood as preaching (see 1 Cor 1:21; 2 Tim 4:17; Tit 1:3). Its corresponding verb form, *kēryssō*, meant to announce or proclaim, and refers extensively to preaching in the NT (see Acts 20:25; 28:31; Rom 10:8; Gal 2:2; 1 Cor 9:27; 2 Cor 4:5; 11:4; 2 Tim 4:2; 1 Pet 3:19; etc.). The other term, *didachē*, specifies teaching or instruction. The NT writers often employ this word to indicate the content of Christian teaching (see Acts 2:42; 5:28; 13:12; Rom 16:17; 1 Cor 14:26; 2 Jn 9–10; Rev 2:24; etc.).

"textbook," the Church has always needed teachers who educate and train the saints from that book, much like Jesus who taught his disciples.[48]

Both Testaments attest to the perverse human tendency to stray from the Lord into false religions, heresies, and apathy. But as the standard of truth, the Bible serves to keep believers on track. Today the Church needs teachers[49] who conscientiously seek to teach accurately the Christian faith as it competes with the truth-claims of other belief systems represented by cults, "New Age" thinking, and other religions, or as it seeks to stake its claim to absolute truth in a postmodern world where "anything goes."[50] These represent major challenges to biblical Christianity, but it may be that "nominal Christianity" poses the greatest challenge of all. One segment of this group consists of people who have grown up as "Christians." They identify themselves as Christian though the Bible or Christian teaching plays virtually no significant role in their values or actions. Others have been advised on some occasion simply to "receive Christ" without any accompanying instruction about what true discipleship demands.[51] Certainly the teaching role requires responsible hermeneutics and courageous proclamation to provide believers with an accurate understanding so they may "contend for the faith that was once for all entrusted to the saints" (Jude 3).

Of course, biblical teaching must go beyond defending orthodoxy—correct beliefs. It should encompass orthopraxy—correct living in the world. Christian lifestyle and ministry require intensive training. To live in a Christian manner, believers need to understand their religion and what it requires of them. In providing instruction to their original readers, the biblical writers also supplied guidance for all their successors in the faith. Both Testaments contain numerous examples of Israelites and early Christians who were misinformed or stubborn about what they were to believe or how they were to live. The Israelites supposed that huge sacrifices would please God, but Micah informed them what qualities God really sought in their lives: "And what does the Lord require of you? To act justly and to love mercy and to walk humbly with your God" (Mic 6:8). Israel also assumed she would win a great victory on the "day of the Lord," but Amos brought her up short with the warning that that Day would bring her God's judgment for her sins (Amos 5:18–20).

---

48 The etymological meaning of the Greek word *mathētēs* (disciple) is "learner," although in Christian usage in the NT it came to mean much more—a committed follower of Jesus Christ. D. Müller says, "Following Jesus as a disciple means the unconditional sacrifice of his whole life (Matt. 10:37; Lk. 14:26f.; cf. Mk. 3:31–35; Lk. 9:59–62) for the whole of his life (Matt. 10:24f.; Jn. 11:16). To be a disciple means (as Matt. in particular emphasizes) to be bound to Jesus and to do God's will" ("*mathētēs*," [*NIDNTT* 1: 488]). See the articles on "disciple" in *NIDNTT* 1: 480–98 written by C. Blendinger and D. Müller.

49 We do not presume to limit who teaches to professional professors and clergy. The Church has always depended upon the faithful work of committed lay teachers. One who helps such lay teachers is L. E. Coleman, Jr., *How to Teach the Bible* (Nashville: Broadman & Holman, 2000).

50 A helpful guide in this task is P. Copan, *That's Just Your Interpretation: Responding to Skeptics Who Challenge Your Faith* (Grand Rapids: Baker, 2001).

51 In Jesus' words, "If people want to follow me, they must give up the things they want. They must be willing even to give up their lives to follow me. Those who want to save their lives will give up true life, and those who give up their lives for me will have true life. It is worth nothing for them to have the whole world if they lose their souls" (Mt 16:24–26, NCV; cf. 10:37 and Lk 14:26–27). Whatever else these difficult words mean, they clearly affirm the seriousness of following Jesus.

Similarly, Jesus taught clearly: "You cannot serve both God and Money" (Mt 6:24). In addition, James instructed his early Christian readers: "Religion that God our Father accepts as pure and faultless is this: to look after orphans and widows in their distress and to keep oneself from being polluted by the world" (Jas 1:27). With sobering words Jesus warned: "Not everyone who says to me, 'Lord, Lord,' will enter the kingdom of heaven, but only those who do the will of my Father who is in heaven" (Mt 7:21, TNIV).

Cultural values and false teaching can lull Christians today into a false sense of what God expects of them, as if he simply smiles upon whatever behavior or attitudes they adopt. Christian teachers need to understand what the biblical directives meant when first written and then explain how believers can fulfill God's expectations for his people today. Instructors need to advise believers how to serve Christ in the Church and in the world. If we are to be biblical Christians, we must obtain our agenda from God's Word. Skillful hermeneutics, again, guides our quest for what is truly God's will for his people. Ferguson reminds us that it is necessary "that the teacher preserve the delicate balance between being faithful to the intent of Scripture and allowing at the same time the Scripture to give perspective and guidance on current issues and problems."[52]

TO PROVIDE PASTORAL CARE

The Bible has always been a source of positive guidance as well as comfort and consolation for God's people. While the next section will examine the Bible's role in personal spiritual formation and in providing instruction for godly living, here we focus on its provision of care or guidance to people in times of need. We acknowledge the truth in Jesus' words, "In this world you will have trouble" (Jn 16:33). He was not unreasonably negative or unduly alarmist; his words simply state the human condition, not only for humanity as a whole, but also for disciples. Life is difficult. Moreover, as if that were not enough, the world is often especially hostile to Jesus' followers. Yet Jesus added a crucial and comforting assurance to that verse: "But take heart! I have overcome the world." What comfort or support exists for strugglers in the midst of life's trials and tragedies, not to mention its doubts and dilemmas?

Whether pastoral caregiver, close friend, or relative, the Christian has many resources available to help others in need. As Clinebell puts it, "Pastoral counseling draws on the rich wisdom and authority of the Hebrew-Christian tradition, as these are available through prayer, scripture, sacraments, liturgical practice, and the disciplines of the church."[53] The Bible stands as the major resource that empathetic helpers may use to provide relief for sufferers.[54] Using the Scriptures, we can remind those who despair

---

52 Ferguson, *Biblical Hermeneutics*, 122.

53 H. J. Clinebell, *Basic Types of Pastoral Counseling*, rev. ed. (Nashville: Abingdon, 1984). The quality and quantity of resources it encompasses increases all the time—particularly with the growing application of psychology to pastoral theology. A standard treatise that also covers the history of the discipline is C. V. Gerkin, *An Introduction to Pastoral Care* (Nashville: Abingdon, 1997). One finds many abundant specialized helps for various maladies and age groups. To mention only one of each: W. E. Oates, *Grief, Transition, And Loss: A Pastor's Practical Guide* (Minneapolis: Augsburg Fortress, 1997); and D. H. Grossoehme, *The Pastoral Care of Children* (*Binghamton*, NY: Haworth, 1999).

54 Observe, for example, how sensitively D. J. Tidball brings biblical insights and perspectives to bear in his excellent book on pastoral theology: *Skillful Shepherds* (Grand Rapids: Zondervan; Leicester: InterVarsity, 1986).

or grieve, who are lonely or in agony, that God does care for them; he shepherds them through their dark valleys; he remembers that they are dust and are frail (Psa 23:4; 103:14). In the Scripture's teachings about God's love and provisions, in the stories of men and women of faith, in the songs of comfort or prayers for deliverance, God's people can discover a sympathetic God who cares. Hannah's example of persevering prayer in the midst of childlessness (1 Sam 1–2) and Job's trust in God's character despite his painful plight (recall Job said, "Though he slay me, yet will I hope in him," 13:15) speak to the troubled today.

Jesus' comforting words to Martha—in the midst of his own pain over Lazarus' death—have provided hope for grieving loved ones ever since. He affirmed, "I am the resurrection and the life. Anyone who believes in me will live, even though they die; and whoever lives and believes in me will never die" (Jn 11:25–26 TNIV). In life's desperate misfortunes, when pain and agony impel us to cry out for explanations, and even in the silences when no answers appear, we take courage in Paul's assurance: "And we know that in all things God works for the good of those who love him, who have been called according to his purpose" (Rom 8:28). Moreover, to the Corinthians he wrote, "No temptation has overtaken you except what is common to us all. And God is faithful; he will not let you be tempted beyond what you can bear. But when you are tempted, he will also provide a way out so that you can endure it" (1 Cor 10:13 TNIV). Though the Bible may not depict the exact situation or dilemma we encounter today, it teaches such values and principles that promote comfort or healing or give guidance and hope.[55]

When dealing with the raw edges of human suffering, caregivers want to give as much hope and promise as possible. In such situations they may be tempted to abuse the Bible; so we must insist on responsible hermeneutics as much here as in all our uses of the Bible. We desperately want to assure a parent grieving over a wayward child that all will be well. Therefore, we may be tempted to turn the well-known proverb into a definitive promise: "Train children in the right way, and when old, they will not stray" (Prov 22:6 NRSV). However, sound hermeneutics forbids such an error because proverbs state general truths, not specific promises (also see 3:5–6). Alternatively, we may seek God's will in some situation and sincerely want to follow a path that honors him. Those are fine motives, but we cannot quote Jer 29:11 ("For I know the plans I have for you," declares the Lord, "plans to prosper you") as a specific promise of financial gain. Jeremiah referred to God's unique plans for Israel's return from exile; we cannot apply this across the board. Though God indeed seeks to "prosper" his people, we dare not read in the adverb "financially."

Other sections of the Bible suffer similar misuse in our well-meaning attempts to provide guidance or comfort. Indeed, such exploitation of the Scriptures is all too common. For example, some mistreat the story of the stilling of the storm on the Sea of Galilee (Mt 8:23–27).[56] Matthew surely intended the story to highlight the wonder

---

55 Outstanding examples that seek to understand the Bible's perspective in the midst of suffering are P. Yancey, *Disappointment with God* (Grand Rapids: Zondervan, 1997); and D. A. Carson, *How Long, O Lord? Reflections on Suffering and Evil* (Grand Rapids: Baker, 1990). Also see C. J. Van Der Poel, *Wholeness and Holiness: A Christian Response to Human Suffering* (Franklin, WI: Sheed and Ward, 1999).

56 See the discussion of how to interpret miracle stories above under Gospels.

and power of Jesus. It seeks to call attention to Jesus and elicit faith in him as the Lord of all. Yet we hear people treat the story as if it taught, "God will calm the storms of your life." This may be a true sentiment, but surely, it does not emerge in any hermeneutically defensible way from this passage. Equally, we cannot promise food or money to those going through economic hard times with Paul's words, "And my God will meet all your needs according to his glorious riches in Christ Jesus" (Phil 4:19).[57] This is not a universal promise. Paul's words followed his glowing commendation of the Philippians who generously supported his ministry (vv. 15–18). They gave sacrificially, and so Paul assured them that God would not abandon Christians who demonstrate such faithfulness. He would meet all their needs. Paul articulates the same principle when he says, "Whoever sows generously will also reap generously" (2 Cor 9:6). Worse yet may be those "counselors" who urge people to trust God for healing *rather than* seek professional medical help. We insist that it be both.

Again, we can confidently promise people from the Bible only those things that God has in fact *intended* to say. A responsible system of hermeneutics will restrain well-intentioned but misguided help. Caregivers dare not take texts out of context or make them say what God never intended they say. They subvert the function of God's Word when they make false promises or give false assurance in the name of God and the Bible. When such mistaken words prove to be empty, those in need of help may come to discount the value of the Bible or, worse, become disillusioned with God himself.

FOR SPIRITUAL FORMATION IN THE CHRISTIAN LIFE

As we have seen, people respond to the Bible's message in worship and praise, and the Bible's teachings provide comfort and hope. In addition, the Bible helps to build up the spiritual life; it provides motivation and guidance for living a life that pleases God. Personal spiritual development must rest upon correct and valid interpretations of the Bible. It is almost axiomatic to Christians that the Bible stands at the core of spiritual growth: to grow in the Christian faith mandates some regimen of Bible study.[58] In their earnest grappling with biblical teachings and their implications, Christians have a prime resource for becoming *spiritual* men and women of God.

This brings us back once again to one of the basic Christian presuppositions. If, indeed, the Bible represents God's revelation—his written communication to his people— then when they listen carefully to his voice on its pages, they encounter his very presence.

---

57 If this strikes readers as unduly harsh, we can only ask them to read our succeeding discussion on determining valid applications of Scripture. The two examples in this paragraph illustrate a point. We might want to add that the theology underlying both may support extended applications, but they must be more general and less authoritative, as we will explain below. To promise one who is suffering, "God will calm the storms of your life" because of Mt 8:23–27 may be cruelly hollow.

58 Note the primary place given to input from the Bible in such helpful books as B. Demarest, *Satisfy Your Soul. Restoring the Heart of Christian Spirituality* (Colorado Springs: NavPress, 1999); L. S. Cunningham and K. J. Egan, *Christian Spirituality. Themes from the Tradition* (New York: Paulist Press, 1996); M. J. Thompson, *Soul Feast. An Invitation to the Christian Spiritual Life* (Louisville: Westminster John Knox, 1995); H. Baker, *Soul Keeping. Ancient Paths of Spiritual Direction* (Colorado Springs: NavPress, 1998); not to mention recent "classics" as R. J. Foster, *Celebration of Discipline*, 3d ed. (New York: Harper and Row, 1988); and D. Bonhoeffer, *Meditating on the Word* (Cambridge, MA: Cowley, 1986). The literature on "spiritual formation" is growing rapidly, and these volumes constitute a small and valuable sample of the ones that show the place of the Bible in the process.

The Holy Spirit uses the Bible it inspired to speak to God's people. This is not "bibliolatry"; Christians do not worship the Bible itself. We believe that the Bible stands as God's written Word to us. So as we listen faithfully and expectantly to its Spirit-mediated message, we believe that we hear his voice. In Scripture we sense the supervision of a loving Parent whose instruction and counsel we seek and welcome.[59]

How may the Bible so form the inner being of the believer? First, the approach we have defended for understanding the intended meaning of the biblical texts provides the central input for this task. When we engage in a careful and faithful reading of the Bible, God nurtures our spiritual lives. Our minds grasp the meanings and principles, we see the examples to follow or to avoid, we exult in God's works on our behalf, we reflect on their implications for our lives, ministries, and relationships—all these and more provide instruction for the person who seeks to walk with God. We perform our Bible study with all due diligence, using sound principles of biblical interpretation, and we embrace their significance for our own walk with God.[60]

Yet for too many, this remains on an overly cognitive a level—what Robert Mulholland calls the "informational" level. Therefore, we suggest a second approach to pursue. Sometimes called *lectio divina* (sacred reading), this way of reading of the Scripture charts a different course.[61] Instead of being in control by seeking the author's intended meaning in the text, we let the text itself control the process—under the prayerful guidance of the Holy Spirit. More meditative, this kind of reading does not seek so much the meaning in the text as the meaning of our lives *under* the text's mastery. In the historic four stages of this type of reading, first one *reads* in a reflective, gentle, slow manner; the goal is to listen carefully, not to get through a body of text quickly. Second, one *meditates* on the significance of the text; meditation seeks to engage what one has read with the heart, thoughts, feelings, motivations, and the like. Third, one responds to this meditation in *prayer*—heart-felt cries to God that emerge from our meditation on the Word. Finally, one rests in quiet *contemplation* in the presence of God; it is a time of rest and peace with our God. These are not mechanical steps nor a set formula but a holistic attempt to engage God in his Word.

We do not offer these approaches in opposition to each other; reading the Bible for "information" is important—as we have demonstrated above. But we dare not allow this informational approach to crowd out the Bible's "formational" role—to allow God's Spirit to speak at the core of our being. However we do that, it must be done! We ought not merely to "know" what the Bible means; we need to ingest it internally. The goals of both informational and formational Bible reading are that we be motivated spiritually and

---

59 One senses the beauty of the connection of God and his people through the Bible in T. Longman, III, *Reading the Bible with Heart and Mind* (Colorado Springs: NavPress, 1997).

60 B. K. Waltke, "Exegesis and the Spiritual Life: Theology as Spiritual Formation," *Crux* 30 (1994): 28–35; E. H. Peterson, "Eat This Book: The Holy Community at Table with the Holy Scriptures," *Theology Today* 56 (1999): 5–17; and N. Vest, *Knowing by Heart: Bible Reading for Spiritual Growth* (London: Darton, Longman, and Todd, 1995).

61 A very useful explanation of this is M. R. Mulholland, Jr., *Shaped by the Word. The Power of Scripture in Spiritual Formation*, rev. ed. (Nashville: The Upper Room, 2001). A NT scholar by trade, he outlines the values of this "non-cognitive" approach to using the Bible in spiritual formation. For other useful insights and guidance on *lectio* see M. Casey, *Sacred Reading: The Ancient Art of Lectio Divina* (Liguori, MO: Triumph Books, 1996); Demarest, *Satisfy Your Soul*, 135–38; Cunningham and Egan, *Christian Spirituality*, 38–40; and Thompson, *Soul Feast*, 17–30.

directed by internal biblical principles, not simply those of the culture around us. We desire to grow spiritually and grow more Christ-like. We apply the principles we discover in Scripture, and we become more conformed to the image of Christ. The Bible shapes and colors our values and attitudes. With God's aid we apply what we learn—to grow in our devotion to serving God and other people. And our sense of God's presence and work in our lives deepens; an unbelievable calm enters—we feel his delight in us.

Often "God's aid," mentioned above, takes the form of God's agents—others on the spiritual journey with us. How to apply biblical principles must often be caught by observing it in the lives of others. An important concept to embrace when we think of spiritual formation is the need for mentors and mentoring.[62] This obviously overlaps several topics we have covered already—teaching, preaching, or pastoral care. On one side, we must seek mentors in our lives—to help impress on us God's ways and show us the "how to" of applying the Bible to our lives. On the other side, with spiritual maturity comes the responsibility and privilege of being a mentor in others' lives to enable them to live out the Bible's imperative for their lives. It means applying more broadly to the entire Church the principle involved in Paul's counsel to the older women in Crete: "But to teach what is good. Then they can urge the younger women to love their husbands and children, to be self-controlled and pure" (Titus 2:3b-5 TNIV).[63] In true biblical mentoring the mentor must assure that he or she imparts *biblical principles* into the life of the mentee.[64]

In short, as we interact with Scripture we engage in a two-way conversation with the Bible's Author.[65] As we understand what God says to us, we progress in our relationship with him and gain increased motivation to grow spiritually. The more we advance in this process, the more spiritually mature we become. Indeed, as Christians, we will develop and promote a spiritual life only by regular interaction with God through such disciplines as Bible study and prayer.[66]

Personal spiritual formation can never remain a private inner issue because the complement to spiritual *formation* is spiritual *living*, and the Bible functions significantly here, too. How do we know what lifestyle pleases God? Which actions demonstrate and grow out of the life of the Spirit and which are antithetical to that life? In the midst of

---

62 The literature on the topic of mentoring also grows rapidly. For helpful perspectives see P. R. Wilson, "Core Virtues for the Practice of Mentoring," *Journal of Psychology and Theology* 29 (2001): 121–30; B. Biehl, *Mentoring: Confidence in Finding a Mentor and Becoming One* (Nashville: Broadman & Holman, 1996); C. Kent, *Becoming a Woman of Influence: Making a Lasting Impact on Others* (Colorado Springs: NavPress, 1999); R. D. Reese and K. Anderson, *Spiritual Mentoring: A Guide for Seeking and Giving Direction* (Downers Grove: InterVarsity, 1999); and H. and W. Hendricks, *As Iron Sharpens Iron: Building Character in a Mentoring Relationship* (Chicago: Moody, 1999).

63 For other NT examples of mentoring and training in Scripture see D. E. Lanier, "The Multiplication of Disciples," *Faith and Mission* 16 (1999): 5–15.

64 J. M. Houston makes this important point in "Spiritual Mentoring in an Age of Confusion," *Crux* 30 / 4 (1994): 2–11.

65 One can even pray the Scriptures. See, inter alia, M. L. Smith, *The Word Is Very Near You. A Guide to Praying with Scripture* (Cambridge, MA: Cowley, 1989).

66 Of course, we do not intend in any sense to limit the means to spiritual formation to Bible study and prayer. The books noted in the previous two footnotes, to name a few, pursue a more full-orbed discussion of this crucial issue. We simply want to underscore here the crucial role the Bible ought to play.

the perplexing decisions of life, which options please God or promote his purposes for our lives? God's Word gives principles and instructions to guide us. We do not suggest that the Bible provides "ten easy steps" to attaining God's "perfect will" for our lives. The Bible does not speak specifically to all the personal decisions—either major or minor—that life demands of us each day. Neither do we suggest that it is always a simple matter to know what the best decision in a given situation is. Yet as the next chapter on application demonstrates, the Bible provides positive guidance so that we can act confidently and responsibly in compliance with God's purposes. The spiritually minded person—one whose heart and motivations are permeated with God's principles and purposes—will interact with this guidance in the decisions and activities of life. To obey God requires an act of submission, and the biblically informed believer has the resources to submit in ways that fulfill God's will.

How important it is then to handle the Bible with accuracy! If we desire to please God and do his will, we need a valid interpretation of the Bible. If we do not understand accurately what God intended to say in his Word, or if we read in our own subjective prejudices without any safeguards, we risk abusing the Bible for our own ends rather than using it with God's intentions. How tragic when, instead of following God's principles and will as clearly taught in the Scripture, people twist or reject its teachings to condone or even promote their sin. To illustrate, it is easy for us to condemn what we consider blatant sins, such as murder or adultery. But responsible readers must also acknowledge that the Bible insists that gossiping, greed, envy, and boasting are abhorrent offenses to God (Rom 1:29–32)! In reality, when Paul lists the kinds of lifestyles that disqualify people from entrance into God's eternal kingdom, greed is prominent on the list (1 Cor 6:9–10). How easy it is in our western affluence to turn greed and boasting into virtues. We envy what others possess, we believe the advertisers who assure us that "we deserve it," and we justify luxury, materialism, and often its accompanying bondage to debt.

All Christians, however sincere, face an ever-present tendency: to mold the Bible's teachings to promote their values instead of allowing the Bible to transform them. The Bible condemns many practices that we have come to accept and even recommend! Without doubt, we require a responsible hermeneutic to guide our interpretation and to assure its objectivity. We dare not make the Bible say what we want it to say or have it approve the activities that we want to pursue. The Bible, as God's revealed truth, demands that we submit to its teaching, not make it fit our desires. Of course, even after the best interpretive work is complete, the ultimate question remains: will we submit to God's requirements that we have discovered in his Word? Not will we do the ones we prefer as we prefer to do them, but will we satisfy the requirements of God? If we do not, we risk God's indictment on us, as on the Israelites of old. As one example, Amos paints the picture of God's response to Israel's injustice against the poor in their midst: "I hate, I despise your religious feasts; I cannot stand your assemblies. Even though you bring me burnt offerings and grain offerings, I will not accept them. . . . Away with the noise of your songs! I will not listen to the music of your harps. But let justice roll on like a river, righteousness like a never-failing stream!" (Amos 5:21–24). Being spiritually formed requires inner transformation that also transforms our lifestyle—precisely what the Spirit seeks to accomplish in concert with the Scriptures.

FOR AESTHETIC ENJOYMENT

In addition to all its other virtues, the Bible delights the people of God. Its pages brim with adventure, humor, and pageantry. It is a book of aesthetic beauty. Surely, God gave us this marvelous message to *enjoy*! God's message has come to us in various kinds of highly crafted literature. It would be difficult not to appreciate the Bible's assorted literary qualities and genius.[67] Though we do not limit the value of the Bible to being great literature, many people appropriately acknowledge the "Bible as Literature" and expound its literary excellence.[68] People savor the artful narrative of the intrigues of Joseph and his brothers, and they admire Nathan's cunningly simple parable to King David. They appreciate the masterful poetry in the Psalms and delight in the parables of Jesus. The Bible's diverse literature—OT epics, strange apocalyptic prophecy, tightly reasoned epistles, the skillful sustained argumentation in Hebrews—inspires and captures our interest. The Book itself arouses intellectual and emotional enjoyment. It invites us to appreciate its multifaceted beauty. But above that, the Bible's beauty and the pleasure it promotes reflects the beauty and personality of the God who inspired it. Its beauty sings his praises just as the stars and planets do (Psa 19).

SUMMARY

The Bible is a collection of remarkable writings of great consequence to all people. For believers it constitutes God's written revelation to his people. Moreover, as in any kind of communication, understanding the message is critical. Whether one communicates with a wink, a word, a picture, or oral speech, if the message gets garbled, the point is lost. Obviously, the results of a muddled message can range from inconsequential to tragic.

The Bible communicates in various ways and serves many purposes (as we have just reviewed). But if the Bible is to retain its integrity and potency as God's communication to his people, we must understand the intention of its message. We must not settle for muddled messages. To impose our own meaning is not a valid option. As we have argued, only a responsible system of hermeneutics gives us confidence that we have understood God's message. We must know the meaning of the Bible's message before we can expect that meaning to perform what God intended. That people misuse and misconstrue the Bible's teachings every day (as some have throughout the Church's history), does not invalidate the relevance of hermeneutics. That God may work through or even in spite of faulty interpretation is beside the point. If a child asks for arsenic and her mother hands her an apple, things may turn out well in that instance, but we dare not argue that to understand the correct meanings of the words "arsenic" and "apple" is irrelevant. So it is in the application of the Bible: correct meaning is paramount. We must always affirm that the best outcomes result from the most accurate interpretations—and outcomes constitute God's purpose for the Bible.

---

67 See the section on "Literary Criticism" in the bibliography for resources on investigating the literary dimensions of the Bible.

68 On this topic see L. Ryken, *How to Read the Bible as Literature* (Grand Rapids: Zondervan, 1985); and J. B. Gabel et al., *The Bible as Literature: an Introduction*, 4th ed. (Oxford, UK: Oxford University Press, 1999).

12

APPLICATION

In previous chapters we have described and defined how an interpreter deciphers the meaning of the text. Yet for the practicing Christian, the process begun with interpretation is incomplete if it stops at the level of meaning. One must then ask how the text applies to life. Certainly we cannot discover the proper application of a text until we have determined what it means. "Application focuses the truth of God's Word to specific, life-related situations. It helps people understand what to do or to use what they have learned."[1]

The terminology adopted for the stage of application varies. Some speak of application as part of interpretation, while others think of it as a separate step. Some talk of what the text *meant* versus what it *means*.[2] One of the most popular distinctions that evangelicals have utilized follows E. D. Hirsch's discussion of meaning versus significance.[3] "Meaning" refers to the ideas the biblical text originally intended to communicate to its readers; "significance" refers to the implications of that meaning in different, later situations. From this vantage point, therefore, the meaning of any given passage of Scripture remains consistent no matter who is reading the text, while its significance may vary from reader to reader. Quite recently various scholars have applied "speech-act theory" to distinguish the locutionary from the illocutionary or perlocutionary forces of a text—distinguishing, respectively, what a text says, what it does inherent in its speech, and what it subsequently accomplishes.[4]

But whatever the terminology employed, the issue is clear. How do we who believe the Bible remains relevant for people beyond the first audience determine that ongoing relevance? We might ask, "What bearing does the biblical message have on life today—on life in general and on my life in particular? How does God expect *me* to respond? What actions am I to *perform*?"[5]

---

1 D. Veerman, *How to Apply the Bible*, 2d ed (Wheaton: Tyndale, 1993), 15.

2 See esp. K. Stendahl, "Biblical Theology," in *Interpreter's Dictionary of the Bible*, ed. G. Buttrick (New York: Abingdon, 1962), 419–22.

3 E. D. Hirsch, Jr., *Validity in Interpretation* (New Haven: Yale University Press, 1967). For a somewhat technical and philosophical defense of this distinction against its critics, see G. R. Osborne, *The Hermeneutical Spiral* (Downers Grove: InterVarsity, 1991), 397–415.

4 See esp. A. C. Thiselton, *New Horizons in Hermeneutics* (Grand Rapids: Zondervan, 1992); and K. J. Vanhoozer, *Is There a Meaning in This Text?* (Grand Rapids: Zondervan, 1998); and the entire unfolding *Scripture and Hermeneutics Series* (Grand Rapids: Zondervan; Carlisle: Paternoster), esp. vol. 2: *After Pentecost: Language and Biblical Interpretation*, ed. C. Bartholomew, C. Greene, and K. Möller (2001).

5 S. C. Barton ("New Testament Interpretation as Performance," *SJT* 52 [1997]: 178–208) argues powerfully for this understanding of application as the necessary culmination of the interpretive process.

THE IMPORTANCE OF APPLICATION

Since not everyone shares our conviction that God intended his people to apply the Bible outside its original setting, we will discuss briefly two factors that support our conviction.[6] First, the Scriptures themselves repeatedly claim that people glorify God by obeying—that is by applying—his Word. After Moses reviewed the Law at the end of the wilderness wandering, he concluded by promising the people blessing and prosperity if, and only if, they obeyed the laws (Deut 30:11–20). Here blessing and prosperity are conditional; they follow only if people "apply" the laws to their daily lives. The historical and prophetic books of the OT in large measure describe the cycles of faithfulness and faithlessness that caused the Israelites alternately to receive God's blessing and judgment. The Assyrian and Babylonian captivities thus served as vivid reminders of the serious consequences of failing to live consistently with God's Word. In the Sermon on the Mount, Jesus reiterates the necessity not merely to hear his words but to put them into practice (Mt 7:13–27). James echoes Jesus' words when he reminds his audience, "Do not merely listen to the word, and so deceive yourselves. Do what it says" (Jas 1:22).

Second, the Bible claims that its message is relevant for later generations, not just its original readers. After Moses wrote down the Law and assigned the Levites as its custodians, he gave instructions for them to read it every seven years before the assembled people (Deut 31:9–13). Individual parents, however, were to teach the Law to their children on a regular basis (Deut 6:7–25). After centuries of relative neglect, Josiah obtained a copy of the Law, recognized its continuing authority, and led the people in renewing their commitment to God's covenant (2 Kgs 22–23). Over a century later when a remnant returned to Jerusalem from captivity in Babylon, Ezra the scribe reaffirmed the relevance of the Law for his generation by calling the people together to hear God's Word read and explained (Neh 7:73b–8:18). Later prophets applied to their own generations the messages given by earlier prophets. Jeremiah, for example, recalled Nathan's promises to David to assure the exiles that God would restore them to their land after seventy years in captivity (Jer 33:19–22; cf. 2 Sam 7:12–16). He also built on Isaiah's prophecy that a righteous branch would sprout from David's line (Jer 33:14–16; cf. Isa 11:1).

The NT contains equally striking evidence confirming that God's Word was designed not only for the original readers but also for subsequent generations. Note that just as Jesus commands his disciples to teach their disciples "everything I have commanded you" (Mt 28:20), he also prays not only for his immediate followers but also for all those who would believe in him through their message (Jn 17:20). In addition, Paul warns the believers in Corinth, who were emphasizing their freedom in Christ, of the dangers of idolatry and immorality by reminding them of God's judgment on the Israelites in the wilderness. Despite recognizing that these believers lived in a different age and era in salvation history, he nevertheless states, "Now these things occurred as examples to keep us from setting our hearts on evil things as they did" (1 Cor 10:6). He makes a similar point later to Roman believers but generalizes to include

---

6 For more detail, cf. W. Henrichsen and G. Jackson, *A Layman's Guide to Applying the Bible* (Grand Rapids: Zondervan, 1985), esp. 17–140.

all the OT: "For everything that was written in the past was written to teach us, so that through endurance and the encouragement of the Scriptures we might have hope" (Rom 15:4).

We understand that people who do not share our presuppositions about the authority of Scripture are not always as concerned to apply it. But in light of the Scriptures' own witness,[7] we find it more difficult to comprehend why many who claim to be Bible-believing Christians read and study the Bible so minimally and are so little concerned to apply it correctly.[8] And even among those who do seek to implement God's Word, many do not consistently heed "the whole counsel of God" (cf. Acts 20:27). Certain parts of the Psalms and Proverbs, the Gospels, and Paul's letters are well-known and applied, while much of the rest of Scripture remains virtually untouched.

This leads to an important theological conviction. *All* Scripture is both inspired and relevant ("useful for teaching, rebuking, correcting, and training in righteousness, so that all God's people may be thoroughly equipped for every good work"—2 Tim 3:16 TNIV). This does not mean that we will find a personal application in every phrase or sentence in Scripture, because the amount and kind of application of a passage will vary from genre to genre. We must interpret and apply each text in its context as part of a larger meaningful linguistic utterance. Tightly packed didactic, epistolary texts may place demands on our lives in virtually every phrase and clause. At the other end of the spectrum, we may read several chapters of genealogical material (e.g., in 1 Chr 1–12) before finding much of relevance, and even then only broad principles—about God's providence, his plan of salvation, his concern for individuals, and so on. But every sentence, indeed every verse, appears as part of a larger, coherent unit of thought that has some relevance for us.[9]

AVOIDING MISTAKES IN APPLICATION

Despite the importance of application, few modern evangelical scholars have focused on this topic. In fact, most hermeneutics textbooks give it only brief coverage, and many major commentary series only mention application with passing remarks to help readers bridge the gap from the biblical world to the modern world. Perhaps many assume that sound application is more "caught than taught." This is probably true, but sound application often seems hard to find, much less to catch! Fortunately, recent studies are helping to rectify this error of omission. Anthropologists, linguists, and missiologists are engaging in intensive discussions of contextualization: how to apply the

---

7 On the significance of the Scriptures' own claim to their authority more generally, see W. A. Grudem, "Scripture's Self-Attestation and the Problem of Formulating a Doctrine of Scripture," in *Scripture and Truth,* ed. D. A. Carson and J. D. Woodbridge (Grand Rapids: Zondervan, 1983), 19–59.

8 On Bible-reading habits among American Christians in the early 1990s, see G. Barna, *What Americans Believe* (Ventura: Regal, 1991), 286–91. An update (G. Barna and M. Hatch, *Boiling Point* [Ventura: Regal, 2001], 213) shows that such habits have continued to deteriorate in the following decade.

9 See further K. J. Vanhoozer, "The Semantics of Biblical Literature: Truth and Scripture's Diverse Literary Forms," in *Hermeneutics, Authority, and Canon,* ed. D. A. Carson and J. D. Woodbridge (Grand Rapids: Zondervan, 1986), 49–104.

Bible cross-culturally from a Western to a non-Western context.[10] And the principles involved prove identical to those needed to apply the Bible from its original non-Western context to a Western one such as ours (or any others, for that matter).[11] Several recent commentary series are working more self-consciously and with greater sophistication to meet the need for application. By far and away the most helpful of these is the NIV Application Commentary Series from Zondervan, which organizes all of its comments on each text under three headings: "original meaning," "bridging contexts," and "contemporary significance."[12] Nevertheless, much more work remains, for Christians today still encounter widespread misapplication of Scripture. Though we could readily multiply and categorize examples in detail, we will point out three of the most common here. [13]

Total Neglect of Any Context

We might term this the "ouija board" approach to guidance. Christians who want to base their decisions on the will of God may be tempted to use the Bible as if it were a magical book. For example, often after a prayer for divine help they might open the Bible at random and accept the verse their eyes fall on as God's guidance for the decision they are making. While God might conceivably accommodate a sincere but misguided Christian through this method, he never promises to do so; consequently, serious mistakes with damaging consequences inevitably occur when people persist in this approach. One of us, for example, knew a young man who had to decide whether to enlist in the armed forces or go to college. Opening his Bible at random, he saw the passage in Ezekiel that speaks of people coming from Tarshish to Tyre in ships (Ezek 27:25). Although this passage contains no command for anyone to go anywhere in a ship and has nothing to do with becoming part of the armed forces, this young man interpreted the text as a call to join the Navy. Chances are good that he deprived himself of a college education by making a decision he thought was God's will but perhaps was not. More seriously, though, he completely misunderstood what role the Bible should have in the Christian decision-making process.

---

10 Two of the most well-known are C. Kraft, *Christianity in Culture* (Maryknoll: Orbis, 1979); and O. Costas, *Liberating News: A Theology of Contextual Evangelization* (Grand Rapids: Eerdmans, 1989). Recall our earlier discussion under historical-cultural background. Two good, succinct, recent surveys on the connection between contextualization and hermeneutics are D. Sanchez, "Contextualization in the Hermeneutical Process," in *Biblical Hermeneutics*, ed. B. Corley, S. Lemke, and G. Lovejoy (Nashville: Broadman and Holman, 1996), 293–306; and T. E. van Spanje, "Contextualization: Hermeneutical Remarks," *BJRL* 80 (1998): 197–217.

11 A point stressed by Osborne in his helpful chapters on application, both labeled, somewhat idiosyncratically, "Homiletics" and subdivided into "Contextualization" and "The Sermon" (*The Hermeneutical Spiral*, 318–65).

12 The next best three are *The Bible Speaks Today* and *The New Testament Commentary*, both from InterVarsity Press, and *Interpretation* from Westminster John Knox Press.

13 As, e.g., in J. W. Sire, *Scripture Twisting: Twenty Ways the Cults Misread the Bible* (Downers Grove: InterVarsity, 1980), which covers errors of interpretation as well as errors of application (errors that, unfortunately, are by no means limited to the cults!). Cf. also T. Longman, III, (*Reading the Bible with Heart and Mind* [Colorado Springs: NavPress, 1997], 53–56) who discusses the "distorting lenses" of treating Scripture as a "treasure chest of golden truths," "grab bag of promises and comforts," a compilation of "riddles and secrets," or "a talisman with magical power."

A more unfortunate incident was recorded a number of years ago on the front page of the sports section of a major Chicago newspaper under the bold headline, "God's Orders Send Pitcher Packing." The story explained how the Christian owner of a minor league baseball team decided to release a pitcher who had requested a raise in pay. She opened her Bible at random, again to Ezekiel (no doubt because it comes roughly in the middle!), and read the phrase, "prepare thee stuff for removing" (Ezek 12:3 KJV). This became her guidance "from God" for dismissing the pitcher. Had she read the context, she would have discovered that these instructions from God to Ezekiel concerned an object lesson Ezekiel was to give the Israelites. He was to pack as if going on a long trip, but he was not actually supposed to go anywhere. Had the owner of this team really wanted to imitate Ezekiel (which would still not have been a correct application of the passage!), *she* would have been the one to make preparations for leaving rather than firing someone else.[14]

Partial Neglect of the Literary or Historical Context of a Passage

Fortunately, most Bible readers usually avoid the extreme errors of the ouija board approach. Much more common, however, is the proof-texting error that is often unwittingly encouraged by Bible memory systems that focus primarily on individual verses. To their credit, those who use this approach at least read entire sentences as meaningful units of thought, but often they fail to observe the larger contexts that appear to limit the application in important ways. Phil 4:13, for example, suffers regular abuse. Christians often announce, "I can do everything through him who gives me strength," to reassure others (or themselves) that they can succeed in undertakings for which they may or may not be qualified. Subsequent failure leaves them distraught with God as if he had broken his promise! But had they read vv. 11 and 12, they would have seen that the application of this passage is limited to contentment regardless of one's economic circumstances.[15]

In other instances, such readers miss important contextual or historical-cultural background insights. Psa 127:3–5, for example, reads:

> Sons are a heritage from the Lord, children a reward from him. Like arrows in the hands of a warrior are sons born in one's youth. Blessed is the man whose quiver is full of them. They will not be put to shame when they contend with their enemies in the gate.

This is a popular passage for wedding ceremonies, perhaps because Christian couples think that God is thus commanding them to have large families. If so, they need to look more carefully at the historical context. Contending with their enemies in the gate of an ancient walled city refers either to military battle or to legal action (which took place near the city gate). The language here is exclusive: "sons" does not include "daughters" because in ancient Israel girls could be neither soldiers nor legal witnesses. In an age when infant and child mortality rates were high, large families ensured that

---

14 For details of this example, along with a discussion of inappropriate uses of a "fleece" to determine God's will, see K. A. Ecklebarger, "Are We Fleecing Ourselves?" *Moody Monthly* 85 (Nov. 1984): 26–28.

15 Cf. further R. R. Melick, *Philippians, Colossians, Philemon,* NAC (Nashville: Broadman, 1991), 154–55.

sufficient sons would survive to care for aged parents in their declining years. While there is at least one clear principle in this passage that Christians can apply (e.g., about the need to care for one's elderly parents, cf. 1 Tim 5:8), Christians dare not use this verse to assert that all couples must have large families.[16]

Insufficiently Analogous Situations

The most subtle of all misapplications of Scripture occurs when readers correctly interpret passages in their literary and historical contexts but then bring them to bear on situations where they simply do not apply. The temptation of Christ well illustrates the subtlety and sinister nature of this misapplication. Using a cunning ploy, Satan quoted Psa 91:11–12 and challenged Jesus saying, "If you are the Son of God . . . throw yourself down. For it is written, 'He will command his angels concerning you, and they will lift you up in their hands, so that you will not strike your foot against a stone'" (Mt 4:5). Here Satan asks Jesus to display God's miraculous ability to preserve his life. Certainly Jesus himself had such power. What is more, the psalmist states that God promises safety and protection to anyone who "dwells in the shelter of the Most High" (Psa 91:1). The problem here is that the devil's challenge confuses the psalmist's reference to "unintentional stumbling" with taking a *deliberate* jump off the Temple pinnacle. The psalmist's intent here is not that we test God's faithfulness to his Word by manufacturing situations in which we try to force him to act in certain ways. Rather, it points out his providential care for his children. Jesus thus refutes the devil with another text of Scripture that strictly forbids presuming on the grace of God (Deut 6:16).[17] No passage of Scripture can be casually or carelessly applied to any and/or every situation.

A FOUR-STEP METHODOLOGY FOR LEGITIMATE APPLICATION

What then should we do? It is always easier to spot fallacies in wrong methods than to formulate sound principles. The very nature of application—which varies from individual to individual in ways that meaning does not[18]—indicates that we probably cannot create a comprehensive list of foolproof principles; however, we can formulate some general and workable guidelines. The preceding examples of how *not* to apply passages remind us that all applications must be consistent with the meaning of passages arrived at by means of the sound hermeneutical principles we have already discussed in this book.[19] Legitimate application requires the use of both the general hermeneutical principles (establishing an accurate text, the correct meaning of words, the historical-cultural background, the larger literary contexts, and the like) and also special hermeneutics or genre criticism. In other words, we must also ask of historical narratives if various char-

---

16 Cf. further L. C. Allen, *Psalms 101–50*, WBC 21 (Waco: Word, 1983), 180–1.

17 Cf. further C. L. Blomberg, *Matthew*, NAC (Nashville: Broadman, 1992), 84–85.

18 A point no more strongly stressed than by W. C. Kaiser, Jr. "The Single Intent of Scripture," in *Evangelical Roots,* ed. K. Kantzer (Nashville: Nelson, 1978), 123–41, and elsewhere. Rather than speak of single intent or single meaning with multiple applications or significances, however, it seems to us better to speak of fixed meaning with varying significances. Kaiser's language could wrongly suggest that certain passages originally intended to communicate only one idea when in fact several are present.

19 Cf. B. Ramm, *Protestant Biblical Interpretation,* 3d rev. ed. (Grand Rapids: Baker, 1970), 185.

acters represent good or bad examples or if they merely describe what happened as part of some larger theological point about God's working in the world. We must inquire if prophecies were pointing to current events in the biblical writer's day, to the First Coming of Christ, to his Second Coming, or to some combination of the three. We must inquire whether proverbs are descriptive or prescriptive and, if the latter, to what extent they teach absolutes or mere generalizations. We must also determine in what ways OT laws were fulfilled in Christ. In short, most of the principles and many of the examples already discussed in this volume suggest legitimate applications.

But we can say more. Recent evangelical analysis has come to a consensus that the key to legitimate application involves what many writers call "principlizing."[20] This may be defined as "an attempt to discover in a narrative [i.e., a text] the spiritual, moral, or theological principles that have relevance for the contemporary believer."[21] How one develops this process ranges from the relatively simple to the relatively complex. Jack Kuhatschek's excellent *Taking the Guesswork Out of Applying the Bible* boils it all down to three steps: understand the original situation, determine the broader principle that the biblical application reflects, and apply that general principle to situations we face.[22] Ramesh Richard, on the other hand, enumerates six steps that move from biblical statements to implications, extrapolations, applicational interpretations, interpretive applications, and finally to significance.[23] We propose the following four-stage model that we believe incorporates all of the major elements of these and other paradigms currently used:

1. Determine the original application(s) intended by the passage.
2. Evaluate the level of specificity of those applications to their original historical situations. If the original specific applications are transferable across time and space to other audiences, apply them in culturally appropriate ways.
3. If the original applications are not transferable, identify one or more broader cross-cultural principles that the specific elements of the text reflect.
4. Find appropriate applications for today that implement those principles.

To explain these steps further, we will briefly elaborate on each.[24]

---

20 E. E. Johnson, *Expository Hermeneutics: An Introduction* (Grand Rapids: Zondervan, 1990), 229. For a curious exception, see P. Enns, *Exodus*, NIVAC (Grand Rapids: Zondervan, 2000), who disputes the legitimacy of doing this and thus uses the "Bridging Contexts" section of the NIVAC's format not to discuss cross-cultural principles as other volumes do, but to present the rest of the Bible's teaching on the same theme (which, of course, is an important check and balance in the applicational process). E. A. Martens ("How Is the Christian to Construe Old Testament Law?" *BBR* 12 [2002]: 199–216) explicitly pits this approach of "biblical theology" against "principlizing," but this would be to contrast apples and oranges, as the former is not an alternate method to the latter but one important tool in determining timeless principles.

21 H. A. Virkler, *Hermeneutics* (Grand Rapids: Baker, 1981), 212.

22 (Downers Grove: InterVarsity, 1990), 33.

23 R. P. Richard, "Application Theory in Relation to The New Testament," *BSac* 143 (1986): 211.

24 Cf. also J. S. Duval and J. D. Hays, *Grasping God's Word* (Grand Rapids: Zondervan, 2001), 204–12.

Determine the Original Application(s)

In this step the interpreter asks questions such as: How did the biblical author of a given passage want his hearers or readers to respond? What did the author intend the readers to do? To answer these questions the interpreter asks a series of additional questions. Is there a command to obey, an example to follow or to avoid, a promise to claim, a warning to heed, a teaching to act on (even if not phrased as a direct command), or a truth to believe?[25] We can suggest other queries such as: Is there a need that prompts prayer or a blessing that motivates praise? Sometimes contemporary applications will be identical to the originally intended responses, though often they will differ in some ways.

For example, obeying the *command* not to covet a neighbor's wife or house remains as timely today as it did when Moses received it on Mount Sinai (Exod 20:17). But this verse also prohibits coveting a neighbor's manservant, maidservant, ox, or donkey. The principle that prohibits covetousness finds its appropriate application in specific areas. The text identifies those possessions of their neighbors that the Israelites might be most tempted to desire. Most Western urban dwellers do not have to worry about the last four of these. The interpreter needs to ask what might be the relevant possessions today and include these in the application: a car, a home entertainment center, or a computer, and so on. In fact the text of Exodus specifically justifies such generalization by concluding "or anything that belongs to your neighbor."

Changing the example, to apply correctly the early church members' practices of sharing their faith, modern readers need to focus on marketplace evangelism (Acts 17:17). Many groups automatically assume that identical practices are both appropriate and necessary today. In certain contexts and certain cultures this may be true, but the interpreter must inquire why the first Christians gravitated to the central squares of Asian and European towns to preach. The answer is: public arenas were the socially acceptable places to consider new ideas (cf. Acts 17:18–21). That is where they applied the principle of evangelizing the world. Many Third-World villages today have similarly structured communities whose central plazas make ideal settings for preaching the gospel. But most Western cities have no such centralized location, and the nearest equivalent—a shopping mall, park, or an airport terminal—is not a place where people go to hear the latest news or to hear visitors publicly greet the town. In fact, because non-Christian cult members often conduct their evangelism in these arenas, Christians have to overcome a cultural stigma to witness effectively in such places. Sensitive application of Acts 17 may motivate believers to look for better, more suitable forums (in colleges and universities, through radio and television, and the like) while not neglecting legitimate opportunities for "street evangelism."[26]

Asking if there is a truth to *believe* and a teaching to *act upon* from Acts 16:25–34 would certainly yield the identical answer Paul gave to the Philippian jailer: "Believe in the Lord Jesus, and you will be saved" (v. 31). This example differs from the previous two since the application is already at the level of a general principle, so we need not pursue the remaining steps in the process. However, since many readers of this

---

25 T. N. Sterrett, *How to Understand Your Bible* (Downers Grove: InterVarsity, 1974), 172–78.

26 For a sensitive treatment of the topic, see M. Green, *Evangelism in the Early Church* (London: Hodder and Stoughton, 1970). See also throughout A. Fernando, *Acts*, NIVAC (Grand Rapids: Zondervan, 1998).

passage are already believers, they simply need to consider how they can help others apply its message. These three examples have taken us through the entire process of application, but we need to go on to itemize what we have done and give further illustrations.

Evaluate the Level of Specificity of the Original Application(s)

This step was a fairly easy task for the passages on coveting and on believing in Jesus that we just discussed. The command against coveting a neighbor's wife or husband clarified that this was a specific example of the more general prohibition against coveting what belongs to others (the precursor to theft). In the Acts 16 example of believing in Jesus, anyone at all familiar with the Bible or Christian teaching recognizes this as the foundational principle of the NT that is repeated in many different ways and places. But in the example of marketplace evangelism, not every reader will realize this is a specific example of a broader principle that may vary from one context to the next. Those familiar with biblical examples and commands concerning evangelism will realize that the methods vary while the mandate to share the faith widely remains consistent. Even then, further historical and cultural background information may help readers to understand what functional equivalents to the marketplace may be available for believers in other times and places.

The issues raised here revolve around a major topic in the study of hermeneutics, and, more specifically, of application. How does the interpreter know when certain biblical commands, examples, promises, warnings, and so on, are "culture-bound" (i.e., limited to their original context, not timeless or universal)? To answer the question, we suggest further questions: When can the interpreter rightly assume that the text presents a specific *form* (example) of a more general *principle*? When does the principle remain timeless and unchanging? How may the form of implementing that principle change from one context to the next?[27]

Perhaps no more controversial example of this dilemma afflicts Christianity today than the issue of women's roles in the home and the Church, given, on one hand, the stance of the "historic" churches (Orthodoxy and Roman Catholicism) and other traditionalists, and, on the other hand, the recent impact of "women's liberation." Although key texts (e.g., 1 Cor 11:2–16; 14:33b-38; Eph 5:18–33; 1 Tim 2:8–15; 1 Pet 3:1–7) indicate certain timeless elements and certain culture-bound elements, sorting out which is which proves immensely difficult. Take 1 Tim 2:8–15, for example. Many would agree that it is possible to pray in a godly fashion without necessarily "lifting up holy hands" (cf. v. 8), and that braided hair for women is not always (or often) immoral (v. 9). The principles involved concern praying and dressing appropriately, not how that may have looked in the Ephesian church. Similarly, few would challenge that it is always appropriate for men to pray without anger or disputing (v. 8) and that women should always perform good deeds (v. 10). But what does the interpreter do with vv. 11–12, in which women are commanded to learn in quietness and full submission and not to teach or have authority over men? In addition to questions about the translation of key words in this passage and their grammatical relationship to one another, the debate over the function of vv. 13–14 looms large. To many interpreters,

---

27 Cf. esp. D. J. Estes, "Audience Analysis and Validity in Application," *BSac* 150 (1993): 219–29.

v. 13 grounds Paul's commands in God's order of creating man first and then woman. They see this as a natural indicator that they should apply his teaching universally. Verse 14, however, seems to base those same commands in the events of the Fall, in which case we would expect the redemption in Christ to reverse its effects.

While we do not propose to take a stand on the foregoing passage,[28] we do note that many hermeneutics textbooks use passages like this to illustrate the principles they outline, and if readers disagree with their particular interpretations and applications, unfortunately, they question the principles employed.[29] We must admit that the passages involving women's and men's roles are among the most difficult in Scripture, and this accounts for the sincere disagreement of godly, well-educated and intentioned interpreters. Consequently, these passages are examples of the difficulty of positing universal application except perhaps to rule out some of the most extreme and unlikely positions. Individual preunderstandings almost inevitably color interpreters' approaches to these delicate texts.[30]

We purpose here to list a variety of criteria that will enable most interpreters to reach a fair measure of agreement on a wide variety of less complex texts, which they can employ with the more complicated passages. Before doing so, however, we must introduce one other preliminary matter. Many passages in Scripture do not clearly indicate whether they convey universal principles or only culture-specific applications. As a result, on one extreme some interpreters argue that unless something in the text specifically indicates that the passage teaches a timeless truth, we should assume it to be "occasional," that is, limited in its specific application to its original context.[31] On the other pole, other writers assume that the reverse is true: unless specific textual data support a "culture-bound" perspective, we should assume the originally intended application remains normative for all believers of all times.[32]

We detect problems, however, with both of these views. The former makes it difficult to establish the timelessness even of fundamental moral principles such as prohibitions against theft or murder;[33] the latter would seem to require us to bar children

---

28 For a recent juxtaposition of egalitarian and complementarian perspectives, see J. R. Beck and C. L. Blomberg, eds., *Two Views on Women in Ministry* (Grand Rapids: Zondervan, 2001).

29 E.g., D. A. Carson, *Exegetical Fallacies*, 2d ed. (Grand Rapids: Baker, 1996), 108–12 (but this feature is noticeably lessened from the first edition); Osborne, *The Hermeneutical Spiral*, 328–30; G. D. Fee and D. Stuart, *How to Read The Bible For All Its Worth*, 2d ed. (Grand Rapids: Zondervan, 1994), 74–75.

30 On which, see esp. R. K. Johnston, "The Role of Women in the Church and Home: An Evangelical Testcase in Hermeneutics," in *Scripture, Tradition and Interpretation*, ed. W. W. Gasque and W. S. LaSor (Grand Rapids: Eerdmans, 1978), 234–59; and A. J. Köstenberger, "Gender Passages in the New Testament: Hermeneutical Fallacies Critiqued," *WTJ* 56 (1994): 259–83. But in principle, we should be able to bracket our powerful presuppositions and make progress, as recent research in fact suggests is occurring.

31 See the discussion of and response to this and related perspectives in J. R. McQuilkin, "Problems of Normativeness in Scripture: Cultural Versus Permanent," in *Hermeneutics, Inerrancy, and the Bible*, ed. E. D. Radmacher and R. D. Preus (Grand Rapids: Zondervan, 1984), 222–27.

32 The view McQuilkin himself presupposes ("Normativeness," 230) and defended by W. J. Larkin, Jr., *Culture and Biblical Hermeneutics* (Grand Rapids: Baker, 1988), 314–18.

33 McQuilkin, "Normativeness," 225–27. This may account for some clergy defenses of abortion.

born outside marriage from our churches (Deut 23:2), to greet one another with a holy kiss (1 Thes 5:26), and to drink wine for upset stomachs (1 Tim 5:23).[34] This debate in fact reminds us of the polarization of perspectives on the application of OT Law in the NT age. As with our resolution of that debate, we believe the fairest and most scriptural approach assumes neither of the above perspectives, but rather a mediating one. With 2 Tim 3:16 and related texts, we affirm that every passage (a meaningful unit of discourse that makes one or more points that can be restated, if necessary, in a proposition) has some normative value for believers in all times and places (recall Rom 15:4). But we presuppose nothing about whether the application for us today will come by preserving unchanged the specific elements of the passage or whether we will have to identify broader principles that suggest unique applications for new contexts.[35] Instead we ask a series of ten questions of the text:[36]

1. *Does the text present a broad theological or moral principle or does it give a specific manifestation of such a principle, which another book of Scripture elsewhere embodies in one or more different forms?* Nine-tenths of the Decalogue (minus the Sabbath command) clearly illustrates such broad moral categories (Exod 20:2–17). Much of the rest of the Law gives specific ways of obeying and disobeying these principles. In the NT, both Jesus and Paul reaffirm the continuing relevance of all nine.[37] The same is true of the so-called double-love command (Deut 6:4–5; cf. Lev 19:18), which Jesus brings together in Mk 12:29–31 ("'Love the Lord your God' . . . . 'Love your neighbor as yourself'"). Romans 12:1–9 presents fundamental ethical obligations for believers: transformation of body and mind; use of spiritual gifts; and, again, love. A theme that recurs in the Law, Psalms, Proverbs, the Prophets, the Gospels, and the Epistles is the prohibition against partiality and the need to show mercy to the poor and dispossessed, to the outcast and the stranger.

On the other hand, numerous specific texts illustrate *applications* of this principle that may need to change if the principle is to be successfully implemented in new contexts. For example, OT Law commanded farmers not to harvest the very edges of their field or go over their land a second time to glean what they missed in the initial harvest. This enabled the poor to gather freely the leftovers (Lev 19:9–10). These commands presuppose a rural, agrarian society in which the poor have access to the fields. Such an application would scarcely help the vast majority of urban poor in our world today. Instead, those who seek to apply this text must find new ways to prevent the wasting or hoarding of surplus food in our world and to give some of this away to the poor. Restaurant owners might willingly restrict their profits for the sake of such redistribution. One Christian businessman in the Denver area, for example, tried repeatedly and finally succeeded in getting a major airline to donate its unused meals to a local clearinghouse for Christian charities, which in turn distributed them to needy people.

---

34 A. Johnson, "A Response to Problems of Normativeness in Scripture: Cultural Versus Permanent," in Radmacher and Preus, eds., *Hermeneutics, Inerrancy, and the Bible,* 277–78.

35 Similarly Osborne, *The Hermeneutical Spiral,* 326.

36 The list of ten does not purport to be exhaustive but illustrative. It shares important similarities with that of Johnson, "Response," 279–80, but is by no means identical.

37 For a justification of treating the Sabbath command differently, see esp. D. A. Carson, ed., *From Sabbath to Lord's Day* (Grand Rapids: Zondervan, 1982).

We may need to find equivalents to the effort expended in gleaning so that poor people today have to expend some effort for their food rather than simply receiving it free. Many charitable food banks have allowed the poor to retain their dignity and incentive to work through charging a nominal fee for commodities. The laws of gleaning are thus relevant as a specific example of the broader principle of concern for the poor, even if we do not imitate exactly their ancient formal application.[38] Certainly the Scriptures themselves exhibit a diversity of responses to the problem (cf. Mk 10:21; Lk 19:8; Acts 4:32–35; Jas 1:27).

2. *Does the larger context of the same book of Scripture in which the passage appears limit the application in any way or does it promote a more universal application?* This question concerns information that might be near to the passage or separated from it in another part of the book. For example, the interpreter might read Jesus' warning to Peter that he would have to die for his faith (Jn 21:18–19) and wonder how widely it applies. Even if not every Christian is martyred, should all believers at least be prepared for someone to lead them "where [they] do not want to go" (v. 18b)? Reading further in the context leads the interpreter to see that Jesus predicts a quite different kind of destiny for John (vv. 20–23). In fact, some later misinterpreted Jesus' words as implying that John would live until Christ's return (v. 23). But Jesus did not say that. In fact he spoke positively enough about John's future to clarify that his words to Peter applied to Peter alone and could not be generalized to include anyone else.[39]

On the other hand, the book of Ecclesiastes is more difficult to assess in places. It is clear that the author has indulged in most of life's pleasures and found them to be futile. Even though periodically he punctuates his narrative with seemingly positive principles such as, "A person can do nothing better than to eat and drink and find satisfaction in his work" (Eccl 2:24a TNIV), ambiguity clouds his statements. Although he immediately adds, "this too, I see, is from the hand of God" (v. 24b), he ends the paragraph with the conclusion, "this too is meaningless, a chasing after the wind." We detect his purpose only when we recognize chaps. 11–12 as the concluding lessons that "the Preacher" has learned. Here he presents without any qualification similarly positive commands to enjoy life in wholesome ways while one is able (11:9–12:1; 12:13). This suggests that passages like 2:24a have a timeless, normative value.[40]

3. *Does subsequent revelation limit the application of a particular passage even if the book in which it appears does not?* Obviously, the interpreter must ask this question of every OT text. As discussed above, we can assume neither that all of the OT carries over into the NT without any change in application nor that none of it carries over unchanged. Rather, we must examine each text to discover how it has been fulfilled in Christ (Mt

---

38 An excellent, recent resource for implementing these principles today is T. Sine, *Mustard Seed vs. McWorld* (Grand Rapids: Baker, 1999). Cf. also J. Ronsvalle and S. Ronsvalle, *The Poor Have Faces: Loving Your Neighbor in the 21st Century* (Grand Rapids: Baker, 1992).

39 Cf. further D. A. Carson, *The Gospel According to John* (Grand Rapids: Eerdmans, 1991), 679–82.

40 Though even then interpreters do not all agree. We have followed the perspective we believe to be ably defended in M. A. Eaton, *Ecclesiastes* TOTC (Downers Grove: InterVarsity, 1983); and W. C. Kaiser, Jr., *Ecclesiastes: Total Life*, LBC (Chicago: Moody, 1979). For a more pessimistic perspective, see T. Longman, III, *The Book of Ecclesiastes*, NICOT (Grand Rapids: Eerdmans, 1998).

5:17). But the same test must be applied to NT texts, not because we live in a new period of salvation history but because the NT itself sometimes revokes earlier commands or presents alternate models. In such cases earlier applications of the principles were not intended to be normative for every place and time.

A well-known example is Jesus' command to his disciples to take along no money or provisions for their itinerant preaching but to rely solely on the generosity of those to whom they minister (Mt 10:9–10). Later, however, Jesus refers specifically to these commands (Lk 22:35) and then says, "But now if you have a purse, take it, and also a bag" (v. 36). Paul does this, too, changing or reversing early practices later on in his ministry. On occasion he relies on other Christians for financial support; at other times he makes tents to finance his ministry. The rationale in each case is what most effectively advances the cause of the gospel (1 Cor 9). It is thus inappropriate for Christians today to assume that all full-time Christian workers must be paid by other believers or that none may be so remunerated. We must ask which option will bring the most number of people to Christ (or most effectively accomplish the ministry objectives). Which will avoid putting the gospel into disrepute? Which will not overly burden God's people? Given the abuses of fund-raising by so many in ministries today, we could make a good case for promoting far more tent-making models than currently exist![41]

4. *Is the specific teaching "contradicted" elsewhere in ways that show it was limited to exceptional situations?* In a sense this is simply an important subquestion of the previous one. Because Scripture portrays Abraham as a paradigm of faith and obedience, we must ask how we can apply the story of his willingness to offer up his son Isaac on the altar (Gen 22). Although we will return to this example later, one thing seems clear here: God does not want us to sacrifice our children (as did many early Canaanite—and a few contemporary pagan—religions). Later laws make this abundantly plain (e.g., Lev 18:21; 20:2–5). We cannot know whether Abraham realized that in his day, but we need not vacillate. As the narrative shows, God never intended that Abraham kill his son. Surely the test was a unique one, not repeated elsewhere in Scripture and not to be repeated by any subsequent believers.

Another inimitable example is God's unusual call to the prophet Hosea to "go, take for yourself a wife of whoredom and have children of whoredom" (cf. Hos 1:2). While some first-time readers of this passage might question why God appears to condone prostitution or at least tells Hosea to marry an apparently unrepentant prostitute, this situation is unique and bears closer study. To begin with, it is unclear if this text originally meant, as is usually assumed, that Gomer already was a harlot, or if it merely anticipated her later adultery.[42] But even if the former, other Scriptures unequivocally state that prostitution is sinful (Lev 19:29; 1 Cor 6:15). What then are we to make of Hosea uniting again with his wife after her later adultery (Hos 3:1)? Jesus indicates that reconciliation is not always possible or necessary following marital unfaithfulness (Mt 19:9).[43] But unlike the Judaism of his day, he never mandated divorce, even in the case

---

41 On this theme, cf. further J. M. Bassler, *God and Mammon: Asking for Money in the New Testament* (Nashville: Abingdon, 1991); C. L. Blomberg, *Neither Poverty nor Riches: A Biblical Theology of Possessions* (Leicester: InterVarsity, 1999).

42 See D. L. Hubbard, *Hosea,* TOTC (Downers Grove: InterVarsity, 1989), 59–60.

43 On which see further C. L. Blomberg, "Marriage, Divorce, Remarriage and Celibacy: An Exegesis of Matthew 19:2–12," *TrinJ* n.s. 11 (1990): 161–96.

of infidelity. Hosea's actions were object lessons intended by God to illustrate the spiritual infidelity of his people Israel and God's unfailing love for them in spite of their disobedience (Hos 1:2; 3:1). Since God did not command this as a general principle, we cannot apply these specific instructions from Hosea to our contemporary situation. In other words, we find no mandate here either to marry prostitutes or to preserve marriages ruptured by adultery. Still, the Bible does defend the broader principle of faithfulness in the face of faithlessness; it may suggest that in some circumstances these actions are acceptable, perhaps even on occasion preferable. More importantly, they should cause us to seek other applications of the broader principle, such as ways of continuing to love prodigal children or friends who have wronged us, and so on.[44]

5. *Are cultural conditions identified in Scripture or assumed by its authors that make it inappropriate always to apply a given text in the same way?* One of the few things widely agreed on by interpreters of the "problem passages on women" is that veils (or long hair) on women and short hair on men (1 Cor 11:2–16) are not universal absolutes. A key to this understanding is Paul's own statement that a woman who prays or prophesies with her head uncovered might as well shave her head (v. 5), which is a "disgrace" (v. 6). These remarks drive the contemporary reader to ask what was disgraceful about shaved heads among women of Paul's day. Numerous possibilities exist. For Jewish women shaved heads may have suggested that they were guilty of adultery. For Greco-Roman women shaved heads may have indicated that they were the more "masculine" partner in a lesbian relationship. So unless short hair or uncovered heads send similar signals in modern-day cultures (as, for example, in certain parts of the more conservative Islamic world), the specific practice here is irrelevant. On the other hand, any dress or grooming, behavior or conversation that suggests sexual unfaithfulness or deviance should remain as wrong for Christian women today as it was in first-century Corinth.

An examination of the rationale for Paul's commands to the men in this passage might at first glance suggest a different conclusion. At least in v. 14 Paul writes, "Does not the very nature of things teach you that if a man has long hair, it is a disgrace to him?" Currently most of us, if honest, would quickly answer the question, no. But Paul's use of the term "nature" suggests that he is appealing to some timeless principle unknown to us. Here knowledge of Scripture and of some historical background helps. Paul, raised as a devout Jew, knew of one major category of Jewish man whom God praised for never cutting his hair—the one who took a Nazirite vow (Num 6:1–21). Paul himself had practiced similar vows on a temporary basis (Acts 18:18). So "the nature of things" in 1 Cor 11:14 must mean something like "the common custom throughout the first-century Greco-Roman world," which in turn explains why all the churches of that time had adopted this practice (v. 16). We see again the need to understand the culture of the time to find the rationale. The best recent research suggests that long hair (perhaps resembling an external head covering) on a man likely made him appear too much like Roman priests officiating at certain pagan rituals. Once again, if long hair is inextricably

---

44 Cf. esp. R. C. Ortlund, Jr., *Whoredom: God's Unfaithful Wife in Biblical Theology* (Leicester: InterVarsity, 1996).

bound up with non-Christian religious practice in some modern culture, then it, too, should remain taboo. But if not, then hair style is not a moral issue with God.[45]

6. *Is the particular cultural form expressed in the biblical text present today, and if so does it have the same significance as it did then?* The two examples from 1 Cor 11 could illustrate this criterion as well. But we may move even further to examples in which certain cultural forms no longer even exist, at least not in all cultures. For example, few of us have ever considered if we should or even could bring a sheep or goat to church and slaughter it in front of the pulpit, letting the blood run down the sides! Of course, the sacrificial laws of the OT were fulfilled in Christ and no longer require our literal obedience, even if we could (Heb 4:14–10:18). But we can still learn principles about the costliness and purity demanded by those laws as we read the opening chapters of Leviticus. Do they not say to us that we should be equally devoted to Christ and should seriously embrace moral purity (2 Cor 6:14–7:1) and sacrificial giving (2 Cor 8–9)? Just as poor people could offer less costly sacrifices in those days (Lev 12:8; cf. Lk 2:24), so Christians should not expect identical levels of giving from all believers today. In fact, the NT does not promote a fixed percentage of giving. We may better capture the spirit of NT giving through what R. Sider calls a "graduated tithe," by which the more one makes, the higher percentage one ought to give to the Lord's work, and especially to helping the poor (1 Cor 16:2; 2 Cor 8:12–15).[46]

Other religious practices exist among Christians in certain parts of the world but not in others. For example, few North Americans trouble themselves over the fact that they do not greet each other with a holy kiss (1 Thes 5:26). Southerners in the United States, however, do at times greet each other this way. While living in Florida, one of us had a pastor who greeted almost all the women who came to his church with a kiss on the cheek, and the practice was largely accepted and appreciated in that context. In the Middle East, however, men commonly greet other men with a kiss on each cheek. In the republics of the former Soviet Union it is common for men to kiss other men on their mouths. The ancient biblical practice most resembled modern Middle-Eastern behavior, i.e. same-sex kissing on the cheek.[47] No sexual connotations were associated with it; it was the acceptable convention for greeting a good friend warmly. The identical form of application can therefore be preserved in some modern cultures but not in others. Opposite-sex kissing should probably be discouraged in most modern contexts, where sexual desires are often too easily aroused. The Living Bible's paraphrase offers an acceptable alternative: "shake hands warmly." *The Message* reads, "Greet all the Christians there with a holy embrace." More abstractly, the NLT translates, "Greet each other in Christian love."

---

45 On the meaning and application of 1 Cor. 11:2–16, cf. further C. L. Blomberg, *1 Corinthians*, NIVAC (Grand Rapids: Zondervan, 1994), 207–26. For a brief supplement, see id., "Neither Hierarchicalist nor Egalitarian: Gender Roles in Paul," in *Two Views on Women in Ministry*, 341–47.

46 See esp. R. J. Sider, *Rich Christians in an Age of Hunger*, 4th ed. (Dallas: Word, 1997), 193–96, even if the specific figures need modification from one setting to the next.

47 See further L. Morris, *The First and Second Epistles to the Thessalonians*, 2d ed., NICNT (Grand Rapids: Eerdmans, 1991), 185–86.

Most readers could correctly infer the significance of 1 Thes 5:26 even if they do not customarily kiss others in church. However, we might not realize that it was usually limited to men with men and women with women. In other cases, the significance of biblical practices may escape us altogether. Why, for example, were Israelites not permitted to clip the edges of their beards or tattoo their bodies (Lev 19:27–28)? Bible students need to consult commentaries or encyclopedias to learn about these customs. They will discover that the two practices proscribed in Leviticus, like many mentioned in the OT laws, formed part of Canaanite religious ritual.[48] So is it acceptable for Christians to be tattooed today? Some say no, simply because the Bible forbids it. Others simply assume it is all right because it is an OT prohibition. Both of these approaches are inadequate for they fail to distinguish the underlying principle from its specific application. Instead, a Christian who considers getting a tattoo must ask: Would someone who saw me sporting a tattoo be likely to assume that I participated in some cultic or pagan practice (as occurs in some Satanist cults)? If so, it remains equally abominable to God. If not, it remains a matter of moral indifference.

Perhaps the most famous example of a practice from biblical times that has largely vanished in Western cultures (though by no means in other parts of the world) is the custom of eating food sacrificed to idols. We include it because it illustrates principles widely applicable to our society. In both 1 Cor 8–10 and Rom 14:1–15:13 Paul enjoins his readers to exercise mutual tolerance on this and related issues. In other words, numerous morally neutral practices in the world can lead some people but not others into sin. In the case of food sacrificed to idols, some could not disassociate eating the meat from their own past pagan practices, namely, fellowship meals with various deities (1 Cor 10:14–22). Paul counseled the "strong" brothers and sisters in Christ not to flaunt their freedoms in these areas if this would cause "weaker" ones to engage in actual sin—and potentially abandon Christ. He also admonished the weaker ones not to pass judgment on the stronger for their practices.

While modern equivalents abound,[49] perhaps the best known involves the consumption of alcohol. One Scripture passage recognizes wine, for example, as a gift from God that gladdens human hearts (Psa 104:15), but another earnestly commands believers not to get drunk (Eph 5:18). This latter verse obviously counsels moderation rather than debauchery. Some people, however, often because of their prior experiences with drinking, cannot imbibe without being tempted to consume to excess. They are wise to abstain altogether. Those who can avoid drunkenness may choose to drink discreetly—and moderately; however, their primary concern should be to seek the filling of the

---

48 See, e.g., G. J. Wenham, *The Book of Leviticus*, NICOT (Grand Rapids: Eerdmans, 1979), 272. Wenham goes on to note, however, beyond what most commentators say, that this was an inappropriate defacing of God's image in humanity—the purity of the external should correspond to the purity of the internal. Even if this is so, it is still doubtful if tattooing is automatically sinful in the NT age in which external, ritual purity laws have been abolished. But to the extent that it, or any other practice, damages the body, it is not exercising good stewardship of the "temple of the Holy Spirit" (1 Cor 6:19).

49 See the lengthy and sadly amusing list in G. Friesen with R. Maxson, *Decision Making and the Will of God* (Portland: Multnomah, 1980), 382–83, a list we could greatly expand since its publication.

Spirit and not to hurt their weaker brothers or sisters. Those who abstain, in turn, should not pass judgment on those who choose to drink in moderation.[50]

The same principles apply to the entire process of determining legitimate applications. Since applications may vary from individual to individual, even though meaning remains fixed, numerous biblical passages require Christians to express mutual tolerance. It is unfortunate that Christians often explain their different interpretations of the meaning of a text by saying, "this is what this passage means to me," as if that justified any preferred interpretation. Often, however, when people speak of the *meaning* of a text "for them," they may be referring to legitimate *application*, which can vary from person to person. For example, Deut 6:6–7 establishes the fixed principle that parents have the responsibility to teach God's commands to their children. But in applying this principle to grade-school education, one couple may use it to explain why they chose home-schooling; another to justify Christian schools; and a third to support sending their children to public schools while teaching them about the Bible at home and in church.

7. Is the rationale for the application rooted in a creation ordinance, in the character of God, or in part of his redemptive plan for humanity?[51] Such principles remain timeless even while their applications may differ. Creation ordinances refer to principles for how people should live that God established prior to the Fall of humanity into sin. Presumably, such principles remain part of the redemptive ideal for Christians as they are progressively renewed in God's image after their salvation. A classic example is monogamous marriage. Both Jesus (Mt 19:5) and Paul (Eph 5:31) reaffirm Gen 2:24 as the rationale for strict standards on sexual ethics. Intervening biblical tolerance of a wide variety of divorces (Deut 24:1) or of occasional polygamy,[52] therefore, does not legitimize divorce or polygamy as valid applications of these texts of Scripture for Christians today. At times these practices might reflect the lesser of two evils, as in the case in certain non-Western cultures where a polygamous husband becomes a believer. In such instances the less evil action may be to keep the extended family intact and spare the "extra" wives the tragic circumstances that would occur should he divorce them.[53] But that is a quite different matter from telling a Christian who has only one spouse that it could be acceptable under certain circumstances to take more than one!

Other scriptural commands reflect the nature of God himself. In Lev 19:1, Yahweh commands all the Israelites to "be holy because I, the Lord your God, am holy."

---

50 For a good study of the biblical data, see N. L. Geisler, "A Christian Perspective on Wine-Drinking," *BSac* 139 (1982): 46–56. Geisler goes on to argue for teetotaling as an appropriate contemporary Christian response to the excesses of our culture. This is one understandable response, but it is not the only legitimate application of the relevant texts (see below). For further reflection on the meaning and significance of 1 Cor 8–10, see Blomberg, *1 Corinthians*, 159–206.

51 Larkin, *Culture*, 109. K. Giles ("A Critique of the 'Novel' Contemporary Interpretation of 1 Timothy 2:9–15 Given in the Book, *Women in the Church*: Part II," *EvQ* 72 [2000]: 195–200) argues that the criterion of creation order is largely a modern German invention, though he concedes partial precedents in Luther and Calvin. The precise terminology may be new, but it is hard to see what else one should call the logic Jesus explicitly employs in Matt 19:1–12.

52 We must realize how rare polygamy was even in OT times; almost without exception it was limited to kings or very wealthy aristocrats who could afford more than one wife. See esp. W. C. Kaiser, Jr., *Toward Old Testament Ethics* (Grand Rapids: Zondervan, 1983), 182–90.

53 See, e.g., Kraft, *Christianity*, 362–64.

Centuries later, Peter quotes these words to justify his commands to "prepare your minds for action; be self-controlled; set your hope fully on the grace to be given you," and "do not conform to the evil desires you had when you lived in ignorance," but "be holy in all you do" (1 Pet 1:13, 14, 15). We can be sure that the pursuit of holiness is a timeless, universal principle applicable for all believers everywhere, even as specific illustrations of that holiness at times vary.[54]

Gal 3:27–28 illustrates a passage grounded in principles of redemption: "For all of you who were baptized into Christ have clothed yourselves with Christ. There is neither Jew nor Greek, slave nor free, male nor female, for you are all one in Christ Jesus." While this passage by itself cannot prove that Paul envisioned no functional distinctions between categories of people in the Church, neither can it be limited to equality in opportunities for salvation. Baptism reflected an outward, liberating rite for women that put them on equal public footing with men in a way that the corresponding OT initiation ritual of circumcision could not. So, too, at the very least, the Church of Jesus Christ should seek outward, public signs to affirm the full equality of the sexes and also of races and classes.[55]

8. *Is the command or application at variance with standard cultural norms of the day?* If so, it likely indicates a transcultural or timeless mandate. In all the discussion of women's roles, many often forget that what would have stood out as most noticeably radical in the various NT domestic codes (see above) were the commands to the *men*. A few partial parallels, for example to "husbands, love your wives" (Eph 5:25), exist in the ancient world, but none enjoins as sacrificial an abandonment of men's own rights and privileges as Paul's statement, which goes on to add, "just as Christ loved the church and gave himself up for her to make her holy" (vv. 25b–26a).[56] Similarly, in the Greco-Roman world few voices were as blunt and sweeping in their condemnation of homosexuality (or, for that matter, of heterosexual sin) as Paul's in Rom 1:18–32. He adopted a far more countercultural stance in his day than is held even today in an age of highly visible and vocal gay-rights lobbies. This makes it unlikely that Paul's views were in any way intended to be limited to first-century Roman society.[57]

To understand how to apply the OT so-called *lex talionis*—"an eye for an eye and a tooth for a tooth" (cf. Exod 21:24)—we must read it against its cultural background. To us it sounds like a vindictive call for revenge, but in its day, it was a radically limiting law that prevented an individual from exacting *more* than equivalent compensation and, for the most part, limited retribution to a legal court.[58] Jesus goes further and prohibits personal retaliation altogether (Mt 5:38–42). Both of these principles remain

---

54 Significantly, Kaiser (*Ethics*) sums up OT ethics under this very heading of holiness and then divides his thematic studies into holiness in various areas: e.g., family and society, marriage and sex, wealth and possessions, and so on.

55 See esp. B. Witherington, III, "Rite and Rights for Women—Galatians 3.28," *NTS* 27 (1981): 593–604. R. N. Longenecker reveals some of these possibilities by organizing his discussion of *New Testament Social Ethics for Today* (Grand Rapids: Eerdmans, 1984) around the three parts of Gal 3:28.

56 E. Best, *Ephesians*, ICC (Edinburgh: T. & T. Clark, 1998), 539–44; A. T. Lincoln, *Ephesians*, WBC 42 (Dallas: Word, 1990), 373–74.

57 See further D. F. Wright, "Homosexuality: The Relevance of the Bible," *EvQ* 61(1989): 291–300. Cf. esp. J. B. DeYoung, *Homosexuality* (Grand Rapids: Kregel, 2000).

58 A theme helpfully expanded by C. J. H. Wright into an entire book, *An Eye for an Eye: The Place of Old Testament Ethics Today* (Downers Grove: InterVarsity, 1983).

timeless, but their specific applications continue to vary. In the first century, striking someone on the right cheek (v. 39) was typically a backhanded slap meant more to insult than to injure; taking one's cloak was a form of legal collateral (v. 40); and going the extra mile referred to forced Roman conscription (v. 41). Legitimate application of these passages does not require Christians to put themselves or their loved ones in positions that deliberately risk injury or nakedness. It does require them to renounce retaliation and to find ways of loving their enemies (v. 43)—giving them what will help them become better individuals.[59]

9. *Does the passage contain an explicit or implicit condition that limits its application?* Conditional promises are valid only if the conditions are met. In the Sermon on the Mount, Jesus promised his followers: "Ask and it will be given to you; seek and you will find; knock and the door will be opened to you" (Mt 7:7). Many today treat this promise as if it were a contract from God guaranteeing that God will give to them whatever they request, particularly in the areas of health and wealth. Others add the qualification, based on passages like Jas 5:15, that if they ask in faith (or with "enough" faith) they can be sure this will happen.[60] But after reading this book, hopefully, no one will try to interpret Mt 7 without first reading Mt 6; or Jas 5 without first reading Jas 4!

In these larger contexts of Jesus' and James' teaching, we learn about the most important condition of all for God to answer prayer: it must first be in accordance with his will (Mt 6:10; Jas 4:15). Jas 4 helps us to understand better why God grants some and not other requests. On the one hand, even when certain good gifts do accord with his will, God has determined to give them only if we ask (Jas 4:2). That alone should be a powerful incentive to pray. On the other hand, sometimes we ask for things with wrong, selfish motives and therefore do not receive them (v. 3). But in other cases, even when our motives are pure, we need to remember that our desires do not always conform to God's. Particularly in the area of physical healing, Jesus' reply to Paul may also apply to us: "My grace is sufficient for you, for my power is made perfect in weakness" (2 Cor 12:9). In light of these various scriptural conditions concerning prayer, Douglas Moo well defines the prayer of faith in Jas 5:15 as that which "always includes within it a tacit acknowledgment of God's sovereignty in all matters; that it is *God's* will that must be done."[61] First John 5:14 makes the same point even more explicitly, that "if we ask anything according to his will, he hears us."

Not only do promises in Scripture often have conditions attached, but so also does prophecy. It is not always easy to sort out which OT predictions concerning Israel's future have conditions and which do not. Historically, dispensational theology has tended to emphasize numerous apparent unconditional promises to the Jewish people, while so-called covenant theology has stressed the unfulfilled conditions attached to

---

59 A theme desperately in need of additional application to the Church today. See esp. G. H. Stassen, *Just Peacemaking* (Louisville: Westminster John Knox, 1992); and J. C. Arnold, *Why Forgive?* 2d ed. (Farmington, PA: Plough, 2000).

60 For a good survey and sympathetic critique, see B. Barron, *The Health and Wealth Gospel* (Downers Grove: InterVarsity, 1987).

61 D. J. Moo, *The Letter of James,* TNTC (Grand Rapids: Eerdmans, 1985), 182. Cf. his expanded remarks in id., *The Letter of James*, PNTC (Grand Rapids: Eerdmans, 2000), 243–45.

many of those promises.[62] The promise of land for the nation of Israel provides an excellent illustration of this debate. In Gen 15 God renews his covenant with Abraham made in Gen 12:1–3 and specifies that he will give to Abraham's descendants "this land, from the river of Egypt [the Nile] to the great river, the Euphrates" (15:18). In neither chapter do any conditions appear, unless one interprets the call to Abraham to "go" in Gen 12:1 as a condition, but Abraham did indeed leave his home in Ur and travel to the Promised Land. On the other hand, when the Israelites under Moses were ready to occupy Canaan, God declared all of the blessings of the land to be contingent on their obedience to the Law (Deut 28). One plausible way to resolve this tension, which fits the rest of OT history, is to state that the promise always remains available in principle but that the opportunity for the people of each generation to appropriate that promise depends on their obedience.[63]

The plot thickens, however, when we ask if God's promise to Abraham and to Moses has ever been completely fulfilled. The largest known territory occupied by Israel occurred under Solomon. Apparently that land included up to the Euphrates (1 Kgs 4:24), but no Scripture indicates that it ever went all the way to the Nile. Still, Solomon himself could praise God by saying, "Not one word has failed of all the good promises he gave through his servant Moses" (8:56). So if God's promise to Israel was fulfilled, then we need not necessarily look for any further fulfillment. This interpretation would obviously have direct bearing on the view that sees a modern-day Jewish nation in the land of Israel as the fulfillment of Scripture.

On the other hand, even if we assume that the people of Israel never fully occupied all the land God had intended for them, this does not automatically mean we should look for a complete and literal fulfillment in our, or some subsequent, day. The NT applies to the Church many OT passages that originally applied solely to Israel (see esp. 1 Pet 2:4–10). In fact Paul specifically quotes from God's initial covenant with Abraham (Gen 12:3b)—"All nations will be blessed through you" (Gal 3:8)—as part of the "gospel," which foresaw Gentiles coming to faith in Christ. So it seems highly incongruous to take the first half of the verse out of Genesis and assume that "Israel" still means a literal Jewish nation. Although it is popular among conservative American Christians to cite Gen 12:3a ("I will bless those who bless you, and whoever curses you I will curse") as a reason for supporting the current state of Israel, legitimate principles of application would seem to require that the "you" in this text now refers to the Church of Jesus Christ. In other words, God will bless those who support Christian causes and will not bless those who attack them.[64]

But are there no unfulfilled promises to Jewish people? Some would say not, but various NT passages seem to hold out hope for a more glorious future for the Jews. The most well-known of these is Rom 11:26–27: "And so all Israel will be saved, as it is written: 'The deliverer will come from Zion; he will turn godlessness away from Jacob. And this is my covenant with them when I take away their sins'" (quoting Isa 59:20–21). Since

---

62 The debate is well represented in J. S. Feinberg, ed., *Continuity and Discontinuity: Perspectives on Relationship Between the Old and New Testaments* (Westchester: Crossway, 1988). A significant collection of essays representing the shift toward mainstream evangelicalism among the current generation of dispensationalist scholars is C. A. Blaising and D. L. Bock, eds., *Dispensationalism, Israel and the Church* (Grand Rapids: Zondervan, 1992).

63 See esp. W. C. Kaiser, Jr., *Toward an Old Testament Theology* (Grand Rapids: Zondervan, 1978), 110–13.

64 Cf. esp. B. K. Waltke with C. J. Fredricks, *Genesis* (Grand Rapids: Zondervan, 2001), 206.

Paul contrasts Jews and Gentiles throughout Rom 9–11, it is not likely that "all Israel" means "the Church" here. Neither is it likely that Paul means every single Jewish person will be saved irrespective of his or her attitude toward Jesus. The context refers to the coming Messiah (the deliverer) and speaks of banishing godlessness and of forgiving sins.

The most likely interpretation of this passage is that there will be an outpouring of faith in Messiah Jesus among large numbers of Jews at the time of Christ's return.[65] But that does not suggest that the overwhelming majority of Jews in the land of Israel, who are not currently Christians, is a necessary fulfillment of prophecy. Paul implies a clear condition in Rom 11:26–27—for Jews now to experience God's blessings they must have faith in Christ. At best, we might say that current Jews in Israel comprise a precursor of such fulfillment. What is more, nothing in this or any other NT passage refers to a *nation* of Israel—that is, a political state that occupies certain boundaries. Romans 9–11 could just as conceivably be fulfilled among Jews and Gentiles scattered throughout the world. In fact, Jesus takes language from the Psalms about Israelites living in the Promised Land and applies it to all true Christians inheriting the entire earth ("Blessed are the meek, for they will inherit the earth" Mt 5:5, quoting Psa 37:11).[66]

So it is hermeneutically naive to claim that the largely secular nation of Israel today necessarily occupies any privileged position in God's scheme of things. Worse still, such a view often leads to uncritical political support for Jews against the Palestinian people, even though a sizeable majority of our Christian brothers and sisters in Israel today are Palestinians, not Jews. We realize this may be a controversial example for some of our readers;[67] however, in light of our emphasis on the commitment of Scripture to social justice we feel it is important to raise this issue here. Hermeneutics can literally make the difference between life and death for multitudes of people on our globe!

10. *Should we adopt a "redemptive movement" hermeneutic?* By far the most significant and sophisticated reflection on the issue of sifting the cultural from the timeless in Scripture is the recent work of William Webb.[68] Webb presents eighteen potential criteria for the task under the headings "persuasive," "moderately persuasive," and "inconclusive." The heart of his argument (and the gist of a majority of his "persuasive criteria") is that just as one can trace developing understanding of various topics within successive stages of OT revelation as well as from the OT to the NT, so also there may be places where the "trajectory" of biblical thought implies that Christians today should move beyond NT teaching. Webb believes Christians have already done this on the issue of slavery. He convincingly shows that the biblical data on homosexuality do *not* fit such a trajectory. Homosexual practice is equally condemned throughout both

---

65 The classic example is W. Ramsay, *St. Paul the Traveller and Roman Citizen* (London: Hodder and Stoughton, 1895; rev. and upd. M. Wilson [Grand Rapids: Kregel, 2001]); cf. Hemer, *Acts*.

66 On *The Gospel and the Land* in these and other passages, see esp. W. D. Davies, in his book so-titled (Berkeley: University of California Press, 1964).

67 For a vibrant defense of the position adopted here, see esp. C. Chapman, *Whose Promised Land? The Continuing Crisis over Israel and Palestine*, 2d ed. (Grand Rapids: Baker, 2002); and G. Burge, *Who Are God's People in the Middle East?* (Grand Rapids: Zondervan, 1993).

68 *Slaves, Women, and Homosexuals: Exploring the Hermeneutics of Cultural Analysis* (Downers Grove: InterVarsity, 2001). A briefer precursor with a similar perspective is D. L. Thompson, "Women, Men, Slaves and the Bible: Hermeneutical Inquiries," *CSR* 25 (1996): 326–49.

Testaments. But he believes biblical teaching on women is more akin to that on slavery. He does not interpret biblical teaching on gender roles, as biblical feminists do, as clearly promoting egalitarianism, but he does see development of thought moving in a direction that would support Christians today going beyond the NT to support complete interchangeability of gender roles in home and church.

Webb's study deserves a careful and thoughtful response. Most of the volume proves extraordinarily helpful. But a few nagging questions remain. Webb correctly points to 1 Cor 7:21 on slaves taking advantage of opportunities for freedom as the kind of "seed" thought that set the stage for the later abolition of slavery (p. 84). But there really is no analogous text encouraging women to become elders or heads over their husbands if the opportunity arises.[69] Two of Webb's "persuasive criteria" appeal to extra-biblical bodies of knowledge—when the basis of an instruction cannot be sustained from one culture to another (p. 209) or when a component of a text "is contrary to present-day scientific evidence" (p. 221). But both cultural practice and scientific evidence have proved remarkably changeable over time, particularly in the "softer" social sciences—the very ones involved in the gender roles debate. Once one opens the lid to going beyond Scripture, even based on trajectories seemingly present in Scripture, a Pandora's box of problems may emerge (cf. also 1 Cor 4:6).[70]

The only other fully "persuasive" criterion for sifting the timeless from the cultural that Webb presents, unrelated to our comments thus far, is that of "purpose / intent statements" (p. 105). Scripture itself may give a reason for a command that requires a different application in a different culture precisely *to preserve* the original rationale. Thus 1 Peter regularly gives evangelistic reasons for its commands to citizens, slaves and women to submit to the authorities over them (2:12, 15; 3:1, 16). In a world that without exception took submission to authorities as a cultural given, to deviate from this behavior as Christians would place unnecessary obstacles in the path of non-Christians coming to Christ. But what of application in a world where many take egalitarianism equally for granted? Might the same rationale argue for treating one another entirely as peers?[71] In this case Webb's criterion could be seen as supporting the egalitarian agenda, though its application is further complicated by the diverse mix of cultures in many parts of our world today. However one answers the question, the issue (and the criterion on which it is based) is clearly worth raising.

Identify the Cross-Cultural Principles

We have already illustrated this step with most of the examples discussed above. Can we deduce a broad principle that a specific biblical text promotes as timeless even

---

69 On the other hand, while less specific, many believe that Gal 3:28 forms precisely such a precedent.

70 E.g., early feminist claims about minimal psychological differences between the genders have been substantially toned down after further studies. A particularly detailed survey of gender roles and the social sciences appears in S. Clark, *Man and Woman in Christ* (Ann Arbor: Servant, 1980), 369–570. Helpful updates and a different overall perspective appear in M. S. van Leeuwen, *My Brother's Keeper: What the Social Sciences Do (and Don't) Tell Us About Masculinity* (Downers Grove: InterVarsity, 2002).

71 For two opposite answers to this question, see S. Dowd, "1 Peter," in *The Women's Bible Commentary*, ed. C. A. Newsome and S. H. Ringe, 2d ed. (Louisville: Westminster John Knox, 1998), 462–64; and J. H. Elliott, *1 Peter*, AB (NY: Doubleday, 2000), 585–99.

if we cannot apply universally without alteration the particular command, example, promise, or warning of the text? If we discern such a principle, we must then devise new illustrations or applications of that principle for new situations. For example, with Paul's teaching on food sacrificed to idols, we proposed the broader principle of "freedom for Christians on morally neutral practices while they weigh how their freedom might affect fellow believers." For tattoos, the principle was not to imitate pagan religious practices that call one's allegiance to Christ into question. For women's head coverings, we generalized to encompass any forms of appearance or behavior that would suggest sexual infidelity. In other words, in each case we want to know why a specific command was given or a particular practice adopted or shunned. What did it mean in its particular cultural or historical context? Sometimes Scripture tells us directly in the immediate or larger context of a passage, or at least gives hints. Sometimes we must do our own historical and cultural research, or, more typically, rely on the best work that others have done.

But we must address here another issue involved in this third step in the process of application. When Bible students generalize or principlize from a specific application, how generally should they phrase the overarching principle? Consider again the story of Abraham's near-sacrifice of his son Isaac. Since God does not expect Christians to kill their children, what broader principles can we deduce from this passage? Someone might propose, for example: "Obey God in whatever he commands you, even to the point of trusting him to get you out of seemingly intractable moral dilemmas." After all, Scripture consistently reminds us of the positive, purifying value of trials and temptations (e.g., Jas 1:2–18; 1 Pet 1:3–9). But God does not promise to "get us out" of all situations in which we might be tempted to sin. In 1 Cor 10:13 Paul suggests that, more often than not, God leaves us in those situations but provides the power not to sin (a power we can choose or refuse to accept!). Moreover, the text never hints that Abraham recognized he was being tested, although in retrospect the biblical narrator explains that he was (Gen 22:1).[72] On occasion we, too, cannot be sure if difficulties in our lives reflect testing from God or temptation from the devil—or are simply the results of our own poor choices or the actions of others.

So perhaps we should advance a still broader principle from Gen 22: "Trust in God's sovereignty." This principle lies behind numerous passages of Scripture, most notably in the OT historical narrative. Its truth is impeccable. But then we must raise the question: Is that *all* the passage intends to teach us? A specific application for our lives based on this general principle might bear little resemblance to the specifics of the story of Abraham and Isaac. For example, we might decide to trust that God will provide us an adequate job after months of unemployment. But this application does not in any way link with the specifics of the Gen 22 passage.

We might settle for a mediating solution, perhaps based on the reflection of Heb 11:17–19 that Abraham believed God could raise the dead, so he trusted that even if he killed his son, God would bring Isaac back to life. Our timeless principle then becomes, "We will not overly grieve or worry when death threatens us or fellow believers, since we know that even if it comes, we will be resurrected on the last day." This

---

72 On this literary device, in which the narrator knows more than the characters throughout Gen 22, see J. H. Sailhamer, "Genesis," in *Expositor's Bible Commentary*, ed. F. E. Gaebelein, vol. 2 (Grand Rapids: Zondervan, 1990), 167–70.

principle has solid NT support (1 Thes 4:13–18; 1 Cor 15:20–28) and fits several of the particulars of the passage in Genesis. Even if we limit ourselves to Genesis, we can conclude that Abraham took God with the utmost seriousness, believing that he was able to keep his promise about supplying numerous descendants for Abraham, through whom all nations on earth would be blessed (Gen 12:1–3)—which encourages us to trust in the other as-yet unfulfilled promises of Scripture.

Levels of Authority

This process illustrates that applications possess different *levels of authority.* The closer the modern application corresponds to the application in the biblical text, the greater the degree of confidence we have that our application is legitimate. Usually, the specific application will be close to the text only if the broader principle it teaches specifically incorporates elements from the text. More general truths, like "the sovereignty of God" in our example above, will not regularly yield specific, contemporary applications that closely resemble the original ones.

So we may not, therefore, always assert with the same level of confidence that we have correctly applied a passage. How confident can we be? (1) When we can employ the originally intended response in our situation with little or no change (and that response validly applies the timeless principle in the passage),[73] we have the highest level of confidence that our application is valid. (2) When we can derive a broader principle, whose application incorporates greater or fewer particular elements of the passage, then we have the next level of confidence that our application is legitimate. But we have to be sure we have derived a valid, timeless principle. (3) When we back off still further to the level of applying more general truths from a passage, our applications may well reflect good Christian things to do, but we cannot be as confident that they are actual applications *of the specific text at hand.*[74] As Millard Erickson nicely phrases it, we should "look for principles of the maximum degree of specificity that meet the criteria for generalizability."[75] Webb speaks helpfully of a "ladder of abstraction, in which the most abstract ideas are at the highest rungs of a ladder, whereas it is our task to climb only as high as the text requires us."[76]

We confront this issue particularly when we seek to address contemporary situations to which the Bible does not directly speak. What, for example, is a Christian position on the possession or use of "weapons of mass destruction"? While the Bible says nothing about nuclear or biological weapons, it does record much about war (mostly in the OT). Yet Christians disagree on whether or not war is ever appropriate in the NT age.[77] Few in the history of the Church, however, have espoused full-fledged pacifism. Be this as it may, do

---

73 It is crucial to add these words since we may directly apply an instruction in a text and actually miss the principle that instruction conveyed in the text. For example, we might very literally wash another believer's feet in applying Jn 13:14 and miss the point of humble service. The practice of foot washing does not convey in our culture the meaning that the practice did in Jesus' world.

74 For further discussion of these distinctions, see esp. Kuhatschek, *Applying,* 56–57.

75 M. J. Erickson, *Evangelical Interpretation: Perspectives on Hermeneutical Issues* (Grand Rapids: Baker, 1993), 65. C. Kraft ("Interpreting in Cultural Context," *JETS* 21 [1978]: 357–67) makes much the same point using the language of "levels of abstraction."

76 Webb, *Slaves, Women and Homosexuals,* 54.

77 See, e.g., R. G. Clouse, ed., *War: Four Christian Views* (Downers Grove: InterVarsity, 1981).

the principles of "conventional warfare" necessarily carry over to the nuclear era? Some think not, alleging for example, that the historic principles for a just war (trying to avoid civilian casualties, etc.) cannot be applied to even the most limited of nuclear wars.[78] But were we to grant, for the sake of argument, that all nuclear war is immoral, does that prohibit even the possession of nuclear weapons? Does their benefit as a deterrent outweigh the dangers of a nuclear accident that could trigger such a holocaust? Obviously, we do not answer these questions by citing chapters and verses of Scripture!

That does not mean, however, that the Bible is irrelevant in a debate on nuclear weapons.[79] Interpreters can bring broader principles or general truths to bear on the topic. They need to balance the teaching of Scripture about the sanctity of life with its concern for justice. They need to raise questions about the eternal destiny of people who might lose their lives in a nuclear holocaust. They may also apply teaching about the role of government in enforcing the law, and about Christians not demanding their rights or seeking to retaliate against wrongs done to them. The issue is complex and we understand why Christians disagree. We cannot directly use specific passages in the same way that they were used in biblical times. And even the general principles we adopt will tend to be broad. So we must temper our discussion with humility. Although we may feel strongly about one side or the other in the argument, we dare not claim the same level of certainty that we have when we quote Jn 3:16 as the basis for trusting in Christ for salvation![80]

Find Appropriate Applications that Embody the Broader Principles

We have been illustrating this final step all along. The following diagram illustrates the process.

THEN   NOW

Principles   Principles

Application   Application

Having found the principles(s) that led to the specific application "back then," we seek to translate the principle(s) into appropriate and corresponding applications "now." Thus, we may give a hearty handshake instead of a holy kiss; we may set up inexpensive food banks instead of leaving our fields to be gleaned; and we should be concerned about the effect of consuming alcohol in the presence of a recovering alcoholic, even if we are never faced with the dilemma of whether or not to eat meat sacrificed to idols. Most of these applications probably seem straightforward and reasonable to our readers.

---

78 E.g., R. J. Sider, *Completely Pro-Life* (Downers Grove: InterVarsity, 1987), 159–63.

79 Or on modern warfare more generally. For a representative range of perspectives, see J. A. Wood, *Perspectives on War in the Bible* (Macon: Mercer, 1988).

80 A good resource for how to think "Christianly" about contemporary issues is H. Blamires, *The Christian Mind* (Ann Arbor: Servant, 1978). Excellent illustrations of applying the broad themes of creation, the fall, and redemption to ethical dilemmas appear in J. R. W. Stott, *Decisive Issues Facing Christians Today* (Grand Rapids: Baker, 1996). Less methodologically sophisticated but also quite helpful on a variety of contemporary topics is K. S. Kantzer, ed., *Applying the Scriptures* (Grand Rapids: Zondervan, 1987).

Greater sensitivity is required, however, when Christians wish to live responsibly in cross-cultural contexts. Whether a white person of European descent ventures to minister effectively in a Muslim community in Jordan, or whether people of two different races try to get along in the same American city, differences between cultures increase the possibility of gaffes in communication. Some conservative Christians in Scotland might find it appalling that Americans would participate in or even watch sports on Sunday. Many older Russian Christians find it outrageous that North American women wear make-up. Some American evangelicals cannot understand the freedom that C. S. Lewis felt in England or many north German Christians today feel to smoke. In each case scriptural texts are marshaled to support these particular applications. Thoughtless Christians who carelessly flaunt their freedom or quickly impose their conservatism will quickly lose the respect of their acquaintances in other cultures, even if their applications could prove defensible.[81]

Scripture provides many examples of cross-cultural contextualization. When Paul encounters those who teach that circumcision is mandatory for salvation, he resists the teaching rigorously even at the risk of severe schism (Gal 2). But when this issue concerns merely a better reception for the half-Jew Timothy to minister among Jews, he happily circumcises him (Acts 16:1–5).[82] Indeed, Paul himself justifies such behavior, noting that it is a characteristic of ministry:

> For though I am free with respect to all, I have made myself a slave to all, so that I might win more of them. To the Jews I became as a Jew, in order to win Jews. To those under the law I became as one under the law (though I myself am not under the law) so that I might win those under the law. To those outside the law I became as one outside the law (though I am not free from God's law but am under Christ's law) so that I might win those outside the law. To the weak I became weak, so that I might win the weak. I have become all things to all people, that I might by all means save some. I do it all for the sake of the gospel, so that I may share in its blessings (1 Cor 9:19–23 NRSV).

If 1 Cor 8 and 10 stress the need for believers to consider the feelings and convictions of other believers, 1 Cor 9 certainly underscores the need to consider what will most likely help or hinder *unbelievers* in the process of coming to the faith.

One final difficulty preachers have in coming up with legitimate contemporary applications of biblical texts stems from the appropriate desire not to be overly repetitious. How many times have seasoned churchgoers heard a message about drawing near to God in which the same handful of spiritual disciplines—esp. prayer and Bible

---

81 Perhaps the best existing work on contextualization in cross-cultural settings is D. J. Hesselgrave and E. Rommen, *Contextualization: Meanings, Methods, and Models* (Grand Rapids: Baker, 1989). For a good, though much briefer update, see Sanchez, "Contextualization in the Hermeneutical Process."

82 Cf. W. O. Walker, "The Timothy-Titus Problem Reconsidered," *ExpT* 92 (1981): 231–35.

study—are about the only applications the speaker makes? Listeners wonder if they are missing other dimensions of "significance." Daniel Doriani has recently written a wide-ranging volume on *Putting the Truth to Work: The Theory and Practice of Biblical Application*,[83] the heart of which addresses this question by proposing seven "biblical sources" for application and four "aspects" of application. The seven sources correspond in part, but not completely, to the diversity of literary genres, as Doriani identifies "rules, ideals, doctrines, redemptive acts in narratives, exemplary acts in narratives, biblical images, and songs and prayers" (p. 82). One text may in fact contain several of these components. The four "aspects" Doriani labels "duty, character, goal and discernment" (p. 98). Thus for every "biblical source" in a given passage, one may ask what one should do, what one should be (the kind of person to become), to what causes one should devote oneself, and how can one distinguish truth from error. Consciously thinking through all twenty-eight potential combinations of "sources" and "aspects" will normally give an interpreter plenty of diverse applications.

In conclusion, faithful application of the Bible to new contexts requires that we become as earnest in our study of the contemporary world as we are of Scripture itself. That is to say, we must learn not only to exegete the Scriptures but also to exegete cultures. Many who preach or teach the Bible to others eventually learn this lesson,[84] but in fact everyone who seeks to apply the Bible to his or her life in a valid way must discover it. Thoughtfully reading and listening to news; judiciously watching movies, listening to music, and monitoring other organs of popular culture; traveling, and, if possible, living for a while in different cultures; sharing with Christians across denominational and religious lines—all these (and this is merely a representative sample) can enhance our sensitivity. A regular amount of time spent in direct contact and friendship with unbelievers is also crucial. A study of the full breadth of topics usually included in the core curricula of liberal arts colleges can be beneficial. Full discussions of how to exegete culture might require another book like this one, but we would be remiss if we did not alert our readers to the importance of the task.

THE ROLE OF THE HOLY SPIRIT

We would also be remiss if we did not remind our readers that everything we have taught in this book falls short of the intended goal if interpreters do not simultaneously pray and rely on the Holy Spirit to guide them in the hermeneutical task. We have assumed that point of departure; it is part of our preunderstanding. Yet as we pointed out earlier, an appeal to the Spirit is no substitute for sound interpretive method. Roy Zuck's excellent article on "The Role of the Holy Spirit in Hermeneutics" deserves reading from start to finish; here we can merely summarize his fourteen main points:

1. The Holy Spirit does not give new revelation on a par with Scripture.
2. He does not guarantee that our interpretations are infallible.
3. He does not give one person new insights that no one else has.

---

83 (Phillipsburg, NJ: Presbyterian and Reformed, 2001).

84 See esp. the excellent suggestions of J. R. W. Stott, *Between Two Worlds: The Art of Preaching in the Twentieth Century* (Grand Rapids: Eerdmans, 1982) on "The Call to Study" (pp. 180–210), in which he describes resources and resource people he uses to balance scrutiny of Scripture with an understanding of the modern world.

4. Many non-Christians can apply sound hermeneutics to understand the meaning of Scripture; without the Spirit, however, they refuse to apply it adequately to their lives.
5. Understanding is not the exclusive domain of biblical scholars.
6. Spiritual devotion on the part of the interpreter is crucial.
7. Lack of spiritual preparation can hinder correct interpretation.
8. There is no substitute for diligent study.
9. The Spirit does not rule out study helps.
10. He does not override common sense and logic.
11. He does not normally give sudden intuitive flashes.
12. The Spirit's role in hermeneutics is part of the process of illumination.
13. He does not make all of the Bible equally clear.
14. He does not ensure comprehensive understanding.

In short, the five crucial elements for proper interpretation and application are: (1) salvation, (2) spiritual maturity, (3) diligent study, (4) common sense and logic, and (5) humble dependence on the Spirit for discernment.[85]

We hope this book has demonstrated the necessity for all five of these elements, even if our primary focus has been on (3) and (4). No one should imagine that this textbook presents a foolproof formula for interpreting and applying the Scriptures. That represents a lifelong process—a goal toward which we should strive. But if we have stimulated your desire for reading the Bible more, for tackling some of the more difficult or lesser known portions of it, then we are happy. If we have heightened your awareness of the kinds of questions to ask of the text as you read and to ask of others' interpretations, then we have made progress. If we have encouraged you to use some of the outstanding study tools and resources that are available to Christians today, then we have accomplished some of our goals. Nevertheless, our labor is in vain if we have not awakened a greater zeal to *obey* the Scriptures more, once they are understood, and to know and love the God who inspired them.[86] We live in an age of great biblical illiteracy and even greater biblical disobedience. As a preacher once put it, "When the darkness is very great, even a little light will do." So we conclude this focus on application by encouraging you to put into practice the principles we have outlined in this book. As you do this you will have the ability to handle correctly the Word of truth (2 Tim 2:15). Read the Word, study it, meditate on it, and then apply it. God will bless you as you do!

---

85 R. B. Zuck, "The Role of the Holy Spirit in Hermeneutics," *BSac* 141 (1984): 120–30. Cf. id., *Basic Bible Interpretation* (Wheaton: Victor, 1991), 279–92. Also helpful in many respects is M. I. Wallace, "Performative Truth and the Witness of the Spirit," *SWJT* 35 (1993): 29–36.

86 Cf. the excellent chapter on "Obeying the Word: The Cultural Use of the Bible," in W. C. Kaiser, Jr. and M. Silva, *An Introduction to Biblical Hermeneutics* (Grand Rapids: Zondervan, 1994), 173–90. This chapter addresses a number of the issues we have discussed with respect to application.

ANNOTATED
BIBLIOGRAPHY

HERMENEUTICAL TOOLS

Many books on hermeneutics provide a bibliography. Often such books list a catalog of significant works in the field of hermeneutical theory.[1] We commend such bibliographies and urge readers to consult them for further study. We will not follow their example, though readers interested in further study in the various areas of hermeneutics can pursue those interests by consulting the extensive footnotes provided throughout this text. (Conveniently located in the appropriate sections, these function in lieu of that kind of bibliography.) Rather, we have chosen to provide a bibliography that assists students in the actual practice of interpretation. We are convinced that biblical interpreters require the appropriate tools as much as skilled practitioners in any endeavor.

The bibliographic references are presented here in units based on usage. Brief annotations supply insight into the uses and benefits of the various entries. We have marked those books we believe to be outstanding, indispensable, or at least top priority with an asterisk [*]. As students are building their biblical libraries we suggest these books be purchased early in the process.[2] We have listed only a few out of print titles (though we have removed some of those from the first edition of this book), but only because of their superior worth and because they may be found in libraries or even purchased from book dealers.

Some books included use the Hebrew and Greek languages. This distinction is noted in the annotations. Students who can acquire the use of these languages will have a decided advantage in the process of interpretation, and they should make use of these original language tools.[3] Those who are unable to learn one or both of the biblical languages can

---

1 For example, excellent bibliographies exist in G. R. Osborne, *The Hermeneutical Spiral* (Downers Grove: InterVarsity, 1991), 436-80; A. C. Thiselton, *New Horizons in Hermeneutics* (Grand Rapids: Eerdmans, 1992), 621-61; J. Goldingay, *Models for Interpretation of Scripture* (Carlisle: Paternoster; Grand Rapids: Eerdmans, 1995), 290-316; and K. J. Vanhoozer, *Is There a Meaning in This Text?* (Grand Rapids: Eerdmans, 1998), 469-85. Two regularly updated bibliographies—one for the OT and one for the NT—of tools important for the practice of exegesis are published in the "Denver Journal," an online journal sponsored by Denver Seminary. See http://www.DenverSeminary.edu and go to the link for the "Denver Journal." For a truly comprehensive guide to commentaries and most other biblical and theological resources see J. Glynn, *Commentary and Reference Survey* (Grand Rapids: Kregel, 2003).

2 Obviously, our colleagues in other institutions—including pastors, teachers, and students—who use this textbook may have different preferences. Though individual favorites may differ, we have attempted to provide a list of sources widely accepted as the best currently available.

3 Frankly, we lament the increasing tendency to omit the biblical languages from theological curricula, but that is another matter.

usually omit purchasing most of these volumes. Readers will note, though, in our description of some of these original language tools that we suggest that even students without knowledge of Hebrew or Greek can profit considerably by using them. Where possible, students should attempt to borrow or use such books from friends or theological libraries to gauge their personal value or usefulness prior to purchasing them.

As tools, books are only as good as the scholars who wrote or compiled them. But even scholars and editors are fallible; they can misjudge evidence and draw imprecise or incorrect conclusions. Some may also have an "axe to grind" or be biased for various reasons (recall our discussion of preunderstandings and presuppositions). So recognizing that biblical interpretation will never be a hard and fast process like the sciences whose tables of mathematical formulae are precise and accurate, it is wise to work with a variety of reference works to verify judgments and opinions.

This is especially important on controversial issues where reasonable scholars differ. Readers must ask pointed questions: Is the burden of proof there? Do other reputable scholars agree? Is the evidence upon which the conclusion is based clear? Was the evidence examined fairly and objectively? Though we might like to believe that a reference book contains only accepted "truths," this is not always the case. We are certainly not advocating complete agnosticism or skepticism; clearly the state of our knowledge today exceeds that of any time in human history. The alternative—to reject all resources and tools—would be far more harmful. Rather, we hope to plant seeds of common sense and healthy questioning that refuse to embrace anything less than the best possible answers to the questions of interpretation.

Of course, the references and footnotes in the preceding chapters have already suggested some of the books in the following list. Here we attempt to collate in an organized fashion the better tools for doing biblical research and interpreting the Bible responsibly and accurately. We limit the list to works in English, with a few exceptions (mostly original language tools) as noted. The focus is on the *practice of interpretation*, not on its theory or defense—we have already attempted that and cited many works in the footnotes. Generally, books are listed in order from *less* advanced to *more* advanced (as precisely as possible) and from those based on the English text of the Bible to those that employ or require the original languages. Usually, OT sources precede NT sources. The annotations should make these factors clear. So, for many categories, students with the least background should begin by consulting the initial volumes. Then work down the lists as more expertise is gained and more in-depth information is required.

ANNOTATED LISTING

Biblical Texts—English language

See the discussion in Chapter Three on canon and translations for help here.

Biblical Texts—Original Languages

Old Testament

*Kohlenberger, J. R., ed. *The Interlinear Hebrew-English Old Testament*. Grand Rapids: Zondervan, 1987. This work presents the Hebrew text and the NIV in parallel columns. It also appends English glosses to each word of Hebrew text. Among other uses, it enables readers to locate appropriate Hebrew words for further study. Some computer-based software programs enable users to make their own interlinear texts either of single verses or whole contexts in parallel columns.

Elliger, K., and Rudolph, W., eds. *Biblia Hebraica Stuttgartensia* [BHS]. 5th ed. Stuttgart: Deutsche Bibelstiftung, 1997. Produced by a wide variety of collaborators, this is the standard text of the OT in Hebrew and is conveniently available through the various national Bible Societies. Its footnotes list the important textual variants, including occasional ones from the Dead Sea Scrolls, as well as suggested improved readings by the editors.[4] For students and pastors, we recommend the handy smaller edition of BHS, also now available in paperback.

Rahlfs, A. *Septuaginta* [LXX], 9th ed. 2 vols. Stuttgart: Württembergische Bibelanstalt, 1984. This is the standard complete text of the OT in Greek today. All "editions" since the first in 1935 are actually reprints. The United Bible Societies also issued a reduced-size one-volume edition in 1979. Its major weakness is Rahlfs' use of a limited number of manuscripts—namely, A, B, and S—to reconstruct his text. Yet its convenience has made it the most popular text. In addition to its translation of the OT into Greek, the Septuagint includes the Greek text of the OT Apocrypha.[5]

New Testament

*Douglas, J. D., ed. *NRSV Greek-English Interlinear New Testament.* Wheaton, IL: Tyndale, 1990; and J. Green, *Interlinear New Testament.* Peabody, MA: Hendrickson, 1984. Both works provide in horizontal lines literal English translations for each word in the Greek NT. Some computer-based software programs also perform this function.

*Nestle-Aland *Novum Testamentum Graece.* 27th ed. [NA-27]. Stuttgart: Deutsche Bibelstiftung, 1993. First edited by E. Nestle in 1898 and now revised and edited by B. and K. Aland, along with others, this volume is the standard text used by NT scholars. Representing the latest scholarly consensus of the original text of the NT documents, it records virtually all the most important places in the NT where alternative readings occur in different manuscripts. Its introduction and appendices also provide a wealth of information. It cites the textual traditions in a more limited fashion than the UBS Greek NT (see next entry).

*Aland, K. et al., eds. *Greek New Testament.* 4th ed. [*UBSGNT*]. Stuttgart: United Bible Societies, 1993. The Greek text is essentially identical to that of Nestle-Aland's 27th edition, apart from periodic differences in paragraphing or layout. But unlike its counterpart, the UBS textual apparatus cites only those places where it deems there are variants that significantly affect translation, providing relatively complete manuscript evidence for each alternative reading. In addition, a "rating system" helps readers see the editors' preferences for the various alternative readings. See the next entry.

Metzger, B. M., ed. *A Textual Commentary on the Greek New Testament.* 2d ed. New York: United Bible Societies, 1994. Written as a companion volume and reading like

---

4 Some find the BHS abbreviations obscure, so a supplementary guide was produced by R. I. Vasholz, *Data for the Sigla of BHS* (Winona Lake, IN: Eisenbrauns, 1983). Further help is found in R. Wonneberger, *Understanding BHS: A Manual for the Users of Biblia Hebraica Stuttgartensia* (Rome: Biblical Institute, 1984).

5 K. H. Jobes and M. Silva, *Invitation to the Septuagint* (Grand Rapids: Baker; Carlisle: Paternoster, 2000) describe why and how to study the Septuagint. The most detailed critical edition for scholarly research, still in process, is *Septuaginta: Vetus Testamentum Graecum* (Göttingen: Vandenhoeck & Ruprecht, 1939–).

the minutes of a committee, this manual provides the details and reasoning the textual critics used in resolving the textual problems in producing the *UBSGNT*, 4th ed.

Aland, K., ed. *Synopsis Quattuor Evangeliorum.* 13th ed. Stuttgart: Deutsche Bibelstiftung, 1985. This is the standard Greek synopsis for studying the Gospels. Printed in vertical columns, the Gospels can be studied in comparison to each other. For each section (pericope) of the text, appropriate parallels from the other Gospels are cited as often as they occur. The text and symbols are identical to Nestle's 26th edition. In addition to the texts of the Gospels, this synopsis cites numerous parallels in other early Christian literature, including NT Apocrypha and the works by early church Fathers, plus the entire text of the Gospel of Thomas in an appendix. This tool also exists in a strictly English edition, *Synopsis of the Four Gospels*, ed. K. Aland. 26th ed. (RSV; New York: United Bible Societies, 1985) and a *Greek-English Synopsis of the Four Gospels*, ed. K. Aland (RSV) diglot edition, (5th ed.; New York: United Bible Societies, 1982) with texts in the two languages on facing pages. These latter editions lack the extensive parallels in Christian literature or appendices of the Greek volume.

Textual Criticism

General

The Cambridge History of the Bible. 3 vols. Cambridge: Cambridge University Press. These volumes present the history of the transmission of the text of the Bible from its origins to the modern period. They provide help in sorting out the problems of the texts and ancient versions. Volume 1, *From the Beginnings to Jerome*, ed. P. K. Ackroyd and C. F. Evans, 1970; Volume 2, *The West from the Fathers to the Reformation*, ed. G. W. H. Lampe, 1969; and Volume 3, *The West from the Reformation to the Present Day*, ed. S. L. Greenslade, 1963. A one-volume abridgement, *The Cambridge Concise History of the Bible*, is slated for 2004.

Old Testament

*Brotzman, E. R. *Old Testament Textual Criticism: A Practical Introduction.* Grand Rapids: Baker, 1994. This is a useful, accessible guide both to the BHS textual apparatus and to the process of textual criticism written by an evangelical. Its many examples will especially benefit students who know Hebrew.

See also the survey of the discipline in A. Wolters, "The Text of the OT," in *The Face of OT Studies.* D. W. Baker and B. T. Arnold, eds. Grand Rapids: Baker; Leicester: InterVarsity, 1999, 19–37.

McCarter, P. K. *Textual Criticism: Recovering the Text of the Hebrew Bible.* Philadelphia: Fortress, 1986. A part of the Guides to Biblical Scholarship series, this brief but helpful book provides a good introduction for students to the science of OT textual criticism.

*Tov, Emmanuel. *Textual Criticism of the Hebrew Bible.* 2d ed. Assen: Royal Van Gorcum; Minneapolis: Fortress, 2001. This is the best introduction to the subject of OT textual criticism. The author is an eminent Jewish scholar whose text-critical research ranks him among the subject's leading authorities today. More technical than Brotzman or McCarter, it will primarily interest the more advanced reader. We especially commend its chapter on evaluating variant textual readings.

Würthwein, E. *The Text of the Old Testament.* 4th ed. Grand Rapids: Eerdmans, 1995. Suggests a methodology for deciding which textual variant should be reckoned as the earliest.

Jellicoe, S. *The Septuagint and Modern Study.* New York/Oxford: Oxford University Press, 1968. This work treats the origins of the LXX, its transmission, its text, and its language. It also surveys the modern study of the LXX. Though still a valuable source, it is out of print. A good, more up-to-date replacement is the chapter, "The Current State of Septuagint Research" (239–307), in Jobes, K. H., and Silva, M. *Invitation to the Septuagint.* Grand Rapids: Baker; Carlisle: Paternoster, 2000.

Tov, Emmanuel. *The Text-Critical Use of the Septuagint in Biblical Research.* 2d ed. Jerusalem Biblical Studies, vol. 8. Jerusalem: Simor, 1997. The author discusses such topics as the canon of the LXX, variants, how to reconstruct the *Vorlage*, reconstruction of other elements, variants/non-variants/pseudo-variants, the nature of the Hebrew text underlying the LXX, and the contribution of the LXX to literary criticism. First published in 1981 as JBS 3, it is available from Eisenbrauns.

New Testament

Greenlee, J. H. *Introduction to New Testament Textual Criticism.* Rev. ed. Peabody, MA: Hendrickson, 1995. Not an advanced or technical treatment, this book provides the beginner with an overview of the principles of textual criticism, and how critics determine the original text of the NT. A very brief counterpart is D. A. Black, *New Testament Textual Criticism: A Concise Guide.* Grand Rapids: Baker, 1994. It shows how the original texts were "corrupted," and how textual criticism operates in an attempt to recover the originals. See also P. W. Comfort, *The Text of the Earliest New Testament Greek Manuscripts.* Wheaton: Tyndale, 2001.

*Aland, K. and Aland, B. *The Text of the New Testament.* 2d ed. Grand Rapids: Eerdmans, 1995. A standard text, it presents the discipline and methods of the textual criticism of the NT. These German scholars lead readers through the technicalities of making decisions concerning the many manuscripts and versions to determine what were most likely the original readings (the so-called autographs) of the NT documents. They survey modern editions of the NT and the transmission of the Greek text of the NT through its history. This is an advanced text for the serious student.

Metzger, B. M. *Text of the New Testament.* 3d enlarged ed. New York/Oxford: Oxford University Press, 1992. This is an alternative to the previous volume by the Alands. Also highly recommended, this work introduces readers both to the history and study of textual criticism and demonstrates how its techniques are actually performed. Again, this volume is not for the novice, though those interested in the subject can learn much here.

Versions and Translations

Metzger, B. M. *The Bible in Translation: Ancient and English Versions.* Grand Rapids: Baker, 2001. This volume outlines the development of biblical translation. It includes a careful analysis of more than fifty versions of the Bible beginning with the earliest translations of the Old and New Testaments before proceeding to English. More selective with respect to modern English versions than the next two entries, it is very readable and concise.

Kubo, S. and Specht, W. *So Many Versions? Twentieth Century English Versions of the Bible.* 2d ed. Grand Rapids: Zondervan, 1990. Though now slightly dated, this work frankly assesses fifteen English versions produced since 1900.

*Lewis, J. P. *The English Bible from KJV to NIV.* 2d ed. Grand Rapids: Baker, 1991. Not only does this volume detail the story of the English Bible up to the NIV, but also includes chapters on the NKJV, REV, and NRSV.

Bruce, F. F. *History of the Bible in English: From the Earliest Versions.* 3d. ed. New York: Oxford University Press, 1978. This is a readable, though obviously dated, introduction to the formation of our English Bibles.

Beekman, J. and Callow, J. *Translating the Word of God.* Grand Rapids: Zondervan, 1974. A fine work, it provides an illuminating primer on the process and theory of translation of the Bible into other languages. It also yields numerous insights into various grammatical features of the Greek NT.

For more advanced students, the United Bible Societies publishes an inexpensive series "Helps For Translators" on many individual biblical books in both testaments. A unique kind of commentary aimed for people actually preparing translations, each volume provides linguistic and cultural background useful to translators and discusses how best to render the original text in other languages.

Studying Words and Their Theological Significance

The sources in the following list presume that the user is able to locate the "lexical form" of Hebrew or Greek words. In a later section we include theological dictionaries and encyclopedias that students who do not want to engage the original languages may consult.[6] For students without a working knowledge of the biblical languages, but who do know the alphabet to find Hebrew or Greek words in an interlinear OT or NT, helpful tools exist. For the OT see, e.g., J. J. Owens, *Analytical Key to the Old Testament,* 4 vols. Grand Rapids: Baker, 1990–93; or A. B. Davidson, *Analytical Hebrew-Chaldee Lexicon.* Peabody, MA: Hendrickson, 1984 reprint of 1848 ed. (now out of print). For the NT see W. D. Mounce, *The Analytical Lexicon to the Greek New Testament.* Grand Rapids: Zondervan, 1993. An alternative excellent source is T. Friberg, et al., *Analytical Lexicon of the Greek New Testament.* Grand Rapids: Baker, 2000. All of these volumes list every word occurring in the Hebrew and Greek testaments in alphabetical order. Each term is analyzed grammatically and is listed with the lexical form (sometimes called a "lemma"). The reader needs to know how to locate this form to use the following tools. Beyond these print versions, several computer software products have advanced the ability to discover, analyze, and parse original language forms to a fine art. Often links to other resources enable savvy users to search a multitude of resources.[7]

---

6 We hesitate to mention word study works based primarily on English, not because of scholarly arrogance, but because we sincerely feel that most are horribly outdated or have serious deficiencies. Students ought to learn to use *NIDOTTE* and *NIDNTT* listed below. One that holds promise of being an exception, however, is D. Bock and E. Merrill, eds. *The Bible Knowledge Key Word Study,* projected 6 vols. Colorado Springs: Cook, 2002– . The first volume, D. Bock, *Gospels,* appeared in 2002.

7 It is risky to list specific software products since the market for computer resources changes so rapidly. A short list of notable resources as of this writing includes the Libronix Digital Library System, (www.logos.com), which integrates Bible versions and an increasing number of research sources (and onto which platform many publishers are now writing products) and BibleWorks which integrates many Bible texts and modern versions, in multiple languages, and facilitates complex searches within the biblical texts. Gramcord (Windows) and Accordance (Macintosh) allow sophisticated searches in the Greek and Hebrew testaments, as does BibleWindows (Silver Mountain Software). Other publishers have excellent products, as well, including Nelson and Zondervan, and students should consult the various web sites to investigate which will best meet their needs.

Lexicons

Hebrew, Aramaic, and Old Testament Lexicons

Holladay, W. L. *A Concise Hebrew and Aramaic Lexicon of the Old Testament: Based upon the Lexical Work of Ludwig Koehler and Walter Baumgartner.* Leiden: Brill, 1997. An abbreviated form of KB below, this work provides briefer access to the meaning of OT words. It functions well for students beginning their study of biblical Hebrew and Aramaic.

*Brown, F., Driver, S. R. and Briggs, C. A. *A Hebrew and English Lexicon of the Old Testament* [BDB]. Repr. Peabody, MA: Hendrickson, 1996. The words are coded to *Strong's Concordance* (see below). This has been the standard Hebrew lexicon, the revision and translation of the monumental work begun by Gesenius (1810–12). Showing uncommon thoroughness, BDB gives the meanings not only of individual words but also of common phrases and idioms. It lists related roots and words that occur in the sister languages of biblical Hebrew. To help find words in BDB, some students consult B. Einspahr, *Index to Brown, Driver and Briggs Hebrew Lexicon.* Chicago: Moody Press, 1976. Organized just like the Bible (i.e., by books, chapters, and verses), it gives the meaning and location in BDB of all but the most common Hebrew words (for which BDB gives a biblical reference). Using this *Index* one can locate the page and section in which BDB discusses a Hebrew word, see where it occurs in the OT, and discover its meaning.

Koehler, L. and Baumgartner, W., eds. *Lexicon in Veteris Testamenti Libros* [KB]. 3d ed. 5 vols. Leiden: Brill, 1994–2001; Study edition, 2 vols. Leiden: Brill, 2001. A translation of the most complete, most recent Hebrew and Aramaic German lexicon, this is the modern counterpart to BDB. KB surpasses BDB on two counts: words are listed alphabetically and not by root, and it employs Ugaritic sources to which BDB did not have access. The descriptions are in both German and English, though the English is clearly the weaker of the two. It assumes at least an introductory knowledge of Hebrew. One must constantly use the supplement to augment the main entries. Many consider the Aramaic section superior to the Hebrew sections.

Clines, D. J. A., ed. *The Dictionary of Classical Hebrew.* Sheffield: Sheffield Academic Press, 1993– . Five volumes have appeared of the projected eight. Designed for a contextual and usage approach to understanding the meaning of words. One unique feature is its inclusion of extra-biblical occurrences of words (e.g., Qumran, ostraca, inscriptions, etc.).

For Aramaic words, the best lexicon in English is M. Jastrow. *A Dictionary of the Targumim, the Talmud Babli and Yerushalmi, and the Midrashic Literature.* 2 vols., 2d ed. New York: Pardes, 1950. Most students, however, will find that the Aramaic sections of the first three lexicons will easily meet their needs.

In reading the Septuagint, the best lexicon to use is H. G. Liddell and R. Scott, *A Greek-English Lexicon* (on which see next section); or see J. Lust et al. *Greek-English Lexicon of the Septuagint.* 2 vols. New York: American Bible Society, 1993, 1996.

Greek and New Testament Lexicons

*Louw, J. P. and Nida, E. A. *A Greek-English Lexicon of the New Testament Based on Semantic Domains.* 2 vols. New York: United Bible Societies, 1988. The Society of Biblical Literature published a supplement volume in 1992. As the title implies, these volumes employ linguistic principles to organize the vocabulary of the NT Greek into its various semantic fields or domains of meaning. They provide the best source for actually defining words, seeing the range of meaning of individual words, finding the most likely sense for a given word in a context, and understanding synonyms. This lexicon has assumed its rightful place among the standard, important tools for doing Greek word studies. It is an important companion to BDAG which follows.

*Bauer, W., Danker, F., Arndt, W. F., and Gingrich, F. W. *A Greek-English Lexicon of the New Testament and Other Early Christian Literature* [BDAG]. 3d English ed. Chicago: University of Chicago Press, 2000. This is the standard lexicon specifically devoted to the Hellenistic Greek of the NT and parallel literature. One can hardly overestimate the wealth of information encompassed in BDAG. The authors often provide succinct meanings, trace uses of the words through the Hellenistic period, and dispense perceptive evaluations of the significance of words. The latest revision adds entries for many more words and more than 25,000 additional references to classical, intertestamental, Early Christian, and modern literature. Danker has also introduced a more consistent mode of reference citation, provided a composite list of abbreviations, and extended the definitions of many Greek terms. Words are listed in Greek, and one must know the lexical form (lemma) of Greek words to look them up. It is also available in some Bible software programs.

Moulton, J. H. and Milligan, G. *Vocabulary of the Greek Testament Illustrated from the Papyri and Other Non-Literary Sources* [M&M]. 2d ed. Repr. Peabody, MA: Hendrickson, 1997. This volume provides examples of specific uses of Greek in Hellenistic times from nonliterary papyri. Begun in 1914, it has been reprinted several times. Far from exhaustive, this volume cites only those words employed in nonliterary sources and so sheds light on how they were understood in everyday use about the time of the NT. The editors provide dates for the citations and often translate them into English. The work is somewhat outdated (since many new sources have surfaced since 1930), but a revision is underway.

Lampe, G. H. W., ed. *A Patristic Greek Lexicon.* Oxford: Clarendon, 1985. This work complements NT usage by showing meanings of words in the subsequent era of the early church Fathers (to about A.D. 826). It sometimes proves instructive to see changes in word meanings as the Church developed in its first few centuries, though, of course, later meanings cannot be imposed upon NT uses.

Liddell, H. G. and Scott, R. *A Greek-English Lexicon* [LS]. 9th ed. with supplement, 2 vols. Oxford: Clarendon, 1925–40; repr. 1968. New supplement 1996. This is the standard comprehensive lexicon for the entire range of the Greek language in the ancient world including the NT. It specializes in the classical period of ancient Greek (up until 330 B.C.), but also traces meanings into the Hellenistic period. It provides valuable help in studying the history and etymology of words that occur in the NT. The newly revised Supplement gives the dictionary a date-range from 1200 B.C. to A.D. 600. It is fully cross-referenced to the main text but additions have been designed to be easily used without constant reference to the main text. Some Bible software programs include it among their electronic lexicons. Oxford also publishes *An Abridged Greek-English Lexicon* (1935), a shorter version of this outstanding resource.

Theological Dictionaries

Old Testament

Harris, R. L. et al., eds. *Theological Wordbook of the Old Testament* [*TWOT*]. 2 vols. Chicago: Moody, 1980. This book comprises a compact discussion of key Hebrew words. Its authors are all evangelical scholars, and the work is readily accessible to most readers, even those without a working knowledge of Hebrew. It attempts to investigate each Hebrew word and its cognates and synthesize the meaning of words in context in a concise format. Each entry has a number that corresponds to the numbers assigned Hebrew words in Strong's concordance (on which see below). This makes *TWOT* an easy source to consult, and the student will find it a welcome and useful guide.

*VanGemeren, W. et al., eds. *New International Dictionary of Old Testament Theology and Exegesis* [*NIDOTTE*]. 5 vols. Grand Rapids: Zondervan, 1997. Volumes 1–4 are organized alphabetically by Hebrew words; volume 5, topically around English words or biblical book titles. Many topical entries also incorporate discussion of relevant Hebrew words. The contributors are evangelicals from throughout the English-speaking world, and *NIDOTTE* represents a standard work on Hebrew words. (For the use of Brown and Kittel for OT word studies, see below). English readers may access the Hebrew words by cross-reference numbers in Goodrick-Kohlenberger, *NIVEC* (see below), which also has a *NIDOTTE*-Strong's numbers conversion chart.

Jenni, E. and C. Westermann, eds. *Theological Lexicon of the Old Testament*. 3 vols. Peabody, MA: Hendrickson, 1997.[8] This translation finally makes available to English readers what continues to be the standard theological dictionary of German students and pastors after nearly three decades. Written by leading European scholars, each article thoroughly treats the OT's most important theological words, their etymology, cognates, range of meanings, usage in the OT, LXX equivalents, and use at Qumran. Its higher-critical tendencies notwithstanding, its pages teem with rich literary and theological insights worth mining by the advanced user.

Botterweck, G. J. and Ringgren, H., eds. *Theological Dictionary of the Old Testament* [*TDOT*]. 12 vols. Grand Rapids: Eerdmans, 1974–2002.[9] This is the OT counterpart to *TDNT* (see below). *TDOT* assesses key OT terms and their theological significance—occasionally going on to postbiblical developments (e.g., Qumran and the rabbis) and employing cognate languages where possible (especially, though not only, Akkadian and Ugaritic) to explain the meaning. A knowledge of Hebrew is useful, if not essential, to get the most out of this source. Its orientation is less conservative theologically than *TWOT* or *NIDOTTE*, often building upon literary-critical assumptions. Read critically, however, there is no better source for Hebrew word studies.

New Testament

Balz, H. and Schneider, G., eds. *Exegetical Dictionary of the New Testament* [*EDNT*]. 3 vols. Grand Rapids: Eerdmans, 1992.[10] The most recent addition to the genre that includes *TDNT* and *NIDNTT*, this work, however, presupposes the historical background found in these predecessors. Unlike others in this genre, the authors treat every word in the NT, but theologically significant words have longer entries. In particular

---

8 The original German title was *Theologisches Handwörterbuch zum Alten Testament*, 2 vols. (München; Gütersloh: Chr. Kaiser, 1971, 1984).

9 This English edition translates the German original, *Theologisches Wörterbuch zum Alten Testament* (Stuttgart: Kohlhammer, 1970–).

10 This is the English translation of *Exegetisches Wörterbuch zum Neuen Testament*, 3 vols. (Stuttgart: Kohlhammer, 1978, 1981, 1983).

EDNT traces the development of the meanings of theologically significant words in their NT contexts to assess their significance for exegesis.

*Brown, C., ed. *New International Dictionary of New Testament Theology* [*NIDNTT*]. 4 vols. Grand Rapids: Zondervan, 1975–78.[11] This is a work similar to *TDNT* (below) that discusses the theological significance of words over time. However, the words are organized around semantic fields of meanings, countering some of Barr's criticisms of *TDNT*. It aims to provide help for theologians, pastors, and teachers, and omits some of the depth of historical research that characterizes *TDNT*. Generally, the articles in *NIDNTT* are briefer, more up-to-date, and written from a more conservative viewpoint than *TDNT*. Overall this is a valuable resource and one that is more accessible than *TDNT* to the student who knows only English or a bit of Greek. Like *TDNT*, it is also useful for studying OT Hebrew words since most articles discuss the Hebrew background of NT words. The final volume consists wholly of indexes that expedite a variety of searches. An electronic version exists.

Kittel, G. and Friedrich, G. (since 1954), eds. *Theological Dictionary of the New Testament* [*TDNT*]. English translation by G. W. Bromiley, 10 vols. Grand Rapids: Eerdmans, 1964–1978.[12] It is also available in an electronic version. Knowledge of Greek is very helpful, though probably not essential to obtain its basic insights. Following a discussion of a word's etymology, this "dictionary" traces its uses in its various contexts through the ancient world—classical Greek, Hellenistic Greek, LXX Greek, and Jewish writers—all as background for the uses in the NT. If a Greek word has a Hebrew counterpart in the OT, the authors provide discussion of that too. Indeed, it is often useful for studying OT Hebrew words since many articles treat the usage of their Greek counterparts in the Septuagint. (Of course, this requires the student to find the Greek word for the Hebrew word under study). The words are organized according to their etymological roots, a cause for some criticism among reviewers and users. Though this makes locating some terms in *TDNT* a challenge, the final volume contains various indexes that facilitate various searches in this massive storehouse of research. Not all its conclusions can be taken at face value, particularly in some of the early volumes.[13] Read critically, however, there is no better source for Greek word studies. The translator of this multivolume work, G. Bromiley, has produced an abridged and edited one-volume distillation of the entire work—about one sixth of the original, also called *TDNT*. Exeter: Paternoster; Grand Rapids: Eerdmans, 1985. Known as "little Kittel," users who know little or no Greek will find it easier to use.

---

11 Brown translates, but also provides additions and revisions to, the German work done by L. Coenen, et al., eds., *Theologisches Begriffslexikon zum Neuen Testament*, vols. I, II/1–2 (Wuppertal: Brockhaus, 1967, 1969, 1971).

12 The German original is *Theologisches Wörterbuch zum Neuen Testament*, 10 vols. (Stuttgart: Kohlhammer, 1933–79).

13 Volumes 1–4 were done between 1933 and 1942 and need updating. For an important critique of the methodology employed in *TDNT* see J. Barr, *The Semantics of Biblical Language* (Oxford: Oxford University Press, 1961), especially pp. 206–262. Barr rightly assails the untenable view that in studying specific Greek words employed in the NT one is investigating the stock of key theological concepts of the early Christians, as if there is a direct correlation between lexemes and theological concepts (207). For appropriate correctives in doing Greek word studies see M. Silva, *Biblical Words and Their Meaning: An Introduction to Lexical Semantics*, rev. and expanded ed. (Grand Rapids: Zondervan, 1995).

Spicq, C. *Theological Lexicon of the New Testament*. 3 vols. Peabody, MA: Hendrickson, 1994.[14] Excellent insights on many theologically significant words, though a one-man product—thus we list it last, not because it is more advanced or less accessible.

Concordances

Organized according to the alphabetical order of the words occurring in the Bible or a Testament, a concordance quotes the specific line in which a given word occurs and identifies the reference where the line may b found. Bible students have access to concordances in both the original and English languages. Concordances enable students to study the biblical use of individual words ("sin," "salvation," etc.) as well as phrases ("in the latter days," etc.). Most software programs (e.g., BibleWorks, Logos, Gramcord, and others) allow one to produce concordances on the fly—either of root forms (e.g., all occurrences of "love" or ἀγαπάω) or specific inflected forms (e.g., "loved," "was being loved" or ἀγαπηθήσεται), and this holds true for all versions and for modern and original languages.

English Concordances

Concerning concordances for English Bibles, the student must acquire one (or more) that parallels the version of the Bible used for study. Now the Bible market is such that each translation has a corresponding concordance. To cite three examples, see the *Zondervan NASB Exhaustive Concordance*. Grand Rapids: Zondervan, 2000; E. Goodrick and J. R. Kohlenberger, III, eds. *The NIV Exhaustive Concordance*. Grand Rapids: Zondervan, 1990; and J. R. Kohlenberger, III, ed. *The NRSV Concordance Unabridged*. Grand Rapids: Zondervan, 1991. This latter text includes all occurrences of all words in the NRSV, including the apocryphal books and alternate and literal translations found in the footnotes. All these enable one to discover specific words that occur in these versions in all their biblical locations.

The old "standbys" for the KJV were those by R. Young. *Analytical Concordance to the Bible*, repr. Peabody, MA: Hendrickson, 1993; and J. Strong. *Exhaustive Concordance of the Bible*. New York: Hunt Eaton; Cincinnati: Cranston Curts, 1894. Strong has been upgraded: see *The Strongest Strong's Exhaustive Concordance of the Bible*. Zondervan, 2001; and with significant additions and improvements *The New Strong's Expanded Exhaustive Concordance of the Bible*, Nashville: Nelson, 2001. They enable readers without the knowledge of the biblical languages to correlate specific Hebrew or Greek words with their corresponding English terms in the KJV and to compare in the concordance itself uses of the same Hebrew or Greek terms, not simply English translations.[15]

*As a bridge between Hebrew or Greek concordances and those based on English language versions are two works: J. R. Kohlenberger, III and J. A. Swanson. *The Hebrew-English Concordance to the OT*. Grand Rapids: Zondervan, 1998; and id. et al. *The Greek-English Concordance to the NT*. Grand Rapids: Zondervan, 1997. Arranged the same way,

---

14 The French original is *Notes de lexicographie néo-testamentaire*, and was translated and edited by J. H. Ernest.

15 As we have noted, various lexical reference tools have included Strong's numbering system enabling students who would not he able to do so otherwise to locate words. See descriptions of the tools themselves.

they list Hebrew or Greek words alphabetically and indicate the references where they occur with brief excerpts from the KJV. These works are keyed, like the new BDB and *TWOT*, to Strong's numbering system and other reference works. Many of the computer software programs also key words to Strong's numbering system.

Hebrew and Aramaic Concordances

Davidson, A. B. *A Concordance of the Hebrew and Chaldee Scriptures.* London: Samuel Bagster, 1876. This covers all the Hebrew and Aramaic words of the OT. It is designed for students who know little or no Hebrew and cites texts in English translation.

*Even-Shoshan, A. *A New Concordance of the Old Testament.* 2d ed. Grand Rapids: Baker, 1989. This mammoth work, more comprehensive but harder to use than Davidson's, lists every word in the Hebrew Bible alphabetically under its root. To use it requires at least a seminary-level knowledge of Hebrew because all of its citations are in Hebrew (with vowels) and its meanings are given in modern Hebrew. One important feature commends it over Mandelkern and Lisowsky (see below): it groups together identical grammatical forms, phrases, and words of similar meaning. The introduction by J. H. Sailhamer enables the beginner to take advantage of this remarkable resource.

Mandelkern, S. *Veteris Testamenti Concordantiae Hebraicae atque Chaldaicae.* Leipzig: Veit et Comp., 1876; 2d ed., 1925; reprinted. Graz: Akademischer Druck, 1955; with corrections and additions, New York: Schulsinger, 1955; 3d ed. with corrections and supplements by M. H. Gottstein, Jerusalem/Tel Aviv: Schocken, 1959. This is a massive and outstanding work, more comprehensive but less manageable than Even-Shoshan's. Rather than merely listing citations (which may be all a student wants), Mandelkern lists them by grammatical form (e.g., construct, conjugated verbs, etc.), a useful advantage if one seeks a Hebrew specific phrase or formula (e.g., "angel of the Lord," "X found favor in your eyes," etc.). All the wealth this work has to offer clearly belongs to the advanced student and scholar.

Greek Concordances

Hatch. E. and Redpath, H. E. *A Concordance to the Septuagint and Other Greek Versions of the Old Testament.* 2 vols. Oxford: Clarendon, 1897; volume 3, a supplement, 1906; repr. [with supplement] in 2 vols. Graz: Akademischer Druck, 1954; repr. Grand Rapids: Baker, 1983; Ares Pub., 1995. This constitutes the standard concordance for the LXX. It lists each Greek word in the Greek OT and apocryphal books along with its Hebrew counterpart. Passages are given in Greek. Its drawback is the limited number of manuscripts (four, in fact) that lie behind the citations. This concordance, requiring a working knowledge of Greek, is indispensable for a study of the LXX, and is the standard tool for finding the Hebrew words behind it. To make this work more accessible, use T. Muraoka. *Hebrew-Aramaic Index to the Septuagint: Key to Hatch-Redpath Concordance.* Grand Rapids: Baker, 1998.

Marshall, I. H., ed. *Moulton and Geden: A Concordance to the Greek Testament.* 6th ed. Edinburgh: T. & T. Clark, 2002—available from Continuum in the USA. The original work published in 1897 used the Greek text of Westcott and Hort, but this complete update is based on the latest *UBSGNT*-4/NA-27. It is extremely complete and truly functional for it provides grammatical helps, Greek citations from the LXX and Apocrypha, and Hebrew quotes where a citation comes from the OT. Asterisks and daggers indicate whether the vocabulary items in the NT occur in classical Greek and in the Septuagint. References to the variants in the older Greek NT editions are preserved, so that the student has available every reading which might potentially be regarded as forming part of the true text of the NT. Unlike prior editions, prepositions are included in the main text of the Concordance. Where the same word occurs twice in the same verse, these occurrences are now printed on separate lines and individually verse-numbered so that it is easier to assess all the occurrences of any given word.

Aland, K. *Vollständige Konkordanz zum griechischen Neuen Testament: Unter Zugrundelegung aller kritischen Textausgaben und des Textus Receptus* [*VKGNT*]. 2 vols. Berlin/New York: de Gruyter, 1975–83, 1978. A computer-generated, exhaustive concordance based upon the *UBSGNT*, 3d ed. and Nestle-Aland, 26th ed. Greek NT, *VKGNT* is a standard Greek concordance for serious NT studies, providing all variants for the modern critical editions of the NT. Citations are full, in Greek, and include word frequencies for each word— book by book—and alphabetically. Words are categorized as to uses. A fully serviceable "slimmer" (and less expensive) version is also available: H. Bachmann and H. Slaby, eds. *Concordance to the Novum Testamentum Graece of Nestle-Aland, 26th edition, and to the Greek New Testament, 3rd edition.* Berlin/New York: de Gruyter, 1987.[16] It omits citations for twenty-nine frequently occurring words, though it does list the passages for these words in an appendix. For personal use this vies with Moulton and Geden.

Since citations in all the preceding concordances occur in the original languages, students wishing to use them will need to have language facility or will need to use these volumes along with an English Bible for finding references (a time-consuming but often worthwhile project).

Bible Dictionaries and Encyclopedias

Youngblood, R. F. and Bruce, F. F., eds. *Nelson's New Illustrated Bible Dictionary: An Authoritative One-Volume Reference Work on the Bible, With Full-Color Illustrations.* Rev. and upd. Nashville: Nelson, 1995. Produced by evangelicals, this extensive dictionary provides much help over a full range of topics that interest Bible students.

Butler, T. C., ed. *Holman Bible Dictionary.* Nashville: Broadman, 1991. Providing exhaustive definitions, it is beautifully illustrated with color photographs, maps, and charts. It is the most up-to-date of the semi-popular dictionaries.

Achtemeier, P. J., ed. *HarperCollins Bible Dictionary.* Rev. ed. San Francisco: Harper, 1996. This dictionary reflects mainstream biblical scholarship and was authored by members of the Society of Biblical Literature. It covers the Bible and its world, the Apocrypha and pseudepigrapha of the OT and NT, and the early church Fathers.

*Freedman, D. N., ed. *Eerdmans Dictionary of the Bible.* Grand Rapids: Eerdmans, 2000. The best, most up-to-date, one-volume dictionary. Written by both mainstream and evangelical scholars, this dictionary features well-informed articles on the Bible and the full spectrum of background topics. Its recent publication gives it a slight edge over other one-volume dictionaries in presenting the most recent scholarship.

InterVarsity Press has issued three superb dictionaries devoted to the New Testament that stand as some of the finest available. Written by a wide cross-section of

---

16 The German title is *Konkordanz zum Novum Testamentum Graece von Nestle-Aland, 26. Auflage, und zum Greek New Testament, 3rd edition.*

scholars, mostly but not exclusively evangelicals, these represent extensive and current summaries of the issues reflected in the topics of each volume.

*Green, J. B., McKnight, S., and Marshall, I. H., eds. *Dictionary of Jesus and the Gospels.* Downers Grove/Leicester: InterVarsity Press, 1992.

*Hawthorne, G. F., Martin, R. P., and Reid, D. G., eds. *Dictionary of Paul and His Letters.* Downers Grove/Leicester: InterVarsity Press, 1993.

*Davids, P. H. and Martin, R. P., eds. *Dictionary of the Later New Testament and Its Developments.* Downers Grove/Leicester: InterVarsity Press, 1997.

*The same publisher projects a similar dictionary series for the OT, with the first of its four volumes now available: Alexander, T. D. and Baker, D. W., eds. *Dictionary of the Old Testament: Pentateuch.* Downers Grove/Leicester: InterVarsity Press, 2003.

Perhaps another IVP dictionary also merits inclusion here: Ryken, L. et al., eds. *Dictionary of Biblical Imagery.* Downers Grove: InterVarsity, 1998. As the title indicates the authors explain the background and significance of the images that occur throughout the Bible. Many scholars contributed articles though the editors composed the final versions of the entries. By the way, all five of these IVP dictionaries, plus many other resources, are available on the Logos/Libronix platform as *The Essential IVP Reference Library. The Complete Electronic Reference Bible* (2001). OT counterparts are projected.

*Bromiley, G. W., ed. *International Standard Bible Encyclopedia* [*ISBE*]. 4 vols. Rev. ed. Grand Rapids: Eerdmans, 1979–86. This venerable work's revision makes it an ongoing standard for extensive treatment of virtually every biblical topic. This masterpiece must be consulted in any biblical study. More conservative than its counterpart *ABD*, the next entry, it is available on CD-ROM on the Logos/Libronix platform.

*Freedman, D. N., ed. *The Anchor Bible Dictionary* [*ABD*]. 6 vols. Garden City, NY: Doubleday, 1992. This dictionary provides the scholarly world and the general public a current and comprehensive treatment of all biblical subjects and topics in a readable though authoritative manner. It is both multicultural and interdisciplinary in scope and reflects the current state of mainstream biblical scholarship. Over 800 scholars contributed to this massive work. It is available on CD-ROM on the Logos/Libronix platform.

Keck, L. E., ed. *The New Interpreter's Bible,* 12 vols. Nashville: Abingdon, 1994–2002. Replacing the venerable 1962/1976 original, this cross between a commentary and an encyclopedia has contributions by leading scholars across the entire theological spectrum. Includes numerous visual aids and a "reflections" section based on each commentary. Also available in a CD-ROM version.

Roth C. and Wigoder, G., eds. *Encyclopedia Judaica.* 16 vols. Jerusalem: Keter, 1972–91; repr. Coronet. Annual yearbooks appear. This set is the definitive work on the Hebrew Scriptures and all things Jewish. It contains in-depth articles on a wide variety of subjects in the Hebrew Scriptures as well as information on Jewish holidays, customs and teachings.

Grammatical Analysis

Hebrew

Williams, R. J. *Hebrew Syntax: An Outline.* 2d ed. Toronto: University of Toronto Press, 1976. A standard work, it presents a useful, simple overview of Hebrew syntax. With its user-friendly organization and index, it remains a favorite tool of both beginning and advanced students of syntax.

*Waltke, B. K. and O'Connor, M. *An Introduction to Biblical Hebrew Syntax.* Winona Lake, IN: Eisenbrauns, 1990. Based upon modern linguistic principles, it serves as both a reference grammar and a resource for self-study. Though not as "user friendly" as it might be, it is an indispensable tool for the student with a seminary-level knowledge of Hebrew. It contains numerous examples and excellent indexes. Its somewhat technical language may limit its usefulness to only advanced students.

Van Der Merwe, C. H. J., Naudé, J. A., and Kroeze, J. H. *A Biblical Hebrew Reference Grammar.* Sheffield: JSOT, 1999. An affordable, well-indexed study incorporating recent insights of linguistics.

The standard reference grammar of OT Hebrew in English remains W. Gesenius and E. Kautzsch, *Gesenius' Hebrew Grammar.* 2d ed. Oxford: Clarendon, 1910, 1995, based on the 28th German edition of W. Gesenius, *Hebräische Grammatik* by A.E. Cowley. It is still authoritative for philology and morphology, but its treatment of syntax is outdated in many places. For the latter, see Williams and Waltke-O'Connor.

Greek

Black, D. A. *It's Still Greek to Me.* Grand Rapids: Baker, 1998. Simplest but very useful treatment of intermediate-level Greek.

Mounce, W. D. *The Morphology of Biblical Greek.* Grand Rapids: Zondervan, 1994. Good for learning the basic forms of Hellenistic Greek.

Moule, C. F. D. *An Idiom Book of New Testament Greek.* 2d ed. Cambridge: Cambridge University Press, 1963. This limited work alerts the reader to a variety of Greek idioms. An index of verses helps locate instances where idiomatic uses convey special nuances of meaning. This is not a compendium of Greek grammar. Knowledge of Greek is an important prerequisite.

Porter, S. E. *Idioms of the Greek New Testament.* Sheffield: Sheffield Academic Press, 1992. This is an intermediate-level grammar based on modern linguistic principles. Porter's treatment of Greek tenses as "aspectual" broke new ground when the book appeared. Includes a helpful section on discourse analysis. Some unique but also idiosyncratic features.

Wallace, D. B. *The Basics of New Testament Syntax.* Grand Rapids: Zondervan, 2000. An abridgement of the following volume.

*Wallace, D. B. *Greek Grammar Beyond the Basics.* Grand Rapids: Zondervan, 1996. The most comprehensive intermediate grammar currently available that makes use of the latest principles and insights from linguistics and grammatical functioning. Extensive examples make this a goldmine for understanding how specific grammatical features function in context. A software edition exists.

*Blass, F., Debrunner, A., and Funk, R. W. *A Greek Grammar of the New Testament and Other Early Christian Literature* [BDF]. Chicago: University of Chicago Press, 1961. This is the standard grammar for making exegetical decisions about the Greek text.[17] The indexes often help the student gain assistance in specific verses or grammatical issues. Unfortunately, the work is not "user-friendly," and finding specific help is not always easy. This work requires a good grasp of Greek.

---

17 BDF is a translation and revision of the 9th–10th edition of F. Blass and A. Debrunner, *Grammatik des neutestamentlichen Griechisch* (Göttingen: Vandenhoeck & Ruprecht, 1954, 1959). Translator R. Funk also had access to and employed additional notes of A. Debrunner. He also incorporated his own findings, so BDF goes beyond the printed German edition.

Geography

Though smaller and less comprehensive, two paperback works merit mention as useful for much basic geography: May, H. G. and Day, J. *Oxford Bible Atlas.* Oxford: Oxford University Press, 1985; and Frank, H. T., ed. *Hammond's Atlas of the Bible Lands.* Rev. ed. Maplewood, NJ: Hammond, 1990.

*Beitzel, B. *The Moody Atlas of Bible Lands.* Chicago: Moody Press, 1985. This is similar in size to Aharoni/Avi-Yonah and Rasmussen (see below) but seems the best atlas in its class. Conservative in viewpoint, it also has fine color maps and pictures.

Rasmussen, C. G. *The Zondervan NIV Atlas of the Bible.* Grand Rapids: Zondervan, 1989. This is an excellent volume produced from an evangelical viewpoint.

Pritchard, J. B., ed. *The Harper's Atlas of the Bible.* New York: Harper, 1987. Representing a more mainline scholarly viewpoint, this is perhaps the most definitive atlas to emerge in recent decades and may become a standard. Students must decide, however, if their library can accommodate its large size.

Wright, G. E. and Filson, F. V. *The Westminster Historical Atlas to the Bible.* Rev. ed. Philadelphia: Westminster, 1956. Formerly the paragon of biblical atlases, this work has been eclipsed by the following book. Nevertheless, the student will find useful discussions of historical events and an attempt to integrate the findings of archaeology to clarify the biblical text.

*Aharoni, Y., Avi-Yonah, M., Rainey, A. F., and Safrai, Z., eds. *The Carta Bible Atlas.* Corrected 4th ed. New York: Macmillan, 2002. New edition of a standard atlas that provides individual maps for many significant Bible events. Formerly the Macmillan Bible Atlas, this is now distributed through Eisenbrauns. This atlas takes pride of place as one of the best available. The authors, Jewish scholars, identify biblical sites and events, though evangelicals may disagree at times with their dating. For obvious reasons it concentrates more on Palestine and less on the Roman world and so is less helpful in studying the expansion of the early church.

The most thorough resource for biblical geography, one destined to become a standard for advanced students and scholars, is Mittmann, S. and Schmitt, G., eds. *Tübinger Bibelatlas.* Stuttgart: Deutsche Bibelgesellschaft, 2001. Each oversized, foldout, colored map portrays a region, its cities, roads, and landmarks during a specific historical period in remarkable detail. Though prepared in Germany, the volume has both German and English captions and is available through any United Bible Societies affiliate.

History of the Ancient World

We face a major difficulty in recommending useful volumes that will serve the student in basic research into the history of the ancient world. Simply put, the discipline is as vast as the terrain. Nevertheless, we suggest a basic list. Though we divide the section into several subgroups, various works overlap.

Ancient Near Eastern and Classical Literature

*Arnold, B. T. and Beyer, B. E. *Readings from the Ancient Near East.* Encountering Biblical Studies. Grand Rapids: Baker, 2002. This companion volume to the authors' *Encountering the Old Testament* (see below) offers a balanced selection of Ancient Near Eastern texts for the general reader, each with a helpful background introduction.

Matthews, V. H. and Benjamin, D. C. *Old Testament Parallels: Laws and Stories from the Ancient Near East*. New York: Paulist Press, 1991. This handy paperback offers the general reader brief introductions to and translations of the most important extra-biblical texts that parallel materials in the Bible. Its literary glimpse of the ancient world helps the student better understand both that world and important biblical texts.

Dalley, S., ed. *Myths from Mesopotamia*. Oxford World Classics. New York/Oxford: Oxford University Press, 1998. This is a collection of translations of the most important mythical texts on topics of interest to Bible students (e.g., creation, flood, etc.).

Coogan, M., ed. *Stories from Ancient Canaan*. Philadelphia: Westminster John Knox, 1978. This handy paperback gives the general reader introductory background and the translation of several important texts from Ugarit, the center of pre-Israelite Canaanite culture. It offers a literary glimpse of the religion with which Israel's faith had to contend in Canaan.

*Walton, J. H. *Ancient Israelite Literature in Its Cultural Context: A Survey of Parallels Between Biblical and Ancient Near Eastern Texts*. Grand Rapids: Zondervan, 1989. Organized by genre (e.g., law, history, wisdom, etc.), this volume by an evangelical not only surveys extra-biblical literary parallels but also evaluates the extent of their comparison. Its contents and clear style make it a valuable resource even for the general reader.

Hallo, W. and Younger, Jr., K. L., eds. *Context of Scripture*, 3 vols. Leiden: Brill, 1997–2002. This masterful set presents translations by an international team of scholars of ancient texts of interest to Bible students, including ones recently discovered. It representative selection of texts, use of biblical cross references, and judicious commentary mark it as a standard reference work for this century's scholars and advanced students.

Pritchard, J. B., ed. *Ancient Near Eastern Texts Relating to the Old Testament [ANET]*. 3d ed. with supplement. Princeton: Princeton University Press, 1969. Though somewhat dated, this single volume still offers an enormous collection of ancient writings organized by culture (Mesopotamia, Egypt, etc.) and literary type (law, history, wisdom, etc.). The general reader will probably prefer the handy two-volume paperback set, *The Ancient Near East*. Princeton: Princeton University Press, 1958, 1976, which combines texts from the above book as well as pictures from Pritchard's *The Ancient Near East in Pictures* (see below).

Beyerlin, W., ed. *Near Eastern Religious Texts Relating to the Old Testament*, OTL. Philadelphia: Westminster, 1978. This is the translation of a German original that focuses specifically on ancient religious texts that illumine the OT.

Gould, G. P. et. al., eds. *The Loeb Classical Library*. Founded by J. Loeb. Cambridge, MA: Harvard University Press; London: Heinemann. In more than 450 vols. these works furnish the standard original language (Greek or Latin) editions of major classical works with English translations on facing pages. They include classical Greek writers (e.g., Plato and Aristotle), ancient historians (e.g., Thucydides, Herodotus), Jewish writers (Philo and Josephus), and post-biblical Christian and secular writers (e.g., Augustine, Eusebius, Cicero, and Ovid).

Ancient World History and Near Eastern History

Hallo, W. W. and Simpson, W. K. *The Ancient Near East: A History*. 2d ed. Fort Worth: Harcourt Brace College Publishers, 1998. This work offers an excellent history of the ancient world aimed at the general reader with a particular focus on Mesopotamia and Egypt.

Kuhrt, A. *The Ancient Near East: 3000–330* B.C. 2 vols. New York: Routledge, 1995. This offers a thorough, scholarly survey of the history of the biblical world by a British scholar. It has already become the standard resource for university ancient history courses and offers more detail than Hallo but less than *CAH* (see below).

Nissen, H. J. *The Early History of the Ancient Near East, 9000–2000* B.C. Chicago: University of Chicago Press, 1988. Translated by E. Lutzeier, this book surveys the historical period that saw the emergence of civilization in the Ancient Near East. Since Abraham probably lived ca. 2000 B.C., it portrays the larger historical landscape preceding that biblical figure.

Hammond, N. G. L. and Scullard, H. H., eds. *The Oxford Classical Dictionary.* Oxford: Oxford University Press, 1970. This dictionary provides a reliable window into the world of the classical period.

Edwards, I. E. S. et al., eds. *The Cambridge Ancient History [CAH].* 3d ed. 5 vols. (often in two or more parts) to date. Many volumes/parts of the 2d ed. still in print. Cambridge: Cambridge University Press, 1970– . This represents, without challenge, the most comprehensive study of the political, economic, and social world out of which emerged the OT and NT.

Von Soden, W. *The Ancient Orient: An Introduction to the Study of the Ancient Near East.* Translated by D. G. Schley. Grand Rapids: Eerdmans, 1994. This volume by a front-rank Semitic specialist has become a popular, standard introduction to the Ancient East, its history, peoples, institutions, and culture. The general reader will appreciate its broad overview.

Old Testament History

Shanks, H., ed. *Ancient Israel. From Abraham to the Roman Destruction of the Temple.* Revised edition. Biblical Archaeology Society, 1999. Popular writing with each chapter written by one or two experts in the field.

*Long, V. P. *The Art of Biblical History.* Vol. 5 of *Foundations of Contemporary Interpretation.* Ed. M. Silva. Grand Rapids: Zondervan, 1994. Seeks to show the need to balance historicity, literary art, and theology in understanding the history-writing of the OT.

*Bright, J. *A History of Israel.* 4th ed., greatly revised with an introduction by W. P. Brown. Louisville: Westminster John Knox, 2000. This text systematically presents Israel's history according to the principles of the now oft-maligned Albright school.[18] Highly praised, the book represents an outstanding accomplishment in history-writing. At the same time, some scholars disagree with its stance in several places.

Provan, I., Long, V. P., and Longman, T., III. *A Biblical History of Israel.* Louisville: Westminster John Knox Press, 2003. This marks the first major history of Israel to appear in English in two decades. Its authors are three leading evangelical scholars, and it may become the standard resource for Israelite history written from a moderate perspective.

---

18 Bright sets out his principles for writing the early history of Israel in J. Bright, *Early Israel in Recent History Writing,* SBT 19 (London: SCM, 1956). See also W. F. Albright, *From the Stone Age to Christianity,* 2d ed. (Garden City, NY: Doubleday, 1957); and id. *The Biblical Period from Abraham to Ezra: An Historical Survey* (New York: Harper & Row, 1963).

Coogan, M. D., ed. *The Oxford History of the Biblical World*. New York; Oxford: Oxford University Press, 1998. Each essay by a mainstream scholar treats a specific period of Israel's history.

Miller, J. M. and Hayes, J. H. *A History of Ancient Israel and Judah*. Philadelphia: Westminster, 1986. Here we find a portrait of Israelite history that departs significantly from that of Bright. Conservative readers may find themselves less at home with its treatment of the patriarchs and the conquest of Canaan than with Bright's.

Dever, W. G. *What Did the Biblical Writers Know and When Did They Know It? What Archaeology Can Tell Us about the Reality of Ancient Israel*. Grand Rapids: Eerdmans, 2001. Polemical but useful survey and important critique of some of current biblical historiographic and postmodern interpretations.

Kaiser, W. C. *A History of Israel*. Nashville: Broadman & Holman, 1998. This is a history of Israel by a conservative scholar, as is Merrill, E. H. *Kingdom of Priests*. Grand Rapids: Baker, 1987.

Ahlström, G. W. *The History of Ancient Palestine from the Palaeolithic Period to Alexander's Conquest*. With a contribution by G. O. Rollefson. Ed. by D. Edelman. JSOT Supplement Series 146. Sheffield: Sheffield Academic Press, 1993. Somewhat tainted by the author's occasional idiosyncratic opinions and perspectives.

Miller, P. D. *The Religion of Ancient Israel*. Louisville: Westminster John Knox, 2000. A study of many important topics of Canaanite and Israelite religion by a well-known scholar.

Hayes, J. H. and Miller, J. M., eds. *Israelite and Judaean History*. OTL. Philadelphia: Westminster, 1977. This work surveys the history of Israel from its beginnings to A.D. 132 in the Roman era. These learned articles for advanced readers, written by an international group of fourteen scholars, discuss the sources of historical data and the current state of scholarly discussions about Israelite history. Now outdated, this work's radical departure from the Bright/Albright tradition that relied much on archaeology to reconstruct history will not find favor with those who prize that approach.

Albertz, R. *A History of Israelite Religion in the Old Testament Period*. 2 vols. OTL. Louisville: Westminster John Knox, 1994. This detailed, comprehensive study uses a classic higher-critical reconstruction of the history of OT literature with interaction with recent discussions and discoveries to describe Israel's religion. Read critically, this oft-cited work is a "must-read" for the informed, advanced student.

Smith, M. S. *The Origins of Biblical Monotheism: Israel's Polytheistic Background and the Ugaritic Texts*. New York; Oxford: Oxford University Press, 2001. This provocative book traces the late emergence of Israelite monotheism in the context of West-Semitic polytheism, especially that evident in Ugaritic texts, of which the author is a leading authority. It follows up his earlier stimulating study: *The Early History of God*. San Francisco: Harper and Row, 1990. Both aim at advanced students and scholars.

De Moor, J. C. *The Rise of Yahwism. The Roots of Israelite Monotheism*. BETL 91. Peeters, 1990. Important evidence and arguments for Israel's worship of one God in Mosaic and later times.

Long, V. P., ed. *Israel's Past in Present Research: Essays on Ancient Israelite Historiography*. SBTS 7. Winona Lake, IN: Eisenbrauns, 1999. A variety of experts contribute essays on the writing and interpretation of historical data relating to the major OT periods and genres.

Millard, A. R., Hoffmeier, J. K., and Baker, D. W., eds. *Faith, Tradition, and History: Old Testament Historiography in Its Near Eastern Context*. Winona Lake, IN: Eisenbrauns, 1994. Important articles on the methods and interpretation of various OT passages in the light of ancient Near Eastern comparisons.

History of Intertestamental Times

Nicklesburg, G. W. E. *Jewish Literature Between The Bible and the Mishnah: A Historical and Literary Introduction*. Minneapolis: Fortress, 1981. The title says enough: an excellent list of valuable primary sources (in English translation).

Cate, R. L. *A History of the Bible Lands in the Interbiblical Period*. Nashville: Broadman Press, 1989. A short, popular treatment of this historical period.

Skarsaune, O. *In the Shadow of the Temple: Jewish Influences on Early Christianity*. Downers Grove: InterVarsity Press, 2002. A comprehensive introduction to early Judaism and its contribution to the NT, and early Christianity.

Scott, J. J., Jr. *Customs and Controversies*. Grand Rapids: Baker, 1995. A clear, thorough, evangelical overview of the most pertinent historical and religious background to the NT from the intertestamental period with special focus on social customs and ideological controversies.

*VanderKam, J. C. *An Introduction to Early Judaism*. Grand Rapids: Eerdmans, 2001. An outstanding up-to-date synthesis of scholarship on historical developments, non-canonical literature, and institutional developments of Judaism in the Second Temple period.

Grabbe, L. L. *Judaism from Cyrus to Hadrian*. 2 vols. Minneapolis: Fortress, 1992. A more lengthy and technical overview of the history of Judaism from the end of the OT period to the end of the NT period.

Hengel, M. *Judaism and Hellenism: Studies in Their Encounter in Palestine During the Early Hellenistic Period*. 2 vols. Minneapolis: Fortress, 1974. These volumes provide the author's helpful insights into the interaction between Judaism and the Greek world that set the stage for Judaism as it existed in the first century A.D. Its updated summary is entitled *Jews, Greeks and Barbarians: Aspects of the Hellenization of Judaism in the Pre-Christian Period*. Minneapolis: Fortress, 1980.

History of New Testament Times

*Witherington, B. *New Testament History*. Grand Rapids: Baker, 2001. This work begins with the events that brought about the close of the OT era and traces Jewish and secular history right through the age of the NT events. No other work matches this for readability and concise coverage over this essential terrain.

Ferguson, E. *Backgrounds of Early Christianity*. 2d. ed. Grand Rapids: Eerdmans, 1993. Well organized and providing extensive additional bibliographic resources all along the way, this text gives brief but highly useful explanations of numerous aspects of the religious, political, philosophical, and social world of the NT.

Evans, C. A. and Porter, S. E., ed. *Dictionary of New Testament Background*. Downers Grove/Leicester: InterVarsity Press, 2000. Up-to-date, descriptive, and often detailed articles on a whole range of institutions and developments, beautifully done.

*Wright, N. T. *The New Testament and the People of God*. Vol. 1 of Christian Origins and the Question of God. Philadelphia: Fortress, 1992. A veritable *tour de force* that challenges many time-honored assumptions and "assured results." Describes the history, social make-up, worldview, beliefs, hope, and symbolic world of Palestinian Judaism within its larger Greco-Roman world. Then takes up the genesis of the first Christians within that matrix. Must reading.

Jeffers, J. S. *The Greco-Roman World of the New Testament Era.* Downers Grove: InterVarsity, 1999. Topically arranged chapters introduce readers to major social and cultural practices and developments, particularly for the non-Jewish portion of early Christianity: e.g., government, social class and status, economics, the military, citizenship, slavery, and so on.

Schürer, E. *The History of the Jewish People in the Age of Jesus Christ (175 B.C.-A.D. 135).* Rev. and ed. by G. Vermes, F. Millar, and M. Goodman, 4 vols. Edinburgh: T. & T. Clark, 1973–87. This massive study discusses the entire NT period from both historical and sociological perspectives. It includes extensive bibliographies. The revision has toned down many of Schürer's opinions that did not accord with the best modern scholarship.

Barnett, P. *Jesus and the Rise of Early Christianity.* Downers Grove: InterVarsity, 1999. An excellent evangelical overview of relevant historical first-century background to the life of Jesus and the first seventy years of church history. Equally clearly places all of the NT writings and events referred to in them in chronological sequence.

Barrett, C. K., ed. *The New Testament Background: Writings from Ancient Greece and the Roman Empire That Illuminate Christian Origins.* Rev. ed. San Francisco: Harper & Row, 1995. This is a wide-ranging compilation of sources that provide helpful background for a variety of NT studies. A similar work, Cartlidge, D. R. and Dungan, D. L. *Documents for the Study of the Gospels.* Rev. and expanded ed. Minneapolis: Fortress, 1994, collects texts from pagan, Jewish, and Christian authors to portray form-critical categories employed in modern research on the Gospels. One may then compare other forms with those that appear in the Gospels (e.g., parables). See also Evans, C. A. *Noncanonical Writings and New Testament Interpretation.* Peabody, MA: Hendrickson, 1993.

Klauck, H.-J. *The Religious Context of Early Christianity: A Guide to Graeco-Roman Religions.* Minneapolis: Augsburg Fortress, 2003. A full guide to the religious environment into which Christianity emerged including domestic and civic religion, popular beliefs (e.g., divination, astrology, and "magic"), mystery cults, ruler and emperor cults, philosophy, and Gnosticism.

Koester, H. *Introduction to the New Testament: History, Culture and Religion of the Hellenistic Age.* 2d. ed. Berlin/New York: de Gruyter; Minneapolis: Fortress, 1995. This first volume provides abundant information about the history of the Greek and Roman worlds. The second volume, *History and Literature of Early Christianity* (1982) rounds out the picture. In places Koester's pet theories skew his analyses, and he has received some criticism on that score.

Safrai, S. and Stern, M. et al., eds. *The Jewish People in the First Century.* Section One of *Compendia Rerum Iudaicarum ad Novum Testamentum.* 2 vols. Assen: Van Gorcum; Minneapolis: Fortress, 1974, 1976. One part of a massive project written by Christian and Jewish scholars to study the relationship between Judaism and Christianity through the centuries, this section concentrates on the first century A.D. These scholarly articles are of uneven quality and must be used cautiously.

Customs, Culture, Society

Pre-Christian Era

*Matthews, V. H. *Manners and Customs in the Bible: Revised Edition.* Peabody, MA: Hendrickson, 1991. This offers the general reader a reliable, illustrated guide to the daily world of both testaments. Photographs enhance its value. In addition see id., *Social World of the Hebrew Prophets.* Peabody, MA: Hendrickson, 2001. It covers the prophets' worlds chronologically and seeks to show how their social contexts shaped their messages.

Thompson, J. A. *Handbook of Life in Bible Times.* Downers Grove: InterVarsity, 1986. This is a handy resource for insight to both testaments.

Blaiklock, E. M. and Harrison, R. K., eds. *The New International Dictionary of Biblical Archaeology.* Grand Rapids: Zondervan, 1983. Now somewhat dated, this useful reference book, written by conservative scholars, is organized by subject. Easily accessible, it offers an entrance into the ancient biblical world as illumined by archaeology. A more ecumenical counterpart is Frend, W. H. C. *The Archaeology of Early Christianity.* Philadelphia: Fortress, 1998.

Walton, J. H., Matthews, V. H., and Chavalas, M. W. *The IVP Bible Background Commentary: Old Testament.* Downers Grove: InterVarsity, 2000. Takes a verse-by-verse approach to providing insight into historical and cultural background matters.

Hoerth, A., Mattingly, G., and Yamauchi, E., eds. *Peoples of the Old Testament World.* Grand Rapids: Baker, 1994. An evangelical update of Wiseman, D., ed. *Peoples of Old Testament Times.* Oxford: Clarendon, 1973. This volume contains chapters on the nations with which Israel interacted. Though the authors are all scholars of international renown, they speak to the general reader.

*King, P. J. and Stager, L. E. *Life in Biblical Israel.* Library of Ancient Israel. Louisville: Westminster John Knox, 2001. With color photos and drawings, this is the best discussion of how life was lived in biblical times.

Matthews, V. H. and Benjamin, D. C. *The Social World of Ancient Israel: 1250 – 587 BCE.* Peabody, MA: Hendrickson, 1993. An accessible window into the prominent social institutions of the world of early Israel and the period of the monarchy—and how an understanding of these informs biblical interpretation. Treats politics, economics, diplomacy, law, and education.

Pritchard, J. B., ed. *The Ancient Near East in Pictures.* 2d ed. Princeton: Princeton University Press, 1969. This is a collection of pictures of ancient Near Eastern artifacts with a commentary on each. By stressing daily life in ancient times, it gives an excellent visual glimpse of the ancient world from which the Bible came.

Two books introduce readers to the culture of the ancient world: Bottero, J. et al., eds. *Everyday Life in Mesopotamia.* Baltimore: Johns Hopkins University Press, 2001; and Snell, D. C. *Life in the Ancient Near East 3100–322 B.C.* New Haven: Yale University Press, 1997. A briefer account is also available in several chapters of Von Soden, W. *The Ancient Orient* (see above).

de Vaux, R. *Ancient Israel: Its Life and Institutions.* D. N. Freedman, ed. Grand Rapids: Eerdmans, 1997.[19] Intended for the non-specialist, this text surveys a wide

---

19 This text translates the French original, *Les institutions de l'Ancien Testament,* 2 vols. 2d ed. (Paris: Cerf, 1961, 1967). This ET employs notes, corrections, and additions provided by de Vaux, and is packaged in a one volume paperback edition.

range of topics for understanding life in ancient Israel. It covers nomadism, family structures, civil institutions, the military, and religion—all as revealed in the OT, ancient secular history, and archaeology.

Aharoni, Y. *The Land of the Bible*. Rev. ed. Philadelphia: Westminster, 1979. From the pen of a well-known Israeli archaeologist, this volume offers extensive information about the geography of ancient Israel.

Meyers, E. M., ed. *The Oxford Encyclopedia of Archaeology in the Near East*. 5 vols. Oxford: Oxford University Press, 1997. Organized by sites and topics, this set is the definitive reference work on archaeology of the ancient world.

Sasson, J. M., ed. *Civilizations of the Ancient Near East*, 4 vols. New York: Scribner, 1995. This is the standard, in-depth reference work concerning the major cultural groups of the Ancient Near East.

The Christian Era

Esler, P. F. *The First Christians in Their Social World*. London/New York: Routledge, 1994. This is an extremely readable introduction to a sociological approach to the study of the NT.

Hanson, K. C. and Oakman, D. E. *Palestine in the Time of Jesus: Social Structures and Social Conflicts*. Minneapolis: Augsburg Fortress, 1998, (2002 with CD-ROM). An overview of social analysis and the ancient Mediterranean worldview that systematically presents major domains and institutions of family, politics, and economy, always with reference to biblical texts.

*Malina, B. J. *The New Testament World: Insights from Cultural Anthropology*. 3d rev. and expanded ed. Louisville: Westminster John Knox, 2001. Extremely insightful, this book provides windows of understanding into certain values, practices, and perspectives of inhabitants of the first-century world.

Keener, C. S. *The IVP Biblical Background Commentary: New Testament*. Downers Grove: InterVarsity, 1993. Takes a verse-by-verse approach to providing insight into historical and cultural background matters.

Jeremias, J. *Jerusalem in the Time of Jesus: An Investigation into the Economic and Social Conditions During the New Testament Period*. Minneapolis: Fortress, 1969. In places idiosyncratic, this work offers a wealth of information about the personnel and institutions in the Judea of Jesus' time, focusing on economic and social conditions.

Sherwin-White, A. N. *Roman Society and Roman Law in the New Testament*. Reprint. Grand Rapids: Baker, 1963. This book provides insights into various legal features of the NT world.

*Meeks, W. *The First Urban Christians: The Social World of the Apostle Paul*. New Haven: Yale University Press, 1983. This significant, ground-breaking work takes a sociological approach to analyzing the institutions and practices of the first-century world and the early Christians' presence within it.

Finegan, J. *Myth & Mystery: An Introduction to the Pagan Religions of the Biblical World*. Grand Rapids: Baker, 1989. Finegan surveys the spectrum of religious beliefs in the world during the emergence of the NT.

Theissen, G. *Sociology of Early Palestinian Christianity*. Minneapolis: Fortress, 1978. A sociological analysis of the Jesus movement, this work attempts to describe the social attitudes and behaviors typical of people in Palestine at the time of Jesus' appearance.

*De Silva, D. A. *Honor, Patronage, Kinship and Purity.* Downers Grove: InterVarsity, 2001. Clear evangelical introduction to the most significant distinctive cultural values of the NT world (as reflected in the title) with numerous applications to how the information makes a difference for interpreting texts.

Chronology

*Walton, J. H. *Chronological and Background Charts of the Old Testament.* Rev. ed. Grand Rapids: Zondervan, 1994. Offering attractive, nontechnical chronological tables that cover biblical and ancient Near Eastern history, this text also provides other background charts to help Bible readers sort out complex biblical topics (e.g., Israel's main sacrifices, etc.). The NT counterpart is House, H. W. *Chronological and Background Charts of the New Testament.* Grand Rapids: Zondervan, 1981.

Hoehner, H. W. *Chronological Aspects of the Life of Christ.* Grand Rapids: Zondervan, 1978. This is a helpful guide to the variety of issues and questions of dating events in the Gospels.

Thiele, E. R. *The Mysterious Numbers of the Hebrew Kings.* Rev. ed. Grand Rapids: Kregel, 1995. This work has useful chronological charts for the monarchy period of Israel and Judah and detailed discussions of the major chronological problems besetting biblical dating. Its technical discussions, however, make it more useful for the advanced student than for the general reader.

Hayes, J. H. and Hooker, P. K. *A New Chronology for the Kings of Israel and Judah.* Atlanta: John Knox, 1988. These authors set aside Thiele's solutions and propose an alternative chronology for the same period from a less conservative perspective.

*Finegan, J. *Handbook of Biblical Chronology: Principles of Time Reckoning in the Ancient World and Problems of Chronology in the Bible.* Rev. ed. Peabody, MA: Hendrickson, 1998. The work details both principles for determining chronology in biblical studies as well as attempted solutions to specific problems of dating. It does a better job with the NT than with the OT.

*Bruce, F. F. *Paul: Apostle of the Heart Set Free.* Grand Rapids: Eerdmans, 2000. The product of many years of research and teaching, Bruce presents the best "life of Paul" (what puts it in this category) along with a wise clarification of many Pauline issues.

Galil, G. *The Chronology of the Kings of Israel and Judah.* Leiden/New York: Brill, 1996. In this scholarly book, an Israeli scholar proposes a viable, alternative system to that of Thiele, explaining the few inconsistencies as due to the biblical author's sources.

Introductions and Surveys

These works provide information on a variety of background issues—authorship, recipients, dating, provenance, purpose, and integrity. They collect in single volumes the essential data to begin the study of a biblical book. The wise student will consult several, along with appropriate commentaries or other sources, to secure a balanced perspective, especially where several options exist for issues of interpretation. Some of these go on to survey the contents of the books.

Old Testament

Hill, A. E. and Walton, J. H. *A Survey of the Old Testament.* 2d ed. Grand Rapids: Zondervan, 2001. This college-level survey of the OT emphasizes its content, background, and literary nature. Its perspective is somewhat more conservative than the following volume.

Arnold, B. T. and Beyer, B. E. *Encountering the Old Testament: A Christian Survey.* Encountering Biblical Studies. Grand Rapids: Baker, 1999. An excellent survey of the OT aimed at the beginning student—with a CD-ROM with helpful supplemental graphics and photographs.

Baker, D. W. and Arnold, B. T. eds., *The Face of Old Testament Studies: A Survey of Contemporary Approaches.* Grand Rapids: Baker, 1999. The most important recent work surveying the academic field of OT studies written and edited by evangelicals.

Dillard, R. and Longman, III, T. *An Introduction to the Old Testament.* Grand Rapids: Zondervan, 1994. A helpful up-to-date evangelical contribution. Longman finished the project after Dillard's death. It supplies an up-to-date evangelical introduction with responses to literary criticism.

*LaSor, W., Bush, F., and Hubbard, D. A. *Old Testament Survey.* 2d ed. Grand Rapids: Eerdmans, 1996. Another outstanding introduction produced by evangelicals, this superb text treats issues of OT authority, revelation and inspiration, canon, and the formation of the OT. It also provides specific introductions and surveys of all the OT books as well as concluding background articles.

Anderson, B. W. and Darr, K. P. *Understanding the Old Testament.* Abridged 4th ed. Englewood Cliffs, NJ: Prentice Hall, 1997. Nonevangelical in its orientation, this volume continues to serve students well since its appearance in 1957. The OT books are set against their historical background. The author employs the recent findings of OT scholars and considers the insights of archaeologists. The book uses charts, illustrations, and maps to excellent advantage.

Childs, B. S. *Introduction to the Old Testament as Scripture.* Philadelphia: Fortress, 1979. A very influential general introduction to the Bible that is still much discussed and much misunderstood. Childs here advocates canonical criticism, whereby books of the Bible and indeed the whole Bible must be interpreted in the form in which they are accepted by Jews and Christians: as canonical (i.e., inspired and authoritative works).

Schmidt, W. H. *Old Testament Introduction.* 2d ed. Louisville: Westminster John Knox, 1999. Translated from a German original by J. O'Connell and D. J. Reimer, this introduces the OT from a moderate higher-critical perspective.

Gottwald, N. K. *The Hebrew Bible: A Socio-Literary Introduction.* Philadelphia: Fortress, 1985, 2002. This volume's idiosyncratic sociological approach by a mainstream scholar gives the advanced reader, reading critically, a fresh angle from which to view OT books and Israel as a society. A CD-ROM with charts and aids accompanies its newest (2002) printing.

We also must mention the fine bibliography on this topic: Hostetter, E. C. *Old Testament Introduction.* Institute for Biblical Research Bibliography. Grand Rapids: Baker, 1995.

New Testament

Burkett, D. *An Introduction to the New Testament and the Origins of Christianity.* Cambridge: Cambridge University Press, 2002. Designed primarily for undergraduate courses in the NT, biblical studies, and early Christianity, it could emerge as a standard liberal text.

Elwell, W. A. and Yarbrough, R. W. *Encountering the New Testament* and *Readings from the First-Century World* [with CD-ROM]. Grand Rapids: Baker, 1998. The most user-friendly college freshman-level introduction. Staunchly conservative throughout.

Gundry, R. *A Survey of the New Testament.* 3d ed. Grand Rapids: Zondervan, 1994. This volume includes both brief treatments of introduction as well as a survey of the contents of the NT books. Best basic level survey in terms of pure content.

Wenham, D. and Walton, S. *Exploring the New Testament.* Downers Grove: InterVarsity. Vol. 1: *A Guide to the Gospels & Acts* (2001); Marshall, I. H., Travis, S., and Paul, I., vol. 2: *A Guide to the Epistles and Revelation* (2002).

*Carson, D. A., Moo, D. J., and Morris, L. *An Introduction to the New Testament.* Grand Rapids: Zondervan, 1992. . This work places primary focus on the background issues of the NT books such as authorship, date, sources, purpose, destination, et al. The authors include, as well, brief outlines of each book plus brief accounts of recent studies on and the theological significance of each NT document. The bibliographies are particularly helpful. A revision is in progress.

Achtemeier, P. J., Green, J. B., and Thompson, M. M. *Introducing the New Testament: Its Literature and Theology.* Grand Rapids: Eerdmans, 2001. A competitor to Carson, Moo, and Morris, this study adopts less conservative positions on some points, but it does more with the contents and narrative flow of each book.

*Brown, R. E. *An Introduction to the New Testament.* N.Y.: Doubleday, 1997. The non-evangelical standard. Brown is actually quite centrist across the whole theological spectrum and acknowledges views to both his left and right.

Guthrie, D. *New Testament Introduction.* 4th ed. Downers Grove: Inter-Varsity, 1990. This is the most comprehensive conservative discussion of introductory issues. Guthrie is both more thorough, but also less readable than Carson, et al., above. As well, Guthrie may be inordinately critical of some contemporary NT scholarship.

The New Testament Use of the Old Testament

Students will find this a hotly debated field with abundant articles and essays that present the various perspectives on the discussion. Thus, students should consult bibliographic sources (in the following) for additional entries. The following is a list of helpful books.

*Longenecker, R. N. *Biblical Exegesis in the Apostolic Period.* 2d ed. Grand Rapids: Eerdmans, 1999. This work covers not only Jewish hermeneutical methods but also discusses how the various writers of the NT may or may not have employed such tactics themselves.

Carson, D. A. and Williamson, H. G. M., eds. *It Is Written: Scripture Citing Scripture.* Cambridge: Cambridge University Press, 1988. This volume is actually a wide-ranging collection of essays on various aspects of the topic (esp. pp. 191–336) including each major NT author's distinctive use of Scripture.

Carson, D. A. and Beale, G. K., eds. *Commentary on the Use of the Old Testament in the New.* Grand Rapids: Baker, forthcoming. Most likely this will become the evangelical standard, commenting book-by-book on every quotation of the OT in the NT—and not a few allusions and echoes as well.

Ellis, E. E. *Paul's Use of the Old Testament.* Grand Rapids: Eerdmans, 1957; repr. Grand Rapids: Baker, 1981; and id., *Prophecy and Hermeneutic in Earliest Christianity.* Grand Rapids: Eerdmans, 1978. Both books provide useful analyses of the troublesome issues, particularly in helping to survey Jewish methods of interpretation at the time of the writing of the NT.

France, R. T. *Jesus and the Old Testament*. London: Tyndale; Downers Grove: InterVarsity, 1971. France investigates the various ways in which Jesus used the OT as recorded in the Gospels—how those uses agree with the LXX or the Hebrew text, examples of typology uses, predictive materials, and finally the influences that Jesus' uses may have had on others' uses.

Biblical Theology

Before listing books for each testament, mention should be made of a major reference work edited and written by evangelicals: Alexander, T. D. and Rosner, B. S. *New Dictionary of Biblical Theology*. Downers Grove; Leicester: InterVarsity, 2000. Organized topically, each article surveys its theological subject through both testaments.

Old Testament

Martens, E. A., ed. *Old Testament Theology*. Bibliographies No. 13. Grand Rapids: Baker, 1997. A helpful survey of more than five hundred of the most important works, listed by subject.

Dyrness, Jr., W. *Themes in Old Testament Theology*. Downers Grove: InterVarsity, 1980. A survey of the main theological themes of the OT in a topical format, this well-written volume provides the general reader with an excellent overview of the subject.

*Kaiser, Jr., W. C. *Toward an Old Testament Theology*. Grand Rapids: Zondervan, 1991. Providing a survey of OT theology, Kaiser believes that the OT's central theme is that of God's promise. He traces the development of that theme chronologically through the OT and (more briefly) into the NT.

*House, P. R. *Old Testament Theology*. Downers Grove: InterVarsity, 1998. A narrative approach designed for college and seminary students, this work outlines God's nature and acts in each book of the OT.

*Goldingay, J. *Approaches to Old Testament Interpretation*. Rev. ed. Toronto: Clements, 2002. The author focuses on key questions with which most Christians who take the OT seriously wrestle. He suggests helpful working solutions to them. The book is an excellent answer to the question: How can the OT be a Christian book?

Anderson, B. W. *Contours of Old Testament Theology*. Minneapolis: Fortress, 1999. Themes of the holiness of God, covenants, torah/wisdom, and prophecy/apocalyptic are interwoven in this synthesis by an influential scholar.

Preuss, H. D. *Old Testament Theology*. OTL. 2 vols. Louisville: Westminster John Knox, 1995–6. Following the tradition of classic OT theologies, Preuss sees God's acts of election and covenant and the subsequent human responses to God as the central and unifying theme of OT theology.

Sailhamer, J. H. *Introduction to Old Testament Theology: A Canonical Approach*. Grand Rapids: Zondervan, 1995. An evangelical, structured study on how to do OT theology.

Childs, B. S. *Old Testament Theology in a Canonical Context*. Minneapolis: Fortress, 1986. Classic on canon with a sensitivity to the NT.

Birch, B. C., Brueggemann, W., Fretheim, T. E., and Petersen, D. L. *A Theological Introduction to the Old Testament*. Nashville: Abingdon, 1999. Written by leading mainstream scholars, this book treats the OT's main theological themes in an order approximating the canon's organization.

*Barr, James. *The Concept of Biblical Theology: An Old Testament Perspective.* London: SCM, 1999. The most important survey of OT theologies at the end of the twentieth century, although occasionally confrontational in its perspective.

Brueggemann, W. *Theology of the Old Testament: Testimony, Dispute, Advocacy.* Minneapolis: Fortress, 1997. A provocative approach that structures the discussion around the metaphor and imagery of the courtroom.

Eichrodt, W. *Theology of the Old Testament.* 2 vols. London: SCM, 1961; Louisville: Westminster John Knox, 1967. This is the classic modern OT theology using a systematic cross-section approach to the subject that is centered in the concept of covenant. Its strength is its combination of topical and historical approaches to OT theology. In reaction to this G. von Rad composed his own theology (see below).

von Rad, G. *Old Testament Theology.* 2 vols. Edinburgh/London: Oliver and Boyd; New York: Harper & Row, 1962, 1965. Vol. 2 has just been reissued, Louisville: Westminster John Knox, 2001, with an introduction by W. Brueggemann. In writing this recent major OT theology, Von Rad rejects the ready-made categories of systematic theology and attempts to synthesize the OT's own theological categories within a historical framework. He rejects any possibility for a unifying theology across the entire OT, preferring to elucidate the specific theologies of individual biblical writers or of OT books.

At present, OT theology is the subject of great scholarly debate on many difficult issues. Hasel, G. *Old Testament Theology: Basic Issues in the Current Debate.* 4th ed. Grand Rapids: Eerdmans, 1995, offers the advanced student an overview of the complex discussion as well as his own attractive solution.

Ollenberger, B. C., Martens, E. A., and Hasel, G. F., ed. *The Flowering of Old Testament Theology,* Sources for Biblical and Theological Study 1. Winona Lake, IN: Eisenbrauns, 1992. This book is a reader of important essays on OT theology during the seminal period of 1930–1990.

New Testament

Morris, L. *New Testament Theology.* Grand Rapids: Zondervan, 1990. This is a short treatment of the topic, longer on some issues than others.

Caird, G. B. (Completed and ed. by L. D. Hurst). *New Testament Theology.* Oxford: Clarendon, 1995. Imagines the apostolic authors all participating at a round-table theological discussion and highlights the distinctives each brings to the table. Painstakingly compiled by one of Caird's former doctoral students after his premature death.

*Ladd, G. E. *A Theology of the New Testament.* Grand Rapids: Eerdmans, 1974; rev. ed. by D. A. Hagner, 1993. Ladd compiles the theology of the various sections or writers as they occur canonically in the NT. So, for example, part I treats the "Synoptic Gospels" with individual chapters covering all the theologically significant issues in the Synoptics. Part II follows with "The Fourth Gospel" with its key issues. The remaining parts of the book cover "The Primitive Church," "Paul," "The General Epistles," and "The Apocalypse." Ladd's exceptional volume offers the student a trustworthy guide through the mazes of intricate issues.

Guthrie D. *New Testament Theology.* Leicester/Downers Grove: InterVarsity, 1981. This volume presents the culmination of the lifelong study of this leading, conservative

British scholar. Organized on the basis of theological categories, Guthrie's work lists topics and then his discussion of the theologies of the various writers in the NT under each one. Unfortunately, the work is weakened by this method of organization and by some of Guthrie's rather idiosyncratic views. For us it proves less useful than Ladd.

Goppelt, L. *Theology of the New Testament.* 2 vols. Grand Rapids: Eerdmans, 1981, 1982. Though reflecting Bultmann's influence,[20] this work offers a much more moderate German theology. Vol. 1 covers the theological significance of Jesus' ministry while vol. 2 surveys, in briefer scope, the important theological contributions of various other NT writers, particularly in their testimony to Christ.

Schnelle, U. *The History and Theology of the New Testament Writings.* Minneapolis: Fortress, 1998. Covers the important historical issues describing the range of scholarly opinion and literature.

Strecker, G. *Theology of the New Testament.* Louisville: Westminster John Knox Press, 2000. Beginning with the theology of Paul and adopting history-of-religions presuppositions, this book proceeds through a discussion of Jesus, the message of the kingdom of God, the composition and contributions of the Gospels, the deuteropaulines, and ends with the theology of the catholic epistles. Schnelle and Strecker comprise the standard liberal approaches to NT theology.

*Two other monumental works merit special mention though they do not cover the entire NT in their scope: Dunn, J. D. G. *The Theology of Paul the Apostle.* Grand Rapids: Eerdmans, 1998; Wright, N. T. *Jesus and the Victory of God.* Minneapolis: Fortress, 1997. Neither should be missed.

Literary Criticism

Dyck, E., ed. *The Act of Bible Reading.* Downers Grove: InterVarsity, 1996. Supplying good examples of literary readings, this anthology of different authors introduces a handful of key methods at the most introductory level of any item on this list.

*Ryken, L. *Words of Delight: A Literary Introduction to the Bible.* 2d ed. Grand Rapids: Baker, 1993. This is one of the best introductions to the Bible from a literary perspective.[21] This edition, which combines two earlier volumes, divides the OT into three sections: Biblical narrative, Biblical poetry, and other literary forms in the Bible, and includes a helpful glossary of literary terms at the end. It proceeds to cover specific literary features found in the NT.

Gabel, J. B., et al. *The Bible as Literature. An Introduction.* 3d. ed. New York/Oxford: Oxford University Press, 1996. Approaches the Bible from a literary/historical perspective seeking to show how its forms and the strategies the biblical authors employ convey messages from and to real people.

Ryken, L. and Longman, III, T., eds. *A Complete Literary Guide to the Bible.* Zondervan, 1993. An evangelical counterpart to Alter and Kermode that follows.

*Alter, R. *The Art of Biblical Narrative.* New York: Basic Books, 1983; and id. *The Art of Biblical Poetry.* New York: Basic Books, 1987. These two extremely popular books explain the literary dimensions of biblical narrative art and poetry. Both have

---

20 R. Bultmann, *Theology of the New Testament,* 2 vols. (London: SCM, 1951, 1955) is an older standard presenting radical NT scholarship. We do not list it as a main entry since it is now so dated.

21 See also the earlier work, L. Ryken: *How to Read the Bible as Literature* (Grand Rapids: Zondervan, 1984).

become standard introductions to their respective subjects and both are available in paperback. They represent the perspective of modern literary criticism.

Bailey, J. L. and Vander Brock, L. D. *Literary Forms in the New Testament.* Louisville: Westminster John Knox, 1992. The work surveys the multiple literary features of the NT in three sections: the Pauline tradition, the Gospels and Acts, and other NT writings. This work not only describes the various forms but goes on to show the value of understanding them for interpretation. It provides good examples and bibliographies for further study.

Bar Efrat, S. *Narrative Art in the Bible.* Sheffield: Sheffield Academic Press, 1989. An Israeli scholar discusses the specific techniques of biblical narrative and illustrates his points with numerous biblical examples.

Gillingham, S. E. *The Poems and Psalms of the Hebrew Bible.* Oxford Bible Series. Oxford: Oxford University Press, 1994. This is the best introduction to Hebrew poetry for students. Its strengths are its many examples, its fresh insights, and its incorporation of NT examples.

*Petersen, D. L. and Richards, K. H. *Interpreting Hebrew Poetry.* Guides to Biblical Scholarship. Minneapolis: Fortress, 1994. In touch with the latest scholarship on biblical poetry, it provides the beginning student with an up-to-date introduction to the subject with many biblical illustrations.

Alter, K., and Kermode, F., eds. *The Literary Guide to the Bible.* Cambridge, MA: Harvard University Press, 1990. In this volume specialists discuss the literary aspects of each book of the Bible. The result is a valuable reference book that presents the best fruits of a modern literary critical approach as practiced by internationally known scholars from diverse backgrounds.

Sternberg, M. *The Poetics of Biblical Narrative.* Bloomington: Indiana University Press, 1987. The definitive, technical book on OT narrative, this work makes available for a wide audience a series of influential journal articles by a noted Israeli scholar, but its highly technical discussions will probably scare away all but the most advanced students. For a very useful counterpoint see Gunn, D. M. and Fewell, D. N. *Narrative in the Hebrew Bible.* The Oxford Bible Series. Oxford: Oxford University Press, 1993.

Watson, W. G. E. *Classical Hebrew Poetry.* Sheffield: JSOT, 1984. This is the definitive discussion of its subject, especially since it compares OT poetry to its ancient Near Eastern counterparts. Its thoroughness makes it of interest mainly to the advanced student, but the author's numerous examples and clear writing keep the book from sounding technical. It is now out of print.

Guides to Studying the Bible: Methods and Principles of Exegesis

Augsburg Fortress (Minneapolis) has an ongoing series entitled, "Guides to Biblical Scholarship" (1969–). Edited by D. O. Via, Jr. and spanning both testaments, the series seeks to explain to the nonspecialist the most common interpretive methods of modern biblical scholars. Some provide genuine and helpful insights; others have met dubious reactions from readers, for the methods are not uniformly sanctioned by scholars. Volumes that treat generally accepted methods (e.g., form, redaction, narrative, and textual criticism, NT theology, etc.) provide useful instructions from the perspective of mainstream critical scholarship. Uniquely, there is a volume, *Postmodern Biblical Criticism*, A. K. Adam, 1995, and another *Psychological Biblical Criticism*, D. A. Kille, 2000.

Old Testament

*Stuart, D. K. *Old Testament Exegesis.* 3d ed. Louisville: Westminster John Knox, 2001. This volume explains to the beginning seminary student how to exegete an OT passage. It also offers an excellent bibliography. Though, sadly, many busy pastors will probably find Stuart's procedures too lengthy, there is no better book on the subject.

*Broyles, C. C., ed. *Interpreting the Old Testament. A Guide for Exegesis.* Grand Rapids: Baker, 2001. Evangelical scholars discuss methods of OT exegesis and criticism for interpreting the text.

Gorman, M. J. *The Elements of Biblical Exegesis: A Basic Guide for Ministers and Students.* Peabody, MA: Hendrickson, 2001. Presents the essential elements of the exegetical method in a succinct and incisive way. Designed for students, teachers, pastors, and others wishing to think and write about the Bible carefully. This brief hands-on guide incorporates insights from the field of biblical interpretation into its straight-forward approach to the complex task of exegesis. Gives examples of exegesis papers that students might write in an exegesis course.

Hayes, J. H. and Holladay, C. R. *Biblical Exegesis: A Beginner's Handbook.* Rev. ed. Louisville: Westminster John Knox, 1997. An explanation of the process of exegesis from the perspective of mainline, critical scholars.

Steck, O. H. *Old Testament Exegesis: A Guide to the Methodology.* 2d ed. Atlanta: Scholars Press, 1995. Translated from German by J. D. Nogalski, the book makes available to English readers a well-respected European exegetical guide. Its thorough approach makes it mainly useful to advanced students.

Westermann, C., ed. *Essays on Old Testament Hermeneutics.* Louisville: Westminster John Knox, 1979. Westermann translates a German original in which world-renowned scholars discuss the problems involved in interpreting the OT. Though somewhat dated and highly technical, this is still the best single volume on the subject, and most of the chapters have become classics. It is now out of print.

New Testament

Fee, G. D. and Stuart, D. K. *How to Read the Bible for All Its Worth: A Guide to Understanding the Bible.* 2d. ed. Grand Rapids: Zondervan, 1993. This is a popular-level guide to biblical interpretation with particular emphasis on genres.

Id. *How to Read the Bible Book by Book.* Grand Rapids: Zondervan, 2002. Designed to integrate the Bible as a whole; and even when the whole is narrowed to individual biblical books, this popular volume helps readers to see how each book fits into the grand story of the Bible.

*Black, D. A. and Dockery, D. S., eds. *Interpreting the New Testament.* Nashville: Broadman & Holman, 2001. In this volume many scholars write chapters explaining the various dimensions of the interpretation of the NT. The authors all subscribe to a high view of Scripture and have produced essays especially useful for serious students.

*Green, J. B., ed. *Hearing the New Testament: Strategies for Interpretation.* Grand Rapids: Eerdmans, 1995. Each chapter introduces a particular approach to NT interpretation and demonstrates how that approach can be used by students and pastors in fruitful work with the NT. Five texts from different parts of the NT are used as sample texts throughout the book in order to facilitate understanding of the differences among the interpretive strategies.

Porter, S. E. and Tombs, D., eds. *Approaches to New Testament Study.* Sheffield: Sheffield Academic Press, 1995. This volume features single chapters on most of the newest criticisms. Older methods are often grouped together in single chapters. Both evangelical and ecumenical approaches are treated. In general, the summaries are very nicely done.

Under the rubric, "Guides to New Testament Exegesis," edited by S. McKnight, Baker (Grand Rapids) has published: S. McKnight, *Interpreting the Synoptic Gospels,* 1988; S. McKnight, ed., *Introducing New Testament Interpretation,* 1990; T. K. Schreiner, *Interpreting the Pauline Epistles,* 1990; G. M. Burge, *Interpreting the Gospel of John,* 1992; W. L. Liefeld, *Interpreting the Book of Acts,* 1996; A. H. Trotter, *Interpreting the Epistle to the Hebrews,* 1997; and J. R. Michaels, *Interpreting the Book of Revelation,* 1998. All are highly useful.

*Fee, G. D. *New Testament Exegesis: A Handbook for Students and Pastors.* 3d ed. Louisville: Westminster John Knox, 2002. Fee guides students through a process of doing Greek exegesis in various kinds of NT literature. He presents a systematic approach to exegesis for sermon preparation and includes helpful bibliographies. This is a practical guide, though some consider it unrealistic for the busy pastor.

Periodicals and Journals

Bibliography and Abstracts

These tools enable interpreters to locate items specific to questions or issues under investigation. Indexes in these tools further enable the interpreter to locate articles (and books) on specific biblical texts. Many such tools exist; we list only four we consider to have the most ongoing usefulness.

Old Testament Abstracts [OTA] is published thrice yearly by the Catholic Biblical Association of America (Washington, DC). It first appeared in February 1978. Though less comprehensive than *Elenchus* (below), it provides abstracts of periodical articles and notices of recently published books on the full range of issues relevant to the study of the OT. The entire run of *OTA* for the years 1978–2000 (Vols. 1–23) is now available on CD-ROM from the American Theological Library Association.

New Testament Abstracts [NTA] is published three times yearly by Weston School of Theology, Cambridge, MA. First appearing in 1956, it abstracts all periodical literature on topics relevant to the study of the NT. Abstracts are written in English, though reviewers abstract important articles written in all modern languages. Each issue closes with brief comments on major books recently published in NT studies. One can hardly overestimate the value of *NTA* for researching issues, topics, and texts concerning the NT. A CD-ROM Release 1.0 contains all abstracts and book notices published in *NTA* from 1988 through 1998.

Elenchus bibliographicus biblicus. Rome: Biblical Institute, 1968– . This work catalogs important biblical materials the world over. A massive, annual resource, it can be daunting for the initial user. It suffers from being chronically late (often three or more years late!), so searches of recent literature prove impossible.

The fourth is actually a collection of electronic resources. Again we must limit to a few; no doubt others will prove useful in specific areas of research. *OCLCFirstSearch* is a comprehensive and complete online reference service with a rich collection of databases. It supports research in a wide range of subject areas with well-known bibliographic and full-text databases in addition to ready-reference tools such as directories, almanacs, and encyclopedias. Databases include: *ATLAReligion Index One: Periodicals* (1975–) and *Religion Index Two: Multi-Author Works* (1960–), Evanston, IL: American Theological Library Association; PsycINFO; and ERIC; among others. These serve as excellent sources for resources in biblical studies as well as wider topics in religion. See your local library for print, CD-ROM, and online access. Other excellent online resources include the *Christian Periodical Index* produced by the Association of Christian Librarians: it indexes more that 100 selected publications; the *Philosopher's Index*: abstracts from books and journals of philosophy and related fields; and *Religious and Theological Abstracts*: provides abstracts for periodical literature in the fields of religion and theology from over 400 journals. No doubt entries in this category will continue to increase.

Biblical/Theological Periodicals (with common abbreviations)

The number of journals currently published—even if we limit ourselves to biblical and theological studies—is enormous. Out of that vast number we list the following major journals because of their focus on the study of biblical texts, their popularity, and their ready availability in many theological libraries and whose articles are predominantly in English. They run the gamut from those devoted more exclusively to the technical work of scholars writing for other scholars to those oriented to nonspecialists and practitioners. Their theological orientations also differ—from those with clear boundaries, which publish only work acceptable to their constituencies, to those that publish all work they consider worthy. We list them in two general categories, giving their common abbreviations in parentheses.

For General Readers
1. *Bible Review (BR)*
2. *Biblical Archaeologist (BA)*
3. *Biblical Archaeology Review (BAR)*
4. *Bibliotheca Sacra (BSac)*
5. *Ex Auditu (ExAu)*
6. *Expository Times (ExpT)*
7. *Evangelical Quarterly (EvQ)*
8. *Interpretation (Int)*
9. *Journal of the Evangelical Theological Society (JETS)*
10. *Near Eastern Archaeology (NEA)*
11. *Themelios*
12. *Trinity Journal (TrinJ)*
13. *Tyndale Bulletin (TynB)*
14. *Westminster Theological Journal (WTJ)*

For Advanced Students and Specialists:
15. *Biblica (Bib)*
16. *Biblical Interpretation (BI)*
17. *Bulletin for Biblical Research (BBR)*
18. *Biblical Theology Bulletin (BTB)*
19. *Catholic Biblical Quarterly (CBQ)*
20. *Currents in Research: Biblical Studies (CRBS)*

21. *Filología Neotestomentaria (FN)*
22. *Horizons in Biblical Theology (HBT)*
23. *Jewish Quarterly Review (JQR)*
24. *Journal of Biblical Literature (JBL)*
25. *Journal for the Study of the NT (JSNT)*
26. *Journal for the Study of the OT (JSOT)*
27. *Journal of Theological Studies (JTS)*
28. *Neotestamentica (Neot)*
29. *New Testament Studies (NTS)*
30. *Novum Testamentum (NovT)*
31. *Palestine Exploration Quarterly (PEQ)*
32. *Vetus Testamentum (VT)*

Commentaries

A wealth of information resides in commentaries, which are useful in single volumes or as sets. Hundreds are currently in print from all segments of the theological spectrum and serve a variety of purposes. Bible students must be clear on their purposes in employing specific commentaries, for the commentary genre covers an array of approaches to commenting on the books. All commentaries reflect the presuppositions and theological commitments (or their lack) of the writers. They are written for various purposes. Some are devotional and stress personal application; others aid preachers or teachers by focusing on illustrating truth or on the "preachability" of biblical texts. Some scholars write commentaries only for other scholars and those who want precise and technical citations of parallel ancient literature and sundry such findings. Others write them so lay people, or pastors, or advanced students can understand the meaning of the biblical books. Some commentaries stress history and the technical details of the ancient world; others focus on the texts' theological significance. Some writers attempt to adopt several agendas to provide help for a variety of readers' needs. One ecumenically-produced series projected to cover the entire Bible collates the salient comments of ancient commentators and preachers (the so-called Church Fathers): T. C. Oden, gen. ed., *Ancient Christian Commentary on Scripture.* Downers Grove: InterVarsity Press. 1998– . Commentaries present Bible students with a tremendous variety of choices. Our advice to the beginning interpreter is to know what you need or want and use those commentaries that will meet your needs. Since commentaries represent a major investment, choose wisely— preferably after "hands-on" scrutiny. J. Glynn, *Commentary and Reference Survey.* Grand Rapids: Kregel, 2003, devotes a major section to commentaries, categorizing them in very useful ways. Of use also are T. Longman, III, *Old Testament Commentary Survey.* 2d ed. Grand Rapids: Baker, 1995; B. S. Childs, *Old Testament Books for Pastor and Teacher.* Philadelphia: Westminster, 1977; and D. A. Carson, *New Testament Commentary Survey.* 5th ed. Grand Rapids: Baker, 2002. Both the OT Bibliography and the NT Bibliography in the online "Denver Journal" have recommended lists of commentaries that are updated regularly.[22] Beyond that we will list the major, current, English language series, recognizing that other series and fine

---

22 See http://www.DenverSeminary.edu/dj or look for the link to the "Denver Journal" on the Denver Seminary website.

individual volumes exist outside of series. We will omit older series.[23] Space simply does not permit our listing individual works. Single volume commentaries on the entire Bible suffer in that their enforced brevity often precludes significant help for interpreters.[24] Note that commentary series, understandably, may contain members of varying quality. Simply because one volume is excellent (or poor) does not mean the others will follow suit. Our list will be subdivided to aid in our descriptions.

Series Commenting on the English Bible (practical emphasis)

Motyer, J. A. and Stott, J. R. W., eds. *The Bible Speaks Today* [*BST*]. Downers Grove/Leicester: InterVarsity, 1968– . This is a popular-level, paperback series on selected books in both testaments. Most of the authors are British evangelicals. Not all are well-written, but they consistently provide practical help for living.

Ogilvie, L. J., ed. *The Communicator's Commentary*. 35 vols. Dallas: Word, 1980– . (Being reissued as *The Preacher's Commentary*, Nashville: Nelson, 2003-04.) These commentaries focus on how to proclaim the meaning and application of the text in detail. Profitable for pastors, teachers, and Bible-study groups, they are often written by the best recent (USA) evangelical expositors or preachers.

Anders, M., ed. *Holman New Testament Commentary*. Nashville: Broadman & Holman, 1998– . Typically written by pastors or others who are not NT specialists, these short commentaries based on the NIV are designed for pastors, teachers, and Sunday school leaders. Includes illustrations and discussion points.

*Muck, T., gen. ed. *The NIV Application Commentary*. Grand Rapids: Zondervan, 1995– . The series aims to cover both testaments; the NT is almost complete. The format breaks down the comments on each section to its "original meaning," "bridging contexts" into today's world, and "contemporary significance"—to allow the text to speak with power to the modern world. Due to this approach, the comments on the original meaning are necessarily brief. Probably the premier series in this section.

*Mays, J. L., et al., eds. *Interpretation*. Louisville: Westminster John Knox. This series has volumes on both testaments. Written by mainline scholars, these focus on the meaning and application of the texts for preachers and teachers.

---

23 To omit older series is a difficult decision, but we made it because this bibliography is already lengthy. We urge readers to consult the work of our theological predecessors. Among those we consider worthy are: G. A. Buttrick, ed., *The Interpreter's Bible*, 12 vols. (Nashville: Abingdon, 1954); P. R. Ackroyd, et al., eds., *Cambridge Bible Commentary*, NEB (Cambridge: Cambridge University Press, 1963–1979); W. Barclay, *The Daily Study Bible New Testament* (Philadelphia: Westminster); various authors also contribute to *The Daily Study Bible Old Testament* (Philadelphia: Westminster); J. Calvin, *NT Commentaries* [Torrance edition] (Grand Rapids: Eerdmans); and C. F. Keil and F. Delitzsch, *Old Testament Commentary*, 10 vols. (Peabody, MA: Hendrickson).

24 If you can buy only a one volume commentary the best include J. D. G. Dunn and J. Rogerson, eds., *The Eerdmans Bible Commentary* (Grand Rapids: Eerdmans, forthcoming) written by an ecumenical group of scholars; G. Wenham, et al., eds., *New Bible Commentary: Twenty First Century Edition* (Downers Grove: InterVarsity, 1994) by evangelicals; J. L. Mays, et al., eds., *HarperCollins Bible Commentary* (San Francisco: Harper & Row, 2000); and J. Barton and J. Muddiman, eds., *The Oxford Bible Commentary* (Oxford: Oxford University Press, 2001) by mainstream scholars; and R. E. Brown, et al., eds., *The New Jerome Biblical Commentary*, 2d ed. (Englewood Cliffs, NJ: Prentice-Hall, 1999) for a Roman Catholic perspective. An important new survey of each book of the Bible—providing mini-commentaries—is D. S. Dockery, ed., *Holman Bible Handbook* (Nashville: Broadman, 1992), a feature also (along with other articles) of R. L. Hubbard, Jr. and G. D. Fee, eds., *Eerdmans Bible Handbook* (Grand Rapids: Eerdmans, forthcoming).

Osborne, G. R., ed. *New Testament Commentary* [IVP *NTC*]. Downers Grove/Leicester: InterVarsity, 1991– . This series of brief commentaries links the pastoral heart with the scholarly mind, emphasizing the significance of the biblical text for today's church in its analyses of the NT books.

Krodel, G. A., ed. *Proclamation Commentaries.* Minneapolis: Augsburg Fortress, 1978– . Short paperback commentaries on the NT, they are designed especially for the preacher. They come from the front rank of critical scholars.

Series Commenting on the English Bible with References to the Original Languages

Chadwick, H. succeeded by Hooker, M. D., ed. *Black's* (or *Harper's*) *New Testament Commentaries* [*BNTC*; *HNTC*]. London: A. & C. Black; New York: Harper and Row; London/New York: Continuum, 1957–, some volumes reprinted by Baker and Hendrickson. These volumes were written mostly by British authors of the previous generation though volumes continue to emerge, the most recent being Muddiman, J. *The Epistle to the Ephesians.* London/New York: Continuum, 2002. They contain excellent material designed to be accessible to readers without knowledge of Greek.

Gaebelein, F. E., ed. *Expositor's Bible Commentary* [*EBC*] 12 vols. Grand Rapids: Zondervan, 1976–92. This series includes commentaries on the entire Bible, plus introductory articles. Authors come from the United States, Canada, England, Scotland, Australia, and New Zealand, and from many denominations, including Anglican, Baptist, Brethren, Methodist, Nazarene, Presbyterian, and Reformed, all evangelicals, and write for a wide audience. They aim to explain the meaning of the Bible, not to engage technical or obscure issues. A revision is currently underway to replace some of the entries. Available on CD-ROM.

*Clendenen, R., gen. ed. *New American Commentary* [*NAC*]. Nashville: Broadman, 1991– . A series sponsored by the Southern Baptists but including a few contributors beyond that circle, it is projected to encompass all biblical books in 40 volumes. The target readers are pastors, though students and laypersons alike can profit from these detailed but not overly technical works.

Arnold, C. E., ed. *Zondervan Illustrated Bible Backgrounds Commentary.* Grand Rapids: Zondervan, 2002. This set that helps readers understand the historical and cultural background of the books of the NT including full color photos and graphics.

Martens, E. A. (OT) and W. M. Swartley (NT), eds. *The Believer's Church Bible Commentary.* Scottdale: Herald. 1991– . This important Mennonite/Anabaptist set provides rather substantial comments on the English Bible text, with Greek employed in the background plus extensive applications to contemporary church life.

Harrington, D. J., ed. *Sacra Pagina.* Collegeville, MN: Liturgical Press, 1991– . A multi-volume series on the NT from a Roman Catholic perspective.

Talbert, C. H., ed. *Reading the New Testament.* Macon, GA: Smyth & Helwys. An ecumenical series focusing specifically on the literary flow of the final form of the biblical text against its historical background. Presents cutting-edge biblical research in an accessible language that is both coherent and comprehensive.

Furnish, V. P., gen. ed. *Abingdon New Testament Commentaries.* Nashville: Abingdon, 1996– . Also ecumenical in scope, seeks to provide compact, critical comments particularly for theological students but also for pastors and church leaders.

Several volumes of the parallel *Abingdon Old Testament Commentaries* series have appeared.

Hendriksen, W. and Kistemaker, S., eds. *The New Testament Commentary.* Grand Rapids: Baker, 1953–2001. This is really a "two-man" series on the NT books begun by Hendricksen and completed by Kistemaker. The contents are strongly Reformed in orientation and often major on devotional aspects. Interpretations in the Hendriksen volumes can be very idiosyncratic and are sometimes polemical; the Kistemaker ones are solid though they seldom break new ground.

*Harrison, R. K., ed. succeeded by Hubbard, Jr., R. L. *New International Commentary on the Old Testament* [*NICOT*]. Grand Rapids: Eerdmans, 1965– ; and *Bruce, F. F., ed. succeeded by Fee, G. D. *New International Commentary on the New Testament* [*NICNT*]. Grand Rapids: Eerdmans, 1952– . Work on these volumes is ongoing. All the original NT volumes and some OT volumes are being revised by their original authors or replaced by other authors. The NT set is virtually complete, while gaps still remain on the OT side. They represent a high level of conservative evangelical scholarship, more technical than popular, though scholarly details are often relegated to footnotes. Most readers will discover these to be extremely useful tools.

The New International Biblical Commentary [*NIBC*]. Peabody, MA: Hendrickson, 1988– . Features well-known scholars, including many evangelicals, writing to make the best scholarship accessible to a wide audience. They tend to be much briefer than other entries in this category. The NT series (ed., W. W. Gasque) is complete, and with a dozen volumes of the OT series also available (eds., R. K. Johnston and R. L. Hubbard, Jr.), the entire series nears completion.

Clements, R. E., and Black, M., eds. *The New Century Bible Commentary* [*NCB*]. Grand Rapids: Eerdmans; London: Marshall, Morgan & Scott, 1966–94. They fall in the middle of the theological spectrum—the NT volumes tending to be more conservative than the OT volumes. Brief at some points, they provide many fine analyses of the biblical books. They are written for a wide audience, but the series is now out of print.

Mays, J. L., et. al., eds. *The Old Testament Library* [*OTL*]. Louisville: Westminster John Knox, 1962– . This series includes both commentaries on OT books as well as specialized works on a variety of topics of concern to students of the OT. Some of the commentaries are translations of German originals, some appeared previously in other series, and excellent new volumes and replacements of older ones continue to arrive regularly. Overall these books reflect good mainline scholarship, and most include theological comments useful to teachers and preachers. The *New Testament Library* [*NTL*], 2002– , a new series of clothbound commentaries, general studies, and modern classics, has recently emerged.

Carson, D. A., ed. *Pillar New Testament Commentaries.* Leicester: InterVarsity; Grand Rapids: Eerdmans, 1988– . About one-half complete, this series represents a major mid-range series and spans a perceived gap between most of the series in this category and those in the next.

*Wiseman, D. J., ed. *The Tyndale Old Testament Commentaries* [*TOTC*]. Leicester/Downers Grove: InterVarsity, 1964–99; and *Morris, L., ed. *The Tyndale New Testament Commentaries* [*TNTC*]. Leicester: InterVarsity; Grand Rapids: Eerdmans, 1956–91. They represent mainstream evangelical scholarship from both Britain and

North America, written for layperson and pastor alike to present the theological significance of the biblical books. They include helpful historical introductions and prove to
be reliable guides for interpretation. Many of the earlier NT volumes have been revised,
and both the NT and OT series are complete. They are comparable to the NICOT/NT
in quality, though briefer.

Cotter, D. W., ed. *Berit Olam: Studies in Hebrew Narrative and Poetry*. Collegeville,
MN: Liturgical Press. 1996– . The commentaries in this recently emerging series, with
contributions thus far by both mainline and evangelical scholars, apply the new literary criticism to produce a literary analysis of OT books.

Series Commenting on the Original Languages Texts

Albright, W. F. and Freedman, D. N., eds. *Anchor Bible* [*AB*]. Garden City, NY:
Doubleday, 1964– . This ongoing series will cover the OT and the NT plus
Apocryphal books. Of uneven size, from slim to very detailed, many volumes are high-
ly technical in nature and only for advanced students and scholars. Their quality varies
widely, though several are truly superior. Contributors include Catholics, Jews, and
Protestants. Many volumes appeared in the 1990s, almost all outstanding.

Silva, M., ed. *Baker Exegetical Commentary on the New Testament* [*BECNT*]. Grand
Rapids: Baker, 1992– . This ongoing series, written from a conservative, evangelical
viewpoint, provides in-depth exegesis of the original language texts. Volumes on Luke,
Romans, Philippians, and Revelation have appeared with several others expected soon.

*Hagner, D. A. and Marshall, I. H., eds. *New International Greek Testament
Commentary* [*NIGTC*]. Grand Rapids: Eerdmans, 1978– . This series reflects a high
level of conservative scholarship, though at a level to make the set accessible to all with
a background in Greek. The initial volumes reflect superb scholarship.

*Watts, D. J. (OT) and Martin, R. P. (NT), eds. *Word Biblical Commentary* [*WBC*].
Waco, Dallas, Nashville: Word/Nelson, 1982– . Almost complete, this series comments on all books in both testaments, and revisions of earlier volumes is ongoing. Two
(or even three) volumes are devoted to several of the longer biblical books. Their format includes sections that provide textual and literary analysis, exegesis (occasionally
technical), and conclusions about the meaning and significance of the texts. These are
not for average readers, though almost anyone could profit from the "Explanation" sections to obtain the results of the technical exegeses. A CD-ROM version is available.

Emerton, J. A., Cranfield, C. E. B., and Stanton, G. N., eds. *International Critical
Commentary, Old and New Testaments* [*ICC*]. Edinburgh: T. & T. Clark, 1895– . Begun
in the nineteenth century though never completed, the project ground to a halt when
the volume on Kings appeared in 1951. The project was revived with the revision of
Romans by C. E. B. Cranfield, 2 vols. (1975, 1979), the appearance of the first volume
of Jeremiah (1986), and a sluggish stream of volumes thereafter. Highly technical and
stressing critical and philological matters, the volumes are written by the first rank of
scholars. Cranfield's work on Romans stands among the best single commentaries in
existence. However, the older volumes are rather dated.

Olsen, R. and Hausman, R., et al., eds. *Continental Commentaries*. Minneapolis:
Augsburg Fortress, 1984– . This is a collection of English translations of major
German works—often with important histories of investigation of issues and theolog-
ical excurses. To date most are OT volumes.

Freedman, D. N., ed. *Eerdmans Critical Commentary.* Grand Rapids: Eerdmans, 1999– . With only a couple of volumes appearing to this point and thus difficult to categorize, this series looks to be detailed and technical—and the most "liberal" that Eerdmans has published.

Cross, F. M. and Koester, H., et al., eds. *Hermeneia: A Critical and Historical Commentary on the Bible.* Minneapolis: Augsburg Fortress, 1972– . This series has projected volumes on books in the OT, the NT, plus apocryphal books, early church Fathers, and even one on the "Sermon on the Mount." The most liberal of all the series, it also often provides the most detailed treatment of books available by front-line scholars. The works are highly technical and focus on historical and critical issues with little emphasis on theology. Some earlier volumes were translations of German works, but not so much recently. Due to their high level of scholarship and prohibitive cost, it is likely that only specialists will find much use for most of these.

If students want to buy an entire commentary set (one complete or nearing completion)—given our cautions at the outset—we recommend considering:

1. *Tyndale OT Commentaries and Tyndale NT Commentaries* (for general readers plus pastors, teachers—for exegesis of the texts);
2. *NIV Application Commentary* (for general readers plus pastors, teachers—for an applicational focus);
3. *Interpretation* (for preachers and teachers—from a more ecumenical perspective);
4. *New American Commentary* (for pastors and teachers—for exegesis of the texts);
5. *New International Commentary OT and New International Commentary NT* (for pastors, teachers, and scholars); and
6. *Word Biblical Commentary* (for serious teachers and scholars).

INDEX OF SUBJECTS

INDEX OF SCRIPTURES AND ANCIENT WRITINGS

INDEX OF AUTHORS AND NAMES